Beyond Eurocentrism

Beyond Eurocentrism

A New View of Modern World History

PETER GRAN

Syracuse University Press

Library of Congress Cataloging-in-Publication Data
Gran, Peter, 1941–
    Beyond Eurocentrism : a new view of modern world history / Peter Gran.—1st ed.
        p.   cm.
    Includes bibliographical references and index.
    ISBN 0-8156-2692-4 (cloth : alk. paper).—ISBN 0-8156-2693-2 (pbk. : alk. paper)
    1. History, Modern—19th century. 2. History, Modern—20th century. I. Title.
    D359.7.G73   1996
    909.08—dc20   95-35939

Manufactured in the United States of America

.   .   .

Peter Gran is associate professor of history at Temple University. He is author of *Islamic Roots of Capitalism, Egypt, 1760–1840* and numerous articles on Islamic history and political economy.

Contents

Acknowledgments

For world history to be useful to educators, diplomats, or others interested in the contemporary scene, the field needs by its own reckonings to get beyond Eurocentrism and beyond the narrow study of elites in which it originated. Greater inclusiveness per se will not suffice; more fundamental rethinking is involved. Technical problems, too, must be overcome. Ways must be found to represent differences among cultures without exaggerating these differences, ways to represent similarities without making all human beings into "economic man," ways to introduce complexity and conflict in different locales in accord with the work of social historians without simply falling into particularity. Certainly, it is not a question of whether to use structural analysis or event history, but how to use both. Nor is it a question of whether the position of the historian affects the outcome of the work; this can be assumed. The question is what kinds of history or knowledge about the world more generally can one expect given the existence of the different kinds of modern hegemonies? How useful will they be? What can one learn from them? For the historian focusing on the modern period, these challenges can to a degree be boiled down to the issue of how to follow the mandate of contemporary historical thought and study the world as a whole, that is, as made up of historical actors when the tradition of the field tells one that real power, historical agency, is concentrated in only a few of its countries. In this book I offer one possible solution.

A number of institutions and individuals were instrumental in the production of this manuscript. I would like to express my deep appreciation to Temple University for granting me in 1992–93 a sabbatical leave which was crucial to the research and writing of this book. The Interlibrary Loan Department at our Paley Library has been enormously supportive as have the staff at Van Pelt Library where I also worked thanks to the affiliation granted me over the years by the Middle East Center of the University of

vii

Pennsylvania. I received support from the Social Science Research Council (SSRC) in New York, from the National Endowment for the Humanities (NEH) through the American Research Center in Egypt, and more recently from Fulbright. In earlier work, I was supported by the Iraqi government during visits there and helped by a number of historians, especially in Baghdad University. I was also helped by historians at the Colegio de México in Mexico City and by librarians of special collections, such as those of the Rockefeller Foundation Archive in Tappan, N.Y.

I was more than fortunate to find individuals willing to share their time and expertise by reading my drafts and pointing out to me where I made mistakes. I did my best to profit from their criticisms; I accept responsibility for errors and misjudgments that may remain.

The Russian chapter was read by Martin and Ylana Miller. The Iraqi chapter was read by Abd Al-Salaam Yousif. The Italian chapter was read by Leonardo Salamini and by Grant Amyot. The Indian chapter was read by Partha Chatterjee. The Mexican chapter was read by Lynn Stephen and Scott Cook. The Albanian chapter was read by Arshi Pipa and Nicholas C. Pano. The Belgian Congo/Zaire chapter was read by Bogumil Jewsiewicki. I also received help from V. Y. Mudimbe, Crawford Young, and Janet and Wyatt McGaffey. The chapter on the United Kingdom was read by Keith Nield and the chapter on the United States by Nan Woodruff. I received comments on the work as a whole from Eugene Genovese, Rifaat Abou-El-Haj, Thomas C. Patterson, and Keith Nield. I received comments on the theory from Arif Dirlik.

The opportunity to write a number of articles proved helpful in the development of this book. I thank the colleagues who gave me these opportunities. For the chance to work on hegemony and family structure, I thank Amira Sonbol Al-Azhary; for the chance to work on Shakespeare Reception in different hegemonies on one occasion and on racial hierarchies in different hegemonies on another, I thank Lee D. Baker and Thomas C. Patterson. For the chance to write a chapter on orientalism and democracy, I thank Hisham Sharabi. For the chance to publish an article on the Azhar and the Vatican as "traditional intellectuals," I thank Mr. Hilmi Sha'rawi and his colleagues at the Center for Arabic Studies in Cairo, and for agreeing to publish an Arabic version of this book, Gaber Asfour.

For help with Gramsci material over the years and for the chance to present Iraq as "Russian Road" at the Socialist Scholars Conference, I thank the members of the New York City Gramsci Society, Frank Rosengarten, George Bernstein, John Cammett, and Joseph Buttigieg. For the chance to present my views of the world systems approach, I thank the Fernand Braudel Center, especially Immanuel Wallerstein and Giovanni Arrighi. I also thank Tuomo Melasuo, who took over the responsibilities for me of Working Group 7 (the Imperialism and Revolution Group) of the International Sociological Association, and finally, I thank my friend and colleague of many a year, Anouar Abd Al-Malek, who encouraged me more than once to take a globalist perspective and who gave me the chance in Madrid, Cordoba, and elsewhere to try to develop one over the years.

For help with the argument and for general support and encouragement over these years, I thank Talal Asad, Edward Said, Martin Bernal, and for much encouragement in the production stage, the editorial staff of Syracuse University Press, most notably, Cynthia Maude-Gembler, executive editor, Virginia M. Barker, copy editor, and John Fruehwirth, editor.

Those who bore the brunt of this work and who deserve special thanks are Thomas Patterson, Rifa'at Abou-El-Haj, Amira Sonbol Al-Azhary, and my family, to whom this work is dedicated. In the years I worked on this book my wife, Judith, became a public interest lawyer representing the rights of people with disabilities, my son, Stephen, became a paramedic for the City of Philadelphia, and my daughter, Nora, became a Spanish language major in my university, all of which not only made me very proud but I believe finds its way into what I wrote.

Footnotes, Bibliography, Spelling, Index

The approach to documentation adopted is based on the assumption that world history is an undeveloped field. There is thus no standard bibliography and there is unlikely to be one given the continuing rapid growth of knowledge in the principle field underlying it, social history. This makes the footnote section—and the index—more valuable than the bibliography, the latter becoming more a slightly arbitrary series of suggestions. As a consequence, a full presentation of documentation is to be found in the footnote section and here I wish to thank colleagues James Mall, Kiki Norris, Luise Caputo-Mayr, and my daughter for their help. The system of spelling adopted is a modification of that used by the Library of Congress, the Arabic hamza and 'ayn being identified by the same.[1] Finally, given the current stage of development of the field, it is not surprising that it lacks a useful conceptual vocabulary. For this reason, I chose to make the index a concept index, one identifying the most important terms and showing their interrelationships. A perusal of this index is not a bad way to begin this book.

Abbreviations

ABAKO	Alliance des Bakongos
AFL-CIO	American Federation of Labor-Congress of Industrial Organizations
AGEL	Association Generale des étudiants de Lovanium
AHA	American Historical Association
ALP	Albanian Labor Party
BHU	Banaras Hindu University
BJP	Bharatiya Janata Party
CERDAC	Centre d'etudes et de recherches documentaires sur l'Afrique centrale
CERUKI	Centre de recherches universitaires du Kivu
CIO	Congress of Industrial Organizations
CND	Campaign for Nuclear Disarmament
CNRS	Centre National de recherche scientifique
COCEI	Coalition of Workers, Peasants, and Students of the Isthmus
COMECON	Council for Mutual Economic Assistance
CPI-M	Communist Part of India (Marxist)
CPM	Communist Party of Mexico
CRIDE	Centre de recherches interdisciplinaires pour le développement de l'education
CROM	Conferación Regional Obrera Mexicana
CTM	Confederación de Trabajadores de México
DC	Christian Democrats

EEC	European Economic Community
EIC	L'État Indépendent du Congo
END	European Nuclear Disarmament
FBI	Federal Bureau of Investigation
FDR	Franklin Delano Roosevelt
GNP	gross national product
GRS	General Revenue Service
HUAC	House Un-American Activities Committee
ICHR	Indian Council of Historical Research
ICP	Iraqi Communist party
ICP	Italian Communist party
IHC	Indian History Congress
IMF	International Monetary Fund
INAH	Instituto Nacional de Antropología e Historia
INCE	Instituto Nacional de Ciencias de la Educación
IWW	International Workers of the World
JNU	Jawaharlal Nehru University
KDP	Kurdish Democratic party
MNC	Movement Nationale Congolais
MPR	Movement Populaire de Révolution
MSI	Movimento Sociale Italiano
NAACP	National Association for the Advancement of Colored People
NAFTA	North American Free Trade Act
NEH	National Endowment for the Humanities
NEP	new economic policy
NIEO	New International Economic Order
NLF	National Liberation Front
NLRA	National Labor Relations Act
OAH	Organization of American Historians
OPEC	Organization of Petroleum Exporting Countries
ORTF	Organization de radiotélévision française
PAN	El Partido Acción Nacional
PNF	Partito Nazionale fascista

PRI	Partido Revolucionario Institucional
PSR	Popular Socialist Republic
RAI	Radiotelevisione italiana
RSS	Rashtriya Swayam Sevak Sangh
SOHIZA	Société des historiens Zaïrois
SSRC	Social Science Research Council
STFU	Southern Tenant Farmers Union
SVIMEZ	Associazióne per lo Sviluppo dell'indùstria nel Mezzogiórno
TUC	Trade Union Congress
UCOL	Union for Colonization
UGEC	Union générale des étudiants Congolais
UNAM	Universidad Nacional Autonóma de México
UNAZA	Université Nationale du Zaïre
VARNITSO	All-Union Association of Workers in Science and Technology for Cooperation in Socialist Construction
WPA	Work Projects Administration

Beyond Eurocentrism

1

Eurocentrism and the Study of World History

This book is a work of revisionist scholarship. If today nearly all subjects in history are dominated by social historians, world history remains something of an exception. It continues to be studied in terms
of elites, mainly Western elites. How can one bring the newer logic of
social history to this field? How can one get beyond Eurocentrism?

Social history maintains that history is expressed through the lives of
the majority. This majority in a global sense comprises subsistence farmers
in the countryside of the Third World and casual laborers living largely
from barter in Third World urban areas. If this majority is the center of
human history, one needs to work out a new method to study world
history; at least this is the argument here.

Several attempts to do this have already been proposed, especially in
political economy, and one can learn quite a bit from them. A number of
writers have categorized the Third World as the periphery of world capitalism, but I have found this position to beg as many questions as it answers.
Should the vast majority of the world's population be characterized as
peripheral, or does this assumption simply perpetuate Eurocentrism? If not,
is there a better way for a historian to proceed? In the 1980s political economy took up several themes under the general rubric of globalization of
capitalism, which are of some use. Still, most of the world's population is
only involved in capitalism to a limited degree; world history cannot be
based solely on world capitalism and or claims about its globalism.

Such issues arose for me out of the experience of trying to persuade
college students that they had a stake in understanding Third World social
history. The majority of the students I refer to here took a course called
Introduction to Third World History to pass a distributional requirement
at Temple University in Philadelphia. From what I could tell, most of them
expected to find nothing of importance in the subject matter for a Westerner; among those more sophisticated, even the idea of history itself—any

1

kind of history—was suspect. I could scarcely fault them for making these assumptions; after all, this was and is the conventional wisdom.

Although changes are underway that are undermining this view of the world and of history, they are scarcely visible to the typical student "victimized" by standard thought. To teach against the current, I needed a book to speed up the process of reconceptualization.

In the first part of this chapter I show that Eurocentrism influences nearly all established historical writing, especially that in world history, at least until the recent birth of social history. Evidence for this, I suggest, can be gleaned not only from a consideration of influential texts but from a consideration of the interests of patrons. This first part concludes with the argument that despite its legitimacy, in recent years, Eurocentrism has been increasingly dangerous even for elites, and even for Western elites; and that social history offers a more secure approach to understanding the world. I then outline this alternative approach.

The claim that Eurocentrism underlies the writing of world history can be inferred from a study of the history and theorization of history. Europeans, notably Germans, gave rise to the field of modern history. They divided it into different subfields, world history among them. Thereafter, historical knowledge grew, but the field retained the divisions worked out by the Germans.

The German philosopher Hegel was the preeminent theorist of history in the nineteenth century. In a famous essay on world history, Hegel postulated that civilization followed civilization from antiquity onward until finally they were all worn out, leaving only that of Prussia. The rise of Prussia, by extension Europe, was, thus, the salvation of the whole world. Europe, historians have subsequently claimed, following Hegel, has been and remains the center of world history. Eurocentrism, the division of the world between Europe and the rest, thus became the dominant paradigm for world history.[1]

To legitimate such a grandiose view, Europe had to retain an obvious leadership role. As early, however, as the turn of the twentieth century, Europe had begun to decline. After World War I, it seemed pointless in the view of a number of rather despairing European writers even to claim that Europe was civilized.

Until at least 1945, world history was, thus, a field that concentrated on the expansion of Europe. Europe and by extension the United States— the West—were taken to be the dominating forces in the world, so it seemed logical to construct the subject as a narrative of the major political and diplomatic events that affected them; the rest of the world was added on. As this paradigm hung on in more recent years, it managed to accommodate a trade history approach, dividing the world into core and periphery, and an orientalist one, dividing culture into Western and non-Western cultures. It made space for area studies as a way to understand the non-West, and it even accommodated the early years of women's studies. Recently, it has begun to incorporate the writings of the postmodernist intellectuals in the Third World who are concerned with globalism. Despite these developments, a challenge to this tradition is in progress. Social historians have emerged as an influential part of the discipline. One finds them increasingly upset with various features of the history's dominant paradigm. There are, by my count, at least nine features of Eurocentrism that social historians criticize; these criticisms range from logic to politics.

Conventional world history, as characterized by its critics, claims ⟵

1. that there is a single power center that is defined geographically, for example, Europe, or assuming the weakness of Europe, then

2. the term *West* can be used more or less interchangeably with the term *Europe;*

3. that Europe, or the West, is analytically distinguishable from the "rest" of the world, the Third World, the differences being "real" ones, ones not erased by an abandonment of any particular approach, for example, narrative history;

4. that the rest of the world is either exotic, essentially different, or, alternatively, essentially the "same" as the West, give or take the vast difference in levels of development separating the two;

5. that a major feature of the Third World is its "golden ages," some of which have inspired revival movements as "traditional" peoples seek to find new identities in the modern world;

6. that all or at least most of the well-known events that take place in the modern Third World occur as a consequence of the actions of the West;

7. that the way these events or changes take place is through the interconnections of elites, significant relationships being those that are horizontal and international, not those that are vertical and, hence, local, for example, class relationships;

8. that world history either strongly accepts or strongly rejects the present in either case—I argue—exhibiting severe problems with temporal processes. If it is presentist, this history is deeply committed to the idea of progress, generally to technological progress; conversely, if it rejects presentism, it is likely to be ultraromantic and to be organized around the cultural paradigms of previous millennia, oblivious to most features of recent centuries;

9. that world history in the dominant paradigm is a defense of the status quo. It is useful to hegemonic elements, so they reproduce it.

For social historians, there is by definition no single center of power. If historians have characterized Europe as composed of "great powers" and "great leaders" in certain periods, this is not because Europe was actually the single center of power and other parts of the world were powerless or leaderless. Rather, it would tend to imply certain kinds of social relations, for example, highly developed internal alliances among various groups linked to the state and weak counterhegemonic trends, the combination of the two giving certain states power. To explain how this came to be or what it means scarcely warrants the common and often uncritical preoccupation with great leaders even where they existed. Choices were made by all people. The prominence of a Bismarck in Germany, for example, should be explained not only in terms of what he achieved within the framework of the constraints, but also in terms of the strivings of the many people, which created these constraints. In other words, in contrast to the free will-oriented accounts of the dominant paradigm, social history imposes a mixture of free will and determinism.

Standard world history is, in fact, so focused on the Western countries, their elites, and high cultures, that it does not permit much critical analysis of them. This world history—at the risk of repetition—is still written the way national history used to be written in the nineteenth century—one center—a Europe, a West, a few actors, cultures, or artifacts, eras of war and peace, information on commerce and other forms of interaction, in other words, more like an almanac than an argument. And this seems to be the case whether one looks at William McNeill, *Rise of the West,* Immanuel Wallerstein, *Modern World System,* Eric Wolfe, *Europe and the People Without History,* or Hajime Nakamura, *A Comparative History of Ideas,* to mention four very different but successful works within the field.

By contrast, a social historian might wish for a work that reflects the assumption of the field that the masses make history and that these masses are mostly peasants in the Third World, that they do so not only during the moments of great events but on an everyday basis. How do these daily activities of Third World peasants affect Western history? This is what my students asked when I spoke about the logic of social history. Clearly, the prevailing studies of world history are not the place to find an answer.

What stands out as a consequence of focusing on elites is a dehistoricization of the mass population. One notes as a result an inability to include a significant number of people as actors except impersonally, as in wars, or to allow for a complexity of social relations among the people, who are included, especially if they are poor.

For example, a world systems approach allows for the study of those peoples caught up in the market economy, but it does so rather one dimensionally. Should the study of the market play down the religious, cultural, and political movements because they do not fit? What about the rest? Are not the vast majority still excluded? Are all these people working for capitalism as a "reserve industrial army" or as a part of the "dual economy"? This seems unlikely. Can one logically include the majority into the minority? Consider the fact that the wealthy classes in many countries fear this mass population and fear it seemingly as much or more than they fear the working class and other groups formally integrated into the capitalist world. That means they, "the outsiders," do have power whether through formal alliances as in the Iranian Revolution or more diffusely through "illegal" migration or business activity or whatever.

As suggested in point 2, the dominant paradigm is driven into racism in trying to uphold the notion of a West, racism being an obviously discrediting feature. If the center of power in the world is presumed to be the West, what happens when the West—as in the 1970s—grows weak and needs a Japan in order to appear "Western-like"? At this point, some combination of racism and science collude in the dominant historiography to insist that Japan can be a part of the West but only partly Westernized. If this formulation is unsatisfactory theoretically, it is unsatisfactory empirically as well. Europe was always diverse; parts of it—indeed, parts of the United States and Japan—have long been fairly similar to parts of the Third World. Confronted with such considerations, many historians today equivocate; they want to have a single center—depending on the time period, Europe or the United States. To protect this idea, some are tempted to abandon presentist defenses of Eurocentrism and turn to the ultraromantic idea of the West drawn from Western heritage. Heritage teaches that Europe is the repository of universal civilization, the details of recent centuries do not matter.

Are, then, Europe and non-Europe so distinct? Or is this a function of writing history in a particular form, for example, as a narrative? Many social historians would be inclined to take the latter position, agreeing with the new literary criticism, which Foucault inspired, linking narrativity with a presumption of centralized power. Indeed, as shown in research of this sort now, one major use of the narrative has certainly been as a vehicle for the European writer to assert individual distinctiveness in relation to non-Europe. And, what is the case for literature is certainly the case for history as well. The foreground of a history book, like that of a novel, is where the power is, that is, where the Europeans are; the background is for the other, the powerless, that is, the Third World. The one depends on the other. So, for "Europe" to survive, as Edward Said argues, it has to create a "non-Europe," a collective background, and it has to destroy alternative concepts of the world, which might challenge this dichotomy of Europe/non-Europe. For, in this paradigm, Europe only exists because it is not non-Europe; non-Europe must remain opposite or undeveloped, that is, exotic or primitive. Thus, many historians exoticize the study of non-Europe, creating ethnohistory and Oriental Institutes, or they stratify humanity, creating a world of "interdependent" parts of a "global village," with Europe as the distinctly developed part.

How do non-European scholars participate in the dominant paradigm?

Denied a claim to the present and to the idea of modernity, non-European scholars working in the dominant paradigm have tended to shift from positivism to romanticism and have conjured up images of golden ages as a form of compensation—not deterred in the least, it appears, from supporting a paradigm that marginalizes their cultures but gives them as individuals a certain function as link points.

In the Third World as in the West, Eurocentrism thus has an array of supporters from the Left as well as from the Right. For, if one assumes that everything of importance is controlled by the West and that the local context does not matter, then Third World leaders are no longer responsible for the ills of their countries. Third World Marxist historians—and, one might add, their European sympathizers as well—have used this part of the paradigm extensively. It is, they claim, Western imperialism that causes the problems in these countries.

What is the connection of the past to the present? As noted previously, upholders of the dominant paradigm tend to be committed to an extreme presentism or to an extreme romantic "golden age-ism," extreme because both tend to gloss over a consideration of the contradiction built into ruler-ruled relationships.

For example, upholders of the presentist variant frequently equate historical analysis with an account of progress; they note in their works achievements in science, in weaponry, in the standard of living, or in the growth of knowledge. But, as indicated above, the utility of such an approach is limited, for there has been continuity as well as change throughout the twentieth century. In fact, the main political, economic, and cultural patterns of the late nineteenth century continue for the most part until today. Upholders of the romanticist version suffer from the opposite distortion postulating too little change, too much continuity, too much golden age, and again too little complexity.

Although Eurocentrism clearly has served the dominant interests, it is an increasingly risky doctrine or scientific stance to uphold even for the elite. The belief of Europeans, for example, that being European protects them from each other because they have much in common has, in fact, given them a false sense of security several times in the twentieth century alone. In 1992, yet another war broke out, this time in Yugoslavia, and like the wars in the past, it threatens all of Europe, if not the whole planet.

Danger exists as well in Africa, Latin America, and the Arab world where politicians influenced by the dominant paradigm believed they had some grounds for confidence in their relationships with people of their own cultural background only to find they did not. Needless wars have broken out there as well. These dangers are the Achilles heel of the paradigm. Power structures and even whole societies can perpetuate ideas about the world, which they know are inadequate, for example, if no costs are involved. In a world of diminishing resources, this is not practical; fighting needless wars is becoming a luxury.

If the dominant paradigm seems likely to be eclipsed sooner or later for intellectual reasons or for purely practical ones, why not anticipate this shift and plan for it as rationally as possible? Accept from it that the bedrock of contemporary history is national history, albeit not simply the history of European countries. Accept from social history that national history, in Europe or elsewhere, stands in need of development. It needs to be more diverse and more complicated than heretofore; allow then for a more heterogeneous concept of what is modern.

Putting such axioms into practice, one finds that what rulers of our modern nation-states are doing is disguising class conflict. Some do it by playing off one culture against another; some, one race against another; some, one gender against another; some, one caste against another. Although all these strategies are found in all countries, one can characterize a hegemony and its logic by which one of these strategies the rulers put first.

Ruling, one finds, simply means dividing the mass population of a country against itself, and this is done by manipulating these primordial sentiments and in the process hiding from the masses what they share in common—oppression by class forces.

But how can something as obvious as class oppression be hidden so much of the time? Is it that so many people are so marginalized from even the class order they cannot intuit it? Although this point cannot be dismissed, a close look at modern states reminds one that they are all very powerful in relationship to their citizens and this power differential in and of itself numbs the thought processes of most of the citizens. Most citizens are as a consequence prone to believe what their governments tell them or, at least, to think within the parameters established by the state. As Antonio Gramsci, the Italian Communist philosopher, insisted, most of us are "massified." It is scarcely a secret that all states invest a vast amount of time, energy, and resources in persuading their subjects to accept the logic on which the system is based and to find solutions to problems in terms of that logic. In other words, far more than historians have traditionally allowed, rule involves not just the use of the police, the army, the "dull compulsion" of the economy and of administrative organizations but also agents of persuasion whether in a "dictatorship" or in a "democracy." Recall, for example, the state's interest in the way in which the family is supposed to raise children, in how education is organized, in what the media presents, in what the religious system is teaching, in what people are consuming or not consuming, in what language people speak and how they speak it, in how they use their leisure time, and so on. Hegemony works when most of the population has a stake in the continuation of at least a part of the dominant set of ideas and practices.

Are these hegemonies—and by extension the world order—given all these strategies successful? Do they have what political science would call legitimacy? Here the answer would appear quite variable both among nations relying on the same type of hegemonic strategy and among the different historical periods of any given nation; varying as well according to whether historians take massification to be evidence of legitimacy and whether historians choose to include generally marginalized subject populations in their analyses. What is evident, in any case, when one immerses oneself in the standard secondary literature in social history about any one country is that subject populations resist the hegemony being imposed on them; no one form of hegemony is thus assured of legitimacy.

Still, during the period considered in this book, rulers do appear to have been more successful than not. It was not easy for opposition movements to organize themselves to confront a hegemonic bloc or even to get rid of a colonial power. The revolutions that took place were incomplete ones; they more commonly changed the ideology than they did the hegemonic alliances.

The book begins with a study of Russia, a country perceived by writers in the dominant paradigm as part of Europe but only partly European. Russia is a paradox, technologically sophisticated but not a democracy, a society based on caste as opposed to a mass civil society. For such a country to exist, it must be partly "Asiatic," that is, like Japan or China. This assumption would explain the part that was not democratic. If Russia could be conceived as partly Asiatic, it would permit someone working in the framework of the dominant paradigm to hold onto the idea of a geographical Europe without having to deal with Russia on its own terms.

By way of contrast, in this book I insist that Russia has always made sense to Russians on its own terms and should, therefore, to a historian as well. There is no need to marginalize it, to insist that its history is a paradox, that it is difficult to understand, or that Russians are schizophrenics. Its history must have a general logic, and in the second chapter I spell out this logic. Russian and Soviet histories, I hypothesize, are an example of a common form of hegemony termed in this book the *Russian Road*. And second, in the specific case of Russia/Soviet Union, the state succeeded by the time of Stalin in buying off the working class for a generation or two with momentous consequences on the international level as the Soviet Union became a great power. From Stalin's time, one can trace as well the beginnings of the expansion of the ruling caste, the caste or class segment called in Soviet history the *new class*. This expansion finally led to a possible breakup of the Soviet Union as a greater and greater percentage of the new class were nonethnic Russians. This means, in effect, that there is a precedent, perhaps even a rationale, if one recalls early twentieth-century Russian history, for why ethnic Russians today accept a position as a semicolony of the United States and of Western Europe. Today ethnic Russians are experiencing a decline in worker support, and they feel a need to regain caste power lost through a generation of too much inclusion of other "ethnics" in the ruling caste, decline in power being a central concern.

In the third chapter, I present the example of Iraq to show a Russian Road state where the working class was not bought off so easily. In Iraq, the expansion of the ruling caste took place only in the 1960s and only with great difficulty, the result being the 1990 attempt at great power status reflected in the invasion of Kuwait.

It was not planned this way, but the choice of Iraq seems vindicated by the fact that much of the world would go to war and kill a large number of Iraqis, rationalizing its acts through this internationally shared dominant paradigm: killing is acceptable; Iraqis do not value life because they are a brutal people; hence, the world should not value Iraqi lives. In early 1994, this point retained its salience.

Of course, the Gulf War was just one episode in Iraqi history and should be seen as an aside in this discussion. The more important point is that over the years the dominant paradigm applied to Iraq has never explained very well anything that has gone on there. The twists and turns of Iraqi political history seem always to be a surprise and seem always to remain an enigma to standard historians. As an alternative to the dominant paradigm, I argue for a revisionist approach to Iraqi history, one based on the logic of the internal dynamic of ruler and ruled. The political turnovers, which appear to confuse the writers in the dominant paradigm, seem, in chapter 3, to be fairly straightforward examples of swings between autocracy and liberalism found in any Russian Road regime. The exaggerated focus on Baghdad, like that on Moscow, has skewed the interpretation of the hegemony, making it seem more violent, more secular, and also less logical than it really is.

The choice of Italy for chapter 4 carries forward the task begun in chapter 2, challenging the viability of the idea of a "Europe." The choice of Italy brings to light another feature of established historical practices as well, that while writers in the dominant paradigm accept that Italy is part of Europe, that it is not part of anything else as Russia is, it still is defectively European. Europe is supposed to be homogeneously bourgeois democracy. Because Italy is not, the dominant paradigm has used the instance of Italy to create a gradation within Europeanness of what is more European, the north Italians, and what is less European, the south Italians. In doing this, the dominant paradigm disguises the North's exploitation of the South, construing Italy to be a labyrinth or tapestry, a country without a structure and without a logic. An important consequence of using the dominant paradigm is that one decontextualizes the South and thereby facilitates this exploitation.

Italy, like Russia and Iraq, is examined here in terms of its internal dynamic. In the political economy section, I reintroduce and build on Gramsci's insights about the Southern Question and about fascism, arguing that the specificity of such a country can only be determined by comparing it to countries that also adopted what I call an *Italian Road* type of hegemony. Thus, Italy makes little sense when compared to the northern European democracies as it often is.

Italy, however, makes a great deal of sense compared to India, and this becomes one of the reasons for the choice of India in this book. In both these countries are similarities on the level of political practices, even of political rhetoric. For example, politicians in both countries use the term *democracy* to affirm the Aryan linkage connecting their countries to northern Europe at the dawn of time, a linkage supposedly proving that their "Norths" or "advanced regions" had even a racial connection to the "other" democracies. In both the countries, the North—as noted—exploits the South, and in both the countries, the South fights back. In Italy, the southerners go it alone, the Italian Left—apart from Gramsci—ignoring their struggle; in India, the struggle of the southerners and the Left overlap, Italy becoming a welfare state for the North, India gradually beginning to disintegrate.

The choice of India in terms of the larger argument of the book is also influenced by the fact that India is a Third World country located in Asia. The dominant paradigm, therefore, wants to make Indian history conform to something generically Third World or Asian, something different from European history, hence the common characterization of India as an "Asian democracy." Of course, it is true that many Third World countries, for example, Iraq and India, share much in common. Both India and Iraq were British colonies that subsequently became independent and then joined the nonaligned movement but—and this is the point brought out in these chapters—each long had its own form of hegemony. The choice of India or Iraq here is one way to show that when historians in the dominant paradigm locate a country in the Third World or in Asia or in the West, they thereby explain very little.

The introduction of Mexico as an example of the Italian Road contributes to the foregoing, adding that not all Latin American countries can be lumped together or dumped into a Third World or a New World as is commonly done by scholarship in the dominant paradigm, that to make sense of Mexico, one needs countries similar to it, and that Italy and India can serve this function. Here are three countries, I argue, whose ruling classes adopted the same political strategy of rule. Here are three countries, which differ from each other as a consequence of the course of their counterhegemonic struggles, the Mexican Left and the Mexican Indian populations adopting strategies midway between those of their counterparts in Italy and India, and modern Mexican history developing accordingly.

In the third section of the book I take up tribal-ethnic states. These states, the dominant model of world history has often skipped or relegated to the domain of anthropology and political science. Insofar as such states receive coverage, they do so by virtue of their positions "on the margin" of European history. Yet they are often judged fairly severely for what has gone wrong in Europe. For example, events in the Balkans are held to be responsible for the outbreak of World War I, events in the Congo or in Vietnam are held to be responsible for the collisions of the great powers in those regions.

Social history permits the scholar to integrate the history of tribal-ethnic states into modern history or, more broadly, into the idea of modernity in a less reserved or judgmental fashion. In tribal-ethnic states, social historians have shown, dominant elements on the scene—alone or in collusion with foreigners—set up a strategy of rule in which class conflict is disguised by tribal-ethnic conflict, tribal-ethnic conflict in turn disguising the primary contradiction, gender contradiction. In these countries, some of which are more tribal, some more ethnic, wide strata among the men of even the oppressed tribes or ethnicities accept their plight in the class order because at least they are not on the bottom of the society. Women are. What becomes clear in these chapters is that this form of hegemony has worked and is working in many countries both in Europe and in the Third World, that it is, thus, a real weakness of the dominant paradigm not to find it to be an integral part of world history.

The choice of the Belgian Congo/Zaire as an example of a tribal-ethnic state is justified first, because it is a sub-Saharan African country and sub-Saharan Africa has been given particularly short shrift in the dominant model of world history; second, because it is a large and influential country; and finally, because it illustrates a particular form of counter-hegemonic struggle typical of a large number of tribal-ethnic states in Africa and elsewhere.

Because the dominant paradigm essentially does not consider the Belgian Congo/Zaire to have a history in its own right, the coverage that results tends toward serving the needs of the countries deemed to have a history—hence the importance attached to Europeans in the Congo, to the "Congo Crisis" of 1960, and to the details surrounding mineral exports—and, hence, to the exoticization of the rest. Thus, a writer in the dominant paradigm of world history might well be forgiven for straying from the conventional realm of history and reproducing in the text of his chapter on the Congo a rather terrifying-looking ceremonial mask as if to warn the reader that the Congolese are different. Although, of course, all countries are different, it could be noted—apropos to supposed differentness—that Zairian music inspires people interested in modern music all over the world. Similar exoticizing tendencies replete with such contradictions abound in the treatment of other subjects as well. A standard account of modern political history portrays the political system as detestable, but without Mobutu, the leader, who is detestable, it alleges there would be no system. In standard treatments of Zairian economic history, it does not seem to matter what the author concludes, perhaps because only Zairians are involved. Some conclude that the country is rich, some conclude that the country is poor!

The conclusions reached here about the history of the Belgian Congo/ Zaire suggest that despite its image as a regime that rests on violence evidence abounds to suggest that the state has organized culture successfully and has enjoyed a great deal of legitimacy. Here, after all, was a ruling class, Belgian and Congolese, which had the advantages of coming from a tribal-ethnic background and was, therefore, experienced in that kind of organization of culture. The Congo stands out in this regard from the countries that emerged from English, Italian, and French colonialism. In the Congo, the Belgians and the Congolese were able to work together to adapt Christianity and bourgeois politics to their local needs, developing in the process a unifying approach to the control of culture, an approach that I termed *gnosis,* an approach able to co-opt and then downplay forms of knowledge that could threaten this hegemony. Seemingly, the very success of this ruling class in organizing its hegemony whetted its appetite for more wealth and drove it to exploit its working class to a degree that forces one to look hard for comparable cases. Its greed easily explains the counterhegemonic movements that have arisen.

The use of Albania as an example of a tribal-ethnic state to compare to the Belgian Congo/Zaire reveals another possible variant of counterhegemony in this road. Whereas in Zaire opposition was predominantly secessionist, in Albania it was broader, composed first of nationalists and later of Communists linked to the trade union movement. While no doubt this support for the Communists permitted the latter to come to power, it also seems possible that the Communists once in power found it lacked support. Even the Albanian trade union movement, its basis of support, did not have deep roots, given the ethnically constructed nature of society. There was no way the Communists could uproot ethnic identification.

Albania, to sum up, is a part of Europe although, as I also argue, the general reader of European history would scarcely be aware of that fact. So alien have writers in the dominant paradigm found Albanian history that they have carved out a subdomain of Europe called Balkan history in which Albania could be located. Ironically, this was not necessary; Albania participated in the World Wars, the cold war, and the other major events that make up modern European and world history, but these developments remain unknown. The conclusion follows that despite all the importance attached to European history, Europe is actually an inconvenience for writers in the dominant paradigm.

In the fourth section of the book, I treat the bourgeois democracies. The dominant paradigm takes as its premise that the bourgeois democracies are the model for all of humanity, that all the other countries are yearning to be democracies. This study finds that this claim is among its weak features; it is not one that can be factually supported. It is, in fact, tendentious. It contributes to the oppression of the people who live in democracies, who are made to feel that the world is jealous of what they have and that because of this envy no matter what frustrations they experience they should put them aside and be grateful that they are where they are. After all, nowhere else is there rule by the majority. A stronger definition of democracy than that implied by the dominant paradigm is one based on the idea that bourgeois democracy is a hegemony based on rule by race.

The choice of the United Kingdom and the United States as examples of democracies reflects the importance of these two countries in the overall maintenance of the dominant paradigm. Writers in the dominant paradigm who study these countries make important claims that affect all of world history. They claim to find a consensus or a lack of conflict in these countries, and they argue from this finding how different the democracies are from the other hegemonies because the other hegemonies are known to be conflict ridden. This work does not support such findings; they are too sleight of hand. Conflict is, in fact, endemic in all the hegemonies.

In this work, the United Kingdom represents a variation of democracy in which the working class was bought off in racial and then economic areas and the state was able to develop a "social contract," whereas the United States represents a variation of democracy in which the working class was not bought off in either area and the state used much more regulation and repression.

If, then, the dominant paradigm for writing world history is Eurocentrism, in essence modern European history writ large, then Europe had to be the starting place to explain the problematic nature of the approach. Thus, one example of each of the main forms of hegemonies is drawn from the continent of Europe. How better can one demonstrate the inchoate nature of "Europe"? And, then, because the dominant paradigm poses the otherness of the Afro-Asian World to Europe and of the New World to the Old, how better can one challenge these notions than by coupling the European examples with examples drawn from what is supposed to be these "others"?

What is called for, then, is a rethinking of political economy—a moving away from elites toward mass societies. One could, I suggest, make the study of the ruler-ruled relationship of a country or two represent a given hegemony and thereby shed light not only on the dynamics of those two countries but on all those countries that participate in this type of hegemony throughout the world. One could, then, repeat this procedure hegemony after hegemony until one covers the world. First, one picks several countries in an area assumed to be a cultural unit, for example, Europe or Africa, a unit wherein one expects the countries will be similar to each other in most respects. One then analyzes their ruler-ruled relationships. Soon, it becomes apparent, contrary to traditional wisdom, that some of the internal dynamics, say in Europe, are more comparable to certain countries at a distance, say in Africa, than they are to those nearby. Meanwhile, the ruler-ruled relations of other European countries are found to be comparable to other African countries, and so on. As one progresses the old model of Europe versus the rest, termed here *Eurocentrism,* gives way to a more polycentric world history, to borrow the phrase of the political economist Samir Amin.

I conclude from all this not that an Africa or a Europe does not exist but that, contrary to views common among historians, they are to this day very complex and unstable constructions. Although Europe may have a common market, it remains a continent that scarcely knows itself and that few outsiders know either, an example of the false security theme. This real Europe, which I must deconstruct to write this book, comprises not only the four different hegemonic logics but a whole spectrum of regimes. These regimes ranged from those where the masses collaborated with the rulers, achieving great power status, to those where the masses resisted the policies and initiatives of the ruling class in the manner common to countries on the periphery of the world market; the Soviet Union is a recent case of a shift from the one to the other.

Finally, world history through the lens of social history has something to teach that other kinds of world history do not. If, for example, two countries follow a particular form of hegemony and if the course of struggle in each took somewhat different directions, as one would expect it would, this approach would, then, be the one—and the only one—to identify both what was general to these two countries and what was particular to each one. In other words, not only does national history give rise to world history but world history gives rise to new interpretations of national history.

Given the purpose of this book and also its scope, I envision two audiences: historians and social scientists. By historians, I mean specialists of national histories, as world history, in the strict sense, is the specialty of relatively few people. I hope that historians will find the analogical comparative dimension interesting, that they will be tempted to use their expertise in one country as the basis for reaching out to others. At the same time, I hope that social scientists will look at the book as a text with an argument; for there is an argument. The text is accessible to both kinds of readers. Technical issues are presented, but they are cast or recast in the fairly understandable language of comparative studies.

This, too, merits comment. The language of comparative studies used here and in other books has historically been predominantly grounded, for better or worse, in English and French categories with some German, some other Romance language material and specialized terms from Russian and other languages creeping in. For example, I assume here that I can interpret the organization of culture in all the hegemonies in terms of the way and the degree to which different hegemonies use four main worldviews. I characterize the worldviews in terms of their English language names: positivism, romanticism, Marxism, and anarchism. I assume, however—something few other writers would—that I should be able to distinguish a kind of liberalism or romanticism, and so on, characteristic of each of these hegemonies. Worldviews are in fact important analytical categories. They tend to be part of vertical solidarities and to have different properties than ideologies, which tend more to be part of horizontal solidarities.

Were this an exercise in positivism, this recourse to a given conceptual vocabulary would imply a kind of closure and here one that might impede a project designed to go beyond Eurocentrism. But this is not the case. The choice of terminology is an incipient one. World history is still at the stage of Europe. The inclusion in any future study of a larger number of cases of a given type of hegemony will warrant or, perhaps, necessitate the use of a different one. Perhaps English, as known presently, will continue to bear the burden of comparative studies; this is one possibility. Perhaps it will be eclipsed by a computer language. Alternatively, perhaps English will be or is in the process of being remodeled. Perhaps, onto English Chinese or Japanese philosophers will impose not just concepts but systems of thought, or, perhaps, onto English African writers will impose their languages of aesthetics, and these will make the language capable of serving as the basis of comparative analysis.

In the first part of this chapter, then, I outlined an experiment to determine if by making the different forms of hegemony that appear in the modern world the point of departure, the student of world history can get beyond Eurocentrism. Can world history so conceived become a lingua franca, a part of world culture and not simply a tool that further divides people. In the second half of this chapter, I demonstrate the rationality of this experiment in terms of the wider culture within which it was conceived.

In the 1990s, historians stand on what could be said to be the other side of the Foucauldian watershed, a broad shift in preoccupations that took place in the 1970s and 1980s. In these years, there has come to be a renewed appreciation of deconstruction as a tool, and by extension, of the influence of Michel Foucault in the intellectual life of many countries. Of course, deconstruction is found in all cultures, and it predates Foucault's writings. But the concept of this time period as a watershed is useful because it allows one to think over the recent concern among scholars for problems swept under the carpet during a century in which traditional scholarship had the upper hand in fields such as world history. Now, as this history writing is being deconstructed, academicians are beginning to discuss issues such as Eurocentrism.

While explicating deconstruction, Foucault instructs one to look for the silences in discourses and to see what they mean. Following his dictates, a number of talented writers in what is loosely termed the postcolonial discourse have started to discuss the meaning of the absence of the Indian or of the Middle Easterner in Western books putatively addressing these subjects. As the critiques of these newer writers multiply, it scarcely seems open to doubt that the older Western historiographers before social history had not been able to discuss difference or otherness in a satisfactory way and that much of the time they did not even try. Apparently, there are simply some long-term blind spots.

Foucault further instructs one to distrust linear logic and to use the logic of adjacency in its place, and this admonition has been taken up by feminist writers and by students of peasant studies to challenge the privileging or foregrounding involved in writing the traditional historical narrative. These narratives were generally constructed around a few Western and typically male figures; everyone else served as background. To their critics, these narratives beg the questions, Whose history? or History for whom?— questions that find no satisfactory answers in the traditional history writing.

Foucault further instructs one to question the assumption that states have power and that ordinary people do not. Power, he insisted, is diffused in the society and not concentrated in the elite as has been commonly thought by historians and social scientists. One must, therefore, put aside the elite-mass type of analysis in favor of social history. If power is everywhere, initiatives from small groups and even from individuals can bring about change, and they can do so from anywhere within the system. Taken as a whole, Foucault's theory challenges not only claims of the narrowly conceived Western power structure but also of the closure or fixity of its established fields and literary genres.

Where does this leave history writing? Presumably, the legacy of Foucault for historians encourages a textured appreciation of ruler-ruled relations, of how hierarchy is constructed, and of how it might be disassembled. Equally, it encourages one to rethink the importance of the interventions of individuals and of small groups in this process. It raises the question without fully answering it of how one might evaluate these interventions. Finally, it encourages historical sociology over narrative history.

Antonio Gramsci, a figure whose writings in many ways prefigure those of Foucault, is enjoying a rising prestige in theory circles. Gramsci, like Foucault, was a keen student of the modern state. He, too, had elaborate notions of hegemony and counterhegemony, culture, language, and the formation of the subject. Gramsci adds to Foucault a series of comments on how modern capitalist states actually rule and how this rule is resisted.

As these and other insights drawn from Gramsci attract increasing attention from theorists, one must observe at the same time an increasing politicization of the reading of his writings. Gramsci was a cofounder of the Italian Communist party (ICP), and at the same time he was a "Southerner." Critics who enter his writing in so narrow a manner often emphasize his interest in Taylorism and Fordism and do so in a disparaging manner, as if Gramsci had no reason to bemoan the uncompetitiveness of Italian industry or as if the Bolshevik model of the party was irrelevant in the 1920s. Another important approach to Gramsci with which this study contends argues that he was a Hegelian Marxist formed through his association with the Neapolitan philosopher Benedetto Croce. Leaving open the question of whether the early writings of Croce, which Gramsci read, were Hegelian, one might agree that Gramsci shared with Croce the conviction that Marxism was not a science but a philosophy of praxis. But the praxises adopted by the two seem so different that one cannot carry this point very far. Gramsci was a Marxist revolutionary; Croce sought to humanize the elite through art and ethics. Another approach to Gramsci, a liberal one, emphasizes the importance given in his work to democracy and to civil society. Although all these approaches have some utility, as I show in chapter 4 in the account of Italian history, I find a Marxist-anarchist or "Sardist" reading to be closer to Foucault and other modern writers than the others and it is this that has something to teach our generation.

Gramsci intended in his early journalistic writings to find a formula to free the southern peasantry and to end the Southern Question," to end not just capitalism but hierarchy. His formula was the alliance of the northern workers and the southern peasants. Because this idea was highly controversial, gradually, he had to shelve it, the Southern Question receding in his thought in the 1920s as other issues drew his attention so that by the time of the *Prison Notebooks,* the Southern Question was a bit buried. Still, it is a valuable part of the book—as valuable as the other unique ideas drawn from his early experience, such as how the intellectual learns from the masses and how the state maintains *common sense* and *massification,* all of which are also in *Prison Notebooks.*

For my purpose, Gramsci, also remains important as a critic of the presentism and linearism of the dominant paradigm in Italy. Gramsci believed that history changed when people changed it. In this view, the past is not a line leading to the present but a series of roads not taken. The future in this view is an open book, the one certainty being no deus ex machina, no crisis of capitalism will come and sweep the Communists to power.

In contrast to Gramsci, Italian northerners then and now, like most English and Americans, defend presentism and argue for a rupture with the past on one basis or another. Not all do, however. Some today appear to agree with Gramsci's view that despite the usefulness of modern technology, it remains epiphenomenal. It has not undermined either hierarchy or capitalism, and it seems unlikely that it ever will.

This poses an interesting challenge for historians. If one lived one hundred years from now and looked back on the post-World War II period, would one argue that it was different than all that went before? Would one still call this late capitalism as many theorists are disposed to at the moment? My findings in this book suggest otherwise.

Although Gramsci—from the reading here and from others as well—is clearer about power structures than is Foucault, his work, too, lacks adequate detail about political economy, Italian political economy excepted, and lacks as well the conceptual apparatus one would need to go beyond it to write a world history. What other modern hegemonies resemble Italy but differ in points of detail? What are the other fundamentally different modern hegemonies? How can one in sum have a world history? Neither Gramsci in the 1920s or 1930s nor Foucault in the 1960s could clarify these issues very well. Neither, however, could anyone else.

From fragments and asides derived from Gramsci, I find the point of departure in these matters. I note them here for the reader who is a familiar with *Prison Notebooks*. The hegemony of Italy differs fundamentally (1) from that of Russia/USSR, and this for him has implications for counterhegemonic strategy; (2) from that of the United States, a country where "Fordism" has created a consumer society even within the working class, and from that of the "Maraboutic" states of North Africa, a point that is not elaborated. The hegemony of Italy is similar to that of France during the French Revolution. The example of the Jacobins, Gramsci believes, is an important one for the Italian Left.

Scholars today obviously have more resources than did Gramsci in prison. Still, in the light of what has been achieved, the debt to Gramsci, as to Foucault, remains apparent.

Even Foucault owes a certain debt to Gramsci. Gramsci's approach to hegemony as a destructured struggle of ruler and ruled anticipated and essentially clarified Foucault's idea of the diffusion of power in society. And in Gramsci's working out of the organization of culture, one finds the fullest development as well of Foucault's idea of disciplinary regimes. The ideas of these two men inspired a totally new kind of historical sociology in which structures become dynamics.

In the broad outline of world history reconceived, it is apparent that all countries, regardless of their hegemony of choice and of the relative disjunction of politics, economics, and social order within, appear to enter a formative period around the 1860s to 1880s. At this point, capitalism gained the upper hand for the first time, forcing states to adopt distinct political strategies, which would assure their continued control. Everywhere in this period, modern bureaucracies emerged as enough unity existed at the top to permit the delegation of responsibility.

After the formative moment, all countries experienced the same three main economic phases in the same order: first, a classical liberal phase, one-class rule dominated by finance capitalists from approximately the 1870s to some time between 1917 and the 1940s; second, a corporatist phase, marked by cross-class alliances and sometimes by industrialism from the end of the liberal phase to the late 1960s; third, a second liberal phase that began around 1970 and lasts to the present. Much of what commentators—post-modernist and others—found unfamiliar in the 1970s and 1980s, had ante-cedents in the first liberal phase, not in the immediately preceding corporatist phase.

Several general questions arise at this point. Most importantly, How does an approach to history, even one making fairly minimal concessions to the traditional political economy of capitalism, escape from the problems of teleology and developmentalism common to the older Eurocentric models of world history criticized above. The answer worked out in the chapters that follow on an empirical level is that the events described are not reducible to—or wedded to—a single telos. They could be taken to show an evolutionary development in a period; equally they could be taken to be elements that are recurring cyclically within the framework of modern history. Alternatively, these events could be shown to be moving sideways around the world analogically through a logic of adjacency à la Foucault. Finally, they could be construed as a series of lost opportunities for revolution, an approach termed here the *historical road.*

Historical road is used here as a metaphor; a literal interpretation would reopen the door to a linearist history. *Road,* thus, comes to mean a way and a set of potentialities for that way, the two together at the same time, the two together producing a characteristic form of hegemony with its common sense. Where the road leads is open, but not entirely so. Given this common sense, one possible direction the road will lead is to revolution. It is not at all unlikely that one day a revolutionary leader may be able to bring together the mass population to overcome and even take apart the hegemony, thereby creating something new—perhaps a more egalitarian order. There is, of course, no necessity that this will ever happen, but if it does, it conforms or would conform to elements of the common sense, albeit elements, which lie half buried in popular consciousness awaiting the project of emancipation.

Perhaps, given the huge investment made by the elite in establishing certain kinds of bonds and, perhaps, given the risks inherent in change for very wide sections of most societies, change on the level of the hegemony and, thus, of the road was not encountered very often in the period under consideration. Empirically, at least, few countries altered their hegemony/ historical road in the time period studied here. Apparent hegemonic changes generally are not that; they usually are shifts, such as those between liberalism and corporatism, moves designed to head off change.

The subject of historical roads is large and complex. For that reason, the most useful place to discuss it is in the text where it can be made as concrete as possible. Thus, the chapter on Russia and the Soviet Union takes up as not just a particular history but also the sociological model of the Russian Road that applies to many other countries as well. The two parts of the chapter reinforce each other and clarify in the process the attributes of the model, the origins of its name, and the rationale for choosing first Russia and then Iraq as the illustrations. Similarly, subsequent chapters present an account of the Italian Road, the Tribal-Ethnic Road, and Democracy.

The Foucauldian watershed, and beyond that the influence of Gramsci, appears potentially to free historians from much of the baggage of the past and, hence, to permit ventures such as this one. One could not effectively criticize Eurocentrism earlier with or without the findings of social history. Second, it elevates the importance of history in a way seldom before done. At the same time, it imposes a much more complicated epistemology on the would-be historian. Teleology, narrativity, linearity, elite analysis, and other shortcuts, which permitted writers to get through their material must be abandoned. In its place come the logic of adjacency, the decentering of power, the concern with the observer and with language itself, which makes for long paragraphs and, yes, a long book.

In the process of arguing for and of presenting a restructured view of modern world history, I argue that history as an academic discipline plays an important role in all the hegemonies, albeit the concept of what history is and its role may vary appreciably. This makes the public lives and writings of what I term the doyens of the profession a matter of some importance both because of the views they uphold and because of the role their views play in various hegemonic discourses. A consideration of academic history, therefore, becomes a part of the book as well. What emerges from this consideration is the conclusion that while participation in state-related organizations such as history associations is wittingly or otherwise a form of contribution to the hegemony, the individual scholar in the instances surveyed is rarely if ever a protagonist of the dominant ideologies, such as racism and sexism. Seemingly, the state simply takes what it can get in the way of support.

Another point. Academic history is by no means equally distributed throughout all the hegemonies. Some employ far more historians than do others. This disparity has implications here. After all, is not social history much more rooted in the democracies than in the other hegemonies? Is there a touch of Eurocentrism in the reliance on this genre? The answer is a negative one. All the hegemonies are hierarchical and have no great use for the masses as part of their histories. The social historian, like the scientist, despite appearances to the contrary, is a critic everywhere—even in a democracy. More social history may be written in the democracies, but that does not mean it is being assimilated there.

In fact, as the profession shifted away from political and diplomatic history to social history in the democracies, it experienced extreme division.

But the question of Gramsci remains. After all, Gramsci is not commonly linked either to the issue of Eurocentrism or to problems of world history. For this reason, his current popularity is probably less among historians than among scholars in other fields. Would there not be more appropriate choices? Here, it is important to admit that Gramsci's influence on the paradigm conflict addressed in this book has, no doubt, been indirect. Nonetheless, more than other figures, Gramsci's political economy serves as a legitimation for social history and for a social historical view of world history, certainly more so than that of many writers who invoke the problem of Eurocentrism only to make a slogan or a cause of it. After all, it was Gramsci who reintroduced politics into political economy along with local capitalism and precapitalism, and much follows from such moves. With politics comes the local national dynamic; with local capitalism comes the realization that most capitalists function in local and national contexts and not international ones. The reinsertion of politics and local economics into the conceptualization of political economy moves world history to the national level. This explains why Gramsci.

But behind Gramsci, one might suppose, is Marx. Why not base this work as a whole on Marx and not limit the use of Marx to the Russian Road theory? As readers will recall, Marx went through several phases in his thought, all of which are of value. At no one point, however, could they either theoretically or in practice be brought together. Marx began as a philosopher in the 1830s. By the 1840s, as late as the *Communist Manifesto* (1848), he was writing about politics. By the 1860s, Marx grew more involved with the logic of capitalism, and it is this later part of his life that is best remembered by political economists today. By this point, Marx wanted to restrict and redefine class conflict to mean only the struggle of trade unionists, a marked retreat from the position he held in the philosophical writings of his youth. This shift in his thought limited his usefulness for my work.

The chapters that follow build on this one. Each begins with an account of the dominant paradigm as it is manifested in the study of the country in question. This initial section serves as the background for the discussion of the political economy and of the historical road. The third section is devoted to the organization of culture and and how the ruling classes attempt persuasion. Each chapter concludes with a section on history writing and historians in the country in question. This section, logically a part of the preceding one, is developed independently to bring together the reproduction of the dominant paradigm with the subject of hegemony in these countries.

The study of Russian history is a fair place to begin this venture. "Semi-European, semi-Asiatic," the very location of the country, not to mention its internal logic, appears to elude traditional expertise, making it a transhistorical phenomenon. What then is the Russian history?

2

"Russian Road"

The Russian and Soviet Experience, 1861–1990

ate nineteenth-century Russian history is usually portrayed in the dominant paradigm in terms of its failure to develop as it did in the Western countries or in terms of its embodiment of Slavophilism; Soviet history is often portrayed in similar terms. While drawing on these well-known approaches, in this chapter and the ones that follow, I adopt a different one. I take up the history of modern Russia and the Soviet Union as an example of a general type of hegemony termed *Russian Road*.[1] In so doing, I overcome some of the problems historians encounter in specialized studies by emphasizing the broad comparability of Russia to other countries. What do such countries share? How do they differ? What sort of roles do they play in world history?

The chapter contains four sections. In the first, I identify the major features of the Russian Road. In the second, I undertake a political economy analysis of Russia and the Soviet Union as Russian Road. In so doing, I divide 1861–1990 into three periods: during the first, 1861–1932, capitalism, spread a weak liberal age regime rose blessed by extensive oil wealth but challenged gradually by the rise of a lower middle class; during the second, 1932–56, corporatism and power sharing formed during the third, 1956-present, a movement back toward liberalism began. In the third section of the chapter, I take up hegemony in terms of the organization of culture for the period 1861–1990. In the fourth, I discuss history writing in Russia and the Soviet Union as a part of the organization of the culture.

The general approach to Russian and Soviet history in contemporary scholarship, as suggested in the last chapter, is driven by the logic of the dominant paradigm. Social historians rooted in Russian peasant studies have begun to challenge the dominant paradigm, widening the historical

23

canvas and imposing new interpretations on the major events from the revolution of 1917, to Stalinism, to World War II.

In this section I codify some of the insights found in this new scholarship to make of them a Russian Road, that is, a distinct modern form of hegemony that stands on its own and for which there are numerous examples, one in which the ruling class disguises class conflict by caste. In the case at hand, the ruling caste, or nomenklatura, the inhabitants of Moscow, Leningrad, the Russian-speaking elites of the nationalities, segments of the ethnic Russian strata overlap with the economically dominant class, the two each in their own way being played off against the rest of the population.

A close study of this dualism reveals not just issues of class, language, and residence but of marriage, of culture, and more broadly of rituals of inclusion and exclusion. Although the idea of dualism conveys well the appearance, the more precise term for a comparative study is *caste*. The outstanding feature of the ruling strategy is that it disguises class conflict and the other crises that came with the spread of capitalism through rule by caste.

In the Russian Road, civil society is not developed. Research shows that the vast majority of the people adopt strategies resembling more those of peasants than those of citizens. Like peasants, they evade the state by paying bribes rather than by trying to influence it from within as citizens do by participating in the dominant institutions.

The Russian Road is further distinguished by the role of a tsar or commissar as unifier of a two-part power structure: a secular bureaucracy, actually in charge, admittedly remote, authoritarian and coercive, and a religious bureaucracy, for example, the Russian Orthodox church, in appearance separate from the state, immediately accessible, merciful, and redemptive.[2] This division of the secular and the religious led by a tsar-type figure survived even the generation in which the Bolsheviki tried to outlaw religion. After the restoration of the church in 1943, the religious leadership has once again been a visible part of hegemony. At times, when the church was oppressed, Bolshevik leaders initiated and participated in popular celebrations in which the two faces of rule became fused to compensate for the fact that one was missing.[3]

Another distinguishing feature of the Russian Road is the pattern of its historical development, a pattern marked by an oscillation between liberal and authoritarian phases. From the mid nineteenth century onward, Russian leaders cautiously pursued capitalist development. In *liberal periods,* or *reform periods,* the political leadership openly encouraged economic development along open market lines and profited from it. Open market capitalism led to class formation, however, and class formation to class conflict. Faced with deepening class conflict, Russian Road ruling classes, doubting their hold on the mass population, abandoned liberalism for autocracy, trading in profit for security. This tendency toward oscillation between liberal and authoritarian periods gives the Russian Road a certain complexity. On the one hand, the long-term political economy phases of liberalism and corporatism are those familiar to countries of all the hegemonies. On the other hand, the more short-term oscillations, which cut through and across the long-term phases are not.

While modern capitalism raised the level of political risk for rulers in all the political systems, the risk, other factors being equal, was greater for rulers in Russian Road regimes than elsewhere. In Russian Road regimes, the working class had an unusual space for maneuvering. It was on the border between outside and inside in terms of caste position, and it had something the state needed, its labor. Revolution in Russian Road regimes is common. Although scholars have argued that the 1917 revolution reflected a special inability of the Romanov dynasty to confront the risks of development, in fact, most Russian Road regimes, for example, China, Iran, Turkey, Nicaragua, and Iraq, have experienced revolutions, whereas fewer regimes in other historical roads have had them. Japan is an exception for a Russian Road regime, because it industrialized without a political revolution, but Japan is not a pure Russian Road regime.

Russian Road systems are also noted for the intensity of their class conflicts. During periods of overt class struggle, Western workers look to the legal system and to a culture shared with their bosses to aid them; Russian Road workers do not. Put another way, class conflict in Russian Road regimes is not blunted. When consensus breaks down, the ruler can be almost isolated from his population. In such a situation, his main hope is that violent repression will quickly end a strike before it can spread. The eighteenth-century Pugachev peasant revolt, the one that got out of hand, haunts the Russian imagination until today.

Russian Road regimes also face problems stemming from the nature of their political culture. How can a dualism be maintained if serfdom is abolished and a growing percentage of the population can make claims against the system?[4] In point of fact, the ruler has no ideological justification for emancipation as a general principle. Thus, to keep the dualism of the Russian Road, emancipation has to be counterbalanced by maintaining a culture of servitude.[5] In Russia until the 1950s, this took the incongruous form of the retention of corvée labor for agriculture and industry.

Oscillation of historical phases in Russian Road regimes helps forestall revolutions; it results, however, in a great turnover or waste of leading personalities, who are forced with each swing of the pendulum into exile or retirement. From Alexander Herzen in the nineteenth century to Lenin, to the recent refugees, political refugees of the Russian Road are notable among political refugees and emigrants of the world for their life-long feeling of political involvement, for their awareness, often quite valid awareness, of not having completed their historic role.

With their small political elites and weak civil societies, Russian Road regimes are more visibly bureaucratic than are the other hegemonies. Political systems that are bureaucratized are generally noted for several specific features. Seen from the perspective of writers in the democracies, these features include pervasive corruption on all levels, a weak professional ethic, a limited development of law, a cult of the ruler, and factional politics. In the Russian case, both the Tsarist and Bolshevik periods offer numerous examples of these attributes, and attracted the attention of reformers. But given the scale of bureaucratization in Russian Road regimes, efforts to reform have often simply perpetuated the problems. For example, quite reasonably, many who have attempted reforms have done so by promoting their reforms in the name of the leader to minimize factionalism. But, regrettably, this has tended to intensify factionalism; the cumulative effect of factional competition has often been more bureaucracy, not less.[6]

Urbanism is another distinguishing feature of Russian Road regimes. Russian Road regimes emphasize the development of one or two major cities, reducing other cities to backwaters that reproduce national culture on a simplified level. In the Russian case, a major city, such as Kiev, is allowed to be a cultural capital for the Ukraine by default; in Iraq, Sulaymaniya and Irbil have underdeveloped university cultures that do not compete with Baghdad and only to a degree reflect their Kurdish context. The major cities are redoubts of the state; the state commonly prevents free internal migration into them and in some cases forcibly repatriates "illegal" immigrants coming from elsewhere in the country.

Russian Road regimes, like others, organize culture and rely on state intellectuals as their voice of persuasion. The challenge for regimes here as elsewhere is how to maintain the dualism. A number of state intellectuals work in the area of language policy. If prose is the vehicle of the bureaucracy or official urban culture and if poetry has the mass appeal, the state can pursue a policy built around this cleavage. Regime patronage and glorification of the great novelists serves to stratify culture in Russia; regime support of poets serves to acknowledge their place in the hearts of Russians. Each, thus, has its place, but its separate place.

The cultural policy of "folklorification" is another common part of maintaining the dualism in Russian Road regimes. The government opens numerous museums to celebrate provincial culture, ethnic culture, and working class culture as folk culture. In another historical road, the same material might serve as a source for the study of social history, but in Russian Road regimes, social history is deliberately limited because it could undermine the dualism by integrating the society. The study of folklore takes the place of social history. Approved history is mainly political history; it treats the state and the official class. A number of the great historians in Russian Road regimes have pursued world history, the field linking their state and its elite culture to the West.

How does the Russian Road approach work when applied to the history of Russia and the Soviet Union?

The Political Economy of Russia and the Soviet Union, 1861–1990

This section shows how the rise of capitalism threatened the political stability, but how gradually by the twentieth century, the threat diminished as access to the political system widened and the state was able to shift the sites of primary industrialization out of the Soviet Union into Eastern Europe and the Third World. A period of industrial peace ensued with capitalists showing their ability to work as state employees within the framework of a socialist rhetoric and workers accepting the social contract offered them. This industrial peace induced the dominant elements to abandon some of their traditional caution and to permit a catastrophically large number of non-Russians to enter the ruling caste. It also encouraged great powerism. By the time liberalism returned in 1956, the ruler would face major political problems.

Modern Russian history began with a liberal phase in a double sense: in the long-term sense of one-class rule dominated by finance capitalism and in the short-term sense of an oscillation to an open-market economy. The short-term phase is remembered for the abolition of feudalism, which occurred in 1861 and symbolized as much as any other the political changes as capitalism began to function on the level of the nation-state.[7]

In 1861, during the reign of Alexander II (1856–1881), the tsar's liberal advisors, among them Nikolay Milyutin, the new minister of the interior, legislated the end of feudalism in land through the Emancipation Act. By this act, the government undertook to compensate the landlords whose land was confiscated and to collect redemption payments from the peasants who received the land. The primary intent was to stimulate local capitalist agriculture and secondarily to give power to the capitalist farmer within the existing framework. Thus, a few years later in 1864, the institution of provincial assemblies *(Zemstvos)* arose. The liberals began to dream of rule by law.

In Russian Road states as elsewhere, liberal ages have fairly predictable dynamics. They generate wealth, but they have no mechanism for its distribution. They thus produce millionaires and paupers. In the Russian Jewish community, where liberalism flourished, fabulous wealth emerged in such families as the Polyakovs, who built railways, the Brodskys, who were sugar kings in southwest Russia, and the Zaitsevs, the Askenazis, and others. At the other end of the spectrum were those impoverished by the accumulation of such wealth, which included many Jews as well as others.

Liberal phases are also well known for movements protesting the injustice in the society, among which in the case of Russia were the Zionists, the anarchists, the Bolsheviki and the Socialists. From the 1860s onward, the radical tradition pondered how the oppressed of Russia could unite to overthrow the tsar. How could caste and class be allied?

Nor was the aforementioned all the opposition. Liberalism had its opponents even from within the system. From then until today, the hierarchy of the Russian Orthodox church opposed liberal reforms. As a result of their opposition, many liberal reforms failed. Ironically, among the groups that suffered the consequences of this failure were the parish clergy; the hierarchy even blocked their clergy from benefiting from the reforms that the society as a whole was enjoying.

During the years 1867–71, parish priests sought the right to a regular salary, but the hierarchy vetoed the idea. Was not the church the one real institution of the Russian people? This left the parish clergy the laughingstock of the peasants from whom they were forced to go on begging for their living.

In this same period, as the cause of womens' rights progressed, a movement of the widows of clergy failed to gain benefits and rights once again as the result of opposition from the hierarchy, leaving women married to the clergy in fear of their husbands' demise. The insecurity of clerical wives remained a problem into the twentieth century. In the liberal new economic policy (NEP) period, wives again pushed for a more secure status, this time coupling their demands with a threat to leave the church for communism.[8]

To return specifically to the 1870s, one finds that liberal policies led to a crisis in the countryside. As the reforms set in motion by the Emancipation Act progressed, many peasants lost their land or became impoverished. The causes for this upheaval were the unrealistic taxes and rent levels that the government had set in expectation of a rise in agricultural productivity.

As the 1870s progressed, evidence of social dislocation caused by economic stress multiplied; there was, for example, a sharp rise in prostitution. Many families were in a state of crisis. In 1873–74, urban radicals, both men and women, began to organize the rural poor. An image of this type of activity, albeit from a slightly later period, appears in Maxim Gorky's famous novel *Mother*. As radicalism spread in the 1870s, the tsarist police began to crack down. In 1881, radicals assassinated Alexander II, and the liberal phase came to an end.

One wonders how crises could build to such proportions. The apparent answer lies in the odd fact that the Russian state was cushioned more than most in the world by immense revenues from oil. Although there were crises on every level, this cushioning always made the state slow to react.

The period 1881–1905 was an autocratic one. Tsar Alexander III (1881–1894) and his successor Tsar Nicholas II (1894–1917) worked to undo the liberal reforms until this became impossible after the revolution of 1905. With their economic policies, they tried to rein in local capitalists while permitting an increase in the role of foreigners and minorities in trade and industry. In politics, the importance of liberal institutions, such as the Zemstvos, fell, and a number of liberal intellectuals who had supported their development went abroad or retired. They were no longer in demand; the tsars now relied on the advice of conservatives. After 1881, the most influential advisors were Konstantin Pobedonostsev (1827–1907), the procurator of the Holy Synod, and Dmitry Tolstoy, the minister of the interior.

From 1881 onward, Alexander III actively sought to channel the discontent of the peasants into religion and anti-Semitism and away from more fundamental political and economic issues. His policies seem to have been so successful, they were reinstated a number of times in later autocratic phases.

Alexander III manifested anti-Semitic tendencies from the outset of his rule. In an almost immediate reaction, Evzel Ginzburg, a prominent banker and a Jew, headed a delegation of Jews, to meet the new tsar and try to conciliate him. The mission failed; Alexander proceeded to pass legislation that discriminated against ownership of land by Jews. Scholars for some time have inferred from this response that the policy of articulating anti-Semitism from above encouraged anti-Semitic practices from below. This policy seemed to be apparent after 1881. Hooligans and even the local police felt free to victimize Jews and liberals. More recent studies of these episodes, however, show other features. The persecution of liberals and Jews by the police had actually preceded the decisive moment in 1881 when the regime officially began to attack liberals, which led to a revised perspective that the police helped prepare the turn to autocracy. As the writings of the historian Roy Medvedev, cited below, and of other contemporary liberals attest, the police as a popular national institution carry on these practices today.

During the reign of Alexander III, with the liberal capitalist culture under wraps, a religiosity and missionary activity surged upward. Suddenly, the hierarchy felt able to pursue its agenda again, for example, to have the state renew its persecution of the old believers and of the Jews, to have the state promote a further Russification of Poland, to secure for itself control over the primary education system, and, finally, to canonize popular religious figures, for example, Anna of Kashinsk.

In this period, the power of the church crystallized in one immensely prestigious intellectual and beloved figure, the theologian, Vladimir Solov'ev (1853–1900), the one figure in modern history whose prestige equaled Lenin's. Like many leading churchmen of Russia, Solov'ev was a pantheist. As a pantheist, his exposition of the traditional Sophia mysticism brought the knowledge of God home to the ordinary Orthodox Russian, renewing in the process the prestige of the church and underscoring its redemptive power.

In Solov'ev's era in Russia, mass visitations and joinings of monasteries and nunneries, and many poor women turning to icon painting seemingly bore out his claim for the appeal of the redemptive nature of Christian life.

Lower-class women seemed to prefer autocracy or the church to the liberal establishment. Given the inability of the church and later of the party to protect them, however, the record inevitably shows instances of disillusionment and political withdrawal as well. Thus one finds that in the Cultural Revolution, an autocratic period for which information is also abundant, women, presumably many of them poor women, became important at the local level of the party and of the youth movements and then later they withdrew.

The reasons for this politicization seem clear. These women stood to gain something or gain something back. With the coming of the Cultural Revolution, divorce laws reverted to what they had been under Tsar Alexander III, the period under discussion. After 1928, in other words, divorce became less casual. Casual divorce had hurt poor women, they had fought it through the system a number of times, and they had won, in the process inadvertently hurting the urban career woman, who had gained freedom from the more liberal personal status laws of liberal periods such as the NEP.[9] By contrast, during the liberal periods of the nineteenth century, in the NEP and in the recent years of detente, lower-class female membership in governmental organizations dropped. Membership was not in their interest.

It is, perhaps, useful to underscore the point that neither the church nor the tsar could shield the lower classes from the harsh realities of capitalism. Having put the lid on class struggle to a degree, autocracy had performed its role. Liberal profiteering was once again an attractive albeit increasingly risky option. The year 1905 marked a swing to liberalism; it was also a year of violent revolution. As early as 1900, reformers had noted that the peasant was expected to produce more, while having less to say in the matter. Such, however, was a part of the logic of autocracy. Fearing the power of the peasant communes, Tsar Alexander had imposed on top of them a land chief, a figure drawn from the ranks of the local nobility. In doing this, the central state permitted the two fundamental contradictory orientations, the feudalism of the nobility and the capitalism of the rich peasants to surface and to collide with each other. In a fully industrialized country, this might have been unimportant, but Russia in 1905 was still an agricultural country. Even its urban workers still had their roots in the peasantry. It is not surprising that the revolution of 1905 stirred by the crises from above and from below was very radical, that it, in fact, threatened the system.[10]

From 1905, liberalism reasserted itself until 1917. This was the era of parliamentarianism, the heyday of the Duma. In 1905, middle-class privileges were restored. Women once again could attend the local universities, and the wealthy no longer had to send their daughters to Switzerland.[11] But liberalism even in this its heyday experienced its share of setbacks as well, for example, the defeat in the Russo-Japanese War in 1904–5, then the dislocations and setbacks caused by the World War I.

The major liberal economic reforms, the Stolypin Reforms of 1906, once again tried to deepen capitalism in the countryside by strengthening property relationships. Specific provisions sought to overcome the heritage of the commune. These failed as did efforts to stratify further the family by vesting ownership in the head of household. In any case, open market capitalism as in the past wreaked its havoc, paving the way for the next swing to autocracy, which came in the revolution of 1917.

The period 1917–1922, actually three separate periods (the revolution of 1917, war communism/worker's Left, and the transition to NEP) together comprised a swing of the pendulum from liberalism to autocracy. The Bolsheviki came to power replacing the monarchy and the aristocracy. The Bolsheviki came to power as the vanguard of the proletariat. But very soon they found that they could not sustain this image. The Russian working class was far more radical than anything Marx had written about or that they had previously encountered. Thus, on coming to power, they felt they had no other choice than to suppress the working class.

The Bolsheviki had tried to generate their support among the more conservative skilled workers of Moscow and Leningrad, but in 1917, the great majority of the Russian working class was not made up of skilled workers or of conservatives; they still had roots in the countryside and the church and espoused a wide range of radical concerns. In addition, they were not searching for some new leadership; they had long had their own politics and alliances.

Thus from 1917, the party came to represent in embryo the ruling caste to which the working class was an outsider. Lenin alone among the Bolshevik leaders appeared to understand the great tragedy of the party's position. The end of the dream of revolution came under the pressures of war communism; by 1921, the victorious Bolsheviki were confronting both workers and peasants in the manner of previous autocratic phases. Liberalism was soon to reappear.

Before pursuing an account of Soviet liberalism, one must confront one last issue. What kind of interpretation of the Russian Revolution is congruent with a Russian Road form of political economy? Should one stress the continuity of Russian history or the discontinuity? It seems clear that this was a revolution, if not in the sense that Marx envisaged and not in the sense of overturning the Russian Road, then in a more general sense.

For thousands of years, feudalists and capitalists ruled over the masses.

With the bourgeois revolutions, such as those of 1776 and 1798, the middle classes proclaimed the end of history, the "deserving" individual could make it out of the trenches at least in a democracy. The Russian Revolution marked another step forward in human emancipation. It brought a segment of the working class into power and drove out segments of the old ruling class. Whatever its flaws and whatever the failings of its leadership and for however limited a period it survived, it was the first such event. It showed that the rule of property was not eternal, that even bourgeois ruling classes and power structures can be brought down, that, therefore, there was hope that someday there would be freedom for the many and not just for the few who were fortunate in the framework of the democratic systems. It was in this sense that the Russian Revolution shook the world.

From 1922 to 1928, the USSR experienced a swing from autocracy to liberalism, a strange mixture of socialism and liberalism called the new economic policy (NEP). This period was rife with contradictions. It found the Bolsheviki isolated internationally, preoccupied with raising agricultural productivity through capitalist means, and unable to coerce the peasants to bring their food to the market even through capitalism. At best, NEP was a temporary solution; it reached a crisis in the late 1920s. Peasant resistance to state demands induced Stalin and much of the leadership to believe that Kulaks were hoarding or otherwise sabotaging the agricultural production, a belief that appears in retrospect to have been exaggerated. Whatever the case may have been in fact, at this point, the party decided to act. It chose to collectivize agriculture and to push ahead with industrialization at all cost.

The Cultural Revolution (1928–32) is a complex period in Soviet history. It marks a short-turn swing to autocracy, but of a new sort, a much more frenetic sort. It marks as well a new, more long-term change, termed *corporatism,* a change marked by the entrance of the lower middle class into the political arena, an event known generally in historical scholarship as the rise of the New Class. One way to view 1928–32 would be as the last traditional autocratic phase. It was equally the genesis of the contemporary society, a mutation in the Russian Road in which the swing of the pendulum slows and widens, becoming a spiral, which until 1956 was more authoritarian, since 1956 more liberal. The key to understanding these mutations that lead up to corporatism and to the expansion of the political system is bound up with the progress of Soviet industrialization. Industrialization promotes a new class formation; it forces open the political system. If the liberal age ruling class was a small, fairly self-contained group of rentiers, the corporatist ruling class was much larger and less coherent, more spread out across the Soviet Union, a country that was a great power on the rise.

Excursus on Greatpowerism

The Soviet example also exhibits from this point yet another feature of the modern system of hegemonies—greatpowerism. The dynamics sustaining Soviet greatpowerism from the end of the Cultural Revolution to the thaw of the Brezhnev years were those of class collusionism between the ruling class and the working class, a situation that afforded the Soviet nomenklatura an unusual degree of freedom to pursue its interests. As long as the working class was included in the rising standards of living, there would be no challenges. During this period, capitalists were able to reorganize the workplace and update their technology almost at will. Politicians were able to engage in adventurism in foreign policy. In addition, greatpowerism permitted the state much more secrecy in its dealings, opening the door to dealings even with organized crime, what in the United States is now called "deep politics." Greatpowerism began to wane in the period called the Thaw. In this period, the Soviet working class began to withdraw from its collusion, sensing that job flight to the South, to Eastern Europe, and to the Third World combined with the possibilities of automation was weakening its position. The Thaw, a set of compromises with the West, followed.

Greatpowerism, as I show in the following chapters, is an anomaly, one generally characterized by expansionism, militarism, and by a striving for technological preeminence. Great powers frequently are destabilizing forces in the world. They tend to be jealous of their positions and quick to perceive other powers as rivals, a fact that may explain why they are prepared to engage in wars, as Germany and Iraq did, even against numerous enemies at the same time.

Not all great powers arise out of Russian Road hegemonies, but several did. Japan, China, and Iraq can serve as examples. As in the Soviet case, the rise of corporatism as a phase in the history of these countries quickly led to greatpowerism. Of course, not all great powers arose out of corporatist phases, and certainly not all countries that arrive at the corporatist phase begin on a trajectory toward greatpowerism. Most do not.

The United Kingdom and Germany are two examples of great powers that arose in liberal as opposed to corporatist phases.

In the United Kingdom, from the late Victorian period, the working class was an increasingly reliable ally of the state, and this was a time many years before the coming of corporatism. What is most apparent is that the era of great powerism coincided with the peak years of empire and not with the years of corporatism, a phase that lasted somewhat beyond. The breakdown of both greatpowerism and empire took place during World War II by which point the working class sensed that while its wealth was growing, its power was slipping. There was no future for it in greatpow-erism or in empires. Jobs were going abroad, colonial immigrants were coming in; the state was not blocking immigration or erecting tariffs or rebuilding industry.

In Germany, the first signs of greatpowerism came with Bismarck. He appealed successfully to his working class, offering it the welfare state in return for political and economic loyalty. And this he received, at least, from them. Germany, however, was not a democracy at this point, it was Italian Road, the South was a peasantry and a cheap labor market. The working class was a minority of the work force and largely located in the North. The southern peasantry did not respond to Bismarck, which left Bismarck on the sidelines of the greatpower struggles of his day. Germany became a serious participant only in the late Weimar and Hitler years. By this later date, the hegemony of Germany had changed: South Germans had become citizens; the country had become a bourgeois democracy as southern citizens like northern citizens were drawn to the state.

But why consider these countries, and not others? Are only the democ-racies and Russian Road regimes likely to produce greatpowers, and if so, is that impression based on a technological determinist view of the term *greatpower?* Is the claim that Bismarck lacked the equivalent of an atom bomb? Clearly, the capacity to produce advanced weaponry is a form of power. Still, if democracies and Russian Road regimes are likely to produce great powers, most have not done so. The information at one's disposal casts some doubt on the linkage of technology and type of hegemony or type of hegemony and the phenomenon of greatpowerism.

Obviously, there are instances of greatpowerism in the other hegemo-nies. Has not, for example, the Italian Road produced examples such as Mussolini's Italy, or Nasir's Egypt, or Nehru's India, not to mention exam-ples of tribal-ethnic states, such as Kim Il Sung's North Korea or Ho Chi Minh's North Vietnam. Here are countries strong enough to trigger the hostility of the other existing superpowers. Recall the Vietnam War.

Finally, is it useful to consider that greatpowerism is a fixed attribute of a given phase, or is it more a matter of ebb and flow? In the United States, the first wave of great powerism came in the late nineteenth and early twentieth centuries. It produced very self-assured rulers such as Mc-Kinley and Theodore Roosevelt. There was a lull as the Eastern political elite suffered an isolationist backlash. Later, from the 1930s to the 1970s, greatpowerism resumed, first rising and then declining. But it was never easy going. The collusionary relationship between workers and the state was never as developed in the United States as it was in some of the other great powers. Workers were not racist enough or loyal enough for capitalists to trust them. Finally, as the working class grew restless during the Vietnam War, the facade began to give way. Recall the endless "cold wars," "red scares," "wars against crime," and Vietnam War Syndrome, which will not go away.

To sum up the prevailing conceptualization of great powerism remains undeveloped given the needs of political economy and of social history, and-this accounts for this rather lengthy excursus. Clearly collusion, the factor emphasized here, must be further studied. Collusion does not imply conspiracy nor consensus; it is rather closer to class conflict and should be studied in that light. When collusion no longer benefits the working classes, they tend to abandon it, bringing greatpowerism to an end.

Although during the Cultural Revolution rapid political and economic changes and unprecedented violence no doubt occurred, a fundamental break in the hegemony did not occur because the dominant elements were prepared to make the necessary concessions to allow more people into the New Class, the new base of the ruling class. As the industrial revolution grew stronger and the New Class solidified its position, the state put a lid on the violence. The Cultural Revolution came to an end; a new autocratic phase had jelled.

From this period, the regime had for the first time both an incentive and a capacity to deflect class contradictions away from its core lands onto more remote regions, for example, Central Asia and Eastern Europe. The working class and lower middle class accepted these policies, and this was, of course, crucial. Corporatism means power sharing. The factory worker of 1932 was no longer the same factory worker as in 1905. He had enough of a veto that the power structure had to listen to him and listen they did. In fact, by the 1950s, the government was conducting regular opinion polls; by the 1980s, public opinion was forcing change.[12]

The Soviet countryside was also an important part of the transition to corporatism, albeit its role was different than that of the city. One of the priorities of the Cultural Revolution was the collectivization of agriculture. Not only would this give the state control over agricultural production, which it wanted, but it would break the relationship of the Russian working class to its rural roots. It would proletarianize workers, making them more dependent on the wage and, one hoped, then less radical.

To achieve this proletarianization and pacification, the Soviet state was prepared not only to favor industry but to countenance a growing number of exemplary workers entering the New Class. Evidence suggests that as the resistance to the state's agricultural policy rose in the countryside, the state made more and more concessions to the industrial workforce, using where possible corvée labor to spare it, hoping thereby to keep it as an ally.

What stands out then is the amount of opposition that corporatism and collectivism engendered in the countryside. In the face of collectivization, the peasants continuously resisted, clinging tenaciously to their private plots and to whatever livestock they could. When the government demanded livestock for the collectives, the peasants as a last measure slaughtered their animals to prevent that from happening. A study conducted by the government in 1938 revealed that although private plots ammounted to only 3.9 percent of land in cultivation, they produced 45 percent of the output and were, as a result, the mainstay of the Russian family. A common perception in the countryside was that families not in the cooperatives tended to be better off than those in them. A gender aspect emerged in rumors that peasant women did not want to go to the collectives because there was free love. A recent study indicates that overall party membership fell in the countryside precipitously between 1927 and 1939.[13]

Despite or, as I am also suggesting, because of the resistance in the agrarian sector, industrialization proceeded rapidly. Corvée labor clearly played a role in this rapid development. Here the interests of the rulers and the working class seemed to converge. First, corvée labor disposed of critics such as Ukrainians, Poles, and even prisoners of war. Second, corvée labor accomplished the most difficult of the industrial work. Third, corvée labor was also somehow acceptable to the Russian working class. This is, of course, an extrapolation from the fact that the workers did not fight it. To the extent that the working class would fight in this period, it would be over the methods of decision making that affected production norms, the use of disciplinary measures, and the control of media by management, but it would not be over corvée.[14]

In the 1930s as well, small but important groups of workers, mainly men employed in heavy industry, challenged the daily production rates, insisting that the rates were artificially low. These small groups were the Stakhanovites. The Stakhanovites appear as workers on the rise. Praised by the hierarchy in Moscow and cursed by the local managers and more lumpen ordinary workers, their rise betokens a part of the reformulation of the social structure termed the rise of the New Class.[15]

Finally, however, one should note that the growth of the working class, the growth of the New Class, or even the growth of cities all represent in their way challenges for a Rusian Road regime. New loyalties arose; they had to be controlled.

In the period 1926–39, the Soviet Union's urban population rose from 18 percent to 24 percent of the whole population. In approximately the same period, the university student population rose from 169,000 to 812,000.[16] These are examples of gains of the working class or of the inability of the state to hold the line. As this growth continued, consumer demands rose; gradually, once again, autocracy began to unravel.

In the 1930s to 1940s, however, with its working class bought off, the Soviet Union was playing an important role in international affairs. Much scholarly commentary would claim this was the heyday of Soviet greatpowerism.

After World War II, the Soviet Union continued to have the power to deflect its problems onto Eastern Europe, using it as a shield against the West, as a region to plunder for industrial spare parts, as a source of skilled labor, and as a captive market for its own products. Between 1945 and 1953, the Soviet Union imposed a *command economy* onto these countries, and they shone in "a reflected light." After 1956, de-Stalinization brought a repudiation of the excesses of this process but no real break with the pattern.[17]

Throughout the whole period 1928–56, regional issues were a source of strain for the hegemony. A price had to be paid for the deflection of class conflicts from the heartlands to the peripheries.[18]

In political terms, the price paid was that the ruling class became less unified. There was not just ethnic differentiation somewhat related to the growth of the system outside of ethnic Russia, but a youth crisis. Youth, especially urban youth, the beneficiaries of the Revolution, could not be motivated to make the sacrifices their parents had. Why should they?

After 1956, the spiral shifted in the direction of liberalism. Splits within the leadership and alienation of the working class were its cause. As a consequence, the Russian capitalist class no longer wanted to share power. More profits were to be made through venture capitalism, and this was more important to them than was maintaining the country's international position or the heritage of the Revolution.

In fact, with neoliberalism in the ascendant, a really considerable repudiation of the past took place. In the Twentieth Party Congress of 1956, Stalin was accused of crimes. This event was unprecedented in Russian and Soviet history.

After 1956, as in earlier liberal periods, middle-class women benefited. Feminism became important; women were identified as important participants in the underground economy, the civil rights movements, the movements of the New Right, the ecology protest, and the protests for new improved consumer goods.[19]

By the 1970s, the international finance economy began to accelerate the impact of neoliberalism in the Soviet Union. Marginal members of the New Class, frustrated by their inability to control Moscow's decision making, could turn to international banks and businesses or to other outside interests. Southerners did this, turning to Muslim countries; ethnic Russians did this, one suspects, to gain the support needed for some future project of recentralization of the union on terms more favorable to themselves. In the short term, the unity of the country and the preservation of its ideology was abandoned. Still, there is little sense that the Soviets have left the Russian Road. Neoliberalism here as in the other countries studied in this book appears to be laying the seeds of its own early demise by fostering chaos and, thus, opening the door to a return of corporatism without bringing any real change. In the Soviet Union as in many other countries, the group that stands to benefit from the breakdown of a productive economy, today as in the past, is the religious right.

What then of counterhegemony? Why has it failed? In the nineteenth century, the radicalism of the Russian working class had few equals; peasant struggles were important as well. By the 1950s, the terrain of counterhegemony had shifted, but it did not result in the kinds of new alliances that the working class would need to confront the system. For one thing, the working class was somewhat a part of the system. Many workers, as a result, probably failed to see their class interests in political terms. They could not, for example, see their interests in allying themselves to youth. The youth in question were middle class. Their revolt was a revolt against the future, not the present. Nor could workers see their interests in allying themselves to the ethnic national communities. Shared oppression was overshadowed by the pride felt by the ethnic Russian worker in his mastery of the Russian language. Russian was, after all, the language of progress and development. A similar blindness is evident in the relation of the worker to the church. In light of all these divisions, one is driven to take yet another look at the state and examine the way in which it has organized culture and persuasion. It is not an accident that the progressive trends are so fragmented.

The Organization of Culture in Russia and the Soviet Union

Hegemony in Russia as in all countries involves coercion and persuasion. Older works of scholarship on Russia and the Soviet Union appear to acknowledge this but mainly emphasize the mechanisms of coercion, underestimating not only the role of persuasion but underestimating as well how problematic it is to assume that an army or a police force, and these are the two examples always raised, must be by the definition of their function the major vehicle through which coercion is exercised by the ruling class.

In Russia and today in the Soviet Union, the regimes have all perpetuated the old Russian tradition of domination based on caste; in this arrangement, Moscow and Leningrad are the center of an elite culture and the rest of the society is a periphery to it.[20] In this section I explore the problems of organizing culture, in the first part emphasizing the state's efforts to organize mass culture, efforts that developed appreciably in the twentieth century, and in the second part emphasizing the state's attempts to organize ruling caste culture, attempts that extend far back into the nineteenth century.

The issues considered here are thus of two sorts: those surrounding the control of the modern mass society involve, for example, the organization of sports, the promotion of literacy, the promotion of a prose culture as the national culture, and coping with the problem of the popularity of poets and musicians; by way of contrast, the issues in the second part involve the state's policies promoting bilingualism, the state's use of folklore studies, archeology, ethnography, and natural science. The section concludes with a discussion of the role of Stalin and of the church in spanning the two.

In the late nineteenth and early twentieth centuries, the picture of the countryside that comes to us from novels such as Gorky's *Mother* conveys a picture of the great gap between the secular state and its policies and the lives of the ordinary people. No doubt where liberal reforms brought schools, this picture was modified; no doubt on certain estates the nobility organized culture; no doubt the royal family was visible to some peasants as they made their way around the country, but throughout most of the country most of the time, the role of the state as police, tax collectors, and army introduced a contrastive note in the lives of people in otherwise fairly self-sufficient towns and villages.

As Gorky and, subsequently, social historians have made clear, the state sought to maintain this status quo. This was the least expensive way to maintain its dualism. It was others who were dissatisfied with what amounted to a stasis and tried to overcome it. From the nineteenth century onward, urban reformers went in small groups to the countryside to educate the peasants politically, to find out what was going on, and to side with them on their issues. It is hard to be sure what weight to give these acts, what weight to give the Russian Revolution, what weight to give the many years of open-market capitalism before the revolution and in the NEP period in terms of the state's gradually deepening involvement in the organization of rural mass culture. The Cultural Revolution of 1928 is chosen here because from that point what was implicit became explicit, what was an unneeded population became a rural and a potential future urban work force, its culture organized, its mobility controlled.

In nineteenth-century Russia, caste privilege came through aristocratic birth and high social status in commerce. A few commoners could rise through the church. After the revolution, caste privilege was open to those who could rise in the party, the church being put under wraps. After the NEP period, a number of people from provincial backgrounds sought to climb the party hierarchy into the New Class through the secret police. If one was a successful informer one could rise. If huge numbers of people tried to be informers, however, destabilization could follow. One could also rise by challenging production norms and getting promoted into the managerial class. As this took place on a growing-scale, it, too, led to chaos.

A brief aside about the police and the army and about coercion more generally might be in order here, given the revisionism implied in these lines. The army and the police are the official coercive apparatus. Whether the officially coercive is the really coercive is a point that needs to be explored as what coerces one class may not coerce another. In the Russian case, in any event, the secret police was an important instrument of the Tsar and then later of the Communist Party. To be efficiently coercive, common sense has it that such organizations must be highly efficient and this means—another assumption—they are highly centralized. Of course, any large organization, such as the army or the police, is likely to have important internal divisions and this appears to be the case here. The secondary literature on the army and the police notes these divisions.

In fact, it seems that since the nineteenth century, a conflict has existed within the circles of the leadership of the army between appointees of the state and military professionals, favorites of the Tsar, or the party versus officers. The police, especially the secret police, were also deeply divided, although along different lines. In the secret police, the demand for total loyalty was often sufficient to outweigh the claims of professionalism. This produced cliques. Another equally divisive tendency was opportunism. Many policemen were simply out for themselves. The more powerful the secret police became in the Stalinist period, the more opportunistic its members.

The high points of influence of the secret police forces were the autocratic periods from the tsarist period onward. For the NKVD, it was the Cultural Revolution and the ensuing years of the purges through the mid-1930s. In this period, many of its officers used their influence to work their way into the New Class. Some did so by marrying into middle-class families.

An example of a prototypical figure, one who rose through the NKVD, was Karl Pauker. Pauker became Stalin's right-hand man, the man who organized his bodyguard. In the 1930s, it was rumored that Pauker could buy and sell death sentences; for many others, responsibility for the organization of the forced labor camps opened the door as well to personal advancement. Of course, the career had its risks. Even the secret police did not escape unscathed from the Great Purges of 1936–39. Numerous established members of the police lost their lives when unknown junior officers from provincial backgrounds rose as their accusers.[21] With the resurgence of liberalism, professionalism and rule by law slowed the attempt of police and military officers to jump into the ruling caste in this way. The death of the notorious Beria in the early 1950s was a turning point.

The question suggested above, however, was what sort of impact did the secret police and the army have on the masses of Russian or Soviet people and on hegemony? Although the police and the army appear to have intimidated the middle classes and segments of the privileged caste, they appeared to be less intimidating to the masses. From the perspective of defending the regime against threats, this was not necessarily too useful, as the major fear of the state was that of its mass population.

A piece of evidence that tends to support this class perspective is that the lower classes held the police and the army in high esteem. Recall that a very large number of ordinary people, especially in Russian Road regimes, volunteered to serve as informers and took pride in giving tips to the regular police; whom they knew.[22] This is not to doubt the role of coercion but to suggest that if one follows the prevailing scholarship, its real locus of effectiveness was limited to the upper half of the social order; for the lower classes, the police were in effect also persuaders.

Coercion for the lower classes, however, is no doubt greater than it is for the middle classes. This "real" coercion is the impact of daily life on the poor under capitalism. It is the political economy. If, thus, one wants to identify the range of agents of coercion that served the hegemony in Russia and the Soviet Union, one might do well to add to the list other types of government employees as well, for example, teachers, social workers, agricultural extension agents, functionaries who, for the middle class, would be simply persuaders. It was they as much as anyone who drove home the necessity for the poor to behave in one way and not in another.

Persuasion, although not thought in a common sense way to be a part of the study of Russia, is thus crucial. This is the case whether the government can claim credit for it or whether it arises from the perpetuation of local customs and traditions, which the government made use of.

In the nineteenth century, one area of important government involvement in the organization of culture in the sense of persuasion, was in sports. Through the organization of sports, the state promoted the idea of the hero and the spectator and promoted as well the virtues of competitiveness.

In liberal periods, the tsarist governments promoted sports aimed at the middle classes; after 1922, the Bolsheviki encouraged hygienist movements in the NEP Period. In autocratic periods, the state placed a heavy emphasis on the militarization of sports. With the mutation brought about by the rise of the New Class, sports policies also changed as sports were introduced into the nationalities. As one would expect, the nationalities tended at first to resist activities organized by Moscow. Gradually, however, the appeal of organized sports increased, especially following their incorporation in the workplace. Thus, the regime succeeded in inculcating new social attitudes. In more recent times, the Soviets sought world supremacy in sport.[23] The political and hence hegemonic dimension of sports policy seems quite clear. The high achievement on the part of so many women suggests a gender dimension as well.

In language policy, Russian and Soviet regimes have used prose as the basis of their elite culture, relegating much of poetry to the domain of folk culture. This has not been one of their more efficient strategies. Many poets are popular across class and caste lines, and as more and more schools opened in the countryside, the knowledge of prose became more and more widespread. To compensate for the weaknesses in their chosen strategy, Russian and later Soviet regimes have alternately courted and persecuted famous poets. Anna Akhmatova, Alexsandr Blok, and more recently Andrei Vosnesensky and Evtushenko, were all popular poets and they all suffered some persecution as their careers threatened the maintenance of dualism.

Russian and Soviet regimes began to encourage a particular kind of prose literacy. For example, from the period of the rise of the New Class, the regime sought to socialize the population through the social realist novel. To do this, the state sponsored contests and awarded prizes. The author of the typical Stalinist novel was thereby encouraged to depart from the form of the classical novel, to place his or her story in an ordinary context, such as a farm or factory, and to depict life without too much specificity, creating, in effect, a universal story of ordinary man and distant Moscow. The sacralization of Moscow meant that few stories after the 1930s were situated in Moscow, even if the cultural ideal, as one could infer from other sources, had clearly become an urban one.[24]

For those concerned with the issue of national language policy, the problem became one of how far could the New Class go toward creating prose as a universal cultural medium without threatening the policy of cultural dualism?

The availability to the Soviets of the new mass media also affected their approach to language policy and to cultural policy more generally. With the advent of the media, the Soviet government, like many others, turned from poets to singers. Singers, it was thought, could be controlled more easily and would be just as popular with the mass audience. Indeed, singers quickly gained popularity at the expense of poets. When the old poetry was recited, it required the involvement of the audience; popular music, on the other hand, was more consumerist. The changing nature of the audience from participant to consumer appears to warrant the common perception that with the death of Anna Akhmatova in 1966, the great age of Russian poetry had passed.[25]

Was the cause of the hegemony really advanced by such policies toward poetry? It is not clear to scholars and it was not clear to the Soviet government either. It would appear that recent regimes are still of two minds about poetry. The complexity and therefore the limited accessibility for the masses to the great poet, especially the art poet, served one set of needs, but this had to be balanced against the possible ill effects of the listener being exposed to what the poet was saying. Here one might choose to recall the propensity for criticism, if not for nihilistic anarchism, of Russian poets, a propensity that perhaps would be accepted in a tribal-ethnic state but certainly not in a Russian Road one. Was it not the case that in the 1920s and 1930s, Trotsky and Zhadanov criticized feminist and anarchist strands in the poetry of Alexandra Kollantai, and a generation later, critics found the unrepentant individualism and religious mystical anarchism of Akhmatova difficult? From all this emerged the rationale, initially at least, for the attraction of the state to promoting popular music.[26]

Popular music, especially guitar music, however, has also been difficult for the state to control. Learning to play the guitar is too easy; too many people know the Russian language. Not surprisingly, popular music is becoming a vehicle of mass expression. Much of its sentiment is anarchist; since the 1950s popular musicians have been supporting a new type of "mass poetry." More recently, guitar players have been drawing from the nihilistic Western rock music. Russia, however, is not the United States. Whereas in the states rock music is regulated but encouraged as business unless it introduces racial themes, in the Soviet Union the state draws the line more broadly, as what is a threat to caste maintenance is not so clear. Rock music, in any case, is coming to be perceived more and more as a threat. Rock music and in fact any guitar music could serve as an integrative language for counterhegemonic movements. Thus musicians are now facing the kind of scrutiny and persecution that once was reserved for poets. Guitar players, such as Bulat Okudzhava, (b. 1924), Aleksandr Galich (1919–77), and Vladimir Vysotsky (1938–80), the nongovernmental "tolerated amateurs," have achieved heights of popularity, according to one writer, not achieved by the leading traditional literary figures, for example, Yevtushenko and Solzhenitsyn.

A few years ago, before the age of the mass media and mass literacy in Russia, art music, such as the operas of the "Russian Five," served the elite; popular music was local.[27] Today popular music is driving the national culture. The strategies to organize mass culture are not all working very well. Let us examine the strategies used to organize the culture of the privileged caste.

In turning now to consider this aspect of the subject, one finds a complex set of projects designed to separate the dominant caste and its concerns from those of the society at large. These projects ranged from matters of language to those of science.

A major feature of Russian and then Soviet cultural policy was the promotion of bilingualism. This meant, for the elite, the knowledge of Russian, especially the dialect spoken in Moscow, and for the rest of the Society, a more colloquial form of Russian. In the twentieth century, however, more people read; journalism became important. To be understood, journalists had to include colloquialisms; this, in turn led to the creation of a wider and wider *colloquial standard* a language pushing aside any other second language.[28] How much colloquial could the state allow to be included? Where does the function of language as a communication device conflict with its role in maintaining cultural dualism? The question keeps coming back.

And it is a difficult one. One can see how it was approached by noting differences in language policy between the liberal and autocratic phases. In the liberal phases, the Russian language rapidly acquired foreign loan words. In the autocratic periods, the rulers pursued Russification more aggressively, not only by diminishing the use of loan words but by increasing the use of classical Russian as opposed to colloquial Russian among the nationalities. In the period 1946–55, the Struggle Against Cosmopolitanism was a well-known campaign to limit word borrowing from the West. Word borrowing by Russians from other languages of the USSR has always been limited in any case. One of the rare categories of terms that Russians have borrowed from the languages of the nationalities deals with criminals. The influence of Russian on other national languages, however, has been considerable, as one would expect.

A policy of cultural dualism begins with language forms; it ultimately must have a specific content as well. The state must be able to portray itself as the embodiment of the high culture and to portray the masses through folk culture, that is, to "folklorify" them. Not surprisingly, for all Russian and Soviet regimes, the study of folklore and the development of folklore museums have been important projects for the elite. Russian and Soviet regimes, however, have faced various pressures when carrying out their policies. Dominant groups have usually wanted their regions to be prominently represented irrespective of other considerations. It was only with the rise of the New Class that "rational," if overly centralized, policies for fields such as folklore and archeology were enacted.

In the nineteenth century, Russian scholars concentrated on the folklore of the South, emphasizing its exotic quality. During the years after Bolshevik Revolution, the emphasis became "popular culture," specifically that of the politically important regions of Old Russia, Belorussia, and the Ukraine.

During the same period, the emphasis in the related field of archeology was also on the South; among issues that interested scholars was the possible link between Russian, Hellenistic, and Scythian civilizations. In the twentieth century, archeology, like folklore studies, moved North; the new concern was to unearth the antecedents of the modern Russian state.

The gradual movement to the North in these fields is reflected as well in the scholarly institutions and journals. In 1867, Tsar Alexander II sanctioned the publication of an ethnographic journal by the Imperial Geographical Society to cover all of Russia. Later, in 1883, Alexander III opened a historical museum in Moscow dedicated to the artifacts of the Russian upper classes. In the 1890s, exhibitions, new professional organizations and, even a new museum in Petrograd (Leningrad) came into existence to study the life of the Russian upper classes. In 1917, the Bolsheviki enlarged this museum so that it would contain forty-seven halls depicting the history of the Russian people.

With the rise of the New Class during the Stalinist period, a trend toward centralized institutions developed. Examples of centralized institutions from this period include the Central Museum of Nationality Studies in Moscow, founded by the early Bolsheviks but reorganized in the 1930s, the Museum of the Peoples of the USSR, the State Museum of the Ethnography of the Peoples of the Soviet Union in Leningrad, and the Scientific Research Institute for the Methodology of Regional Studies, organized to replace the Central Bureau for Regional Studies founded in 1920, to oversee the work of the local museums.

By the 1960s, with liberalization progressing and with nationality questions requiring more and more concessions, the urge to control local cultural representations from the center slackened. Popular open-air museums began to flourish around the country.[29]

In science, another area of concern since the nineteenth century, the state has had a distinct policy as well. In the liberal phases of the nineteenth century, the Imperial Academy of Sciences turned to the contemporary international trend of pure science. With the coming of the more inward-turning and autocratic phase of Alexander III, the government criticized the director of the academy for allowing foreigners to dominate it and for failing to serve the nation. Leadership of the academy fell to the minister of the interior. In summarizing the history of the academy and of Russian science before the Revolution, a recent writer suggested that through its shifting policies the regime tried to resolve its own conflicts among its objectives. It needed science, but it did not want to be controlled from abroad. Basic research was increasingly carried out in smaller institutes tied closely to the new industrial centers, and the academy permitted itself to become the symbolic center of science.[30] Science remained elite culture.

In the period after the Revolution, the Academy of Sciences of the USSR (1917–1925) carried on developments in probability theory and in other areas of mathematics that received international recognition but that were at odds with dialectical materialism as it was coming to be understood. A collision course was set. The early Bolsheviki, as if in the footsteps of Alexander III, increasingly sought to define a national science policy and to impose their methodology on it as well. They sponsored conferences to illustrate the link between scientists and other workers who faced common problems. During NEP, the level of conflict abated. The government recognized the Academy of Science's function and M. N. Pokrovsky, the president of the Communist Academy, stressed how the Russian Academy of Sciences had a function complementary to that of his own academy.

When the Cultural Revolution began, A. M. Deborin, the leading advocate of dialectical thought, called for a "Soviet science" freed from mechanism. By 1929, the academy had become a target for the Deborinites. The academy did not have a single member who was both a scientist and a dialectical materialist, and, furthermore, by 1929, scientific work was carried on in a large number of institutions. An attack on the academy could, thus, be an assault on a symbol without jeopardizing required work or Russia's standing in world scientific culture. In 1929, Deborin's influence resulted in the formation of party-related groups composed of New Class technical workers, especially workers from the All-Union Association of Workers in Science and Technology for Cooperation in Socialist Construction (VARNITSO). These party-related groups launched a smear campaign that led to a purge of academy officials.[31]

In the twentieth century, Stalin as much as anyone embodied this organization of culture. If one examines the logical structure of Stalin's writing, one finds a functional if "illogical" positivist Marxism. Language, he claimed, was neither base nor superstructure; language was, therefore, outside of the dialectic.[32] Language could be organized as science could be organized.

Positivism seemed to grow in popularity with the rise of the Soviet Union. Stalin gained great popularity by attacking the excesses of the Cultural Revolution in the name of positivist values. The voodoo of dialectical materialism and romantic metaphysics was interfering with engineering and slowing down industrialization. Socialism, Stalin insisted, could develop scientifically and in one country (through positivism and not through metaphysical philosophy). While Stalin's faith in engineering and his generally pragmatic line of thought struck a deep chord, ever mindful of the possible weakness of the hegemony, he also chose on occasion to legitimate his policies through romanticism, for example, through the cult of the personality and through appeals to tradition.

The attempt of Stalin and the New Class to create an elite culture based on science and tradition ultimately gave the Orthodox church its chance to seize back its traditional role of preserver of worldviews and most particularly of romanticism. How did the Church exploit its opportunities in modern times? How, in other words, did its struggle return to it its role in the organization of hegemony?[33]

To begin this discussion, one must recall that hegemonies are not comprised of just a secular hierarchy but of a religous one as well. This appears to be the case in all the hegemonies even at times when the church is proscribed. In Russia, the weakness of the elite secular culture in the late nineteenth century and the power of the church in relation to the people made it a dangerous rival for the secularists.

With the 1917 revolution, the Bolsheviki tried to push the church underground.[34] But it was too powerful; by 1943, it was Stalin who was asking the church for help.[35]

This paver of Russian religion in the nineteenth century is, of course, part of the explanation. As noted before, Vladimir Solov'ev (1853–1900) was the most influential Russian intellectual of the nineteenth century to the average Russian. Solov'ev was an advocate of Christian theocracy for Russia, his ideas based at one time on church teachings and at another on love mysticism. An important moment in Solov'ev's life took place in 1881 when he demanded that Tsar Alexander III from religious conviction should pardon the assassins of Alexander II. The tsar, of course, indignantly refused, and it spelled the end of Solov'ev's academic career and the breakdown of his relations with the *slavophile,* or romantic intellectuals.

In his mature philosophical writing, Solov'ev's master concept was Godmanhood, the ultimate synthesis of all reality, an essentially pantheist idea that could threaten not only the policy of the tsar but of the church and even of Russia's cultural dualism. Underlying Godmanhood was Solov'ev's claim to a knowledge of God through intuition. Knowing God, he implied was personal; it did not depend on church tradition.

Solov'ev's pantheism emerges clearly in his treatment of the theme for which he became most famous, Divine Sophia, the Eternal Feminine, the active force in cosmology, the transmuter of man's earthly love "for the feminine spirit, who was the Divine Wisdom of God." Even those who were not so radical found Solov'ev moving. Dostoyevsky created a major character in one of his novels based on Solov'ev, and among the leading writers of the early twentieth century, such as Alexsandr Blok, Andrej Belyj, and Sergej Bulgakov, his influence was acnowledged. In fact, these and other writers belonged to a salon in which his ideas were discussed.[36]

History Writing

Over the twentieth century, historians have served the hegemony by reinforcing the idea of the gap between the elite and the mass. In the process, Russian and Soviet historians have made major contributions to the study of political history and to fields related to political history, such as diplomatic history, political biography, and world history. The one area of history that Russian historians have eschewed is social history, which emphasizes social integration. Methodologically, Russian and Soviet historians are most at home in liberalism; politically, they have tended to be liberal even when they use a few Marxist phrases.[37] Ironically, Marxist historians actually play a more influential role in many other countries than they have played in the Soviet Union, contrary to common thought.

The major school of Russian history writing from 1861 to 1917 was the State school; its main figures were all liberals. As the name suggests, their focus was on the state and its institutions, whose evolution, they believed, embodied the nation itself. In its earliest phase, the writers in this school simply regarded the subject of society and of the nationalities of the empire as footnotes to the study of the great Russian elite. The school had a great Russian outlook. A writer in the school reveals this chauvanism: "Russians could obey; Ukrainians were individualists and could not." Among the important institutions in which the State school was influential was the Russian Historical Society (1866–1917), which collected sources from the archives of the world for the study of the Russian state. The State school historians also played an important role in the project of the Russian Historical Society to publish major reference works. Between 1896 and 1918, twenty-five volumes of the *Russian Biographical Dictionary* appeared under the society's auspices.

Two of the three founders of the school, K. D. Kavelin (1818–1885) and B. N. Chicherin (1828–1904), wrote for the ultraliberal journal of Alexander Herzen, *Voices from Russia,* published in London. Like many liberals, they favored the emancipation of the serfs, but beyond that, they opposed the anarchists and radical populists as threats to the interests of the state. Their political stands led to problems for them in autocratic periods. For example, in 1883, Chicherin, in his capacity as Moscow's municipal head, made a speech praising popular representation. The autocratically inclined Alexander III removed him from this position. The third founding member of the State school, S. Solov'ev, escaped these difficulties, but his leading student at Moscow University, V. O. Kliuchevskii (1841–1911), was not as fortunate. When Kliuchevskii opposed the domestic policies of Alexander III and Nicholas II, he incurred their wrath and had to take precautions to survive, but survive he did by shifting from writing national histories to writing local histories. In 1905, with the rebirth of liberalism, Kliuchevskii emerged as a supporter of the Duma. His shift in focus was shared by a number of the prominent liberal intellectuals. These liberals could survive if they avoided direct clashes over national policies. Local history served them in this respect yet permitted them to draw attention to important and unresolved problems in, for example, of agricultural administration on the local level.[38]

Sergei M. Solov'ev (1820–1879), a history professor at the University of Moscow and tutor to the royal family, is best known for his monumental and still influential study, *History of Russia from Earliest Times* (St. Petersburg, 1851–1879) in twenty-nine volumes. Modern scholars, Soviet and Western, state that he maintained standards equal to those of leading international scholars. Solov'ev focused on the seventeenth and eighteenth centuries. One contemporary scholar notes his strong support for Peter the Great, ever under attack by Slavophiles for his Westernizing policies. By praising Peter and the role of the state that Peter exemplified, Solov'ev was directing a criticism at certain liberal reformers of his own time who advocated that the tsar play a lesser role. Like many nineteenth-century historians, Solov'ev grounded his thought in Hegel. Solov'ev took the Petrine reform movement to be the Hegelian spirit realizing itself. The forces of progress are portrayed in mortal conflict with the customs of old Muscovy. As the embodiment of the Spirit, Peter was the hero. The high level of official corruption of the era, Solov'ev postulated, must have been for Peter a source of anguish.[39]

Historians, as liberals, were often ignored in the autocratic periods. Thus, one finds in the periods of Alexander III and Nicholas II before 1905 and later in the Cultural Revolution that politicians took their own initiatives to change the image of the past almost without reference to existing historical scholarship.[40] For example, Alexander III and Nicholas II more or less on their own opened museums and formed historical societies designed to emphasize particular issues. These practices continued in the autocratic periods after 1917 as well.

In 1899, Nicholas II opened a Museum of the History of the Don Cossack Host by the Society of the Antiquities of the Don designed to glorify feudalism. Only in the post-World War II period did the Soviet regime, in a liberal phase, seek to dilute the glorification of feudalism embodied in this institution by adding various other museums to it.[41]

Seven years earlier, in 1892, Alexander III had encouraged the formation of the Imperial Orthodox Palestine Society (IOPS)(1882–1917), a scholarly organization designed to study the history and culture of the peoples of the Middle East and to serve Russian policy objectives. In the liberal reaction brought about by the revolution of 1905, the institutions of the preceding period lost prestige. Despite royal patronage, the membership of IOPS fell sharply, but thanks to the patronage, it continued to sponsor research. By 1907, the society had published 347 books on Palestine. With the breakdown of liberalism after the Russian Revolution of 1917, the Bolshevik government renamed the society the Russian Palestine Society, and connected it to the Academy of Sciences of the USSR. At this point, the society apppeared to regain a trace of its original messianism. The Bolsheviki demanded that the society undertake to study and foster a rapprochement with the people of the Middle East. This objective underlay the opening of the Russian Institute in Constantinople in 1894, a major center for Byzantine studies until 1917.[42] It, too was tinged with religious messianism and colonial expansionism.

The problem for historians in autocratic periods was not just their convictions but their goal of combining government service with objectivity. For example, in 1884, a professor of the Kazan Theological Academy wrote a letter on behalf of K. P. Pobedonostsev (1827–1907) and the government, stating that the students and faculty of Oriental Languages of St. Petersburg and of the Lazarev Institute in Moscow did their work objectively and, thus, would not be reliable for missionary or governmental service. This was the logic of autocracy. During the Cultural Revolution, Pokrovsky, had a similar view of such figures as the Arabist, I. Iu. Krachkovskii; Krachkovskii, nonetheless, retained his position.

Autocracy was an specially strong opponent of social history. The well-known social historian, M. M. Kovalevskii, (1851–1916) was forced out of Moscow University in 1887 during a period of autocracy. Social history had made him vulnerable. The government could single him out because public opinion in the wider sense would acknowledge that his work threatened the long-standing policy of cultural dualism. He survived, however, even without the vast range of international supports that the later figure Roy Medvedev received.[43]

For the historians that remained in the Soviet Union after 1917, life was marked by an expectation of coexistence with the new regime; there was little anticipation of the decimation that would occur after 1928. For scholars, the period of the civil war was more chaotic than authoritarian. Liberal bolshevism, the era of Marxist tolerance during the NEP period, induced a considerable number of the traditional liberal scholars to remain.

In 1921, the Bolsheviki founded the Institute of History as part of the University of Moscow and reasserted an older pattern. Politicians once again were attempting to influence the content of history writing by modifying its institutional structure; as in the past, however, historians persisted in writing largely in the tradition of their teachers. The early leadership of the institute perforce included non-Marxists. In 1925, the Soviet social science consortium (RANION) took over the institute from the university; liberals kept their places and continued to publish.

In 1929, the Cultural Revolution struck the field of history when the Institute of History was transferred from RANION to the Communist Academy, and the government changed the institute's official function from research to buttressing the positions espoused by the political elite and contributing generally to the agitation and propaganda for Marxist-Leninism. A historian close to the power structure, Pokrovsky, ran the Communist Academy. He made no effort, however, to protect his colleagues in the institute. To the contrary, he expelled and drove into exile a number of prominent historians, and in the process some of these historians met their deaths. Evidence from the period suggests that for all Pokrovsky's prestige, many of his fellow historians did not respect him. They continued to pursue their traditional liberal historial scholarship by paying lip service to Marxist-Leninism and by avoiding domains of special concern to the party. Pokrovsky, nonetheless, was the dominant historian of the period in the view of many scholars and warrants the extended treatment he receives here.

In 1934, government objectives for history writing once again changed as did the institutional arrangements. First, the government encouraged historians to make history entertaining and memorable so that students would more willingly learn the broad outline of their national development; the abstract schema of Marxism-Leninism had not served this purpose. By 1936, the Communist Academy was defunct, and the government transferred the Institute of History to the Academy of Sciences of the USSR. The institute's functions in its new location included scholarship, once again, and the training of scholars to which was added the production of popular works. Professionalization and more precise job definitions re-emerged. Scholars who undertook extra burdens for the state were compensated for assuming them. The historical canvas once again widened. While scholars continued to study the 1917 revolution, the regime sought justification in the more remote Russian past for its current policies as well. To this end, it encouraged work on Russian heroes such as Peter the Great and Ivan the Terrible. The individual as a part of history returned.

Still, in the 1930s, the Old Guard criticized later historians for failing to fit Russian history into a convincing Marxist-Leninist scheme; elements of the New Class in the same period complained that the textbooks did not reflect the Soviet Union as a whole; the new nationalities criticized the whitewashing of Russian and Soviet imperialism; historians defended these policies, arguing that Russian imperialism had been a civilizing mission, that it had laid the groundwork for the great friendship of the Soviet period.[44]

M. N. Pokrovsky (1868–1932) is an indispensable element in any portrayal of modern Soviet historiography for the years leading up to the age of corporatism. Additionally, he is one of the most famous figures and one of the most difficult to interpret. The scholarship of the cold war period has found him to be a powerful figure, whereas the view that emerges from the more recent studies in social history is one of a rather weak, old-fashioned figure, not politically adroit.

During the cold war, Western scholars viewed Pokrovsky as Stalin's henchman, as an instrument in the purges of his fellow historians, and then as a mysterious victim of Stalin's wrath during the later days of the Cultural Revolution. Pokrovsky's rehabilitation in the 1960s thus fit the model of de-Stalinization. But a closer look suggests that the cold war paradigm left out much of importance about his career while it emphasized features of secondary importance. The cold war view, in general, has been predisposed to overrating the importance of historians. Not too surprisingly, scholars took Pokrovsky's formal titles, such as deputy people's commissar of education (1918–32), his ties with Lenin, and his achievements as a reformer in such areas as workers' education and the Communist University to be all of a piece with his career as a historian. According to a recent study, the two roles were, in fact, separate. As a historian with political connections, he managed to grab various offices; for example, in 1925, he became the first president of the Society of Marxist Historians. But it is quite a jump to argue that his criticisms of various rivals written from that post were responsible for the fate that befell them after 1929. A close look shows that what was more important, given that he was in politics, was that his views did not please Stalin.

Pokrovsky was a scientist. He believed in universal laws and particular applications. He studied modes of production. He did not place much weight on the role of the individual or even the force of nationalism. In addition, Prokovsky was rooted in his craft; he saw the virtue of many liberal historians of the nineteenth century, historians whom he found to be good artisans. He valued their objectivity and careful use of sources. Although he believed that historical study was useful for policymakers, and this emerges in his *Russia in World History,* he was not capable of being flexible or eclectic. Like Trotsky, Lenin, and many other early Bolsheviki, Pokrovsky was internationalist and world oriented, an easy target in the Cultural Revolution. By 1929, Pokrovsky was in a position similar to that of the liberal and slavophile "world historians" of the nineteenth century in the reign of Alexander III. Although he was useful to autocracy, he was not sympathetic to its premises. Here, the comparison breaks down; the majority of the older liberals survived, but Pokrovsky, confronted in the Cultural Revolution with enemies from both above and below and with cancer, did not.

The events after Pokrovsky's death but related to it provide some final evidence of the fragile position of those who were not part of the liberal tradition and attempted to keep up with the shifts in communism. In 1934, two years after Pokrovsky's death, the government attacked those historians who followed his line, accusing them of creating abstract, anti-Marxist, and untrue history. A number of historians lost their positions; some lost their lives.

Stalin's "favorite" historian, Anna Pankratova, led the attack. The contrast between her and Pokrovsky is one more indication of caste antagonism in the purges. Where Pokrovsky and other leading historians were the product of the Moscow scholarly elite who had, in effect, created the modern profession of history; Pankratova came from a poor family far from Moscow and worked her way up through the party in the provinces, breaking into the ruling caste and classes only later.

In 1961, Pokrovsky was officially rehabilitated and he was exonerated for his "errors." It was noteworthy on this occasion that it was once again a political decision. A number of historians opposed the rehabilitation; perhaps they, too, only recently had made it into the system.[45]

In 1956, permissible cultural trends gradually widened; it was the year marking the beginning of the current long swing toward liberalism. De-Stalinization brought into question the utility of a personality cult in the age of collective leadership, but the question could not be pursued because politicians did not want the cult to be dismissed entirely. Academic freedom was praised; Stalin had clearly abused the universities. But even in this period, historians could be dismissed for political reasons. In the 1950s, the state did not hesitate to dismiss Burdzhalov, the well-known historian and critic, and in the 1970s, it dismissed P. V. Volobuev, a specialist on the Russian Revolution.

As one examines Russian and Soviet history after the purges, the continuation of liberal positivism is apparent. Trends from the interwar period that arose in reaction to the Cultural Revolution continue through 1956 and beyond. They remind one of the trends in history writing that predated corporatism altogether: among others, the modern State school, the regional historians, peasant historians, and historians interested in the philosophy of history and Byzantine studies.

Romanticism, too, had its place. In 1939, a Byzantine Section at the Institute for History opened, but as official instructions of the period made clear, and they are in place today, the section was not to evoke romantic nostalgia that would make religion the key to modern history.[46] Still, what else could it do!

The best-known work of historical scholarship in the new liberal period was produced by Roy Medvedev. In *Let History Judge* (Moscow, 1968), the parallels to Solov'ev are striking. Both works are state centered, both take up the dialectic in terms of good and evil, and both serve a contemporary purpose through a focus on a great figure of the past.

The personal context of the two men is obviously quite different. Where Solov'ev was a much-favored academic historian who created a school in Moscow University, Medvedev was until quite recently on the margins. He was as well known as a human rights advocate as he was as a researcher of history. He was a man whose scholarly life was overshadowed by the fact that his father had been a victim of the great purges. Yet, Medvedev is the author, almost accidentally, of what many regard as the most important single contemporary Soviet study of history.

Let History Judge is a stinging indictment of the crimes of Stalin written from within the Soviet academic discourse. Medvedev does not espouse capitalism; he defends freedom as socialist collectivism. From this, one would expect a book in the Marxist tradition. Yet an epistemological analysis reveals that this is not the case. There is no examination of social structure, and little that is materialist. The work happens to be biographical, but the biographical content is decontextualized. The main contention is that Stalin was always bad from his youth to the day he seized power. With this premise and with a definite mastery of documentation, one is simply overwhelmed by the empiricism. Granting Medvedev his thesis that here was an evil genius, how did Stalin differ from his contemporaries? How can one explain his rise? Medvedev himself is struck by the irony of the rise of an individual who encountered no opposition. The dialectic demands opposition and contradiction, the Hegelian one, included. Stalin is the actualization of individual will, but as if in a posthistorical, postdialectical time. What about the working masses? Medvedev argues that because the masses are remote from the actual centers of power, they passively worshipped Stalin as God. Medvedev recognized in an aside that a lower middle-class bureaucracy would have no interest in democracy and, thus, might not believe that Stalin's actions were crimes. This insight did not lead him, as it did Trotsky, to the issue of whether Stalinism was a collective phenomenon. His conclusion returned him to the theme of the power of Stalin and the powerlessness of the society leading him to raise questions about religious cultism. The book ends with an enumeration of Stalin's crimes. How would Solov'ev have dealt with Stalin? Would he not have had a similar approach?[47]

A deeper critique of the past no doubt came from fields other than history. The historians themselves up to the end of the 1980s were too much a part of the establishment.

A general strategy of hegemony in the modern world is rule by caste; it is, contrary to common impression, dependent on persuasion as well as on coercion. A range of cultural projects maintain this form of hegemony in place. Historians participate in these projects. Among their major contributions are those in the area of political history.

There are advantages for the student of Russian and Soviet history in adopting this approach over others. It is holistic, comparativist, and at the same time internalist. In chapter 3, The comparativist dimensions emerge with the portrayal a Russian Road state only able to buy off the working class in the last couple of years. Its rulers have thus virtually never been able to dispense with the strategies of the tsars; for example, diverting discontented workers with anti-Semitism and with pogroms. In this country, the religious structure has spawned a revolutionary wing and not simply a mystical critic. The country is Iraq.

3

The "Russian Road" in the Middle East

Iraqi History, 1869–1990

In this chapter, I develop the thesis that the modern history of Iraq is an example of the Russian Road model of hegemony introduced in chapter 2. In the first section I link this approach to the paradigms conventionally used by scholars to interpret Iraq; in the second section, I take up the political economy of Iraq through a Russian Road approach in point of detail.[1] In the third section, I deal with hegemony in Iraq in the more restricted sense of the organization of culture and, in the fourth section, treat the writing of history in Iraq as part of the organization of culture.

The most influential paradigm for the study of modern Iraqi history has been liberalism. Around the time of World War I, liberals, among them Arab nationalists and British colonialists, began to argue that their own arrival from the Hidjaz marked the birth of a new era in Iraq, that the preceding Ottoman period was a morass of anarchism, that the great reformer, Midhat Pasha, was in 1869 no more than a harbinger of the days to come, that the dominant culture of the country was not just a traditional religious one but a mystical one as well, entirely different from the modern culture found in Baghdad under the British.

In their study of Iraqi history, liberals postulated a medieval Golden Age in the 'Abbasid period, a subsequent period of decline under the Ottomans during which Iraq became essentially tribal; then came the discovery of oil and the birth of modern times. The Ottoman era ended for all intents and purposes with the British occupation in 1917; a British protectorate was formally installed in 1923. In 1932, Iraq became a state independent of direct colonialism, subsequently in 1958 a republic, and in 1968, a socialist state.[2]

55

The great virtue of the liberal school has been its portrayal of the unfolding of Iraq's history in a somewhat comprehensible manner. No other school has an interpretative schema that is so clear. There is much, however, that the emphasis on developmentalism cannot explain, and this seems to predispose the liberal school to pessimism and to an emphasis on failure. Some writers, for example, emphasize that the South of Iraq has simply failed to develop. The most sophisticated study of modern Iraq to date, that of Hanna Batatu, adopts the premises of the liberal school but modifies them through a recourse to political economy. Batatu argues that development, the primary concern for liberals, does not necessarily lead to a modern society but to a mixture of modern and archaic structures, for example, communal ones. The Russian Road approach adopted here owes much to his work.[3]

Over the twentieth century, the main opposition to liberalism has been romanticism. Writers in the romantic trend emphasize the force of long-term continuity in Iraqi history. For romantics, continuity explains the existence of classical or archaic forms in modern times.

In Iraq, the leading romantic trends have been the "Pan" movements. In the nineteenth century, pan-Islamism was important at the same time that pan-Slavism was in Russia. The more secular but equally messianist pan-Arabism came to occupy a major place after World War I at about the time when bolshevism was going through its romantic phase.[4]

According to pan-Arabist writers, Iraq is a part of the larger Arab history. This is a romantic argument rooted in a view of the past as shared heritage. It can be distinguished from other forms of Arab and Iraqi nationalisms that are presentist or futurist and are rooted in positivism and the idea of progress. Today on a political level, the leader of the pan-Arabist trend is the Ba'th party of Iraq.

The other romantic reactions to liberal positivist history include the Mesopotamian Civilization school based on archeology and the recently renewed Islamic trend. Writers of the Mesopotamian school emphasize the unchanging character of Mesopotamian Iraqi culture from ancient times to the present as evidenced by particular features that they research, for example, colloquial proverbs, irrigation practices, peasant rituals, and so on.[5]

The Islamic trend in Iraq tends to emphasize communal differences as the basis of the Iraqi political order; its scholars adopt views compatible on the whole with Western orientalism.[6] For the Islamic trend, modern secular culture is an imposition of Western colonialism abetted by a Sunni ruling class in Baghdad; the real culture of Iraq is Shi'ism.[7] Iraq for them has, thus, been pushed out of its true course, a Shi'a democracy, into a Tribal-Ethnic Road.

A Marxist school of interpretation of Iraq has also influenced Iraqi history writing. Following the ideas of Lenin, Iraqi Communist scholars have pursued such themes as imperialism, oil, the working class, feudalism, and the rise of capitalism. Non-Leninist Marxism has done less well. The historical role of the peasantry, of the "non-vanguard" working class and of race and gender oppression, remain undeveloped in Iraqi Marxist thought as they remain undeveloped in Soviet Marxism. A few writers appear troubled by the lacunae in Leninism; they postulate that the "archaic" may not simply be archaic or "pre-capitalist" but a byproduct of uneven capitalist development.

The claim that Iraq is Russian Road is an argument against the romantic claim that Iraq has been pushed into being a Tribal-Ethnic state and the liberal claim that Iraq is more like the Italian Road. Iraq, however, has features that Tribal-Ethnic states do not have, which would be dysfunctional if they did. Among these is a paramount city, Baghdad, the center of a high culture rooted in positivism, a culture particularly strong in the study of political history. Iraq has shrine towns that tribal-ethnic states do not; they have museum cities. The ruling classes in Tribal-Ethnic states use tribes and ethnicities as the apparent organizational basis of the state. In Iraq, rulers appeal to communal sentiment sometimes, but the nature of political organization in modern history reflects the urban and rural dichotomy of the Russian Road, not the communal one. Finally, in Tribal-Ethnic states, the real contradiction is gender, the condition of women is frozen. In Iraq, gender is not the primary contradiction; the condition of women is variable.

Equally, it can be shown, even on the basis of the points introduced thus far, that the Iraqi ruling class did not pursue an Italian Road approach; it did not exploit the poverty of the South the way the Italian ruling class exploited its South. Thus, in Iraq, the organization of culture was not set up to create the southerner, a type who was to be racially and culturally inferior to the rest of the Iraqis. Perhaps the Iraqi ruling class chose the Russian Road because the economy could not absorb the southerners as they came off the land searching for other work the way the Italian economy could. This is speculation. What is well-known is that in the 1950s, the state forcefully repatriated a number of southerners who lived in shacks on the outskirts of Baghdad back to the countryside.

The date 1869 in Iraq parallels 1861 in Russia. This is the point at which the Iraqi ruling class had resolved how to deal with the crises accompanying the spread of capitalism to the country as a whole. From this point, power could be delegated to the bureaucracy. This point is considered here to be the birth of modern Iraq.

Using a Russian Road approach to political economy in Iraqi history, one finds a first liberal phase (1869–1963), a corporatist phase (1963–68), and a new liberal phase (1968–present). As elsewhere, so in Iraq, the liberal phase was characterized by a one-class rule and the dominance of finance capitalism. In 1963 came corporatism. The political bases of the system widened with the entrance of the New Class, and the ruling class committed itself to pursue industrialization. The lower middle class played an active role in the politics. During the third and most recent phase, the neoliberal phase, Iraq returned to one-class rule.

In Russian Road regimes, the complicating factor in the political dynamics is that there are not only long-term phases interrelating the dominant caste to world capitalism but also short-term phases that reflect efforts to control the local class conflict. Again, as in Russia and the Soviet Union, so in Iraq, the two kinds of dynamics overlapped as the following periodization for the short-term cycles makes clear: 1869–76 liberal; 1876–1908 autocratic; 1908–23 liberal; 1923 autocratic (momentarily); 1924–36 liberal; 1936–37 autocratic; 1937–58 liberal (except briefly in 1941); 1958–63 autocratic; 1963–68 liberal; 1968–75 autocratic; 1975–90 liberal.

Differences emerged between the Soviet Union and Iraq and from a consideration of them came the specificity of each. The Soviet ruling class managed to co-opt its working class, whereas its Iraqi counterpart did not. As a consequence, the short swing of the pendulum in the USSR gradually widened into a long, slow swing, a spiral. In Iraq, class conflict is still quite open. As a result, the swing of the pendulum is still short. Iraq developed as a "crisis" state, its politics more violent and its knowledge production less stable than was the case in the Soviet Union.[8]

In Russia, oil wealth began in the nineteenth century, much earlier than in Iraq, and although the ruling class was very slow to develop a strong secular culture and seize the power from the religious bureaucracy, it escaped from much that beset Iraq, enduring a period of only semicolonial control.

Colonial regimes usually retard the development of industry; this was the experience in Iraq. By contrast, in Russia, industrialism developed over many years; when the working class began major strikes in the early twentieth century, the ruling class could take it in stride. By the 1930s, it was placing much of the primary industrialization in the South. Later it placed it in Eastern Europe and the Third World. This strategy left the Russian workers with the better-paying, more skilled jobs and made them appreciate that their jobs depended on a certain level of Soviet power in the world. The working class was somewhat dependent on the state. In Iraq after 1958 and more so after 1963, the state poured money into industrial development; it could not, however, gain the working class's support. It was too obvious that the state could just as easily use its oil revenue to import what it needed. It was equally apparent that whether the products made were sold really did not matter. This sort of interaction between ruler and ruled, of course, bred distrust.

Iraq thus developed as a crisis state. The ruling class constantly had to divert the working class from economic issues by attacks on Jews, Kurds, or Assyrians, attacks reminiscent of the pogroms used by the tsars before Russia industrialized. Only recently, in the years before the Gulf War, could one speak of Iraq taking on the attributes of greatpowerism.

The Political Economy of Iraq, 1869–1990

The year 1869 marks an important change in Iraqi history and is the point of departure here. In the early nineteenth century, the ruling classes in Iraq blocked the entrance of a wider capitalism to protect the old East-West caravan trade. With the rising value for agricultural products on the world market, merchants and tribal chiefs were induced to undertake agricultural production and to allow a wider play of capitalist forces.

The reign of Midhat Pasha, 1869–1872, thus marked the birth of the Russian Road in Iraq. Its first phase (1869–76) was a liberal one. The rulers attempted to impose a constitution on the country and to tie the rural power structure to the state. Midhat's vehicle to achieve this was the Ottoman Land Code; through it, the Baghdad government awarded property ownership, urban residences, and titles to the shaykhs in return for the shaykhs' cooperation in the sedentarization of their tribes and tax collection. Shaykhs and their descendants, who cooperated, have figured prominently throughout modern Iraqi history. Midhat also played a role in the history of modern education. He founded military schools, introducing in the process secular educators to Iraq. He even tried, albeit unsuccessfully, to impose secular authority in the Holy Cites, beginning construction of new government buildings in Karbala'.[9]

From the mid-1870s onward, the liberal phase produced a reaction. Poorer tribe members resisted the peasantization forced on them, often rising up in the name of old tribal solidarities. The resistance of the poor tribe members to their shaykh's affiliation to the government created insecurity in Baghdad. The government quickly resorted to meting out new, severe punishments to what was becoming a more homogenized rural underclass. Servitude, collective punishment, and "tribal" levies were features of the swing to autocracy in 1876.[10] Liberal phases often enough end in this manner as the state clamps down on class conflict.

From 1876–1908, an autocratic phase ensued in which a powerful Ottoman sultan, Abdul Hamid II, in Istanbul ruled Iraq by proxy. As in the autocratic phases in Russia, the rulers of Iraq in this period amassed vast landholdings. In 1908, the empire collapsed and a liberal regime arose in Iraq; royal control of these lands came to an end. Several other features of a Russian Road regime and, more specifically, of an autocracy stand out in this period: the rise to preeminence of Baghdad, the increased power of the religious hierarchy and foreign and minority businesses, and the rise of a liberal Arab culture in opposition to the ideology of Pan-Islamism.

The long-term rise of Baghdad at the expense of other cities can be inferred from the fact that through this period, 50 percent of tax revenue collected in Iraq was sent to Istanbul; 50 percent remained in Iraq. Of the latter, 25 percent was spent on local security and 24 percent on administrative salaries, the remaining 1 percent on social services.[11] Although Baghdad was the center of administration and security, the city was also the site of the new bridges and prisons constructed in the 1890s. Put another way, the lack of tax revenue sharing was among the main causes of the decline of other Iraqi cities.[12]

During this period as well, the rising power of the Shi'a hierarchy was reflected in the development of a new office, the Marj'a at-Taqlid, whose holder claimed that believers had the duty to obey the living clerical authorities, to treat as myth the older doctrine that required obedience to the Hidden Imam. The prestige of the Marj'a al-Taqlid rose in 'Abd Al-Hamid's reign but then declined with the resurgence of liberalism during the Mandate. In the 1890s, during the heyday of its influence, the Shi'a hierarchy had the power to forbid its followers to attend schools that were run by Sunnis or were based on a secular curriculum. In addition, the Shi'a hierarchy had the power to impose a major economic boycott on an imported product, tobacco.[13]

Autocratic phases present more opportunities for foreign businesses than for local ones because security of the realm takes precedence over profit maximization. Rulers calculate that foreigners can always perform needed functions and then be dismissed. Profit for foreigners, however, depends on local contacts; in this situation, the Iraqi Jewish community found it had an important and lucrative function as an intermediary. Wealth for the wealthy, at least, increased as exports from Iraq increased and as Europeans became more involved in Iraqi affairs, and this they did. For example from 1885 to 1891, French engineers overcame a crisis in the Hilla River irrigation system and helped to expand the base for export agriculture in that part of the country.

The sum of these developments led to other changes as well, not the least of which were in culture. Although pan-Islam was the dominant trend in culture, by 1900, segments of the middle classes, Muslims, Christians, and Jews began to support a modern and liberal Arabic culture.[14] Governmental policy was not affected; the state's involvement in the field of education was limited to military education and religious education. More than one thousand secondary-level students graduated from military schools between 1881 and 1913.[15]

The 1908 revolution of the Committee of Union and Progress in Turkey brought in its wake changes across the Ottoman empire. It brought a liberal phase to Iraqi politics that lasted despite repression during the World War and the onset of British colonial rule until the military coup of 1936. Its main feature was the ascendancy of the secular culture in Baghdad over the religious culture in the Holy Cities and the expulsion of members of the Shi'a hierarchy, who refused to accept the Anglo-Iraqi Treaty of 1923.

At the onset of the liberal phase, politicians in Baghdad proclaimed the principle of freedom of the press; newspapers began to espouse the cause of Iraqi nationalism and pan-Arabism.[16] The Wali, Nazim Pasha, who arrived in Baghdad in 1910, established a Chamber of Commerce, built the first modern street of that city, and a dam that saved the city from flooding.[17]

In the next few years, the British protectorate of Iraq emerged. For the British, the protectorate was to protect the oil. The British depended on oil. They feared that without it the Germans would capture the oilfields and deny them access. Colonization, especially the onset of colonization in the years 1917–23, was not easy for the British; peasant and tribal uprisings in the Middle Euphrates and in Kurdistan surprised them. It was only by means of aerial reconnaissance and bombardment and by using the Assyrian levies, spies, and informers deployed against Iraqi tribes that the British succeeded in crushing their opponents. In so doing, the die was cast; local support for a British presence would be more urban than rural. The British would have to rebuild their relations with their erstwhile allies, the shaykhs of the Middle Euphrates.

The year 1920 was the high point of this uprising and of the political struggles of the period 1908–36. In the so-called Revolt of the Middle Euphrates, or Thawra Tishrin, the nationalist movement reached its zenith but then split. All during that year, public opinion in the Middle Euphrates favored greater freedom than any foreign regime would allow; it opposed a British mandate on principle and opposed as well the imposition of King Faysal as the British puppet in Iraq. During this struggle, for reasons that are not entirely clear, the religious hierarchy, a key part of the nationalist alliance, also split. One part provided leadership for the revolt and allied with the leadership in Baghdad, another part abstained. This split contributed to the defeat of the nationalists and ended the liberal phase for a brief time, which-permitted the British to come in through a military conquest. Perhaps the Shi'a leadership reasoned that autocracy would come with a British victory, and autocratic periods were better for the hierarchy than were liberal periods. In any case, they made a serious misjudgment. The new government, in a manner reminiscent of the Bolsheviki of the same period, was quite prepared to try to rule without them. It was much more committed to liberalism than the Shi'i leadership may have calculated. After the uprising, the power of the hierarchy plummeted for a generation. By the 1950s, the body of religious students in Iraq had shrunk from several thousand in the 1920s to a few hundred. For this reason, commentators on

Iraq as early as the 1920s, in much the manner of the commentators on the Soviet Union after 1917, concluded that religion would no longer be politically important.[18]

After the victory in World War I and the crushing of the liberation struggle of Thawrat Tishrin, the British, represented by such figures as Lady Gertrude Bell, the oriental secretary, set out to formulate Iraq's political identity.[19] They believed they were making a fresh start. Because they thought there was no country, simply the region of Mesopotamia, they decided to impose a tribal-ethnic state. Their choice for ruler was King Faysal (1921–1933), a tribal leader from the Hidjaz. When Faysal came to Iraq to be king, he may have expected to carry on the Arabian tradition of tribal and ethnic communities, but this was not to be and he adjusted quickly. To rule, Faysal had to deal with caste groups and not tribal ones. Iraq was not a Tribal Road regime but a Russian Road one. Tribalism, as such, was vestigial; the urban-rural dualism was more important.

The justice system of Iraq in the 1920s illustrates neatly the gap between the British master plan of tribalism and the Russian Road reality of Iraq. The British had set up tribal councils to handle criminal cases and disputes in rural areas and appointed tribal shaykhs to the council offices. These shaykhs naturally gained, or regained, great power, but the results were not what the British tribalists had foreseen. The shaykhs became a new gentry; their traditional tribal ties weakened as they came to rely on the central government.

Another surprise for the British was that King Faysal adjusted to Iraq as he did, that he pursued policies that actually reinforced a Russian Road-type hegemony. For example, he sought to build an army through universal conscription. The British opposed this, preferring to depend on "martial races," for example, the Assyrian levies. In addition, Faysal appointed his friends to the leading positions in provincial government, and many of his friends were "new men" who had been army officers and nationalist politicians. As noted, the British preferred to appoint existing shaykhs than to form a new political group.

Liberal phases create new wealth and new poverty in Russian Road regimes. Commercialization of agriculture greatly benefited the land-holding shaykhs of the Middle Euphrates. Some of them followed the path of the earlier tribal shaykhs, moved to Baghdad, and left a functionary stratum, the *sirkal,* to run their estates. The social bonds between ruler and ruled became weaker and weaker. By the 1930s, the impact of the Great Depression began to be felt in the Iraqi countryside. A mass exodus of the landless poor from the countryside to the cities and towns of Iraq began.

Even before the Great Depression, an organized labor movement arose, responding to the inequities of the new world of wealth and poverty. In 1931, Muhammad Salih Al-Qazzaz, an early leader of this movement, led a strike against the imposition of new taxes through a Municipal Fees Law of that year.[20] The government arrested Al-Qazzaz and outlawed his movement. In 1934, organized labor was joined by the Iraqi Communist party, which arose to challenge the legitimacy of the Iraqi political system. In the countryside, there was strife as well. Peasant struggles, "tribal" conflicts, confronted the state throughout the early 1930s.

By 1934, the social crises found their way into the political process. In the 1934 electoral maneuvers, Prime Minister 'Ali Jawdat Al-Ayyubi was an urban politician obliged to rig the election to the Chamber to the point of excluding all but his own followers. Those excluded included the representatives of the countryside and among them a very powerful figure, 'Abd Al-Wahid Sukkar, a Shi'i and the shaykh of the Fatlah "tribe" of South Iraq. Opposition quickly arose in the South and in the North of Iraq to Al-Ayyubi's government; the leading Shi'ite figure, Shaykh Kashif Al-Ghita', issued a *fatwa,* or religious opinion, criticizing the government. Al-Ayyubi's actions had betrayed the political understandings worked out by King Faysal and the British.

By 1934, the structural limits of liberalism had in essence been reached. There was little future for a liberal politician who wished to promote capitalist development in the countryside. The 1932 Land Law had already granted more land to the shaykhs loyal to Baghdad, and the 1933 law had tied the peasant with debts to these lands, thereby blocking their employment elsewhere in the country.[21] In 1934, Al-Ayyubi was facing the fact that except in limited areas of the Middle Euphrates, political support for liberalism outside of the city was very limited. How else could capitalism be promoted except through autocracy?

A crisis brought down liberalism and brought in an autocratic phase. King Faysal died in September 1933; he was succeeded by the young, inexperienced Prince Ghazi, which, in essence, created a political vacuum. Shortly thereafter, in 1934, came the Assyrian crisis. Before commenting on this crisis, one other change must be noted. An Iraqi lower middle class was emerging: junior army officers, small merchants, journalists. For the first time in modern history, the size of this class made it something the political system had to respond to; for the first time, therefore, Arab nationalism became an ideology with which to reckon.

By the early 1930s, the leaders of the Assyrian community realized that their service to the military as levies would not continue in an independent Iraq. In an independent Iraq, the power of nationalism would be such that they would lose not just their special position but even their raison d'être. Not surprisingly, as the nationalist movement made more and more progress, the Assyrians pressed the colonial state more aggressively to secure a lasting niche for them. In 1934, while their efforts were proceeding, a group of Assyrian villagers encountered the Iraqi army; a massacre ensued.

General Bakr Sidqi, who carried out what amounted to a pogrom, emerged as the "savior of Iraq." From the perspective of the Chamber of Commerce and the landed elite, the pogrom served to deflect popular concern from labor questions mentioned above to national questions. By 1936, as the political crisis of liberalism deepened, Sidqi's leadership position became unassailable.[22] The Assyrian community began to disintegrate.

Bakr Sidqi's ascension to power in October 1936 brought to the fore groups that were more sure of their opposition to liberalism than they were of their commitment to one another. What began as a diffusely nationalistic political move fell apart when details had to be worked out. The alliance lasted one year. The high point of that year was the passage of a law supporting the rights of workers. Influenced by his allies in the Ahali Group, Sidqi legalized trade unions. Influenced by his ties to the Kurdish community, Sidqi used administrative power to halt the state's drive to Arabize Kurdish culture and personal influence to persuade the principal Kurdish leader, Mulla Mustafa Barzani, to remain in Sulaymaniya in 1936 and not to launch a new campaign.[23]

Modern Iraq in both its liberal and autocratic phases had grown up under the aegis of colonialism. To Sidqi fell the unexpected task of improvising a political style for a now "independent" Iraq. Sidqi and his minister of the interior, Hikmat Sulayman, were impressed by Iran and Turkey, two nearby Russian Road states, and wanted to further produce one like them for Iraq. In Iran and Turkey, what appealed to them was that poor officers from provincial backgrounds rose to take wealth from the affluent liberal families of the capital city, and they did this on behalf of the nation. For Sidqi and Sulayman, such figures as Ataturk and the Pahlavis symbolized national salvation. Although this subject has not been well explored, the influence of this model on Iraq may conceivably explain certain obscure but perhaps important features of this period, notably the attack on several well-known wealthy liberals in Baghdad by unidentifiable gangs.[24]

By the end of 1936, Sidqi had become vulnerable; his coalition was in disarray. He was forced to base his rule on his own personal popularity. His initiatives were thwarted even by his own supporters. For example, when Sidqi tried to expand welfare benefits, he faced opposition from within his own coalition. Even a hint of land reform antagonized the shaykhs, some of whom abandoned their support of him. In early 1937, strikes in Kirkuk, Basra, and Baghdad threatened major industries; Sidqi employed the army to repress them. The use of the army against the workers outraged his allies, the Ahali Group, and they resigned from his coalition. Social reform was soon shelved altogether, and without the likelihood of social reform, Sidqi's authoritarianism became less and less popular.

In 1937, a soldier with pan-Arabist sympathies assassinated Bakr Sidqi, and a liberal regime headed by Jamil Midfa'i came into power.

For twenty years until the revolution of 1958, liberal regimes, with one brief interruption in 1941, strove to combine open market development with putting a brake on social changes that would give power to the nationalists or to the Left. In 1937, for example, Midfa'i tightened the laws against "communism, anarchism, nihilism or similar movements." In addition, he welcomed home the liberal statesmen exiled by Sidqi. The Palestine Uprising, 1936–39, was a challenge for the liberal politicians. The Shi'i hierarchy seized the opportunity to issue fatwas calling for a jihad, or Holy War, in Palestine; Midfa'i and the other secular leaders denounced their interference in politics and increased the protection of Jews in Baghdad. Might not Iraqi soldiers return home from Palestine to attack the government in Baghdad? So thought the politicians.

In 1938, another military coup brought in yet another politician, Nuri Sa'id, but without shifting the orientation away from liberalism. Nuri Sa'id promised the country new electoral laws and democracy. To achieve this, he, too, outlawed the Communist party. His policy and that of his successors was to press the regent, 'Abdul-Ilah, to form a government that could divert the army's attention from the Palestine Question and to keep Iraq tied to its treaty obligation to England. Nevertheless, by the late 1930s, the army, public opinion at large, and nationalist politicians, such as Naji Shawqat and Rashid 'Ali Gaylani, were increasingly pan-Arabist, pro-Axis and pro-Palestinian.[25]

The Rashid Gaylani coup of 1941, yet another military intervention, marked a brief return to autocracy. Rashid Gaylani installed a new regent and turned for support to the Axis. His goal was to make Iraq truly independent. To do this, he tried to limit the movement of British troops in Iraq, a move so frightening that some U.S. and British citizens, as well as some local Jewish merchants, moved into the embassy compound. As fighting between the British and Iraqis commenced, Gaylani received support from some of the religious hierarchy. Hajj Amin al-Husayni from Palestine and various 'Iraqi 'ulama' declared a jihad against Britain, repeating a traditional pattern of the Russian Road of clerical assertiveness in autocratic phases. Relations between Baghdad and Kurdistan improved, again a part of the pattern. Gaylani even appealed to Barzani, the Kurdish leader, to join the side of the Iraqi government. By May, however, it was clear that no shaykh supported the government, that Gaylani's Youth movement was no military asset, and that public opinion had swung against Gaylani and the Iraqi army as the hardship of daily life grew.

The Gaylani regime, April–June 1941, however important for the future of Iraqi politics, was unexpectedly short-lived. In the moment of its collapse and before the new government of the liberal Jamil Midfa'i was fully in place, another event occurred that was equally important for the future—the Farhud, a pogrom against Jews and Jewish property in Baghdad. The Youth movement and military officers were clearly involved but the returning British, counting their blessings, turned a blind eye.

From late 1941 to 1948, Iraq experienced a period of guided liberalism in the service of British war aims not unlike that of World War I. After the war, 1948–58, liberalism of the more traditional market-driven sort returned.

During the period 1941–48, the rulers once again built their hegemony on a policy of singling out "undesirables" and arresting them. Politicians believed that the existence of a "Red Peril" would make the British-Iraqi alliance more palatable to public opinion. Under the pretense of ridding Iraq of dangerous individuals, the British justified the expulsion of Palestinian and Syrian teachers and the closing of the Italian legation. In 1942, the government expanded this "purge" to include the Ministry of Education. Ministry officials, they claimed, bore some responsibility for the sympathy of urban youth for the Axis and for immediate political independence. In the same year, the British sentenced three Iraqi politicians active in the Gaylani period to death and executed them. In this atmosphere, the Iraqi government felt secure enough to declare war against the Axis and to receive economic and logistical support for the duration of the war from the U.S. Lend Lease Aid.

In 1945, with the war over, the government began gradually to abandon guided liberalism and to return to laissez-faire. In the same year, the government initiated as well a policy of political decentralization; it set up Provincial Councils, rewarding the shaykhs, who stood by the British during the war, by giving them more power. The shaykhs, especially those of the Middle Euphrates, seized this new political authority and pushed forward with the development of capitalism in agriculture. Once again, a vast tide of peasants began to leave the land in search of jobs in the cities. In the North, another Kurdish uprising was underway.

In 1945, class conflict reemerged in the open in strikes.[26] In the oil fields, Iraqi troops fired on Iraqi workers to protect British-owned oil works; the workers fought back. A Rights of Workmen movement demanded its own newspaper, an insurance system, and wage-arbitration boards. A strike among port and railway workers followed on the heels of the oil workers' strike. It, too, took a political turn. Communism, declared illegal in 1938, resurfaced among the railway strikers, and from there it spread rapidly. In the early 1940s, government employees began to suffer severely from the inflation brought on by war profiteering. By the mid-1940s, many of these employees nearly engaged in class conflict with the government itself, becoming Communists or at least Communist sympathizers.

On January 12, 1948, the Iraqi delegation signed the Treaty of Portsmouth, renewing the Iraqi-English alliance. Coming at a time of inflation and of labor unrest, the signing of this antinationalist act fueled the opposition political movements. In April 1948, as a reaction to the signing of the Treaty of Portsmouth, the oil workers of K3 pumping station near Haditha went on strike and proceeded with popular support to march on Baghdad. This Great March was blocked by the police 70 kilometers from the capital; it remains, however, in the popular imagination, the outstanding symbol of Iraqi labor militancy.[27] From June 1948, the government had to rule by martial law until early 1949. Demonstrations of the opposition parties, of college students, and of workers continued to attack the renewing of the treaty during this period; these demonstrations are known by their Arabic name, Al-Wathba, meaning literally political uprising. In the face of this uprising, the government gradually panicked; the police were ordered to restore order and they did, but in doing so, they fired indiscriminately at demonstrators. Public opinion held the police responsible for the injuries that ensued. So strong was public opinion that the regent and the prime minister, Salih Jabr, were forced to disavow the treaty; the opposition movement celebrated the event as a major triumph. On January 6, 1949, the government, weakened by the events surrounding the treaty, fell[28] over a disagreement with the army concerning intervention in Palestine. The last act of Prime Minister Muzahim Al-Pachachi was another purge of the Communists.

By 1949, laissez-faire liberalism was, however, still assured; major political problems, such as the Iraqi role in Palestine, were resolved by the Arab defeat. The army withdrew, removing an important point of conflict between the liberals and the pan-Arabists. The passage of the Law of March 1950 diminished another major source of friction in Iraq by regularizing the departure of Jews from Iraq and by recruiting Pakistanis to fill the positions that Jews had previously occupied. As in previous liberal ages, decentralization of power continued to be a favorite theme; regional political power as defined by the Liwa Administration Law increased.

The novelty of the post-1949 period was the abundance of wealth in Iraq generated from oil revenues. The government set up a Development Board to identify worthwhile projects that the state could undertake. Not surprisingly, the Development Board recommended a number of projects primarily of concern to the large landholders. These projects included the construction of dams and the solving of various irrigation problems.

Liberal economic policy encouraged the concentration of land in private hands; a consequence of this on several occasions was the growth of more and more landless people, a phenomenon that in turn often resulted in a forced exodus of starving peasants toward the slums of the cities. This period proved no exception. In the decade from 1947 to 1957, Greater Baghdad's population rose from 593,000 to 793,000. The arrival of this large mass of peasants led to repression by the city police; it also served to further depress urban wages. As the 1950s progressed, strikes grew more numerous and increased in intensity; the Left began to anticipate revolution.[29]

When it finally came in 1958, the revolution was the greatest upheaval in modern Iraqi history; it also marked the start of an autocratic phase that lasted until 1963. The 1958 revolution has also been a very difficult event to interpret. Although most of the population of Iraq was rural, the best-known events of the revolution took place on the streets of Baghdad. In addition, although the Communists took credit for many of the events of this period, it was widely acknowledged by observers that most workers and most of the urban poor seen on the street did not belong to parties. In addition, it is obvious that the struggle was ongoing in the countryside. These well-known facts have yet to be used very well.

The figure who came to power in 1958 was a charismatic military officer, 'Abd Al-Karim Qasim. Qasim's politics, not unlike Bakr Sidqi's before him, were nationalist, progressivist, and eclectic, torn by the conflict within his alliance between the liberal nationalists and the Communists, on the one hand, and pan-Arabists, on the other.[30]

Following the example of previous rulers in the autocratic mold, Qasim expanded the power of the state through the growth of administative centralization. In 1958, the state entered such areas as public health and primary school education on a large scale. Again, in line with the previous autocratic phases, Qasim sought to solve the Kurdish Question administratively through granting the Kurds internal self-government.[31] Pressure from the peasant leagues forced Qasim to undertake some land reform as well. He acknowledged the existence of a rural crisis but sought solutions to it short of large-scale land reform. Without large-scale land reform, however, the large landholders retained their lands and their influence; not surprisingly, only a few of the landless received lands. In areas such as oil and other modern industries, Qasim was likewise unable to make many reforms.

In 1959, Qasim made his famous tilt to the Left, that is, in the direction of his allies among the Communists and the women's movement. He passed a law outlawing polygamy, another law unifying Sunni and Shi'i laws of inheritance, and a third law granting equal rights of inheritance to women.[32] Qasim's right-hand man 'Abd Al-Salam 'Arif, an Arab nationalist, opposed these laws, finding support for his opposition among liberals, the landlord class, and fellow officers, economic liberals often enough being social conservatives. Emboldened by this support, 'Arif instigated a coup with the help of a military leader, Ahmad Hasan Al-Bakr, but Qasim foiled it. After that, Qasim included a sampling of parties in his cabinet but made himself the sole leader.

Another serious challenge to Qasim from the pan-Arabists was the uprising in Mawsil in March 1959; this time it was led by a military figure, Colonel Ahmad 'Abd Al-Wahhab Al-Shawwaf. Again, Qasim survived.

Kurds loyal to Qasim on ethnic grounds and Communists loyal to him on ideological grounds combined to defeat Al-Shawwaf. In the process, class hatred surfaced. Qasim's supporters, many of whom were from the lower classes, extracted a heavy toll in life and property from the wealthy classes of the city. When such attacks spread to Kirkuk and Baghdad, they cost Qasim support among the urban middle classes. How could he choose such fanatic allies? they wondered. This loss of support hurt. What he lost was not compensated by the support that came his way from 'ulama'. The 'ulama' were not real allies. Many were simply more hostile to pan-Arabism than to Qasim's liberal radicalism, liberal radicalism being less antagonistic to religion than pan-Arabism.

A distinctive feature of the Qasim period was the purge trials, the Mahdawi Court. In contrast to the famous purge trials of Stalin, those of Qasim were all orchestrated from above; there was no purge from below, no Stalin-like insanity, and no Reign of Terror. Furthermore, the purge trials were only in an incipient sense a part of the rise of the New Class. The rise of the New Class on a large scale, at least, came in 1963. Nonetheless, for the comparative studies of Stalinism, this use of the legal system by Qasim is important.

The Mahdawi Court, variously known as the Special Supreme Military Court or the People's Court, dealt with conspiracies against the safety of the country or those that contributed to its corruption. Colonel Fadil 'Abbas Al-Mahdawi, the government prosecutor, became well known from the television coverage of the trials for his satire, verbal abuse, and colorful methods. In the tradition of the Cultural Revolution, he arraigned the liberal leadership of the pre-1958 period, the military officers who had opposed the leadership, even the youth who plotted to assassinate Qasim in September 1959.

Pan-Arabism did not end in the early 1960s with the fall of 'Arif or with the Mahdawi Court but carried on, becoming focused around an old hero whom Qasim permitted to return from exile, Rashid 'Ali Gaylani. Under Gaylani's aegis, the pan-Arabists grew more moderate; they even sought rapprochements with the liberals. Gaylani's own house served as a meeting place for such diverse elements as tribal shaykhs of the Middle Euphrates and Ahmad Hasan Al-Bakr, a future leader of the Ba'th party. Times were right for these meetings. In the early 1960s, the traditional quarters of Baghdad's middle class, Karkh and A'zamiya, quarters known for the their sympathy to religion, began to turn against Qasim and to show more support for pan-Arabism. Qasim's move to the Left combined with economic hardship were factors. Feeling their power, the pan-Arabists began to out-maneuver Qasim; Qasim became isolated. He no longer appealed to the liberals; he also lacked deep ties to the religious establishment. Like Bakr Sidqi, Qasim was part Kurdish by birth. The pan-Arabists used this biographical fact against him. Like Sidqi, Qasim was executed or murdered by a pan-Arab nationalist.

In 1963, in the wake of Qasim's death came the First Ba'thi Revolution, the so-called Ramadan Revolution, an event I argue, that was of greater importance to modern Iraq than the 1958 revolution. In this year, 'Abd al-Salam 'Arif, a pan-Arabist, ushered in corporatism. The long-cycle liberal age ended; the New Class arrived and with it the new ideology of Ba'thism. The political system widened as it kept its open-market approach to the economy.

The rise of the New Class under such conditions resulted in numerous contradictions. For example, usually liberal ages favor the aspirations of bourgeois women, but these women supported Qasim. 'Arif thus began by reintroducing polygamy and by modifying inheritance laws making inheritance for Shi'i women much easier than for women of Sunni families. This was an attempt to capture the feudal and peasant women women away from the Qasim legacy; these women were 'Arif's best option because they were less involved in the careers opened by Qasim than were the Sunnis. Generally, the autocrat in both Russia and Iraq aligns himself with poor women rather than middle-class women. The affiliation of the middle-class women with Qasim's alliance stands out as a new kind of politics. 'Arif's personal status law can be seen as a kind of retaliation.

The shift to liberalism within corporatism makes class conflict unusually apparent. 'Arif's regime attempted to deflect popular attention away from class issues by setting out to purge the Communists. His attempt was clumsy. The National Guard, a civilian militia loyal to the Ba'th party, undertook violent attacks on civilians, often civilians previously uninvolved in politics who simply had the misfortune to be labeled as Communists. Given the corporatist context, the campaign backfired, tarnishing the regime's reputation.

As one might expect in liberal regimes, 'Arif attempted the full range of usual reforms. He modified Qasim's land reform laws to favor the owner class; redefined the Kurdish Question to be one of individual Kurdish rights rather than collective rights; then, swayed by the New Class around him, emphasized Arabism and allowed Iraqi-Kurdish fighting to break out again. In 1963, 'Arif led the Sixth Congress of the Ba'th party in adopting a Soviet-style concept of collective leadership. In 1966, 'Arif's successor, 'Abd al-Rahman 'Arif, who had become president in that year with the death of 'Abd Al-Salam 'Arif, tried to end the fighting by offering the Kurds a nationality in a united Iraqi homeland. Viewed in a comparative perspective, this was essentially the Stalinist solution. Viewed in terms of Iraq, a nationality-type solution, especially in a liberal phase, was not entirely realistic. In fact, it hurt 'Arif's regime. All the liberal phases in the past had been predicated on Arabism; for liberal politicians to encourage

Kurdish nationalism was counterproductive. A real nationality solution, judging from the experience of the Soviet Union, depended on a high level of industrialization. In Iraq, this was lacking; one could not simply move primary industrialization to Kurdistan.[33] A provincial ruling class in Kurdistan might simply use economic power given to it to secede. Having antagonized the Left, the liberals, and the Arab nationalists with his policies, 'Abd Al-Rahman 'Arif, in his turn, grew more isolated. Like many of his predecessors, he had to depend on his personal political skill more than on the strength of the system. Never cohesive from the start, his regime collapsed precipitously in 1968.[34]

The rise of Saddam Husayn in a duumvirate with Hasan Al-Bakr in 1968 during the so-called Second Ba'thi Revolution marked the swing of the pendulum toward a new seven-year phase of autocracy. It was, however, more than a simple return to autocracy or to an autocracy modified by the presence of a "New Class"; it marked an attempt to hold the line, to break down once and for all the corporatist alliance. It was a period of purges, a period of crisis in secular culture, a period marking the rebirth of a challenge by the religious hierarchy for control of the state, and, finally, as the decade progressed, a period of rebirth of neoliberal economics.

From 1968 to 1971, the Ba'thi leadership supported a policy of purges not dissimilar to that of Stalin after 1928; this was the heyday of the notorious head of the security forces, Nadhim Kizar, a confidant of Saddam Husayn, a figure one could term the Pauker of Iraq.[35] For middle-class Iraqis in those years, the daily events were nightmarish as they had been for the Soviet middle class in the purges.

In 1968 also, Saddam Husayn declared that Islam was the religion of the state. Perhaps overreaching his actual power, he named a secretary of the Organization for Religious Orientation in Najaf to run the traditional hierarchy.

In reaction to these initiatives, the Shi'i elite set out to strengthen its power base. Iraq was becoming more urbanized; many peasants had been unjustly forced off their lands and driven into the urban slums. With this consideration in mind in 1968, the Shi'ite hierarchy launched a semisecret, urban-oriented evangelizing movement, Al-Da'wa Al-Islamiya (Islamic Mission). The results were impressive even if, as critics have maintained, the movement clearly undertook too much too quickly. Where in Iran, the Shi'i opposition to the shah took control of the mainstream culture, in Iraq this was impossible or, at least, more difficult. The Ba'th party did not repudiate Islam as the shah had done in Iran. Control of mainstream culture, thus, had to be contested with the Ba'th party. One wing of the Iraqi clergy, including the famous *'alim* (theologian) Muhammad Baqir Al-Sadr, nonetheless, began openly to support Khomeini's call for *wilayat al-faqih* (political rule by theologians). Quietism and secrecy were no longer necessary; in a time of such oppression, the logic of an Islamic revolution would become obvious. However progressive Sadr's theory was, and this it was, the organizational base for a revolution of any sort in Iraq was not prepared; there was no rapprochement of the Shi'a with the Sunnis of the middle classes or with the working class and no mass following for religious leaders. Possible linkages with the Left had not been forged. Thus, nothing prevented the Ba'th party from arresting and executing Sadr, his famous sister, Bint Al-Huda' and a number of other religious leaders as traitors to the state. This tragedy, a lost opportunity for counterhegemonic struggle, happened in 1980.[36]

After 1968, Ba'thi policy toward the Communists and the industrial working class changed in keeping with the logic of autocracy. Where from 1963 to 1968, the Ba'th party was a virtual enemy of the Communist party and the working class, after 1968 and at least until 1975, the Ba'th party sought to incorporate them into the state and to co-opt their politics. Thus, between 1969 and 1971, as heavy industry developed, the Ba'th party passed a number of laws to protect the rights and health of industrial workers. In this period also, workers were unionized, and finally the Communists were allowed a token presence.[37]

After 1968, the logic of autocracy required centralization of political control in the countryside and collectivization of agriculture. In 1969, the Governorates Law abolished the independence of the village. All power was returned to the provincial governor. In 1970, the Ba'th party proposed a program of agricultural cooperatives borrowed essentially from Qasim's Land Law of 1958, but predicated on their own much-higher level of political authority in the countryside. The party anticipated (incorrectly) as Stalin once had that higher productivity in agriculture would result from agricultural cooperatives than from land reform. Productivity does not rise when the state tries to control the peasant. Even if the legal rights of peasants were greater under the laws governing cooperative agriculture than ever before, as the Ba'thi's claimed, peasants claimed that their actual freedom of choice declined. Not surprisingly, production levels stood still or declined.

Were the Ba'thi officials as persuaded of collective agriculture as their Soviet counterparts? It seems unlikely. As of 1972, 3 percent of the owners still owned 30 percent of the land, and there was no move on the part of the state to change matters. If anything, with the swing toward liberalism after 1975, signs appeared that Iraq was beginning a trend back toward private ownership of farms. In fact, by 1980, the family farm unit essentially replaced the collective farm. And through this period, much evidence exists to suggest that peasant resistance to collectivization was forcing the state's hand, a point one could easily infer, on the one hand, from the official tirades against farmers and, on the other, from the intense distaste peasants evinced toward the employees of the agricultural extension service.[38]

After 1975, the private sector, buoyed by oil wealth, grew especially in construction and contracting. The growth of the private sector helped to reestablish regional and communal life that had been downtrodden since 1968. The state, however, did not relinquish its controls. Liberalism was once again "guided" liberalism. During this period, the state continued to invest in heavy industry.

Oil wealth and a growing power of the state after 1975 began to erode the political position of the organized Iraqi working class and lower middle class. Gradually, they allowed themselves to be bought off economically in return for their political quiescence. As in the Soviet Union and in other countries, this freed the hand of the ruling class to experiment with pieces of neoliberalism and even with greatpowerism.

In 1980, Iraq attacked Iran. It was destined to be a very long war. Russian Road analysis sheds some light on what took place. In the early phases, Iraq had the initiative, but it missed a major military opportunity. Saddam Husayn hesitated to attack Iran, and thereafter lost the initiative. There is no surprise in this. At least since the first Palestine war of 1948, Iraqi military strategy has been to keep the troops under tight rein; strategists have emphasized defense over offense.[39] Offense is more costly. The reasoning behind this approach seems irrefutable. The infantry was drawn from the lower classes and from the countryside; under Russian Road conditions, its loyalty to the government was never predictable. Thus, even when Iraq had the upper hand, the battle of Stalingrad served as the model for the strategists. By contrast, after 1979, the Iranian alliance between the Mullas and the slum dwellers, albeit a very unusual populist development in what was also a Russian Road system, permitted the Khomeini regime to risk offensive campaigns. The reliance on young children, however, suggests some reservations.

War for the Iraqi state seemed to become part of the reproduction of life. Oil money came; some of it could be invested, but most of it went to weapons for the war. The existence of a war drained off many lower-class men and permitted a certain level of social control the regime needed if it was going to prolong liberalism and not have unmanageable levels of class conflict. By 1990, the war was over and the Ba'this needed another war, so they invaded Kuwait. The American government needed a war, too, because a similar kind of economic dislocation was affecting its politics. This led to the Gulf War. Iraq was defeated, losing many lower-class people from its slum population during the bombing. In the aftermath, liberalism seems quite secure.

The rise of the Russian Road hegemony in Iraq did not have the same consequences that it did in the Soviet Union. First, the working class of Iraq was only very recently and never so fully incorporated by the state. Second, the middle strata was not fragmented in the pursuit of nationality questions as it was in the Soviet Union. Rather, the Iraqi middle strata have always supported broad-gauge integrative trends, such as liberalism, communism, and Islam.

Herein lies the specificity of each country. The Soviet Union developed essentially unchallenged for many years; as a consequence, the state permitted a deep institutional structure to flourish until it finally woke up to the crisis of an overly large New Class. Iraq developed as a crisis state, its middle strata and working class a potential challenge to the ruling group. As a consequence, the state blocked the development of middle-strata institutions on the assumption that they would serve the interests of its opponents.

The Organization of Culture in Iraq

The general features of a Russian Road type of organization of culture were in place in Iraq by the turn of the twentieth century. Some of these features were much older; some presumably newer. To maintain the cultural dualism, rulers promoted an urban prose culture rooted in Ottoman Turkish and classical Arabic. This culture was played off against a rural culture more oriented to poetry, especially to colloquial poetry and to popular music. The field of history recorded the activities of the dominant and mainly urban caste; folklore and folklore museums recorded those of the rest.

Features of the organization of culture are special to Iraq or, at least, to a crisis state in the Russian Road of which Iraq is an example. Of governmental paranoia about the evolution of middle class cultural organizations, two examples especially stand out: the governmental response to the professionalization of education and the governmental response to the activities of the literary salons.

Education policy in all the hegemonies is a terrain of controversies. In a Russian Road state, these controversies include the issue of whether there should be universal education and, if so, how it should be managed. First, if there is to be universal education, how can it be implemented without jeopardizing the social dualism of city and countryside? Second, if there is to be universal education, can the state allow a body of professional teachers to come into existence?

Although the common view in this century is that each specialty in education and in knowledge more generally benefits from professional organizations to organize its progress, politicians in Iraq have been circumspect about the functioning and even about the existence of such professional organizations. A professional organization might, after all, serve as a locus of power that could threaten the state. This concern grew, naturally, with a crisis state situation.

From 1923 onward, the Iraqi state encouraged professional education; at the same time, it blocked the professionalism that normally accompanies such developments. Legal education, was one of the most important fields in Iraqi higher education. Although Iraq had the first law school in the Fertile Crescent, it lacked an institutionalized bar until 1933, long after other countries had theirs; it also lacked a firmly established law journal until 1942 or a pension system for lawyers until 1960. Even after the formation of the Bar Association, lawyers did not have a free hand in its operation. This state of affairs was paralleled in such areas as the Medical Syndicate formed in 1952 and in that of other guilds formed even after the revolution of 1958.[40]

Where professional organizations are strong, they regulate entrance to the profession. This is not the case in Iraq. Entrance to professional life is regulated by politicians. For example, the criteria for admission to law school in the liberal phases were different from those in the autocratic phases. In the liberal phases, at least before the rise of the New Class in 1963, the policy was to reach out and accommodate; in autocratic phases, narrow criteria of selection were in place. Thus, in liberal phases, the regimes tried to enroll Shi'ite students in law school despite their lower level of preparation, avoiding possible quarrels with them by narrowing the domain of legal education, making it more technical, and diminishing thereby the contact with politics and critical thought they found controversial. During autocratic phases, the regime solved the problem differently. The curriculum was widened, but entrance to law school was more controlled.

Where professional organizations meet too much resistance, one response by scholars has been simply to avoid them and to carry on their work in the traditional literary salons and coffeehouses. In Iraq, these institutions have played a vital role in Iraqi culture until quite recently, and the state has long sought ways to control them.

For many centuries, in fact, educated Iraqis have belonged to private literary clubs, the salons, or *majalis*. There, poets recited poetry and scholars did research. From the 1930s, one notes the serious efforts of Iraqi governments to control these organizations. To this end, the politicians encouraged and praised those salons that adopted patriotic positions, for example, clubs such as the Nadi Al-Qalam Al-'Iraqi (Iraqi Writers' Club). From 1945 onward, the government began to create cultural institutions of its own, for example, in 1945, Lajnat al-ta'lif wa al-nashr (Committee to Promote Writing and Publishing) and in 1947, the Iraqi Scientific Academy.[41] In the long run, governmental fear of the salon and the coffeehouse led to a policy of circumventing them by forming more and more official institutions, including professional organizations and even universities.

The government's fear of the salon and of the coffeehouse had two bases: first, a fear of the knowledge that might be produced in them or the opinions expressed in them and second, a fear of the free assemblage of influential people in them. In 1934, The Iraqi Writers' Club, for example, had as members several well-known poets, historians, and educators. When two major figures of the Shi'ite establishment, Baqir and Muhammad Rida Shabibi also joined, the club instantly took the spotlight. Was a political agenda underlying all this cultural contact?

If, during the interwar period, the salons of Baghdad were a center for the middle strata and their culture, the coffeehouses served as the cultural centers for the rest of the urban population. With much of the power structure resigned to or even sympathetic to nationalism in this period, it became increasingly possible for even the greatest poets, figures such as Maruf Al-Rasafi and Jamil Sidqi Al-Zahawi, to recite nationalist poetry to coffeehouse audiences. It was also in coffeehouses that poets raised social problems in their poetry. Not surprisingly, it was there as well that the left-wing intelligentsia, poets such as Muhammad Mahdi Al-Jawahiri (b. 1900), held court.

Al-Jawahiri and his circle are a probable example of what made the government nervous about coffeehouse and salon culture. While in literary terms, Al-Jawahiri was a part of the conservative classical tradition, politically he was a radical. Al-Jawahiri was not only a great poet but a great inspirer of the poets around him. As a teacher, Al-Jawahiri was the inspiration for three of the most famous poets of the entire Arabic language of our times, all three Iraqis, all three political critics. One of these was Badr Shakir Al-Sayyab. Originally, Al-Sayyab was a Communist; later he embraced modernist criticism in postwar Iraq and went on to play a role in the Arab world not unlike the role that Bertolt Brecht has played in Europe.[42] Another one of these poets was 'Abd Al-Wahhab Al-Bayyati, also a Communist, author of an extraordinary poem anticipating the revolution of 1958 and of a famous ode to the Russian people at Stalingrad. The third poet was Naziq Al-Mala'ika. Her fame came from the postwar revolution in free verse and her subsequent contributions to modernism.[43] More recently, the popular colloquial opposition poet, Muzaffar Al-Nawwab, emerged from the coffeehouse culture. With the gradual politicization of the coffeehouse, subsequent Iraqi regimes of the postwar period have searched for new strategies to control of culture. From this postwar period, one can date an increase in official patronage in cultural fields: Baghdad University opened in 1957; the growth of radio and television followed.

Official preoccupation with the control of culture reaches its high points in the autocratic periods. In Iraq, one such high point was reached in 1968. In 1968, the Ba'th party set out to control not only the institutional culture of the university but poetry and prose itself. And, in a moment of good luck, it did so: first, by direct patronage, exiling or buying off well-known poets, for example, Muhammad Mahdi Al-Jawahiri and Muzaffar

Al-Nawwab, and second, by sponsoring youth poetry, especially youth poetry that lacked any social content.[44]

One can control prose writers sometimes, but can one really control poets? In the Ottoman period, politicians obliged poets to be court poets, to carry on poetic traditions of use to the court, such as the traditions of praise and mourning. Their rationale was that if poets can communicate with the masses, this skill should be used in an appropriate way. Literary critics point out that officially sponsored poetry is insincere, that it represents a debasement of the language, but seen from the point of view of strategic practice or of bureaucratic needs, this is not an issue.[45] The trouble has always been, in countries such as Iraq, rebel poets. Certainly, there is poetry praising Saddam Husayn. The problem for Saddam Husayn is that Iraq has poets who will not praise him.

Prose serves as the more reliable basis for an urban and literate culture. Not surprisingly, Iraqi leaders from the Ottoman period onward have encouraged prose writers. As early as 1917, John Van Ess, an American missionary in Iraq, published a grammar book, *The Spoken Arabic of Iraq*, facilitating the development of the prose language. As the years went by, an immense number of prose works have appeared, especially in Baghdad and Najaf. Since the 1940s, the Iraqi government, as indicated, published prose works and even sponsored a weekly radio program drilling its listeners on proper prose usage.[46]

Furthermore, as the power of the state developed, the state became increasingly more careful about what it would sponsor. Van Ess's book was discarded as too tolerant of the spoken language; more useful were grammars and glossaries explicitly sharpening the cultural dualism.[47] After the 1968 revolution, the state again reevaluated its role as a sponsor of prose. By this time, with literacy spreading fairly rapidly, the party feared that excessive access to prose would permit too much social integration. The Ba'this, not unlike the Soviets, reacted to this by encouraging socialist realism for the masses and an elliptical political prose only really accessible to the political insiders of the city. *Al-Thawra* became the Iraqi *Pravda*.

Since the 1940s, as was also noted, politicians have made use of the mass media on a very considerable scale, first radio and then television. Liberal regimes saw the media as a way to promote their philosophy of the development of the educated citizen. By contrast, autocratic regimes placed great hope in the media as an instrument for controlling the citizen's thought. In the National Action Charter of 1971, the Ba'th party defined the role of the media as a "collective persuader, educator, agitator, reformer and mobilizer . . . to be closely supervised because of its relation to the masses."[48] For both the supporters of liberalism and autocracy, poetry recitals would always be a part of Iraqi television programming; prose, however, would be the dominant language form.

After 1975, Iraq swung from an autocratic to a liberal phase, and the corporatist age as a whole faded. At this point, the Ba'th party's activism diminished. The party acknowledged that its own shows on the media had few watchers; most Iraqis preferred the traditional music shows and even the private sector movie productions to the shows of the government.[49]

In Russian Road regimes, the religious hierarchy plays an important role in the hegemony and the organization of culture. In Russia and in Iraq, this subject remains understudied. A partial justification for scholarly neglect is that in the two cases at hand, the religious leadership made miscalculations that lost it power vis-à-vis the secular structure. This explains why the two examples of Russian Road regimes in this book are so secular.

Among other miscalculations made by the Iraqi hierarchy, after dissuading their followers from pursuing secular education, the Shi'ite elite found that few in their community possessed the necessary qualifications for the new government jobs that became available in the twentieth century. As a result, students abandoned the religious schools for the secular ones. After half a century, the religious structure shows signs of making a comeback. Today, it is the main challenger to the continued dominance of the Ba'th party and to secularism.[50] How did this come to be?

The organization of culture undertaken by different regimes over the twentieth century has succeeded in dividing the opposition. Perhaps, however, just barely. The Ba'th regime was more than lucky that it was able to isolate and assassinate Sadr. His challenge was formidable; it combined Islam with leftist secularism.

History in Russian Road regimes is a strong area of the hegemony. It reveals the prowess of the leadership. Iraq is no exception.

Historians and History-Writing in Iraq

As in Russia and the Soviet Union, the main point of emphasis in history writing in Iraq has been the state. Historians study the state through political and diplomatic history and in the context of world history. Notwithstanding the importance of history to modern Iraqi regimes, for a generation or more, the politics of the crisis state effectively blocked the development of a professional organization until 1970. Yet as early as the 1960s, Iraq had historians with international reputations and even before that time had historians who were well known in the Arab world.[51]

Between 1869 and 1963, history writing evolved from the town chronicles of local littérateurs to national political history of the sort identified in the chapter 2 as state school liberalism. Shunned by the state itself during both the colonial and the postcolonial era, the best-known historians of those eighty odd years worked in the literary salons or on the periphery of state employment.[52]

In contrast to the professor of history in the corporatist era after 1963, the historian of this period trained himself to write for the general educated public. Several major historians from the early twentieth century were actually lawyers or journalists who managed to write studies, even multi-volume works, in their spare time.

One particularly celebrated work composed in this period recounted the history of Baghdad from 1257 to 1917. The work was nationalist in tone; it commanded a considerable audience. Its author was a lawyer who was also a historian, 'Abbas Al-'Azzawi. He began this work in the late 1930s and saw its last volume appear in 1956.[53]

In contrast to history writing in Russia, history writing in Iraq has tended to be on the medieval state. Political conditions appear to be the obvious explanation. A generation or two of a crisis state dating from at least 1923 onward has made the terrain of modern Iraqi history less appealing for writers capable of deep interpretations. Many historians adopted themes about medieval Baghdad that hint, however, at life in modern Baghdad.

In the late 1950s and early 1960s with the rise of the corporatist state, history writing shifted from the salon to the university history department. Social history emerged briefly; monumental works ceased to be produced. The number of monographs increased. During this transitional period, an influential scholar was the economic historian Muhammad Salman Hasan, author of *Al-Tatawwur al-iqtisadi fi al-'Iraq* Sayda: Al-Maktabah Al-'Asriyah, (A study of the economic development of Iraq from 1864 to 1958 with emphasis on foreign trade)(1965). Hasan showed how Iraq's economy was caught in the world economy and how the development of capitalism changed the country. During the same period, Salih Al-'Ali published a history of medieval Basra, which emphasized its social and economic features.[54]

The Ba'thi Revolution of 1968 marked a swing back to autocracy. Not only social historians but all the liberal members of the profession suddenly began to experience a lot of pressure against them. One professor in Baghdad University, Fadil Husayn, a political historian, and the author of a very objective study on the fall of the monarchy became a symbol of the liberal will to survive.[55]

After the 1968 revolution, history once again became political history; social and economic analysis was driven out of history into fields such as sociology. Figures such as Muhammad Salman Hasan were marginalized; Salih Al-'Ali survived after 1968 but did not publish another major work for years. Even a historical sociologist, 'Ali Al-Wardi, a scholar whose career was well launched before the 1968 revolution, was "put on the shelf" thereafter. Al-Wardi had published numerous studies on Iraqi society; he was also known for his interest in world history.[56] Yet in sociology, as events showed, a writer with a historical bent could encounter political problems. Al-Wardi's penchant for objective descriptions of Iraqi society led him to insist on the importance of Iranians as part of Iraqi history. This subject made him controversial; consequently, the Ba'th party pushed him away from the university into retirement. Al-Wardi's interest in the historical model of Ibn Khaldun probably helped him survive these setbacks because the party was also interested in Ibn Khaldun.[57]

In 1969, a number of the prominent historians aligned with the state managed to form a professional organization. Trends in Iraqi historiography at odds with the dominant pan-Arab nationalism of the Ba'th from this point began to appear as challenges and not simply as alternatives.

On an intellectual level, professionalization brought little that was new. As early as the generation of World War I, the pan-Arabist paradigm had a wide appeal in Iraqi thought albeit as opposition ideology. In the 1940s, pan-Arabism even gained a measure of international validation when the well-known British historian, Arnold Toynbee, granted Arab culture a distinct position in his schema of world history. A distinguished Iraqi archeologist, Taha Baqir, translated Toynbee into Arabic in 1946. From the 1940s until today, at least in pan-Arabist circles, there has been a virtual Toynbee cult in Iraq. After 1968, this trend was accentuated.

Medieval Iraqi history had been a terrain for the pan-Arabist trend in the preceding generation and this continued. The leading medievalist of this past generation, 'Abd Al-'Aziz al-Duri, was, in fact, a pan-Arabist. In the 1960s, he had risen to be president of Baghdad University. In one of several well-known books, he characterized medieval Arab culture, especially that of Iraq, as the point of origin of the modern field of history writing. In another, he drew attention to the threats to the Arabs throughout history from their enemies and notably from the so-called Shu'ubiya (Persian-leaning) trend. Although Al-Duri himself went into exile as the Ba'th party rose, his ideas are still current. Probably, they have more influence today than they did in the 1960s. Faruq 'Umar, a chairman of the history department at Baghdad University in the 1970s-1980s and also a specialist on the 'Abbasids has adopted many positions identical to those of Al-Duri.[58]

The novelty surrounding the professionalization of history was that it led to the persecution of non-pan-Arabists, meaning, of course, liberals and Communists. Surviving professors tell of violent oppression, scapegoatism, purges in the university, censorship, and an all-pervasive atmosphere of bureaucratic pressure. For the first time, the liberal majority turned in on itself and ignored modern changes in professional trends simply to survive. When most of the profession of historians in the world moved toward social history in the 1970s, making it the dominant and fastest-growing part of the field, Iraqi historians shunned it, not for scientific reasons but because it was associated in the mind of the Ba'this with the breakdown of the social dualism and, hence, with class conflict.

In 1969 as professionalism began, Husayn Amin, a historian with ties to the party, was chosen to be the first editor of the organization's new journal. Under Amin's editorship, the *al-Majalla al-ta'rikhiya (Historical Journal)* published its first issue in 1970, beginning with an editorial introduction praising the party and by implication criticizing the work of earlier Iraqi historians in the liberal tradition (3). Amin called for scientific research that would evoke the role of the Arabs and Muslims in the construction of society.

The party obviously hoped that the *Historical Journal* would help incline the Iraqi historians toward Ba'thism. They saw the development of professionalism in much the same light. It was part of the autocracy.

Who were the historians drawn to the party? What can one learn from a glance at their careers? Two of the three Ba'thi historians whose careers took off after 1968 are easy to interpret. Husayn Amin, a *Seljuq* specialist, and A'ala Nurus, an Ottomanist, emerged from historical specializations usually perceived as unimportant by the mainstream of the profession. The Ba'thi Revolution gave them new career opportunities through an interface with the party. The third, Faruq 'Umar, was born into the Revolution as the son of an army officer. He managed a career both as a diplomat and as a scholar. 'Umar was a specialist on the 'Abbasid period, useful because the Ba'th party wanted to be pictured as the continuators of the great caliphs of medieval Baghdad. 'Umar's article in the first volume of the *journal* on medieval Iranian subversive movements in Baghdad fit the party's needs; Iranian subversive movements in Baghdad were a danger for the Ba'th party as well.

Amin's incorporation of non-Ba'thi trends in the *Historical Journal* seemed to parallel the incorporative approach of the hegemony as a whole. Even religion could be a legitimate, albeit a subordinate, part of Arab history. This point was underscored in the very first article of the first issue, Amin's own essay on the rise of the institution of the teaching assistant in the medieval madrasa education system in Baghdad. Amin had deliberately chosen a subject containing an Islamic element alongside an Arab element. In the same year, Amin published an article by 'Abd Allah Fayyad on the Buwayid period. In a commentary one year later, the *Journal* reported that Professor Fayyad had given a speech in Karbala' on the role of the guerilla in Islam in the past and in the present. The speech was well received; Amin accepted it, too, for publication because it combined Arab and Islamic themes.

Amin also published articles by liberal and Marxist writers. He showed some deference to the most famous modern historian, Fadil Husayn, publishing his essay on the Arab historian and the Palestine Question, a theme that was in any case greatly appealing to the pan-Arabists. Two articles appeared by another prominent figure, Faysal Samir, once a politician of the Left, later a history professor. One of Samir's articles was on modern

Iraqi history, and the other was on movements of religious and secular renewal in Indonesia.[59]

From the mid-1970s as economic liberalism began to reassert itself, the Ba'th party still sought to control the writing and teaching of history although from this period, it permitted a wider range of trends. Among the main initiatives of the period after 1975 were the publication of a book on how the government wanted historians to write history, the production of reference works and encyclopedias codifying the official worldview of the party, the opening of new institutions in which the Ba'th Party would have more academic as opposed to merely bureaucratic influence, the shift to sponsoring large-scale projects more easily controlled from the top than small-scale, single-scholar research projects, the regimentation of the work day of professors effectively to discourage small-scale private research, and the creation of a new pan-Arab history organization, the Union of Arab Historians, that would bypass the conflicts between liberals and Ba'this that were beginning by the mid-1970s to unravel the first professional organization.

Clearly, the Party wanted a student body with heightened loyalty to Ba'thism. The historians were not producing this loyalty. The solution must be a pedagogical one, so the party decided to instruct historians how to achieve this objective. They brought together a number of senior professors and government officials and produced a collection of essays that they published in the name of the president of the country, Saddam Husayn, entitled *Hawla kitabat al-ta'rikh* (On the writing of history)(Baghdad: Al-Maktaba Al-Wataniya, 1979). From this work, one learns that while the liberals, for example, Salih Al-'Ali, study the past for its own sake, the Ba'thi's study the past for its utility to present politics. In the spirit of the Soviet Institute of Red Professors, the Ba'thi's called for the historian to manipulate and not merely mold knowledge. Nizar Al-Hadithi, a historian, party official, and director of a Ba'thi Research Center noted in his essay how the study of history could help to achieve desired goals. Al-Hadithi praised the Prophet Muhammad for using history in this way.[60]

Governments weigh the benefits and liabilities of cultural patronage. If researchers in modern or medieval Arab history tend to be fairly self-sufficient, it no doubt often follows that the government can have but little influence over them. In archeology, however, practitioners have always maintained that they cannot move forward without significant patronage. In this case, patronage means real control, and real control was what the party sought. Although budgetary figures are not available to show how much money was spent to promote the study of archeology compared to other kinds of history, the Ba'thi's decision to promote large-scale archeology was a conspicuous one if for no other reason than that for the past generation, world trends in archeology have emphasized small-scale, cost-saving work. It was in this context the Ba'thi's set out with a limited trained staff to excavate and reconstruct the most spectacular planned city of antiquity, Samarra', an 'Abbasid capital.[61]

While the expansion of the New Class in the 1960s and 1970s diminished the utility of purges, the Ba'th party did its best to regiment the life of the professors. In this, they succeeded. University professors are often physically tired from the mandatory forty-five week per year attendance in the university and from teaching schedules that can range from ten hours upward. In 1978, these requirements actually became formalized in a law regulating university service, a law passed on the pretext that the government had the right to curb teachers and professors from spending their time giving private lessons. Because most of the professors do not have private offices but sit twelve in a room until 4:00 P.M., individual work is difficult or impossible. Thus, the government can pay a substantial amount for publication, but few publish with any regularity. There are simply too many obstacles. Shopping for necessities takes a great deal of time in Baghdad. The city lacks enough modern stores, and there are constant shortages even of necessities. If necessities are in short supply so, too, are new books and periodicals from abroad, whether in Arabic or European languages. In addition, the price of books is high; the quality of photocopying is very low. For the younger generation, developing in the 1970s and thereafter, the results have been devastating; for the older generation, the situation has not been much better; many try to live off their past.[62]

By 1975 the Ba'th party's attempt to impose its controls was weakening. The attempt to impose a profession on the historians had failed; conflicts between the liberal and the Arab trends were too deep. Shortly thereafter, in what appeared as a fall-back position of the party, Husayn Amin began a new journal called *Al-Mu'arrikh Al-'Arabi (The Arab historian)*. It continues to this day. This journal was the project of a hand-picked group who also ran a new professional organization, the Union of Arab Historians. The editorial board of the *Arab Historian* had, apart from Amin himself, only one other Iraqi member, 'Abd Al-Amir Muhammad Amin, a member of the party and a professor in the College of Education. In this new journal, Husayn Amin continued to emphasize the rational progressive and Arab character of Islam and Islamic history. Amin's contribution as an editor lay in his focus upon Arnold Toynbee's contribution to understanding the Arabs. As a number of articles made clear, the Ba'thi's understood Toynbee to be interested in an Arabo-Islamic personality as opposed to a Persian one. In issue 7 (1978), the chair of the history department at Algiers University took up the theme of Toynbee and African history while Derek Hopwood, the English scholar, addressed the subject of Toynbee and anti-Zionism, linking this subject to Toynbee's attraction to civilization as a unit of study. Finally, Muhammad Tawfiq Husayn of Baghdad University wrote an article on Toynbee's pro-Arabism and summarized his debates about Jewish history with the English-Iraqi-Jewish scholar Elie Kedourie. In number 9 (1978), Jawad 'Ali, a historian of the pre-Islamic period, wrote on Toynbee's cultural morphology approach, noting as well the latter's long opposition to Anglo-Saxon racialist theories of civilization, among them Zionism.[63]

By the end of the 1970s, a new figure from the party was on the rise in the history profession of Iraq, Mustafa 'Abd Al-Qadir Al-Najjar. Al-Najjar had risen rapidly in party politics in Basra. The party appointed him director of the Gulf Study Center of Basra and editor of its journal. When Al-Najjar moved to Baghdad, he had a firm foothold in the party and succeeded Husayn Amin as the head of the Union of Arab Historians.[64] Al-Najjar's rise has signaled a gradual acceptance of more diversity. The Islamic, the Iraqi Civilization school and the communist trend are once again in evidence and growing in importance within the history profession.

By the late 1970s, 'Imad Ad-Din Khalil, a history professor at the University of Mawsil, had become an important representative of the Islamic trend in history writing. Khalil's career is an interesting one. In 1965, Khalil wrote his master's thesis at Baghdad University on a medieval military and political figure who lived in the North of Iraq, 'Imad Ad-Din al-Zankhi. In an atmosphere strongly favoring military and political history and with a subject that lent itself to such genres, Khalil nonetheless treated his subject without much reference to them but rather as a way to raise contemporary problems of ethics. Khalil approached Al-Zankhi as a Muslim forced to choose between good and good. This theme, which one associates with tragedy, pervades a number of Khalil's books of the 1970s and 1980s on such subjects as nature in Western art, the problem of freedom and determinism in contemporary Arab theater, a miracle on the West Bank, social justice, the life of the Prophet, and even criticism of contemporary Islam.

Historical methodology occupied an important place in Khalil's writings as well. In an article in the early 1970s, Khalil argued for a holistic approach to teaching. He criticized the exaggerated emphasis placed on memorization in the teaching of history at the expense of comparison and analysis. He suggested that teachers should give one hour a week to a theorist, for example, Toynbee. They should also spend some time helping students overcome negative feelings about being Arab and Muslim brought by the Western influence in Arab universities.[65]

In a 1975 book on the connection of historical study to religion, Khalil argued that the interpretation of history comes from the vision of God; the division of reality into past, present and future is much less important than another dimension, that which probes the depth of the human soul. God reaches humans through their souls and molds them. Khalil compared the movement of history to that of a waterwheel that goes round and round; states rise and fall in their turn as bearers of values and principles.[66]

By the end of the 1970s, the Iraqi Civilization school was once again in evidence as well. Among its major protagonists was Ahmed Sousa *(sic)* (d. 198?), a historian of the Iraqi-Jewish community. In several well-known books written over a long lifetime, Sousa emphasized the cultural unity of Iraq from ancient to modern times.[67]

Syriac studies underwent a brief revival as well. The year 1975 witnessed the founding of *Majalla Majma' al-Lughah al-Suryaniya,* a journal of the Syriac Language Academy. It appeared for several years and then was subsumed for political reasons by the party and put under the trusteeship of the state-controlled Iraqi Scientific Academy. The journal had had an English language section and an Arabic section. In the first volume (1975), two European Orientalists praised the glories of the Chaldean church, and Faruq 'Umar, the 'Abbasid specialist, wrote an essay on the attitude of the early 'Abbasids toward Christians and Jews. They were well treated, he maintained. Restrictions placed on minorities were matters of Caliphal expediency to curry favor with the masses and the *'ulama'* against political enemies. Such pressures forced the Caliph al-Mutawakkil to invent customs with no grounding in the Qur'an. This, of course, was the Ba'thi line, and it is not inconceivable that they had an interest in Syriac studies, possibly an interest in driving a wedge between the Syriac-speaking Christians and Kurds. Articles by local Christian scholars, however, challenged the party line, albeit indirectly, imputing rationalism to the religious tradition and historicity to miracles. One such article took up Syriac scientists and the rationalist tradition; another studied a Christian miracle at a time of Roman persecution.

Among other projects promoted by local Christian scholars of the academy during its short life was an attempt to make Syriac a living language and to make a modern dictionary for it. This last may have been their undoing.[68] Not only did the party stand for Arabic but the words, which were chosen to start the dictionary, did not appear to be chosen from traditional philological concerns but from those of oppositional politics. One group of words to be Aramaicized included *military dictatorship, state, salary, capitalism, reactionary, administrator, cheap prices, political views, international oil monopolies, humanitarian ideas, fraternal,* and so forth. Not only were the Ba'this alarmed but so were European classical scholars.[69]

In the same time frame, a Confessional school of Iraqi historiography emerged, emphasizing ethnicity and religious sectarianism, some of which was being produced abroad in the West among Orientalists and in Beirut among the Lebanese.[70]

Finally, in the late 1970s and early 1980s, a communist trend among the historians appeared. The Baghdad history professor, Ahmad Kamal

Muzhar, in his *Dawr al-sha'b al-Kurdi fi thawra Tishrin al-'Iraqiya* (On the role of the Kurdish people in the Iraqi revolution of 1920)(Baghdad: Ministry of Information and Culture, 1978), conformed with the liberal age assumption of the assimilatability of the Kurds into Arabic culture. But he gave it a new twist, challenging the presumed Arab character of the revolution of 1920 and reopening, thereby, the unresolved political problem of minority nationality. Such a book was naturally controversial for many Baghdadis in the late 1970s. It was the Arab Iraqis, who were nationalists; the Kurds at best were a backward people and probably were a fifth column. To believe otherwise forced one to go beyond governmental propaganda, to rethink the idea of Kurdistan and ultimately the logic of the hegemony itself.

The dialectics of class struggle in the 1920s and 1930s is the subject of Ahmad Kamal Muzhar's more recent book, *Al-Tabaqa al-'amala al-'Iraqiya: al-takawwun wa bidayat al-taharruk* (The Iraqi working class: Its formation and the beginning of its movement)(Baghdad: Ministry of Information and Culture, 1981). This work sheds light not only on its own period but indirectly on the contemporary one as well.

Seen in a comparative light, Soviet and Iraqi history writing appears quite similar. In Soviet history writing, there has been a long-term tension between the romantic dialectical side and the positivist side, with most historians coming down on the positivist side. This tension appears in Iraqi history writings as well. Where Kamal Mazhar's work exploits the romantic dialectical side, others reflect the positivist side. An example of the latter is the well-known book of 'Isam Khafaji on state capitalism.[71]

One more comparison between Iraqi and Soviet historians remains. A number of Iraqi historians have chosen to, or been forced to, pass most of their careers in exile. Like their Russian and Soviet counterparts, they have, nonetheless, remained intellectually tied to their country of birth; some have even had influence in Iraq. Majid Khadduri (b. 1909) is a well-known liberal who taught and wrote extensively on Iraqi history from various academic positions first in Iraq and then in the United States. Even in the United States, Khadduri has remained sufficiently connected to Iraq to serve as an advisor to the Iraqi government.

If one were to choose representative figures for different eras of modern Iraqi history-writing, one would choose liberals and romantics as in Russia, noting, however, the influence of the crisis state on their careers. A leading State school figure of the liberal tradition was 'Abbas al-'Azzawi. For the period coinciding with corporatism and the rise of the New Class, one would choose a liberal pan-Arabist, for example, 'Abd Al-'Aziz al-Duri. During the transition to neoliberalism, Iraqi history is dominated by organizational figures such as Husayn Amin. The differences between these three men and their Russian counterparts appear to be the wider range of issues they are free to raise and the lack of a position of power on the scale exercised by the likes of a Pokrovsky or a Roy Medvedev. Samir Al-Khalil, author of *Republic of Fear,* is an exile.[72]

In this chapter I argue that the Iraqi ruling class adopted a Russian Road hegemony, that this is a new and plausible way to look at the subject, that it serves to highlight the salient features of the subject, and that this strategy, however, failed to diffuse opposition trends from the middle strata and the working class. As a result of this failure, the rulers of Iraq were forced to develop the country as a crisis state, continuously carrying out pogroms or violent acts of deflection. Institutional development in a crisis state carries with it certain risks for the rulers because it gives a structural context to potential regime opponents. Not surprisingly, organizations, such as middle-class professional organizations, came late to Iraq and often took oppressive forms when they were permitted to function. Despite these objective difficulties, scholarly and popular interest in fields such as history in Iraq has been immense as it often is in Russian Road states. This makes the study of the history profession worthwhile; it is a true mirror of the hegemony itself.

The internal logic of Italian history is entirely different from that of Russia or from that of the northern European states to which it is often compared. I argue that just as Russia can be compared to Iraq, so Italian history can be fruitfully compared to that of other countries of the Third World, including India and Mexico.

4

The "Italian Road" in Italy

The Risorgimento to the Present, 1870–1990

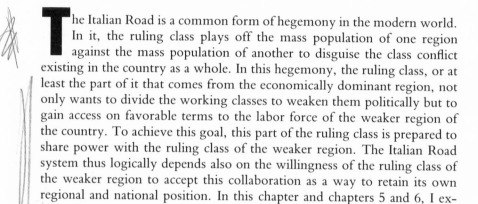

The Italian Road is a common form of hegemony in the modern world. In it, the ruling class plays off the mass population of one region against the mass population of another to disguise the class conflict existing in the country as a whole. In this hegemony, the ruling class, or at least the part of it that comes from the economically dominant region, not only wants to divide the working classes to weaken them politically but to gain access on favorable terms to the labor force of the weaker region of the country. To achieve this goal, this part of the ruling class is prepared to share power with the ruling class of the weaker region. The Italian Road system thus logically depends also on the willingness of the ruling class of the weaker region to accept this collaboration as a way to retain its own regional and national position. In this chapter and chapters 5 and 6, I explore three variants of the Italian Road as they appear in Italy, India, and Mexico.[1]

This chapter has four sections: (1) to introduce the Italian Road as a historical model and relate it to the more specific historiography of Italy proper; (2) to employ the model to study Italy from the Risorgimento, or founding of the modern state, in 1870 up to 1990; (3) to treat hegemony in Italy in the more restricted sense of the organization of culture; and (4) to treat history and history writing in Italy as a part of the organization of culture.

Italian Road hegemonies are political strategies to disguise class conflict by emphasizing the idea of regional difference. In Italian Road regimes, the ruling classes exploit to the hilt the existence of an "advanced," northern region. In Italy, the North includes the Center and the Northeast, the regions that are more urban and more industrialized than is the South. The North possesses, consequently, more of a bourgeois legal culture than does the South; the South is more feudal, agrarian, and culturally rooted in custom.

Given the disparate nature of the regional cultures perpetuated by Italian Road hegemonies, politicians seeking office present themselves as personalities more than as bearers of specific ideologies. Once elected, they leave the actual decision making to the bureaucracy, which has the advantage of functioning behind closed doors.

Italian Road regimes are typically characterized by one dominant party accompanied by a plethora of minor parties, some of which are allied to the dominant party. The one dominant party is umbrellalike; it straddles the whole country, North and South. Some observers believe that a one-party predominance safeguards an Italian Road hegemony better than a functioning two-party system. With two parties, one of them might tend to be more concentrated in one region than the other, which could tear the system apart.

Italian Road regimes go through predictable historical phases. They arise under conditions of nineteenth-century liberalism. When confronted by demands from the lower middle class, they collapse into corporatism. When the pressure diminishes, they return to liberalism. This course of events took place in Italy, India, Mexico, and other Italian Road states as well.

In the Italian Road hegemony, corporatism has essentially two main forms: corporatism of the Right, or fascism, for example, Mussolini's Italy and corporatism of the Left sometimes called *state socialism,* for example, Nehru's India or Cardenas's Mexico. Both forms of corporatism blunt class struggle by at least token integration of groups in civil society into the state. In so doing, corporatist regimes tend to outlaw strikes and other autonomous collective actions typical of the liberal phase of the hegemony.

To generalize very broadly, the specificity of fascism within corporatism is that it tends to favor the interests of the landlord class and of small and middle-size capitalists. It takes the Left and the trade union movement as its special bête noire. It attempts to reorganize the work force through syndicates.

The specificity of state socialism within corporatism is that it benefits the organized working class and, of course, the interests of large-scale capitalism. State socialists take feudalists as their special bête noire. Often, state socialist regimes engage in extensive programs of land reform to destroy the feudalist class. Neither variant of corporatism departs from the logic of the Italian Road; neither uproots the peasantry. In this basic way, fascism differs from nazism, the movement to which fascism is most frequently compared in conventional scholarship. Where fascism as a political movement contented itself with a small political following typical of a country with a large peasant population, nazism was a mass movement, a part of democracy, that is, part of a totally different hegemony. Leaders risk mass movements in democracies when they cannot do so in Italian Road regimes because in democracies, the mass is composed of citizens, individuals integrated into the legal and cultural order. This difference in the organization of the hegemony explains the totalitarian quality of German nazism and the piecemeal quality of Italian fascism.

In Italian Road hegemonies, the leaders tend to organize culture on a regional basis, reinforcing the regionalism emphasized on the political and economic level. Thus, typically, one finds a southern metaphysical tradition and a northern liberal positivist tradition. In this chapter, a certain weight is given to the career of the Italian philosopher, Benedetto Croce, the major example of a southern intellectual.[2] In the following chapters, a certain weight is also given to the analogous figures of Mexico and India, José Vasconcelos and Krishnamurthy. My rationale is that the southern intellectual plays a key role in the hegemony, persuading those in the oppressed region to accept the national culture.

As in the case of other hegemonies, so with the Italian Road, the hierarchy of the dominant religion is an integral part of the power structure. From the late nineteenth century onward, an alignment of the secular and the religious is, thus, apparent as the Catholic church undergoes a seventy-five-year process of delinking and relinking in various ways with the Italian state. The Lateran Accords, 1929–31, was an important moment in that process. As a result, the church has been able to promote its program in civil society through Catholic lay organizations fully protected by the law. In Mexico and India, similar developments took place at the same time.

Given the difference in regions, the role the church plays differs in the North and South. For example, lay Catholics in the North play an important role as reformers. By contrast, in the South the major religious figure is the village priest. In Carlo Levi's famous novel, *Christ Stopped at Eboli,* the author makes clear the limited role the priest plays. To the Italian peasant of the South, Jesus Christ is God and not just his son; Mary is a Goddess; Saint Joseph is a God as well. Furthermore, God is present and not in some remote heaven, and as a consequence, one surely gets one's just deserts. Although such ideas are probably common to many peasantries, what is unusual about Italian Road regimes is the state's response to them, that is, its attempt to reform the North, but not the South.[3] This has been the case not only in Italy but in India as well. Hindu reformists, especially in the North, have long battled the folk ideas of God as an Avatar found in the Rami cults, reformers urging on the Hindu masses a respect for the Sanskritic tradition and with it for the more remote deity Vishnu. This type of reformism is much weaker in the South.

For the study of Italian Road regimes, the most developed trend in historiography is the liberal one.[4] This school dominates history writing in

Italy and on Italy and can, thus, be classified as one of the attributes of the hegemony. Its main premises are that Italy is European and democratic but with some Mediterranean and traditional features, especially in the South; that, however, the South has developed steadily since World War II so that whatever truth there once may have been to the Marxist contention that the South was deliberately held back to provide cheap labor, this is no longer the case today; that in sum, Italy is a liberal democracy, fascism was an aberration.

The liberal school identifies itself with the rise of the modern state and especially with the unification in 1870. It sees liberal ideas and liberal scholarship as the main force overcoming clericalism and provincialism. Although Mussolini gets credit for the Lateran Accords, the solution to the Roman problem, the liberals claim credit for making modern Italy a modern secular country. The inspiration for this achievement they find not only in their links to northern Europe but in the classical past of Italy.

Not surprisingly, there are problems for the Italian Road analysis in the liberal historiography. Liberals assume that Italy is part of "Europe" or European history. On the surface, this view seems unexceptionable. It is, in fact, a rather particular ideological proposition. The European-ness of Italy implies for Italy that the real country is the North, that the South by virtue of being more Mediterranean is less European and by extension, therefore, is less Italian. If one leaves the South out of history and simply considers it the land of folkore, Italy so understood is—or is on the road to being—a democracy as Germany is a democracy. In fact, Europe is really another word for democracy. I would postulate otherwise; for democracy to be a valuable designation of a hegemony, it has to have a fairly precise set of characteristics (to return to the comment about the difference between fascism and nazism). By fairly standard concept, peasant-based societies around the Mediterranean are not democracies unless one exaggerates the role of particular regions within them.

The Marxist tradition in Italian historiography has had the greatest influence of any of the main trends of historiography on the model of Italian Road presented here. This is especially true for the Marxist tradition before 1945; for the Marxist tradition of the post-1945 period, the Italian Road model appears obsolete. At this later date, many Marxists in Italy moved closer to the liberal position outlined above, leaving behind the Italian Marxism of the 1920s and 1930s used here.

That the model of the Italian Road goes against the dominant contemporary version of Italian Marxism is not insignificant. It casts at least the presumption of doubt on the adequacy of its use of Gramsci. Nonetheless, I assume in what follows that it is still useful to distinguish between the long-term validity of Gramsci's insights and what I take to be the tactics the party chose to adopt in his name when accepting the liberal state after

1945, tactics that I believe ultimately to be at odds with Gramsci's approach to Italian history.

To recapitulate, the Italian Road approach, as I use it, maintains that there still is a Southern Question, that when liberalism fails another round of corporatism is probable, that the contemporary liberal age, is in large part a throwback to the era of nineteenth-century finance capitalism, that the old imbalance in power between the North and the South has not been fundamentally modified by the postwar economic growth because this growth has not redressed it, that movements, such as the Movimento Sociale Italiano (MSI) in which Southerners have been important have never been more than a minority force within the status quo, that, while the state does—as part of its hegemonic strategy—make use of appeals that have nothing to do with region, for example, its cold war appeals to beware of the Soviet Union or its appeals to Italian patriotism or even more subliminally, the appeals of seeing the Italian team compete for the European Cup on Italian TV or seeing attacks by racists against foreigners in Italy again on the Italian news, these appeals are less important than what the state also upholds and appeals to: the laws, the customs, the organizations of the political and economic structure that, taken collectively, make regionalism central to the hegemony.

Having made these claims, it must however be admitted that the subject of the South as a part of modern Italian history remains an undeveloped one in contemporary scholarship. The fact that the important writers in the dominant paradigm have assumed that "underdeveloped" means unimportant has no doubt had a large influence on scholarly priorities in general.

In trying to reassert the logic of taking Italian national dynamics as a whole, the South included, the most appropriate tack in this type of study seems to be one of stressing that what information there is available about the South, for example, in migration studies, in peasant studies, in gender analyses, in the study of family structures, in the study of the regional high culture and finally from politics, take for example the Mafia and the northern "leagues" in recent years, all point toward the continuation of the Southern Question and thereby cast doubt on the adequacy of the dominant paradigm, the dominant paradigm being that Italy is a democracy.

The Italian Road approach, whatever its debt to writers in the other world views and whatever the stance of the PCI at a given moment, derives most of its inspiration, even its comparativism, from Marxism. Marx commented on the similarity of India and Italy; later on, so did Gramsci.[5] According to the contemporary Marxist scholar Victor Kiernan, Gramsci had keen insights about the struggle for independence in India. Although most Marxists dismissed Gandhi out of hand, Gramsci saw revolutionary possibilities in Gandhi's movement. True, he ultimately judged Gandhi to be a naïve theorist, not because of his religiosity or because of the spiritualism of the Orient, but on strategic grounds. In Gramsci's view, India was like Italy a country where the nationalists were elitists and afraid to mobilize the masses. Today in India, this type of Italian Road reading of Indian history is alive and well in certain circles.

Romanticism constitutes a force in Italian historiography and in the ✓ influential writing on Italy by non-Italians. It, too, contributes to the model of the Italian Road along with liberalism and Marxism. Where positivism and Marxism emphasize change and progress, romanticism emphasizes continuity and tradition. If Mussolini built up the city of Rome and created for it a pseudolineage linking it back to the Roman Empire, this best makes sense as a part of a prevailing attraction to romanticism. If southern nationalists in Italy or if foreign scholars studying the South find continuity this, too, is justified by romanticism and it plays a role in the modern hegemony.[6]

The Political Economy of Modern Italy, 1870–1990

The nineteenth-century movement for the unification of Italy was led by the North and coincided with the rise of capitalism there. It resulted in the establishment of the Kingdom of Italy in 1861. In 1870, the Kingdom of Italy annexed Rome, bringing together the new configuration of southern and northern elites, which has lasted to the present day as Italy.[7]

For most of the period from 1870 to the present, the Italian ruling classes have faced few insurmountable challenges to their hegemony despite the weakness of the economy and the endless conflict of leading personalities. As a result, rulers generally have been prepared to risk the booms and busts of the market cycles, and there have been many of them. What has also worked to their favor has been the extent to which they have been able to induce lower-class southerners to emigrate and not simply to migrate North to the slums of the major cities as happened in India, Mexico, and Egypt. One might add to this their good luck that the Left has tended to favor a liberal approach to social change.

In the years after World War I, the political situation underwent a qualitative change for a brief period. During this time, the Italian Socialist and Communist parties adopted a strategy new to the history of Italian radicalism. They tried to unify the struggle of workers and peasants. The reaction of the ruling class to this challenge was panic; many erstwhile liberals embraced fascism, shifting back to liberalism only in the election of 1948.[8] The existence of this unusual period should not obscure the larger point about the 120 years under consideration that finance capitalism has played a dominant role in the economic sphere and that liberalism combined with feudalism has played a dominant role in the political and social spheres.

From 1870 onward, with the basic questions of hegemony resolved, the bureaucracy began to function. Decision making was centralized; the provincial prefects oversaw the decisions of the commune; the civil service oversaw the decisions of the prefects. Careful choice of the key functionaries assured the hegemony of the North. Most of the functionaries came from the same background as the political elite, that is, from the Piedmont. In the shadow of this imposing bureaucracy came the one literally new institution, the parliament.

To the dismay of the church and the feudalists, liberals gained the upper hand in this system. To the dismay of the liberals, however, Italian politics came to reflect their concerns only to a limited degree. The system had many checks and balances.

Thus, for example, although the liberals used the state to expand their overall power vis-à-vis that of the church, their successes were more formal than real. True, the anticlerical laws of the 1870s closed religious establishments, required military service of priests, and made inroads into the church's traditional right to make its own appointments and to enjoy the revenue attached to its property. Not surprisingly, the church was fundamentally alienated by these initiatives. Catholics asked each other if the Pope was to be reduced to the "chaplain to the House of Savoy." Would Catholicism eventually lose all its influence? With the growth of civil society and with the growing power of the Catholic laity in it, the church found its way to strike back.

The liberals also controlled the finance capitalism of the period, that is, the banks and insurance companies. Not surprisingly, one finds them embroiled in tariff wars throughout the 1880s and 1890s. Commentary on the period notes that first one sector of the Italian economy and then another was affected by the changes in tariffs. Eventually, the most secure investments were those in banks with overseas interests. Not surprisingly, investment banks came to play a leading role in the country. But, for better or worse, these banks were also the ones most prone to speculation. This was especially the case in the economic crises of the late 1880s; speculation also played an important and unfortunate role in stimulating the colonial adventures of the period.

Was the end of the Liberal Age in sight? Would the instability in the domestic economy lead to an ever-increasing social upheaval that would bring down the regime? The answer for the first generation was a negative one. After 1896, came a period of greater calm, especially for the industrial North. What saved the liberal age at this point was the sudden unexpected growth of the economy as it began to move from textiles and food processing to engineering, chemicals, metal making, and luxury automobiles. Demand generated by wartime needs after 1914 was, perhaps, the single greatest boost to this development. Significantly, nearly all the development took place in the North. Poverty in the South grew worse.

Sudden growth sooner or later has its political consequences. In this case, political movements born of the new prosperity arose from among its beneficiaries in the North, especially the urban North. These new movements lacked a connection to the past, and they began to demand a more open system. The state found their demands for a more open system unnerving and tried to offset their influence by extending the suffrage in 1912 to include many conservative rural and illiterate people. The state hoped that they would oppose the new *radicalism* of the cities.

By the eve of World War I, the efforts of the state notwithstanding, the liberal age system was not working smoothly. Too many unreconcilable political groups had gained a foothold in the political arena, making it too large to control through the traditional maneuvers.

As argued in previous chapters, however, political systems can lose their ability to function and even their legitimacy, but unless they are effectively challenged, they simply carry on. As far back as the 1860s, there have been protests by the Italian peasantry of the South, but these protests did not lead to a change in the system. Against such upsurges, the state could and did deploy its army and, on a more quiet level, permitted the rise of the Mafia as a countervailing force.

Slowly after 1890, however, one can discern a qualitative change in the opposition. In this period, peasant leagues with socialist leanings appeared in Sicily and began to garner support from urban areas. In a few such instances, when the army intervened, the national political order was exposed, and the Crown and the elite politicians had to bear the brunt of public criticism of the conduct of the army. These events took place in the youth of Antonio Gramsci and made a great impression on his later political thought.

By the early years of the twentieth century, emigration from the South brought a significant number of radicalized, landless laborers to the Po Valley in the North. The new rapidly modernizing economy of that region needed these workers. At the same time, the political experience of these workers from the South made them extremely class conscious. In some instances, the most politically conscious among them simply refused bad working conditions and turned to organizing peasant leagues. In 1919, the struggle of the migrant laborers in the Po Valley gained the support of the more urban Socialists. In May 1919, the Socialist party in Turin offered a new political line. Influenced by Gramsci, the party paper proposed its famous strategy of the factory councils. The party envisaged that factory and farm councils would be the first stage toward worker government. By 1920, as worker struggle increased, the state was obliged to occupy the factories of Turin to regain capitalist control.

This dramatic crisis of the liberal state was visible to all, and although it was the Left, which was instrumental in forcing the state to make its move, it was the Fascists who seized it as their opportunity. It almost seemed that the more the Socialists organized in the Po Valley and south into Tuscany, the more the Tuscan landlords turned to fascism and to its "goon squads." Gangs of rural thugs appeared at night in these regions, attacking union organizers and forcing the workers into the syndicates organized by the Fascists. Meanwhile, through the early 1920s, Mussolini himself remained in Milan remote from the actual scenes of violence. As liberalism collapsed, he could watch with satisfaction as the ranks of his National Fascist party grew and grew. In desperation, liberals found it strategic to bring the Fascists into Parliament to trap them. By the 1920s, however, it was too late; the strategy backfired, and it was the liberals who were gradually entrapped. In his speech of January 3, 1925, Mussolini announced the takeover by his party; henceforth, press freedom would be curbed as would opposition parties; the state would be—at least according to his claims—a strong state.

What is a strong state? Writers have reached wildly different conclusions. For those who are inclined to "great man" theories of history, great men produce strong states. But as shown in this analysis, this is not too precise. Under Mussolini, Italy simply entered a corporatist phase, a cross-class alliance from which it would eventually emerge again. The rise of a strong state, I prefer the term *great power,* does not necessarily require a dictatorship or even a new form of hegemony, but class collaboration. To the extent that Italy was a great power, this was the reason.

In important ways, life under Mussolini continued as before. For example, it did not entail a mobilization regime designed to disrupt ordinary life. Thus, even the chief of police retained his post as a career prefect, for, there were no political police such as the SS. There was a Special Tribunal for the Defense of the State—the tribunal that convicted Gramsci—but Mussolini never sought to use the Special Tribunal or other such bodies to convert the existing Italian judiciary to a fascist one. By and large, he accepted the traditional professions as they were, including the military.

The big gainer in the shift to fascism, one could argue, was the traditional bureaucracy more than the party. Thus, for example, the Prefectoral Corps retained its power in provincial administration because Mussolini needed it. There was always the possibility of the resurgence of rural radicalism, or *squadrismo,* and Mussolini feared this possibility. Of course, the party itself, the Partito Nazionale Fascista (PNF) grew when it took power, but in growing it became diluted, attracting job seekers more than it did Fascists. Thus, for example, by accident or by design, many nonfascist writers and professors flourished; some even received subsidies. Parliament still functioned; Italy was still a monarchy; governmental support to the Catholic church even increased.

In the urban economy, the innovations of the fascist period were on two levels: state-run unions, or syndicalist movements, and state-run industry. Both were important, but their long-term influence was not sufficient to alter established regional patterns of power distribution. In point of detail, the Fascists were initially able to depress the wages of the industrial work force by breaking their unions, but wartime conditions soon made the government dependent on them again for production. By 1943, the Communists and others who supported the workers were able to force up the wages, which the Fascists had earlier depressed.

In the rural economy, the major innovation of the fascist period was land reform. Through land reform, the Fascists won some support among the peasants, but not enough to achieve their ends. When, for example, Mussolini launched his well-known Battle for Wheat drive, a drive designed to free Italy from its dependence on food imports, he ran into problems with the peasants. Once the government began to ration food, and this became necessary when the costs of importing it rose, peasants were obliged to sell their crops to the state at a fixed rate. Many peasants subverted this system either by consuming the crops themselves or by selling them on the black market. This was especially the case in the South.

By the 1930s, the black market in agricultural products began to have a political impact. The state reluctantly gave up its land reform project and encouraged a return to sharecropping as a way to assure control of the crop. This was one of Mussolini's boldest repudiations of the broad trajectory of the Italian ruling class toward capitalism.[9] Perhaps it clarifies the real nature of that class in Italy.[10]

The role of the of the church in the hegemony is important to the analysis of the period. A close look at the late 1920s shows that for both the church and the party, the Roman Question was still a matter of frustration; both wanted to resolve it. Rome was, after all, Mussolini's capital; his support was weaker in the cities of North Italy because they were the heartland of the liberals and the Left. Mussolini, thus, needed Rome. He also needed the church; its location and ideology ovelapped with that of his own. Fascism like Catholicism rested on the maintenance of tradition. This was one of its great appeals to the mass population in the face of the modernism of the liberals. The Vatican, too, needed Rome and needed a guaranteed legal status. Thus it was that Mussolini as well as the Pope could reach the most far-reaching agreement between church and state in modern history, the Lateran Accords (1929–31). But it was as well that once these accords were in place, the Vatican, as the only institution legally functioning independently of the Fascist regime, could oppose fascism.[11] After all has not the church always opposed the ruling party?

Too much that is written about hegemony suggests synthesis and harmony, too little suggests conflict. In the power struggle between Mussolini and the church to dominate the direction of culture and politics, clearly

Mussolini had the upper hand but still could not bend the religious structure to his will. He could threaten the church, and this he did, drawing some members of the church hierarchy to him as a result, but he could not win over the church as an institution, much less gain the support of the Pope. Thus, when Mussolini closed some of the theological faculties in the Italian universities and forced the less-cooperative clergy to shoulder the financial burden of supporting the others, he appeared to gain some influence in Catholic education circles, but, as his critics were quick to point out, the success was only skin-deep. He did not really gain the allegiance of the clergy.[12]

On the defensive during the fascist era, the Pope adopted the posture of a mystic and simply waited out the Mussolini era. It is difficult for a state to persecute a mystic. Catholic doctrine of the era adopted a suitably mystical tone.[13] In the influential work *Principi,* by the Dominican Giorgio La Pira, the author called for a re-Christianized fascism. In this work, La Pira replaced the mysticism of fascism with the mystical idea of the union of the soul with God. To this theme he appended an assortment of earlier church condemnations of the evils of the twentieth century: worship of the state, adherence to racism, and support for the proletariat.

The church did not come to use mysticism without some trial and error. During the early 1930s, the church had sided with the Fascists in the name of traditional values in opposing the Partito Populare, a Catholic political party with liberal leanings. By 1939, Pope Pius XI acknowledged that his silencing of Catholic liberals was an error; fascism was a worse menace. Still, however, these ten years appeared to seal the possibility of a Catholic Left-antifascist alliance.[14]

Yet despite this fact, the church remained active in areas of concern to the Left. For example, in the last years of fascism before the return of liberalism in 1948, labor struggle in the North reached a high point. The church chose this period to gain influence by promoting a reconciliatory approach to labor problems through Catholic trade unionism. Here the church had a trump card; the reconciliatory approach was a particularly appropriate one at a time when neither labor or capital could prevail.[15] Reconciliation thus carried the day redounding to the credit of the church leadership, restoring prestige to the church in social policy. The Italian church could, thus, plausibly argue that its traditional doctrine of reconciliation was a rational and less-wasteful approach to labor market problems than the fascist one of subsidizing Italian peasants in Libya or permitting them to emigrate to other countries or the Marxist one of class war.[16] At the same time, the party gained one of its objectives as well; a reconciliatory approach to labor opened the way for northern capitalists to use cheap southern labor on the farms and in the factories.

The Catholic Church also was able to exert power in education, welfare, and law. In theory and sometimes in practice, fascism was a threat to them. Of course, Mussolini was not the first nor the last politician who would, for example, try to ignore the legal system. But, even for him, particular issues would arise revealing the limitations inherent in functioning above or outside the law.

The Fascists wanted Jewish help in sustaining their international financial connections. To receive this help, Mussolini would have had to guarantee the rights of the Jewish community, in other words, to adhere to the legal and financial order. This he could not do, however, because of his alliance with Germany. Not surprisingly, Mussolini failed to garner much support from the Jewish community, and, in fact, he opened himself to criticism for what he was trying to do. Even the Vatican could capitalize on this faux pas and on his treatment of Jews more generally and do so in the name of Italian jurisprudence as well as Christian morality.[17]

By 1942, military setbacks, economic stagnation, and the lack of a political program to free Italy from its commitments to Germany and the colonies were all factors contributing to a growing disenchantment with fascism from above and from below, going far beyond the conflicts within the ruling circles of party, church, parliament, and throne.

In 1943, the king arrested Mussolini and appointed Marshall Badoglio to head a transition government to return Italy to a system based on rule by law. The transition would be a difficult one. Italy was becoming for the first time a real battleground. No longer allied to Germany, Italy was occupied by Germany. Mussolini, freed by the Germans in a daring raid, moved to the North, ending his political career as the leader of the Republic of Salo, a small town on a lake under German occupation.

In March 1944, the USSR recognized the Badoglio government in Rome. This decision had a profound influence on the events that followed. The Communist party in Rome led by Palmiro Togliatti offered its support to the government. This, in turn, entirely undercut the possibility for a socialist revolution. Given a free hand, the Partisan movement in the North of Italy might well have been strong enough to carry on. Perhaps Italy would have become socialist. With the Communists supporting the state, however, the final denouement of the corporatist age took place, the election of 1948. The Christian Democrats emerged victorious; the liberal age had returned.

Liberalism in Italy, 1948 to the Present

The election of 1948 marked the "official" rebirth of the Republic, of the old party structure supporting liberalism and of finance capitalism, features found here to be the hallmarks of the liberal age. With the Left as a part of the system, liberalism in Italy took the form of a welfare state, the state playing a continuing role in development as well.

From the vantage point of 1990, the election of 1948 marks the birth of a new era, but an era that has more links to the past than the prevailing scholarship allows. Granted, after 1948, one finds an impressive resurgence of civil society and its institutions. But, to what extent does this establish a break with previous Italian history or simply reassert the prevailing regional differences of the country? Looking closely, one finds that in the North, the resurgence was an important phenomenon. Institutions in civil society shared in the rule. In the South, this was not the case. Civil society remained weak there; land reform policies were never implemented. Civil society in the South was essentially a contradiction in terms.

For those who argue that 1948 was even more, for example, the end of the aberration, two problems remain: how to explain all the continuity, for example, in the careers of the bureaucrats and all the change. The fascist period had opened the door to southerners in significant numbers. Many of the important positions of the judiciary and of the civil service and the lower military officer ranks remained in southern hands after 1948. In other words, the social changes of the fascist period remained in place.

With the election of the Christian Democrats, what happened to the church? One would think that a party of believers would open the door to the Vatican; the war of church and state would end. Although this was, indeed, partly the case and the church gained considerable power, especially in the postwar years, still the conflict of church and state continued as in the past, but it reverted to the form that it took in the earlier liberal phase. The new Italian constitution confirmed the privileges of the church, making it, in effect, a quasi state within the state. If, however, priests' salaries and Catholic schools were subsidized by the state, the state could then exercise some control over appointments of the upper clergy and could then veto the acquisition of gifts to the church. It was, thus, clear that the conflict would go on; Catholic lay organizations and anticlericals would once again fight each other.

In the postwar period, many countries sustained growth; Italy, too, experienced growth. It soon experienced as well the problems of a liberal regime undergrowing growth, problems reminiscent of those at the turn of the twentieth century.

By 1963, labor union activity was growing. Migrant workers coming from the South into the northern labor market had made their presence felt as well. Wildcat strikes and struggles in the informal sector were becoming stronger. As this took place, capital flight to northern Europe also became noticeable; capitalists were not going to be caught napping as they had been in World War I when many of their assets were trapped with the rise of Mussolini.

Still, it was the northern middle class that was benefiting. It was northern women who pursued education and careers and did so to a degree theretofore unknown. By 1974, educated women in the North gained the power even to affect the political process, spearheading a drive to legalize divorce. In 1978, at least in certain parts of the North, women could receive an abortion on demand.

In the same period, the northern middle class as a whole was able to assert itself in wide areas of culture. It broke the monopoly of Radio televisione italiana (RAI) on radio and television. Large numbers of northern middle-class listeners and viewers secured the freedom to choose what they wanted to listen to or to watch. For some writers, these changes mark a part of the postwar revolution that symbolizes the break with the past. I argue that it is more precise to see these changes as part of the tradition of Italian Road regional differentiation, which if anything was reinforced by the laws of regionalism passed between 1968 and 1970.

Is there regional oppression or simply regional lag?[18] Certainly, after World War II, some of the traditional surface features of the Southern Question were pushed out of sight for a few years. Pockets of the South under the aegis of a "new" state bourgeoisie industrialized; a number of southerners who migrated found for the first time fairly remunerative positions in northern Europe or even in northern Italy. The remittances of these workers to their families permitted a significant rise in consumption in parts of the South as well. These changes have not, however, been permanent nor structurally transformative ones. Despite the prosperity of some, the majority of the migrants have tended to remain unassimilated in northern slums, outsiders in northern Italy almost as they were outsiders to Germany and to other parts of northern Europe. Evidence of this nonassimilation in recent years is the phenomenon of return; southerners who went to the North have begun to return as the economies of the northern regions contract. Today, many are where they began—unemployed and in the South. They are still the labor reserve awaiting the next expansionary cycle of the economy, still potential migrants.

One must wonder about the "new" ruling class imposed on the South after the war to modernize it. Although a few well-known figures, such as Aldo Moro, catapulted from their work in the South to national careers, most of the bureaucrats were absorbed into the South, developing their patronage networks and local ties.

All observers agree that the South retains its distinctive cultural and social system. This persistence cannot be an accident. If the South were simply underdeveloped, the South would have welcomed the northern culture. This, however, did not occur.

For example, the South preserves its dialects despite the fact that these dialects connote low prestige to other Italians. In addition, anthropological research shows that the South preserves an oral tradition eventhough the written tradition carries the most prestige.

What supports this persistence? The persistence of a dialect may have many explanations; oral traditions, however, do not last unless they are institutionalized in cultural organizations. If in the North, the centers of culture are public institutions, in the South, this is less the case; the family is more important. It, therefore, seems reasonable to hypothesize that southern family life supports an oral tradition, whereas the northern family life does not.

In both the North and the South, men have public power, so it would be reasonable to hypothesize that women have private power. If one divides up the hours of the day, women outnumber men in many domestic contexts during the important daytime period, and where this matters, in the South, oral tradition and the role of women become interrelated.

Men who grow up in southern families and who become intellectuals eventually attend universities in Naples or Rome after spending their formative years in what one now recognizes are women-dominated institutions. It seems reasonable to hypothesize further that intelligent but untutored women not only produce an oral folk tradition but an intuitive way of thinking, a way of thinking one associates with a Croce, a Gramsci, or a Pasolini.[19] And because the state needs intuitionism to offset the dominance of the positivism of the North, the southern home, contrary to the thinking of the dominant paradigm, is not something to be reformed.

In disputing the continuing existence of the Southern Question, the liberal developmentalist school does not argue that there is no southern culture or that women have not had or do not have an influence in the South or on their sons' development. Simply put, these exist, but they have no wider import because what is important is development. This means money, and women do not earn money. Given a money-based economy, liberals believe, life in the family and even gender issues more broadly understood are simply part of the background. Thus, if the South failed to develop as fast as Italy as a whole, which liberals agree is the case, southern women would likely become more dependent on men than before and the culture as a whole would likely be more atomistic or amoral than it had been a century earlier. This setback caused by the failure to develop rapidly, the liberals conclude, is regrettable but temporary. It reflects the fact that national development is inherently uneven. Over the long run, this will change. Southerners as a whole and southern women in particular will better themselves through local development or, if need be, through migration.[20]

But does this jibe with what liberal scholars know is actually occurring? An actual gender-related issue drawn from anthropological research in the 1960s, some years after the official end of the Southern Question, may elucidate whether there is a dichotomy between an amoral, atomistic, underdeveloped South and a more developed North, a dichotomy that would support the liberal assumption of the difference between modernity and tradition. An issue related to gender other than that of the childrearing culture, that is researched enough to permit a comparison of conditions in the North and the South could be that of marriage. Is the southern approach to marriage evolving? Will it one day be the same as the northern approach?

According to postwar social science research, the marriage of the modern educated girl of the North is a matter of "her will"; yet northern society approves of this decision without the slightest intention of ending the institution of marital patriarchy. There must be more to the subject of the northern marriage in Italy than is embodied in the concept of "her will." There must be the role of tradition or custom that supersedes in a girl's thought what she might as an individual will. Freedom must contain here some calculus of risks related to the above. A man or his family could turn against a too-emancipated woman in preference for a more traditional, perhaps less-demanding one. In most cases, this may not happen; the man may not literally turn against such a woman if he has chosen her, but his manner of relating to her will confirm her intuition that even modern marriage does not contain the equality for which she was hoping.

If marriage in the North does not conform to the liberal stereotypes of modernity and rationality, what about marriage in the South? Whereas engagement in the South is "early," courtship is often "long." According to one study, peasant girls marry at age twenty to twenty-one. During this long period of courtship, the couple is obliged to get to know one another well and to plan realistically because the logistics of finding a home are difficult. Thus, contrary to the stereotype of traditionalism in the South, the prevailing custom implies some real social maturity. For example, if the bride's older sister is still unmarried, the prospective bridegroom is expected to delay the marriage until his fiance's older sister marries. Although in both the North and the South each family contributes specified articles to the formation of the new home, the consequences of this social merger is somehow different in the two regions; the result in the South more than in the North is a unity of the two families, which speaks to the needs of the possible children who will be produced.[21]

Examined from the perspective of political economy, the existence of this southern ideal of marriage is very much a part of what one can rightfully call the Southern Question. The selflessness implied in the southern ideal of traditional marriage taken in a manipulative way out of context becomes a reproach to a Northern woman, who in choosing for herself is made to feel that she is being selfish. The traditionalism here of the South is made to serve the needs of Northern patriarchalism. Southern women, of course, do not plan their marriages to thwart social change in the North. There is a local rationality, and they are rewarded for using it.

In both regions, marriage brings status although people choose to define status differently in the South and in the North. According to the dominant paradigm, the status that most educated northern women bring to their marriage comes from their jobs because the job market is as open to women as to men. For most women, however, even in the North, the job market is open in a way that makes their value demonstrably less than that of their husbands or brothers. This is, of course, also the case in the South. There is, thus, a certain shrewdness on the part of the Southern woman who avoids defining her status through education and the job mill. One asks the liberal historian, therefore, Where is the lack of rationality? Where is the atomism? Where is the lag in the South? Can one really dismiss the Southern Question and the resistance to it so easily? There has been an ongoing struggle over the late twentieth century, especially in the South, to the imposition of the Italian Road. What was presented as issues in economics and then gender are equally those of politics.

Counterhegemony in Modern Italy

The linkage of the northern worker and the southern peasant in common struggle against the state has been a dream of the Left all through this century. In the brief interlude of the Workers' Councils in Turin in 1920, the dream started to become reality. Before it did, the Fascists took over. Counterhegemonic struggle for the entire next generation was preoccupied with the struggle against fascism. It took the form of an alliance of the Left with the liberals.

In a famous exchange shortly after the demise of the Worker Council experiment, Gramsci told Togliatti that the South would be the grave of fascism, but it would be of great use to fascism if the Communists did not seize the initiative there. Gramsci recognized the practical problems involved. To make it the graveyard of fascism, it would be necessary to create a context in which the democratic intellectual would not have to migrate, leaving a void for the Fascists to fill. In the South, Gramsci claimed the priest was corrupt; therefore, the party must turn to the peasant soldier and the officer veteran.[22]

The Italian Communist party (ICP), even the party in the South, however, never seriously attempted to use Gramsci's insights. As it existed under the leadership of Giórgio Amendola in Naples in the interwar years, the ICP was in spirit closer to the accommodationist position of Eurocommunism that emerged after 1945 than it was to the older more radical position of Gramsci.[23]

To the more radical segments of the Neapolitan working class, however, the line of the ICP was wrong, the party had in effect sold out to the North and to capitalism. This idea of the party selling out, which was introduced into public discourse in the 1920s in Gramsci's debates with Amadeo Bordiga, lives on at least in the South until the present day. It seems worth attending.

In the 1940s, opposition to the ICP from among the more radical workers of the South was apparent in such movements as the Montesanto Federation, a splinter group that broke off from the Communist party. Typical of the Montesanto Federation demands was that for more democracy within the ICP. Policy in the ICP was imposed from the top down. In the 1950s, Amendola's leadership in Naples was challenged by yet another radical trend, the Communist Youth movement. By the 1960s, the ICP membership in the South had declined appreciably from the levels reached in the interwar period. By this period, radicalism was beginning to find its own voice in the South in an ICP journal, *Crònache Meridionali*. The writers for this journal were almost all critics of the ICP's main lines. One of their bête noires was the adherence of the party to the two-step solution." The two-step solution upheld the idea that no socialism was possible until capitalist development throughout the country had created contradictions that would lead to the struggle for socialism. Because the South was years from such a stage of economic development, this deferred the socialist agenda almost indefinitely. This critique appears and reappears in the South. In the 1960s, the Ingrao Group, another radical splinter group from the party ennunciated these ideas. According to the writers of the Ingrao Group, the key to the Southern Question was anticapitalism, not capitalist development as the ICP and the Christian Democrats (DC) argued.

In September 1970, the Ingrao Group began to merge with the Manifesto Group. It continued to engage the ICP in theoretical debate. It argued that Western society was now developed; revolution was possible. The party must abandon the ideology of the Vanguard party and become a mass party in a true sense, using Workers' Councils. The two-stage solution was irrelevant. The response of the ICP was to expel a number of well-known figures associated with the Manifesto Group from its ranks. Those expelled included Màssimo Caprara, Luìgi Pinto, Rossana Rossanda, and Lucio Magri. The position of the ICP leaders was that the party already was a mass party. The original Ingrao Group decided to stay in the party at this point.

As one might imagine, such measures as expulsion from the party had little impact on radical thinkers. They simply proved their point. The party lacked democracy, not just in the occasional instance but as a matter of course. Amendola, for example, a leading figure of the party, ran the Neapolitan branch of the ICP in the typically corrupt manner of the official parties, that is, through clientelism and personalism.[24] By the late 1970s, criticism of the party was once again on the rise. The Manifesto Group had grown into what is now the Partito di Unità Proletàrio per il Comunismo (contemporary party). On a more regionalist level in the North, a group of intellectuals, inspired by the philosopher Antonio Negri, a part of the extra-Parliamentary Left, had also arisen to denounce the failure of the ICP to challenge the system.[25]

According to the American scholar, Sidney Tarrow, who studied the communist leadership in the North and the South, it was the southern leadership who, despite their wealth, were closer to the people, albeit in a more paternalistic way than their northern counterparts, and they were, perhaps, more honest and more predictable in their dealings as well. The northerners were career politicians. They tended to be married to party members, thereby living their whole lives within the party. Southern leaders usually were traditional intellectuals, often landlords; wives tended not to be members.[26] By contrast, the northern leadership is much closer in terms of social background to its constituency, but this fact does not seem to have made it more effective as an advocate of its concerns. This is Sydney Tarrow's argument. The example that he and other writers give is the relationship of the party to feminist issues. An important part of the party's membership is also part of the Italian Woman's movement, but feminism has succeeded in making few inroads into the party's platform. After 1973, Berlinguer, the leader of the party became increasingly obsessed with the idea that the DC would make a center-right coalition as Pinochet did in Chile. To forestall this possibility, the ICP reached out to the church, putting its support of the feminist agenda on hold.[27] One can only conclude from this that if the DC does make a center-right coalition and fascism reappears, however remote this chance may be, the struggle against fascism will once again take years and years.[28]

The Organization of Culture in Modern Italy

Up to this point, my approach to the study of hegemony has concentrated on politics and economics by implication, at least, on the more coercive side of hegemony. In this section, I examine the culture that the Italian state inherited, successfully molded, and still uses in its project of rule. I emphasize the role played by persuasion in hegemony. Language, literature, folklore, anthropology, and religious politics illustrate the broad outline of the strategy of organization of culture. These fields lay at the heart of the cultural policies of the modern state.

What was the language policy followed by the state after the Risorgimento? At that time, Italy was a polyglot of regions and dialects with a classical literary language known to a small number of people. One school of thought concerned with language policy advocated the use of the classical literary language as the language of the new country. The leading representative of this position was the famous writer Alessandro Manzoni (d. 1873). Manzoni argued that the classical literary language should be made the national language and should be spread by the government from above through the education system. His doctine, Dirigìsmo-Populìsmo, was not suitable for the regime's political agenda, so despite Manzoni's tremendous prestige as a writer and intellectual, the regime bypassed him on questions of policy, turning instead to a linguist who accepted the theory of regional divisions of the Italian language. This linguist, Graziano Isaia Ascoli (d. 1907), emerged as one of the main cultural architects of the new state. Ascoli's journal, *Archivio Glottòlogico Italiano,* emphasized dialectology, and this remained the most important area for Italian linguistics up to World War I. Ascoli believed in the unification of the language but argued that it would take a long time and would not come about artificially. His model was the spread of English and French. They began as administrative languages, and over centuries, they gradually became widely accepted.[29]

The state also needed a standardized prose language for everyday communication that would be simpler and more accessible than the language of the littérateur. This, too, it developed and incorporated into its language policy. According to Bruno Migliorini, a specialist in language history, Italy developed a practical standardized prose language from its bureaucracy. The bureaucrats homogenized the language and simplified it. Because they had access to the mass media, they posssessed as well the power to introduce it into society at large. Migliorini, who approved of this process, tended to see the major literary writers, Alessandro Manzoni, Giosuè Carducci (1835–1907) and Gabriele d'Annunzio (1863–1938) as a problem. They exoticized language. There is some truth to this point; Carducci and d'Annunzio introduced rare unused words and classicisms seemingly almost in reaction to the march of bureaucratic simplification. And why not? To the partisans of the older literary language, especially those from Florence or greater Tuscany, the Roman bureaucratic colloquial on Italian television to this day constitutes an affront. Herein, one can observe the conflict between the objective of maintaining a hegemony based on region and the logic of development and homogenization.[30]

As Rome grew in importance in the late nineteenth century, the bureaucracy wanted to limit the North's influence. It made a number of specific choices in language policy that cumulatively were very important. For example, it chose French loan words; in doing so, it avoided a reliance on classical Italian from Florence, in other words, North Italy. German and English loan words were also available, but in each case the bureaucrats had reasons to avoid dependence on them. The feudal aristocrats were increasingly turning to English and the state did not want to ally with them. Dangers existed with German as well. Germany university culture was spreading in the North, and German was becoming increasingly familiar to Italian workers. French had the least risks; it was in any case the language of the legal system.

During the fascist period, the government continued to stress the practicality of language to the point of making practicality a part of regime ideology. Mussolini, after all, wanted to be able to mobilize Italian society. In point of fact, this was not possible. In 1939, Bruno Migliorini undertook with the regime's blessing the editorship of *Lingua Nostra,* a journal devoted to scientific and, thus, practical use of language. Migliorini's initiatives, however, placed him in direct opposition to Croce, and Croce had much the greater claim to authority in linguistic matters. Migliorini wanted to compose an Italian dictionary. For languages to be practical, they have to be accessible, and to be accessible there must be dictionaries. Croce was an opponent of dictionaries. Languages, he believed, are in continuous motion; no word truly has a synonym, nor is it truly used twice in the same way. The Italian language is like the Mediterranean Sea, its depths, its crests, its beauty are all interconnected, the one part making the other. In this encounter, Migliorini and by extension the state may be said to have lost outright. Croce induced the Accadèmia della Crusca in Florence to abandon its unfinished dictionary project. Even today, Italy has no satisfactory dictionary or, for that matter, grammar book, and this as well has a connection to Croce.

Despite some setbacks the fascist state did finally succeed in gaining a measure of autonomy without disrupting the existing regionalism. Archeology provided a way as did folklore and anthropology. From the first years of the fascist period, the Italian government relied heavily on archeological findings from the excavation of Rome to argue that the identity of Italy, its alliance with Germany notwithstanding, did not depend on the Aryan links of the Italian North but on the Roman links to the Roman empire.

Folklore studies provided the regime with legitimacy as well, but here the terrain was more contested than in archeology, as there was less pure state autonomy. As early as Gramsci, writers on folklore in Italy had noted the subject's political nature. Gramsci himself introduced the idea that the state was permitting the North to "folklorize" the South. What were the trends in folklore studies and the implications of their claims for an Italian Road hegemony?

During the twentieth century, the leading Italian folklorists had two main preoccupations: the classification of folklore by region of origin and the collection of folklore, especially from the South. The late nineteenth-century founders of the modern field, Constantino Nigra, Ermolao Rubieri, Alessandro d'Ancona, and Giusèppe Pitrè created the conceptual basis for what today is called the Mediterranean Honor and Shame school.

Nigra was a friend and collaborator of the nationalist hero Camillo Cavour. Like Cavour, he was from the Piedmont, but unlike Cavour, he was more of a Piedmontese nationalist than an Italian nationalist. Nigra was the first Italian folklorist to be concerned with the geographical diffusion of folklore. He divided Italy into two zones; North Italy was the lyrico-narrative zone (children's ballads), Middle and South Italy contained songs and dances. The form of folklore for Nigra was crucial. The South was unique in its forms, whereas the North was not. The form of folklore for Nigra was defined in its genetic period, and its transfer thereafter was limited to similar cultures. Nigra assumed a Celtic origin for North Italy, hence an Aryanized folk culture, an Aryanized philology, and Aryanized aesthetics.[31] Nigra's views were of some use to Italian hegemony, but it would be difficult for him to play the role of a national intellectual. He was too much of a regionalist.

Another leading folklorist of the same period was Ermolao Rubieri. In contrast to Nigra, Rubieri found a unity of the Italian people, placing more weight on their poetry than on their folksongs; he conluded that the regional differences that distinguish the Piedmontese narrative poetry from the Sicilian Madrigals were not absolute.[32]

A third folklorist of the same period, Alessandro d'Ancona, appears to be close to Rubieri. He emphasized that the gulf between high culture and folk culture extended across the country as a whole and did not divide the North and the South. He also believed, however, that most of the high culture was in the North. D'Ancona like Rubieri was much more a supporter of the Risorgimento than was Nigra.

A fourth early example of an influential folklorist was Giusèppe Pitrè, (1841–1916). Pitrè was a medical doctor known for his support of the Risorgimento as well as for his work as a compiler of Sicilian folklore tradition. In 1882, Pitrè started the journal *Archivio per lo stùdio della tradizióni popolari*. In the journal, he noted that folklore was the collective element of history. Left unrecorded, it would disappear as Sicily entered modern times and ceased to be an isolated collectivity. Like many other folklorists before and since, Pitrè found the folk to be "a great source of sentiment, thought and image."[33]

When examining the needs of an Italian Road hegemony, one finds that the theory of a shared national high culture is necessary to permit the entrée of the southern intelligentsia. It also legitimates the interest in regional variations in folk culture without region being used as the sole basis of culture. As the North developed into the main region of high culture, the South and the southern folklorist rose in importance in folklore studies. All of this is clarified through a consideration of the work of the Neapolitan philosopher, literary critic, and folklorist, Benedetto Croce (1866–1952), the figure known to political economy as the great intellectual of Italy.

In folklore, Croce's work ranged from gathering examples firsthand to developing a theory of folklore criticism. In his folklore criticism, Croce pointed out the defects of the naïve positivist methodology dominant in northern Italy. He termed pseudoscientific the claims implied in their works about the origins of folklore, claims, he noted, that permitted their authors to accord privilege to the narrative as the highest developed form of folk culture. He replaced this positivist evolutionary approach with more genuinely historical and aesthetic criteria, validating in the process intuitionism, metaphysics, and even Marxism. In the 1880s and 1890s, Croce contributed proverbs, popular poems, songs, and tales he personally collected to the Neapolitan folklore journal, *Giambattista Basile*. He also studied "folk manifestations"; his first scholarly research was an investigation of one, the Leggènda di Cola Pésce. He once stated that he took part in this work both as a discipline and for the pleasure it gave him. He loved folk art for its immediacy, its ambience, its character, and its life.[34] Croce's research always had its politics, so if a regime depended on southern intellectuals, such as Croce, it would have to permit them to influence the definition of bourgeois culture, and this it did. In a famous article in *La Crìtica,* Croce once stated that beauty and ugliness were to be found in both high art and folk art and that the best folk poetry is no different than artistic poetry. Nor was this his only critique of the hegemonic framework of high versus low. In the introduction to an early historical work on the Neapolitan Revolution of 1799, he argued that history involves both ruler and ruled.

Italian anthropology, like Italian folklore studies, has played an important part in hegemony, and often the two overlapped.

Three kinds of anthropology rose with the modern Italian state and have performed some services for it: the oldest and least formalized trend was ethnology; the second trend was the history of popular traditions; the third and most recent trend was cultural anthropology. Cultural anthropology emerged during the 1960s coinciding with the peak of the mass migration from the South to the northern Italian cities, a movement so massive as to have rendered the older regionalist schools of ethnology and of the history of popular traditions with their Mediterranean School of Honor and Shame orientation out of date.[35]

The available evidence suggests that the cultural anthropology of the post-1960 period was the high point of anthropology's contribution to hegemony. In the 1960–1970 period, what stands out is that cultural anthropologists more than others were able to promote a picture of the cultural whole into which all Italians, newcomers included, could be suitably assimilated. One cultural anthropologist, T. Tentori of Milan, actually emerged as a television and mass media personality; politicians began to use terms from anthropology. Gradually, as the 1970s progressed, however, a major debate arose among professors of anthropology, leading many to question the role they had been playing. As a result of this debate, a number of the professors came to realize that anthropology contributed to the imperialism of the North over the South or worse that the Southern Question had become American neocolonialism. Some then decided to cease lending their names to the state development schemes in the South. At this point, the state turned from its use of anthropologists to the use of littérateurs, figures such as the popular southern writer Danilo Dolci, seemingly because Dolci was prepared to romanticize Sicily, a function that the anthropologists refused to perform.

These changes should be seen not just as choices made by small groups but as part of a larger picture of changes taking place in the period that affected the organization of culture. Since the fascist era, the South has had more power in the system than earlier; not surprisingly, its voice has become louder. It may still provide the romances of a Dolci, which the state can use, but alongside them comes the biting satire of figures such as a P. P. Pasolini. The unwillingness of anthropologists in northern universities to participate in the old form of the hegemony is another reflection of this southern power.

The rise in southern power dates from the fascist era. When, for example, the Fascists wanted star personalities, athletes, and popular idols, they turned to the South. The Fascists did not want to remain prisoners of the North or of liberalism. Whereas before World War I, a few figures emerged to national prominence from the South, they did so on northern terms; from the interwar period onward, this changed. A number of figures emerged. Some continued to use the South as their subject matter, following what earlier generations had done. Others, however, imposed the southern dialect on the nation through film and radio, and still others criticized the culture of the North as outsiders to it. An example of the latter was P. P. Pasolini, *A Violent Life*. Examples of the former are Italo Calvino, *Italian Folktales* and, of course, the writings of Danilo Dolci.[36] Whereas Croce criticized the positivist trends of northern culture by implication, Pasolini was able to do so directly. By his time, the South was in the North, a part of the sweatshop economy, a part of everyday life. The vast South to North migration began to bring the Southern Question into the North.

The Catholic church, as any reader of Gramsci would know, was a formidable part of the organization of culture. Gramsci, in fact, coined the phrase "traditional intellectual" to characterize it, and although the phrase has crept into social science literature, still not enough has been done with the subject of the church as a part of political economy.

In this work, I prejudge the outcome of future sociological research and sketch what I take to be the role of the Catholic church on its elite level in the organization of culture. An important and widely diffused piece of knowledge about the church in different periods is the description of the official persona of the pope. I assume that this persona is a conscious political construction, that it is not the sum of the accidental qualities of some individual. By studying the persona, one can glimpse the praxis of the church in a given period. Following this approach, one finds that during liberal phases, when the church had an entrée to civil society, popes were activists. They adopted theological stances to confront the challenges that liberalism represented. During the corporatist phase, in this case fascism, the popes, although by tradition the providers of church dogma, adopted as noted above the stance of a love mystic. The Church was weak vis-à-vis the party; it had to avoid a direct conflict while it continued to serve the state.

An important example of a Pope of the liberal phase in the years after the Risorgimento was Pope Leo XIII (1878–1903). According to the *Catholic Encyclopedia,* Pope Leo XIII was the son of a nobleman from central Italy; he actively asserted the rights of the church in the temporal domain, commented on colonial issues, and condemned the rise of liberalism. His stands were carried on by his successor, Pope Pius X (1903–1914). Pope Pius X, like his predecessor, had ties to the land system. He was the son of a village official; he rose through the church hierarchy to become the bishop of Mantua and the cardinal of Venice. He manifested a distaste for interconfessional groups; he supported missionary expansionism. Pope Pius X was followed by Pope Benedict (1914–22). Son of a patrician from Genoa, Pope Benedict fought the liberals and the socialists, but seemingly in a way his predecessors did not, through humor, humanism, and personal popularity. Here one senses the crisis of the liberal age encoded in the biography, the weakness of the church as one of the constituent elements in that hegemony.

Of the Popes of the fascist era, one should begin with Pope Pius XI (1922–39). He was also born in the North; his education prepared him for a career in two fields that became important to the Fascists: Christian archeology and diplomacy. When Pius XI became Pope, his major goal was the unification of humanity under Christ out of the ashes of the old order of the nation-states. As noted before, his demeanor and his actions had long been those of a mystic. In 1922, he had founded Italian Catholic Action as a nonpolitical organization to offset worldwide misery. He called for love, prayer, penance and devotion to the Divine Heart of Jesus. His successor, Pius XII (1939-), was from Rome, the son of a lawyer there. As noted before, in the waning years of fascism, he took up the issue of the persecution of the Jews as one of his major preoccupations. After the war, he was concerned with communism, adopting, at this point, the positions of his predecessors of the liberal phase. In recent years, all the popes have been attacking liberation theology and, once again, Catholic liberalism.

History Writing in Italy

Over the twentieth century, most Italian historians were drawn to study the affairs of their own regions or cities as opposed to those of the nation. The professionalization of the field of history in modern times highlighted this fact. In the fascist era, the preoccupation with the local as opposed to the national was upsetting to the regime because the state then wanted nationalist history. But, in general, Italian regimes have used literary figures and philosophers to characterize the nation as a whole, leaving history to professionals and to amateurs on the local level. Over the long run, subordination of a field gives space to amateurs and to writers in more important fields to dabble in it as the philosopher Croce did. It also encourages technicianism as manifested in the publication of document collections.

Among Italian historians, the study of medieval and classical subjects has long commanded prestige. Most historians, at least until World War II simply continued older traditions in these specializations, studying some old theme from their regions. The outstanding writers generally came from the North. The fascist drive for self-determination and national integration found expression in a wholesale reinterpretation of established subjects and in a widening of the regional base of historical studies. From the fascist period, one finds studies of the House of Savoy and of the Roman past cast in national terms and conceived as antecedents or models for Mussolini. For the first time, the scholarship of Italians on Italy was held up by the Italian government as equal to that of foreigners. In the postwar period, classical and medieval subjects continued to have prestige but so did modern history. By the late 1950s, a Marxist school of historiography challenged the dominant liberal school's interpretation of modern history.

Typical of a large number of continuators of classical and Renaissance studies who tended to write on their regions were Mercurio Antonelli (1863–1940), Geròlamo Biscaro (1858–1937), and Cèsare Imperiale di Sant'Àngelo (1860–1942). Antonelli was a medievalist born in Montefiascone in Latium in central Italy; his most important research was on his own region. The same was true for his contemporary, Biscaro, who devoted his research in the Vatican Archives to Renaissance subjects, including the cathedrals and tombs of his own region, Lombardy. The third example, Cèsare Imperiale di Sant'Àngelo, was born into a Genoese patrician family. In Parliament, he represented maritime interests; on a cultural level where one would expect him to have been an internationalist, one finds instead that his allegiance was to provincial cultural organizations, especially those specialized in medieval themes.[37] Although in their choices of local Italian religious subjects, historians such as these were continuators of older trends, they also prefigured a modern trend that would develop during the fascist period "to Italianize" Italian history. Thus, although Biscaro was a liberal nationalist, his reputation rose to its highest point in the fascist period.

Although fields such as Classical, Medieval, and Renaissance Italian history and culture have long commanded great prestige among Italian historians, the recent commentary literature makes clear the degree to which these fields have been dominated not only internationally but in Italy itself, not by Italians but by German and English historians and classicists. For this to be the case, one can scarcely avoid the conclusion that it was acceptable to the Italian state for whatever reasons. If it was not in the interest of the state, leading politicians would have rejected foreign claims and emphasized local self-sufficiency as Mussolini briefly did. Did the state fear that Italian classicists would use their field as a vehicle of criticism? Did the state accept foreign scholars for the sake of its political relationships? This is difficult to judge. One must acknowledge, at least, that over a long period foreign scholars have been permitted to blame Italian scholars for the latter's interest in Roman over Greek studies and to find "especially reprehensible" the fact that Italian students of Roman antiquity often take an essentially national as opposed to a classicist interest in the field. Why should criticism of Italian scholars be tolerated, even celebrated? Why, for example, should the German scholar Ritschl, who was in the forefront of nineteenth-century developments in the critical treatment of texts, be remembered for singling out the work of the Italian classicist Vallauri, (1805–1897) on Plautus as an example of this form of "incompetence?"[38] To the eye of an outsider, at least, Italians have played a major role in the development of this field. Italian scholars have directed the excavation of Rome from the nineteenth century onward; one thinks, for example, of the work of Lanciani and then later the more famous G. Boni (1859–1925), and of P. Orsi (1859–1935), best known for his rediscovery of prehistoric Sicily. Still the "major" intellectual debates, syntheses, and interpretations of Roman history were and are made by non-Italians. According to the North European Classics journals, the Italian contribution appears to be no more than that of coordination and bibliographical compilation, as one finds for example in such journals as the *Rivista di Filologìa* (1873-), *Atène e Roma* (1898-), and *Il Móndo Clàssico*. Institutions such as the British School at Rome, however, marginal and undersupported by England, are even today accorded prestige by the Italian state.[39]

A willingness to accept cultural subordination, a propensity to study local subjects, and an incapacity to confront the problem of foreign control of much of Italian historical studies were, then, some of the main features of the old Liberal age that have to be considered as part of the hegemony.

Last but not least, it could be argued that the fascist era arrived during a particularly stagnant period in the history of Italian history writing.[40] The backbone of the Italian historical profession, the provincial committees for local history (Deputazióni di Stòria Pàtria), were not accepting the work of younger scholars; a similar schlerosis was manifest among the journals. *Rivista Stòrica Italiana* and the *Archivio Stòrico Italiano* were declining, leaving only the *Nuòva Rivista Stòrica* (1917–) as a journal of modern ideas. In addition, in the early twentieth century, the older generation of scholars began to retire without creating important students. For example, by the time of the rise of fascism, Nino Tomassia (1860–1931), the eminent legal historian, was nearing the end of his career at Pisa and Padua. Alessandro d'Ancona (1835–1914), the folklorist and historian noted above, had recently died.

This state of affairs gave the Fascists some freedom to use history. History as a field was suitable to serve in the struggle for national integration over provincialism. In addition, it could evoke the glories of the present-day Italian state, linking them to those of the past. If the liberals looked back to the Risorgimento of the nineteenth century, the Fascists could claim the Renaissance, a far more illustrious age. This approach to co-opting the past was actually tried. In two well-known examples of Fascist revisionism, the author, Pasquale Villari, dated Italian nationalism back to the origins of the House of Savoy (*Savanarola* and *Machiavelli*). The liberals responded to this initiative with indignation, and Villari was no match for their counterattack. In a definitive reply, Benedetto Croce in his study of the Baroque in Italy emphasized its decadence, despair, and exhaustion in contrast to the birth of hope in the nineteenth century.

Fascist historians were more successful in medieval and ancient studies. Gioacchino Volpe (b. 1876), a professor at Rome, gave importance to the medieval commune as an antecedent of the modern corporatist state.[41] For other historians with fascist sympathies, the Roman empire provided a model for fascism. Not surprisingly, Fascists supported Roman studies lavishly. Much was done to study the harbor town of Ostia, ancient Rome itself, Pompeii, and Roman culture in North Africa, especially Libya. The uncovering of glorious historical antecedents obviously contributed to the regime's standing, and this was its main objective. Judging, however, from an article by British classicist A. H. McDonald, Mussolini's classical studies failed to gain him prestige abroad.[42] In McDonald's opinion, the field of Roman Studies as created in the nineteenth century underwent few changes into the 1960s. At least for northern Europeans, the scholarship of Mommsen, Eduard Meyer, Beloch, and Niese continued to hold sway.

What stands out, however, is the contestation. For the first time, history was sufficiently important to the hegemony that the state backed a historiographical paradigm. As a British writer noted, Italian classicists mounted a challenge to the North European hegemony of the field of classics. It may have been a limited challenge, but it was a challenge, and it lasted well into the postwar years. The name most associated with this challenge was that of the Italian classical scholar Arnaldo Momigliano. Momigliano was the first classicist to take stock of the implications of classical studies for modern Italians; for his pains he has been called the (de-)"colonizer of German Hellenistic Studies."[43] But, he was not alone. Following him in the postwar years, several other writers have taken up the same or similar tasks. S. Mazzarino and J. Carcopino both wrote critically on the subject of Caesar's dictatorship. In the postwar years, however, the Italian state was no longer so interested; neither writer gained a reputation similar to that of Momigliano.

One obvious target for Italian nationalists was the writings of the German classicist Werner Jaeger, the leading scholar of the last generation. Jaeger's greatest work was *Paideaia,* a study of the aristocratic educational program of classical Greece. In *Paideaia,* Jaeger rejected the idea that all the ancient countries had culture; only Greece, he claimed, had a culture. To understand Greek culture, it was best to think in Greek, failing that, in German. Momigliano countered this position, putting forward the claim that classical studies ought to apply modern forms of analysis, for example, anthropology and sociology. Momigliano hesitated slightly over whether he would also endorse social science generalizations, but this was implied.

Another obvious target for the Italians was *The Civilization of the Renaissance in Italy,* the work of the great Swiss historian Jacob Burckhardt that defined Renaissance studies as Jaeger's defined classical studies.[44] The Renaissance, Burckhardt believed, was another period of universal importance in human history; it was the precursor of modern secular culture. This view, popular with some, was inevitably unacceptable for others. Religiously inclined historians, even in northern Europe, could never fully accept the proposition that the religious spirit of the Middle Ages had no bearing on the creativity of the Renaissance. Thus it was that beginning in the late nineteenth century with the art historian Adolfo Venturi, years before the rise of fascism, Italian scholars began to put forth arguments on behalf of an Italian interpretation of an Italian Renaissance. In the fascist period, when there was more general support for a nationalist history, the state built on this trend. In the interwar period, two major books appeared, arguing for an Italian-Christian interpretation of the Renaissance, one by Vladimiro Zabughin in 1924 and the other by I. Siciliano in 1936. But as Momigliano showed, even with the assertiveness of the fascist era, the major books of the leading Italian historians appear to have sought legitimation by basing their findings on non-Italian writings. This too, he found to be the case, even for the most-famous Italian historians, for example, Federico Chabod (1901–1960) and Croce.[45]

Although the fascist period was the high point of history's contribution to hegemony, not all historians active in those years were destined to side with the Fascists. In the area of modern history, the influence of the Fascists was distinctly weak. Perhaps as a consequence, the party's policy there became one not so much of promoting scholarship but of hampering the careers of those who were holding sway in that specialty. Whether or not this was actually a policy, it perhaps suffices to note that only one important scholar of modern Italian history, the German-educated Federico Chabod, survived in Italy in the fascist period, all the more remarkably because he was a liberal, an opponent of fascism, and not even an Italian nationalist. Perhaps he was simply lucky, or perhaps he survived because he represented something useful for the Fascists, possibly a link for Italy to the German academic scene. This is speculation because there is no easy way to judge how the state viewed him. All that is really known is from the chronology of his career. When he returned from Germany to teach in Italy, he, like his teacher Meinecke, dwelt on the conflict between ethics and power and on the problems of linearism and positivism as one finds them in English historiography.

Chabod was fairly lucky in his career; several well-known historians who were antifascist, including Luigi Salvatorelli and Gaetano De Sanctis, lost their jobs; one well-known liberal historian, Gaetano Salvemini, was forced into exile.[46] The communist historian Emilio Sereni spent time in jail; Nello Roselli, a specialist in Mazzini studies, was assassinated by the Fascists in 1937.[47]

Ultimately, however, the intellectual marginality of fascist scholars in fields such as modern history had political consequences for the party. Leading liberals, such as Croce, were able to align the majority of those specialized in the field against fascism. What the regime had to offer scholars was too little. Among the most famous of Croce's "conquests" was Chabod. Croce invited Chabod to leave Turin to be the director of his historical research center in Naples, and he accepted.[48] Adolfo Omodeo (1889–1946) soon followed Chabod.

Croce's conquest of Omodeo must be ranked alongside his conquest of Chabod as among the high points of the liberal struggle with fascism. Omodeo had begun his career as a student of Gentile's in philsophy at Palermo, in other words, in fascism, and Gentile remained a lifelong influence on him. With Gentile's patronage, Omodeo ultimately achieved the position of professor of church history at Naples. Along the way, however, Omodeo served as a soldier in World War II and was very embittered by the experience. Much as Omodeo despised the antiwar sentiment of the North, and he did, the war experience was so traumatic for him that it led him to a break with Gentile and with fascism in later years and permitted his turn to Croce and to liberalism.

Was Croce an important element in the struggle against fascism? Radical critics, including Gramsci, have not accepted this interpretation of Croce's role. Discounting his role as critic, they accused him of a de facto collaboration with the regime. After all, Croce pulled the intellectual youth of the South into the circle of his journal, *La Critica,* thus drawing them away from the radical peasantry, a practice Gramsci and others saw as contributing to the regional solidification of the regime.[49] But surely whatever support Croce brought to the regime, he undercut with his criticism of positivism and of the vulgar racism of fascist social science. When Mussolini's scholars harnessed biological theories of race and ethnology for colonial ends, Croce opposed their premises. These fields, he argued, do not produce true knowledge. Even natural sciences and mathematics, he claimed, lack the character of true knowledge. Human life is surrounded by mystery; human intelligence given by God's grace permits people to grasp individual situations; humans do not have access to a larger picture. For a regime that sought to make the structure of knowledge serve as propaganda, Croce was an albatross. He could not be attacked for indifference as one could attack a liberal positivist or for opposition as one could a Marxist; he forced the regime to carry around its neck the unending complexity and thoroughness of his method.

Croce wrote several works of history, including the attack on Villari and the defense of the Risorgimento. He contributed institutionally to the development of an independent center of historical studies at Naples. But Croce's even greater contribution to history was his attempt to liberate history from positivism by making positivism no more than a methodology of history. To the extent that he could force his contemporaries to question the assumptions of positivism, he was able to diminish the likelihood of the historian serving as a propagandist.[50]

The Postwar Years of Italian Historiography

To Momigliano, the most ardent supporter of positivist history, the postwar years brought no real changes in Italian historiography.[51] He attributed this inactivity to the lack of any real disruption in Italian intellectual life by the end of the war. In one sense, he was right, and in two senses, he was wrong.

Momigliano was absolutely correct when one considers the kinds of projects undertaken in the postwar years by the liberal mainstream of the history profession and even when one considers the continuing rootedness of the profession in its own traditions. For example, when Italian historians evaluated the merits of the Annales school, which was suddenly rising in prestige in the postwar years, they recoiled because of the need for quantification. There was no base in Italian historiography for quantification.[52] They were equally put off by the concept of the *longue durée;* the Italian historians preferred their own more anarchistic particularism of time and place. Thus, what continued to thrive was the traditional study of local history. As in earlier periods, so in the postwar period, the writing of local history provided an agreeable context for both professional and amateur historians. Often, it provided a source of income from the local audience. So if, during the fascist period, the emphasis on things Roman induced the professors at the University of Rome in the Istituto Stòrico to produce a thirty-volume history of Rome, after the war, another group of professors went on to produce a quite similar multivolume history of Milan.[53] Where was the change?

Change in Italian intellectual life did occur and did affect the history profession after World War II. First, the state no longer sought to use history as part of the hegemony in any important way. Historians were, thus, clearly not as important as they had been in the fascist period. Second, change is observable in terms of who the history profession had to or wanted to confront in an intellectual sense in this period. If, since the nineteenth century, the principal critics of the liberal positivist historiography had been the southern metaphysical philosophers, after 1948, liberal historians had to confront Marxism.

Although one could dispute the newness of debates between liberals and Marxists in this period in an absolute sense, one must still admit some change had taken place. After all, the Communists had accepted the premises of liberal society, and their ideas had gained respectability. With its newfound freedom, the Communist party was able to publish its important writers in complete editions. Gramsci's works, among others, became accessible; historians began to use them. By the late 1950s in historical circles, research increased in labor history, the nature of Jacobinism, the agrarian question, and the nature of retarded capitalism—issues that could be profitably examined through a Gramscian approach. The success of Marxist scholars in these areas induced a number of liberal historians to take up socioeconomic themes as well. The chief debate of the period was between a noted, liberal historian, Rosàrio Romeo, and the "Gramscians," concerning the nature of the Risorgimento and the Southern Question.[54]

Another debate in this period concerned the nature of fascism. In this area, the Italian liberals received a big boost by the sudden impact of the Anglo-American liberal scholarship on Italy. Writers such as Dennis Mack Smith and Edward Banfield, who did much to shape the position of Italy in the historiographical imagination, asserted in influential books that the liberal elite in Italy, although destined to triumph was incredibly incompetent and, thus, in part brought fascism and other ills on itself. Adopting the view that the national character of Italians was to be anarchic, it was natural that liberals would always have to contend with authoritarian countertrends such as Fascism.

If foreign liberalism could content itself with arguments made in a vacuum on the supposed national character of Italy, Italian liberals had to confront the intellectual legacy of the Left more directly, for example, the claim that the stagnation leading ultimately to the emergence of fascism was brought on by socialist struggle. This view was disputed by Rosario Romeo in his *Risorgiménto e capitalismo* (Bari: Laterza, 1959). In this influential book, Romeo claimed that Gramsci's explanation of modern Italian history was a politically motivated and, hence, not truly scholarly. It was based on an illogical set of arguments by analogy drawn from French history. To be precise, it was too influenced by the model of the French Revolution. In Romeo's opinion, if an agrarian revolution had come to Italy such as that which followed the French Revolution in France, it would have delayed the coming of capitalism. Other factors, such as the strength of the outside world market forces, militated against such a revolution in any case. The Marxists replied to Romeo on all these counts. First, they argued that the utility of agrarian reform had been debated in Italy at the time and was not a communist idea so that there was no—or at least minimal—politicizing of historical scholarship as Romeo had stated. Second, they argued that although the French Revolution was one prototype of the rise of the bourgeoisie, it was not the only one, and it was wrong, therefore, to dismiss Gramsci's theory for overdependence on a given model. Third, Marxist historians argued that Romeo himself made errors in his interpretation of Italian economic history. Romeo argued for the necessity of the accumulation of capital, but he did not emphasize the role land reform would necessarily play in it. Accumulation follows upon the dissolution of the peasantry because peasants contribute little to accumulation. As a consequence of the liberal failure to understand this fact—and Romeo was scarcely alone in this matter—major investments in Italy actually were foreign investments and state investments. Did not Italy suffer from fascism and semicolonialism as a consequence?

It might be recalled that these debates were going on against a background of the ICP's gain in the 1970s vis-à-vis the Christian Democrats. Sensing the rise on both an intellectual and political level of a real challenge, the liberal majority of the history profession dug in its heels, opposing the university reforms of the 1970s and adopting a rather defensive cultural position in general.[55] In a conference held in 1980 at the University of Milan, the historians attempted to doyennize the figure of Federico Chabod. They called him the symbol of the *new history,* a term not even found in Gino Pasoli's manual on the study of history of 1970 that I cited above.[56]

In this chapter, I introduced an interpretation of Italy as Italian Road. Its principal argument is that 1948 is not the total watershed in Italian history as is often maintained but that this date marks instead a resurgence of a liberal phase of the older hegemony. Evidence from economic history, from the sociology of gender relations, and from cultural fields, including history, appears to reinforce this conclusion. Two implications of this revisionist interpretation are important for the larger argument of the book. First is the implication that if Italy is Italian Road as Russia is Russian Road, Europe is more than simply bourgeois democracy; one cannot, therefore, speak of "Europe and the rest," implying some great divide. Second is the implication that to determine specificity one needs comparability; This takes the study once again outside of Europe.

5

The "Italian Road" in Asia

India, 1861–1990

In modern historiography, India is usually presented as an example of failed development, as a country too large to study as a whole or as a culture composed of unchanging religious and communal relationships. In this chapter, modern Indian history (1861–1990) is an example of an Italian Road hegemony.[1] What stands out in this optic is the ruling class's use of regional difference. Equally marked is the counterhegemonic struggle and the ensuing political crisis.

The chapter is divided into four parts: the Italian Road model relative to the dominant paradigms of interpretation of modern Indian history; a history of modern India as Italian Road; hegemony on the level of the organization of culture; the writing of history as a part of the organization of culture.

Since 1885, the founding date of the Congress party, liberals have assumed that India was on the road to becoming a modern secular country, a democracy, albeit a democracy beset sometimes by occasional resurgences of traditionalism.[2] After independence in 1948, some liberals began to question this assumption. Could *traditionalism* explain how communalism had power enough to result in the partition of the country in that year or to sustain a religious influence in the affairs of state year after year thereafter?

When explaining the events of 1948 and those thereafter, liberals often found themselves pushed in the direction of romanticism. India is not so much a "modern" country as it is a society that has eternal cultural differences between Muslims and Hindus that simply well up now and again.

For romantics, the major concern has long been the one about decline, about the supposed gap between current caste practices and the ideals that caste practices are thought to represent. Because the caste system is the essence of Indian history and culture, modern history in this view becomes a footnote to medieval history.[3]

For the study here, the entrance of caste into a prominent position in the dominant paradigm as it relates to India poses the problem of how to make caste an institution of the Italian Road.

Caste as a Part of the Italian Road: An Aside

It stands to reason that caste should play different roles in different hegemonies.[4] In Russian Road states, as argued in the previous chapters, caste is central. One does not find in Russia as one does in India the proliferation of subcastes, groups that tend to make caste more equivalent to class. Still, caste is clearly more important in India than it is in Italy or Mexico, which requires an explanation.

Under the British, the codification of caste practice led to the identification of certain quite contemporary groups as "backward classes and castes" who were, thus, in need of legal redress. And, indeed, a close look at who they were is quite revealing. It appears that the government's strategy in this matter has long been to support the claims of the *Kulaks,* or rich peasants, of the South over others, a strategy obviously designed to maintain a southern wing of the ruling class.[5] In fact, in a classic account of the nature of caste written by a scholar in Calcutta one generation ago, the author argued forthrightly for a North-South division underlying caste. Brahmins, he argued, are whiter and more in the North, whereas the Sudra and other lower castes are blacker and more in the South. Practices associated with ritual purity follow from the need of those who are whiter to keep their purity because so many blacks coming North as migrant agricultural laborers now inhabit even the Gangetic Plains.[6]

It becomes apparent that whatever caste in India is at different points and at different times, it is useful for the state and at the same time popular. Through it, the state has been able to curtail the influence of saints and of *swami* and to gain control over temple employees. Today, these temple employees are employees of the central government; fifty years ago, they were not. At that time, saints and swami freely issued opinions; today the semiofficial Banaras Hindu University is the center of validation of religious thought. Support of caste permitted the state these gains.[7]

Caste serves the needs of society as well. Middle strata and even Subaltern groups identify their projects with caste and often manage thereby to get them accepted. For example, since the midnineteenth century, the Arya Samaj, a middle class reform movement not unlike the Catholic reform groups discussed in chapter 4, achieved its objectives largely by promoting caste.[8] Still that leaves the question Why is caste so prominent in India?[9]

And, what deeper theory is there beyond various correlations suggested by an Italian Road interpretation?[10]

For political economy, one can establish the relationship of the history of a particular phenomenon to that of capitalism. How, for example, did caste develop as capitalism and the state become modern? What is different about the development of the state and capitalism in Italy that might explain why caste plays a more reduced role there?

In sixteenth-century Mughal India, caste was weak. At this point, the state, which was strong, controlled its own commercial sector and promoted a mercantilist market-based form of autochthonous capitalist growth.[11]

In the seventeenth century, the state grew weak, and caste in civil society grew strong. In the eighteenth century, caste became weak. At this time, regional politics and economies flourished; *bhakti* (mystical) cults grew in importance, challenging caste. In the early nineteenth century, as the central state began to redevelop, caste once again grew strong. In the late twentieth century as Hindu involvement in capitalism grew stronger, again as in the sixteenth century, caste grew weaker. Later, in the early twentieth century, caste continued to weaken among Hindus as their capitalism continued to grow in strength. For example, in the 1940s and 1950s, intermarriage among Hindus of different castes and even between Hindus and Muslims took place as it had in the sixteenth century. As in Mughal times, a syncretist cult, the Qadiyaniyya movement, sprang up, which combined elements of Islam and Hinduism. Finally, as capitalism among Hindus grew in strength, the Raj experienced its final crisis; caste was at a low ebb. The British left; their allies, the Muslims, Parsees, and Jews saw their communities fragment. As more recent events show, however, this efflorescence of the Hindu political economy did not mark the end of caste ideology. In the 1970s and 1980s, when the international market reasserted itself, the capitalism of the Hindu majority in the North faltered. Once again caste ideology rose in importance.

From the late nineteenth century onward, the Islamic community, which had lost its control of the commercial sector, also lost its caste structure, the correlation being reversed. Muslims of various castes drifted toward a class-based version of ethnicity either more modernist or more conservative. Here one thinks comparatively of the Jews and Protestants of countries such as Mexico or Italy. In India, the Muslim modernist trend collaborated with the Raj and opposed partition. This trend was embodied in the thought of Sayyid Ahmad Khan and in the evolution of Aligarh University. Today, the modernists are Indian nationalists. A second trend, the conservatives or Deoband school, also arose in the nineteenth century but not so much among the wealthy urbanites, who followed Sayyid Ahmad Khan, as among the smaller more puritanical merchants of North

India. The Deobandis presented a major challenge to the modernists. In the interwar period, The Deoband trend was partitionist; later, after 1947, it was a critic of secularism in India.

As with the Indian Muslims so also with the other commercial groups, the Jews and the Parsees, one finds a caste-to-ethnicity mutation as Hindus established their predominance in modern capitalism. Wealthier Indian Jews, like their Muslim counterparts, allied themselves to the Raj in the nineteenth century as Indians. The Jewish leader Sir Albert Sassoon serves here as a historical parallel to the Muslim Sayyid Ahmad Khan. As the Raj declined in this century, the Jewish community, like its Muslim counterpart, divided according to class interests. A turning point in this process came in 1919. In 1919, the Race Laws of India codified in the Montague Chelmsford report, lumped all the Jews of India into a low category, non-Muslim. Conscious of themselves as Jews, the increasingly more threatened middle-class Calcutta community contested this designation, but by the time it was able to secure a remedy, it was too late to matter. By contrast to the Calcutta Jews, the South Indian Jews, led by a few wealthy families, were more conscious of themselves as Indians than as Jews and made little protest over the rulings of 1919.

Similarly, during the later years of the Raj, an important segment of the Parsees, this time mainly in the North, evolved into a modernist ethnic group. Their position, however, by this point was quite tenuous. Parsee children from this period emerge with names such as Readymoney and Sodawaterwalla, suggesting the community's utter dependence on the British. As Hindu capitalism evolved and British capitalism continued to retreat, their position, even their culture nearly collapsed.[12]

What upholds caste and caste legislation today is, thus, perfectly clear. It is modern India; it is the state, the army, the university, and the political parties.[13] Given the power of these institutions in India or elsewhere, one can scarcely imagine caste reform.[14] Caste may change with historical conditions, but it is useful. This leaves open the question of why this is so much the case for India. What is driving scholarship to focus on the subject of caste?

Sati, Bride Murder, and Purdah

Much of the contemporary interest in caste in India is associated with the analysis of the oppression of Indian women, aspects of which have a clear link to caste, for example, *sati,* bride murder and *purdah*. A brief analysis of these phenomena to learn about caste and gender oppression concludes that none of these singly or together shed much light on either. One must look elsewhere.

As mass market capitalism expanded in the last century, sati declined soon to be replaced in those places, where it appears to have been the most widely practiced, that is, among the property-owning classes of North India, with an increased tendency toward bride murder. To proceed rigorously, it would, thus, be necessary to know if this is really a constant connection. If, for example, the emergence of a capitalist sector earlier, during the Mughal period, accompanied a similar decline of sati and increase in bride murder or if other features unique to the nineteenth century must be emphasized.[15] This at present is not known.

As recent scholarship does, however, make clear, there is more to bride murder than its correlation with the development of capitalism. To be more precise, it is actually a part of it. Bride murder is from an economic perspective a form of plunder or primitive accumulation, a very generic part of capitalism, not something long gone, but something ongoing, like an investment is ongoing. If one fails to realize this and interprets such practices primarily as a representation of gender oppression, as is common enough, then these practices become incomprehensible and India as a whole becomes incomprehensible and, therefore, unique.

For example, if sati is to be defined through gender, then the writer is prone to find that there is more violence against women in India than in other countries and against women in Italian Road countries than against women in other hegemonies, claims based, I suggest, on fairly shaky evidence.[16]

Although the subject of violence against women is poorly studied, one can safely claim that it is a worldwide problem. A recent study in the United States showed that during the height of the Vietnam War (1967–73) some 39,000 men died in combat. During the same interval, 17,570 women and children were victims of domestic violence. Current statistics for violence against women in larger countries, such as India, do not record such high figures; perhaps they are not complete. For the years 1976 and 1977, the home minister of India placed the number of women burned to death at less than 3,000 each year.[17]

From what is known, the form of violence seems to correspond to the economics of marriage. Spousal violence in the United States, for example, appears to be a consequence of the nuclear family form and of the system of inheritance through wills, which commonly goes along with it. If spousal violence—in the expanded sense—includes a range of acts from nonsupport of children to wife beating, but does not include bride murder, this appears to follow from two factors: the nuclear family structure and inheritance through wills. If bride murder is a common form of domestic violence in India, it appears to follow from the cousin-based family form and the dowry system. What a bride can get from her family is what she gets initially. After the nuptials, little more is expected, so the bride's utility as a source of wealth goes down. Given an Italian Road family structure prone under certain conditions to plundering projects, the bride has reasons to watch her husband's family.

Today, in North Italy, the custom of dowry is in a state of decline. Property is now more commonly passed on through wills. The new priority of the women's movement there now is for the end of violence in society and against women.[18] The Italian movement in this instance is coming to resemble in its concerns the American feminist movement, that is, it is no longer signaling a fear of crime passionelle or of machismo but a fear of unchanneled aggression in what is now often a more nuclear type of family setting.

Dowry as a system is not responsible for the abuse of women in India or in any other country. Dowry is the dominant practice in many countries, not just in India but in Russia and even in Zaire, with such variants as one finds in the cross-generational Russian Road families and the clan-based families of the tribal-ethnic states. Gender friction related to dowry may occur; overt violence is abnormal.

How then, does a pathological phenomenon such as bride murder become sociologically prevalent?

Seemingly, the most persuasive explanation for the higher rate of bride murder in North India over that of a potentially comparable region, for example, North Italy, would be bound up with an explanation of how North India differs economically from North Italy. Such an explanation would undoubtedly note that from the midnineteenth century onward, the distinguishing feature of the history of these two regions appears to be that of the resources available to each to deal with periods of economic stagnation.

Close examination shows that the impact of stagnation in North India was greater than in North Italy because in North Italy an alternative exists for maintaining one's family status under such conditions, working abroad in a wealthier country nearby. This can be done strategically and conditionally, and it is an option that is immediately accessible. Migration, of course, is not unknown in India, but the lack of a predictable and suitably wealthy host country nearby has meant that the decision to migrate has tended to be an all or nothing one that attracts the poorest of the poor more than anyone else.

Indian women in property-owning families of the North are seemingly caught in a double bind. Their identity comes from their social status, from their regional identity, and from their family's participation in capitalist consumerism. But this identity, given the frequent stagnation of North India in the face of world capitalism leaves them vulnerable at the very least to the frustration of their spouse's kin. It is little wonder that women from these families have been vocal in their demands that the government protect them in a world where the ups and downs of family status are outside their control. In the 1950s, the Indian government passed a Hindu Code Bill, which ought to have assured women rights of property and personal status. The Indian women's movement, however, reports that this law often has had no force until today even in wide parts of the North.

Purdah, like sati and bride murder, is a subject area where a political economy could develop in a similar way. Certainly, tendencies to sequester women have existed in a number of countries. Ancestral ideas of purity commonly figure in the rationale, thus creating a link between purdah and caste, but political economy offers more specific reasons for why, when, and where it occurs.

In an Italian Road regime subject to colonialism, for example, late nineteenth-century India (or Egypt), purdah was an observable phenomenon. Under conditions of colonialism, Indians found that the job market for upper-class women led nowhere, that it was in a sense a polluting one. Although the ruling classes did not want to oppose the work ethic, they wanted to carve out an exception for themselves. Poorer women could still work because they had to survive. Later, with the coming of independence and the regaining of indigenous control over the local economy, opportunities improved, and as they did more women entered the job market and purdah declined. As purdah declined, the situation of women came to approximate that of the women of Italy or Mexico, Italian Road countries that were not colonized in recent times.

To write about sati, bride murder, and purdah as caste practice seems misleading, whereas to write about them as defining gender practice simply seems ineffectual. The question of gender in political economy is quite crucial not just for the study of India but for all other countries as well. As it applies to India, however, my assumption is that whatever one's choice of method, gender analysis is going to be an independent subject. If it is to be reduced to the minimum for the sake of a brief discussion, the analysis must shed light on the issue of patriarchy.

Patriarchy touches all women. The vast majority of women in India are poor. They are, thus, less affected by sati, bride murder, and purdah than they are by the oppression of the state. The state upholds the rights of men in the economy and in the legal system against those of women. Because they are poor, these women can bring little as a counterbalance.

Arguing from an analogy to the idea of a working class, one might, thus, claim that although the experience of poor women does not exhaust the reality of gender contradiction as a subject nor is the witness of poor women necessarily the most profound, the struggle of poor women would still be the most fruitful locus for an analysis aspiring to go beyond Eurocentrism. It is easier to argue from the experience of this majority to the rest than it is to argue from the few to the many.

The conflictual interaction of poor women and the state, which is the direction I recommend for gender analysis, can be inferred from scholarship in a number of fields. It is not a special field. For example, a researcher can draw information from studies of social work, public health, criminology, and so forth. The best-studied example of poor women's relations to the state in existing scholarship is probably found in the history of prostitution. Beginnings exist elsewhere, for example, in the work on the Self-employed Women's Association of Ahmedabad. Clearly, prostitution history, too, can only serve as a beginning because most poor women are not prostitutes and not all prostitutes are poor women, but in terms of contemporary scholarship it is the best-researched area. Researchers from numerous countries confirm that a significant number of poor women earn their living whoring, that states oppose prostitution in theory, but they condone or encourage it in practice, that women working as whores try to earn their money and stay free from state controls, and that whores do not want or do not have the option of state-approved family structures. Herein lies gender as a contradiction. States have the power to describe this commerce as a feature of the immorality of these women rather than that of their customers or of the state, itself. Under such conditions, whores are obliged to resist.

A sceptic might object here, pointing out that prostitution is more economic than it is gender specific. Emma Goldman's famous essay, "Traffic in Women," makes just this point. The gender dimension of prostitution is, to my mind, established by looking simultaneously at the life of the prostitute and at the behavior of the state toward the prostitute. The general tendency of states is to impose or reimpose dependence on the women convicted of prostitution. Whores are put in the custody of police and social workers, functionaries whose job it is to restore male dominance. One scarcely expects a whore to be sentenced to pay back taxes. The threat whores represent to society is not what they earn but what they represent as a challenge to those upholding the virtues of the traditional family and, thus, by extension, the state itself. If whoring was a viable option for women, would families survive? If the family did not survive, would the hegemony survive? Another telling argument for a gender-based analysis of prostitution is that states commonly choose the possible existence of prostitution as their pretext for why they need to mount antivice or pro-family campaigns, strategies designed to strengthen the hegemony. In the process of attacking vice or protecting the family, the gender contradiction dimension of prostitution, of course emerges, but the state camouflages it by the focus on the economic or moral aspects of prostitution that it is not actually concerned with at all.

Marxists are often among those most insistent on an economic interpretation of prostitution, ignoring thereby the possibilities offered by gender analysis. In this regard, Marxism appears to follow the lead of liberalism. One can see this in the choice of terms. A writer who accepts gender as a contradiction would tend to use the term *whore* because whore is a more active term. Few Marxists do; most prefer to start from class analysis or from the more state-oriented lingo about individual morality. This leads them to use the more passive term *prostitute*.[19]

The Italian Road state, the concern here, has traditionally been characterized by its upholding of two main forms of ideology about prostitution: regulation and the double standard. In Italy, these ideologies were enshrined as policies in the formative legislation about prostitution, the Cavour Law of 1860, which, despite the opposition of the Catholic church, gave whores some limited forms of legal protection. In 1982, violence by American soldiers against whores at Aviano triggered the formation of a Committee for the Civil Rights of Whores.[20] Public opinion quickly turned against the Americans. In a second Italian Road state, Mexico, the double-standard approach has been the more dominant. There is an obvious link, at least in Monterrey, between the border tourist trade and the well being of the national economy.[21] The choice of a strategic location empowered these women. Still other examples could be drawn from India. In Calcutta, whores have successfully opposed registration attempts by the state. One author writing about the conflict in Bombay ruefully admitted that the police could be easily bribed. In one famous episode of double standard practice in 1921, Gandhi requested that prostitutes, who were members of the Congress party and who were among his financial supporters, not seek office. It is not known how they responded. The request itself reflects the power these women had.[22] The phenomenon of the educated call girl is thought to have increased after independence.[23] The double standard made this possible.

In democracies, gender contradiction appears to be more important than it is in the Italian Road. In democracies, prostitution is perceived to be not only illegal but immoral; it is common for whores, therefore, to need the protection of a pimp, a male. Prostitutes without pimps would certainly risk the violence the Italian women mentioned above experienced. In addition, in democracies one finds mass murderers of women thought to be prostitutes, the so-called Jack the Rippers who appear as a sociological type. Such figures are accorded media attention as if to intimidate women from being about and from seeking to work in any domain, which underscores the link between the fate of prostitutes and all other women.[24] Again, only in democracies do reformers recurrently launch crusades, albeit unsuccessful ones, to end prostitution.

In the Russian Road states, the gender contradiction is less important to the maintenance of the hegemony than it is in the democracies, and, perhaps, as a consequence, the struggle of whores at least in Russia itself has been able to spark public debates. Is the state to be a guardian of public safety defined as protecting its citizens against syphilis or AIDS or is it to provide what its citizens want? In both Russia and the Soviet Union, the government acquiesced to prostitution to "serve the needs of armies" because masturbation was "debilitating." To deal with this contradiction of how to uphold public morality while maintaining a "healthy army" to safeguard the country, the state from the late nineteenth century onward encouraged Jewish businessmen to run bordellos. The existence of legal bordellos left open the question of who was to regulate them, a code phrase for how much gender freedom had been won. Could the state "entrust" its medical profession with the responsibility of regulation with the implication that it favored women's health more than the needs of the state? or Was it necessary to leave the responsibility to the ministry of the interior?

In 1917, the Russian Revolution occurred; gender freedom was proclaimed as an objective of the Bolsheviki. In the long-run, however, the relationship of prostitutes and the state remained the same. Looking more closely, one finds that the Bolsheviki did not really develop gender as a part of their ideology but simply carried on older ideas that prostitution had its roots in capitalism not patriarchy. Operating on that assumption, the party attempted to correct the situation. But, as an account from the Stalinist period by a devoted Communist suggests, this effort had only the slightest impact. After five years of trying, Stalin managed to reemploy only 575 former whores retrained by his prophylactorums. Apparently during the Stalinist period (1928–56), even with prostitution outlawed, the number of whores increased. In the wake of the AIDS epidemic come reports that the state is approaching the problem by fining whores who are not registered.

The USSR is not unique in its tendency toward inept regulation; similar practices can be found in Iraq, another Russian Road state. A literary depiction of the red-light district in contemporary Baghdad by a well-known male writer reveals the pretensions of the police and the hypocrisy of the religious officials.[25]

In the tribal-ethnic states, gender is the primary contradiction of the hegemony; the institution of prostitution is absorbed into the system in a way that at first glance appears to differ from that of other historical roads; Brussels, for example, is the capital of the World Whores Organization. In Kinshasa, a recent study of prostitution suggests that the older manageress of the bordello creates a fictive kinship relationship between herself and her younger women workers because if the bordello takes on a tribal-and gender-appropriate format, the state ignores it. Any assertion by women against the ideology of tribalism or against gender apartheid more generally —and there are examples of these—immediately reveals the willingness of the state to uphold the hegemony. Thus, even the suggestion that a woman is adopting a male role as, for example, when a whore becomes a political confidante, makes her a target of suspicion. This suggests that the semi-legality of the bordello in countries such as Zaire, Albania, Belgium, and so forth, reveals not freedom but the relative centrality of the gender contradiction in those hegemonies.[26]

The romantics are right to insist that violence against women in India is a major theme and that it has deep historical roots. This is the extent to which they can go. To go further, they need a framework of analysis that is more historically specific than they can provide. Here, a study of the struggle of prostitutes in the different hegemonies could help to lay a general foundation from which to judge gender struggle in a given country such as India.

Clearly, to make sati typify gender oppression against women is illogical. To explain sati in terms of religion is equally illogical, by so doing one ignores the economic components which have nothing to do with gender or religion. Sati, or in modern times bride burning, emerges from this long set of preliminary comments as a problem associated with Italian Road capitalism, a capitalism in its North Indian context frustrated by stagnation, a capitalism prone to wars with neighboring Pakistan but often forced to turn in on itself and often violently so. In short, purdah, sati, bride burning, and caste in India represent what in comparative studies one terms *specificity* or *difference* and not what romantics believe it to be, something unique or fixed in time and space.

The Political Economy of India, 1861–1990

From 1861, a hegemony based on alliances, which the British called indirect rule, prevailed in large parts of India, and these played a dominant role in the semicapitalist/semifeudalist economy that evolved. One century later, political reforms had shorn the feudal wing of its aristocratic titles, but they could not paper over the dependence of the hegemony on a southern part of the ruling class. From the 1970s until today, the state has been seriously challenged by the South, bringing into question not just the continuation of various governments but of the hegemony itself.

In the years before 1861, political power was embodied in loose alliances made up of the merchant classes of the coastal cities, of the northern landlords, and of the royal satraps. The British were prominently represented in each of these constituent parts. From the India Act of 1858 onward, a passive revolution began. The British and their Indian allies amalgamated the lands of the East India Company with those of the princely states into one country from above, creating a hegemony with a built-in North-South division.[27]

In 1861, codification of the penal and procedural law symbolized in important ways the takeoff of the modern state. Bureaucracy, too, was on the rise, which signifies that the hegemony was in place, for only if some agreement existed among dominant elements could the problems of policy implementation be delegated.

The year 1861 also serves as a dividing point after which a civilian police emerged, taking over functions previously performed by the military. Thus, for example, during 1861, the police no longer collected revenue. The pay of police chiefs was raised. But, as is common in Italian Road states, the North-South regional differential was maintained. The Police Act of 1861 was not applied to the South. Only in 1882, did the state invest in a southern armed reserve, after a riot there.

For the more reform-minded among the British and Indians of the period, the discrepancy between the North and the South was difficult to accept, especially in such areas as law. It was intolerable that given the same facts judges in two different parts of the country could reach entirely different decisions. In 1861, the government thus sought to paper over this problem by reserving all the high judicial offices for members of the India Civil Service and by widening the power of the magistrate to include both judicial and executive matters at the same time.[28] In this year, also, an India High Courts Act led to the establishment of high courts in Calcutta, Bombay, and Madras. But still, critics of the new order could detect southern exceptionalism in the slowness with which legal reform actually progressed in that region.

From 1861, a weak parliamentary tradition became visible as part of the new bureaucratic edifice. The India Councils Act of that year mandated an enlargement of the size of the Viceroy's Executive Council and of the Legislative Council. It called for nonofficial native members. Definite limits remained, however; the governor general exercised veto power over council measures.

In 1864, centralization and recomposition of the army made it theoretically more reflective of national than of regional interests. The new army was 40 percent smaller than before the 1858 mutiny and 60 percent more British despite the White Mutiny in which ten thousand Europeans had to resign from the army.

During the 1870s, the trends of the 1860s deepened, the new hegemony was sinking roots. On an economic level, the state sponsored a successful program of rapid development of the infrastructure of Western India; more products began to reach the coast and to find their way into the export trade. On a political level, the princely states flourished.[29]

Opposition, of course, arose, and the state confronted it. Some came from among establishment figures; some was subaltern. In 1871, the governor-general could justify a Criminal Tribes Act because the police needed extra support as they confronted criminal groups and not just ordinary criminals.

In 1873, in what could be taken as a sign of the success of the hegemony, the lieutenant-governor of Bengal opined that the prestige of the law and lawyers was rising. He was naturally pleased that it was rising among the *zamindars* (landlords); he was concerned that it was also rising among the moneylenders. He was worried that the moneylenders would use the court system against the peasants and that the peasants would lose their land.[30]

In 1876, manifestations of a civil society were evident. The nationalist hero Surendranath Banerjea founded the Indian Association in Calcutta. In 1878, the newspaper *Hindu* began in Madras. In 1883, rule by law, a cardinal feature of civil society, was strengthened by the withdrawal of the Ilbert Bill. Henceforth, at least in theory, a European could be tried by an Indian magistrate. In 1885, the Congress party was founded.

After 1880, the contrast between the North and the South was an accepted part of the national culture. A common-sense understanding of India indicated that the modern institutions in India were mainly in the North, that modern institutions even in Madras were less evolved than their northern counterparts.[31]

By the late nineteenth century, the modern economy was led by its export sector. The social structure came to reflect this change. A considerable middle strata arose in North India; increasingly, it was Hindu, educated and bilingual. In the early twentieth century, industrialization began in Bombay around cotton and in Calcutta around jute. The urban population grew rapidly; a home market began for locally manufactured products.

The political consequences of these socioeconomic changes were far-reaching. The Muslims, Jains, and Parsis mentioned in the previous section pressed the government for guarantees of their traditional privileges, but by the year 1900, the government could no longer meet this demand. The economy no longer depended simply on exporting raw goods, but on expertise in exporting combined with skill in selling to the home market. In a dramatic if ill-conceived move, Lord Curzon, the viceroy of India, called for a partition of Bengal in 1905 to assure the Muslims a political base. This move backfired. A compensatory attempt to widen the political framework to include more Hindus, the dyarchy idea of the Montague-Chelmsford report of 1918, backfired as well, as the British officials in their turn felt betrayed.

Lord Curzon's policy decisions in the early years of the century pointed toward something else as well—that the interests of the ruling class in India, whether English or Indian, and its counterpart in England were diverging; they were, after all, functioning in two different hegemonies.[32]

An early example of this divergence appeared in 1905. The English in England were seeking to conciliate the Russians, who were at that time a potential ally. They were embarrassed by Lord Curzon's sudden statement that Russia's expansion was a threat to India. As time progressed, the divergence deepened. With labor colonialism on the rise in England, Curzon in India seemed out of step with English politics. The English in England wanted to find an accommodation with Indian nationalism; Curzon did not want to bend.

Strained relations between India and England from this time forth belie the more commonsensical expectations one might have of the harmonious connections between a mother country and its chosen ruling elite in a colony. Yet, for example, in World War I, scandals in Mesopotamia over the English use of Indian levies added to the sense of exploitation felt and expressed not only by nationalists but by the government of India to its counterpart in London. After the war, India suffered economic crises that led to food riots and trade union agitation. Politicians in India attributed these events to the sacrifices India had to make for Great Britain during the war. In the Great Depression, British dumping practices led the government of India to pass tariffs to protect Indian cotton, paper, and sugar products against the home country. This action drove the English in England to circumvent the tariffs.

Partly as a result of the rivalry between mother country and colony, business in India, including Indian business, began to gain more and more political influence with the government of India. Was a class of national capitalists, the steel magnate Tata, for example, becoming the spearhead of the national movement? Seemingly, this was not the case. Tata was clearly not anti-British. What drove businesspeople such as Tata and, increasingly, the state as well to pursue a course of collision with Great Britain was more a matter of economics than of politics.

As early as World War I, the conflicts between India and England were destined to be political. The Congress party, led by the likes of Gandhi, would have it no other way. After all, it was Gandhi, like Gramsci in Italy, who grasped how the Indian state ruled.

If the Indian state had found ways to divide North and South, then Gandhi found a way to overcome these divisions. He used radical symbolic protests that permitted millions to participate in nationalist politics in a coordinated fashion. In the Rowlatt Satyagraha of 1919, a nonviolent protest against the Rowlatt decrees, regulations that were perpetuating wartime restrictions on civil liberties, Gandhi brought his political strategy to fruition. In this protest, Gandhi shifted from an approach during which he fasted and called for self-purification to an approach during which he called for voluntary work resistance. Through this change of strategy, Gandhi received wider and wider support even from among the generally more secular urban lower middle class of North India.[33] So successful was the work refusal approach that by the early 1920s, this experience led him to extend the noncooperation movement even to the South. Gradually, however, by the middle 1930s, Gandhi's call to refuse modern work in favor of traditional practical manual labor began to collide with the interests of the Indian industrial class, and it was the latter who tended to have the ear of Congress party politicians.

As if this were not enough, by the 1930s, two new trends had arisen that threatened to undermine the noncooperation movement or, at least, its connection with the Congress party: the communalist trend, and the peasant movements. The government—and much subsequent scholarship—held Gandhi responsible for the former. Although this may not be fair, it is correct to claim that the implication of his message was to cause his followers to distinguish what was Hindu from what was not Hindu. Although this differentiation could serve nationalist interests to a certain extent, it ultimately served to retard it, given the large number of Muslims in India. Of equal importance for the outcome of the Noncooperation movement was the rise of the peasant movement. Wide segments of the peasantry wanted land and food. For better or worse, neither the Raj, nor Gandhi, nor the secular nationalists could accommodate their needs. Peasant uprisings added to the environment of crisis without contributing to Gandhi's prestige. Corporatism would soon come to India.

Gandhi's decline became apparent in the early 1930s with the rise of industry as the real backbone of the Indian economy. Before that time, Gandhi could impose strategies on the Congress party that were arguably hurtful to the industrialists. Between 1932 and 1935, however, the industrialists became too strong. Even the government of India began to support the industrialists, imposing duties on foreign cotton products, including cotton goods from Lancashire, and on paper and sugar as well. A shift in the economy in the direction of industry was becoming apparent even in the old South.

As industrialization progressed and attracted the support of the state, the landlord class experienced a decline in official support. Labor relations in the countryside went from bad to worse. Agitation in the form of peasant movements grew. The Indian landlord class, like its Italian counterpart of the 1920s, prepared to give up liberalism to hold onto its land if it had to. Soon, it would have to do so.

During the crisis of liberalism in these two countries, Italy ultimately went to a rightist form of corporatism and India to a leftist one as outcomes of the choices made not only by the state but also by the principal counterhegemonic movement. As the previous chapter made clear, in Italy, despite Gramsci's attempts at a Workers Councils strategy and his attempts to recruit the rural migrant labor in the Po Valley into the party, the party chose to retreat and to support only the urban working class just at the time that liberal capitalism was facing a real crisis in the countryside. The crisis and the retreat of the Communists gave the Fascists not only their chance to come to power but their chance to co-opt the left's program. In India, in the long term, the historic link between a part of the Left with the peasantry forced the Indian ruling class to acknowledge its vulnerability and to seek a mass base for its programs. In the short term, however, the path of least resistance for the bourgeoisie was to choose the urban working class as its ally. This it did. The result was state socialism.

In 1948, the quintessential year of conjuncture in modern India, corporatism emerged as state socialism; so, too, did political independence and partition. State socialism lasted almost unchallenged until 1970. It survives in a weakened form today. I term the first twenty-two-year period the *corporatist period par excellence*. During this period, both capitalists and trade unionists collaborated to rule India under the umbrella of the Congress party. In the process, the images of both, however, were tarnished by the party's numerous setbacks.[34] By the 1960s, critics of the Indian system used such terms as *disarticulated state, state monopoly capitalism, Eurocommunism,* and other such phrases to characterize the distortions that were appearing.

Through the 1960s, the regime aspired, however unrealistically, to make India an industrial country. Industrial productivity did not rise; land reform was not proceeding either, the landlord class was too strong. The latter was, if anything, making a political comeback through alliances with the communalist parties at home and with the United States abroad. Landlordism was functioning even within the Congress party itself. From the general election of 1968 onward, the party became more and more divided between industrial and agricultural interests. Thus 1968 was the end of the coherent corporatism era.

After 1970, India entered the era of neoliberalism, but it did so gradually. The rulers were too divided to allow one-class rule. The Congress party remained in power with its cross-class alliances intact but weakened. The Indian industrialists in the party retained their alliance with the representatives of the trade union movement, much as had been the case in earlier years, but as the continuation of the industrial economy came more and more to depend on the state, changes were noticeable. In the public sector, the Communists began to perform capitalist functions, which made it easier for the state to force the working class to accept wage freezes and give-backs to protect jobs, and easier for the state to use inflation to diminish the buying power of the public sector while it protected the higher bureaucrats with cost-of-living increases. During this period as well came the largest growth in indirect taxation.[35] As neoliberal economics and finance capitalism more generally gained ground, classical liberal political practices resurfaced. Clientelist politics came out in the open.[36]

The most important initiative of liberalism in the 1970s was the introduction of a high-technology approach to agriculture, the so-called Green Revolution. In due course, the benefits of the Green Revolution came and went, and as it did, the competition between the bureaucracy and the landlords for profit continued and probably intensified.

As the 1970s progressed, the state began to be seriously challenged by the South. For the first time, it was obliged to strengthen itself with new short-term alliances, for example, the women's movement, northern ethnic groups, and so forth, to survive.

The alliance of the state with the feminist movements of the 1970s-1980s in India has given feminism a degree of visibility unheard of before. It appears that as long as feminist activists were prepared to emphasize middle-class ideals and to lean toward secularism, they had the freedom to explore social problems and to raise the consciousness of segments of the population, especially of the North, and to do so with official blessing.[37]

The alliance of the state with specific ethnic communities brought the causes of these groups into prominence as well. Rulers in countries such as India, Italy, and Mexico appear to calculate today, as they did in the last third of the nineteenth century, that a strategic release of ethnic tension serves to distract and divert without resulting in change. Thus, the national media gives space to the complaints of small groups in such discrete regions in North Italy as the Valle d'Aosta or to groups such as the Sikhs in the Punjab or the Kashmiris in Kashmir.[38] In Mexico, the state appears to promote Yaqui ethnicity in northern Mexico.[39] In the face of these moves, Communists appear caught off guard. Class analysis scarcely applies.[40]

The Southern Question in Modern India

A common view in India is that India is a democracy, just as a common view in Italy is that Italy is a democracy, but as in the foregoing, a little reflection forces one to realize that such a use of the term *democracy* is imprecise. It covers over the role of regional oppression that lies at the heart of the hegemony. Thus, the Southern Question in India as in Italy, although often overlooked, nonetheless exists and is, in fact, an important subject for political economy.

There is nothing particularly complicated in describing issues of unequal regional development or retardation in general; what makes the Southern Question in India somewhat more complicated is that in different periods of modern Indian history, it manifested itself in different parts of the country. One needs, consequently, to divide the history of the South into at least two phases. The first phase extended from the midnineteenth century to the interwar period. During this period, the South was the rice culture region of Tamil Nadu.[41] The second and current phase began in the late 1930s. At that time, one finds a relocation of the Southern Question from the geographical South, the old Madras presidency, to the impoverished regions of the Bengal presidency. The western parts, which remained part of India after independence, are of the most concern here.[42] Concurrently, from the mid-1930's onward, a Northern-type capitalist development starts to take place in at least some parts of the old, or geographical, South.

The South of India as a geographic or political economy region between the 1860s and the 1930s was more dependent on rainfall than on irrigation and on manual agriculture more than on mechanized agriculture.[43] By contrast, the North of India in that period, as typified by the Gangetic plain, relied on irrigation-based agriculture, using first the plough, later the tractor. Both plough-based agriculture and tractor-based agriculture tend to result in male-centered forms of economy. By way of contrast, in the old South, the wet-rice rainfall-based agriculture required a vast amount of manual labor, for example, weeding and transplanting, work conventionally done both by men and women. Social organization was, not surprisingly, more gender equal in the South; it was also more tribal than familial, again in contrast to that in the North.[44]

The explanation offered by economic geographers to account for the difference in family structure between the two regions is that the plough produces higher yields than does nonmechanized agriculture, higher yields, in turn, permit denser populations; denser populations, given the division of labor, mean more stratification; more stratification permits a dowry system, arranged marriages, seclusion of women, veiling, an honor and shame ideology, and so forth.[45] When Tamil Nadu industrialized, kin structure began to change as well.

In the years after 1930, the industrialization of the geographical South and the involution of the economy of the old West Bengal had consequences for India as a whole. In the nineteenth and early twentieth centuries, the large numbers of peasants who left South India tended to migrate abroad and to remit money home, thereby raising the standard of living in their region. By the interwar period, overseas opportunities were fewer, and the chief hope for avoiding starvation and unemployment was through internal migration within South India or to the marginally more prosperous North. Over the next generation, this internal migration had three broad consequences. For the segment who chose the slums of the northern cities, the principal consequence was the opening of the door for the contemporary wave of petty commodity production. For the segment who moved to predominantly rural areas, such as Bihar, the principal consequence was the reopening of the sharecropping option and of other often exploitative forms of agricultural production. Finally, for Madras and other parts of Tamil Nadu, the outflow of surplus population coincided and, perhaps, contributed to the beginnings of industrialization and a rising level of prosperity.

In an account of the Southern Question in the transitional phase of the 1930s, one starts to find changes in the way the North was perceiving the subject of North and South. From this period, northern intellectuals began to abandon the traditional distinction used to separate North and South; the Aryan and Dravidian cultural line ceased to be important. When a "neo-Tamil" literature emerged, it was recognized as such by the Indian Literary Academy in New Delhi. No longer regarded as vernacular writing, neo-Tamil works had begun to be part of the national literature.

From the 1930s onward through the years of partition and beyond, the region of old West Bengal began to feel the brunt of growing exploitation and to turn in on itself. In this period, Calcutta professionals moved to find work in Bihar; Hindu communalists came from Bihar to build their base in urban Calcutta. Nevertheless, in Bihar, one finds an unprecedented involution away from the secular politics of the early part of the century to religious neotraditionalism. Finally, in Calcutta, a new kind of left-wing radicalism arose, new in its openness to the peasant question.

In more recent years, this involution led to a communalist trend spearheaded by the owners of the new petty commodity production and by the landlord class. The reasons seem obvious enough. First, communalism creates a bond between employer and employee that blunts class conflict and pushes into the background the inequities of who got backward caste and class benefits and who did not. Second, by promoting religious bonds among Hindus across the region and then across the country, communalists had a strategy they hoped would bring an end to the system of regional exploitation.[46]

Just as Gandhi faced opposition in the first liberal age, however, so do communalists today. Peasants, feminists, and the Left are then as now opposed to communalism. Neo-Hinduism was oppressive for feminist women; it was equally oppressive for peasants. For the peasantry, oppression in the countryside became extreme; the shift to sharecropping in the 1970s lowered risks for landlords by placing more and more of the burden on the backs of the direct producers. Superexploitation in economic and gender terms eventually began to produce a reaction.[47] Ironically, both women and peasants appealed to the state as did, of course, the communalists. Today, the liberal state is in crisis. Currently, it is hiding behind emergency measures necessary to counteract terrorism.[48]

Challenges to Hegemony In India

A major thesis in this chapter is that India differs from Italy and Mexico in that after a phase of unsuccessful challenges, important elements among India's oppositional trends began to overcome the oppression of the South, first from the Left and later from the Right. Individuals such as M. N. Roy and Ambedkar struggled in the early twentieth century to construct a worker-peasant alliance; in later years the Communist Party of India

(Marxist) (CPI-M) and the Bharatiya Janata Party (BJP) emerged as the beneficiaries of these earlier efforts, bringing about the modern crisis of the state.

From its first congress in 1928, the Indian Communist party was not only factionalized, a trait shared with the other Italian Road communist parties, but nearly split. As early as the 1920s, Communists such as M. N. Roy, objected to collaboration with the Indian bourgeoisie, Lenin's so-called two-stage strategy. In one famous episode resulting from Roy's continuing opposition, Lenin went so far as to forbid the Indian party from allying the peasant with the worker, demanding instead that the party ally itself with the "progressive bourgeoisie." Roy disputed whether such a thing existed, and eventually was expelled from the CPI. Outside the party, Roy continued to function as an counterhegemonic intellectual.[49]

With the movement of the Southern Question to old West Bengal, the Communist party of India split. By 1964, its mass following and a few of its leaders went to the new CPI-M and thereafter actively attempted through electoral politics in West Bengal to displace the existing Indian hegemony; that is, CPI-M attempted to confront the Italian Road approach with an immediate communist alternative.

Seemingly as a result, the Indian government entered the crisis in which it has remained since the late 1960s. Gradually, it tolerated the rise of communalism, in general, and allowed communalists to become a leading force in the oppressed Hindi-speaking areas, in particular.

Communist parties in the Indian context cannot all be seen as counterhegemonic. With National Democratic Fronts, People's Democratic revolutions, and New Democratic Revolutionary movements, communism in India is, in fact, hard to characterize.[50] For example, where the CPI was successful, as in Kerala, even the party's Central Committee was not impressed. Thus, Kerala, the premier early success of the CPI, does not even figure in a history of antihegemony because the party there collaborated with its rival the Congress party as much or more than it challenged it.[51] Victory did not even entitle Kerala Communists to claim a high percentage of the membership in the Central Committee.[52]

The one important communist personality from the South, E. M. S. Namboodiripad, was an organizational man, a moderate at heart, much like his Neapolitan counterpart, Giorgìo Amendola. In later life, Namboodiripad took advantage of the split in the party to rise to general-secretary of CPI-M as the Southern Question moved to Calcutta.

Another major struggle that contributed to the crisis of the state in the 1960s was that of the Untouchables. It was originally led by Bhimrao Ranji Ambedkar (1891–1956) among the Mahars of Maharashtra. Because the Untouchables were both urban and rural and in different social classes, Ambedkar's movement constituted, as did M. N. Roy's and the CPI's, an important challenge to hegemony in India, all the more so because Ambedkar's demands were those to which the state itself was theoretically committed, social democracy.

Skilled as a lawyer and parliamentarian, Ambedkar was able to work with the British and the Indian elites to mitigate casteism from within the system, all the while fighting for the abolition of caste from without. Although caste still remains and is even enshrined in the Indian Constitution, Ambedkar managed to impose onto casteism its image as a fundamental national problem. He did this in the face of considerable opposition. Gandhi, for example, fought to preserve caste, opting to simply rename the oppressed Untouchables Harijans or Children of God. When Ambedkar supported separate elections for the depressed classes, Gandhi opposed him, arguing that separate elections would split Hinduism as Luther split Christianity. Gradually, Ambedkar came to realize that working within the system for radical change was reaching a point of diminishing returns. In electoral politics, the Congress party always had more clout than his All India Scheduled Caste Federation. The turning point in his strategic thought came shortly after independence. At that point, Ambedkar was a member of Nehru's cabinet. When the cabinet failed to pass the Hindu Code Bill, which Ambedkar was advocating, he resigned from the government and from involvement in the establishment. In the last phase of his career, Ambedkar converted to Buddhism, despairing of reforming Hinduism. From this phase comes his book, *The Buddha and His Dharma* (1957). From this phase as well comes the mass conversion of his Harijan followers to Buddhism accompanied by renewed conflicts with the Nehru regime. In point of fact, when large numbers of Harijans converted to Buddhism, the Nehru regime responded by denying Buddhists the status of scheduled caste, a status that carried with it significant benefits. This, in turn, forced Ambedkar's following to turn to a dual identity of Buddhist-Harijan.[53]

Ambedkar was both a public figure and a scholar. In a major study on untouchability, he proved that the Untouchables were not racially separate from the Hindus, that Hindu scholars have portrayed a false picture of Buddhism, and that original Buddhism, freed from its later more reactionary commentary literature, was a progressive creed, especially as regards women. In contrast to the Brahmanic ideal, Buddhist teaching encouraged women to have knowledge; it did not celebrate virginity nor encourage women to be recluses.[54] With the death of Ambedkar came the rise of CPI-M and other empowerment movements, heirs in their way to Roy and Ambedkar.[55]

Deindustrialization appears to be having an important bearing on the counterhegemony.[56] Seemingly, it explains why the traditional politicians in the 1990s were able to rebuild the hegemony through an alliance with the Right. As early as the 1970s, reports indicated that petty commodity production or informal sector work had began to increase in importance at a precipitous rate. Traditional union organizers lacked the skills and often the motivation to organize the new sweatshops with their disproportionately female and Harijan work forces with their animist and pantheist beliefs. By 1990, it was apparent to political observers that the communalists were able to benefit more than the Communists by these changes.[57] They could provide a range of social services that the Left would not or could not provide and could thereby claim a measure of popular support.

The Organization of Culture

Since the nineteenth century, the Indian state sought to maintain a differentiation between the secular and positivist intellectual high culture of the North and the more religious metaphysical high culture of the South. This section begins with the impending crisis of the state in the area of culture as it fails to sustain the southern intellectual and becomes increasingly entwined with a populist communalist South.

For Gramsci, the cultural symbol of the Southern Question was Croce. In India, the Croce of the old South was the philosopher and politician Sarvepelli Radhakrishnan (1888–1972). Radhakrishnan's fame rests on his contribution to Hindu modernism and to his opening the door to an idealist critique of the liberal positivist state. Like Croce, Radhakrishnan had a number of important colleagues and collaborators in his own region.

Radhakrishnan, again like Croce, had several careers at the same time. In his political career, he rose through vice-chancellorships of universities to become ambassador to the USSR, the vice-president and, finally, the president of the Republic of India. In his scholarly career, Radhakrishnan took up the critique of positivist science and behaviorism from the perspective of a romantic; he affirmed the existence of the Absolute or God where "will, intellect and emotion are integrated." He criticized contemporary philosophers for not approaching the practical problems of modern life. Again like Croce, he believed that philosophy needs a program for action; otherworldly philosophy, such as Advaitism, was simply inadequate.[58]

Perhaps as a consequence of the changing location of the Southern Question, Radhakrishnan never occupied quite the position that Croce did in Italy. He was, for example, never India's only Southern Intellectual. He never totally dominated fields of learning as Croce did. Among several other southern intellectual-type figures, one might recall Annie Besant, an Irish woman transplanted to South India as a leader of the Theosophy movement. In the highest phase of theosophy, Besant claimed, Hinduism is unified not with God but with universal reason.[59] In their various stances, Besant, like Radhakrishnan and Croce, represented the antithesis of the real mass culture of the South dominated as it was by its folklore, carnivals, and cults.[60] They also were all arguably subverters of a southern political consciousness.

In the politics of the the Southern Question—old and new—the question of language was important. With skill and determination, southerners have exposed the inadequacies of the language policy of the state as part of their struggle to overcome their own oppression. In both Italy and India, the success of the southerners is all the more remarkable given the opposition of wide segments of the population of the North to them. Even Communists tend to be among those siding with the North in language policy, and this is the case not just in India. For example, in Italy, the Italian Communists have sided with the Florentine high language against Sicilians; nonetheless over twentieth century, the southern Italian dialect has made steady progress in terms of its impact on the country as a whole. In Mexico, the Communists have generally had "Castillianist tendencies" and again to little avail; in India, English, the bureaucratic language championed by Tamil Nadu, was the first official language of the country. In more recent years, with the formation of a new South, Hindi, the language of the religious trend of the new South is rising to challenge the use of English not only in the English-speaking North but more generally as possibly the most dominant language of the nation.

The success of the contemporary southern offensive in language in India no doubt results from the linkage of language and religion. Through religion, the South in India has gained important allies within the North. If the southern offensive one day prevails, one of the figures most responsible will have been a conservative northern philologist, Acharya Raghuvira, a leader in recent years of the Hindi resurgence movement. Raghuvira has produced or standardized one hundred thousand modern words from classical Sanskrit for the Hindi Translation Committee of the Constitution of India and for the Ministry of Education. Of course, his work has often been perceived as controversial. Not only do people in technical fields, who rely on English, object to what he is trying to do but so do even students of literature. Will Hindi grow and remain a creative medium, they ask? Does Raghuvira seriously expect to achieve the social integration of India blocked by the use of English?[61]

As in Italy and Mexico so in India, an important part of southern influence in language has come from the prominent role of southerners in the mass media. At least in the period of the old South, Madras was a film production center of great importance, especially from the 1930s through the 1960s. One commentator surveying this period wrote of a southern "assault" on the northern market with waves of popular movies filled with singing and dancing with a story line drawn from mythology and legend. A famous early example was the film *Chandralekha,* a movie produced by

Gemini Studios. Later, when Madras began to lose its position as the capital of the South, its directors made changes. In 1947, a nationalist film, *Nam Iruvar,* produced in Madras made box office history. Gradually, however, Madras began to aim increasingly at an elite audience, having lost its identity as cultural integrator to the stage in Calcutta. From the 1950s, movies without music began to emerge, and in the 1960s an international style New Wave cinema in Tamil was in vogue.[62]

In light of the state's difficulty in sustaining the southern intellectual, the activities of the religious hierarchy inevitably begin to assume considerable importance. What sort of identity does it have, what sort of political praxis has it been following?

Unlike the Catholic hierarchy in Italy and in Mexico, the traditional intellectual in India is a university, not a spiritual person. Of course, India is replete with spiritual persons. For example, the Sankaracharya, or religious personage, who lives in Varanasi, offers opinions on canon law as an expert, but he does not have the linkage to the state that Banaras University (BHU) does.

What did the state want and what did it get from its support of this university? Arguably, what the state sought in turning to Banaras was a manageable appendage that would defend state policy in the name of religion. What they got, however, was something less. Spokespersons emerged, but they were not regarded as particularly important by the society because Hinduism under the Raj was less hierarchized than its counterparts in most other lands. And, even if they had wanted to, rulers could not have hierarchized a religion while relying so heavily on indirect rule. So, *perhaps* for this reason, Hinduism remains in modern times without one unifying deity. Rama remains an Avatar and not a prophet, such as a Christ or a Muhammad. Hinduism remains a bundle of religious traditions and practices not reducible to a single orthodoxy, its mystical path a more pronounced part of the system than the mystical path in the other Italian Road regimes.[63] This line of thought, in any case, meshes with important details of recent years. In the postindependence period, with the abandonment of indirect rule, dogma became more apparent. As this occurred, Hindus became more accepting of hierarchy and of proselytizing activities than they had been theretofore.

The thinking of Madan Mohan Malaviya, the founder and first vice-chancellor, has influenced the precise role that the university played in relation to the state since its founding in 1916. It was his choice to place Banaras at some distance from the early Congress party and, thus, from secular nationalism to forge a sort of "Lateran Accords" with the state. Malaviya carried this notion of separation of religion and politics to the point that Banaras became the first "Indian" Indian institution to welcome the English Royal family on a visit to India, the first educational institution in India to propagate the ideology that life, for example, the life of faculty, staff, and students, could be divided into the political and the nonpolitical. In this formulation, Banaras was staking out its own autonomous position. Like the Italian Catholic church, it did not want to espouse causes that would make it an appendage to other institutions.

However fictive this autonomy may seem from a distance, seen from close up, it seemed real enough as it permitted the university to play the role of the traditional intellectual and to receive the appropriate rewards for doing so. Being the traditional intellectual brought the university added prestige, but it also involved it in the preservation of archaic and extreme ideas and practices as a supposed part of tradition. Tradition, after all, was not something to be interrogated by modern critical thought. Partly as a consequence, Hindu communalist politics emerged at Banaras early and by the 1930s, even gained the blessings of the administration. Soon thereafter, BHU was proclaiming that communism and Islam were the enemies of Hinduism. Fights on the campus between more-mainstream and more-extremist Hindus became common.

As time progressed and as the struggle against the Southern Question took on a more and more communalist orientation, Banaras became more and more difficult to govern. After the retirement of the founding generation of its leadership, the university underwent ongoing bureaucratic turmoil. Distinguished chancellors came and went, victims of backdoor politics that forced them out before the completion of their normal terms, a phenomenon that lasted to the present day.

It was not the intention of the secular part of the state to sit idly by and see Banaras be a niche for the development of communalist movements such as the Rashtriya Swayam Sevak Sangh (RSS). Thus, the cabinet mandated that regulatory committees go to Banaras and investigate the violence. Although these committees—and there were several of them—have at times intimidated the extremists, they have not really been able to bolster the position of the university leadership.[64]

Indeed, partly as a result of their failures at Banaras, parliamentarians have considered a number of other initiatives, believing it to be their function to take the middle ground between religious pressure and the more secularist needs of a multigroup society. One parliamentary proposal urged the government to drop the word *Hindu*. On a more practical level was the Hindu Code Bill of the 1950s. This bill facilitated divorce, forbade polygamy, and opened the door to intercaste marriage. Related legislation opened the door for women to inherit property.

To examine the more explicitly secular components of hegemony, one must return to the question of language, taken this time from the perspective of the dominant elements as opposed to that of the southern ruling class.

The traditional scholarly view of the language question emphasizes the colonial strategy and its postcolonial breakdown. During the Raj, according to many writers, the British attempted to draw the subcontinent together through language and by extension through law, an attempt that was noble if ultimately unsuccessful. But was this what was being attempted? Integration, one might argue in opposition to this view, was only a limited goal of the English and its allies; if it proceeded too quickly, it could have made the Raj irrelevant. The role of the English language under the Raj, then, was more precisely that of a bureaucratic language; like its Italian counterpart, it was useful but it was not meant for everyone. Its extensive spread in Tamil Nadu may even have have worked against official policy.

In the long run, challenges to the use of English gave the state a chance to modify its language policy. In the interwar period, nationalists sought to challenge English with Hindustani. But this failed. Not only did it fail because of opposition from Tamil Nadu but also because of opposition from Banaras. Tamil speakers did not want to be marginalized, whereas for the power structure at Banaras, Hindustani was too far from Scripture. In the postindependence period, supporters of Hindi mounted a powerful challenge to English. But at least in the short run, it was doomed to failure. The success of Hindi—given its diffusion across regional lines—might undermine a system in which Madras was becoming part of the North. Thus, when the Hindi campaign began in earnest in the postindependence period, New Delhi was disposed to grant minority language speakers a chance to redraw state boundaries to protect them from being "overrun."

This is the background to an important piece of legislation, the Official Language Act of 1967. By means of this act, there seems little doubt that the government circumvented certain conflicts by giving the non-Hindi-speaking states their own language plus English; in doing so, however, it merely intensified other conflicts. Each state was authorized to interpret the 1967 act in its own way. Bihar, a leader of the Hindi challenge movement, chose Sanskrit alongside Hindi, making English an elective.[65]

In addition to looking at language policy, one must also examine the policies toward the sciences, literature, and the arts to understand the organization of secular culture.[66]

With the rising power of the North during the corporatist period, science in India underwent rapid development. Moving from a long-term isolation inside teaching institutions, the scientific community increasingly adopted a research orientation in the 1950s. Its need had long been to demonstrate its utility, and this finally was achieved thanks to the rise of brokerage institutions such as the Council of Scientific and Industrial Research and the Indian Council of Agricultural Research, which were founded in New Delhi in this period as a result of the new emphasis on technical growth and self-sufficiency. As science grew in India, both theoretical and applied fields advanced in the North while in the South, as one would expect, a few applied centers emerged in textiles, foods, and public health.

The Indian novel, the chief exemplar of the prose tradition, like its Italian counterpart, was also a product of the North, meaning in recent years the North plus the neo-Tamil literature of the geographical South. One can extrapolate this both from studies of the novel and from government initiatives toward prose literature more generally. Although, of course, prose exists in all major languages, patronage and other forms of official attention determine what is important, for example, the awards given out by the Sahitya Academy in New Delhi. Thus, in modern times, Punjabi and Gujerati prose literature appears to be on the rise while Bengali and Hindi literature appear to be on the decline. By way of contrast, commentaries on the literature in Assamese over the past generation stress poetry. The novel was emerging in that language but much more slowly than in, say, Punjabi.

In recent years, an example of what is taken to be significant is the Indian feminist novel. The feminist novel has become to an important extent the bearer of social realist and modernist themes in contemporary North India. Well-known feminist novelists include Anita Desai and Kamala Markandaya. One contemporary Indian author, Romen Basu, a male writer but a realist, deserves particular mention in this study. His novel insists on the similarity of family life in North India and North Italy.[67]

Modernism—the dominance of form, subjectivity, and language—tends to be an important force in the North in Italian Road regimes. Its rise often comes when liberalism is failing but when the state is still strong enough to channel protest into symbolic forms of protest. India has had some modernist writers, such as the Bengali Sudhindranath Datta (1901–1960) and, more recently, some of the neo-Tamil writers, but in all not a large number. More Indian modernism is reflected in music. As one might expect, Italy and Mexico have had more coherent modernist trends in the arts, for example, the Pirandellist trend in both countries, the Italian literary neoavantgarde, and so forth.[68]

Modernism in Indian culture is arguably more important in the Raga than in prose. It is there one finds more of the anarchistic spirit, which is at the heart of modernism.[69] Raga lends itself to centering more on the performer and on his sensibility than on the composer's notations or leadership as is common in most other music. Raga is, thus, like other forms of modernism, a self-conscious revolt against form.

Although the role of music in hegemony is not well studied generally, in India at least, there is evidence that the state has long been involved in its support. During the Raj, for example, the state took over as the major patron of classical music from the princes as the latter increasingly faced financial difficulties. All India Radio broadcast some classical music. By the 1930s, a second phase arrived in the relationship of the state and music. The film industry arose and soon producers began to make use of flashy, fast-moving songs. Problems of royalties arose. For awhile, the government banned these songs from the radio, only to find people listening to them on Radio Ceylon. The government relented. In the 1970s, a third phase began with the government launching of a music appreciation campaign to widen the audience for classical music. Today, the appreciation of classical music is now a status marker for the cultivated middle classes, many of whom are in the North or today in Tamil Nadu. It divides them from the larger mass who prefer film music.

Examined in comparative terms, the case of India does not seem particularly unusual. For example, in Italy, Umberto Eco, the well-known cultural critic, is particularly interested in the break with notationalism. In one of his studies, he identifed a break with notationalism in such composers as Karlheinz Stockhausen, Luciano Berio, Henri Pousseur, and Pierre Boulez. Eco noted how these composers gave their performers a considerable autonomy to choose the way to play the piece. As could the performer of the Raga in India, so, too, could any performer of this music become a "creator."[70]

The North of India is also the traditional home of the social sciences and of history. Where hegemony is strong as in Italy and Mexico, political science, economics and sociology have had the wider utility for the state; where the hegemony has been weaker as in India in recent years, and the state has had to appeal to the mass population, history and particularly social history has had the greater utility.[71] In the former case, the state did not need mass support; society, therefore, could be studied ahistorically; in the latter, it did. Challenged by a political resurgence of the South, the Indian state needed to make alliances in the mass population, especially in the North. Here social history and even political economy were more efficacious.[72]

Anthropology, folklore, and archeology, are also important fields in India, each illustrating a different facet of the hegemony. According to the leading student of the subject, L. P. Vidyarthi, the early anthropology in India under the British concentrated on tribal studies. Because many of the tribes were in the old South at one point, a noncontradictory approach to cultural interpretation emerged, which allocated the South to anthropology and the North to history. As the South and the country as a whole evolved toward a more industrial culture, one could have expected that anthropology would have been eclipsed by sociology. In India, this did not happen. Sociology did rise but anthropologists shifted from tribes to peasants and continued to enjoy considerable prestige.

In 1968–72, with the transition to the crisis state in Indian politics, anthropologists turned their attention to the problem of the spread of neo-Hinduism in West Bengal. A leading anthropologist, Biswanath Banerjee, warned the government that Hinduism could threaten the "integrity" of the tribes. After many years of attempting to modernize the backward classes and castes, the government, according to anthropologists, now confronted a backward-looking Sanskritization campaign sponsored by the Kulaks, a dangerous one given that the non-Sanskritized folklore was actually the basis for higher culture.

Folklore studies under the Raj were dominated by British civil servants; missionaries, and Indian writers, most of whom believed in an Indo-Aryan mythology that linked the Indian and British elites at the dawn of time through a supposed Greek migration to the North of India. In 1871, a professional folklore organization emerged in India and published the *Indian Antiquary;* in 1878, it was joined by one in England that published the *Folk Lore Record.* From the 1870s, the South of India received attention in the works of such pioneering folklorists as William E. Marshall, *The Todas* (London: Longmans, Green, 1873), and Edward Jewitt Robinson, *Tamil Wisdom* (London: Wesleyan Conference Office, 1873), works drawn on in a later generation by the well-known regional novelist Narayan, the best-known storyteller about village life in South India.

Folklore study in recent years continues to be concentrated in the main northern university centers. As in Italy, southerners play a significant role. Since 1950, a folklore journal has been appearing in Calcutta. Around 1970, the editor of *Folklore,* Shankar Sengupta, began to publish prolifically about the folklore of Bihar. When one turns to the geographical South, one finds that less work has been done recently, much of what exists dates back to the interwar period or even earlier. In more recent years, translations of South Indian material into North Indian languages are appearing, a trend obviously congruent with these regions becoming a part of the "North."[73]

Archeology is another branch of the social sciences that rose up under the Raj and lives on as part of the hegemonic culture in independent India. Among the major contributions to Indian hegemony by archeologists is the creation of the image of the North as Aryan and the image of the South as Dravidian. In the 1860s and 1870s, the Indian government sponsored an initial survey of archeological sites in India. In the next generation, the details of middle-class life replaced the concern with imperial edifices. A number of museums opened in North India. The automatic preference for Greek and Buddhist-influenced sites gave way to a wider criteria of selection. Finally, archeologists turned to South India. Sir Mortimer Wheeler, the famous British archeologist, found Roman coins near Pondicherry and established a chronology of events in South India from the known dates of these coins. This research facilitated the writing of an integrated national history of India North and South. With the partition of India and Pakistan,

much of the Indo-Aryan heritage found itself in Pakistan, and this component of Indian identity fell into abeyance. In 1959, a School of Archeology
opened in New Delhi to train Indian archeologists, partly to overcome the
dominance of North European archeologists, a concern in India as in Italy.[74]

History Writing in India

History writing in India assumed its modern form in the North with
the rise of a positivist culture in the late nineteenth century. During the
better part of the first liberal age, that is, 1860–1960, most historians of the
North wrote political and diplomatic history. In the old South, history
gradually came into being as well, but as a part of cultural studies. After
1930, there were changes. Historians in Tamil Nadu began to address issues
in political and diplomatic history of the sort in vogue in the North. One
generation later, Calcutta stands out as a center of oppositional thought as
its intelligentsia resisted southernization by developing a historicized view
of the peasant. Faced with this continuing challenge, the state through
Jawaharlal Nehru University (JNU) in New Delhi turned to a social history
that emphasized the working class as a way to reach out to society.

To see all these changing functions of history over the twentieth century at a glance, an obvious place to begin is with the institutions which
support the research. In the Liberal Age in the three countries studied here
as examples of the Italian Road, the most prestigious institution was the
scientific academy. Although history was not a priority for the scholars
associated with the scientific academies, it had a place.

In 1922, the poet Rabindranath Tagore founded a scientific academy,
the Visva-Bharati Center, outside Calcutta. Its ideal of the disinterested
pursuit of learning, the ideal of Plato's Academy, was broadly the same
ideal as that of its counterparts worldwide, including the academies of Italy
and Mexico. All these academies sustained the traditional belle-lettrism
common in most history professions of that period. In addition, mutual
contacts among academies was common; Tagore, for example, visited Italy
where he met Croce and discussed philosophy.[75] The fact that India was a
colony and Italy was not did not seem to have been an issue.

A second type of scholarly institution, which produced historical
knowledge, was the Indian History Congress (IHC) founded in 1935 in
Pune by a local cultural organization, the Bharata Itihasa Samshadhoka
Mandala. Where the Visva-Bharati served the needs of universal cultural
scholarship, the Congress was an obvious vehicle for the nationalists of
North India. Many of its members were journalists, lawyers, and later
college professors. Its rise presaged the rise of the corporatist state after
independence.

From the outset, the IHC was able to petition the colonial government about questions concerning archives, monuments, and curriculum, and it often got its way thanks to the support it received from the larger nationalist movement and from the Congress party.[76] In this respect, Indian historians have had an advantage over those of many other countries. In neither Mexico nor Italy, for example, does one find a group of historians organized on a nationwide basis and enjoying national recognition until the present day.

The third type of scholarly institution was the government-sponsored data centers of the 1970s, examples of which include a Center of Advanced Study in History at Aligarh Muslim University and a Center of Advanced Study in Ancient History and Culture at Calcutta. JNU was developed as a major center for historical study in the late 1960s. A few years later, the government set up the Indian Council of Historical Research (ICHR). This body funded a number of individual researches, published a newsletter, and since 1974, a journal, the *Indian Historical Review*.[77]

As the twentieth century progressed, the center of gravity of historical writing shifted from a focus on ancient studies in Pune to one on modern studies in Calcutta and then in Delhi, a shift broadly coinciding with the socioeconomic changes in different regions and these institutional changes.

The record shows that scientific historical studies evolved from the work of R. G. Bhandarkar (b. 1837), the founder of two pioneer research centers, one in Bombay University, one in Poona, and the teacher of several students who became well-known historians in their own right. A. Nilakanta Sastri, for example, became a famous historian of South India, and Bhandarkar's own grandson, became a major Indologist.[78] What historian today has not heard of the Bhandarkar Oriental Research Institute of Poona University?[79] In Bengal, nineteenth-century scholars also paved the way for the more modern work carried out in Calcutta University and Visva-Bharati Academy, which were opened in the early years of the twentieth century.

The study of modern history as a discrete field may have had its roots deep in the nineteenth century as contemporary writers claim, but the significance of modern history or even of national history within the Indian cultural scene only began to rival that of ancient history in recent years. It did so far more in Calcutta than in Bombay, the latter remaining a center of classical studies. Even in Calcutta, however, there were few jobs for modern historians.

The most eminent of this pioneer generation of modern historians was Sir Jadunath Sarkar (1870–1958), the so-called Columbus of the Mughals. Sarkar was the son of a Zamindar from Bangladesh. He received his education in Calcutta. Despite his privileged background, he lived his life in hardship with many responsibilities. In an intellectual sense, however,

Sarkar had the leisure and the distance from his own times to undertake major research. He has been compared to Gibbon as a political and intellectual historian; he was the author of a multivolume history of Aurangzib. What made him so important was not only his immense productivity but that he was a Bengali not biased against Shivaji; this capacity for detachment and for a widening of the historical consciousness made possible a history of modern India.[80] Another historian, also the son of a Zamindar from West Bengal, Biman Behari Majumdar (1899–1969), followed the path of Sarkar to Calcutta University for his education. Majumdar, however, eventually moved to Bihar "helping to give the region a historical consciousness." Over a long career, Majumdar wrote on ancient and modern political thought and on nationalism.[81]

Two other major scholars in history who came from Bangladesh through Calcutta University were the epigraphist Radhagovinda Basak (1885–1982) and R. C. Majumdar (1888–1980). The most important of the two was R. C. Majumdar. Majumdar was born to an aristocratic family that was downwardly mobile. He attended Calcutta University on a scholarship. Later, he taught periodically at Dacca, Banaras, and the University of Chicago while making his career at Calcutta. From several publications in political history, one might conclude that in his earlier years, Majumdar was more of a nationalist, whereas in his later years, he became increasingly a communalist, undergoing a change not unlike that of K. Datta, the historian from Patna. Majumdar's doctoral dissertation, *Corporate Life in Ancient India,* was published (Calcutta: S.N. Sen, 1918) he followed this with a history of the Freedom movement.[82] But in the 1960s, his criticism of the Indian state and its nationalism led him to resign a prominent editorship. In *India at the Cross roads* (Calcutta: Contemporary, 1965), his main work from that period, Majumdar criticized India's industrialization policy, favoring in its place small-scale industry and farming. He attributed India's policies to the "tyranny of the Congress Party."[83] In the 1970s, Majumdar became involved in a communally oriented historical group, the History And Culture Society. With Majumdar as editor, this group published a text, *History and Culture of The Indian People,* (London: G. Allen Unwin, 1951–1974) which had enough prestige to compete even with the texts of the ICHR. In the 1970s, Majumdar seemed to be able to push the mainstream of historical thought somewhat to the right. Perhaps, one reason for his being able to do so was the rise of ultraright groups, such as the fascist-oriented Institute for Rewriting Indian History in Delhi, which frightened the mainstream.

When examining Calcutta's extraordinary importance to the rise of professional history, one must note not just the scientific academy and the university but the unique clustering of high-quality journals. Two of these particularly stand out: *Bengal Past and Present* published by the Calcutta Historical Society and the *Quarterly Review of Historical Studies* published over the past generation by the Institute of Historical Studies. On close inspection, it is surprising to find that these two major institutions are heavily based on single individuals whose death or declining influence in the 1970s fundmentally altered these journals. In the first, the important figure was Narendra Krishna Sinha (1903–1974), son of a famous judicial official in West Bengal. Sinha's education at Calcutta University led him to study Ranjit Singh, the famous Sikh. In later life, he wrote on the economic history of Bengal and edited the journal. The second was S. P. Sen (1914–1979). Sen was born in Bangladesh and went to Calcutta University; his career included a sojourn at the University of London and a professorship at Visva-Bharati, by then a university until 1972. In 1961, Sen founded the institute, serving as its director and journal editor until 1979. This culminated for him many years of work for the Indian History Congress and the Indian Historical Records Commission. Over these years, Sen made his mark by publishing reference books on Indian historians, Indian historiography, and leading Indian personalities.[84] In his later years, Sen too veered from nationalism to communalism along with several of his generation discussed here.[85] And in deed, Sen's later support of regional history provides a good example of the hazy terrain between the communalist right and establishment history writing. Regional history could be a useful corrective to an overly general national history but it could just as well promote communal thought against the nation.[86]

By the 1970s, a left-oriented peasant history had emerged in the world as a whole and in India. In India, it became concentrated in Calcutta and was by 1990 arguably the most important trend in Indian historiography.

No doubt the idea of the peasant as an agent of history could be found in the writings of the previous generation of historians but only in the form of passing comments. The Subaltern Studies Group, as it came to be called, made this their mission. No longer were the peasant masses to be portrayed as led by the progressive working class, they were to have their own history with its own logic and with its own cultural praxis.[87]

As Calcutta became the capital of the new South, history there underwent major changes. The older form of positivist history writing declined. In its place emerged a Subaltern Studies Group owing a clear debt to Gramsci and a belle letristic tradition owing a clear debt to Croce, the former in the Centre for Studies in Social Science and in the Subaltern Studies Group, some of whose members are from Calcutta, the latter in the Center for the Comparative Study of Literature of nearby Javadpur University and in the Visva-Bharati Academy, now university.[88] Finally, there are the communalist historians R. C. Majumdar and Datta.

During the past generation in New Delhi, one finds developmentalism to be the dominant ideology, each of its two variants, capitalist and Communist, present, both represented as well in the academic history writing of the city's universities. The more capitalist variant was represented by the Delhi School of Economics in such figures as Dharma Kumar, the editor of the *Indian Economic and Social History Review,* whereas the more communist variant was represented in JNU and through journals such as *Social Scientist.*

Several prominent historians at JNU were members or affiliates of the Communist party of India, and it is they who present the hegemonic interpretation of the history of the country. As noted before, they tend to emphasize the role of the working class led by the progressive elements of the bourgeoisie engaged in a long-term struggle to triumph over feudalist Kulaks, rich peasants, and communalists. The development of capitalism in modern India and the struggle against British colonialism are major themes in their writings.[89] Both JNU and Delhi oppose not only communal and idealist views of history but neocolonialism as well.[90] They do so not only in their writings on modern history but in their writings on the ancient, medieval, and Mughal periods as well. Romila Thapar, the leading specialist on the ancient period at JNU, identified the communalist school of thought with a racialist colonial view of India. Her research shows that communal identity did not even exist in ancient and medieval India.[91] Her findings dovetail with those of Utsa Patnaik, Bipan Chandra, and others, who specialize in the modern period and who also argue for the more recent provenance of communalism.[92]

Along with Delhi University and JNU is Aligarh University. One must include some account of Aligarh University especially for the contributions of its historians to the study of the Mughal period and to Muslim history more generally.[93] Historians at Aligarh, such as Irfan Habib and Nurul Hasan, provide the contemporary hegemony, a suitable backdrop for its secular outlook. In their scholarship, Mughal history transcended communalism but eventually foundered because of its failure to develop economically.

Politicians in Italian Road states want to balance the region, the nation, and the heritage, often creating thereby an essential but often difficult task for state intellectuals of rationalizing and integrating culture on these different levels. In India, these tasks in recent years more often than not fell to historians. How should a historian treat the development of the old South? How long is the old South part of folklore? How and when does it become history and to what extent? What does one do with modern Bihar? The historians of old South India did much to resolve these problems for their region.

If, at the beginning of the century, a southern intellectual such as the philosopher Radhakrishnan had imposed a concern for cosmopolitanism, democracy, and art, one generation later with the changes that permitted history to emerge, a number of southerners were able to impose a concern for modern history. One of the first important modern southern historians was Sardar K. M. Panikkar (1895–1963). His writings through the 1930s, such as his *Malabar and the Portuguese* (1931), revealed his own cosmopolitan orientation. Later in the 1940s, Panikkar became more of a nationalist. He supported independence for India. From this period also came *The Foundations of New India,* a reflection on the meaning of the citizen, of democracy, and of oppression in a Hindu context.[94] Another well-known historian of the formative generation of modern Southern historians, S. Krishnaswamy Iyengar (1871–1953), was also concerned with democracy and oppression. Iyengar was educated as a scientist in Bangalore but changed to epigraphy. In his best-known work, the *Evolution of Administrative Institutions of South India,* he made a point of praising those Tamil rulers who carried the devolution or decentralization of power the furthest.[95]

Another feature of southern historical writing has been its preoccupation with research on Indian aesthetics and art history or, even more broadly, on world culture. Where Radhakrishnan wrote about values and by implication would thereby criticize the Philistine character of the more dominant North, a few years later southern historians would write concretely how values in India are revealed in Indian art, using examples from South Indian art. An example of this newer more contextualized historiography could be taken from the writings of K. A. Nilakanta Sastri (1892–1976). Sastri is of particular importance for this study because in his later years, he happened to move from the Old South to the New South, to Patna in Bihar. From his lectures at Patna, Sastri produced his *Cultural Contacts Between Aryans and Dravidians* (Bombay: Manlaktalas, 1967).[96] This was his mature work; a work actually begun years before in his *Development of Religion in South India* (Bombay: Orient Longmans, 1963). In both of these books, he rejected the premise of Tamil nationalism and argued with increasing forcefulness for a profound Aryanization of Tamil culture. Here, paradoxically, was a turning point in Indian historical thought. Here was a South Indian Brahmin, writing on the shared nature of the elite high culture of North and South India, writing both an epitaph for his class and an essay of legitimatization for the growth of a new North-type culture in Tamil Nadu.

The movement of the Southern Question to the old West Bengal also brought a change to historical thought in Bihar. By the 1960s, Bihari historians had become preoccupied with local issues after a period in the early twentieth century of scholarly involvement in the national struggle. Examples of contemporary pursuits can be drawn from the Ranchi school of historians, a school that has as its focus the history of the Chotanagpur region. Equally localist has been the production of Professor A. L. Thakur of the K. P. Jayaswal Research Institute in Patna. Professor Thakur's main work was a three-volume general history of Bihar from ancient times to the present of which he was the general editor. The third volume of this series was authored by a well-known scholar of the region, the aforementioned Kalinkar Datta.[97] The career of K. Datta better than that of many others serves to illustrate the progressive dehistoricization of Bihari thought. Datta's career began in the interwar period. From a committed reformer of that period concerned with sati and other national social problems, Datta went on in later years simply to produce a number of decontextualized works. One was a textbook, another a rather dull *Survey of Recent Studies on Modern Indian History* (Patna: Patna Univ., 1957), and a third, the most recent, an equally colorless history of the Freedom movement in Bihar for Thakur. His career fits the breakdown of historical imagination common to Bihar as a whole. During the years of his declining commitment to a nationalist ideology if not to historical analysis itself, he attracted the attention of the Rockefeller Foundation in whose correspondence one finds the opinion, couched in the quaint lingo of the Green Revolution, that Patna, that is, Datta, and Delhi will "bring alive" modern Indian historical studies.[98]

Indian historians have molded the dominant culture and participated in politics far more dramatically than their Italian counterparts or for that matter most others as well. Their power to do so seems to come from the particular challenges to hegemony in India, challenges not yet experienced by any other Italian Road state, challenges the Indian state has tried to confront by privileging historicism. These counterhegemonic challenges came from the rejection of Eurocommunism by important segments of the Left. Contrary to what the dominant paradigm of world history might suggest about the distance between Third World and European history, this exercise has shed light on what is specific about modern Italian history and about modern Indian history. Would there not be a middle ground in counterhegemonic struggle against the Italian Road falling between these two cases, one in which the party does not split but vacillates between the South and Eurocommunism? An example of this vacillation is Mexico.

6

The "Italian Road" in Latin America

Mexico, 1876–1990

In this chapter, I present modern Mexican history, 1876–1990, as a Latin American example of the Italian Road. In four sections, I situate this approach in relation to those that dominate Mexican historiography, provide evidence from Mexican political economy, take up the organization of culture as a part of this political economy, and discuss the role of history writing as a part of the organization of culture.

In Mexican historiography, liberals and Marxists vie with romantics over the interpretation of the past one hundred years. For liberals and for Marxists, the goal of the Mexican Revolution (1912–17) was to emancipate the country, bring education and suffrage, and thereby develop a new people. In their view, the Revolution was thwarted by the strength of the traditional feudal and conservative interests. For romantics, not only the Revolution but the liberal Madero dynasty and the Marxist Cárdenas period that followed were symbolic of the crisis of Mexican Catholicism, a crisis that the Mexican people overcame through their bravery during the Cristero Revolt in the 1920s and 1930s.

After the 1950s, none of the older positions in historiography seem adequate. Migrants flooded out of the countryside into the city, altering the old social dynamics. For historians, revisionism became obligatory, whether in the form of microhistory, Braudelianism, dependency theory, or neo-Marxism. What follows draws on some of this revisionism.

A recent work by Barry Carr, an Australian historian, introduced the concept of a Mexican "Piedmont," or advanced part of the North. Since 1876, Carr argues, Mexico's Piedmont was a triangle composed of the Federal District of Mexico City, the State of Mexico, Veracruz and Monterrey, whereas Mexico's North in a broader sense, the Piedmont being simply one part, includes not just this triangle but Chihuahua, Sonora, and parts of all the north-central provinces as well. The South, meaning the southern states and the Central Highlands, also constitutes a distinct region. The South can be identified not only geographically but also in socioeconomically. The southern states are poorer than their northern counterparts, more rural, and more Indian.

According to Carr, the peculiarity of the Mexican North lies in its features as well. It is more secular, meaning that the church is weaker. One does not find concentrations of Indians in the North as in the South. Capitalist farming has not resulted in debt peonage as in the South. Wages are higher in the North as is the level of foreign investment. Not only has a recent border industry developed but there are more long-term mining and cotton interests as well. In the North, again in contrast to the South, Mexican capitalism competes with U.S. capitalism. The North is, not suprisingly, more politicized over the question of imperialism than is the South.[1]

The South in Mexico, as in Italy, serves as the place in which cheap labor is produced and exported through migration to the North. The density of population in the South is higher, the level of amentities lower, and the rate of infant mortality higher. Differentials in literacy, houses with running water, and the existence of usable roads should also be noted. Over the twentieth century, the major statistic that shifts is the percentage of the total population resident in the South (including here both the peninsula and the Central Highlands). Through the interwar period, the South had more than one-half of the population, but with the intensification of internal migration after the war, the balance shifted so that the South had 49.3 percent of the population in 1960: many southerners at that point were counted as northerners.[2]

If in the North the development of capitalism fostered the social structure, in the South it destroyed it, thereby creating the context for the outward migration of populations to the urban slums. In the major southern cities such as Puebla and Mérida, the agents of this capitalist development, the local landlord class, can be said without exaggeration to have plotted this destruction. Sometimes their plots succeeded, sometimes they failed. When they succeeded, the Indians were literally driven off their lands, their social structure and way of life collapsing around them.[3] Through the late nineteenth century and through much of the twentieth century, struggle to control the land remained intense.[4]

Mexico is, of course, quite different from Italy or at least the Italy that Gramsci experienced. The hegemony in Mexico is weaker. The South in Mexico, although oppressed by the North, is a great deal stronger politically than its Italian counterpart. This somewhat greater parity results in the formation of *contested* regions. Put another way, in Mexico, one finds regions that are continuously resisting Southernization, such as Morelos, the home of the famous peasant revolutionary Emiliano Zapata. Nothing like Morelos is found in the central South of Italy or India. Other examples of contested regions include the environs of Cuernavaca, regions along the upper Pacific Coast and some new style industrial sites as far south as Oaxaca. During the twentieth century, Mexico City has become an increasingly contested region as well.

Another element of the Italian Road model is the southern capital. A strong hegemony, such as Italy, has a well-defined southern capital, such as Naples. A weak hegemony has a less well-defined southern capital. This is the situation in Mexico and accounts for the more indistinct character of cities such as Puebla and Mérida. By the 1960s, these cities had become university centers; earlier, they were simply centers of southern provincial culture. To compensate for this weakness, the southern intellectuals of Mexico live conspicuously in Mexico City, both disguising and reflecting the mass migration out of the South.

Migration, thus, has had a major influence on the political economy. In India, migration, especially the migration of southerners, was multidirectional, the South retaining much of its population, whereas in Mexico much of the southern migration moved in only one direction, out of the South to the United States or to Mexico City. As Mexico City absorbed a larger and larger southern rural population, it became more "southern" than the other capital cities considered in this book, that is, Rome and New Delhi. Is it on the way to becoming a southern city? One hundred years ago, it was the capital of the positivist, científico culture, which one associates strictly with the North; today, it contains much of the romantic traditionalism and cosmopolitanism associated with a southern capital.[5] The crude, optimistic positivism is all but gone. Liberals appear depressed; history for them has become a labyrinth and no longer a straight line.

Another main element of the Italian Road model is the party system. In Italian Road regimes, the party system is based on a single dominant party stretched over the North and the South. In Mexico, this has long been the Partido Revolucionario Institucional (PRI). In recent years, the PRI has steadily lost ground. Will it suffer the fate of the Congress party in India? How well can it hold together given that the northern ruling class identifies with democracy, that is, European or U.S. democracy, whereas the southern ruling class identifies with Catholic Europe, believing itself to be a "pure Spanish" caste in a society of mixed-blood and Indian people?

How long can the party keep on proclaiming that the number of Indians is dwindling as they become mestizos when anyone who understands marriage patterns knows better? Two people who get married want to speak the same language and eat the same food. A veneer of Mexican culture scarcely overcomes the distance between the Mexican peasant and the Mexican citizen. The Mexican peasant, like peasants everywhere, lives in one world, the Mexican citizen in another. If the peasant survives by

avoiding taxes, the draft, the legal system, and the national culture represented by the PRI, these very skills make him a problem for the citizens,
those who are part of the class order and who, therefore, stand to benefit
by acquiescing to these more official institutions.

Whereas in Italy, the rulers were able to divide clearly the working
class and the peasantry into a quiescent welfare state and a secure Southern
capital, in Mexico, the rulers lacked the capacity. Internal migration is
leading to political struggles, which potentially may unify workers and
peasants. The ruling class remains in control but in a state of crisis, it
appears to be losing control of its national capital as happened in Brazil. In
desperation, it is mortgaging its work force to North American capitalism
through the "fast track" scheme.

An Italian Road interpretation of modern Mexican history is a new
hypothesis created in the 1980s. It would not have been warranted much
earlier given the then prevailing knowledge about Mexican regional history
or assumptions about the state as an actor in the political process, or about
the Indians as part of history past or present. At least until the 1980s,
liberalism or a dependency school version of it had too much legitimacy.
If development was going awry in Mexico, this was the result of U.S.
imperialism, something the Mexican elites were powerless to prevent.

As regional studies have grown, so, too, has an appreciation of the
importance of local ruling classes, local politics, regional culture, and the
role of the central state as an actor on local and national levels. Writers now
think the state selectively invites in North American influence. If the state
allows North Americans the opportunity to exploit sectors of the economy;
there is until now at least a certain logic to it. Large numbers of dissatisfied
Mexicans blame North America and not the Mexican ruling class for the
consequences.

Although 1876 as a takeoff point for the study of modern Mexican
history is and has been a part of the dominant paradigm for a long time,
having gradually eclipsed the Mexican Revolution; from an Italian Road
perspective, the right year was thus chosen but for the wrong reasons.
What is missing in the dominant paradigm is the role of the South and of
the Indian population as operative parts of the national history. Consequently, as a date in political history, 1876 represents the birth of the
Porfiriate, meaning his reign, not the birth of the new social dynamic of the
capitalist nation-state. Porfirio Díaz here is much more than a stereotypical
southern autocrat, and his system is not one that was antithetical to the
values of modernism, as historians used to maintain, at least before 1968.
Nor was the Porfiriate an autocracy, which historians, being so demoralized after 1968, found acceptable.[6]

Today, I believe, the preconditions for the acceptance of 1876 as the
birth of a new social dynamic are starting to fall into place in a more

positive sense. First one finds, for example, a textbook on Mexican history that mentions parallels between the Aztecs and the Italians of the Renaissance. By implication, the Indian population of the "New" World is now accepted as part of comparative world history. Only a few years ago, the dominant paradigm would still have insisted that the Indians of the New World were outside history until they became Mexicans; the permissible scope of comparativism for Mexico was limited to the Hispanic world.[7] Today, this is no longer the case. Second, Gramsci is used as a theorist in Mexican historiography.[8] Third, one finds developments within Marxism and liberalism that tend to be supportive; studies, for example, of capitalist development, of the bourgeoisie,[9] of the working class, and the peasantry.[10] Meanwhile, liberals are making new studies of indigenism.[11]

Mexico took the Italian Road, as much as anything, as the result of a series of particular choices made by the church and the state. To retain its power, the church hierarchy had to stand with the landlord against the Indian or accept the risk of an anticlerical regime, such as Cárdenas's. In so doing, the hierarchy had to remain Criollist, ignoring the real piety of the Indians in the South, on the one hand, and the indifference to religion of its preferred middle class and landlord class constituency in the North, on the other.[12] Meanwhile, to retain its power, the party had to be pragmatic. Mestizoism was useful to the party's progressivist image. If, however, the southern wing of the party and the church refused mestizoism, then indigenism was a necessary fallback. This synthesis of North and South forms the basis of the political economy of Mexico.

The Political Economy of Modern Mexico

In 1876 when Benito Juárez returned to Mexico City and Emperor Maxmillian was executed, the modern state of Mexico emerged. It took a liberal form from this point to 1934, the year in which corporatism appeared in the form of a state socialist regime led by Lazáro Cárdenas. From 1940, the date of Ávila Camacho's accession to the presidency, liberalism reappeared and has dominated Mexico to the present day.

In 1876, Mexico was a land with rich agricultural possibilities and mineral wealth but with a limited infrastructure. As in India, so in Mexico, the development of modern capitalism resulted in the rapid growth of the railroad, which, in turn, facilitated the development of an export-oriented economy and, in its wake, the formation of a proletariat. From 666 kilometers in 1876, rail mileage increased to 20,000 kilometers in 1910. With the spread of the railroad came a communication revolution, for example, in telegraphy. A more broad-based development of the infrastructure followed the development of a modern communication system. As this occurred, the state gained the power to control wider and wider areas of the country. Banditry was suppressed; urban centers were constructed around rail depots. Foreign investment followed, and with the rapid influx of currency that accompanied investment, social change became noticeable. The traditional *caudillo* families, who had some money to begin with, now amassed considerable property. Ownership of the means of production by a few families was particularly pronounced in the South and in key sectors of the economy: land, textiles, and mines.[13] It was this trend toward concentration of wealth that provided the original impetus for the internal migration.

The rise to power of Porfirio Díaz (1876–80, 1884–1911) brought a regional hero to national prominence.[14] As was the custom of the period, Díaz primarily relied on a number of those who were close to him from his own region, which happened to be the South. Díaz, survived for years and years in Mexican life; there are no parallels to him in this book. The Raj in India and the Unification movement in Italy introduced changes that led more rapidly to protest and to political turnover.

Díaz was unusual in another way when compared to his contemporaries in Mexico, Italy, and India; he relied on his wife Carmelita to perform many roles, some political and ceremonial and some that bordered on diplomacy. Most importantly, Carmelita maintained good relations with the church hierarchy, which no doubt lengthened Díaz's reign by diffusing some of the natural opposition of the church to any Liberal Age-type regime.

Was Díaz so different from the politicians who followed him? This is the common assumption in traditional scholarship. Díaz was a dictator; later rulers were not. Recent scholarship makes the picture more gray. While Díaz's public persona was dictatorial, perhaps more so than was the case with others; in practice, he left much of the decision making in the hands of his subordinates, which suggests that he was not so dictatorial. Díaz's hallmark was (a stereotype about southerners) his skill in backroom conciliation of the powerful regional families and caciques of Mexico, which was possible because of wide personal contacts among them. A structural analysis of his system might easily lead one to conclude that he brought into existence a rudimentary one-party system consisting of an outer circle of his contacts and an inner circle of his confidantes.

Who were the inner circle of his confidantes? Little question exists of the great importance of his minister of finance, José Yves Limantour, and his chief of cabinet, Rosendo Pineda. Limantour made technical decisions that perhaps few in the period even understood. As chief of cabinet, Pineda made many decisions related to personnel choices and procedures that had far-reaching implications as well. Two other figures with whom Díaz was close and on whom a great deal of resposibility devolved were the historian and journalist Justo Sierra and Joaquin Baranda (1882–1901). Sierra's newspaper, *La Libertad,* was a mouthpiece for the government and a former of public opinion. Baranda, Díaz's minister of justice, also came to have great power.

Scholars examining this group of people note that what they have in common is that they were all southerners, whereas, the membership of the later PRI was more northern than southern. Yet Díaz was not a prisoner of the South. His system opened the way for important northerners, for example, Ramon Coral, to reach the top as well. Indeed, Díaz promoted Coral's career, often to the surprise of public opinion. For example, in 1904, Díaz named Coral to be the vice-president of the Republic. In 1910, Díaz named the Chihuahua millionaire Enrique Creel to be ambassador to the United States. Northerners also occupied the highest ranks of the army and were the most important local capitalists.[15]

But did not Díaz block the development of the North? Standard accounts of Díaz mention his period as one that retarded the development of the middle class, the class taken to be crucial to the rise of the North. Yet examined comparatively, the point, if true, does not seem very important. Neither in Mexico, in Italy, nor in India was there a large northern middle class until late in the century.[16]

To see Díaz's period as the birth of modern Mexico, one begins by considering law. Mexican law after 1867 clearly reveals to students of its history important aspects of the rise of a nation-state and with it the spread of capitalism. Law during the Porfiriate balanced the needs of the northern and southern wings of the ruling class, defending private property in land, even absentee estates, while supporting the centralization of the administrative power of the state.

Among the most important examples of legislation during the Porfiriate that facilitated capitalism were the so-called Colonization Laws (1875, 1883, 1889), which empowered surveying companies to check land claims, thereby often facilitating land expropriation and the development of latifundism. Indians who resisted the Colonization Laws confronted the feared Ley Fuga, a law used by rural police to shoot convicts on the grounds, often false, that they had tried to escape. By 1910, 80 percent of the farmers of Mexico were landless; three thousand families controlled most of the land.[17] The Colonization Laws had performed their function.

Among other examples of law during the Porfiriate were those facilitating political and administrative centralism. Here, one might note the overturning of the older nonreelection laws, the rise of a modern patent law, the codification of military law, the development of a water law, the abolition of state privileges to issue their own stamps, and the passage of a uniform commerical code based coincidentally on its Italian counterpart from the same period.

Taken as a whole, these laws appear to be the legal basis of the modern state. Looked at closely, the much commented on Constitution of 1917 is more a moment of consolidation than a break with the past. Even the issues it raises, which are new thematically, such as oil or secularization of education, can easily be perceived as emerging out of the logic of the existing body of law.

As the North continued to rise, it simply continued to solidify its power. In 1917 the Family Relations Act mandated that men and women have equal authority in the home and made divorce permissible. In the same year, the Labor Law called for a minimum wage, maximum hours, and the establishment of a Court of Arbitration and Conciliation Boards to deal with work conflicts. Although these laws, like the Constitution itself, were obviously important as a clarification or an amplification of earlier laws, most of which appear to be Porfirian. The only real novelty was a return to the older practice of limiting the term of the presidency.

From the Porfiriate until today, not only the legal system but the Mexican Catholic Church has played an important role in the political economy. According to a standard account of church-state relations, Porfirio Díaz, a one-time grandmaster in the Freemasons, rose to power, thanks to his wife, with the help of the Mexican church, and in return, allowed the anticlerical laws of the Reform period to fall into disuse or, at least, to be interpreted according to local understanding. From economic ruin in 1870, the church, according to one estimate, came to control 10 percent of the wealth of Mexico in 1910. Its wealth today is still formidable.

Much to the consternation of the liberals, Díaz never did much to control the church. The church controlled the education system; Díaz appeared to acquiesce. For Díaz, the only issue seemed to be that of political loyalty. Díaz did insist that the Mexican church be a national church and resist papal interference. Because the clergy had a major stake in the continuance of the system, when Díaz made his demands known, the church bowed to them.

In the period of the Revolution, the position of the church took a temporary nosedive, leading some interpreters to define hegemony in modern Mexico as secular. Here, of course, I mean interpreters who take the Mexican Revolution to be the beginning of modern history. A longer-term view of Mexican hegemony reveals that this assumption is unwarranted. It is true that during the years of the Revolution when the clergy supported Victoriano Huerta against the liberal, Venustiano Carranza, the constitutionalist, this led to many setbacks for them. The Sonoran dynasty, however, once firmly ensconced in the years that followed, refused to enforce the more anticlerical provisions of the Constitution of 1917 and despite some exceptions this became the pattern as it had been in the Porfiriate. Thereafter, whenever the state verged toward anticlericalism, the church was more than able to strike back on its own. For example, in 1926 in the Calles presidency when the state began to "nationalize" property that the church believed it owned by right, this led to the beginning of a long revolt.[18]

Yet another feature of the Porfirate that lives on to the present day is civil society. Most commentators pay little attention to civil society during the Porfiriate because the dominant image of the period is a dictatorship. Nonetheless, civil society was important at that time, especially for northerners.

For example, in 1893, the famed anarchist journalist Ricardo Flores Magon enjoyed sufficient legal protection to serve on the editorial staff of a well-known opposition newspaper *El Demócrata*. And although much of the older scholarly evidence of open and legal opposition is restricted to Mexico City, some is now beginning to appear for other northern cities as well. For example, in San Luis Potosí in the 1890s, a Liberals' Club flourished around Camilio Ariaga, a local mine owner. A recent study suggests the probable existence of more such clubs.[19]

Although *El Demócrata* was a well-known newspaper, it was by no means the first newspaper that flourished in Mexico from within civil society. In fact, as early as the 1870s, radicals published newspapers in Mexico City and circulated them there fairly freely. Without the existence of civil society, it seems reasonable to postulate that nothing would have protected the freedom of speech of their editors. In addition, between 1876 and 1882, radicals played a role in labor congresses. For example, Soledad Sosa, an anarchist, emerged in this period as the first woman to participate in the industrial and urban labor leadership.

In fact, such was the power of civil society and of rule by law that although the state opposed radicalism, its opposition in the Díaz period generally was constrained by it. When Díaz intervened in labor politics in the North, he was obliged to do so in a legal way. Relying on his personal popularity, Díaz was able to draw enough workers to him to set up a progovernment union to encourage foreign investors and to undermine the power of the more anarchist antistate unions.[20]

As the years passed, these older trends continued. In 1916 at Querétaro, Carranza, the leading liberal politician of the era, felt obliged to acknowledge the legal rights of the small farmer to have land for his subsistence, a prudent move that no doubt lengthened the Liberal Age.[21]

In the South, by contrast, the imposition of law had a radicalizing effect on the peasantry. By the early years of the twentieth century, it is clear that most southerners realized they were on their own, unprotected by the system as it was known in the North. It was this insight that gave Zapata and his movement its enormous importance in Mexican history.

Had Zapata's challenge been, as liberals maintain it was, that of a unique figure, he would rate no more than a footnote. But Zapata is not that unique, and even as a failure, he is still a clue to how counterhegemonic struggle could proceed. Of course, liberals are correct to point out that by the time of Zapata's challenge, Mexican industry was profiting from World War I and in doing so was deepening the wedge between the northern industrial workers and the southern farm workers, making Zapata's task that much more difficult. The same applies to the intertwining of the Mexican with the U.S. economy. But does this add up to the conclusion that Zapata was a unique if belated figure? Are others more accurate who insist that with the defeat of Zapata the Revolution was simply "interrupted"? What, after all, had the Revolution given the South? Would not one logically expect continuing uprisings? What did southerners stand to lose?[22]

With the South in effect defeated and with the marginalization of Pancho Villa, the secularly oriented Sonoran Dynasty that came to power chose to use the next few years to take on the church. Its attempt, however, backfired and ultimately proved its undoing as the Liberal Age as a whole began to collapse. First, the Cristero movement arose. So fierce was this movement that it effectively stalemated the Federal Army for several years, and as it spread, it came more and more to resemble the much-dreaded Zapata movement.

As the state's confrontation with the Cristero movement dragged on, the Great Depression in 1929 suddenly emerged. Starving peasants demanded land redistribution, not simply land sequestration. Trade unions emerged as a powerful force. One of their most famous leaders, Vicente Lombardo Toledano, found support for his movement in both rural and urban areas and began to follow a strategy not unlike Gramsci's Factory Council strategy in Turin. It was this pressure, the economic crisis and the struggle against the state, that brought Cárdenas to power in 1934 over Calles, the latter still wishing to hold firm.[23]

Corporatism in Mexico: The Cárdenas Years of the 1930s and Its Neoliberal Aftermath

In Mexico, the left wing, or more accurately, state socialist version of corporatism came to power.[24] This can be attributed to several factors. First, the popularity of the Cristero movement frightened the landlord class. Second, even the state had to recognize that this time there was the possibility that the working class might make the North-South alliance that Zapata and Pancho Villa had failed to make. Third, there was the role of the church. The Church in Mexico might well have pushed for fascism as preferable to state socialism, but in the crucial interval when its opinions solidified, fascism suddenly appeared too risky. Radical peasants were beginning to seize land in its name, and the hierarchy did not have the capacity to stop them.[25] It thus was safer to support workers than to support peasants. A few years later, the Cristero threat passed and the church rethought its position and turned against Cárdenas and state socialism.

A corporatist system depends on political inclusion. When Cárdenas came to power in Mexico, he showed considerable skill and determination in incorporating diverse groups into the state. He proclaimed to the Mexican people that his role was to carry forward the Mexican Revolution; the memory of the Revolution was to be the vehicle of inclusion. This was an astute way to legitimate his alliances.

Cárdenas started with a circle of acquaintances from his native state, Michoacán; to this he added alliances from among unions and parastatal organizations. Everywhere he turned, mainly to the North, he found talent. From his own state, one might single out the particularly dedicated political figure General Francisco J. Mugica, who became his minister of communications and public works.[26]

Cárdenas also sought and received the support of women's movements. He did so by initiating a challenge to the more traditional domesticist ideology of the first liberal period by opening the door to careers for women. It would be wrong, as noted above, to construe this as revolutionary; more properly, it fit his basic strategy of appealing to the Mexico citizenry. But whatever interpretation one places on his motivations, in his first years, he had mass support and the public sector became a major employer of women.[27]

Not suprisingly, the church fought this change in Mexican hegemony because it did not benefit from it, and it did so by creating a separate Catholic women's movement and by holding mass protest marches against the government. From this resistance, it became clear that Cárdenas's policy was not without risks. He had to face both the opposition of the church and the opposition from elements in his own immediate ranks such as the trade union movement, which also were threatened by women's liberation. Equalization of gender rights was thus not an issue he could use beyond a certain point; making women's liberation a major part of his political struggle was out of the question.[28]

When, for example, Cárdenas argued that suffrage was a part of the Mexican Revolution, the traditional conservatives violently disagreed, rallying around Saturnino Cedillo, the minister of war and Portes Gil of the National Executive Committee, arguing back that a premature granting of suffrage could result in another tragedy "like Spain." After the collapse of corporatism, the state dismantled Cárdenas's Women's movement, turning it into a Feminine Technical Commission (1946) while quietly agreeing to suffrage on the level of municipal elections, again mainly in the North.[29]

Like all other rulers, Cárdenas not only needed to make specific tactical alliances with, for example, the women's movement to build up his power but he needed a wider if more diffuse support from the society for his program as a whole, and this, in turn, obliged him to portray his program as traditional. To this end, he welcomed Spaniards, refugees from the Spanish Civil War, who were sympathetic to his programs and who were products of the Spanish belletrist tradition so respected in Mexico. Several major scholars such as the historian Ramón Iglesias, the writer Victor Alba, and the social commentator Salvador de Madariaga served his regime.[30] They failed, however, to serve the ideological function Cárdenas needed. The Mexican church managed to portray them as leftists and to ignore them as Spaniards. Give or take segments of the artistic community, Cárdenas's corporatism can be said to have generally lacked intellectuals, and this was a major problem for it.[31] Emboldened by this fact, opponents of Cárdenas increasingly took the initiative against him, exploiting the new mass media of the period, for example, *Excelsior* and *Universal* as their voice of criticism.[32]

How did the collapse of Cárdenas and of corporatism come about? To move from a discussion of the existence of critics to an explanation of Cárdenas's collapse requires a more detailed look at Cárdenas's relationship to his mass base. In general, if politicians support the workers, should not one postulate that this would place them in fairly strong positions in a country of workers? Was Cárdenas really, as some commentators claim, a prisoner of non-reelection laws in 1940? Concerning the first point, the answer hangs on the meaning of the word *support*. To support the workers on his terms, Cárdenas had to incorporate them into the state. This he did, and in so doing, he had to destroy what remained of the tradition of trade union autonomy. This led Cárdenas to undermine the independent trade union movement in this period, the Confederatión Regional Obrera Mexicana (CROM) movement led by Lombardo Toledano. In essence, by controlling Lombardo Toledano, Cárdenas split the opposition to the state, but in doing so, he also split the potential social base for his own reform program. Cárdenas no longer had to fear unincorporated unions or even personal rivals, but he also no longer had a mass base. Thus, when he attempted to carry out reforms, for example, his famous *ejido,* or land redistribution cooperative scheme, he did not have the mass base of a worker-peasant movement that he would need to withstand the opposition of the landlords and the church. This issue stands out because Cárdenas faced problems in land reform that, for example, a Nehru or a Nasir managed to avoid; he had to take land from a class that claimed a right to it, whereas in the other countries, land could be taken from a dieing aristocrary or a departing monarchy. This issue made the process of land reform in Mexico more difficult. Brave young teachers sent to the countryside as part of the reform program were assassinated and, finally, when state socialism collapsed, the landlord class was able to take control of the ejidos. Haciendas became common again.

Yet the landlord class in Mexico was not large. With a popular program such as land reform, Cárdenas might well have calculated that he would ultimately prevail. What could not be calculated was the talent and the determination the church would bring to bear to thwart and overthrow him.

Who exactly opposed Cárdenas? Two figures stand out in the historical record. Their prominence no doubt implies the involvement of many others about whom less is known. A particularly famous and outspoken critic of Cárdenas was the archbishop of Guadalajara, Mons. Francisco Orozco y Jimínez. Born in Oaxaca in a family claiming a Castillian pedigree, he adopted a number of extreme antiregime positions.[33] It can also be shown that he had a major impact on the direction that the church took in the 1930s, that he, along with several other leading figures, inspired the church to undertake to woo the urban working class and to break Cárdenas's alliance with the Women's movement. To achieve these ends, the church chose Luis Martínez (1881–1956), a second major opponent of Cárdenas, to be the primate of Mexico in 1937.

Martínez differed markedly from the typical specialists in theology who dominate the upper levels of the hierarchy. He was a love mystic, well known and much liked by most Mexicans, workers included.

In addition, Martínez had particular luck as a spiritual advisor to women. Biographical reasons offer part of the explanation for this. With the death of his father at an early age, Martínez grew close to his mother. When he chose religion as a vocation, she followed him from seminary to monastery through the early part of his career. Later, Martínez became known for a celebrated vision, and still later, perhaps because of this upbringing, he was known as the spiritual mentor of distinguished women. Whatever the reason for his success, it seems reasonable to suppose that he could use such opportunities to limit the growth of Mexican feminism in influential circles and possibly to blunt Cárdenas's other initiatives as well.[34] This is, of course, a speculation. What seems less open to question in that the church chose this popular love mystic over many others schooled in the minutiae of the Cárdenas era and that he had the skill to prevent the regime from finding the hierarchy an easy target. All the while, in the countryside, the church and the landlords fought land reform, gradually draining and finally undermining Cárdenas.

With the rise of Ávila Camacho to the presidency in 1940, Mexico veered sharply toward liberalism. Camacho's retrenchment toward religion and away from state socialism was a victory not only for the church but for the southern upper class as well. At this point, foreign investment began to pour into Mexico.

From 1940 to 1992, Mexico experienced liberalism. There were inevitable similarities to the earlier liberal period, but there were also some new neoliberal features. True enough, the state reverted to one-class rule, abandoning much of its alliance with the working class. True as well, politicians proclaimed the virtues of capitalism and the evils of socialism. But equally true was the fact that the state did not sever all its connections with the public sector and the union movement. Was it because it did not have to? Were unions and the old public sector simply atrophying as the restructuring of the economy progressed? Whatever the case, by the 1960s, sweatshop production began to predominate. Factory workers were a privileged remnant of the past; they could only keep their privileges by being quiet and quiet they tended to be.

During the period from the 1940s to the 1960s growth was very rapid. It warrants more study than it has received. Perhaps it was here in Mexico that post-Fordism, so much discussed in the United States in the 1970s and 1980s, made its start. Perhaps the United States even had a hand in this through its large foreign investments of the period and through the encouragement it may have given to factory managers, who adopted the putting-out system. Put in other terms, perhaps it is in Mexico that one first finds the ideology about a "transition from authoritarianism to democracy" now widely found in many other Third World countries. Or put in still other terms, perhaps it was as a result of neoliberal policies that capitalism started to become a working-class ideology in Mexico.[35] These hypotheses, of course, need to be researched.

What is more certain is that as in the nineteenth century, the postwar mass society never accepted the setbacks to their well being brought by open market capitalism. Movements espousing the rights of Christians, peasants, and others downtrodden by the new economic forces were a continuous feature of the years after World War II as they had been earlier. The massacre of the students in 1968 pointed backward to the nineteenth century as well. In the nineteenth century as in the 1960s, students were among those occupying center stage. The Marxist Left and the trade union movement, which were so important under corporatism, were fairly marginal. Today, these older movements are called "new" social movements, but many of them as this makes clear are an echo of the protest movements in the late nineteenth century.[36]

Thus, despite some changes brought by neoliberalism, the period after 1940 may be compared to the old Porfiriate period. Control of the nation's land once again was in the hands of a few landlords, and the estate system returned. As in the nineteenth century, the process of land acquisition in the 1940s and 1950s was violent, this time leading not to a trickle but to a dramatic flood of people into the urban slums from the countryside. Once again, export agriculture soared; once again, food production dropped and the government had to import food. Those with money found this satisfactory, but for those without money, poverty led to malnutrition and a shorter life cycle.

Although one century's growth in population no doubt helps explain the rise in the level of struggle, so, too, does the logic of social dynamics. For example, small farmers found that they could profit by growing food and hoarding it until the government was forced to pay exorbitant rates for it. Migrants to the city found they had squatter power, the capacity to demand entitlements not provided by the state in rural areas.[37] A recent study of Mexican politics that surveyed the last generation characterized the government's policy as one that increasingly confronted struggle through "crisis management."[38]

As migration from the countryside to Mexico City increased, the Southern Question in its new form, municipal expenses also rose. As municipal expenses rose, municipal authorities tried to limit their expenses by forcing new arrivals into immediate self-sufficiency in the informal sector of the economy. In Mexico City, Indian women newly arrived from the countryside are in effect forced to stand and sell in the street of the city where, according to various accounts, they are persecuted by racist, abusive police and male street class. But this, too, has gradually brought a counterreaction. New forms of social resistance are springing up. In 1985 in Mexico City, to give one example, women garment workers formed a solidarity group, the Nineteenth of September Garment Workers' Union.[39]

Not surprisingly, despite all this outward migration, the South remains a crisis area. In recent years, the army has shifted from making occasional attacks on southern regional movements such as the Coalition of Workers, Peasants, and Students of the Isthmus (COCEI) to becoming an army of occupation.

Why? What has happened to the capacity of the state to govern? Where is the church today? What role does it play in the maintenance of hegemony in Mexico? Does the church play the same role that it did in the Porfiriate? Will it throw its weight against the state and bring down liberalism again? Today, this last possibility, at least, seems unlikely; the church is weaker than before. It is divided; a number of priests are sympathetic to liberation theology. As the authors of a Latin American collective report point out, the church has not been able to adjust to the new mass poverty of Mexico. Forty percent of women cannot afford the legalization of marriage in Latin America. Not only do these women lose what benefits accrue from a legal marriage, the church and, thus, the state lose an important linkage to these women and to their families as well. Perhaps this will be the era for evangelical Protestantism, or perhaps as in the past, the church will open the door to more saints and popular miracles and stage a comeback.

In the 1970s and even in the 1980s, some writers claimed that the policy of repressing the South was rational. Through this period, a new invincible agricultural technology was emerging that would make the capitalist agriculture predominant in the North self-sufficient. Soon the North would not need the South, meaning it would not need a whole region simply to produce more labor. Today, of course, there are all manner of doubts about the Green Revolution, as this new agricultural technology was called. Ecological concerns about what the Green Revolution does to the soil abound. Costs are an issue as are politics. The beneficiaries of the Green Revolution are not those the United States wishes to support; rich peasants are often quite critical of the United States and latifundists, the most pro-American group, are far more concerned with maintaining the status quo than with revolutions green or otherwise.[40]

What then of counterhegemony in Mexico? What is there beyond the new social movements of today and the traditional leftism of the past? The answer seems twofold. First, there are splinter movements on the margins of the labor movement and of the Communist party that took up the Indian Question, and second, there are cross-cultural populist movements. An example of the first was the CROM movement led in its early phase by Vicente Lombardo Toledano (1894–1968), which contributed importantly to the breakdown of the first Liberal Age.[41] More recently in the early 1990s, a second movement is emerging led by Cuauhtemoc Cárdenas, the son of Lazaro Cárdenas. It appears to be trying to resurrect some of the cross-cultural features of CROM.

As in Italy and India, so in Mexico, most of the early radicals were anarchist and there was certainly some element of anarchism in the radicalism of Lombardo Toledano and today in that of Cárdenas, Jr. Among the most famous of the early Mexican anarchists were the brothers Ricardo and Jesús Fores Magon. Biographical accounts show that these two radicals were sons of the provincial middle class from a rural Indian milieu in Oaxaca, that they moved to Mexico City to carry on careers of protest as journalists, and that they hoped to steer, perhaps, toward becoming leaders of the working class. Clearly, they had great influence during the years of the Revolution when they were instrumental in persuading the working class in Mexico City *not* to support Zapata. Later, however, in the 1920s their influence dwindled as the labor movement became increasingly organized and consolidated under the aegis of the state.

When CROM, the trade union headed by Lombardo Toledano, rose in the 1920s, a tug of war ensued between the state and the remaining anarchist radicals of the labor movement to influence its direction. As noted in the last section, the state gradually was able to exert more and more influence over the movement. As this took place, the anarchist movement began to despair of influencing the urban workers. One of the principal collaborators of the Magon brothers, Díaz Soto y Gama, eventually abandoned urban protest altogether to support the peasant movement in Morelos. There he formed a group to carry on agitation where to his credit, according to a recent commentator, he had a number of continuous years of agitation exceeding even that of Zapata.[42]

There is little doubt about Lombardo Toledano's service to the cause of labor from the 1920s to the 1960s. What eludes the bulk of the commentary literature is the significance of the contribution of the early years of his career. What standard accounts miss is that his struggle in this period took the form of a challenge not just to modern sector capitalism but to the hegemony or North-South strategy used by the ruling class.[43]

Lombardo Tolendo was born in the South in Puebla to middle-class parents and received an elite education, culminating in his attendance at the Law School and the School of Higher Studies of the National University of Mexico.[44] In his student days in Mexico City, a formative influence was the philosopher Antonio Caso. Caso taught him the intuitionist theory of Henri Bergson, a theory that shielded him against the positivism of the official culture and of the orthodox Marxism of the World War I period as well. Upon graduation, Lombardo Toledano's career began as an employee of the Mexican government charged with distributing land to peasants. Here, as he noted in later writings, he saw all too clearly the corrupt side of the Mexican Revolution's aftermath at close range.[45] His views swung toward what would today be Maoism. One of his positions became "All, who do not own the means of production should rally against imperialism."

Experience, power, and insights made Lombardo Toledano a critic of the Communist party of Mexico (CPM); in turn, the CPM dubbed him a "chauvanist nationalist," criticizing his emphasis on philosophy as a key to social change.[46] This is an obvious parallel to Gramsci and very reminiscent of Gramsci's own problem with the ICP. Lombardo Toledano, however, did not draw on the Italian experience but came up with his own characterization of the South as suffering in Mexico from an internal colonialism. He took Stalin's idea of autonomous nationalities and called for the creation of Soviets in Mexico. This would require, in his view, a political reorganization involving a decentralization of power in the country. Empowerment would not be simply political but cultural as well. It would be the obligation of the government, he believed, to conceive of socialist construction as creating alphabets and spreading literacy in Indian languages, ending the folklorification of Indians, promoting aesthetic, physical, and military education among the different ethnicities, and linking them to the industrial proletariat.[47] What worked against Lombardo Toledano was that the trade union movements with which he became involved did not embody the range of ideas or experiences that he did and could not be made to see their virtue. A mass of recently urbanized workers formed the membership of the unions; it was, perhaps, too much for them to look on that which they had recently repudiated to gain upward mobility as somehow still necessary for their well-being.[48]

One can summarize the highpoints of Lombardo Toledano's career as follows: as the leader of the trade union movement (CTM) in the 1930s, he was first a major ally and then a rival of Cárdenas. Functioning from a base among urban workers, he set out in the mid-1930s to unionize the rural sugar, cotton, and hemp producers. Cárdenas thereupon organized counter-erunions and exerted legal pressure, which gradually forced Lombardo Toledano to choose between the urban workers and the rural workers, in effect preventing him from organizing both. Lombardo Toledano finally chose urban workers. His more original ideas thereafter he expressed in his essays and not in his practice, which became that simply of a trade unionist. Thus, one can only read in *Futuro,* his journal, about his plans to organize the unemployed, his argument for daycare centers for children, his stand on equal wages for men and women, his support of consciousness raising, his strategies to overcome bureaucratic tendencies in the trade union movement, his encouragement to teachers to use evocative pedagogical techniques, and last but not least, his idea of a workers' militia, an idea that was crushed by the Mexican army.

Between the 1940s and the 1980s, there were many political movements in Mexico, but none took the specific form of a challenge to the hegemony. What did take place in this period was the mass migration of southerners to Mexico City. As this occurred, it became clear that the struggle over the maintenance of a South would now take place not only in the South but in the slums of Mexico City as well.

In July 1988, the son of Lazaro Cárdenas, Cuauhtemoc, running at the head of a coalition of groups espousing the Indian cause received 31.1 percent of the vote for president. Is Mexico heading for a new era of counterhegemonic struggle? Many think so.

The Organization of Culture in Mexico

As one finds in India and Italy, so one finds in Mexico that throughout modern history the state has organized philosophy, literary criticism, the social sciences, and other aspects of culture as part of its effort to maintain hegemony. And once again, one finds as well a built-in conflict between the romantic metaphysical worldview represented by southern intellectuals and the positivist worldview represented by northerners.

According to Leopold Zea, author of a standard text on the history of philosophy, Mexico has had few positivist philosophers, and those they have had have generally been reluctant to justify what the army and business elite have done in the name of positivism. As a consequence, after the initial generation of the científicos in the first years of the modern state, the economically dominant North has had to function almost defensively on a cultural level. Where one finds pockets of almost militant positivism in North Italian and North Indian culture until the present day, this is not the case in Mexico. In Mexico, positivism is only accepted on utilitarian grounds, that is, faute de mieux. The history of philosophy is to a large extent that of the history of the romantic metaphysical tradition associated with the southern intellectual.[49]

Perhaps it had to be that way. Here was a ruling class determined to support business and progress but unable to rely on positivism and developmentalism as ideologies. How was it to defend itself against the claims of religion? After all, wide segments of the population might well have preferred a religious party over the one they had. To defend itself against such threats, real or otherwise, for example, the Partido Acción Nacional (PAN), the state gradually came to rely on the metaphysical tradition. Of course, this was produced where positivism was the weakest, which was the South.

Porfirio Díaz tried to be an exception to this; he ruled by allying himself to the church and to positivism. This approach produced a revolution. Cárdenas tried to be an exception as well. He ruled by opposing the church and romantic metaphysical philosophy with socialism. He lasted six years.

In Mexican philosophy from the beginning of the twentieth century, one finds a growing disillusionment with the hold of positivism as represented by the científicos of the Porfiriate. A few years later cames the decisive break in Mexican philosophy with positivism, termed the *turn to neo-Kantianism,* a turn associated with the spreading influence of the Spanish philosophers Miguel de Unamuno and Ortega Y Gasset, and of the French philosopher Henri Bergson, in Mexican thought. Spain, is Italian Road as were France and Germany until the turn of the twentieth century. Italian philosophy does have its place in Mexico, but it comes less through Croce than through Vico, the figure who inspired Croce.[50] In Mexico, Vico influenced the contemporary writer Carlos Fuentes and certain eighteenth-century writers introduced to his works by Lorenzo Boturini, a Milanese disciple of Vico, who traveled to Mexico.[51]

José Vasconcelos, (1882-) the first major modern philosopher of Mexico was a Catholic modernist, a metaphysical thinker, and an important politician of the revolutionary period through the 1920s. Born in Oaxaca in the South, he grew up in the generation in which a liberal metaphysical philosophy served as the main alternative to the positivism of Díaz for the Mexican middle classes. The centralization of cultural life progressing during his youth caused him to come to Mexico City and to the National University. As a member of the Atenistas, a philosophy group, Vasconcelos taught and carried on studies of Croce, Nietzsche, Schopenhauer, Bergson and the Catholic modernists.[52]

Like Croce, Vasconcelos was involved in national affairs, often at a very high level; for example, he was minister of education in the 1920s, the period when the country was forming its modern education system.[53] During this period, he propagated his own version of indigenism, his Cosmic Race doctrine. The Cosmic Race doctrine—along with other forms of indigenism—affirmed the spiritual as opposed to the biological unity of the Mexicans. By contrast, the position most supported by the northern capitalist interests was mestizoism, the position making of the Mexicans an interchangeable work force and consumer market. Vasconcelos's position was, thus, a political middle ground between mestizoism and Criollist or Hispanicist racist sentiment. Ever the elitist, Vasconcelos appears more as a cosmopolitan who is above it all than as a nationalist, again like Croce. This image of him grows during his later career, which was largely that of a diplomat for the Mexican government.

In the writings of another southerner, the philosopher Antonio Caso (1883–1946), metaphysical Catholicism gave way to phenomenology and to a neo-Kantian critique of science in the doctrine of Cosmovision. Yet, during a number of years of his career, Caso was close to, yet highly critical of, Cárdenas. Such was the power of the southern intellectual in Mexico that this was possible.[54]

The third major figure of Mexican philosophy, Samuel Ramos, also espoused idealist positions. Born in 1897 in Zitácuara, Ramos was a student of Antonio Caso and of Vasconcelos. Although he criticized his teachers' use of intuition, he pursued the somewhat similar perspectivist philosophy commonly associated with Ortega Y Gasset. Perspectivism gave him his vocabulary to criticize the socialist education of the Cárdenas period. No new method of education, he claimed, can be imposed inorganically on a people, that is, in a way that is outside their experience. During the period when Cárdenas was propagating the concept of the new Mexican and Mexican socialism, Ramos emerged with his analysis of the actually existing Mexican personality, a personality, he claimed, which fit Adler's concept of the inferiority complex.[55] Here was indigenism used against socialism.

With the rise of the neo-liberal regimes after 1940, the state sought to confront problems in both the city and countryside that required more and more social engineering. Social science becomes a part of the southern intellectual. An important figure of the period was Alfonso Caso. As the director of the Instituto Nacional Indigenista, Caso had influence in policy circles and more broadly as the author of a best-seller *People of the Sun*. Along with Caso came two other important figures, Ignacio Bernal and Miguel Léon-Portilla.

The rise of these figures marks an important break in the history of Mexican anthropology and archeology. From 1877, the year of the opening of the divisions of anthropology and ethnology in the National Museum, the year of the first official archeological expedition (Oaxaca) and the year of the birth of the museum's journal *Anales,* these fields had been historicist. The main figure of this earlier period was Manuel Gamio, and, indeed, his theories play a role even today. Gamio saw the Aztecs as the forerunners of the modern Mexican state. With all their faults, the Aztecs promoted racial integration or mestizoism, which he claimed, was a precondition for the rise of the modern nation-state. In the context of Cárdenas' problems with the Cristeros, the idea of the Aztecs as forerunners to modern Mexico was useful. It bolstered a left-wing version of indigenism, and it bolstered as well the regime's anti-Criollist sentiment. The school of Manuel Gamio was also a major source of support for Lombardo Toledano, the trade union intellectual mentioned above.[56] But, there were limits beyond which Cárdenas, at least, could not go, and Gamio, and those who used his ideas, challenged Cárdenas to go further, Aztec origins becoming a two-edged sword. Thus, through the Cárdenas period, the state accorded public prestige to the philosophers, and Manuel Gamio remained in relative obscurity.

By 1940, with the resurgence of liberalism, a not insignificant development in the social sciences was that Mayan studies began to displace Aztec studies in terms of perceived prestige and relevance. Where Manuel Gamio, one generation earlier, had portrayed revolutions, Ignacio Bernal, a leading figure in the new Mayan Studies, an archeologist from a wealthy southern landlord background, presented the development of Mexico as a long, slow evolution. Bernal's career coincided with the rise of stratigraphy, a methodological technique quite appropriate for an evolutionist, and he used it. Thus, one finds Bernal arguing that the current migration of southerners North should be looked at positively. The South was a worn-out region. Eventually, through reacculturation in the North, the remaining Indians would become Mexicans.

Background matters. Like Vasconcelos before him, Bernal was a diplomat and a factotum of prestigious institutions in Mexico City such as the National Museum of Anthropology. In his best-known book, *A History of Mexican Archaeology: The Vanished Civilizations of Middle America* (London: Thames and Hudson Ltd., 1980), he included a map of old Mexico that showed no important ruins in the geographical North, few in Veracruz, but a great many in the Yucatán peninsula, Oaxaca, and Chiapas. The North for Bernal was "history," the South was "prehistory."

From figures such as Bernal, his influential colleague and teacher, Alfonso Caso, and his colleague, the archeologist Miguel León-Portilla, a picture of the Mexican past emerged among influential social scientists that made the Aztecs, located near the present-day national capital, a part of the historical experience leading to modern Mexico. Like modern Mexican civilization, Aztec civilization was religious and warlike, more so, at least, than that of the peaceful Mayas in the South, who were now to become the ultimate object of folklorization.

However appealing to some, the model of a civilized but disappearing Indian population largely of southern background was not one that all Mexican social scientists would accept; it certainly did not really address the needs of the state given the ever-increasing urban immigration of unassimilated people, arguably Indian in culture. Among the critics of Caso and Bernal, were the anthropologist Arturo Warman, the political scientist Pablo González Casanova, and the sociologist Rudolfo Stavenhagen. The Indians, Warman argued, were growing in number, they were not a residual culture but were built into the reproduction of the social structure. Siding with Warman was González Casanova; he insisted that the Indian Question was actually a form of internal colonialism. To these discordant notes, Rudolfo Stavenhagen added his impression that it might be incorrect to assume that miscegenation changed social structure. It is not surprising in the face of this onslaught, given as well the failure of social scientists to provide practical help to the state, that politicians in the 1960s began to bypass social science and to look for cultural spokespersons elsewhere. Following the same path as the Italian politicians of this period, their search ended in the choice of literary writers.

According to a recent commentary on contemporary Mexican literature, during the postwar years, the period of concern here, social realism declined sharply from what had been produced since the late nineteenth century. Romanticism combined with anarchism was reasserting itself. Art, a number of prominent writers came to believe, was the only way to escape from the nightmare of history. Inspiration comes from within oneself, from within language or from cosmopolitanism. The leading figures of the postwar period mainly upheld this version of romanticism and in so doing were of some use.[57]

The turn to literature by the state has to be understood, however, as a not altogether free choice and certainly not an entirely satisfactory one. Perhaps it was not a defeat, but it was a setback because what the state received for its patronage was alienation more than inspiration or social direction. After 1968, this was, perhaps, all that one could expect. In Octavio Paz, the most celebrated contemporary writer, these ingredients combined in disturbing ways in *The Labyrinth of Solitude* (New York: Grove Press, 1961) and in *Claude Levi-Strauss: An Introduction* (New York: Dell Publishing, 1970).

Paz performs, I nonetheless suggest, a traditional role in the history of Mexican hegemony, that of the southern intellectual. As such, he has clear antecedents in Vasconcelos and others, some of whom have been discussed above.

Like much of the southern diaspora, Paz was born in Mexico City and thereafter spent important parts of his life abroad. These points, especially the latter, have influenced interpretations of his work to this point. Still, it is reasonable to assume that his formation in Mexican society ought not to be overlooked. Mexico made a vast amount of difference to him; each trip out ended with a return to Mexico, a *Revuelta,* the name he gave to the well-known cultural periodical that he edits. From a biographical point of view, it is not insignificant that Paz spent his youth in Mixcoac in the Yucatán, attending secondary school in Mexico City from the age of thirteen. In his youth, Paz was raised by his mother, an aunt, and his paternal grandfather, an accident of circumstances, but not an uncommon one among the southern intellectuals surveyed in this book. Paz's father, a lawyer, was absent, defending Zapata and promoting agrarian reform after the Revolution; still he had his influence, as one of Paz's earliest poems shows. Some years later, in 1936–37, Paz returned to work for the Revolution in Yucatán. This decision involved, among other things, a flight from life as a university student, a life to which he never returned.[58]

Labyrinth of Solitude is a work of national character analysis. Like that of Samuel Ramos mentioned above, it offers a much more evolved image of racial integration or indigenism than that officially proclaimed by the government of the day, but, of course, it is not mestizoist.[59] Paz surprises the reader by taking up Mexicans in the United States as his point of departure. He calls them *Pachuco,* a word meaning, inter alia, a cultural orphan, and used by Paz as a metaphor for Mexico as a whole and to make the Mexican personality a mask. From the mask that Paz believes Mexicans wear, whether in the United States or in Mexico, Paz derives his explanation for the fulfillment Mexicans obtain from festivals, notably from the Day of the Dead festival when what is inside is let loose cathartically. From this, Paz's argument moves to history. Paz finds the meaning of modern Mexico in its initial identity as the sons (and daughters) of Malinche, the Indian mistress of Cortés, betrayer of her people yet founder of her country. Paz concludes his work by drawing these ideas together with the argument that authenticity comes in solitude.[60]

Paz is a novelist; he is also an anthropologist, following the traditions of southern intellectuals already familiar from this and previous chapters. Where much of Mexican social science is influenced by North American developmentalism, Paz's thought is not. Paz chose the anarchist metaphysical anthropologist, Claude Lévi-Strauss as his model. The impact of Lévi-Strauss on him, Paz reported, was "anthropological, philosophical." Two points stand out in Paz's study of Lévi-Strauss that tend to support this claim: first, Paz's acceptance of the postulate that a one-way observer-observed relationship is illegitimate and second, Paz's sympathy for the Mayan's attempt to "abolish history," an attempt Paz found similar to that of the Buddhists in India, whom he also admired.

In these claims, one returns to the Southern Question and to the cosmopolitanism, which is against national history. In the subordinate positivist tradition, two fields that are important in Mexico are associated with positivism: medicine and the new mass communication.

In Italian Road regimes, Mexico included, because of the weakness of positivism, the internationally dominant biomedical model in medicine has lower prestige than it has in countries where positivism is more secure, notwithstanding that the government promotes this model and the country has certainly produced its share of internationally renowned doctors.

Lower prestige makes medical institutions more open to criticism and challenge; criticism and challenge permit over time the development and legitimization of more than one medical system. This change has occurred. Conversely, efforts to professionalize medicine in modern Mexico, meaning to legitimate a single system, have not paid off, notwithstanding the common-sense assumption that would make any modern professional organization a bulwark of state power, hence something the state would have an interest in promoting. Rather, one finds that the political efficacy of professionalism for the state is actually more limited. The state has an interest in a situation in which there is only one dominant orthodoxy. When an alternative concept of a field not only exists but is legitimately institutionalized; the state gains no administrative or regulatory influence for the expenses it shoulders in supporting one system against the other. This is actually the case in India and potentially the case in Mexico.[61]

In Mexico, the biomedical or allopathic model is, of course, in charge but as the wider comparative literature suggests it is also on the defensive. Reference to India helps clarify this point. In India in the 1970s, when counterhegemony developed, the state had to recognize and even support *ayurvedic* medicine. In Mexico, much to the frustration of the biomedical doctors, spiritualist healers and *curanderos* are now starting to present a challenge similar to that of the ayurvedic practitioners. Indeed, even in Italy where the opposition parties support the state and its "national" health program, spiritual healers are quite in evidence.[62]

A glance at commentaries about Mexican medicine suggest that although the utilitarian achievements of positivism in medicine are appreciated by educated people, positivism itself is resisted, especially the effort of positivists in medicine to enter the philosophical terrain traditionally dominated by metaphysicians. If in countries such as the United States psychiatry is highly regarded, in Mexico, it is not; medical doctors tend to refer their patients to neurologists rather than to psychiatrists. The most reasonable explanation for such practices would once again bring one back to the strength of metaphysics and the weakness of positivism in Mexico. In Mexico and in Italy, even doctors believe in a mind-body dualism, that the mind is spirit and the body matter and that mental ailments simply are outgrowths of neurological disorders. Although for some doctors, the humanism of the psychiatrist Erich Fromm might overcome their negative assumptions about postivist psychiatry, for most, this is not the case.

The available evidence suggests that in countries such as Mexico and Italy not only do psychiatrists feel themselves to be déclassé among doctors but they suffer from their image in society at large. The combination of these pressures on the lives of a few psychiatrists in these two countries has led them to become critics of the regime, even counterhegemonic ones.

Why do hegemonic intellectuals shift and become counterhegemonic? With the growth of civil society in Italy and Mexico, especially in the years after World War II, an increasing number of people began to demand health services, including mental health services. Faced with rising costs, the government adopted the approach of providing mental health services by constructing asylums. The number of asylums grew rapidly as did the tendency to pronounce patients' ailments chronic and, hence, in need of such institutionalization. A few psychiatrists and community activists in both Mexico and Italy rose in opposition to this abuse of professional power by the mental health establishment. The most famous figures in what has now become an important struggle were an Italian medical couple, Franco (1942–1980) and Franca Basaglia. Directly influenced by the Gramscian ideas of empowerment of the oppressed, this couple launched a drive to unify the struggle of doctors, staff, and patients against asylums and to bring back people to their communities.[63] This agenda, naturally, met opposition. The Mexican counterpart to this movement, the community-centered approach to psychotherapy, was also encountering opposition by the late 1970's.[64]

The second technical field associated with the development of positivist science is communication. Here positivism dominates, but again it is clear that the domination is contested.

Information about the communications industry in Mexico suggests a strong influence not only of the South but of southerners. The reason for the first is essentially the same as it was for medicine. The prominence of the media, like the prominence of medicine, means that its programs are very much in the public eye. Predictably, then, media programs succeed or fail in proportion to their conformity to existing norms laid out by the dominant culture. The reasons for the second, for the actual presence of southerners and their possible predispositions to excel in the communication field, is a somewhat separate matter.

Given the organization of society—half peasant, half citizen—the communication industry in a country such as Mexico or Italy is more challenged than it is in a country such as the United States. In contrast to U.S. networks, networks in Mexico cannot assume that viewers trust their veracity but rather that they are looking for occasional services or entertainment.

Under such conditions, both the political and economic value of the communication industry is more limited.

By contrast, in the United States the predisposition of citizens, i.e., the entire population, is to identify with the government. Thus, for the United States, one can reasonably speak of media as "mass media," implying the probability that a viewing audience will be "massified." For Mexico, one cannot reasonably speak of the communications industry as a mass media because it does not have, by virtue of its rather tentative acceptance by the society, the power to perform this function.[65]

Specific examples from Italy and Mexico of attempts—especially unsuccessful attempts—by politicians to influence public opinion by controlling the mass media may help clarify this point. What the examples show is that their media simply is not able to do what the media has been known to do in the United States.

In the 1930s, Mussolini turned enthusiastically to the new communication systems in Italy; he hoped thereby to be able to bypass the university system with which he was at odds. His efforts did not work. Public opinion was not swayed by his attempts on radio or in news films. Lazaro Cárdenas had similar experiences. He, too, was frustrated by his inability to achieve results from the mass media; he, too, tried unsuccessfully to dabble in university reform. For example, in the 1930s, Cárdenas demanded that the university teach Marxism. He was rebuffed by the professors, and in the long run, his efforts undermined his own popularity. Opposition to Cárdenas's demand was spearheaded by the southern intellectual Antonio Caso. Under Caso's influence, and here one thinks of the role of Croce in Italy, the university's faculty withstood government financial pressure to do its bidding and by 1944 was able to erode government-sponsored reforms that had given a voice to students in the university council.

Are there sociological reasons suggesting that southerners would have advantages in the communication industry? Is this field heavily populated by southern business people and entertainers? If so, what is the advantage southerners have in entertainment? In other words, could the new scientific technology of the twentieth century—radio, television, films—enter Mexico and simply reinforce the traditional hegemony of romanticism over positivism?

A definitive answer to these questions is obviously not available. But what is suggested gives this hypothesis more than a little plausibility. To compete in the communication and entertainment industry, one needs the special knowledge and exposure to the society that southerners tend to have or tend to have more of than northerners do. Migration trends suggest that few northerners know the South but that many southerners know the North. In addition, southerners who become successful make language changes. Linguistically, they are coming from the outside in. This permits one to hypothesize that southerners in the communications industry would tend to be more conscious of who the audience is and how the audience can be addressed than their northern counterparts would be. This kind of knowledge is power.

Can it be shown that southerners really play a role in these industries where they have the potential to do so? The answer is yes. Within the communications industry, radio has historically had the largest audience. The most influential radio stations of the 1930s–1950s were Emilio Azcarraga's station XEW and the chains of stations owned by Romulo O'Farrill, both from Puebla. These stations emphasized popular music and soap operas because such programs had the best market potential. The most popular Mexican comic book has long been owned by a conservative southern businessman, José Garcia Valseco. In 1970, the president of Radio Systema Mexicana S.A. was also a southern businessman.[66]

The film industry is yet another area in which the South has influence. Film is primarily an entertainment medium; secondarily, it is a medium that disseminates some information. To the northern eye, the contemporary movie houses show nothing but third-rate Hollywood reruns, the reason being imperialism. An equally valid interpretation is profit. These films are chosen by people who know which films will draw the most viewers.

Earlier, and especially in the years from the 1940s to the 1960s, the South had a weaker hold on the film industry. A northern-oriented public sector was producing films. A neorealist trend dominated the Mexican film industry much as it did its counterparts in Italy and India in this period. Locally produced films that often emphasized socialist themes dominated the market. In this "Golden Age" of Mexican cinema, talented Mexican Indian actors appeared, their very appearance almost a challenge to the regime's attempt to make the Indian question invisible. A symbol of the Golden Age was the great actor-director Emilio "El Indio" Fernandez (1904–1986). He directed forty-two films and won sixteen international awards, including one at Cannes. Of Indian origin, he often portrayed the situation of Indians in his films.

By the 1970s, considerable evidence suggested that the state at least thought that the film industry was not serving its needs and, therefore, ought to be moved back to mass-market entertainment. From this period come the major policy changes toward film: the gradual discontinuation of public sector involvement in local film production, the growing policy of state censorship and review of local films, and the state's continuing collusion in the 1970s and 1980s in what one writer termed "Hollywood film-dumping practices."[67] Given the choice of developing a local industry, which might be critical, or of importing foreign films, which were not, the state opted for the latter, giving the nod to the use of film for mass-market entertainment and, therefore, for southern taste and commerce.

The organization of culture in Mexico reflects the realities of the Italian Road. The relative weakness of the hegemony in Mexico has forced the ruling class to give more authority to the southern intellectual than was the case elsewhere. The consequences were a stronger hold of the romantic metaphysical worldview and a weaker hold of the positivist one.

History Writing in Mexico

In an Italian Road regime, when the Southern Question was deflected by regional issues as in Italy, history writing remained useful as elite chronology or as local particularity. Where the South surfaces and becomes a threat, states may see a need or an opportunity to widen and deepen their bonds in civil society by encouraging social history, in which case, the field's prestige as a whole may actually rise. This happened in India; it is beginning to occur now in Mexico.[68]

History Writing: The First Liberal Period, 1876–1934

During the period from 1876 to 1934, liberals and conservatives both played a role in the rise of the modern history profession. According to a recent study, the scientific apparatus of periodization and a careful if partisan use of chronology arose among liberal historians in the 1880s.[69] Conservatives made their mark in the production of works of distinction and in the formation of scholarly organizations.

In this period, no doubt the majority of historians were Christians and conservatives. Some wrote about their region, often doing so without too much reference to the nation or to its progress. Others accepted the fact that the nation had come into being but regretted what was lost in the process. From this last group, perhaps the most famous was Orozco y Berra. With the rise of Porfirio Díaz, Orozco y Berra took up the study of the pre-Hispanic and colonial periods as a statement about Mexican Independence and what had followed from it. A second historian with similar Hispanist leanings was Joaquin García Icazbalceta. A biographer noted that he was a beneficiary of the new state. He was a landlord whose holdings greatly expanded during his lifetime at the expense of Indians.

Orozco y Berra and Icazbalceta have had their continuators among conservatives in the twentieth century, especially among the historians of religion, such as, Mario Cuevas and José Bravo Ugarte.[70] Among other conservative historians with strong Hispanist leanings was Atanasio Saravia y Aragon (1888–1969). In 1919, Saravia y Aragon formed the Mexican Academy of History, making it a branch of the Royal Academy in

Madrid and then appointing himself the first editor of the Academy's *Memorias*.[71]

With the rise of a more secular northern culture among liberals came the modernization of the National Museums, the National Archives, and the study of history in the National University.[72]

Examples of the early liberal historians include Luis González Obregon (1865–1938), a long-time employee of the Museo Nacional, author of a number of books on old Mexican customs and anecdotes and on old Mexico City as well. Late in his career, Obregon wrote a history of the National Library (1910), finally winding up as a member of the Academia Mexicana de la Lengua y de la Historia and as the first editor of what today is one of the oldest, most influential journals, the *Boletín,* journal of the National Archives.[73]

Juan Bautista Iguinez (1881–1968), an editor of documents, was a bibliographer for institutions in his native Guadalajara; later in his career he moved to the Museo Nacional. From provincial concerns, Iguinez's career changed to national ones. His later works included a bibliography of Jesuit writings, a manual for the application of the Dewey Decimal System to Mexican libraries, and collections of documents for provincial history.

Fernando Ramírez de Aguilar (1887–1953) from Oaxaca was a third figure who parlayed regional cultural knowledge into a career as a professional historian. Along the way, he worked as a journalist and a municipal politician in Mexico City and taught folklore. In 1933, he helped organize the first national congress of Mexican History.[74] This congress met thereafter every two years in provincial capitals, serving as a stimulus for many years for the publication of regional histories and for the gathering of source materials.

In 1914, the Escuela de Altos Estudios of the National University became a research center. By 1927, it offered programs leading to masters and doctoral degrees. After that, gradually, the center of gravity of historical research began to shift to academic institutions, but the transition was slow given the problems of academics in the corporatist period. Dissertations begin to appear in measurable quantities only in the 1940s.

The first generation of university professors no doubt found it still easier to work around the university than through it. For example, Emilio Rabosa, a constitutional law professor, and his colleagues from the law faculty of the National University played a leading role in the 1920s in the formation of the Academia Nacional de Historia y Geografía.

The figure in whom liberal historiography of this first phase reached its culmination point was Justo Sierra (1848–1912). A southern intellectual and an idealist, previously introduced as an intimate of Porfirio Díaz, Sierra as a historian, however, was closer to the the everyday world of the people than to the metaphysical philosophic tradition of his region and his class. In his most famous book, *Mexico: Su evolución social* (1900–1902), Sierra revealed himself as a nationalist conveying the spirit of the Mexican people on the rise. Speculation exists how, given his social background, he knew so much about the details of life in Mexico. One view is that his knowledge came from his years of service to the Mexican judiciary, which provided him his main career. Whatever the reason, Sierra became well known in public life and for his writing without becoming controversial as liberals tended to be.

History Writing in the Corporatist Era

As in Italy, the vast majority of Mexican historians were opponents of corporatism. To their admirers, these figures appear in retrospect as heroes and, in some cases, as founding figures of the field for the neoliberal period. It is certainly possible to follow this type of formulation and to compare the role of the prominent Mexican scholar Daniel Cosío Villegas (1898–1976) with that of Federico Chabod or even of Croce in Italy because Mexicans like Italians look back on these figures in this way.

Cosío Villegas, like Croce, falls into the category of the great figure who came to the study of history during an important career in several other fields, in his case, economics, publishing, and diplomacy. During his work in these other fields, corporatism emerged, and he opposed it. In opposing it, he set out to draw from it its cultural resources, much as Croce tried to do in Italy. Among Cosío Villegas's successes was his separation of the National School of Economics in 1933 from what would be the more socialistically inclined National University (UNAM). He also founded the important publishing house Fondo de Cultura Económica, which translated and published many books from the United States; in the 1930s, he was among the founders of the private university, El Colegio de México, and still later, a founder of the faculty of economics of the University of Nueva León.

In Cosío Villegas, one finds an unchanging old-style liberal nationalism as a core ideology. Although he was anticlerical, like Sierra and the other liberals of the end of the Díaz era, and, thus, could survive both then and during the Cárdenas period, he differed fundamentally from the neoliberals of the generation emerging in the 1940s. Thus, his career ended with him increasingly a critic of the different postwar regimes.[75] With the swing to the right in the 1940s, Cosío Villegas was too much an older generation liberal positivist. At this point, he turned to writing history. Deeply rooted in documents and archival sources, he was able to sustain his famous Seminar in Modern History out of which came the ambitious multiauthor, multivolume *Historia Moderna*.

At the other end of the spectrum from Cosío Villegas, one finds two historians who supported Cárdenas and his programs: Luis Chávez Orozco (1901–1966) and Alfonso Teja Zabre (1888–1962). In their writings, Marxism and left-wing indigenist thought entered Mexican historiography.

Somewhere between these two groups one finds a third stance toward corporatism among historians, especially conservative historians, that of self-exile. For example, José Bravo Ugarte (1896–1968), a Jesuit and the leading historian of the Mexican Catholic Church, took teaching jobs during the Cárdenas years first in Guadalajara and then years later in Ibero-American University in the capital. Another eminent church historian, Mariano Cuevas (1879–1949), also a Jesuit, chose to teach abroad in the Cárdenas period before coming to Mexico City.[76] In the waning years of corporatism, the private university, El Colegio de México emerged, giving a career to the historian Ramón Iglesia Y Pargo (1905–1948), a Spanish refugee and Hispanist.

The Writing of History in the Era of Neoliberalism

Postwar historical scholarship in Mexico revealed the evolution from liberalism to neoliberalism, the integration of Marxism into the profession as a subordinate trend, and the rehabilitation of local history also as a subordinate trend. The growing crises after 1968 offered historians new opportunities. The state turned to them, hoping to forge deeper links in the civil society and with the United States.

The early years of neoliberalism found the Congress of Mexican History and its constituency in the national museums, archives, and provincial universities, that is, the old institutional structure within the history profession that the Cárdenas regime used to promote national integration, in disarray. No other constellation of institutions and organizations, however, came into being.

Judging from the titles of theses and dissertations accepted by Mexican universities between 1941 and 1968, the twentieth century rose in popularity, but after 1968, it fell. After 1968, the adoption of the theme of civil society is noticeable.[77] The younger generation appeared worried about whether it still existed.

A recent study, which surveyed trends in the study of the conquest of Mexico and the early colonial period written by Mexicans after 1945, concluded that the writing of institutional history declined in these two specialties. Institutional history, was a main genre of the older liberal positivist history, and this was especially the case in these two specialties, thanks to Silvio Zavala and his colleagues, the scholars who dominated these fields for decades.

This study also found that the growing attraction to neoliberalism in the younger generation seemed to incline historians to present subjects in a more fragmented way than they had theretofore, that in addition, the post-1945 historians tried to avoid issues or to restructure issues that had divided their ranks in the Cárdenas era. They stressed the influence of the Indians and the Spanish on each other rather than adopt the older, more partisan and, thus, divisive positions. Another example of restructuring is drawn from an article by Edmundo O'Gorman, a noted representative of perspectivism, one of the forms of neoliberalism. In the article, O'Gorman comments on the somewhat positivist and rather judgmental claims of the American historian Lewis Hanke about the Spanish role in Mexico, and he concludes by noting that the Spaniards did what they did in accordance with the morality and values of that period. One cannot judge the Spaniards according to the mores of one's own day.[78] This perspective was new. An earlier generation of scholars might have reached the same conclusions, but they would have done so in terms of nationalism or religion or on technical or factual grounds.

In a recent study on the interpretation of the Mexican Revolution in Mexico, the author shows that it also underwent a dramatic shift after 1940 that became all the more pronounced in the wake of the disillusionments after the student massacre of 1968. What declined at that point, the author found, was the positivist belief that the Revolution was a fixed point, a great beginning. As an example of the new type of scholarship on the Revolution, the author pointed to the work of Luis González, a historian of the younger generation best-known for his book *Invitación a la Microhistoria* (Mexico City: Secretaría de Educación Publía, 1973). This work shows that for the region of Michoacán, the Revolution was far less a watershed than was the later Cristero period. This insight drawn from personal experience brought into question the whole scaffold that held together the more stageist version of the official history.[79]

After 1968, the status of history once again rose, and as it did so, a deeper set of linkages between historians and the bureaucracy appeared. Several historians whom I interviewed in 1980 in Mexico City characterized the organization of the profession at that time in terms of cliques, the quintessential social grouping in a bureaucracy.[80] Of course, professional organizations continue to exist as well, but for these respondents, the dominant reality was the Left, Right and Center factions of the ruling party around which one could find groups of scholars and their journals. They pointed out a leftist grouping around the journal *Nexos,* including the historian Enrique Florescano, his wife, the historian Alejandra Moreno Toscano, who is the daughter of a PRI senator, and the political scientist Pablo González Casanova. This circle produced the highly critical book by Carlos Pereyra et al., *Historia para que?* (History for whom?)(Mexico City: Siglo Veintiuno, 1980). A centrist element of Mexican historiography led by Edmondo O'Gorman but including the writer Octavio Paz is identified with the journal *Vuelta*, whereas the right of the profession is represented by Silvio Zavala and other El Colegio de México professors and their publications.

The predominance of cliques is something new to the 1970s, and it deserves a special study. Clearly, membership in a clique is different than the affiliation of historians to parties as in India or to the older scholarly organizations of Mexico or of other countries. It seems to imply a higher level of political connection. It does not necessarily imply new thought. Membership in a clique may be taken to be evidence of clinging—in an intellectual sense—to the status quo. This view is sustained indirectly, at least, by the findings of the two leading studies of the philosophy of history in postwar Mexico. The authors of these works argue that historical thought between the 1940s and the 1970s has scarcely broken with that of the preceding period. One of these studies stresses the importance of the romantic metaphysical worldview; the other stresses the emergence of cosmopolitanism or neoliberalism.[81]

The year 1968 can also be seen as the point when the historian's contribution to Mexican-U.S. relations begins to pay off. Long years of holding binational conferences—the Encuentras—made a difference.[82]

In the Encuentra conferences, which had been held regularly since 1949, what was politically significant was the idea that the United States and Mexico are partners. The ability of a group of Mexican historians to project this idea no doubt explains the interest of the PRI in the history profession. How did they do it? Obviously, in the whimsical—and political—world of academics, partnership is not something that comes automatically with colleague relations, so it is made to emerge indirectly from the structure of the conferences themselves. For each conference, the organizers chose a theme. Participants naturally offered multiple interpretations of the theme; the multiplicity of interpretations neutralized any one of them, diminishing the authorial presence and thus the significance of the author's nationality. What stands out in the printed version is simply the list of subheadings under the theme. The table of contents shows that the real divisions are not between Mexicans and Americans but between individuals of either nationality concerned with these subheadings. In sum, Mexico and the United States are partners.

In searching for a general way to characterize the contemporary generation of Mexican historians who participate in these conferences, one is struck by the deep long-term contact that these particular Mexicans have had with the United States or with Western Europe or with both. Two figures for whom biographical information is available who epitomize this more general phenomenon of elite cosmopolitanism are Josefina Vázquez and Ernesto de la Torre Villar. Born in 1930 in Mexico City, Josefina Vázquez was educated at Harvard, Louisiana, Spain, and UNAM; she was one of the first and very few Mexicans to specialize in the history of the

United States. For some years, she has been a professor and director of the Center of Historical Studies at El Colegio de México. Her publications include the Latin American section of the *Encyclopedia Brittanica,* a translation of John Phelan, *The Millenial Kingdom of the Franciscans,* and a book on the U.S.-Mexican War of 1847. Ernesto de la Torre Villar was born in 1917 in Mexico City. He, too, had an international education and thereafter made his reputation as a director of the National Archives and as a professor at El Colegio de México.

Hegemony in Italian Road regimes requires the reproduction of a southern intellectual not only on the national level but on the local level as well.[83] Given a weakness in the hegemony, however, the southern intellectual may be elevated to the national capital to cover the loss of authority on the local level in the South. In the actual South, one notes a gradual abandonment of the world of folklore and myth and a turn to the production of history as southernization weakens.

Beginning with leading historians who left the South, one finds Angel María Garibay K. (1892–1967), a cleric, and a student of Nahuatl culture, who followed a career line that took him from parish priest to UNAM professor extraordinaire in 1952. In the process, he lived twenty years among the Indians of the Central Plateau and published extensively on their history.[84] Agustín Cue Canovas (1913–1971), a teacher for many years in local southern schools and polytechs, made his reputation as a member of the Socialist party from Tabasco. Long known for his Zapatista sympathies and for his interest in the cause of Mexican independence, he concluded his career studying the fate of liberal constitutionalism as a UNAM professor.[85] These figures were, of course, exceptions. Almost by definition, the route out of the South into the historical mainstream in the North was difficult; specializations and worldviews in the North are too different from those in the South. Only Silvio Zavala, the colonial period specialist, did it easily. His personal wealth, his political connections, and the nature of his specialization contributed to his success.

Less often discussed in works on history writing are the scholars who live and work in the South. Examples of such figures from the contemporary Mexican context would include Alfredo Barrero Vásquez (b. 1900), who has worked mainly in Merida compiling a Maya-Spanish/Spanish-Maya dictionary. Some years ago, he served as chair of the Department of Philology and Linguistics of the South East Regional Center of Instituto Nacional de antropología e historia (INAH). A painter and a poet, and here the polymathic character of the southern intellectual comes out, he was also the founder of the Institute of Fine Arts in the Yucatán. A second such figure is Humberto Lara Y Lara (b. 1906), a journalist and history professor of Oriental cultures and world literature at the University of Yucatán. He also manages a publishing house.[86]

Mexico was presented in this chapter as a Latin American example of the Italian Road. Its salient characteristic was the long-term internal migration to the capital city, a migration that distinguished the history of the country from the other examples of the Italian Road considered in this book. I now examine a third major form of hegemony found in the modern world, the tribal-ethnic state. Chapters 7 and 8 provide two of its major variants.

7

The "Tribal-Ethnic Road" in Europe

Albania, 1878–1990

One of the fundamental forms of hegemony in the modern world is the system of political domination based on the use of gender as the major disguise of class relationships, one commonly organized around tribal or ethnic divisions. Although all hegemonies use gender, here meaning biological distinctions and blood-line solidarities, as part of domination, the tribal-ethnic states are the only ones essentially based on them. The ruling classes of many countries—European, Southeast Asian, Arab, African, and Pacific Island—have adopted this strategy.[1]

In this chapter, I present the history of Albania, a European tribal-ethnic state that is predominantly Muslim, and in so doing, seek to challenge three important features of the dominant paradigm: its claim that Europe is secular or if religious then Christian and Jewish; that Europe is a democracy, and even more important, its claim that a tribal-ethnic state is by definition more or less not modern, that it can be given over to anthropologists and political scientists or to such spare time as a historian may have.

In the first part of this chapter, I enumerate the most common attributes of this form of hegemony, providing as well an overview of how scholarship in the dominant paradigm treats this country. In the second, I provide a political economy interpretation of its modern history from 1878 to the present as an example of a tribal-ethnic hegemony. In the third, I deal with the organization of culture as a part of that hegemony, and in the fourth part, I take up the writing of history in Albania and by Albanians living abroad as a part of that organization of culture.

In a tribal-ethnic hegemony, a paramount chief, his allies and kin, dominate a society. Workers and peasants belong to less-favored tribes or ethnic communities. Thus, on the surface, at least, and certainly in terms of the received scholarship, the principal disguise for class conflict is, as the name implies, tribal and ethnic ideologies. Looked at more closely, however, this view although correct is incomplete. Why would less-privileged tribals and ethnics accept such an ideology? The apparent reason is that even oppressed men have a stake in a system that gives them a higher public status than that accorded to women, whereas even oppressed women have a stake in a system that accords them a particular place and beyond that a space to maneuver through male relatives.[2]

Is, however, the common view correct, that the actual situation of women is worse in the tribal–ethnic states than elsewhere? This is a possibility, but it seems unlikely. The evidence from the cases considered in this book is mixed. In the 1940s and in the years thereafter, Albanian women seized on the prevailing ideology of developmentalism and found opportunities in the modern sector work force. In Zaire, this opportunity did not present itself, but reports indicate instances of middle-strata women launching out, forging fictive kinships, opening all-women businesses, or joining opposition church movements.

Hegemony in tribal-ethnic states rests on an organization of culture termed here *gnosis,* a way of controlling culture that gives a fairly unlimited authority to the arbiter over the text, a way that reaches its full development only through anarchism as a worldview.

Specialists on Albania refer to gnosis as Albanology; some in the dominant paradigm take it to be merely the ensemble of various fields of learning about the country, others take it to be a methodology, such as deconstruction or hermaneutics, a means of attacking positivism, whereas those more attuned to anarchism take it to be an alternative form of modernity altogether.

The concern here is more with the latter, gnosis perceived as a technique to prevent the development of a controlling positivist high culture, its adepts devoting themselves to undermining such knowledge by resubmerging it into the folk culture out of which it came. In the words of one of its protagonists, it (gnosis) is a way to overcome the "false essentialisms of home/world, spiritual/material, feminine/masculine propagated by [Western] nationalist ideology."[3]

Historical scholarship on modern Albania usually begins with the year 1912. If it takes 1878 as its point of departure—as I do in this chapter—it does so merely to note the rise of the nationalist movement as an antecedent to the actual birth of modern history in the later year when the country became independent. Thereafter, historians in the dominant paradigm note phases of liberalism, 1920–24, of dictatorship under King Zog, 1925–39, of communist rule 1944–90, and thereafter once again of liberalism.

This picture of change found in familiar works of historical scholarship contrasts with standard ethnographic accounts for the same period. Ethnographers in contrast to historians make modest claims at most for change even up to the present. One finds in their works accounts of the northern Ghegs and the southern Tosks, the two main tribal-ethnic groupings, and of the religious communities found in and between them: Sunni Muslim, Bektashi, Greek Orthodox, and Roman Catholic.

The juxtaposition of these two bodies of scholarship establishes for those so persuaded that countries such as Albania are not at all like the truly modern nation-states in which state and society seem more as one.

In a political-economy interpretation, the country appears neither to be so static nor so constantly changing as it does in the ethnographic and historical works alluded to above; a middle position between these two emerges from a focus on class and gender struggles. For political economy, the most useful periodization would be 1878–1944 as a liberal age, 1944–90 as a corporatist period, 1990-as a neoliberal period.

In a tribal-ethnic hegemony, as in others, crises can destroy a state. What is to prevent ethnic group conflicts or revolts from splitting the leadership, creating a crisis of law and order, or worse? To diminish the prospects of such conflicts and revolts from reaching this point, the state tries to incorporate the dominant elements of all the ethnicities into a super-grouping, making of them the followers of the supreme ruler and members of the ruling party. Failing to achieve this, options are more limited. War may become a necessity. What other options are there? This predicament leads observers to perceive this type of hegemony as violence prone. Without a great deal more study, however, it will remain uncertain whether violence plays a greater role in this hegemony on the average than in others. It seems fair enough to point to the magnitude of the problem of conflicting loyalties and identities. Although multiple loyalties and identities exist everywhere, can ordinary persons carry on when they are in conflict, as, for example, when clan opposes state? Would this not lead to schizophrenia or violence or other seemingly modern pathologies?[4] Still, the larger point remains open. Researchers in democracy have not done an adequate amount of research on the role of coercion and violence. Thus we are left to suppose some hegemonies use coercion, others persuasion. This can't be!

Today, all states feel the pressure to develop. For the states following the tribal-ethnic hegemony, this pressure, the common claim goes, is more distressing than it is for other states, judging from the fact that the ruling classes of many of these states tend to avoid it by focusing instead on elite consumerism. If such states develop a modern work force, this line of thought goes, the risks for them are higher than for others; tribal and ethnic solidarities are put at risk by the advent of other forms of solidarities and identities. And, indeed, until the recent efflorescence in East and Southeast Asia, this notion of risk remained hard to assess: communist Albania was among the few tribal-ethnic states, that had attempted development.

In tribal-ethnic states as elsewhere, language policy plays an important role in the maintenance of hegemony. How far can a state encourage linguistic integration for the sake of development before it undermines tribal-ethnic boundaries? Should the state support higher education? Should the state encourage its scholars to produce facts accessible to all people, or would the availability of a common patrimony of knowledge undermine the necessary social differences? Should knowledge produced by emigrants be allowed in and if so in what form?[5] Does not science need to be controlled by philosophy and linguistics? Such are the typical concerns of many tribal-ethnic states.[6] It explains the power accorded to the students of language over others.[7]

In all the hegemonies, the development of education corresponds with —perhaps even causes—the rise of a culture based on prose. Poetry loses some of its hold. Tribal-ethnic states appear on the whole to be something of an exception. In most such states, the most famous intellectuals today are still poets. The common observation is—and it seems correct—that the vertical bonds within ethnic communities or tribal groupings assure the linguistic intimacy necessary for poetry and more generally for an oral culture.[8]

In the tribal-ethnic states, culture is also more "performative" than it is in the other hegemonies. In the absence of a traditional "high culture," with its dichotomy of performers and audience, text and reader, art forms —dancing, singing, poetry—writing, and recital—are skills diffused to an extent unknown in the other hegemonies. In modern times, states typically encourage participation in these art forms through competitions, some of which are now telecast.

Tribal-ethnic states play two main roles in international relations. First, they support in a fairly unconditional way one or another of the Great Powers. Examples include Albania's support of Italy, the Soviet Union and China and Zaire's support of the Belgians and more recently of the United States. In the 1970s, the Zairian government was obliged to finance projects all over the world in return for U.S. backing. Although this role is possible when the ruling class is unified, it can backfire if it is not. Overtures by an unraveling leadership to more than one Great Power can turn a country into an arena of Great Power conflict. Given that the Great Powers assume that the support they are receiving is unconditional, changes catch them by surprise. For example, events in Albania in the 1870s and 1880s caught Bismarck, the most experienced of politicians, by surprise.[9] Other well-known examples of international crises produced in this way include the crises in the Balkans at the outset of World War I, in the Belgian Congo in 1960, the war in Vietnam, and, more recently, the Civil Wars in Lebanon, in the Horn of Africa, and in Yugoslavia.

The second role in international relations of tribal-ethnic states is withdrawal from the world system. Hoxha withdrew Albania from the world market after the break with China. Amilcar Cabral took Guinea-Bissau out of the world market as did the leaders of various of various other countries, for example, South Yemen after the Revolution and Libya under Qadhdhafi.[10]

A Concluding Observation on Albania's Relation to Russian Road Regimes

An important argument in this book is that Albania differs in important ways from the Soviet Union for the period these professed to follow Communism. This argument is not in line with contemporary scholarship, which tends to amalgamate the study of regimes that take communism as their ideology. The following section addresses what is perceived as a too-great homogenization of Albanian and Soviet history.[11]

The core proposition of contemporary scholarship, Western and Albanian, which I am disputing, is the one claiming not simply that the country had until recently a Marxist-Leninist-Stalinist regime, albeit unique in many ways, but that with its "Russian-style" Revolution in 1944, it made a clean break with its past. My argument is that its history, like that of other countries, is one marked more by continuity than the dominant paradigm allows. There is no question as to the intent of the regimes—which borrowed or whether they borrowed; the question arises as to what actually happened to Soviet practices in their new context.

Clearly, Hoxha invoked Marxist-Leninist-Stalinist lingo throughout his career, yet, a close look at the major institutions in his country does not support the view that the country underwent a transformation to the Russian Road after the communist takeover in 1944. A more temperate position is Arshi Pipa's concept of the nature of politics as "Stalalbanian."

Does the country have Soviet-style institutions? The strongest case for this position can be made from a consideration of the secret police and the armed forces. But even here, the proposed similarity is not strong. It depends on a view of the police in one period, the purges, a very atypical period of police abuse. By contrast, for the past half century, it would appear that the *Sigurimi,* or political police, was notorious for its continuous abusiveness. It was known not only for its large numbers of political detainees but also for its incarceration of innocent individuals on the grounds that they might potentially become dangerous to the regime. Although, no doubt, the use of incarceration as a preemptive device is a universal practice, its form in Albania was far more devastating than that of its counterpart in the Soviet Union. In Albania, it was not unreasonable to suppose that the activity of one member of a family was shared by others or even by the clan. To stop a given person, the Sigurimi reasoned, one may have to arrest a whole family and even the neighbors. This was rarely the practice in the Soviet Union. Another distinctive feature of the Sigurimi was the career instability of its members. Again, this brings to mind the career instability of the Soviet secret police during the purges, but there the parallel ends. Beria, a famous functionary of the Soviet secret police, had a long tenure in his office even during that period as did many others before and after him. By contrast, the directors of the Sigurimi regularly fell victim to purges after only brief periods in office. Koci Xoxe directed the Sigurimi in 1944. In 1949, he was purged and executed. Thereafter, the Sigurimi was controlled by a whole series of Hoxha's men, for example, Mehmet Shehu, Kadri Hasbiu, and Feçor Shehu, all of whom were also purged.[12]

Despite the fairly similar emphasis on political indoctrination carried on by the party inside both armies, a point often referred to by students of communism, the armies in these two countries are far from being identical. The Soviet Union has maintained standing armies, trained by career officers, with professionalism playing an important role. In Albania, the army began as an ensemble of ethnic guerilla groups and thereafter has coalesced uneasily under the aegis of the party. There has been much less room for professionalism as an ideology than in the USSR.

In a discussion of institutions of these two countries other than those of the police and the army, the difference becomes increasingly apparent. For example, the central political apparatus in the USSR, landlords, industrialists, and others possessing wealth and power on the national or provincial level join the party, the bureaucracy, or both to reinforce, even to create, their class position by becoming part of the ruling caste, the nomenklatura. By way of contrast, unless one resided in Tirana and partook on that level of decision-making, membership in the party was simply a further legitimation of power in actuality possessed by virtue of local family and clan connections.[13]

The local power structures in the Soviet Union, for example on the level of the republic, are composed of a "Russified" cadre in an alien ethnic sea. Local government is the central government on the local level where conflicts of interest are fought out in a shared lingo such as that of the Five-Year Plans. In Albania, the relationship of the national level to the local one is quite different. Local leaders function on the assumption that they are part of an ethnic pantheon more than they are part of a chain of command. According to Hoxha, central party directives are often scarcely even noticed.[14]

Yet another important difference lies in how culture is organized. The Soviet Union presents its elite culture as the embodiment of the national culture, whereas Albania, despite having the capacity to do so, presents folk culture as its national culture as the discussion of gnosis makes clear.

Differences between the Soviet Union and Albania exist as well in the organization of religion. Whereas the Soviet Union has relied for most periods on religious hierarchies as a part of rule, officially so in any case after 1943, Albania has not. It is safer for Albania to have a multiplicity of ethnic and religious communities, each with their "museum city," than to have a single hierarchic one, which would a potential rival to the leader.[15] There is, thus, no Russian or Soviet equivalent to these museum cities, which are not capitals such as Moscow, nor shrine towns such as Kazan, nor simply provincial capitals such as Kiev.[16]

Museum cities, rather, are ethnic cultural centers whose collective memory is organized by the regime as a part of the hegemony. There are three Albanian museum cities: Gjirokastër, Berat, and Krujë. In contrast to these cities are others one could term simply important cities because much of the present regime comes from them.[17] Soviet hegemony also uses museums, but most of these are located in Moscow and Leningrad.

Although Stalinism was espoused by both regimes for many years, the practices that followed from it were quite different in each country. If Hoxha espoused "orthodox" Stalinism, his practices to the Soviets, at least, included numerous "deviations." These deviations included a decentralized system of production based on the nature of the locality and of the factory in contrast to the Soviet version's emphasis on maximum centralization, lowering the consumption of bureaucrats and raising that of workers and peasants, and tolerance of the inadequate production and inefficiency of the agricultural sector. Although Albania under Hoxha was not drifting back toward "Titoism," it, along with Yugoslavia and other socialist states with a tribal-ethnic hegemony, was aspiring to a different model of socialism, anarchist Marxism, a model that tended in practice to place greater weight on local self-sufficiency than did its Soviet counterpart.[18]

As the comments about the secret police suggest, this anarchism correlates with a high level of institutional factionalism, including party factionalism. Although factions have always existed in the Communist party of the Soviet Union, they have not been one of its defining features. Service to the party, seniority, or even simply credentials impose their contours on party life. In Albania, this appears to be less so. One rises in the party as in the police through unquestioning service to one's patron and to his faction. For example, Ramiz Alia, the contemporary leader, rose under Hoxha's patronage. In doing so, he played a role in 1981 in the elimination of Mehmet Shehu and his faction, which included the minister of the interior Hazbiu, the foreign affairs minister, the minister of health and the director of the party's ideological school in Tiranë, and other party members of long standing. During this incredible power play, Alia and Hoxha accused Shehu and his faction of being foreign agents.[19] Although this is not unknown in the Soviet Union, the Russian leadership would be more restrained in eliminating party members of thirty years standing for mere personal gain, which was what this really was.[20] Law and public opinion would play a role and some of the worst features of factionalism would be thereby abated, people would recant and be rehabilitated. By contrast, in Albania, standing in someone's way could very well be fatal.

Politics in both systems is influenced by expatriates, however, the role that expatriates play is not the same. Although it is true that Russians live, in a sense, in their country even while abroad, Albanians abroad have almost created their country's modern culture. For example, while abroad Bishop Fan Noli made a major contribution to the development of the literary language through his translations. When he returned to become the ruler of Albania, he accomplished little of comparable importance. The contrast might be to Lenin.[21]

Albania and the Soviet Union have quite different legal systems. The common view that Albanian law is inspired by Soviet law seems misplaced, the issue of the Albanian "Unwritten Law" aside. The Constitutions of 1946 and 1950 ushered in a system based on a political concentration of power that allowed for no opposition. Although most writers attribute this to Stalin, it can be better seen as a continuation of the system of King Zog. In the Soviet Union, even under Stalin, opposition in theory did exist. In Albania in the period of King Zog and thereafter, it did not.

Of course, although the application of law may have varied by period and according to the issue involved, what strikes the eye is the degree of continuity. If one compares the Penal Code of 1952 to the 1928 one, what stands out is not so much change—as from one hegemony to another—as growth of expectation of control on the part of a similar type of state, a trend well in place at least from the 1920's. In 1952, for example, the state demanded control over the estates of people who died intestate, whereas in 1928, such estates were passed on to random collateral relatives. Other examples might be drawn from marriage law, landownership law, child custody law and much else that relates to gender issues.[22]

It appears that although countries such as Albania and the Soviet Union may share a smattering of features, their similarities do not go beyond that. The dominant paradigm that finds Russia and Albania to be "communist" thus does not illuminate very much.[23]

Modern Albania, 1878–1990: A Political Economy Interpretation

Commonly, the beginning of modern history is made to coincide with the date of political independence; in a political economy interpretation, it begins with the political response of a ruling class to the spread of market capitalism, or more precisely, capitalism on a national level, the two events actually being quite unrelated. Here, the logical point of departure for a political economy interpretation is 1878.

From 1878, historians note the rise of liberalism and market capitalism in what had been a largely precapitalist society disposed to communalist political thought. Before 1878, the existing capitalism was the local merchant capitalism of the major cities and of the coast. As this local capitalism coalesced with an increasingly powerful international capitalism and as the landlord class became oriented to the production of crops for export, the country became an example of the elite consumerist approach to modern capitalist development discussed in the previous section.[24]

In 1878, among the landlord classes dominant in the central and southern parts of the country, a split appeared, revealing the initial impact of the new capitalism. The largest landlords, the de facto local authority, retained a desire to hold onto their privileged position in the Ottoman empire. The smaller holders wanted to make a break. The latter, the liberals, resented the high taxes of the empire, the low profits possible to them, and the inadequate access to capital. The former—the dominant element—were content to retain the empire and along with it their consumerism.

Thus, in 1878, for liberals to seek independence and to launch the nationalist movement that they did was distinctly premature. On the one hand, the Ottomans were determined to hold onto Albania, and, on the other hand, the liberals were scarcely in a position to mount a real political challenge isolated as they were from the mass of society because of their class position. Yet, ironically, in this period, nationalism was already at a fever pitch.

Nonetheless, in that year, a handful of liberals founded the League of Prizren, the first modern nationalist organization. The league lasted three years, which was—given the times—quite an achievement. Under the leadership of Abdul Frasheri, the league effectively blurred the differences among its dominant elements, permitting the country to speak with one voice on such matters as political autonomy within the Ottoman empire and on the use of the Albanian language in the schools. Such cooperation and coordination serves even today as an example.

The year 1878 was, however, a year of crisis for national aspirations. Serbia and Greece backed by Russia sought to take pieces of Albanian territory. For the ruling class, this was a perilous moment. War would be very risky, yet a failure to act given the nationalist sentiment could result in their being swept aside. Fortunately for them these initiatives were opposed by the Great Powers and came to naught. Still, all was not well. The Great Powers could not be counted on to be guarantors of Albanian territorial integrity. In fact, international consensuses reached by them on the whole led to more loss of territory, and such losses, if anything, fueled popular nationalism making the position of the local ruling classes less secure.

In 1880, the Great Powers pressured the Ottomans to crush the nationalists involved in the League of Prizren. A number of prominent Albanians favored the move as well. The Ottomans duly invaded the country and imprisoned some of the best-known nationalists. But it was too late; nationalism continued and grew. In 1885, nationalist pressure forced the Ottomans to release their prisoners and suspend their efforts to interfere in the administration of the North.[25]

The intervention did have one lasting effect. Thenceforth, over the next century a local ruling class unable to head off popular protests turned to the outside for help. This, in time, led to a number of alliances with the Great Powers in which the ruling class allowed itself to be a satellite or a colony if it could stay in power. For example, in 1883 as in 1880, the local rulers once again asked the Ottomans to put down a rebellion. This time it took them two years to do so, and it cost them in lives.

In the Greco-Ottoman War of 1897, the Albanian rulers supported the Ottomans, fearing an Ottoman loss would lead to further loss of territory, possibly to an expansion by the Macedonians.

In 1900, an influential figure emerged on the scene, Ismail Qemali of Vlora. Qemali became the leading representative of the nationalist intelligentsia. Caught between rich and poor, he called for the struggle being waged to be lawful.[26]

In 1903, however, the Mirdites along with other tribes rose against the Ottoman government, demanding the return of their chieftain Prenk Bib Doda. In the same year, a tax revolt broke out in Berat. Deeper splits appeared in the ruling class. Some elements supported the tribes and the tax revolt, others felt that these struggles were illegal or still premature. With the Young Turk revolt of 1908, more of the Albanian elite swung toward nationalism.

The gradual conversion of the middle and upper classes to nationalism was the consequence not simply of political and economic struggle but of the development of culture as well. Since the 1870s, the Franciscan seminary in Scutari supported by the Austrians taught its students in Albanian. So did a Jesuit school. In 1899, a literary society, Bashkimi, was founded in Scutari by Monsignor Preng Doçi, the abbot of Mirdita. This society produced an alphabet for the language, using a Roman script. Muslims, however, would not accept it. They demanded an Arabic or Ottoman script. At this potentially divisive juncture, the Bektashi leadership with its ties to both Christianity and Islam played a remarkable mediating role in working out a solution, contributing substantially to the development of Albanian nationalism.[27]

By 1907, military resistance to the Ottomans was taking place inside Albania. By 1911, the Porte began to negotiate directly with the national movement. By 1912, the progress of these negotiations permitted Qemali to return, to openly convene a meeting at Vlora, and to proclaim national independence.

From 1912 onward, the ruling class, pronationalist or antinationalist, had to concern itself with internal issues. Starvation and near starvation prevailed. Most of the best agricultural land of the country was in use to produce products for the world market. What the country gained from this policy was luxury goods for the rich and a lack of maize to feed the poor. To the middle class, the solution was land reform because most of the best land was owned by latifundist feudalists. But when Ismail Qemali and his compatriots proposed this solution, they found themselves opposed not only verbally but militarily by the feudalists. The conflict between liberals and nationalists, on the one hand, and feudalists, on the other, from this point was never reconcilable.

In 1913, Esat Pasha Toptani, a leader of the feudal class, rose in opposition to the new state, and upon so doing, he received the immediate backing of the Great Powers. An International Control Commission determined that the country should become a hereditary monarchy guaranteed by the six powers of Europe. The commission further determined that the appropriate candidate for the office would be Prince Wilhelm of Wied. The latter agreed after being offered various incentives and arrived to assume his duties March 7, 1914. The commission, however misjudged their man; the regency only managed to last a few weeks.

On one level, the departure of Wied made as little difference as his arrival had. On another level, however, his departure had a deeper meaning; it marked the temporary breakdown of the alliance with a Great Power. It was this breakdown that permitted liberals to make some progress. Thus, in 1920, the country became a parliamentary republic and a member of the League of Nations; its capital became Tiranë.

In the new parliament, liberals tended to belong to the Popular party; feudalists tended to belong to the Progressive party. The Popular party was headed by Fan Noli. Curiously, however, the Popular party included in its ranks Ahmet Zog, a tribal feudalist and Xhafer Ypi, a future Fascist. The Progressive party was headed by the feudalist landlord Shevqet Vërlaci.[28]

In 1924, a popular uprising brought Fan Noli to power. This was the highpoint of liberalism; feudalism soon made a comeback and Noli's program, for example, his land reform, like Qemali's before him, was rebuffed. As with previous liberals, Noli and his supporters feared the masses more than they feared the feudalists, a fear that left them paralyzed between talk and action. It was only the feudalists who knew what their real position was, and it was they, who, in any case, still had the ear of international capitalism.

The fall of Noli in December 1924 brought Ahmet Zog to power. He ruled from 1925 until 1939. Standard accounts characterize the period 1925–28 as republican and after 1928 as monarchical, but as political economy shows, these were simply the surface forms of a liberal age typified by one-class rule. Who then was Ahmet Zog? How could he garner the support he did to push the liberal age back toward feudalism? Some writers note his extraordinary personal charm. Not only was his return in 1925 financed by the Anglo-American, Anglo-Persian, and Standard Oil Companies but he was popular on a mass level as well.

Ahmed Zog was the son of Djemal Zogu, a tribal chief of the Mati tribe, and of Sadije Toptani, daughter of the ruling family of central Albania. The family alliance represented by his parents' marriage cemented two significant parts of the country. His mother's influence, however, was most apparent on the son, his father having died in 1901 while he was still a youth. One account portrays the mother as a brilliant, strong-willed woman able to lead troops on horseback, sole leader of her deceased husband's clan for thirty-four years. Her death in 1935 devastated her son; he built for her a mausoleum guarded day and night.[29]

These vignettes are, of course, from an official version of family life, but they show an individual authentically rooted in the life of the country. His principal rival, Fan Noli, may have had intellectual luster, but as a Christian and as a Harvard graduate he always had to overcome the image of a foreigner.

When Zog came to power, he pursued policies favorable to business and to development, widening in the process the base of the ruling class by introducing more of the urban commercial classes. By 1926, deeply overspent, Zog turned to Fascist Italy to borrow money and signed the Tirana Pact. In 1928, he enacted a new law code to replace the Ottoman Mecelle. To allay the fear of the more traditional feudalists, he limited the growth of the political arena, assuming the right to appoint one-third of the members of the Senate and to exercise veto powers over the Commons. Among his other acts were assassinations of various liberal politicians at home and abroad.

In June 1931, to fend off his continuing deficits, he once again borrowed money from Mussolini. One year later, he was again in difficulty. Disagreements with Mussolini in 1933 over repayments worsened his problems. Lacking alternative foreign supporters and a popular base of support at home, he temporized, keeping public opinion uninformed.

In the 1930s, industrial capitalism made a limited debut. The Italian government promoted it as a form of satellite production, that is, production presupposing the existence of finishing processes and market structures in Italy itself. Thus, Italy encouraged industrialists to produce cardboard, cement, cigarettes, soaps, and lumber products for Italian industry.[30] As Italian economic penetration progressed, however, a reaction developed. The working class and the middle class began to unite against foreign exploitation.[31]

Historical studies reveal that, as early as the middle and late 1920s, left-

wing ideas among strikers in the building and mining sectors appeared. In
1929, the first communist group was formed. As elsewhere, it had to face
problems of its actual relation to the working class, but in a remarkably
few years, given the conditions outlined above, the Korçë Group was able
to link itself to the working class through a popular front strategy that
supported workers' rights. From the mid-1930s to the end of the Liberal
Age in 1944, the radical Left dominated by the Communists increasingly
constituted a challenge to the regime. In this situation, the ruling class chose
to deepen the alliance with the Fascists and to drive the liberals and the Left
underground through persecution.

Challenge, it was noted, is something difficult for most hegemonies to
bear. For King Zog, challenge induced a rather high level of paranoia. In
this period, he would only eat his mother's cooking for fear of being poi-
soned. His food arrived in a locked box from his mother each day. His
main trips outside his castle were in her company because custom did not
condone killings where women were involved. Occasionally, he broke the
routine and took with him cavalry and his trusted Mati followers. In his
office, he was never separated from his revolver.

Zog's approach to marriage had some of the same characteristics manifested in his eating habits. After a long search among the daughters of the
lesser nobility, he eventually married a Hungarian woman of the Catholic
faith. Geraldine Apponyi, nicknamed the White Rose of Hungary, was a
natural linguist. She learned Albanian in a few months. Zog was afraid
partly on that account that she would be compromised through Italian
intrigue, so he insisted that she be waited on by her grandmother from
Hungary. His fears seem to have been well grounded because her priest, an
Italian, threatened her the denial of communion for marrying a Muslim and
possibly revealed the contents of her confessions to the Italian government.
Furthermore, Italians tried to bribe Geraldine's Hungarian cook on one
occasion and possibly assassinate her on the royal yacht on another. The
honeymoon of Ahmet and Geraldine took place in Durrës, requiring a drive
from Tiranë. According to a recent author, "a long procession of other cars
followed the royal couple in accordance with the Albanian passion for being
in at the death of such occasions." Zog, however, surprised the Albanian
ruling class. His marriage actually raised his popularity in the country,
especially after he and Geraldine made a successful visit to Vlorë in the
South where he had never been popular.[32]

In April 1939, Italy invaded; the plan was to overthrow Zog and annex
the country. The state of preparedness of the ruling class for such an eventu-
ality can be deduced from the fact that on that day, Queen Geraldine happened to be giving birth; she required a Caesarean operation and then a
way out of the country to some place where medical care would help her
recuperate. These issues totally preoccupied King Zog during these critical

moments. His plans to retreat to the mountains to engage in partisan warfare were, thus, abandoned.[33]

Zog, one might argue, bad luck apart, was typical of many of his counterparts of the Liberal Age in different countries. He, like they, attempted to introduce a civil code to diminish the influence of the clan loyalty system. He, like they, introduced schools, clinics, and other institutions. Yet this is not the whole story. An equal effort was made to hold the traditional system together despite the increasing fragmentation brought about by capitalism. Law codes in Tiranë taking liberal positions on social issues thus coexist with resolutions and pledges made on the local level to uphold the existing system. A famous study of the subject translates the texts of a number of these local resolutions and pledges made between the 1860s and the 1940s in the North.[34]

From King Zog's period comes as well the modernization of the major cities. A visitor of the period noted a Royal Court Orchestra of Tiranë playing the standard European classics, a National Museum, roads and infrastructure, the centralization of police and army and from a foreigner's point of view, the efficiency of the system; foreigners were subject to the same law as Albanians.[35]

The fall of King Zog was not necessarily what the ruling class had wanted, but given the weakness of the regime a reversion into a colonial format that involved some sacrifices was the only way for them to hold their property. Zog was an easy scapegoat. His Civil Code (1928) was too liberal for some, whereas his increasing reliance on loans created constituencies undesirable to others. In addition, Zog's attempts at administrative centralization were not popular because they involved taking power away even from his supporters. Many were upset as well at the continuing growth of nationalism and at the talk of land reform, and they blamed him for that too.[36]

Zog's fall resulted not just from the changing evaluation of him by his class but from his inability to satisfy Mussolini's concerns about the debt to Italy. As the government became dependent on the flow of Italian money, no politician was indispensable and certainly not one who had difficulty handling the debt diplomacy. Its interests threatened, the ruling class demanded nothing less than the unequivocal backing of Mussolini.[37]

Such, however, was highly unlikely. Nationalism was too powerful a force, colonialism too crude and obtrusive, loans or no loans. When, for example, Mussolini began to use Albania as a settler state, sending there the unemployed and the surplus southern population, the effect on the country was maximally disruptive. Not surprisingly, resistance to colonialism and to feudalism deepened and became even more radical. Youth emerged as a political force in this period. Obliged to choose between the Communists and the Fascists, they joined the Communists in large numbers.

In 1940, Mussolini attempted to win support by promising territorial gains in return for support in campaigns to invade Greece and Yugoslavia. The attempt failed; Albanian units of the Italian Army deserted on the battlefield in Greece. Sabotage committed by workers cut into the production of oil and chrome on which the Fascists depended.

In 1940, however, the Communists were still so divided that they could not challenge the Fascists effectively. Those in the more Muslim southern city of Korçë sought a general struggle of national liberation, while those in the more Roman Catholic northern city of Scutari favored a struggle within the context of Italian colonialism to mature further the working class's ideology. In 1941, Enver Hoxha led an anti-Fascist demonstration in Tiranë, embracing most of the strands of the communist movement. The demonstrators in Tiranë called for national independence and democracy. Shortly thereafter, Hoxha emerged as the head of the Central Committee of the party.

In the face of political opposition, even divided political opposition, the ruling class and their Italian allies began to lose their nerve. They decided to "Albanianize" their administration. The colonial option was not working; the National Liberation Front (NLF) was too powerful and too dangerous. To thwart a possible communist victory, the old landed families turned to the British and put yet another coalition of fighters in the field under the banner of anticommunism. This was the Balli Kombëtar or BK National Front.[38] In this context, the NLF began the famous phase of partisan warfare waged from the northern mountains. Eventually, numerous members of the BK and even of the Italian Army deserted to fight for the NLF. One famous group from the Italians was the Antonio Gramsci Battalion.

With the collapse of the Axis came the collapse of the traditional ruling class. Many of its prominent personalities went into exile. England and America had not come to the rescue in any meaningful way. Thus ended the Liberal Age.

Corporatism in Albania, 1944–1990

Corporatism in Albania went beyond the usual cross-class alliance common to the other countries studied in this book. It had some features of revolution. A new ruling class rose and seized power, destroying an old one in the process. Yet in both the short term and the long term, the concept of corporatism rather than revolution seems justified as the prime designation. The core feature associated with corporatism, a reorganization of an already existing hegemony, is what one finds. The tribal-ethnic character of politics and the mixed modes of production character of the economy remained intact. From private-sector capitalism allied to feudalism, the country turned to a system of state capitalism, termed *socialism,* allied to a much diminished private sector and to a somewhat camouflaged rural feudalism that the party either failed or never truly sought to uproot. As in other corporatist regimes, the peasantry lost power as its autonomy in work decisions decreased under the system of collective agriculture. Again, as with many corporatist regimes, the agreed objective among bourgeois and lower middle-class members of the party was industrial development.

In 1945, the victorious Anti-Fascist Council for National Liberation headed by Enver Hoxha introduced the measures, termed here *corporatist.* These included confiscation of foreign property, nationalization of the means of production, and taxation on wartime profiteers. This was followed by still other laws that gave the party control of the wealth of the country previously controlled by King Zog's supporters.

The policies of the Albanian Labor Party (ALP), like those of other corporatist regimes, greatly widened the previous political and economic arenas. This widening brought much new talent into the system, including large numbers of women workers, which, in turn, permitted the country to undertake the industrial development that the party wanted.[39]

Industrialization of a country requires a great deal of coercion. The English uprooted their peasantry by starving them into the factory. The Albanians did not; they offered incentives. Their approach was, however, less successful than that of the English. The peasantry held out. In his writings of the 1950s and 1960s, Hoxha increasingly showed his displeasure with the failure of economic transition, which was apparent on all levels, what with the growth of a bureaucracy made up of party hangers-on and the bourgeois tendencies of the new generation of educated youth.

But what educated youth, bourgeois or otherwise, would want to work in a factory or return to the countryside to work on a collective farm? There was no freedom or expectation of freedom; the party kept close control. Factory jobs were dead ends. Land was awarded only to heads of households and only on a use basis, not on an ownership basis. Transfer was forbidden, and even use-right was eroded as collectivization progressed. For many young people, it became obvious they would be better off in the city even in mediocre office jobs.

Thus, throughout the corporatist period, despite the aspiration of the party to have a self-sufficient economy, dependency remained the rule. The party had to ally itself to a Great Power even to survive. In the 1940s and 1950s, industrial policy reflected the dependence of the country on Yugoslavia and on the Soviet Union for its inputs. As a result, during this period, Albania emphasized its traditional and light industries. In this period came the expansion and rationalization of existing production under the aegis of the Union of Handicraft Cooperatives.

In 1961 in the third period of economic development, the regime shifted to basic industry, benefiting at that time from Chinese assistance.[40] Gradually thereafter it began to strive for economic self-sufficiency, giving it priority over supporting Soviet modernization, the traditional priority of all Council for Mutual Economic Assistance (COMECON) nations.

But as the 1960s progressed, it became clear that economic self-sufficiency would not come cheaply. It would require more sacrifices. For example, to repay the loans and other debts to China, the country had to raise taxes, and to do this, real political choices had to be made.

To the surprise of many observers, the country tightened its belt at the expense of its better-paid workers and bureaucrats, many of whose salaries were diminished. It did so as well through the introduction of large numbers of women into the work force, often at low wages.[41] And, most dramatically, it did so through purges of the military. General Balluku and his group, architects of the concept of a modern professional army, fell in this period, victims of the new politics of the budget. Hoxha had, in any case, wanted to retain the partisan tradition of every man a soldier and the party as part of the army; he feared the professionalization of the army. It gave the Soviets too much influence. The budget crisis provided him with the chance to have his way without a confrontation.[42]

Finally, the party sought to impose its belt-tightening policy on the agricultural sector, which turned out to be a misjudgment. The agricultural sector was already shrinking and suffering from a chronic labor shortage. As the 1970s began, according to one writer, the agricultural part of the work force was down to 49 percent from 74 percent in 1950. Seemingly, as collectivization spread, more peasants stopped farming. In 1950, 1.7 percent of the farmers were in cooperatives; by 1970, all those who still farmed were.

If collectivization of agriculture was not popular with the peasantry, would imposing a belt-tightening approach simply make it more unpopular? It seems so. Certainly, from as early as the late 1950s, significant opposition to the policy of collectivization was in evidence. As did the peasantry of the Soviet Union, many peasants in Albania preferred to slaughter their livestock rather than turn them over to the collective. As early as 1957, some years before collectivization reached its peak, the number of livestock had fallen below the number in existence in 1937. If the government seriously expected the peasants to pay for the industrialization through additional sacrifices, they were truly out of touch with them. Collectivization of agriculture was enough of a cross to bear. It was a negation in many ways of the personal freedom dear to the heart of the peasantry. It is not surprising that the progress of collectivization correlated with the growth of food shortages.[43]

In 1968, the party decided to strike back at its opponents, as it termed those who disagreed with its policies, and it launched a Cultural Revolution. Clearly, there was a clash between the consumerist logic of the hegemony and the developmentalist logic of the party. Some of the well-known aspects of revolution included the repoliticization and deprofessionalization of the army, noted above, the atheism campaign, and the renewed attempt to pursue the further emancipation of women. What the party intended in having a Cultural Revolution has yet to be clarified by scholars; suffice to say that certain details have become well known. For example, Albanian media sought to find and to celebrate instances of the breakdown of arranged marriages, of removals of the veil, and of women entering heavy industry.

Yet in 1968, an ethnographer in Tiranë repeated the point introduced in the preceding section that despite a generation of developmentalism, the Ghegs of northern Albania were still the largest clan grouping of Europe. On the whole, they were organized in patrilineal groupings around household units as they had been for centuries. They continued, as they had in the past, to fight wars over issues, such as family honor, and, as in the past, women could trigger these wars and even fight in them through various strategems. With the centralization of power achieved in the interwar period, the state had begun to make inroads into the marriage system with its campaigns against child brides and with the incentives it offered for youth to leave their clans, but still the traditional system remained essentially intact.[44] Did the state want the system uprooted? It is not clear. With the coming of land reform and with the formation of agricultural cooperatives, clan solidarities in any case survived, reinforced by a state now more dependent than ever on the cooperation of the local power structure.[45] Would the Cultural Revolution take cognizance of these realities?

This returns us to the question: what was the party? One view is that although the party was in theory an "open party" its important membership was, in fact, heavily drawn from one region, the South, and it was isolated from the rest of the society.

Another view is that although the leadership was not isolated, it was simply using the Cultural Revolution to buy time. The Party itself was responsible for the continuation of tribalism. Certainly, by the late 1960s even government officials recognized that centralism was stifling. But to be the bearer of bad news always has a price. By the mid-1970s, a number of officials, including even cabinet members, who were identified with liberalization and, thus, some implied criticism of existing policies, had lost their posts. They were ten years before their time. All during this period, the regime plunged on, insisting on its orthodoxies. Some fourteen thousand youth were forcibly sent to the country to aid in agriculture. A new salary law went into effect lowering, in Cambodian fashion the ratio of office workers' salaries to manual and farm labor salaries from 2.5:1 to 2:1.

Behind the scenes, Hoxha tried to limit the excesses of the structure he had created, but to little avail. Given the developmentalist outlook, the continuous need to show growth, there was a great deal of rigidity. When a contradiction arose for which there was no quick solution, for example, the relationship between manual and mental workers, the regime was stuck; the use of force was counterproductive. Given the emphasis on industry, the party could not be too selective about its allies in other sectors, such as agriculture. From Hoxha's speeches and correspondence of the 1970s come complaints about the complacent attitude in the countryside. Hoxha noted that the party cadre, the workers and the peasants, all feel they possess adequate self-knowledge. This is scarcely the case. There have been serious problems in the "correct execution of directives" as a result of sheer ignorance. On a procedural level, Hoxha discerned chronic lapses, especially in rural areas, from the democratic centralism of communism into bossism and to the acceptance of "officials" and "commanders." Hoxha also discerned instances of illegal activities by party members and of the growth of intellectual revisionism. The new local leadership, Hoxha claimed, was becoming a privileged strata, simply anxious to hold its offices. The local party offices were not distributing central party materials nor voicing any criticisms of central party directives. Evidence of this was the general failure of the local party to activate people on the village level through the people's councils although from all appearances, the local party offices were well staffed and more than able to do so. Not surprisingly, Hoxha blamed the traditional culture, lumping together failures of the party with those still persisting in the society.[46] Of course, he knew as well as anyone that the party had made alliances with the local power structure over the years, perhaps out of necessity or perhaps as a strategy of divide and rule, and the results were not pretty to behold. Traditional clan practices, which had been outlawed, persisted. For example, fathers still sometimes sold their daughters in marriage to get consumer goods. What Hoxha found particularly troubling was that these practices were engaged in even by prominent members of the party.[47]

The breakdown of the Cultural Revolution in the mid-1970s came at a difficult time for the Party. The country was secure. The demands for more consumer goods and more civil liberties began to rise, and from this point, one may date the beginning of the breakdown of the corporatist phase, hence the view of some writers that the Cultural Revolution was a last gasp, an effort simply to buy time.

To many in the 1970s, the party seemed not only clanlike and austere but old. Where had the revolution gone? Urban youth of all classes steadfastly refused to go to work in the countryside, struggling instead to express their feelings of alienation where they were in cities. The incidence of theft and of other crimes among youth rose, even among middle-class youth; factory productivity dropped.

Although there were signs of liberalization throughout the 1970s, officially at least until 1987, the country pursued corporatism. With the passing of Hoxha and the rise of Ramiz Alia in that year, policy began to change, and Albania drifted toward a new Liberal Age. Fresh policies appeared that deemphasized cooperative agriculture, linked industrial wages to a given factory's overall production, and promoted a greater openness about the flaws in the system. In 1988, another new policy led to the replacement of all officials concerned with housing, labor, and residence bureaus at least every five years because favoritism and family connections had become rampant. Responding to the criticisms of the now better-educated and slightly more affluent population, Alia acknowledged the generally shoddy nature of the consumer goods. Public-sector factories simply could no longer produce what the public wanted. By 1990, liberalism was increasingly imposing itself and the country economically was slipping more and more into the orbit of West Germany.[48]

In 1991, it was clear that even communist ideology could not survive the collapse of corporatism. As in the years before 1944, the ruling class appears today to find dependent liberalism a useful way to co-opt discontent; Communist ideology might, thus, be dispensable for a while.

Opposition Movements and Counterhegemony in Albania

In tribal-ethnic states, opposition is commonly manifest in secessionist movement or in populist movements, some organized by heterodox religious groups, some by regional or ethnic parties. Albania is closer to the populist variant. A major vehicle of opposition for much of modern history was popular nationalism. Liberals used it and so did the Communists in their various attempts to come to power.

Still, as shown in the foregoing pages, however revolutionary these movements were, they could not emancipate themselves from the prevailing hegemony. This led in time to new currents of counterhegemony, first expressed as different forms of alienation then as movements espousing democracy and Islam.

Was alienation a result of the low level of urbanization or the rising literacy? Did it arise from the situation of women or from the fact that religious groups, which were outlawed, such as the Bektashis, offered fulfillments that the party did not?

A number of writers refer to the government's supposed antiurbanism as a factor contributing to alienation. The country, they find, is underurbanized by European norms. But, is it so by the norms of tribal-ethnic societies? After all, tribal-ethnic states, being less developmentalist, tend to be more rural than states in the other hegemonies.[49]

Does widespread literacy, one of the consequences of the communist program, generate political alienation? This is possibly the case although whether it would be more true in this kind of hegemony or another remains unresolved.[50]

Does the increase in gender exploitation that accompanies development lead to more alienation? Here the evidence is mixed, as noted previously. The rise of a political movement, like the ALP, claiming to challenge the traditional ethnic and gender lines had the effect of raising women's expectations. And, certainly, development projects required more workers, not fewer. Still, commentators make clear that despite the new opportunities for women, male-female relations did not change that much. Communist family policy, with its radical pronatalism, serves as a stark reminder of that. Thus, the vast majority of women at work lived in one world; on returning home, they continued as before to live in quite another one. A number of women in this period, however, managed to achieve high positions. Those inspired by this fact were likely to have supported the regime. The point so often made in commentary literature on how women got such jobs through their families scarcely seems germane. How else could one get a job?[51]

Finally, since the late nineteenth century, the Bektashis, a heterodox religious community open to men and women, have posed for various regimes a somewhat organized populist-style challenge. Initially, the Bektashis played an important role in the rise of secular culture, education, and nationalism. At that point, they were a thorn in the side of the feudalists. Later, they were allies of the Communists in the fight against fascism. By virtue of their cross-cutting male-female, Muslim-Christian memberships and their influence in the South among the Tosks, however, they became a rival for the Communists.

When King Zog came to power, he was backed by a dominantly Sunni landlord class. Soon, he found himself offended by the Bektashi doctrine of imbibing alcohol, by the openness of the Bektashis to Christian-Muslim intermarriage and to the changing of names. During the fascist period, Zog tried to place the Bektashi hierarchy under the aegis of the Sunnis as a way to gain control of them. In the 1945 Constitution, the communist government gave a status to the Sunnis that was superior to that of the Bektashis. In 1947, in violent but obscure circumstances, the communist regime assassinated, or contrived to have assassinated, the Bektashi leadership in Tiranë, their erstwhile allies, events all the more baffling because Enver Hoxha, the leader of the Communists, came from a family that was Bektashi.[52] In 1967, the Bektashi challenge seemingly came to an end when the regime deported the Bektashi leaders along with other religious leaders. Today, the Bektashi leadership is centered in the United States.[53]

Thus, after 1967 while there was still no organization to challenge the hegemony, democratic sentiment, which the Bektashis and other liberals had fostered, remained. Events suggest, in fact, that democratic sentiment grew, gradually becoming a democratic movement.

As a last gasp to stem the tide, the regime seems to have turned to the Cultural Revolution and to the Atheism Campaign. It made sense to promote atheism and to try to turn religious practice once and for all into folklore, something, in other words, that the state could regulate. It would be a way of dealing with the fact that the country was 70 percent Muslim and that increasing alienation might lead to a resurgence of Islamic ideology. Thus, after 1967, one finds counterhegemonic acts mentioned in official writing as "ethnographic" details, for example, priests secretly performing masses, Sunni Muslims secretly fasting in Ramadan, secretly making pilgrimages, and secretly carrying their rosaries.[54] An article from an official paper in the early 1970s, however, had a more alarmist tone, claiming that even some party secretaries had fallen to religion and concluding that the power of religion was still underestimated. An article in 1976 claimed that the acts of private devotion each year were on the rise; 96 percent of marriages, this same article asserted, came from within the same religion, a very sharp rise in communal solidarity over that prevailing at the time of King Zog.[55] Perhaps, the party was right; the pressure for economic liberalism brought with it a renewal of religion.

In a more general sense, democratic political movements are dangerous for a hegemony, which has no space for rule by law or for a civil society. What can such a hegemony do if a cultural revolution fails to distract its opponents? The situation is not a simple one. Indeed, it is likely that once a leader in this type of hegemony caves in to the demand for civil rights as actually occurred in Yugoslavia, violence might occur among the ensemble of groups on the scene. Albania's way out appears to be through dependency.

The current situation in postcommunist, liberal Albania of the early 1990s seems to be a completion of the political economy cycle. Liberal and feudal elements are once again ascendant; it is too early for opposition to surface.

The Organization of Culture in Albania

The organization of culture in tribal–ethnic states rests on the maintenance of gnosis. In Albania, specialists from the nineteenth century until today refer to this gnosis as Albanology. In this section I take up the identity of Albanology in Albania, how it evolved, producing the intellectuals who managed the culture first in the nineteenth century and then later in the communist period.[56]

The first modern use of gnosis appeared in the Alphabet Question.[57]

This controversy which was dangerous for the ruling class to resolve, was dangerous even to explore, for it pitted a Catholic North centered in Scutari against a Muslim South centered in Korçë, Gjirokastër and Vlorë. The Scutari Albanians sought a Roman alphabet that would link the country to Western Europe, whereas the southerners sought an Arabic or Ottoman alphabet that would link it to the Islamic world. For many years, this matter, as one would expect, was left unresolved. In the famous 1909 gathering at Monastir, the participants, who reflected all these contradictions, broke with tradition and decided that the outcome of their proceedings had to be a unified alphabet, that the country could not progress without one. And at that meeting, the Bektashis "broke rank" and voted with the Christians for a Latin alphabet.[58]

The agreement on the alphabet brought to the surface still other problems, which these intellectuals doubtless foresaw would give them ample opportunity to choose between resolving or not resolving. Should a language with an agreed upon alphabet also have a standardized grammar and set of literary models? In other countries, such as Italy, the unification of the country gave state bureaucrats a chance to impose an essentially new language, but in the case at hand, there was the question of whether it would be in the interests of the state to promote one, thereby turning language into a positive science accessible to everyone. As early as the 1920s, the government experimented with the possibility of trying to use the Elbasan dialect of Central Albania as an administrative language. But the Elbasan dialect could not match the attraction felt for the Tosk of Bishop Fan Noli or for the Gheg by its speakers.[59]

For those seeking to promote the development of a national language policy, the times were not propitious. In the 1920s and for many years thereafter, the ruler, King Zog, and much of his retinue remained Gheg speakers while the majority of the ruling class, who were southern were Tosk-speaking. In the long-run, the power of the Tosks would lead to their predominance, but until the 1940s, the incumbency of King Zog and the importance of the relationship with the Axis through him created what developmentalists regarded as a stalemate in the development of language policy. Put in other terms, gnosis remained the form of control. Inappropriate developmentalism could tear the hegemony apart.

Development, that is, standardization or simplification, would in any case be difficult. As with other tribal languages, Albanian has limited word-stock with numerous meanings associated with each word. As noted in a recent article, there is an unusually powerful vocabulary for wild animals, beasts, and livestock, animals and people all closely linked, and the more the language is tied to poetry as in the Gheg dialect, the more this is the case.[60] Given these features of the language, a standardization or modernization program as proposed by various linguists supporting development would also be an assault on the social structure. Would not developers naturally choose the most modern meanings of words? What then would happen to the rest—the phrases associated with spirits, exorcism, impotence, evil eyes, virtuous rocks, herbs, and heros? If female *Isoglosses* were displaced and, for example, the word *enderre* (dream) was "modernized" would not one lose the role of women as dream interpreters that comes to mind with this word? If the word *dhe* (and) can also mean "that, thence, still, nearby," and so on, what is the point of eliminating these secondary possibilities? Is the goal really to create universal audiences? Would the state benefit from that decision?[61]

In Elbasan in the later years of the Liberal Age, Alexsandër Xhuvani (1880–1961) emerged as the major figure in Albanian Albanology. Xhuvani was a grammarian; he also wrote occasional essays on the authenticity and the purity of language. Just as development demanded a unified alphabet for the language so it would demand, he believed, a grammar. A biographer commenting on Xhuvani's career notes that he was remembered by his contemporaries for espousing "many ideologies but only a few loyalties," that his career could be contrasted with that of the literary figure, Fan Noli, who preferred to freely choose his loyalties even if this meant a life in exile. Through a long life, Xhuvani held many important positions, among them director of the Elbasan Training College for Teachers; later he was an official in the ministry of education where he was known for his sympathies to the Axis. Nonetheless, after 1944 Xhuvani joined the Revolution and was elected to the People's Convention in 1950.[62]

With the rise of Xhuvani and a few other such figures, gnosis was forced to coexist for a period with developmentalism. Pragmatic "resolutions" began to come more quickly. Thus, in 1945, the Communists declared Tosk to be the national language. A school grammar appeared in 1949, emphasizing Tosk usages; in 1954, came the regime's dictionary, again emphasizing Tosk. Naturally, the newspapers and the radio of Tiranë followed suit as did the government bureaucracy. This marked a change in two senses. In King Zog's period, the bureaucracy was solidly Gheg-speaking, and a few years later after the Revolution, it was 90 percent Tosk-speaking. More importantly, in King Zog's period, the strategy of the hegemony was to leave the matter of dialect unresolved, to accept the idea of a degree of indeterminancy in language. Now, for awhile at least, this had changed.[63]

In 1957, with the opening of the university in Tiranë, the question of linguistic and literary policies arose once again with the choice of professors and programs. Here, too, Tosk dominance was quite obvious. Given that fact, it was only a matter of time before the academic establishment would announce "unification" of the language. This took place in 1972. Shortly thereafter, however, it became apparent that the new language policy was not working. Diglossia was on the rise, especially in the North. This raised many questions. Was it in the interest of the state to become a Tosk state? Was there no other way to pursue development than to keep on "resolving" problems? Could not the state eventually be challenged from within by an ungrateful class of Tosk-speakers?[64] From the 1970s, it was clear, in any case, that the North felt the pinch of development the most.[65]

Before turning to consider the contemporary figures who have inherited these problems, it is helpful to widen the discussion of cultural hegemony and consider the "technical intellectuals," the somewhat larger group of poets and figures in other fields, and so on, whose writings and creative output reinforced the status quo. If, in the first liberal period, splits in the ruling class gave unusual power to the northern poets, in the communist period, this trend reversed with, most of the writers coming from the South and from a range of cultural fields that continued to widen as time passed.

A celebrated poet of the early liberal period was Gjerj Fishta (1871–1940). From a village background near Shkodër, Fishta grew up to be a Franciscan priest and founder of the Illyrian Secondary School of Shkodër, the first school to teach all subjects in Albanian, and to be as well the author of *Lahuta e Malcís* (Shkodër: Shtypshkroja Franciskane, 1923), a famous epic poem of massive proportions on nineteenth Albanian history.[66] In later years, Fishta was also a leading participant in the Alphabet Question.

Two figures of the last generation of liberalism for whom Shkodër was famous were first, the writer Luigj Gurakuqi (1879–1925), a political associate of Fan Noli, and second, Ernest Koliqi (1903–1975), a poet and leading literary figure of the 1930s and 1940s and in later years a scholar renowned for his work on the epic. Koliqi served the Fascist Grand Council in Tiranë and when it collapsed, fled to Italy, where he continued to teach for several decades. Among his students in later years was the leading Gheg poet of our times, Martin Camaj.

In the more contemporary generation, one finds some decline. The last Scutari poet noted in the commentaries, Migjeni (1911–1938), had actually died before the Communists came to power. He is remembered as the first to break with romanticism and to take up social themes, a precursor of socialist realism. After Migjeni, there seems to have been a few party officials, for example, Mehmet Shehu, the military hero of the Resistance, and Fadil Paçrami (1922–), a dramatist and one-time president of the People's Assembly.

The best-known intellectuals from the town of Elbasan in central Albania came from the more recent period; several had careers linked to the rise of the Communists. The poet, Qemal Stafa (1912–1942), known in literary circles as an imitator of the poetry of Migjeni, was also the founder of the Communist Youth movement. Ali Abdihoxha (1923–) wrote novels that reflected his participation in the Resistance; Dhimitër Shuteriqi (1915-) emerged as a major literary critic and theoretician of the party. More recently still, emerged Elena Kadare (1943-), the first female novelist and a leading feminist voice. She married the novelist Ismail Kadare.

For the period after 1930, the most influential cities, Tiranë excepted, were those in the South, especially Korçë, the center of the development of the ALP. From this period, the majority of well-known writers from Korçë were the new men and women who rose with the Resistance. The most famous of these writers was the poet Dritëro Agolli (1931-), author of the extraordinarily popular poem *Mother Albania;* others made their names through service in Tiranë after independence. Such figures include Kiço Blushi (1943-), a prose and film scriptwriter employed in later years by the New Albania Film Studios; the feminist poet Natashia Lako (1948-), who works for the same studio; Zhuljana G. Jorganxhi (1946-), a poetess and journalist who rose to be a literary editor of Albanian Radio and Television after 1975; and Skënder Drini, a writer who later became a teacher.

The city of Vlorë, although in the South, has suffered a relative decline since the era of Ismail Qemali before World War I, whereas Gjirokastër, next to Korçë, has been the major feeder city of the cadre of the Revolution. In addition, it has a longer history in terms of cultural development.

Gjirokastër was the home of Naim Frashëri (1846–1900), an architect of the Albanian language, an author of more than fifteen books on cultural subjects, and a leader of the nationalist movement. From Gjirokastër came Eqrem Çabej (1908–1981), a German-educated linguist, lexicographer, and Albanologist, and Pano Çuka (fl. 1925), a poet and prose writer who represented the bridge between Albanian and Greek culture.

With the rise of the generation of the Revolution came a group of figures with important national reputations: Vedat Kokona (1913-), a writer, a translator of French literature, and a professor at the University of Tiranë. Dalan Shapllo (1928-), a literary critic and editor of the literary magazine *Nentori* (November) in Tiranë, and Zihni Sako (1912–1981), a prose writer and the director of the Folklore Institute until his retirement in 1979.

The capital city of Tiranë achieves its importance during the communist period. Before that point, two writers of traditional Islamic books are noted. Since the rise of the ALP, the city became the center of the control of culture. Many of its personnel migrated there from the politically privileged southern towns, including Kolë Jakova (1916-), a partisan and an ideologue who became the director of the People's Theater; Agim Cerga (1935-), a writer known for his concern with youth problems and, more recently, the literary secretary of the Union of Writers and Artists; Jorgo Bulo, a literary critic who was appointed head of the section of Prerevolutionary Literature at the Institute of Linguistics and Literature of the Academy of Sciences of

Tiranë; Koço Bihiku (1927–), a literary critic and the head of the section for Postrevolutionary Literature at the same institute and author of the *History of Albanian Literature* (1980).

For those born and raised in Tiranë in the communist period, access to the outside world afforded by their location also made some important careers. For example, Diana Çuli, a prose writer, became a senior employee of *Les Lettres Albanaises,* the main link to Western European culture. Hasan Petrela (b. 1927–), a writer, made a career in journalism working for *Zëri i Popullit* (The People's Voice) and became its correspondent in China.

When reflecting on this tableau of poets and prose writers in terms of the objectives of the state, one must recall that what was wanted was not so much their work as a certain effect within the society that their work would evoke. Looked at in these terms, King Zog, who wanted to preserve the status quo, had more intellectuals than did the Communists with their continuous developmentalism.[67]

The application of gnosis in archeology and ethnography was in the forefront of the regime's concern in this period. Archeology did not have a long or distinguished history before the 1940s. According to Muzafer Korkuti, a one-time director of the Center of Archeological Research before 1948, there was not even a specialized institution in the country. During 1948, however, the Ethno-Archeological Museum opened and followed in 1976 by a Center of Archeological Research attached to the Academy of Sciences.[68]

In the years between 1948 and 1976, the government funded numerous archeological missions. The goal of these missions was to establish what historical studies alone could not or would not establish about the origins and early development of the country and most specifically about "Illyrian culture," the putative basis of the modern culture and indeed of all-Albanian culture from Greco-Roman antiquity to the present. Archeologists succeeded in their work. From the 1970s, it thus was possible to make an ethnogenetic interpretation across the ages. This was useful. History had become too confining. In addition, it emphasized other countries coming to Albania and not what Albanians themselves were doing. Archeology could destabilize history and vice versa.

Archeology had other advantages as well. It was expensive; the patron, thus, had a real say. Consequently, the state, like so many others, seemed more than eager to use it to get away from history.[69]

Albanologists also turned to the fields that make up ethnography— folklore, music, art, and dance—whose works were valuable for social engineeering and for offsetting the claims of history. Their study had begun in the nineteenth century, but it was from the contemporary perspective then simply a pastime. In the communist period, ethnography became useful; its study grew more rigorous.

According to an ethnographer who was in Tiranë, during this period of development, by 1960, the cumulation of work by folklorists and ethnographers over the twentieth century justified the creation of an Institute of Folklore. By 1972, the year of the first national conference on folklore, this institute had collected some ten thousand folk songs and published some forty works on folklore.[70]

In 1976, an example of the continuing use of gnosis emerges in the report of an ethnographer critical of the positivist claim of the existence of an ethnographic polarity between the Ghegs and the Tosks. This way of framing the issue is not adequate, he insisted. Both of these two larger groupings are composed of dozens of smaller ones. As ethnographic research progesses, this is becoming clearer and clearer. The implication of this article, it seems, was that the door was open to new types of initiatives from above. A policymaker aided by an ethnographer would never be facing immutable social groups.[71]

Dance, a party writer had once proclaimed, is a living source of creativity; it is annunciatory and not archaic as some folklorists and musicologists believe. But which dance is annunciatory and from what point of view? A leading figure in the Marxist-Leninist generation of gnosis, Zihni Sako, tackled this question and came to the following conclusion. There are, he claimed, two distinct approaches to folklore: the socialist one, which seeks to discern the "genuine popular culture at the core of folklore," and the bourgeois, or Nazi one, which ignores this in favor of a tranquil, conflict-free, infantile image.[72] Herein lay a resolution porous enough to leave the question essentially unresolved, awaiting the next occasion for intellectual intervention.

Cultural hegemony in Albania, as in other countries, is promoted through the mass media and the educational system. In Albania, as in many other tribal-ethnic states, rulers have long taken the view that these mediums should reflect official thought. Since the turn of the twentieth century, when newspapers became important, they have often exercised the power of censorship with a heavy hand to ensure their loyalty.[73] In more recent years, radio and television have experienced the same fate. Advances in archeology, outstanding folk cultural performances, poetry, and music are all used as propaganda. Pedagogy, however, has been more of a problem area. Can one separate people from their milieus, make them competent in positivist sciences and avoid creating a new class?[74]

History Writing in Albania

Historians in Albania have composed genealogical accounts of different rulers. They have also written diplomatic history. Some of their important work of a more specifically positivist nature has been carried out, however, by émigré scholars in countries that encourage that sort of scholarship. In recent years, studies of local history have appeared, suggesting the influence of the Annales school.[75]

The contribution of history to the gnosis is circumscribed by the rather ambivalent attitude toward positivism, the worldview on which historians have traditionally depended the most. Although history offers a hegemony some degree of certainty, in doing so, it imposes some strains on the gnosis by saddling it with a truth to uphold and by challenging the status of the epic and, more generally, of the role of myth, memory, and, by implication, of orality. Not surprisingly, history has been most successful where it deals with externalities such as foreign relations or where it accommodates myth as in genealogy.

The turn to Marxism does not seem to alter the status of history. A class analysis approach to history could be as threatening to a tribal-ethnic polity as the more traditional narrative. Thus, it is not encouraged. To accommodate the hegemony, historians in recent years turn to a Stalinist "history of peoples" shorn of its larger positivist underpinnings, ethnogenesis replacing diffusionism, modernity emerging from a Germanic mode of production.[76]

A major theme in historiography from the nineteenth century to the present day has been that of the hero, for example, Skanderbeg. The explanation for this selection seems clear enough: although many kinds of historical study are detrimental to the hegemony, genealogies of heros are not. Among the advantages for a historian to take up the subject of Skanderbeg, he would include, for example, that Skanderbeg in his own life transcended the Christian-Muslim division as the party itself does and that Skanderbeg, like Enver Hoxha, was anti-imperialist.[77] Finally, he would not challenge the place of epic literature.

Historical scholarship without positivism is difficult. Fortunately, the country had poets who dabbled in history and scholars working in it abroad.[78] In the late nineteenth century, the most famous Albanian historian apart from Fishta was the poet Naim Frashëri (1846–1900). Among Frashëri's poems were some that adopted historical themes, such as *Skenderbeg* (1899), and some that formed pageantries based on the *Qur'an* and the *Gospel*.[79] As the twentieth century arrived, there was still little opportunity to do original research; the country continued to lack an archive policy. Thus, one finds the two major pieces of historical scholarship written by Albanians—Fan Noli's study of *George Castrioti Skanderbeg* (New York: International Universities Press, 1947, microfilm) and Athanase Gegaj's study of the Turkish invasion of Albania, *Albanie et l'invasion Turque au XVe siècle* (Louvain: Bureaux du recueil, bibliothèque de l'université, 1937) —basically were works written abroad. The main developments in the country were the publication of textbooks and the opening of the National Museum in Tiranë (1922).[80] Historical study, however, had no institutional foundation of any consequence before the communist period. Nazi Germany had maintained an Institute for Sciences and Arts briefly, as had the Italians, but it is with the creation of the Institute of Sciences in 1947 by the ALP that one can speak of an institution that at least included the concerns of historians.[81]

This institute undertook the organization of the National Archives, the opening of a wing of the National Library to be devoted to Albanology, the creation of a History and Linguistic Institute, and the writing of a national history. Progress was slow. The study of ethnography remained a major part of the work of the new Institute as it had of the old one. During the early years, the staff devoted its attention more to collecting objects, training functionaries in museum work, and carrying out planning studies than to history per se. In 1960, with the opening of the Institute of Folklore, the historians were freed for other work.

In 1957, when the State University of Tiranë opened, one of its seven departments was History and Philology. The chairman and main influence of this department, A. Kostallari, was, however, one of the country's leading specialists on "Standard Albanian" more than he was a historian.[82]

In the 1960s, Franco Prendi emerged as the leading figure in the new field of Illyrian studies, a field comprising the Bronze and Iron ages. Some of Prendi's conclusions—already presented in this chapter—struck scholars at the time as surprising. If, as Prendi claimed, the origins of the country was the Illyrian Coast noted in Greek writing, then it had an autonomous existence during the Classical Age of Greece, making the modern inhabitants heirs to glories far older than those of Skanderbeg, the acknowledged point of departure for Albanology in the 1960s.

By the 1980s, history writing does not appear to have gained much ground; the major project which the historians set themselves was to produce a series of more up-to-date textbooks.[83] What can one learn from these efforts? Although textbooks on the whole are not generally the easiest of books to dissect, given the homogenizing and simplifying that goes with the genre, one such book that emerges in this period does permit some commentary. It is the *History of Albania* by Pollo and Puto noted above. Written in cooperation with the Historical Institute of the Science Academy, this work appears to be trying to open the door for the country's move toward liberalism and for its hoped-for ties to the West. In different eras, the authors claim, Albanian civilization was a part of Western civilization while having its own identity. Thus, there was a Golden Age, a decline and a rebirth through interaction with the modern West. Skanderbeg is no longer a folk hero embodying justice but a Renaissance warrior. Scanderbeg's mixed religious identity, the theme of such fascination for Fan Noli in the Liberal Age and for many writers later in the Corporatist period, is no longer of interest. By the 1980's, the Ottoman period in which Skanderbeg lived, could be termed the post-Renaissance period of decline, a designation seemingly drawn from Italian history. Here ethnogenesis, once conceived as a way to free the country from the West, is made to conform to modernization theory to tie it to the West. Other mutations are also apparent. The authors raise the generally closed subject of Albanians whose lives were spent abroad, even noting the influence of Italy and Italian-Albanians on modern Albania. The authors' choice of illustrations for their text—two churches in the Berat area—could almost be construed as a return to the communalism of the first liberal phase. The striking feature of this work like others commented on in this chapter is its intellectual porousness. Here, even a history book is written so as to be rewritten.

In this chapter, I presented modern Albanian history, 1878 to the present, as the history of a tribal-ethnic state. This was a revisionist interpretation of the subject. The main arguments were that the hegemonic culture, Albanology, is a form of gnosis not unlike that of other tribal-ethnic states, that the organization of culture in countries, such as this one, reflects the preeminence of anarchism as a worldview.

History writing plays a limited role either as a consequence of the deployment of gnosis or as a precondition for its deployment. Whichever the case, the relatively marginal position of historical thought contributes to the maintenance of the dominant paradigm, which assumes that such countries do not have much of a history.

Albania's specificity as a tribal-ethnic state emerges from the form of popular response to this hegemony. Since the nineteenth century, the masses perceived—for diverse reasons—their interests to entail an independent country. This made the country among the most nationalistic in the world. A series of regimes from the nineteenth century onward, culminating in King Zog, each of which failed to maintain independence, opened the door to more and more radical forms of nationalism, and, finally, to the ALP. After 1944, The ALP's advocacy of industrial development met with widespread satisfaction for some time. In recent years, following problems of integrating developmentalism into the logic of the system counterhegemony has been renewed.

In most tribal-ethnic states, in contrast to Albania, the mass population, for better or worse, has not perceived a threat to the state or even a threat to one of its ethnic components as a threat to the whole, which would demand action. In crisis situations, logic dictated to these masses, here by way of contrast, that resistance should take the form of an ethnic secession movement or of a movement based on religion. The case of the Belgian Congo/Zaire is presented in the next chapter as a representative of this larger group.

8

The "Tribal-Ethnic Road" in Africa

Belgian Congo/Zaire, 1885–1990

The historical development of the Belgian Congo/Zaire is an African example of the tribal-ethnic hegemony. Taken in conjunction with chapter 7, this chapter is intended as a challenge to the scholarly dichotomizing of Europe and Africa.[1]

In the first part of the chapter, I situate this interpretation of the Belgian Congo/Zaire in relation to others. In the second, I consider the history of the Belgian Congo/Zaire from a political-economy perspective. In the third, I discuss the organization of culture as a part of that political economy; and in the fourth, I examine history writing as a part of that organization of culture.

The liberal school interprets the subject of modern history as a progression from the Free State (1885–1908), to the Belgian Congo (1908–60), to the Republic of the Congo (1960–64), to the Democratic Republic of the Congo (1964–71) and, finally, to the Republic of Zaire (1971–).

According to political economy, modern history begins with the spread of capitalism and with the political resolution that followed from it, a phase of liberal hegemony—or one-class rule (1885–1944)—in which the dominant elements, capitalists and noncapitalists working together, built a system based on tribal and ethnic divisions. The Congo thus arose through class collusionism, locals and foreigners. (In a few countries, this never worked out and the state was formed as in the case of the United States and Libya through settlerization).[2] With the emergence of the petty bourgeois class as a political force in the years 1945–71, modern Congolese history continues through a failed attempt at corporatism. Finally, in the period 1971–90, liberalism returns as international capitalism and the local ruling class combine to beat down the challenge of the petty bourgeoisie.

As was the case with Albania, the explanatory models that that have the most prestige in the country itself are those influenced by anarchism. Examples of well-known works include those of the anthropologist Luc de Heusch, author of *The Drunken King, or, the Origin of the State* (Bloomington: Indiana Univ. Press, 1992), or those of the philosopher V. Y. Mudimbe, author of such books as *L'Odeur du père: Essai sur des limites de la science* (Paris: Présence Africaine, 1982).[3]

As was the case with Albania, so with the Belgian Congo, contemporary scholarship paved the way for the kind of reinterpretation undertaken here with its very broad understanding of what constitutes hegemony and counterhegemony, with its theorization about lineage modes of production, and with its reconsiderations of the changing meaning of terms such as *ethnicity*.[4] It is also assisted by studies of the political opportunities afforded the different ethnic regions of the country.[5] These newer developments permit one to go beyond the more externally-oriented lines of analyses focused on colonialism, economic dependence, or the community of all African countries, permitting one to make the argument which runs through this chapter that Zairian specificity or authenticity emerges from class analysis.

Political Economy of the Belgian Congo/Zaire, 1885–1990

This section surveys the three main phases of the political economy noted in the previous section—a Liberal Age (1885–1944), a failed attempt at corporatism (1945–71), a neoliberal phase (1971–90).

In economic terms, the beginning of the Liberal Age in the nineteenth-century Congo came about from the entrance of a fairly dynamic capitalism into a largely precapitalist area, one that had in the Congo Arabs at most a fairly stagnant and regionally contained capitalism. In political terms, the beginning of the Liberal Age was marked by the formation of an alliance between Europeans, mainly Belgians, and Congolese, the latter mainly from one northern province. The two together through this alliance gradually were able to expand their joint control over a wider territory and to thus form a nation-state.[6]

In the middle of the nineteenth century, there was no single movement or regime in the Congo river valley, but several regional powers. Thus, in the 1880s, as the country was being united by capitalism, it is not surprising that alliances grew up between the Belgians and all those along the line of penetration, the Congo river basin. So it was that the dominant elements from the Mongos of Equateur Province became the principal allies of the Belgians and have remained the backbone of the ruling class until now.[7] The Belgians received their help and access to the riches of the country in return for guaranteeing support to the chiefs. Others, however, joined in among them, wealthy Bakongos from Lower Zaire and Lunda aristocrats from the southeast. The mass population of the new country was composed of the Kiswahili-speaking masses of the East and parts of the Bakongo population in the West and Southwest.

The factors that coincided in the 1880s, permitting the Congo basin to evolve toward one nation, still need elucidation. The major states of Europe, such as Germany, perceived the possible development of a Congolese state as of secondary importance for them, and they did not block it. The Belgians who came to the Congo were a skilled group of people. What they lacked in economic stature, they made up for in political know-how acquired from their experience in ruling a tribal-ethnic state, their own country, Belgium.

Belgian internal politics also played a role. In King Leopold's period, Belgium was beginning to take on some attributes of bourgeois democracy. Civil society and rule by law were more pervasive than they were earlier in the nineteenth century. This hemmed in royal authority at home, disposing the ruler to turn his energies outward into faraway schemes. In the era of King Leopold there were several such schemes, the Congo being the most important.[8]

Another factor to consider was the disposition of Belgian public opinion toward colonialism. Belgians, it seemed, demanded for themselves bourgeois liberties and social welfare at home. What King Leopold did abroad to raise the money needed to pay for these did not matter to them. Thus, only in 1908, after thirty years of "slash and burn" economy did the Belgian government under heavy international pressure come to the rescue of the low status Congolese and formally begin a colonial order, bringing to an end the era of pure rapacity.

When reflecting on the reason for the prolongation of the free state approach to building the country, one must note that it served not only Belgian interests but also those of various local chiefs. It was cheap, and this was an important factor. Belgium was too small to compete in the industrial products market, where the great profits of the era were being made. She could, however, thanks to well-developed maritime and banking institutions, compete in the area of extractive industries, industries, such as oil, rubber, copper, and ivory, an area where a market was assured if labor costs remained low. The chiefs, for their part, could guarantee a supply of cheap labor if they received a percentage of the profits, and this could be assured if the costs of maintaining the state were kept minimal.

The colonial conquest—and the evolution of state formation—went from West to East. It depended not only on alliances with major groupings in the western part of the country but on the day-to-day cooperation of many peoples along the Congo River who also became allies. Many of this latter group spoke Lingala, the most widely understood language of the river basin region.⁹ After French, Lingala became and remains today the most important language of the country.

The conquest depended as well on the construction of the railroad. By World War I, the railroad from Matadi on the Atlantic Coast extended to Leopoldville (Kinshasa). This gave the allies a base for further penetration through the Congo River basin (Cuvette). The next point of consolidation was Stanleyville, the city later renamed Kisangani. Rail transportation finally reached Bukuma and then Elizabethville, the southeastern city later renamed Lubumbashi.

Through the 1890s, the allies directed themselves against the challenge to their hegemony from the East. There, Congo Arabs, among them bands of well-armed merchants, were functioning. They might, the colonialists thought, try to expand. A propaganda initiative was called to arouse public opinion for a confrontation. To this end, the Belgians and their allies began to proclaim their attachment to the cause of antislavery and to the propagation of Christianity. This campaign seemed to succeed; one wonders how. Who would have freely done the porterage, built the railways, mined the ore, or carried out agriculture? It is difficult to imagine anyone but slaves.¹⁰

The challenge of the Congo Arabs apart, the task of state formation for the new rulers remained formidable for other reasons as well. They were divided among themselves on most issues. If, at Boma in 1885, King Leopold confidently proclaimed the birth of the Free State of the Congo (EIC), his supporters soon found that such confidence was not really appropriate. To the Europeans, it soon became clear that the local chiefs had too much power, that it was an obstacle to European profit making. One finds an immense amount of jockeying for power among all the groups on the scene. Although some local rulers, such as the son of Msiri, a Yeke potentate, needed help from the Belgians to suppress his subjects, and thus was manageable, many others, especially in the East, were not. Among the latter were the Swahili-speaking Muslims, the erstwhile Congo Arabs, some of whom had changed sides. Thus, as late as 1892–94, the dominant alliance found itself deposing its erstwhile allies and trying to replace them with more pliable subordinates.

From 1885, the most important elements of the modern state had made their appearance, not just rulers but bureaucrats as well, secular and religious. Alongside Catholic missionaries—much to their dismay—were Protestant missionaries, and although religionists, mainly Catholics, controlled education and culture, administrateurs généraux known for their secularism and anticlericalism controlled everything else.¹¹

By 1900, the first phase of state formation was drawing to a close. The "slash and burn" approach to primitive accumulation from rubber could not be sustained ecologically; more profit and more stable profit could be assured only through the development of mining. Mining, however, required a larger, more rationalized political order than the one that thereto-fore had existed. In 1906, the Belgian ruling class and its local allies made the required transitions; new institutions emerged in politics, culture, and law, and along with these came new industries led by the famous mining company, Union Minière du Haut-Katanga. [12]

On the whole, old problems of all sorts continued. Changing the political status of the country from a free state to a colony did not alter the hegemony. The Europeans continued to regard chiefs' attitudes toward questions of land rights and toward crime as lax. Europeans thought that "vacant" land should be state land, and Europeans should have access to it, African objections notwithstanding. By this time, however, enough cohesion of the ruling class existed to permit political problems to become bureaucratic ones. In May 1910 came an important administrative decree; chiefs were to be rated and paid salaries. Their powers as police agents and enforcers were defined, and they were then duly invested with them. [13]

In 1914 came the recognition from Brussels that administration was too centralized to be efficient and that the lower rungs lacked power commensurate with responsibility. This recognition, or at least this way of framing the issue, suggests that little progress had been made toward resolving the real question of the division of power between Belgians and Congolese. Another continuing problem was the rivalry between the religious and the secular power structures. Both had their own agendas; the secular structure wished to maintain a laissez faire culture, the church wanted social and cultural development. Congolese in this period, finding few opportunities in the secular sphere, redoubled their efforts in the religious one.

With the growth of the modern economy during and after World War I, now increasingly based on mining, a working class emerged. In 1919, mine workers struck the Union Haut Minière. The strike was crushed ruthlessly by the company. This proved to be a decisive moment in labor relations. It led to the flight of the white work force. [14] Thereafter, mining was done only by blacks.

After this defeat in 1919, demoralization among the mine workers was quite noticeable. Disease became a major problem as well. In the years after the strike many secretly fled. Initially, fleeing workers were hidden by the traditional chiefs. Later, by the end of the 1920s, with the creation of an African quarter in Elizabethville, workers began to be able to care for each other. And soon they were able to use the quarter as a place from which to launch their struggles. Lodges and friendly societies developed there as well, spreading in time to the other major cities.

With the growth of capitalism in the 1920s, the ruling class, meanwhile, appeared more and more divided along political lines. Conservatives, by which I mean nineteenth-century liberals, continued to see the chiefs as too numerous and too weak. Fewer chiefs would be better because they would be stronger; an évolué in place of an unsuitable traditional chief would be even better.[15] This was the gist of the so-called Louis Franck reforms.

By the 1930s, conservative Belgian administrators, such as Katanga's Attorney-General Martin Rutten, had come to believe that the liberals, meaning "welfare colonialists" led by British investors, by British colonial officials in nearby colonies, and by Protestant missionaries in the Congo, planned to foment a mass rebellion against the Belgians, their assets, and Catholicism itself. Although this was an extreme view and a biased one as well, it shows in embryo the crisis of the Liberal Age to come. It shows as well the desperate desire to deny that there was change. Change, after all, was dangerous. If it was too quick, it could threaten the hegemony; if it was too slow, it could bring about a crisis as well. Rutten's critics—and these included many churchmen—held the central state and the Ministry of Colonies to be responsible for establishing policies against change; Rutten's supporters, however, took the opposite view. They, like he, wanted to diminish the role of the central state, to leave changes of policy to the local authorities. Their concern was that change, meaning, of course, development would bring a rise in "worker politics." They feared the worker lodges, suspecting they had interconnections with the more rural and hence less-controllable Watchtower Sects and to a certain extent, they were justified in their fears. Such connections did exist. Protestant missionary activity was having an emancipatory impact on the workers as well.

When examining the crisis of the Liberal Age in many, many countries, one finds that the depression played a notable role. The Congo was no exception; export earnings plummeted in the 1930s and political agitation increased.[16] To recover, at least to do so quickly, required greater productivity, meaning for all intents and purposes that the country would simply have to wait out the depression and suffer through it. As a consequence, suffering increased as did resistance to Belgian rule, justifying use of the phrase "crisis of the Liberal Age."[17]

In May 1940, Germany overran Belgium. The erstwhile Belgian leadership was determined to carry on an opposition to the Nazis, and this it did from its colonies. Wartime conditions thus opened opportunities for Congolese in such areas as the military, the bureaucracy, and the mines. Thus, although conditions for the majority grew harder—more and more corvée labor and copal harvesting being demanded—the regime did not fall as it was offering unprecedented opportunities at least to a minority.

In the years 1936–44, the demand for copper and other minerals rose sharply as the major nations entered the war. The companies, in turn, demanded more and more from the miners; labor unrest grew. In 1941, a general strike among miners took place; millenialist ideology, perhaps a product of Watchtower Sect influence, was apparent among the strikers. In 1944, a second major strike took place. This time a more proletarian ideology was apparent suggesting a possible weakening of the rural–urban alliance.

As the agrarian sector continued to stagnate and the pressures to leave the countryside grew stronger, the government appeared nervous about its control there; Catholic schools became an increasingly important bulwark of the rural status quo, Catholic education serving as a means for people to find their way out of the countryside in an orderly way. All this notwithstanding, urbanization grew rapidly as more people left the land to earn the money, which they needed to pay their taxes. One other outcome. For a significant number, urbanization resulted in upward mobility into the petty bourgeoisie, resulting as well in a rising support for nationalism.

1945–1971: A Failed Attempt at Corporatism

For a historian, the period 1945–71 is the most challenging period of the country's modern history. Many events happened at the same time in this period, and most still remain unexplained. What is clear, however, is the broad contours of change that took place. This provides a basis for some interpretation.

In economic terms, this period saw the rise of a petty bourgeois class disposed to pursue its agenda through an alliance with the large bourgeoisie. The large bourgeoisie refused this alliance, choosing instead to play on the divisions within the petty bourgeoisie to outlast this challenge and then simply to carry on as before. The history of the period in many standard texts does not reflect this, historians preferring to organize their works first around the rise and fall of Patrice Lumumba in the years up through 1960, then around the period of anarchy, and then around the return to stability after the rise of Mobutu. From class analysis, it appears that Lumumba's arrest and subsequent execution by apparent agents of imperialism triggered a phase, a "second revolution" during which a segment of the petty bourgeoisie, mainly in the East, linked itself to the rural masses in movements such as Pierre Mulele's in Kivu. As the mid-1960s arrived, however, it was clear that these movements were doomed, no matter how popular they may have been. Mobutu, a politician with close ties to international business, had emerged as the real power in the country; when opposition movements arose, he would receive enough international assistance to put them down. Still, for the first six years of his rule, 1965–71, given the balance of forces, Mobutu had to maintain the trappings of nationalism and other ideologies dear to the lower middle class, feeling secure enough to be open about the one-class nature of his rule only in 1971. It is useful to note that the failure to achieve corporatism here as in many other tribal-ethnic states has been commonly used to deny the modernity of this type of hegemony by theorists. Until recently, with the general breakdown of developmentalism, the elite consumerist approach to capitalism, such as one finds here, has not been seriously reckoned with.[18]

Why corporatism failed, especially given the huge sacrifice of Zairian youth to impose it, is still a question the literature does not fully resolve. Looked at in comparative terms, which is the approach adopted here, what stands out is the difficulty faced by the nationalist movement, the driving force behind corporatism, in developing a mass following. If most tribal-ethnic states have perhaps three or four major groupings, Zaire has dozens. Is it surprising that the rulers have almost always been successful playing one group against another? A second and related difficulty faced by the nationalist movement was language. If a nationalist politician had to carry out his organizing work in French, the only national language, in effect, among the graduates of Catholic schools, those who could be organized would be few and subject to counterpressures from the church, which was deadset against nationalism.

Other reasons for the failure of corporatism exist as well. Generally, one finds that the onset of corporatism takes place against the background of splits in the bourgeoisie. One wing of the bourgeoisie tends to seek an alliance with the petty bourgeoisie. In the case at hand, what is noticeable is that this did not occur. No economic splits occurred, no wing needed such an alliance.

But, despite the failure of the petty bourgeoisie to bring about a corporatist state, the rise of this class and its struggles represent an important phase in modern Congolese history.

In 1945, in the wake of a mutiny of soldiers in a garrison in the provincial city of Luluabourg, the political birth of a new phase and a new class occurred. This class had, as its spokesmen at that time noted, sided with the colonial authority in putting down the mutiny; now, it had the right to make demands on the state in return. Acting on this belief, a group of the évolués issued the so-called Declaration of the Évolués in which they demanded the right to higher education. Such was their strength by this time that the publication of this declaration forced a review of colonial education policy. No less a figure than Joseph Van Wing, the famous Jesuit educator, began to urge the administration to open higher education to the Congolese.

In 1955, more evidence of évolué power appeared when King Baudoin visited the country. Accounts of this visit indicate that he made a point of trying to court the évolués, visiting a number of the Amicales or Belgian-Congolese friendship societies. In the same period, the church sought to advance its relationship with the évolués as well. Thus in 1956, the hierarchy published its Conscience Africaine Manifesto in which it called for a thirty-year program leading to emancipation. The Alliance des Bakongos (ABAKO) was not taken in by these initiatives. Under the leadership of Joseph Kasavubu, it called for immediate political independence, thus marking the moment termed the takeoff of nationalism. By 1958, évolué politics brought about the formation of several parties, a regionalist party in Katanga (CONAKAT) and in Kivu (CEREA) and a nationalist party, the Movement Nationale Congolais (MNC), led by Patrice Lumumba, which assumed the leadership role in the national struggle.[19]

In 1960, independence came and with it an increase in ethnic, tribal, and class struggles. When, for example, the new parliament decided to raise its own salary fivefold to the level of the erstwhile white-held positions, it was surprised at a mutiny arising among the junior officers of the Force Publique, which had similar designs. Lumumba found himself responding to the mutiny in terms of his new class position, urging restraint by officer corps while countenancing a lack thereof in members of his own party.

As the 1960s progressed and the power of the petty bourgeoisie increased, nationalization of industry and state intervention in the economy became commonplace; the results, however, were unexpected. Given the weakness of the central state, many groups found it opportune to rebel. As a result of both the governmental interventions and of the rebellions, agriculture broke down; whole areas were in a state of anarchy. As the period, I term a "failed attempt at corporatism" came to an end in the late 1960s, finance capital was on the rise. There was by this point no compelling reason for a capitalist to invest in production, although the state undeterred continued to nationalize existing industry and invest in new industry even when its programs were based on deficit financing. As a consequence of these policies, a new illegal or no more than semilegal private sector emerged to exploit the wasteful policy of investment. It engaged in such practices as hoarding and smuggling.[20]

During the 1960s, the Party asserted itself radically into fields such as education and culture that were traditionally controlled by the church. As a result of this assertion, tension between the church and party rose when, for example, Mobutu demanded that citizens take African as opposed to Christian names, that they study Mobutuism in school in place of Christianity and that the universities be nationalized. As the challenge of the petty bourgeoisie gradually weakened, so, too, did the party's assertiveness. In the 1970s, the tension declined as Mobutu became increasingly dependent on Europe for loans and the support of the Catholic church became increasingly important to secure these loans. In 1980, Pope John actually visited Zaire.

Neoliberalism, 1971–1990

Mobutu's declaration in 1971 that the country was a republic marked the transition to neoliberalism. Neoliberalism here as elsewhere involved dismantling the public sector and turning over the assets of the country to the friends of the ruler. This program in Zaire was called Zairization. As elsewhere, the stated goal of all neoliberal initiatives was to invigorate the economy. No doubt, in the short term at least, it might have achieved this goal had the timing not happened to coincide with a great decline in the price of copper on the world market. Thus it was that through the 1970s and increasingly through the 1980s, the state's finances were insecure for reasons not directly related to its policies.

Politically, as well, neoliberalism brought insecurity in Zaire, although whether more here than elsewhere is difficult to tell. Those who felt that their human and civil rights were violated by the system began to appeal for outside intervention. After all, there was no one else to whom to turn. Thus the church, the judiciary, the alternative religious movements, such as the Kimbanguists and the Kitawalists, all sought international support and all wound up increasingly at odds with the state.

Here, one might note some parallels to the situation in Albania. To survive, Mobutu, like Hoxha, abolished the office of the prime minister and eliminated the parliamentarian nature of the assembly, creating in their places a unique party, essentially a new tribe. Mobutu criticized his cadre, just as Hoxha did, for its lack of militancy and for its separation from the masses which it was supposed to serve. Mobutu like Hoxha was obsessed with the youth crisis, which arose when the regime solidified its position. His policy, again much like that of Hoxha, was that youth must do one year's work for the state before entering the university and that parents may not send their children abroad for education.

Did the move to neoliberalism thus make Mobutu more vulnerable. The answer would appear to be negative. Despite the political and economic insecurity, the seemingly still underdeveloped quality of the economy, the barely developed "museum cities," the lack of a role for educated women, and so on. Mobutu seemed no more or less vulnerable than rulers of the first liberal age. To speak of political vulnerability, one must find challenge, not just challenge to Mobutu but to the kind of state to which he was heir and which he today maintains. To establish this point, one must consider in more detail the efforts at counterhegemony that appeared up to 1990.[21]

Opposition and Counterhegemony in the Belgian Congo and Zaire

Organized opposition in the Belgian Congo/Zaire has most commonly taken the form of regional and ethnic challenges that varied according to opportunity. The openness of Zaire to the World Market has encouraged even a degree of foreign participation in this opposition. For better or worse, opposition has rarely met with success. Spokesmen for the colonial regime and later for Mobutu insist that the authentic Congolese is a member of his tribe and that revolts against the system are, thus, simply acts of foreign instigation.[22]

The most famous example of a tribal-ethnic secession struggle in the Belgian Congo/Zaire is that of Katanga. From the interwar period, secessionist thought was rife there fed often by the prevailing hardships of the period. For example, in 1932 among the budget-cutting steps made necessary by the impact of the depression, the government in Leopoldville decided to restructure Katanga, removing from it the Lomani District. This district, however, was the chief source of labor for the mines, so the governor-general's decision led to unrest. In the next few years, again in a manner unmindful of public opinion, the government cut costs ever further by reducing the vice governors-general to provincial commissioners. In protest, a number of the key personnel resigned amid widespread demands for secession. Although the threat of secession at this particular point came to naught, the colonial administration felt the need to make some real and some symbolic concessions to the Europeans of Elizabethville and it did so.[23]

Thus, in 1944 in Katanga, Europeans founded the Union for Colonization (UCOL) to press for the restoration of Katangan autonomy and to promote European colonization generally. In 1960, during the rule of Patrice Lumumba, Albert Kalonji from South Kasai declared the independence of his province. Lumumba ordered the army to reestablish order, but the army mutinied. After the mutiny, Moise Tshombe of Katanga joined Albert Kalonji in rebellion. When Lumumba declared martial law and accepted aid from the Soviet Union, Kasavubu dismissed him and permitted Mobutu to come to power. Shortly, thereafter, Lumumba was killed as a prisoner in Katanga.

Patrice Lumumba (1925–1961) marked another sort of challenge, one which, I have argued, was an attempt to transcend the tribal-ethnic character of the hegemony, one which sought to appeal to nationalist sentiment and to class sentiment, one which aimed at corporatism. Lumumba had first gained prominence as the president of a trade union movement; he had also been active in the Belgian Liberal party in the Congo, that is, in two cross-ethnic movements. In 1958, he founded the Congolese National movement. In 1960, he was a national hero and the nation's first prime minister. His execution in 1961 enraged opinion in the country and across the wider Afro-Asian world.

In searching for the reasons for Lumumba's too rapid collapse, one could no doubt look into the role of the Central Intelligence Agency (CIA). This was a factor. But the success of the CIA usually depends on the political context. Here was one, as I note above, where the lower middle class and the working class were profoundly divided. These divisions made political challenge difficult. The state simply had too many options at its disposal.

Equally, when searching for reasons to explain Lumumba's too-rapid collapse, one should also consider the trustworthiness—or lack thereof—of the figures on whom he was depending. For example, Justin Bomboko, his minister of foreign affairs, Joseph Yav, his minister for economic affairs, Antoine-Roger Bolamba, the writer, his secretary of state for information were known Belgian protégés. Other close allies of Lumumba included politicians openly pursuing agendas of their own. Among these, one could include Edmond Rudahindwa, his minister of mines and power, who was also a lobbyist for the settlers of Kivu and Raphael Batshikama, a representative of ABAKO. Among Lumumba's allies also were some who simply happened to rise on his coattails from Stanleyville and who were ideologically of little use. Such figures included Christophe Gbenye, his minister for home affairs, Joseph Lutula, his minister of agriculture, and Alphonse Songolo, his minister of communications. Finally, one can identify choices Lumumba made in his appointments, which were, in retrospect, simply disastrous. One might include among these Charles Kisolokele, whom he brought in as a minister of state because he was a Kimbanguist. Lumumba appears to have thought that by turning to the Kimbanguists he could split the Bakongos and ABAKO and weaken his rival Joseph Kasavubu. A second error was the appointment of Albert Nyembo as his secretary of state for defense. Nyembo worked as a spy for Moise Tshombe, making it impossible for the government to retake Katanga Province once the revolt broke out there. A third error was his break with the Left, for example, with experienced figures such as Antoine Gizenga.[24]

What about the MNC's student base? It is unquestionable that Lumumba had the enthusiastic support of the Zairian students' unions AGEL and UGEC. This support it would appear, however, was both a source of strength and a liability. The unions were united in their willingness to challenge the power structure but scarcely were a match for it, not able to respond to campaigns of arrests nor to cope with the closing of the universities during strikes nor with the drafting of students into the army.[25]

Finally, it might be argued as an explanation for the too-rapid collapse of Lumumba that the MNC failed to prepare the ground along the way in the one area where the ancien regime was quite on the defensive, that is, gender policy. Influential thinkers of the party do not appear to have even been interested in it. For example, *Sans Rancune* (Brussels: Remarques Congolaises, 1965), the autobiography of Thomas Kanza, gives the impression that the author resented the independence of European women, that he would scarcely wish it for Congolese women. Antoine Roger Bolamba, Lumumba's minister of information and author of *Les Problèmes de l'évolu-*

tion de la femme noire (Elisabethville: Éditions de L'Essor du Congo, 1949), in effect rejected the possibility of significant advancement for women at least in his lifetime. At the same time, there is no question that many évolué women supported the MNC anyhow.[26] One might add here that even without support or appreciation, certain groups of women were formidable opponents of colonialism. Contemporary scholarship shows that they created and circulated myths and rumors the effect of which was hurtful to the colonial project. One such myth was that of Mutumbula, the white who eats black. This myth was apparently used as a warning, especially for women, not to be alone at night on auto routes. During World War II, women in Kasai used the threat of Mutumbula to disrupt draft procedures. Outbreaks of real panic about the coming of Mutumbula continued at least until 1960.[27]

The failure of the secular lower middle-class leadership, such as that of the MNC around Lumumba, to transform the old autocracy of the Liberal Age into corporatism left open the door to other challenges, some from entirely outside the system such as the aforementioned movement of Pierre Mulele, others from within the system such as the "populist" challenges. The most important example of the latter is the Kimbanguist church. The origins and early years of this church are tied up with the personage of Simon Kimbangu (1889–1951) founder of the Church of Jesus Christ on Earth through the Prophet Simon Kimbangu and later its messiah. After World War I, the authorities condemned Simon Kimbangu as they did many other independent preachers and had him arrested. He became ever more famous. As time progressed and the Kimbanguist movement did not subside, the authorities arrested a number of its suspected adherents. Thereafter, jail became an increasingly important center of the propagation of the faith. By 1970, the Kimbanguists may have numbered one million. Like their counterparts, the Albanian Bektashis, the Kimbanguists operated an elaborate welfare system. They also were important participants in the politics of the country. Charles Kisolokele, noted before, was a member of the cabinet, and he was by no means the only prominent personality. Still, the countercultural image of Kimbanguism persists. In a well-known incident in Bandundu in 1964, the army gunned down a group of Kimbanguists as "enemies of the state."[28] This suggests that the movement has not lost all of its implicitly "popular-national" character.[29]

The Organization of Culture

The Congolese/Zairian state, like others in the modern world, organizes culture; it does so because it depends on persuasion to maintain its domination.[30] It does so according to a logic characterized in chapter 7 as gnosis. I examine first the role of the religious structure, the contribution of the Catholic church to this hegemony, and then consider representative endeavors of the secular structures, noting policies toward ethnography, language, archeology, literature, music, and medicine. This section concludes with a brief account of two individuals who bring these diverse parts of the organization of culture together in their thought, individuals one could term *great intellectuals.*

Rule through gnosis implies a policy of destabilization. Thus, on the one hand, the colonial administration undertook daily to protect what was particular and traditional to the country, while on the other hand, its indispensable ally, the Catholic church, undertook daily to undermine what was particular and traditional through modernization, education, and development. The church functioned less as a "traditional intellectual" as, for example, in Italy and more as a partner. In the postindependence period, this built-in confrontation between the secular and religious structures continued, the Faculty of Catholic Theology opposing the party, African Christianity and philosophy opposing authenticity and negritude, neither being a prisoner of the other and, thus, a traditional intellectual.[31]

Education was historically a church monopoly, which it used not just to promote religion or even just basic education but to promote acceptance of state doctrines, for example, the absolute difference between men and women.

Catholic education taught that women's obligation was to obey. From obedience comes the good life. This was an absolute obligation unaffected by the growing tide of Catholic modernism in the world at large and unaffected by the liberal and developmentalist tendencies within society or even within the Zairian church itself. Furthermore, despite the growth of an urban culture, Church education stressed the ideal of the rural Christian life, the evils of migrating to the city, the evils of literary societies, and even the evils of secular culture, all of which make women less obedient. Finally, despite the growth of women's participation in the modern economy, the church continued to stress the importance for males to have remunerated work as opposed to females to maintain the natural social hierarchy of men over women. Is it surprising that their schools favored males over females, that more males attended and more progressed further than their female counterparts?

Given the strength of the hegemony, political pressure could not shake the church in these areas whatsoever, even when it came from fairly important segments of the society. In 1952, for example, the Council of the African Quarter in Leopoldville, an important évolué group, demanded better quality education for women. Évolué women, who wanted an education, were finding it fatiguing, if not demeaning, to take the ferry to Brazzaville to get it. The situation was delicate for the church, so it equivocated. It did not agree; it did not disagree. As a result, it managed to forestall significant change. By 1960, eight years later, a few women had joined the university, but statistics suggest there was no overall change. In that year, the high-water mark for women's education, only 1.5 percent of the girls in primary school reached the secondary school.

In the 1970s and thereafter with the challenge of the petty bourgeoisie diffused, Mobutu passed a series of laws further setting back the status of women, in the process making education for them even more difficult. In this period, once again as in the 1920s, it became necessary for women to have their husbands' permission to work, travel, or have bank accounts. In court decisions of the era, widows or women without male relatives appeared to have lost their legal rights. The church had to choose to oppose these initiatives in the name of progress or to support them as central to Christian dogma. It did the latter and benefited from doing so.

As women increasingly resisted this renewed oppression; the church made yet another strategic move, taking up the theme of human rights, positioning itself to judge the values necessary for the hegemony. If, today women turn down an offer of a lawful marriage to be a wealthy man's mistress or if they participate in the contraband economy or in the alternative churches, cannot such acts be said to require a rededication of the country to the teachings of Jesus Christ?[32]

The church serves as well as the bulwark of the state against the Kimbanguists, a mass movement that is indigenous and authentic, but which has so far been no match for it. The church presents itself as African, modern, and pro-state; the Kimbanguists do not. Are they with the state or against it? This is an uncomfortable question. The church chooses for its spokespersons "state intellectuals"; the Kimbanguists do not. This, too, costs them. Thus, in recent years, (Vincent) Mulago (gwa Cikala Musharhamina), a well-known writer on African philosophy and theology spoke for the church.[33] Before Mulago in the colonial period, there was Father Van Wing.

Finally, the church led the state's effort to reincorporate Protestants and popular preachers back into its fold. A recent study published by the theology faculty with this in mind took as its theme the Word as the personal manifestation of God in the Sacrament according to the writings of Martin Luther, defending the latter against the charge that he opposed the Sacrament. In the process, it defended his theology against the tradition that claimed him, the one inspired by nineteenth-century Germans such as Harnack, who believed that the Word was simply the vehicle of the message, defending thus the rights of Protestants to return to orality and to Catholic dogma, defending the rights of charismatic preachers to keep their orality but making it part of Catholic theology.[34]

Secular intellectuals, such as ethnographers, also play an important role in the organization of culture whether creating new tribal identities as for the Luba[35] or creating museum cities out of Kinshasa, Lubumbashi, and Kinsangani[36] or deciding that a certain practice at one moment is primitive, at another authentic, at another foreign in inspiration or, as the case may be, modern and national.

Beginning in the colonial period, several well-known museums for Congolese ethnography such as the Tervueren were established in Belgium. After 1960, the center of museology shifted to Zaire. In 1970, Mobutu created a National Museum Institute. In subsequent years, this institute appropriated tribal artifacts from the countryside and from European repositories and placed them in the country's main museums. In time, the underlying agenda in museology became clear; art from the Eastern part of the country was to be "folklorized." "Modern or international" art was to be reserved for the studios of Kinshasa. Both would have status although, of course, not entirely equal status.[37]

From the 1920s, the leading ethnographers linked to colonialism defined Congolese literature as oral literature, the counterpart to folk art; studies of it appeared in prestigious journals such as *Congo,* the research journal of the Institut Royal Colonial Belge. In 1935, Belgian parliamentary pressure led to the chartering of a commission to protect the traditional arts and crafts, which were perceived to be in danger of disappearing. In this period as well, Belgians began to collaborate with Congolese to form associations of the friends of the indigenous arts.

In odd moments, however, this elite collaboration broke down, permitting a glance behind the scenes, a glance at how gnosis was really working. K. E. Laman, a Swedish Protestant ethnographer somewhat out of step with his contemporaries, requested local Bakongo intellectuals to collaborate with him by submitting accounts of their culture under their own names. Laman's four volumes on Kongo ethnology published between 1953 and 1968 were thus based on the writings and testimony of particular Bakongos. As a result, several Congolese collaborators are known historically from their intellectual work. Even before Laman, moves in this direction appeared. One particularly important figure, David Malangadila (d. 1915), an informant for European scholars, became disaffected and left this work, resenting the nativizing of people such as himself. Why should for the arbiters of gnosis the Congolese always be the anonymous folks and the Europeans always be known by their names?

The Belgian Congo/Zaire is a country in which people speak dozens of languages. This posed the question of how the government should formulate a language policy. The solution was to make French the language of the state but to limit sharply the access of the population to it. Since the country had never been a "mobilization regime," rule through a language that few could speak or read would be acceptable. If language policy would help restrict access to the political arena, so much the better. Thus one finds a colonial language serving the needs of the state even in the postcolonial period, one ironically enough given over to concerns of national identity and cultural authenticity.

According to a recent article, the initial influential commentary on the contribution of language policy to hegemony in the country was a scholarly intervention on this subject that appeared in 1912 by one Count Jacques de Lichtervelde. He first articulated the strategy of permitting the native population restricted access to French in preference to unrestricted access to Kiswahili. The latter option would give the local population too many links to the Arabs in the North, which might be dangerous. A total reliance on French, however, would produce a situation in which African opposition to colonial rule would be more difficult to ignore. Flemish was not a real option either. Although it may have been the first language of many of the Belgians who served in the country, students showed no interest in learning it. Those who wanted outside contact wanted an international language, not another local language. This seemed fairly predictable. When, however, one comes to the postcolonial period, the rationale for the maintenance of French as the language of the state becomes hazier. Passing references suggest that it was a response to modern politics or to the imperatives of developmentalism. This is not quite adequate as explanations go however; there is nothing inherent in French that would lead to developmentalism if one judges from the previous seventy-five years of history. Indeed, in small-scale experiments, scholars have shown that even technical and philosophical issues can be conveyed in the local languages. French is not so indispensable.

What, then, sustains French today? From the party's perspective, at least, the answer seems obvious. Not only does its use separate ruler and ruled but it also throws an obstacle in the way of the church. A common observation has always been that the sheer externality of French for the mass population constitutes an obstacle for the teacher of Christianity. One additional consideration may well be that few women know very much French because few women attend school. Its use ipso facto facilitates the marginalization of women, an unstated but, nonetheless, real goal of the regime.

Thus, French remains for political reasons the language of the state, and other languages serve for practical reasons the needs of those who actually are communicating in the country. One of these languages, Lingala, is more and more beginning to compete with French. Lingala is no longer just the language of merchants in the river basin as it was in the nineteenth century but is the actual normal language of daily intercourse in the capital city, of modern music, of the police, and of the army.[38]

When one examines the features of a language in a tribal ethnic hegemony, certain general points emerge. Language is not a mirror of thought as positivists believe it to be, nor does it suffice to claim it is tonal. Rather it is—à la anarchism—talismanic or iconic. If Western Marxists want to dismiss Hoxha's writings for being chaotic, they should add "chaotic for Western Marxists," for it is not chaotic for the Albanian mass population. Similar points can be made concerning the *Green Book* of Qadhdhafi, the collected works of Kim Il Sung, Mobutu's *Manifeste de la Nsele,* the basis of Mobutuism, and other such works.

Along with ethnographers and linguists, archeologists make important contributions to the organization of culture. Where religionists provide a myth of origins that is fixed, archeologists can always find something new. In the colonial period, archeologists fostered a picture of prehistory that reinforced Bakongo hegemonism, a picture establishing that prehistoric industry flourished in the Lower Congo and around Kinshasa. By the 1940s, East Africans and South African archeologists challenged these claims with their own about ancient societies in the East of the country. Debates among archeologists in different countries raged through the 1940s. After independence, Zairian archeology suffered lethargy from which it recovered in the 1970s in new work in Shaba that linked old Shaba to ancient Egypt.[39]

Why does archeology mirror the politics of the regime so much more than other fields do? It appears that access to archeology is limited by the high cost of research. Only states can afford to finance the research, and if one pays the piper, one calls the tune. Debates, such as they exist in archeology, are frequently carried on among scholars in different countries, and they reflect different national interests. Less often are there competing national traditions in archeology in any one country.

Compared to archeology, literature is more accessible terrain. Authors can easily go astray; constant criticism is necessary. The publication of a recent interpretation of literary history is a case in point. No sooner was it published than it had to be attacked. As critics pointed out, the author chose to organize his history of literature around history, not around literature. The Zairian literary establishment, meaning, of course, those critics close to the state, thus raised an outcry. Where is the literary or artistic space? What sort of criticism is this? If one understands African literature as a response to colonial oppression, as the author appeared to, what would then remain of African literature after the departure of the colonists? Would it not be more acceptable to have as one's critical foundation the ongoing experience created by race? Would it not be preferable to postulate that Zairian literature emerged as a part of the wider Negro-African culture, a culture flourishing between Harlem, the Latin quarter, and Africa?

The outcome of this controversy is not certain. The critic's view does not gibe with Mobutu's ideology of authenticity much more than does the author's view that he was criticizing. Where, after all, does pan-African black culture end and Bakongo culture begin? Mobutuism is certainly not reducible to pan-Africanism. Such thoughts open a wider question than how to dispose of an unwanted work of literary scholarship; they ask what direction the state's functionaries should follow when they themselves make choices about cultural policy.[40] Literature in its various forms is more difficult to control and benefit from than archeology.

A straw in the wind about which way the state may go in fields such as literature, which are widely accessible, may be found in the state's approach to music. Maybe the way to control a field in which masses of people are involved is simply to allow the prevailing diversity of the population to assert itself. This appears to be the policy toward popular music.

According to a history of music, from the 1960s on, the number of musicians in the country grew as did the types of music played. Peak periods included the 1960s when many musicians sided with freedom and decolonization and the 1970s when many musicians reacting to the chaos in the country chose to adopt government themes such as authority and solidarity of the society and respect for women.[41]

A major figure in the development of modern Zairian music was K. Tshamala (1930–1984), the "Grand Kallé," a great musician who was also known for his band African-Jazz founded in 1951 in Kinshasa. This band served as an inspiration for much of the generation that followed, and many certainly followed. If Kinshasa had 20 bands in 1963, it had an estimated 180–200 bands in 1984.[42]

The organization of culture, which is inherently positivist and yet absolutely indispensable to the ruling class, remains to be considered. Here, I do not mean the highly technical fields that permit a government to rent the services of a foreign teacher or technician, but rather fields such as medicine that touch the ordinary life of the society on a daily basis. Against a background of many medical problems, the astonishing feat of the gnosis approach is to turn several entirely unrelated traditions against each other and thereby to reduce the threat posed by any one of them. Allopathic medicine, or "Western" positivist medicine, becomes only one trend among others.[43]

For allopathic medicine to be perceived in Zaire merely as one tradition among several, given its resources and charisma, the intellectual community wishing to sustain such a state of affairs has had to commit itself to an ongoing critique of positivist science. This it has done. Representative of such criticism is a book. *Problemes de methodes en philosophie et sciences humaines en Afrique* (Kinshasa: Faculté de Théologie Catholique, 1986). This work, the published proceedings of a conference on the philosophy of methodology, Semaine Philosophique de Kinshasa, conveys quite clearly the thoughts of an elite faculty about the inadequacies of positivist methodology. One piece attacks Kant's argument that the object could be understood without reference to the method adopted to approach it. Another calls for an African science. A third argues that philosophy, positivism for example, is at its base simply culture. A fourth contends that all philosophy runs a "regime of orality," that all men are philosophers, constituting an attack on textuality and on credentialism within positivism.

As with Albania in the communist period, so with the modern Belgian Congo/Zaire, alliances and ideologies do not always perfectly fit a textbook notion of hegemonic logic. Two of the influential figures who played the role in the hegemony of "organic" or leading intellectuals were Joseph Van Wing and Vincent Mulago. Both these men were known as religious thinkers; both concerned themselves with the dangers of positivism. In considering these two figures, one comes to understand how gnosis can coexist in a power structure with the Roman Catholic Church. The issue of maintaining the museum cities remains, but somewhat in the background.

Joseph Van Wing (1884–1970) was a Jesuit evangelist authority on the Bakongo, well known both as a scholar and as a politician. He was among the early Catholic evangelicals in the Congo, Catholic evangelism being the trend among the missionaries, who rejected the rather deprecatory approach of the older missionaries and who looked forward in the years after World War I to an African modernism. Van Wing was, of course, only one of a number to study the Bakongo, but his major work, *Bakongo religion et magie* (many editions) was among the first to emphasize the rationality of Bakongo theology and ritual. As a politician, Van Wing held various offices and was known for his stands defending Congolese interests. He was, for example, a critic of the "excesses" of colonialism. He viewed the disruption of African economy and social structure as wasteful and unnecessary. By 1948, Van Wing occupied the important position of missionary representative on the Colonial Council. In this period, as earlier in his life, he continued to uphold a number of liberal positions: the right of Congolese to higher education, the right of Protestants to pursue missionary work, and so on. In this period as well, Van Wing encouraged the Bakongo to form an organization to protect their interests. The Alliance des Bakongos (ABAKO) soon became a major force in Congolese affairs. Van Wing encouraged Edmond Nzeza-Landu, one of his students in the seminary at Kisantu, to write a manifesto of Bakongo unity on its behalf. In the last phase of Van Wing's life, he became worried about Bakongo chauvinism, especially with the rise of Joseph Kasavubu.[44]

Van Wing's major work is a fusion of African studies and Catholic theology. Other intellectuals in Van Wing's generation, liberals among them, gained prestige by protesting the inhumanity of the Belgian colonial practices along rationalist lines only to be ostracized. Van Wing remained a champion of the indigenous, but he did so as a believer in progress through the status quo.[45] Van Wing's work lives on in the career of the contemporary great intellectual, Abbé Mulago.[46]

Abbé Mulago, Mulago gwa Cikala Mushashamina, was born in 1924 in the region of Kivu. He was a seminary student in the Congo and, subsequently, in the years from 1949 to 1955 a seminary student in Rome, where he was one of the first Congolese to receive a doctorate in theology. Mulago also received a license in Canon Law and a degree in journalism. Between 1956 and 1962, he taught in Bukavu. In 1962, he became a professor in Kinshasa at the Faculty of Catholic Theology. In 1967, he became the director of the Centre d'Études des Religions Africaines and the editor of the journal, *Cahiers des Religions Africaines*. In 1971, he became vice-dean of his faculty and consultant to the Secretariat in Rome for Non-Christians. In the 1970s, his students, most notably, Alphonse Ngindu and Oscar Bimwenyi, developed the idea of an "incarnation theology." In this theology, God speaks to all human beings, and the need of the church is to adapt to that fact. Mulago did not go this far.

As a scholar, Mulago is known for a number of works on Bantu philosophy, the best-known of which is *La Religion traditionelle des Bantu et leur vision de monde* (Kinshasa: Presses universitaires du Zaïre, 1973). Much like Van Wing before him, he merged African studies and Catholicism, pursuing the theme of the overlap between Catholic mystical theology and Bantu philosophy in the concept of union vitale.[47]

When reflecting on the difference between Van Wing's period and Mulago's what stands out is the growing strength of the gnosis method used by intellectuals in the organization of culture. Progressively, a wider and wider range of fields become open to interrogation and to destabilization; history writing can serve as an example.

History-Writing in the Belgian Congo/Zaire

The main genres of history writing in the Belgian Congo/Zaire from the colonial period until today have been political and diplomatic history and genealogies, works sometimes useful in education and sometimes for government officials.[48]

In the absence of official patronage, which has been the general situation, textbooks have been a predominant form because they pay for themselves.[49] Diplomatic history textbooks and political history textbooks, the commonest genres, usually were chronological. Argumentation was indirect, appearing in terms of the information presented. No claims to scientific finality were presented such as one finds in works rooted in a more developed positivism. Rather, the works stay close to the sources on which they were based.[50] Genealogies, however, took the form of short biographies. Some treat the founding and development of various tribes and ethnicities; others deal with esteemed personalities. Indeed, the largest single work of history in the Belgian Congo/Zaire, the *Biographie coloniale Belge,* 5 vols. (1948–) was a work of genealogy. Writings about Mobutu are often genealogical as well.

As shown in chapter 7, genealogy is the version of history most accommodating to myth and to an oral history methodology. Myth and history in genealogical studies become in certain senses interchangeable, thus giving the wider discipline of history its niche.[51] In fact, oral history, one of the two methodologies referred to here, could arguably be said to have been born in the Belgian Congo in the work of the anthropologist Jan Vansina.

The idea of myth as history is, of course, not new. To the Western reader, it may seem archaic. Should one compare the situation of Zairian historians to that of Herodotus, the Greek historian who wrote his history in a world in which poets and oracles knew not only the meaning of this world but of the next as well? Why not? Why not then accept elements of the archaic as modern, if one must use the word *archaic?* Bakongo cosmology, like Greek cosmology, divides this world and the next while also uniting the two. According to these cosmologies, the next world is filled with the causes of the events of this world. Although, of course, there are seemingly cosmological events in this world, such as an Albanian Skanderbeg or a Beatrice of the Congo, there is not much desire on the part of the society for the kind of truth about this world that positivism alone might aspire to supply.[52] Of greater concern, at least on the popular level, is to know about the power that the other world might exert through witches on this world. Mputu, the other world, is in popular thought the home of the white people, a sort of myth version of Europe and America. The dead go to America; the slave trade was a kind of trivialization of this universal norm, which resulted from the rising influence of witchcraft. Witches had begun to intervene, forcing people to go prematurely. Among these witches may even have been some of the missionaries. Given the dangers inherent in this situation for ordinary people in this world, it is advisable to take certain precautions, to participate in cult rituals, and to take advantage of the power of chiefs to block witches from channeling power to their private advantage and possibly sending people to Mputu prematurely. The movement of history that emerges from this perception of the world is more an oscillation between order and disorder than development or progress of the sort commonly studied by historians. The most popular contemporary "historian," Zamenga Batukezanga, a Bakongo littérateur, appeals to his audience as a storyteller; history comes together with cosmology.[53]

In the colonial period, conditions for modern historical scholarship were not at all conducive. À la Albania, there was not only a lack of specialized institutions but an almost complete lack of funding. This was the case not only in the Congo itself but even in Brussels, its colonial metropole. Although the reasons for this cannot be entirely reduced to the fact of the tribal-ethnic form of hegemony in Belgium, it is worth noting that even the study of modern Belgian history, the centerpiece of the profession, is not as strong a field in Belgium as it would be in any other hegemony.

During the colonial era, Congolese history in Belgium developed as a part of African Studies in the École Colonial d'Anvers. This school, founded in 1920, was, however, so poorly funded that it drew its support from the American Commission for Relief in Belgium.[54] Later, the École, subsequently renamed the Colonial University, widened its basis of support, receiving assistance from an anthropological institution, the Musée Royale de L'Afrique Centrale at Tervueren, and a sociological institution, La Société Belge de Sociologie, and although this support no doubt helped historians, the Colonial University never became a specialized center for history.

Political and diplomatic histories and genealogies were produced in that era. The most important work of the former was R. S. Thomson's, *Fondation de l'état indépendant du Congo* (Brussels: Office de Publicité 1933). The most important of the latter was the *Biographie coloniale Belge* noted above.[55]

In 1954, Lovanium University in Kinshasa was founded. Twelve years later in 1966, a department of history began there, and this department played an important role in the development of the discipline, especially in the early years of independence. Through the 1960s and 1970s, the period in which he taught, François Bontinck, a Belgian historian, retained a considerable reputation for his *Aux Origines de l'état indépendant du Congo documents tirés d'archives américaines* (Louvain: Nauwelaerts, 1966), a work in diplomatic history in the tradition of the aforementioned work of R. S. Thomson. Indeed, a textual comparison of the two works suggests that any difference comes mainly from minor points of emphasis. Writing in the era of American hegemony, Bontinck linked the international affairs of the country more to America than did his predecessor, who, although actually an American, chose to link the international affairs of the Congo more to those of Europe. Bontinck thus began his work with an account of the American role in the creation of the Free State, whereas his predecessor emphasized more the role of Great Britain.

Although, no doubt, diplomatic history has some utility to any government, still a study based on positivism is a threat to domination by gnosis. Thus, it is not surprising to find criticism by government officials of the writing even of diplomatic history. For example, in an essay from the 1970s written by Ndaywel E. Nziem, a professor at the National Pedagogy Institute, the president of Société des historiens Zaïrois (SOHIZA) and the

permanent secretary of the Université Nationale du Zaïre (UNAZA) Con-
seil d'Administration, an implied criticism of Bontinck's approach to history appears. Historians, he argued, ought to accept the Diop thesis of the
African origins of civilization. Diplomatic historians, such as Bontinck, of
course, tend to be Eurocentric. In practical terms, historians ought to gather
information about Zaire first in their own native languages. The implications of this line of thought clearly reveal the author's reservations about the
idea of a national history profession with which Bontinck was concerned or
of a serious foreign interest in Zaire's history.[56]

The study of history was not destined to remain centered in Lovanium
but in the newly founded university in Lubumbashi, especially in the years
1971–76. In this period, social history flourished as part of a broader counterhegemonic political culture of the eastern region. In 1976, Mobutu attacked; Zairization struck the history profession, and the field lost its two
leading figures, B. Jewsiewicki and J. L. Vellut, both of Lubumbashi University. Thereafter, the history profession seemed destined to sink to the
level of inactivity of the colonial period.[57] At least, this may have been the
intent of the government in doing what it did.

Clearly, however, not everything happens as the government wants it
to. The study of Congolese history in the East continued, Zairization or
not. So did even the relationship of history to the social sciences. Thus,
among the special concerns of Centre d'études et de recherches documentaires sur l'Afrique centrale (CERDAC), the Lubumbashi history center,
are those inspired by contact with social science, such as the methods and
techniques of teaching local history, especially of Central Africa.[58] CER-
DAC was something of a model for the newer provincial research centers
that emerged in the 1970s. Thus, for example, in Kivu, Professor Bishik-
wabo of the Centre de recherches universitaires du Kiva (CERUKI) in
Bukavu publishes a journal with some concern for methodology and social
analysis; so does the Centre de recherches interdisciplinaires pour le de-
velopement de l'education (CRIDE) center in Kisangani.[59]

As other sources about the 1970s make clear, the Zairian history organization, SOHIZA, remained for diverse reasons very much on the defensive,
still struggling to establish for itself a more secure role, its leadership still
trying to quell dissident voices. If Zairization gave Zairian historians a few
more jobs, it did little to make history important in the eyes of the regime.
SOHIZA thus sought to lobby for history. It demanded that the state
should create a system of national archives over which historians should
have some say. But it did so to little avail. Through the 1970s, at least, the
National Archives of Zaire were national in name only; SOHIZA only
managed to have authority over the Western part of the country, and even
there, it lacked authority over regional depositories.[60] This seems predictable assuming the maintenance of museum cities.

Toward the 1980s, the profession appears to split. History at Lubum-bashi retains its critical voice; history at Kinshasa continues to serve as a part of the hegemonic African Studies cum Mobutuism.

As one writer from Lubumbashi put it, what is needed is a political history "which publicly accuses the divisions and instability which threat-ens Zaire."[61] To be beneficial, political history must be conjoined with a socioeconomic analysis "to denounce injustice," and it must be conjoined to a cultural analysis to combat "immobilism." It is, this writer continued, unfortunate that the state has chosen to make so little use of the history profession. History has been left purely in the academy instead of encour-aged to undertake needed research.[62]

The state was soon to reply to its critics, defending in effect its own African Studies-cum-Mobutuist vision of the field. The fiftieth anniversary of the founding of the Centre Aéquatoria, a research center in Equateur Province, was taken by the government as an occasion in 1987 for a major international conference. The local organizers were permitted to seek and to receive German funding for the conference and for the publications of the results, an expensive production called *Africanistique au Zaire* (Mban-daka, 1989). As the editors of this volume make clear, the function of this famous historical center was always to safeguard the knowledge of the local culture, and the purpose of the fiftieth anniversary conference was to reaffirm the link between scholarship today and the scholarship of the founding fathers of the center—E. Boelart and G. Hulstaert—both sincere scholars in the quest for such knowledge. In the sardonic spirit that gnosis seems to induce, the editors then went on to note that regrettably in the 1940s, the center's journal published some unfortunately inflammatory arti-cles about local cannibalism and consequently, both were in eclipse. In 1980, circumstances changed, and only since that time have the center and its journal begun to flourish again.

The state had a reply to its critics in another matter that concerned historians, the writing of political and diplomatic history textbooks. The writing of textbooks has been a source of income and of prestige for profes-sors as was noted earlier. In the late 1980s, the state evidenced a wish to distance itself from its own history profession even in this area. Thus, in this period, the ministry of culture and the Zairian ambassador to Paris turned to Robert Cornevin, a European and an author of a traditional text on the Congo, and sponsored his writing of an up-to-date and enlarged edition of his *Histoire du Congo* (1960s–1970s) to be retitled *Histoire du Zaire* (Brussels: Hayez, 1989). The main text of this latest edition does not seem to have changed much over that of the earlier ones. So the initial section still takes up the geography, the riches, and the tourist possibilities, which is still followed by an account of the prehistory, the precolonial history, and so on, arriving, finally, at a lengthy section on the government of the day, that is, of Mobutu. Obviously, this is a book that any Zairian historian could have written, but the government clearly did not wish it that way.

The Belgian Congo/Zaire is an African example of a tribal-ethnic state. Given the highly centralized character of its early capitalist history, the ruling class was able to hold off the political challenge of the petty bourgeoisie. This reached a high point during a *failed corporatist period*. This "failure," however, opened the door to struggles such as those of Pierre Mulele and Simon Kimbangu, which might not have been possible at all had the petty bourgeoisie actually come to power.

In chapters 9 and 10, I turn to an account of the fourth and final form of hegemony, beginning with the example of the modern history of the United Kingdom.

9

Bourgeois Democracy in Great Britain, 1880–1990

The modern history of Great Britain from 1880 to 1990 is an example of bourgeois democracy. The main point of the interpretation here is that in Great Britain, democracy was imposed and resisted in the late nineteenth century and finally installed when the ruling class was able to diminish the possibility of an Irish–British working-class alliance, one that surely would have undermined both the racial and the class order. The ruling class offering the English worker a welfare state, and the British worker accepting this offer. In the United States taken up in chapter 10 as a another variant of bourgeois democracy, the ruling class could not achieve this, which led to other outcomes.[1]

In the first section of this chapter, I identify the common attributes of bourgeois democracy, noting their reflection in the historiography on the United Kingdom. In the second, I discuss the phases of hegemony in Great Britain from the 1880s to 1990 and in the third, present the subject of hegemony in terms of the organization of culture. In the last, I take up the role of history writing as part of the organization of culture.

Democracy is a hazy notion in modern political thought sometimes used to describe systems that are thought to have political freedom, sometimes used to refer to a specific tradition of politics arising in ancient Greece. Historians often use the term *democracy* as the opposite of *dictatorship*. During the era of Stalin and Hitler, this usage had considerable utility and still does for the human rights organizations. In deference to this fact, it seems preferable to use the term *bourgeois democracy* as opposed to simply *democracy* here. But, whichever term one uses, one can still maintain that it is no longer really sufficient to imply that democracy or bourgeois democracy can be equated with freedom. Full stop.

In this study, as made clear in the first chapter, bourgeois democracy is taken to be rule by race, one of the four main strategies for organizing hegemony found in the modern world. In democracies, rulers give the working class legal rights, making them citizens, using bureaucratic and cultural procedures to make sure that despite the granting of such entitlements a permanent racial undercaste is maintained.[2] To succeed in playing race against class, rulers attempt to uphold the image of inclusion of the masses of poor white workers through a white-oriented cultural system while they include small numbers of the racial undercaste into this more privileged world as individuals. It is not correct to claim blacks are a minority; they may be a majority, as in South Africa. The function of this racial undercaste is not predominantly to persecute blacks but to maintain the loyalty of the white working class. As evidence of this intention, the state is willing to encourage blacks to have a cultural life and to develop themselves but to do in terms of blackness, that is, to see themselves as an unassimilable African diaspora. The bone thrown their way is that maybe their ancestors were Egyptians and maybe the Egyptians influenced Greece. This undercaste thus serves as the negative identity for the worker of the dominant race. "Thank God I am not X; my people, my country is white." X is the Catholics of Northern Ireland; the Commonwealth immigrant population or, more generally, the colonial population; U.S. blacks, Hispanics, Orientals, and American Indians; poor Israeli Sephardic Jews and Palestinians. For the blacks and for the Irish, this form of hegemony generally has meant *institutional racism* or *internal colonialism,* and these terms have sometimes been taken to be descriptions of democracies.[3]

Hegemonies have their ruling ideas and their intellectuals who represent them. In democracies, this body of thought is most clearly discerned in national character literature, commentaries on law, liberalism, and parliaments. Writers on the subject of national character, such as the American historian Perry Miller, tend to emphasize the visible fact of social consensus found in bourgeois democracies, its English counterpart being the Whig tradition or the "broad church."

No doubt consensus exists in democracies; whether one finds more there than elsewhere is difficult to know. How it is arrived at and maintained is likewise difficult to know. What can be stated with certainty is that in democracies, consensus is an element of the dominant ideology, an important idea tying together notions of how civil society functions to resolve problems peacefully, how culture and cultural diversity can spring up and still be protected by broad notions of individual liberties.

Democracies also sustain a chosen people ideology. Other societies, such as those of the Russian Road go through messianist phases in which God touches them, and those of the tribal-ethnic hegemony have apocalyptic moments in which they experience the presence of God. The idea of a compact with God that makes one a chosen person, a Westerner, and that gives one a history originating in the ancient Near East is predominantly that of the democracies, give or take its presence as a part of the Middle East itself in the idea of the "people of the book." In comparing several different examples of national character literatures produced by bourgeois democracies, it appears that the idea of chosenness or election is one of the most fundamental cultural idea in these countries, an idea sometimes appearing as science, sometimes as religious gospel. Sometimes, one finds it expressed in terms of the specialness of the West, sometimes as Zionism, sometimes as outright white supremacy, and sometimes religiously, people believing that they are special because they have the Covenant, sometimes secularly, people believing themselves to be different, perhaps simply more modern.

New imperialism & modern warfare

The idea of the chosen people is often thought to have universal appeal. Although this is not the case, even within the democracies, it clearly has more than a one-class constituency. The apparent majority of the dominant racial community grow up in, convert to, or accommodate in one way or another the concept of a chosen people. Consensus ideology offers a way to make sense of this fact.

In practical terms, the concept of chosenness offers a justification for the prevailing separation of individuals, families, and neighborhoods of the dominant race from those of the racial undercaste. In addition, it frees white persons from responsibility for what their ancestors may have done to slaves or Indians or done in spreading Christianity or Anglo-Saxon civilization. What is widely assumed might be stated as follows: the racial undercaste is not made up of chosen people. They may be Christians, but their ancestors did not come fron the Middle East as "ours" did. Therefore, what happens to them may indeed be unfortunate, but such tragedies are simply events and not a reflection on one's own culture or identity. Jews can lose their lives to the Nazis, Indians or Palestinians can lose their lands, the Commonwealth people in London can be victimized by the police daily, but these are somehow remote events even if they are happening one block away. The headline in a Western newspaper, however, expresses the felt concern of today's citizenry for a possible threat to Israel, a fellow democracy, which is halfway around the world but in many ways is much closer than what is down the block.

Thus the British live as chosen people with their John Bulls, their Winston Churchills, their Iron Ladies, and their other symbols of uniqueness and indomitability, while the Americans do much the same with their Monroe Doctrine, Manifest Destiny, their Peace Corps, and their Pax Americana.

Chosen people, in theory at least, know no limitations. They may live in nation-states like everyone else, but these states do not have fixed and final borders. It is ordinary people who live in states with fixed and final borders. In Great Britain, it was long a matter of pride that the sun never

set on the British empire; in the United States, only God and nature created
boundaries. The question of the boundaries of Israel is still unsettled.[4]

Although racism is something commonly found in all the hegemonies,
it takes different forms in different hegemonies. Where racism in the Tribal
Road, Russian Road, and Italian Road is *cultural,* in bourgeois democracies,
it is *scientific,* something taken to be immutable as opposed to constructed
or malleable. Immutable at least in the popular mind because scientists in
bourgeois society are supposed to possess real truth. It is also the case that
sometimes scientists in democracies exploit this aura and carry out rather
questionable research about race, often getting away with it because science
is so unquestioned.

In general terms, science is unquestioned if positivism has no critics. If
positivism has critics such as one would find with an independent metaphysical tradition in Italy or in Russia or with an anarchist deconstructionist
tradition as in Zaire, then it and its ideas of race become a part of what is
true, but not truth itself. In bourgeois democracies, for whatever reasons—
individualism, consumerism, presentism, and so forth—it has no effective
critics. The romantic metaphysical tradition serves to reinforce positivism
more than to challenge it. Thus, it is that bourgeois democracy is the
hegemony that is the most open not only to science as critical inquiry but
to science as dogma, a terrain with its fixed categories. Antiracists are
reduced to arguing that race is a false category because one can not attack
the idea of a category, that mulattos are not lepers, that they themselves are
not "race traitors."

Democracies reveal in their conduct of international relations, to anticipate the conclusion of the book, certain predictable patterns of interaction
that are worthy of note. One might divide this subject into relations with
countries that are not democracies and relations with those that are. With
regard to the former, some would say such relations are predictably violent
and exploitative, and there is certainly truth in this point, especially as
regards Western relations with the Third World. Again, the idea of a chosen
people ideology or identity politics seems to have some explanatory value.
What one does to people who are not chosen does not matter for, one is
carrying out God's work.

Among other predictable patterns of democracies' interactions with
nondemocracies is the one that emerges in immigration policy. Whereas
politicians in some historical roads try to solve their problems by getting
rid of their own people, politicians in democracies try to do so by introducing new cheap labor through immigration mainly from outside the democracies, perhaps because one cannot get rid of chosen people. Whatever the
case, the common pattern is for people who do the cheap labor to come
from the other hegemonies and, if they stay, to undergo a major identity
transformation and become chosen people. Although no doubt the interests

of capitalism are involved, it is again the broader cultural ideology of the hegemony that determines why this should happen to the immigrant, why some groups are perceived to have assimilated simply by having arrived, why other groups are perceived as having difficulty assimilating or as being unassimilatable.

Relations between countries that are democracies have other attributes and other outcomes, sometimes catastrophic ones. Given the feelings of solidarity that chosen people feel for each other, an attack on one, especially an attack by a nondemocracy, is an attack on all. Wars quickly became world wars; Russia, Japan, or the Third World becomes a common enemy. Hitler, an outsider from Bavaria, stole Germany, and the West won it back. The Marshall Plan, the NATO alliance, the aid to Israel, and the sympathy for white South Africa are among examples of this solidarity among the democracies. What seems to follow from the commitment to this form of international relations is that democracies often exist in the world as a group; other nations tend to stand alone. This solidarity tends to make a democracy quite formidable.

Despite this apparent strength of the democracies, their citizens commonly take the position that they are threatened by the existence of the other hegemonies and that they must collectively undertake the task of "making the world safe for democracy."

Making the world safe for democracy has various significations, ranging from failing to understand other countries or their languages to a belief in the need to restructure or destroy them. Somewhere in between is the posture of aggressively flaunting the virtues of democracies. "There may have been blemishes in the past, such as slavery, but today the blemishes are all gone."[5] Such identity politics underlies missionary activity, foreign aid, and even political interventions. And although it may be true that civil society and rule by law are more developed in democracies than elsewhere and that they are, as democratic ideology maintains, independent at least in the formal sense from "politics," as much historical research shows from Gramsci onward, civil society is not a free or autonomous domain, but simply a construction, one which the state penetrates on a regular basis to secure desired outcomes. This fact of *government intervention* makes the issue of freedom as a feature of democracy less clear-cut; democracies in practice are closer to other hegemonies than is commonly thought.

To make this revisionist picture of democracy clear, imagine a family in a democracy who believe that "one's home is one's castle" deciding one day to markedly alter the appearance of their home by adding a couple of rooms in back because they have invited several friends to live with them while the friends are out of work. Suppose they have children. As if from nowhere, such decisions by the family may well bring down upon them social workers, zoning-law specialists, and the like, with the result that the families involved, if not affluent, may face eviction, loss of custody of their children, and so on.[6]

Why then the furor about freedom? Why all the assumptions based on so little compelling evidence? Seemingly, the idea of freedom in a democracy emerges from the the assumption that chosen people are individually responsible for themselves to their creator. To manifest this responsibility, they must make free choices. To make free choices, they, therefore, must be free to make such choices; they must as a consequence be living in the freest of all societies. Capitalists cynically exploit this ideology by arguing that governmental welfare to the poor deprives the poor of the chance to take their lives into their own hands, and such is the power of the belief in freedom that many poor people deprive themselves of possible government benefits in the belief that they should earn their way.

In comparative terms, citizens in a democracy tend to assume a world cultural hierarchy manifested through institutions such as the Nobel Prize, something that is mainly won by people in democracy. Citizens in democracies believe that the reason for this success is that creativity depends on freedom, and because they have the most freedom, they have the most creativity. Whether this is true or not, individual achievements are a conspicuous feature of the democracies. How this is to be interpreted is not so clear. Perhaps capitalism benefits from having a few countries in which new technology is being produced. This, however, seems speculative. Concepts go through many stages to become ideas, then applications, and the actual products. There is plenty of leeway for how one chooses to ascribe credit from witch doctors with their herbs to pharmaceutical houses with pills based on these herbs. Thus, if hundreds of individuals in the bourgeois democracies are identifiable to their neighbors as inventors or achievers of unusual merit, far more so than is the case in the other historical roads, and nearly all of them are white, politics must be playing a role. Perhaps giving an award to a chemist who is English as opposed to a witch doctor who is Zairian is simply a functional thing. In a tribal-ethnic state, it would not be functional for someone to receive such an award, individualism not being promoted there, whereas in a democracy, such as England, it would be.

Finally, citizens in the bourgeois democratic hegemonies share a specific outlook toward history, a surprisingly disinterested one, given their involvement in the affairs of state. Bourgeois governments insist that citizens should know their history as they know the law.[7] And, indeed, history is a major preoccupation of national leaders of education in the democracies. Yet, paradoxically, despite this preoccupation on the official level, a profound tendency remains toward ahistoricism in the culture as a whole. Positivism and individualism seem to promote vast productions of history books by small groups of individuals but the typical student often says thus and so is *history* meaning it is dead, gone, and no longer important. This is, perhaps, one of the most common usages of the word. In recent years, the official media has been expressing alarm that social studies has supplanted history and that students do not know the sequence of events anymore. Reflecting once again on "national character" literature, one finds that because of the chosen people ideology, a wide segment of the educated population turns away from history to heritage or turns to history not so much for understanding but out of nostalgia. The nostalgia trend, currently called "public history," is so large that it threatens to engulf the little world of students and professors concerned with scientific history.

What the flight from real history signifies on a deep level or why there is so much nostalgia, is, naturally, a matter for speculation. The most consistent hypothesis is the one alluded to before, namely, that the chosen people ideology does not fully overcome feelings of discomfort or guilt that the dominant white middle strata feel about race relations past and present and that the stress on identity through heritage as opposed to history is simply the most comfortable way of managing the meaning of the past. Thus, one finds on the grass-roots level, democracies teach their youth Western civilization or Western heritage. They do not place the same emphasis on the knowledge of history. "Youth are left ignorant," the criticism is justified.[8] What educated persons in a democracy come to feel most is an affinity to Greece and the Bible, perhaps to the Middle Ages or the Renaissance, but not to the recent historical past even of their own country. Yet modern history is rich in stories of struggle and of hope far more so than ancient history.

In turning to the case of the UK, what strikes many commentators, nonetheless, is the power of the state vis-à-vis the civil society and the working classes. From the 1880s onward, politicians were able to forge alliances with the working class, which not only blunted much of the industrial struggle but gave the state the freedom to involve itself in many aspects of the life of the country. Stuart Hall, the British sociologist, uses the term *interventionist state* to describe this state. Opposition to it has not been easy; the racial undercaste from the late nineteenth century became separate "nations," that is, essentially excluded from the standard modern history of the country.

Standard historiography, the writings of positivist and Marxist historians on the modern period, usually begin with the industrial revolution of the eighteenth century. For the period 1780–1880, the emphasis is more on economic growth than on anything else; politics and culture are obliged to take a back seat. Somewhat more marginal is the romantic historiography. It treats modern history as a footnote to the Whig tradition that arose in the Middle Ages and has glided on ever since from the Norman Conquest through the events of the early modern period to the culture of the Victorian period. Looked at in a more critical light, much evidence serves to contradict this idea of continuity presumed by the romantics. Victorian culture in the 1870s and 1880s underwent a rupture as it was made to serve the needs of the cultural hegemony of the modern state. It was, as Stuart Hall and others have shown, different than what went before. I work here with the implications of Hall's portrayal of modernity in the United Kingdom.

Since the early nineteenth century, following his approach, the landed, industrial, and mercantile elites in Ireland, Scotland, Wales, and England shared through marriage, investments, and the City of London itself, a United Kingdom. In the late nineteenth century, a perceptible integration of these elites occurred. Horizontal integration from above, combined with a widening suffrage from below, made class conflict a significant possibility. To keep the old order of the *single nation,* the Tories and Whigs gradually abandoned their laissez-faire policies summed up in the idea of the state as a nightwatchman and replaced it with a new bureaucratic structure of control, the *interventionist state.* Between 1880 and 1920, the liberalism that the state sought to uphold, however, played itself out.[9] These forty years are the period in which the modern nation state began. From these years followed a corporatist period termed here *collectivism,* 1920–70, and a libertarian-liberal phase from 1970–90.

The Rise of the Modern State: A Liberal Age, 1880–1920

The attribution of the terms *liberal* and *modern* to the period after 1880 is, in the main, political.[10] Capitalism had long since been a dominant force economically; the political linkages or "interventions" of the state were new. Economic changes are, of course, important to note. During this period, British industry began to face competition on a world scale, and although it continued to expand, its expansion was slower and slower. Increasingly, capitalists fell back on commercial and financial services, the remaining area where they had an advantage. As a result of this reorientation, the white-collar work force and, by extension, the lower middle class more generally expanded, employed both in industry and in the government. As this expansion occurred, political participation widened as well, and new kinds of splits appeared in the dominant Liberal party; a number of intellectuals (T. H. Greene, Hobson, and the Hammonds) defected from the broader consensus supporting classical liberal laissez-faire economics to welfarism. Finally, even well-known politicians began to defect, for example, Joseph Chamberlain. As mayor of Birmingham, Chamberlain abandoned liberal economics and introduced welfare state policies, policies termed derisively by his contemporaries as "gas and water socialism."[11]

An important issue for the new hegemony—or at least so the liberal politicians claimed—was the resolution of the Irish Question. As was obvious even to contemporaries, the Irish Question in English politics had the potential to disrupt the hegemony by challenging the racial hierarchy, introducing socialism or anticolonialism or all three. This did not happen, the "one nation" ideology incorporated it, thereby permitting the eventual breakdown of the Liberal Age to lead to a collectivist phase from within the same hegemony. The historic legislation in 1920, the Government of Ireland Act of 1920, linked six northern counties to Britain as the "one nation." This act, a compromise between the home rule and the union positions, kept the United Kingdom intact, keeping as well a segment of the Irish population as a racial undercaste for the United Kingdom.

Another area of relative success for the state came in its handling of gender policies. At a time when many middle-class women sympathized with poor women, the state succeeded in dividing women against each other, pitting middle-class domesticism against the needs of working women. Operations carried out by the police of London in the 1880s and 1890s were able both to break the economic self-sufficiency of working-class women employed as whores and to separate whores from their neighbors and kin. The attack on prostitution took the form of registry and forced moving of prostitutes to locations separate from those of their families. The campaign was a great success over anything the state had done before in its various campaigns in the name of contagious diseases or public morality. The outcome of this campaign had many ramifications; one of the most important of which was that the state was able to impose the nuclear family as the only acceptable form of the family. Because working-class women did not earn enough to survive by themselves, many were obliged to marry or stay married.[12] From the success of this campaign, it became clear that the state had some basis of support among middle-class women, and this seems logical at least for this time period. These women had had to come to terms with the nuclear family and, perhaps, therefore resented women who did not. These women as well had recently gained an important measure of legal equality in the British Married Woman's Property Act of 1882.

The "success" of the liberal hegemony depended ultimately on how labor would challenge it. Before World War I, the leadership of the Labour party had fallen to men who had grown up under the wing of the Liberal party and who were unlikely to mount a very formidable challenge to the government. To be more precise, labor challenge was possible in matters concerning wages and working conditions, but it did not translate into what the working class might share with Irish nationalists. Even for the Labourite intellectuals, who did challenge the government on many issues, the presence of well-assimilated Irish Catholics in England, carrying on their lives without undue problems, served to confirm the wisdom of the status quo, given even their own nonconformist and anti-Catholic views. Northern Ireland simply needed what the Tories had always claimed it needed, more modernization and fewer papal bulls.[13] A deeper interpretation of the role of the Irish in British hegemony does not seem to have emerged.

The breakdown of the liberal hegemony, the so-called "death of liberal England," defies easy explanation. External setbacks as in the Boer War, in the relative erosion of Britain's industrial position vis-à-vis that of her rivals, and, finally, in the costs of World War I clearly played a role. Of most concern is the internal dynamic because it is here that the basic choices were made in the face of the various difficulties the country may have faced. Internally, it appears the breakdown of liberalism took the form of a drift toward corporatism. Gradually, over twenty or thirty years, the Labour party became an acknowledged part of the ruling alliance. A harbinger of these changes was the welfare program of 1906–12.

A common misconception about the breakdown of liberalism and the rise of collectivism is that it was a project of the Left. This is not illogical because the working class was obviously a beneficiary. On closer scrutiny, however, one finds that the Right as well as the Left had a hand in the move to collectivism. In fact, it appears that the appeal of the political Right to the organized labor movement gave the ruling class more reason to rely on it. The two classes shared similar attitudes about race, at least judging from the support both gave to movements such as the British Brothers League, which was founded in 1902 to limit immigration.[14]

The Collectivist Period: 1920–1970

The collectivist period from 1920 to 1970 followed upon the crucial decision of the English capitalist class to align itself with labor to protect the home market and the industrial base. It followed equally from the crucial decision of the labor movement to move from confrontation to collaboration with the state, a decision that came from both the Left and the Right within the labor movement, a decision that can be said to have been taken almost by inertia with the passing of the threat of a general strike and or of active involvement in the Irish Question in the years between 1919 and 1926.[15]

From this shift in strategy on the part of both labor and capital gradually evolved the social contract and the welfare state. Factors contributing to this outcome included not just the willingness of the working class to follow the lead of the state in the areas of race and gender but something else as well, capitalist tendencies in the working class. Recent studies of the

British working class reveal not only its capacity for militancy but the entrepreneurial tendencies of its penny capitalists, the segment of the working class that as individuals and families was engaged in small-scale production. According to one study, such families brought to their working class neighborhoods much of their conservatism.[16]

Yet another area where state and working class interests overlapped was that concerning the empire. The working class felt an undeniable interest in the progress of empire. In acceding to the common term *collectivist,* one must stress that it was never an alliance of equals but an alliance of classes. In the other hegemonies and, indeed, in other democracies such as the United States, one must use the word *corporatism* because in effect there the state and ruling class fragmented the working class and the lower middle class in the process of allying with it, whereas here it did not or could not do so.

In 1925, the race issue rose to challenge collectivism. White workers in ports such as Liverpool forced the National Union of Seamen to exclude blacks from employment as dock workers. Although there were not so many blacks and this was, in any case, not the first attempt to restrict the immigration of workers, it was at this point that blacks, seeking protection, turned to organizations such as Harold Moody's League of Coloured Peoples, an organization that became important in the years that followed. The black population gradually supplanted the Irish and Jewish communities as the center of the racial undercaste in the United Kingdom.[17] Finally, the challenge of the Commonwealth people, which had begun in 1925, had by 1968 driven the Labour government to pass the Commonwealth Immigration Act, which denied entrance to British passport holders, read "colored" British passport holders, those not born in the United Kingdom.[18] By this point once and for all, blacks took center stage away from other groups in British racial politics.

This is not to suggest that the Irish Question simply went away with collectivism or with the arrival of blacks nor that Jews ceased to be a "Jewish nation" within the United Kingdom. These things live on, and at least the Irish Question remains unresolved. In the Belfast dockyards, "Orangeist" ideology continued as before to divide the working class along religious-cum-racial lines. The Protestant working class clearly benefited from Orangeism. They were not, as many writers have imagined, simply dupes of Protestant capitalists. They would not have gained from class solidarity with their Catholic confrerees because the context held no hope for either. Would a united working class in Belfast be able to hold its own against the larger rural-oriented power structure of Northern Ireland? Thus, the Irish Question simmered on through the collectivist period, gradually declining in importance as the racial undercaste became more and more black, South Asian, and on the mainland.[19]

Viewed in economic terms, the alliances of the collectivist era tended to link the state and male workers, on the one hand, and the state and middle-class women, on the other, at the expense of the poor in general and of the racial undercaste woman in particular. There were exceptions to this and there was change, but this was the general picture. As British industrialists assimilated Taylorism, they, like their American counterparts in the interwar years, began to whittle away at the position of their ally, the skilled worker. Wartime exigencies in both the world wars gave employers added leverage. During these wars, employers were able to use women because there were no men. Employers found women workers to be cheaper and easier to control because the women were in desperate need of income. Fired if they married or joined a union, or, having joined a union, fired if they rejected the agreements reached in their name by the union representative, working-class women were politically isolated. Middle-class women, as Virginia Woolf ruefully noted in a famous novel of World War I, were rewarded for their acquiescence to collectivism with the vote.[20] Feminist initiative still lay in the future. At least for this period, the state could still be sure of its alliance with middle-class women.

The factors contributing to the breakdown of the collectivist era were not new; they had been there from the beginning. For capitalists, collectivism was a structure with which to make profits. When this did not suffice, their tendency was to withdraw from the alliance with labor and try to reimpose classical liberalism. For labor, collectivism fulfilled certain generic needs, such as security of life and welfare. When these needs were met, many members of the Labour party found themselves then wanting much the Party could not provide, whether peace, a clean environment, or suburban amenities. As more and more members of the working class moved to the suburbs, many withdrew from the Labour party, losing interest in the collectivist alliance.

The leverage that labor had was proportional to the level of struggle that they were prepared to engage in. Having accepted the principle of collectivism, the amount of leverage left was proportional to the degree to which capitalists sought to make money through manufactured goods produced in Britain. At the outset of the collectivist period, in any case, it is clear that state policy clearly favored the interests of manufacturers over others. One generation later, priority went to finance capitalism.

In 1919, the government raised death duties. It was one more heavy blow against the agricultural estates of England traditionally inherited from one generation to the next. As land became more costly to inherit, this accelerated the trend toward the breaking up of estates and, consequently, a trend toward owner occupancy, which affected more than one million acres of British agricultural land. In the opinion of a recent author, during the early 1920s, the onset of the collectivist period, the traditional landed class was destroyed and a new one was created, a yeomanry.[21]

Although, no doubt, a few of the old rural families of wealth held on for another generation, most of them succumbed. By the 1920s, these families were faced not just with the death duties, but with a lack of affordable domestic help as well. During this period was a general servants' crisis and the near end of the British nanny. Again, state policy was involved. In the 1920s, the state dismantled the poor law legislation, replacing it with laws that set up public housing and widows' and orphans' pensions. The poor began to have an option other than servitude on the rural estates.[22] In addition to policies against the agricultural elite, which helped industry indirectly, one can identify state policies clearly designed to benefit industry, for example, state policies toward labor "radicalism." Labor radicalism was perceived by industrialists to be a threat to their interests. Given the presence of the Labour party in the ruling alliance, the state could engage in violent repression of the more radical workers in the early years of collectivism, 1918–21, demanding the complicity of the labor officials in the alliance in its policies. In this it succeeded, although when this complicity became apparent, the working class was greatly demoralized. Put another way; a new equilibrium had been reached, one that would last a generation.

By the end of the 1960s, British manufacturing had become a weak sector. It was increasingly noncompetitive. Thus, in this period, the state began to abandon industry; it had become an albatross. The great profit area was becoming once again finance. For finance and for the wider service sector by extension to reach its full potential, it was necessary for the state in the view of various financiers to sell off the industries it owned and stop subsidizing the rest. Capital must be liberated to earn the largest possible returns, and the largest possible returns were no longer likely to be made in the United Kingdom. By the end of the 1960s, not only economic but political strategies needed to be changed.

The Rise of Neoliberalism, 1970 to the Present

The twenty years, from the 1970s to the 1990s, variously termed neo-Liberal, libertarian-liberal and Thatcherite by different writers, marks, however one characterizes it, a rupture with the politics of collectivism. How did it arise? What made British industry so unprofitable? The two questions seem interrelated. One obvious reason for the second was the stiffening of international competition with the rise of Germany and of East Asia. On the domestic front, however, class conflict was taking new and more sophisticated forms. This, in turn, produced reactions from capitalists. Some tried to expand their control over workers by increasing the size of their managerial staffs, only to find that as their managerial staffs increased, their businesses became less profitable. Others tried to use cold war ideology as a form of social control, only to find that in the British case, it did not work very well. Finally, some capitalists responded to the problem of decline by trying their luck in the Third World. Not all, however, had to go so far, for as important segments of the working class became more middle class, they also became willing to abandon the Labour party. In this section, I take up the strategies of the new Tory ruling class that emerged to promote a return to laissez-faire capitalism as the collectivist era fell apart.[23]

As one enters the 1970s, it is apparent that class conflict increasingly turned on middle-class issues; the threat of the strike was more and more a means to an end to sway public opinion. In fact, the struggle between ruler and ruled became increasingly one of swaying public opinion. Numerous commentators have pointed out that from this period, the role of the mass media rose in importance and that Thatcher and the other new Tories emerging on the scene were superb media personalities. They were not isolated from the society as the old Tories had been because of their special education and upbringing. Thus, the new Tories could flaunt their ordinariness. Given who they were in social terms, the sight of them expressing confidence about the national future struck a deep chord with the British middle classes. "Vote Labour, and you are on the road back to where you began. Who would you prefer to guard you against the menaces of terrorism, foreign labor, crime on the street, welfare fraud, and so forth, Labour or Tory?" With its split constituency between blue collar and white collar, the Labour party grew weaker and weaker. It involuntarily began to participate in Thatcher's image of it as the party of the past.[24]

The very quest of the Labour party for a base in the new middle classes, however plausible, tended to loosen the party's ties to the working class and to open the door to voter defection. But this loss was almost inevitable. With the movement of working class voters to the suburbs, new issues arose that divided the party's supporters. Suburbanites were preoccupied with race and crime in different ways than was the old urban working class. For suburbanites, welfare was no longer something to support so enthusiastically. In the city moreover, realities were different than they had been one generation earlier. A new generation of working-class youth was on the rise, cut adrift from the major parties. As one might guess, splits in the working class deepened and cost the Labour party votes if not to the Tories then to the fascist-oriented National Front, which moved in and gained the loyalty of much of this new generation. The fate of the Labour party, like its analogue, the Democratic party in the United States, was to become on the national level the perennial underdog. With the defeat of the miners in the Strike of 1984–85, why would even a miner vote Labour?

Yet why would anyone vote for the Tories? Clearly, to rule in the United Kingdom from this period on meant mastering the art of crisis management, the art of presenting the situation as a crisis and the present ruling party as indispensable to the solution of the crisis. What is important, thus, is not the de-facto shift to a one-party system but the way in which the leading Tory politicians managed to redefine politics away from unsolvable issues to those that could be dealt with in fact through crisis management. By magnifying crime on the street and terrorism abroad, politicians could shift the discourse from the more problematic long-term dimension of the national future to small-scale successes in the present. By defining what the crisis is, the state begins with an advantage. With any luck, a government can manage crises such as youth on the street and claim success after success. As was the case in the late nineteenth century, so in the 1970s, crisis management easily enough led to policies supporting the police and the army and an ever-larger, more vigilant version of the old interventionist state.

Thatcherite politics rested heavily on playing on middle-class sensibilities. Here was a class much affected by images of Britain in the nineteenth century. Once Brittania ruled the waves and was not easily defied, but at that time, things were different. The present Tories could scarcely claim to be the heir to that tradition. The more recent form of Toryism bears little resemblance to the older one. Its relationships to the Third World smack of pure pragmatic interventionism as, for example, in the Falkland Island or Malvina War.[25] Disraeli would have invoked a thousand years of historic precedent. The difference that stands out is that the old Tories and new Tories are truly very different people. Financiers in those days, in contrast to today, sought to marry into the manufacturing elite or the landed aristocracy and to root themselves thereby in the "real" ruling class. This tendency gave British foreign policy a certain fixity through its rootedness in history and tradition in contrast to that of contemporary Britain where any such appeals seem to critics at least artificial.

Still, in manipulating fears over class, race, and gender in a fearful age, the new Tories have demonstrated a comparable level of skill to that of the Victorians in playing one contradiction against another. As in the nineteenth century so today, not only does one find violence and repression on the part of the state but side by side with it a skillful cultivation of a few blacks and a few women, some of whom the Tories even helped get elected to parliament.[26] One recent example of this neoliberal cultivation of select undercaste personalities emerged in Thatcher's decision to guard Salman Rushdie's life at state expense. Rushdie's status today is one of which other South Asians in Britain may only dream.

With regard to gender, there are instances as well where libertarian policies can be shown to have had a "trickle down" effect that benefited the Tories at the polls. For example, under Thatcher in 1983, British women gained the power of passing on the nationality to their children, independently of their husbands. This did benefit a few women, and the media made the most of this fact. Previously, for example, before 1948, women were less free but also a lot less poor. In those days, women's citizenship simply followed that of their husbands. In 1948, women gained their own right to British nationality but marriage with children to a foreigner still had some of the qualities of indenturement. In 1983, Thatcher tried to play on that contradiction and turn more women, especially from the new business strata, into Tory voters.

At the same time, she and those around her found a way to place themselves in the tradition of the Puritans and of leaders such as Oliver Cromwell, insisting in so doing that they were upholding the real English values. Judged by results, Thatcher's regime has made the odd fusion of Puritanism and libertarianism somehow believable. She is as much a part of the chosen people tradition, as much a Whig as anyone. By turns, Thatcher has been able to exploit the coercive totalitarian qualities of Cromwell and then, with equal facility, to embody the values of his critics, picking up on the individualized pragmatist or "remissive" qualities of the anti-Cromwellites. Her opponent is the British Left. Their collectivism, she claims, makes them incapable of understanding personal moral responsibility, and from this comes their failure to appreciate the degeneracy of the welfare state. Thatcher has been able to evoke older habits of British thought, which tend to reduce broad social issues such as mass poverty into moral questions to be judged on the basis of the merit of individuals.[27]

Thatcherism scarcely seems invulnerable. It seems reasonable to imagine that even the Thatcherites and today the Majorites are asking themselves what will happen when Britain joins the European Economic Community (EEC) as a quite weak participant? How will they survive without the revenue of the North Sea oil?

Are there challengers in the modern British experience who are aware of their opportunities? Here, one comes to some disconcerting conclusions. No British movement faced the issue of the racial undercaste squarely or made a deep estimate of the power of the state to extract loyalty from its subjects because of the shared chosen people ideology. Sympathy for the Irish as oppressed workers was a sentiment in the British working class before World War I, but the idea of an alliance with the Irish nationalist movement was something outside its ken. Most movements of opposition in modern times have come from within the working class or the middle class and reflect fairly narrow class and racial concerns, the most prominent example being the British Communist party.

Periodically, however, there have been exceptions or partial exceptions to this general point. Groups arise that make the effort to combine diverse constituencies, for example, the recent left-leaning Campaign for Nuclear Disarmament (CND).[28]

CND's strategy has been to try to claim the ground that the Tories cannot claim. Influenced by the strategic thought of the historian E. P. Thompson and of the sociologist Stuart Hall, the movement has attempted to claim for itself the classical Tory tradition of the broad church. New Tories cannot enter this area. If they stress too much their Puritan approach to Englishness, they lose their libertarian backers and vice versa. They can keep both constituencies only by obscuring the differences. How will the Tories fight the CND? Will the CND push the Tories to allow the development of a National Front-type fascism? Until now, the Tories appear to hope that they can keep the CND split. After all, was not Thatcher Britain's real revolutionary? Was not she the one who freed the masses from the state?[29] The CND, in any case, clearly has its limitations and its divisions.

The Organization of Culture in the United Kingdom, 1880s–1990

Since the nineteenth century, the English state has sought to organize a cultural policy and to carry out projects of persuasion useful for the maintenance of its hegemony. Among the most important strategies adopted in the area of culture was the state's monopolization of the idea of Englishness, of what is acceptably English. To be English is to be acceptable; to be non-English is to be dismissable. By examining the idea of Englishness in some detail, the more abstract concept of a chosen people becomes more concrete. It opens the door to a consideration of fields such as anthropology, literary criticism, archaeology, and the media, all of which have played an essential role in the organization of culture.

It should scarcely be surprising that, given the changing interests of ruling class, the leading intellectuals of the state have had to recast what the term means in each of the three periods surveyed. They have had to suppress parts of the term that were true but not useful in order to exclude the racial undercaste, and they have had to exaggerate parts of Englishness that were, perhaps, fairly shallowly rooted in the British culture of the time but were useful for the regime, such as its regionalist association with Southeast England. In the period 1880–1920 in which the state was rooted in an alliance of the industrialists, the London bankers, and the landed aristocracy, the intellectuals presented Englishness as ethnicity. In the period 1920–70, a social inclusiveness notion of Englishness that corresponded to the strategy of collectivism appeared. In the period 1970–90, Englishness once again was redefined in a more limited way around Puritanism and libertarianism.

In the nineteenth century, Englishness was that which the ruling "plutocracy" could agree on in the face of issues that divided it: Ireland, the empire, the growing importance of London, the politics of expanding education to the masses, and the gradual decline of the economy, to mention a few. A close look at the details of Englishness in this period reveals that what could be agreed on was geographical; Englishness emphasized the politically most influential region of the country, the countryside of the South East. This localism gives to the Englishness of that period its ethnic flavor. Ethnicity is further reinforced by the importance attached to the dominant prose. Mastery of this prose was mainly possible through the public schools, and these schools were open to certain English men. This linguistic-ethnic concept of Englishness is further clarified when one turns to poetry. The poets of the era, even the well-known ones, appear to be outsiders to the dominant idea of Englishness; perhaps as a result, some were avowedly rebels, anarchists, symbolists, and so forth.[30]

Englishness, argues a recent writer, was a production of the last quarter of the nineteenth century. It was a self-conscious attempt to absorb what was English into a mold and to place what was Irish or non-English more generally underneath it.[31] The Church of England and the universities worked in collaboration. Specific features that stand out include the marked preference for the active voice, for the masculine voice, and for the literary canon. This is the period that produced the major reference tool, *The Oxford English Dictionary,* to serve both as historian and arbiter of the language. During this period, study of the folklore of the Celtic fringe as well, increased, of course, as the study of the colonies. A low culture was created and placed alongside the high culture of Englishness. Political shrewdness is apparent in this as well. One finds the traditional Tory concern with breadth appearing in a judicious broadening of what was construed to be English literature so as to include a few works simply because they were beloved by the whole society, for example, *Peter Pan.* Curiously, classics, the area of interest of the older aristocracy, entered the modern period only to decline. It was not included.

Englishness as an ethnically oriented form of cultural hegemony was certainly vulnerable to the assaults of outsiders. What is less well known is that leading English writers felt vulnerable even in their own circles. This last is reflected in the insistence on a somewhat official level that the authoritative dictionary, James Murray's *New English Dictionary,* be not only the record of the language's development but its arbiter as well. Dissenter and Scotsman that he was, Murray, its editor, had originally conceived his project merely to provide a record of usage, but when he sought the backing of Oxford and approached Benjamin Jowett, the master of Balliol College, he found that what the latter would insist on was not just a record of the language but an arbiter of good usage. Thus arose *The Oxford English Dictionary,* a monument of Whig linguistic history from 1150 onward.[32]

The major assault on Englishness in this period, no doubt, was the one from without. The Irish avantgarde writers, in particular, disrupted the attempts to institutionalize an English traditionalism; Joyce, for example, broke with the conventional narrative strategy, Yeats with the division between history and myth, Shaw presented the English public with an alternative to what they read from the writers trained at Oxbridge. The Irish avantgarde were not alone; in retrospect they were part of wider currents of literary modernism that included even some of the leading English prose writers such as E. M. Forster and D. H. Lawrence. Writers who emphasized acceptable subjects such as imperialism, for example, the historians and a few literary figures such as Kipling, were too limited to serve as a counterweight.

The collectivist period saw a shift in the foundations of Englishness from language and folklore to science, economics, political science, sociology, and even to social history, fields facilitating greater inclusiveness. In this period, Englishness in fact reflected the cross-class alliance, which brought together the Labour party and the representatives of the traditional upper classes led by the industrialists. Classical liberals and segments of the religious establishment were marginalized. But as Perry Anderson, the political economist, showed, rather than collapsing they strengthened their position by importing or attracting a range of brilliant intellectuals from the Continent who were all antagonists of collectivism and of the metaphysics and holistic thought that tended to go with it. In Anderson's interpretation, the last great English intellectuals—Bertrand Russell, John Maynard Keynes, and D. H. Lawrence—all matured before World War I, leaving the interwar stage, Keynes and Russell excepted, to imported figures such as Ludwig Wittgenstein, a philosophy professor from Austria, Lewis Namier, a historian from Poland, Karl Popper, a social theorist from Austria, and Isiah Berlin, a political theorist from Russia.

The economist John Maynard Keynes arguably was what Gramsci would term a "great intellectual." He combined the philosophies of manufacturing capitalism and workerism in his thought, this combination being the basis of the regime's hegemony. As an economist, Keynes was a scientist, thereby tapping into another form of legitimacy in English culture. In his career as economist and economic advisor, Keynes found a way within the inherited categories of neoclassical economics to construe Englishness to mean the need for state intervention of the sort that would avoid social crises. Keynes master concept, demand management, was the bridge between the idioms of capitalism and workerism; it led in practice to governmental control of wages and prices.[33]

How far should state intervention go and to what end? Politicians in this period involved the state in deeper and deeper interventions into the organization of culture and of society. As they did so, social workers, sociologists, and academic professors in many other fields were needed. State patronage grew perceptibly, and the groundwork for this patronage was laid by legislation. Examples of laws that influenced the direction of state policies include the Public Libraries Act (1919) and the Physical Training and Recreation Act (1937). After World War II, the state opened numerous Red Brick universities, but contrary to its expectations more was not better; new universities did not strengthen the hegemony. Indeed, they often proved divisive. Conservatives who were part of the collectivist coalition did not see the need to educate the working class. Radicals did not want the state to directly influence the working class by providing entertainment and education for it. Thus, for example, as early as the depression, the Communist party of Great Britain turned to the organization of sports and academic life as did the British Fascists, making the organization of sport culture and even higher education less rewarding for the state.[34] The Communists, for example, eventually opened a Communist University.

With Britain's decline after the Great War, a number of intellectuals were cast adrift. As Anderson noted, they chose to leave the center stage to foreigners who came to the British universities, but nonetheless, they continued to play for many years a major role in British life. An important example of such a figure was the philosopher Bertrand Russell. From World War I onward, Russell concerned himself with the issue of world peace. Other British intellectuals served the League of Nations; still others served the international humanitarian organizations and the church. What is extraordinary through the collectivist era and even during the Great Depression was the staying power of writers who directly or indirectly continued to espouse the older ideology of laissez-faire capitalism.[35] Extraordinary also under such circumstances was how long collectivism lasted.

Englishness after 1970 was the Englishness of *neo-Puritanism*. For the first time, Englishness really lost its specific class appeal. Gone was the aristocratic Englishness of the nineteenth century and the upper-class paternalism of the collectivist period. Not only does Thatcher's Englishness appeal to the banker concerned with inflation but to the British worker concerned with the threat posed by the immigrant worker.[36] In this period, the basis of Englishness is found in fields such as archeology, which reveals a heritage for all classes in England, and in fields such as literary criticism, which makes the speech and taste of the ordinary man equal to that of Oxbridge. Englishness is revealed as well in the rising influence of religionists among whom for the first time are fundamentalists. The fields supporting social engineering declined as the state no longer perceived social differences to be a problem.

Since the 1970s, a Selsdon Group of "radical" Tories, among whom were Margaret Thatcher, Sir Keith Joseph, and Nigel Lawson, arose calling for a return to classical liberalism, not to the decadent classical liberalism of the old Tories but to an evangelical version that drew its roots from as far back as the Puritans. They insisted that not only the Labor party but the Tories, for example, former Prime Minister Harold Macmillan, author of *The Middle Way,* had misread the meaning of the Great Depression in emphasizing employment over control of inflation.[37]

External pressures played their role in the evolution of this hegemony, but what finally mattered was how the British politicians of this era chose to use them. Thus, one finds that a far-sighted Conservative government used the crisis of the 1973–74 Organizatoion of Petroleum Exporting Countries (OPEC) oil embargo not to make military cutbacks but to borrow money from the International Monetary Fund (IMF). By 1976, the pressure of the IMF on successive Labor governments had taken its toll, and the mainstream Labourites had to give up their goal of full employment. Subsequently, the Conservative government was able to use the Miner's Strike of 1984 to make public opinion at large come to see the ultimate irrationality of the whole collectivist tradition.

When, for example, Thatcher wanted to cut income taxes, which she claimed were a hindrance to entrepreneurs, she extolled the British tradition of private initiative. These cuts hurt the working class, but this was never articulated. Through a series of media appearances, Thatcher could speak of inefficient business numbed by a too-long and too-intimate relation with an expanded state structure without intending in the slightest that backdoor relations should come to an end, merely that some public sector concerns should be put up for sale. What Thatcher's performance showed was that politicians could say what they are doing while not saying it at all. Thus, Thatcher could speak of abolishing tenure in the university and of the retrenching of professors as a way of freeing up talent locked up for life in the public service when it should, in fact, be serving the British private sector in its time of need. Similar initiatives against the principle of a minimum wage or of cheap housing in the English North appear in media performances as yet other expressions of the national interest. Because struggles against Thatcherism have often had to proceed on a local level, Thatcher—especially the Thatcher of television—has had an almost free hand to claim the mantle of Englishness, for example, in the Falkland War.[38]

When examining closely the construction of Englishness in this period, what stands out is the success of the political elite in forging significant alliances with influential segments of the middle classes without offering the benefits of collectivism. Thus, not only could elements of Thatcher's ideology enter general culture but eventually even academic culture. In this period, some major changes in academia occurred. Anthropologists, who had enjoyed a high level of prestige through the 1960s, lost out to literary criticism, which suddenly became an influential field. Archeology also underwent a considerable rise in its fortunes.

The decline of anthropology was a trend new to the 1970s, and it sheds some light on the reorganization of culture in that period. In this period, several writers came to regard anthropology as spurious or as an outgrowth of the colonial order. Although this, perhaps, was a fair-enough criticism, it was not one to be expected so many years after the colonial period nor one that could explain anthropology's continuing vigor in the postcolonial period. One thinks of Mary Douglas. Coinciding more precisely with the decline of the prestige of anthropology were two other events, both of which were closer to home and more disruptive of hegemony in the United Kingdom than one would glean from what was being written in academic journals. First, the resurgent feminist movement was now intent on maximizing the freedom offered by libertarianism, and with the resurgence of the movement came a renewal of the critique of the family. Second, one finds the struggle of the Commonwealth people in the United Kingdom for civil liberties and for the *decolonization* of the knowledge that pertained to themselves and to their ancestors. Anthropologists, who had been useful to the hegemony in the previous period for precisely the reasons implied in the foregoing, suddenly became controversial. Perhaps the idea of family or tribe was relative or was constructed after all. With the rise of such thoughts, the government appears to search for new fields through which to articulate its ideas of being Western, civilized, and English.

One of the fields to which the government turned to promote an articulation of its hegemony on an intellectual level was literary criticism, and it was there that the new Tories gained their initial foothold in academic culture, which, however, they found would cost them dearly. From the outset, literary criticism had its drawbacks. First, the Tories had to acknowledge that the literary criticism to which they were attracted was not English but an import from the Continent, and second, in embracing continental literary criticism, they placed themselves in the position of having to deny the validity of earlier British literary criticism. This was not easy for any British politician, much less for a Tory. British literary criticism, as I noted before, has enjoyed prestige, and at times has been able to claim for itself even the credentials of science. The new literary critics, the poststructuralists, however, have shown extraordinary ability in performing a useful function. Not only did they attack literary criticism for being scientific, they attacked the idea of science itself. Typically, the new works all followed a pattern: find, then exploit the "symptomatic trace" on the margin of a text to break down a text's more central logic or authority. From a closed text with a single meaning that one can determine comes an irreducible plurality. The appealing aspect of this for the Thatcherites was that the interpretation of the strongest may thus be the strongest interpretation.[39] The difficulty, however, was that literary criticism or any field allied with poststructuralism was not only foreign in appearance and in its language but also in its basic demands that its users abandon a concept dear to Britain, the concept of science.

Archeology was another field that saw a meteoric rise in its fortune thanks to the new Tory hegemony. In examining this phenomenon, two main explanations stand out. First, is a structural explanation. Archeology is useful in the way that the new mass media is useful. Archeology, like the new mass media, requires large-scale financing, which permits total control. Under conditions of total control, results can be manipulated according to need. Archeological work on British heritage, for example, offered the Thatcherites a way to control the past without dealing with historians or, more broadly, with objectivity or science.

The second explanation for the increasing utility of archeology must put more emphasis on issues such as luck and timing and, to a lesser extent, subject matter. After near total dominance of archeology by the Marxist Left in the interwar period thanks to the writings of the famous archeologist V. Gordon Childe, archeology in the postwar period fell into the hands of narrow technicalists, who given what was frequently their more conservative politics, were open to collaboration with a Tory government.

The most prominent British student of the "New Archeology," Colin Renfrew, is also, coincidentally, a well-known Tory. In academic circles, Renfrew is an Indo-Aryanist. Within this important but traditional field, Renfrew is a trendsetter. He upholds the division between the Aryan and the Semitic worlds, but he argues for it from new grounds. Whereas most Indo-Aryanists are philologists, Renfrew is not. He is closer in his approach to the Annales school in history. Thus, he takes up the theme of the westward spread of farming from Turkey into other Aryan lands with quantifiable evidence. Renfrew dismisses the usefulness of his predecessors' work rooted in comparative philology. Archeology for Renfrew is more rigorous than philology. It is a science. In fact, archeology is more than that. It is the most rigorous of scientific enterprises. Through sampling and the use of the computer, the archeologist can carry out scientific mathematical tests to validate hypotheses in ways that traditional philology and traditional science cannot do because archeology is more sophisticated than these other fields. Archeologists can, according to Renfrew, turn when they choose to the insights of poststructuralists and semiologists, whereas scientists cannot. Put another way, archeologists can be quite malleable.

In a recent book which Renfrew coauthored, archeology as science and as hegemonic politics is clearly on display. On the scientific side, the authors praise the importance of radiocarbon dating. Much of the old Europe thought to be Mediterranean or Near Eastern, Renfrew claims, actually predates these civilizations. Welcome news!

The success of archeology goes much beyond the career of Colin Renfrew. The television program *Animal, Vegetable, Mineral?* won for two other well-known archeologists, Glyn Daniel and Mortimer Wheeler, the awards of Television Personality of the Year in 1954 and 1955. And, no doubt, the major proof of success is that British archeologists have come to enjoy an enormous endowment through the government-funded English Heritage, a fund dwarfing the state monies that might find their way to the study of history proper.[40]

Thatcherism has been more than a match for its opponents. Its co-optation of the idea of Englishness has never been seriously challenged. If today Englishness is defined by Thatcher to permit a tokenistic freedom of existence for her opponents, it appears her opponents are willing to accept what they can get, reinforcing in the process her logic of Englishness as libertarianism. Witness the space afforded the Liberal party, the New Left Marxist establishment, and the National Front. True, the Thatcherites have had some difficulty legitimating the escalation of their political repression and racism in the name of Englishness, but they have managed. On occasion in recent years, the government has had to concede at least by implication the illegality of some of its initiatives or, at least, to countenance investigations of such operations as Clock Work Orange, an illegal attempt to discredit Labourite politicians, but these all have passed until now without tarnishing the essence.[41]

In 1992–93 Britain's participation in the Common Market began. Tory politicians will be expected to accommodate the collectivist tradition of the Continent, to share responsibility with Socialists, and to diminish their relationship with the United States. What will they turn to in their arsenal to do this?

Several times in this book, I have alluded to the great importance of the mass media for hegemony. The argument posed in chapter 6 was that for media to be mass media, as in the United States, it had to be able to find broad acceptance and not be perceived simply as the voice of the government. In the United Kingdom, it now may be noted that this occurred as the collectivist era came to an end, that when the working class had some organized power they could still resist massification, but when that broke down, they could not.[42]

As this took place, the state appears to shift its emphasis in persuasion, from directly educating the student through the school to indirectly educating the youth through the mass media, the video game, and the comic book. As that momentous shift was taking place, the role of the traditional institutions, Oxford, Cambridge, and the newer universities following in their wake simply declined in importance. Education and scholarship continued, but much of its role was nonspecific, reinforcing the existing social stratification. Going to a university did not assure one a prestigious job. Increasingly, as the century progressed, the crystallization of and communication of hegemonic thought was shifted to the media.

A quick glance at the British media substantiates this shift. Among the well-known features of the British Broadcasting Company (BBC) are the special programs, which suggests the breakdown of attempts at social integration through education of an earlier era. Now one finds special programs for the Cockney-speaking working class and for the traditional upper classes in Oxbridge English. Age, gender, race, and social class are also targeted by the media as constituting particular audiences. Other features of the organization of the British media include a specifically Scottish media for Scotland while the more heavily populated ethnically English Midlands and North of England are accessible by satellite to the media of London and the South. Yet when it so chooses, the state equally has the capacity to use its media to overcome these cleavages that it created and to generate a wider audience. It does so, as the career of Thatcher shows, by presenting shows that blur issues. The media even has the power to blur a particular issue on one show for the wider audience and to clarify it on another show for a specialty audience.[43]

Although it is easy enough to speculate about why politicians did this as the new communication technology became available, it does not jibe with the fact that over the long term, the education budget was also rising. Why has the government of the United Kingdom supported the universities on the scale it has, especially if it gets better, more predictable results from investing in the media than it does from investing in the unversity system? What, after all, is the state seeking in its support of education? The apparent answer is the control of science. Arguments turn on what is scientific. Progress is thought to depend on science. The scientific community, much of which is in the university, is, thus, inevitably worth supporting.

Yet in both the United Kingdom and the United States, this support brings with it its share of frustrations. Many academics, scientists included, in contrast to the media personnel, do not uphold the state's doctrine of racial and gender differences; some go so far as to criticize the edifice of science.

In the years 1880–1920, the state organized culture to defend an ethnic concept of Englishness. Language, folklore, and anthropology came to the fore. With the rise of collectivism in the period beginning in 1920 and extending to 1970, language and ethnicity were too narrow. Englishness was defined around the English economy and the English society. In this period, economics was an influential field as was sociology and social history. In the period since 1970, the state has turned instead to fields such as archeology and to an anarchist form of literary criticism when it began to lose control of economics, sociology, and social history.[44]

In the next section, the writing of history in the United Kingdom is taken up in detail. Fields, such as history, although sometimes co-opted by the dominant chosen people ideology, have also been able on occasion to criticize it by including what it leaves out—by writing what historians call *scientific* history. The state, as a consequence, has long had a love-hate relationship to the field.

History Writing in the United Kingdom

All the hegemonic constructions require history writing in one form or another. Most make use of a *tableau* approach to the past, containing an origin giving rise to heritage, a golden age, a period of decline, and a modern period characterized by a revival. By contrast, the hegemonic elements in the democracies promote an image of continuous progress across the centuries in line with their chosen people ideology. In Great Britain, this image is found in the Whig view of history.

In all the hegemonic constructions, historians chafe at the demand that they serve as propagandists. A large part of the history profession of modern Great Britain is, not surprisingly, critical of the Whig view of history that is upheld as the standard view in school texts. From the nineteenth century to the present day, British historians, like their American counterparts, have often reacted to the expectations of chauvanism imposed on them by extolling the virtues of "scientific" history, that is, the tradition of Leopold Von Ranke and the method he proposed of studying the past for its own sake. In recent years, the Annales school or Marxism has served a similar purpose.[45]

In the first Liberal Age, the professionalization of history occurred more slowly and less completely than it did in many other countries and in other fields of scholarship even in the United Kingdom. Beyond the first Liberal Age, one finds even today the criticism that historians deserve their relative obscurity because they have failed to organize themselves as a profession in order to capture a large audience.[46] Historians can, conservative critics of scientific history maintain, always solve their problems by writing "public history," that is, history for whoever pays.[47]

In the United Kingdom in the late nineteenth century, several important factors weighed on the development of professionalism. First, elements in the state wanted a history profession and a greater concern with the study of modern history as opposed to medieval history. Second, a number of important historians were prepared to study modern history but did not want to have anything to do with the state. Third, obstacles to professionalization of history were imposed by the Whig tradition. In due course, thus, a "bureaucratic," solution emerged, one accommodating as many of these concerns as possible.

The first factor in a discussion of the development of a history profession is that nineteenth-century culture in Britain favored classical and medieval historical subjects over modern ones. The sudden expansion of the suffrage and the formation of modern Britain created the need for a modern history. It was this new need above all that the state hoped that professional historians would fill. As late as the 1880s, however, history in general, but especially modern history, was an "inferior and insecure" academic discipline. The reigning tradition in history was the one established by T. W. Arnold, a classicist. From the perspective of the modern state, this was unfortunate. Classics were too much of an encumbrance. Universal suffrage had created an electorate, few of whom knew or cared about Latin and Greek.

The second factor affecting the development of the history profession was that although Britain did have historians interested in the modern field, they had no desire to have anything to do with the government of the day. Thus, there was an influential history journal, the *Economic History Review*, founded and maintained by a small group of private individuals. These individuals chose to publish articles in the Rankean mold and to eschew Whiggism, and it was they who were gradually gaining the upper hand over their critics and not vice versa. In fact, scientific history, as championed by the *Economic History Review*, eventually triumphed and became the accepted way to write history. Manchester, the leading center in which these individuals taught, even gained a brief notoriety, but the Manchester historians remained as did the *Economic History Review* and history writing as a whole, at least from the point of view of the state, disappointingly unorganized.

A third factor bearing on the evolution of professionalism was the Whig tradition, Whiggism providing the dominant perception of the function of history in the traditional elite universities. In universities such as Oxford and Cambridge, the idea of history as a science or of historians serving the growth of knowledge as scientists collided with the established belief that the true function of history was to build moral character. The charge of the most elite professorship in history, the Regius Professor of Modern History at Oxford and Cambridge, was to speak to the world about larger moral issues, not to contribute to a discrete field of specialized knowledge that a history profession would be interested in promoting.[48] It was only with the development of a modern history program at Cambridge in the late nineteenth century that the Whig tradition ceased to be an obstacle to professionalism.

A fourth factor, the bureaucratic imperative, finally led in due course to the formation of a professional organization. In 1906, the Historical Association began. From that year until the end of World War II, this association succeeded in bringing together through its openness the diverse communities of historians in the United Kingdom, and did so by focusing on issues that the majority in these communities would find noncontroversial, such as the empire and the problem of upgrading history education in the schools. With the breakup of the empire and the breakdown in the United Kingdom of the spirit of collectivism, the Historical Association seemed to lose its importance. In recent years, it has clung to its past, pursuing such themes as decolonization.[49]

Fifth, although the state had long proclaimed its need for modern historical knowledge and the need for a professional organization to promote it, at the same time, from the day it began, the state claimed that the Historical Association was a controversial organization. Such, at least, was the opinion of many individual historians in the early twentieth century. Whiggist sentiment, no doubt, was a factor in this, but more specific political considerations perhaps played a role both for the state and for these individuals. A feature of the association was its openness. For some, this was a strength; for others it was not. Openness carried with it some degree of endorsement of diversity. Thus, the work of small groups of historians in sensitively placed fields, with views that were not necessarily representative of those of the majority in the organization, could affect the credibility of the organization and even of the discipline as a whole. A particular example comes to mind in which the organization's reputation was tarnished by the work done by a small group of its members. Not surprisingly, the example concerned Ireland. A tiny historical community in the United Kingdom in the early twentieth century cultivated the study of Irish history. This tiny community was welcomed by the larger guild on scientific grounds and welcomed in the Historical Association, no doubt as part of its policy of openness. When one particular historian, Eoin Macneill (1867–1945), however, began to publish works establishing that the Celtic domain had a history before the Anglo-Norman invasion of 1169, the association felt that it was, in effect, endorsing the use of scientific historical methods to challenge Englishness. This paradigm challenge was not appreciated. Englishness specified that one would approach the Celtic fringe as folklore, not as history.[50] The association suffered from its inclusion of the likes of Eoin Macneill.

Evidence of the rather negative attitude of many historians in the United Kingdom toward professionalism—and thus by implication, the Historical Association—can be extrapolated from the rather endless stream of historians who espoused the Whig ideology, who eschewed the profession and sought to establish themselves as amateurs. These historians are still remembered even today, for example, H. G. Wells, author of *Outline of History* (1920), for his commercial ventures, Sir Karl Popper, author of *The Poverty of Historicism* (1957), for his intrusive kibbitzing.

In the long run, weak professionalism definitely had some positive as well as negative consequences. It, among other things, freed historians who had controversial ideas, such as Arnold Toynbee, to produce their books. It also served the needs of historians sympathetic to the Peace movement and to other counterhegemonic trends.[51]

The first important modern historian was Sir John Robert Seeley (1834–1895), author of the *Expansion of England* (1883) and *The Growth of British Policy: An Historical Essay* (1895). According to his most recent biographer, Seeley was a well-known public figure credited both with transforming British public opinion into loyal support for the empire and with modernizing Cambridge University's history curriculum in the years after 1869, the year he was appointed Regius Professor of Modern History there.

Seeley's contribution to Cambridge's history program had an impact that was wider than simply that of Cambridge itself. By introducing a concern with scientific history among the students of an Oxbridge university, Seeley helped to remove a major obstacle to the growth of professional history in the United Kingdom that is, generally, Whiggism. Seeley's influence at Cambridge can be seen to the present day in that University's concern with modern history. History should be rescued from the hands of littérateurs and pursued by those who were serious in a professional sense, separate from popularists. History, Seeley persuaded the elite, was a useful science; its subject was ultimately bound up with the state.[52]

Seeley himself was a "new man." This had a bearing on his views on history. He came from the middle classes; he was an outsider to the wealth of Cambridge. He was a new man in a second sense as well; his family were Evangelicals. He rebelled against them joining the broad church.

As a marginal member of the elite, Seeley was alert to its frailties and excesses. He saw what they could not always see. He, thus, worried about the spread of secularism and doubt among the intellectuals, which was taking hold among the English upper classes. He wrote about British religious history. He was also concerned with and aware of the developing class conflict. Along with others of his generation, such as T. H. Greene and B. Bosanquet, he shared a concern that Britain be an "organic nation-state." From this broader concern, Seeley arrived at his positions on various specific issues. For example, he supported the British empire and the union with Ireland, but on domestic issues, he supported higher education for women.

In Seeley's time, professional organizations were weak, and important scholars had direct relationships with politicians. During Seeley's career, the government honored him for his achievements and for his political views with the appointment of K.C.M.G. He appeared as a spokesman for the Unionist cause and as a figurehead for the Imperial Federation movement. Yet as a closer view reveals, Seeley held views that would be problematic for ruling class ideology. The state accepted him no doubt because it had no one else to whom to turn who had his skills.

If one places Seeley among his contemporaries, his importance appears to come from his stance interrelating history with hegemony. If one compares Seeley to his well-known contemporary Mandell Creighton, a Dixie

Professor of Ecclesiastical History at Oxford, a founder of the *English Historical Review,* this stance becomes clear. Where Creighton was a pure Rankean, Seeley was not. Seeley attempted to occupy what he perceived to be a middle ground. Thus, he argued that the conditions permitting the study of history scientifically included political conditions. For Creighton this sounded evasive. For any pure Rankean, history was either to be studied for its own sake, or it was not.

Seeley, however, like other scientific historians, was an outspoken critic of the Whig view of history. In his own work, he took on the Whigs in one of their most central domains, constitutional history. Seeley found that the Victorians, who could find modern British democracy a thousand years in the past, lived in a myth world. A particular target was Seeley's eminent contemporary, W. Stubbs, the Oxford medievalist. Seeley tried to refute Stubb's contention that there was essential continuity in consitutional development since 1066.[53]

Modern history was not the only field of interest to the state. If classics was on the decline, ancient history was on the rise. There were lessons to be learned from the Greek and Roman empires. According to a recent study of trends in ancient history over the twentieth century, the author found that the figure of Julius Caesar was viewed in the late nineteenth century as a savior of democracy for the middle classes. By contrast, in the collectivist era, the Augustan Dyarchy that linked the ruler and the Senate rose in prestige among scholars. More recently, the impact of libertarianism can be shown. In the writings of the British classicist, Ronald Syme, author of the still influential *The Roman Revolution* (Oxford, 1939, 1979), the morality of Augustus is no longer upheld. The classical world is shown for all its cold pragmatism devoid of higher values, ancient history in the process appearing more malleable than modern history.[54]

In the late nineteenth century, Anglo-Norman England was the subject of great sweeping narratives; it was dominated by masters of Whig historiography such as F. M. Stenton, author of *Anglo-Saxon England.* Today, as the author of a recent survey of historiography acknowledges, the field of Anglo-Norman history is pluralistic to the point of being fragmented and takes a back seat to other specialties. The dream of medieval order, so much a part of nineteenth-century imagination, evaporated in the age of collectivism and neoliberalism.[55] Apparently, not even the money of the Heritage Trust can put it back together.

History Writing in the Collectivist Period, 1920s–1970

The growth of the Labour party led to the formation of a cross-class ruling alliance. In the United Kingdom, it also happened to coincide with major external changes, notably the breakdown of the empire.

Evidence from the field of history writing suggests that the rise of collectivism was clearly unnerving to the Whigs; liberal history became unmoored, even eclectic. Its terrain changed; its struggle was no longer against scientific history but against Marxist history. A Marxist political economy and labor history arose and on some issues gained the upper hand.

Liberal historiography, of course, still dominated; its two main features were its cosmopolitanism and its "trench warfare" defense of traditional Whig positions. A trend, represented by the prosopography of Lewis Namier, emerged in the profession toward the end of this period. Namierism foreshadows the later attempts by liberals to regain their lost authority.

In the interwar period, the now somewhat marginalized liberals produced a number of prominent eccentric but cosmopolitan historians, mainly in political history, who stayed aloof from daily politics. Probably the most famous of these was A. J. P. Taylor, a historian who adopted an ultrarevisionary position on the origins of World War II. Geoffrey Barraclough, a historian, took up the sensitive subject of British decline.[56]

Most of the liberal establishment found themselves drawn into confrontation with labor and forced to fight for their paradigm in "trench warfare conditions" in subject areas that labor chose. Whereas earlier liberals sometimes became embroiled with labor over the interpretation of the English Civil War, with the rise of the Labour Party, the main subject became the industrial revolution. Two topics connected with the industrial revolution came to dominate some of the best minds of the period: the aristocracy of labor and the standard of living during the industrial revolution.

It seems reasonable to surmise that the Marxist historians, such as E. J. Hobsbawm, influenced by Lenin, chose the issue of the aristocracy of labor as a way to insert the idea of a socialist future into the analysis of history. Predictably, liberals rejected out of hand that possibility. For liberals, a labor aristocracy arose from the unequal skills of the individual workers. During the collectivist period, this view did not seem persuasive.

From 1949 to 1954, Hobsbawm attempted to make the term *aristocracy of labor* a fixed part of the logic of capitalism to remove it from the serendipity domain of worker motivation à la liberalism. His point of departure was a historical study of supply and demand in the labor market. From the general picture of supply and demand, Hobsbawm demonstrated the logic of the rise in the nineteenth century of a system of subcontracting work to workers. Workers, he argued, who ran these subcontracting ventures objectively shared some interests with capital. They were a labor aristocracy. Hobsbawm's analysis of labor aristocracy was time specific, related to the era of partial mechanization in the new factories in which the skilled worker was still in demand, an era that ended by the 1890s. Hobsbawm's analysis by any intellectual standard was brilliant; in political terms, however, it failed to give liberalism a place and probably for that reason failed to penetrate it. Evidence for this can be drawn from the fact that in the 1970s and thereafter with the weakening of the alliance between labor and capital, liberals were able to reassert their position on labor aristocracy in terms of the "science" of industrial relations. By this point, the Left, too, had other objectives than those of Hobsbawm's during the cold war. Some of its social historians, writing from the perspective of labor, began to examine the relation of labor aristocracy to the politics of hegemony.[57] Does the idea of a labor aristocracy suggest an accommodation to the Whig idea of an aristocracy? Might it be inappropriate for a Marxist?

The other subject of importance to the historical debates of the collectivist era was the standard of living during the industrial revolution. The Marxist Left led by Hobsbawm established that the revolution was brought about through a net decline in the standard of living in the British working class. Once again, the political power of labor and the intellectual authority of historians such as Hobsbawm ensured that this view would dominate. But, once again, its domination would not be eternal. Lacking a mechanism to co-opt the positivist view of progress, or in one way or another to make use of it, the Marxists failed in the end. By the 1970s, the ahistorical economics of the Marshall School at Cambridge University had made a comeback. Its influence could be easily discerned in the weighty tomes of the rising doyen of economic history from that University, Sir John Clapham.[58]

In seeking to explain how "losing" ideas, such as racism or liberalism become "winning" ideas, one must return to the domain of national politics. First, the decline of the empire long sought by the Labour party did not benefit party fortunes when it occurred. At that point, the party's anticolonial rhetoric collided with the economic interests of the membership. This point is driven home if one juxtaposes calls for welfare colonialism by Labourite intellectuals next to calls from the Trade Union Congress (TUC) to limit the number of Commonwealth immigrants. Clearly, the concern of a few intellectuals in the party for the rights of the colonized was not shared by the rank and file. In essence, the politics of race gave liberal positions, including liberal positions in such areas as historical research, a new lease on life because the difference between labor and liberalism in such areas was not that great. Second, in the postwar period, much of the Labour party leadership appeared to confuse the welfare benefits that it had won with actual power, which, of course, it had not won. During this period, the leaders appeared complacent. The benefits of U.S. foreign aid and a short-term boom induced many Labourites to think of the period, in much the way liberals did, as one of sustained growth. The Labour party showed signs of losing its class perspective, of taking on a liberal way of thinking without being aware of it. This, too, affected its historical thought.[59]

In 1952, the "fusion" of a group of leading Marxist historians, including E. J. Hobsbawm, and non-Marxist historians resulted in the publication of the most celebrated journal of the late collectivist period, *Past and Present*. It was a remarkable platform of opposition to the cold war, the opening riposte of neoliberalism in its struggle against the welfare state. The journal's existence forced some eminent historians to decide either to write for it or to acknowledge to themselves their rightist political affinities. The trajectory of the journal in terms of internal balance of editors and articles published is also of some interest. After 1958, the influence of the Annalistes rose and that of the Marxists fell. More recently, in 1976, *Past and Present* was joined by *Social History*.[60]

History Writing in the 1970s and Beyond

After 1970, heritage and public history projects increased greatly in the field of history and traditional multivolume productions poured from Oxford and Cambridge. These activities, which catch the eye of any observer, reveal the power of the Whig comeback from something approaching exile in the age of collectivism to relative predominance.

Equally notable is that this vast resurgence has not led to the formation of a new dominant school of historiography. The reason for this appears to follow from what has been said before. For a liberal or libertarian regime, preoccupation with the historical past is not particularly rewarding. In the main, the historical past is a bit too factual and, therefore, too constraining to be useful.

When one looks closely at what was funded and what was not, one finds that governmental monies supported the development of historical museums, the restoration of old homes, of public buildings, of monuments and the expenses of journals, which required subsidies. Government funds supported the Cambridge Center for Population Studies, the British version of the Annales school, the trend in history most congenial to libertarianism. At the same time, the arguably most interesting and most discussed trend of the period the popular culture school, arose and flourished with little or no public funding. The trend reflected, some writers believe, the delinking of the lower classes of the postindustrial economy from the national culture.[61]

In the 1970s, partly as a consequence of the government funding, there was a considerable resurgence of liberal historiography of different sorts after a generation of two of decline. Much of it appeared to have been directed against Marxist labor history. The aloof cosmopolitanism of earlier periods came to an end, and liberals made a great effort to reconquer the terrain of modern British social history. Because theory belonged to the Marxists, the logical strategy was to show that theory was of no avail to a historian. To do this one need only fragment reality sufficiently to eliminate the larger picture and then point out that there is no larger picture and, hence, no need for theory. Thus, in this period, articles in the *Economic History Review* began to show a rejection of the assessments of the size and importance of the industrial revolution advanced by scholars in the previous generation. As statistical regional histories appeared, a historian could argue that Lancashire's textile industry was simply atypical. Most of the country did not show the growth that the Marxists were assuming. Gone, too, was the assumption that the British industrial revolution was a watershed in human history. The image of Britain as a universal model for later industrial experiments was similarly put under wraps, such was the impact of libertarian pragmatism even on traditional Whiggism.

Among the trends of liberal historiography that flourished in this period was the trend I term the British version of the Annales school, the trend of history arguably most congenial to a libertarian regime because it is the trend furthest from traditional history. Arguably, if a state is weakly connected to the society, as is the intent of the British state, it will not seek to keep on widening the traditional narrative history in the manner of the earlier liberals. Political chronology or elite genealogy would suffice. To be more specific, social history endlessly produces new facts. These facts are shared property and imply the need for sharing among people. A state of the sort just mentioned may not want to engage in sharing; to avoid having to do so, it may prefer that knowledge be data because data can be locked up in a data bank as it is today at Cambridge. In addition, if history can be turned into data, it can be manipulated when manipulation is needed and, therefore, it is less dangerous than a field such as traditional history, which is entirely based on facts. Facts from a libertarian perspective are dangerous because of their aura of finality. It is difficult to manipulate facts; it is easy to manipulate data.[62] Thence comes the attraction of the state to the Annales school.

The Annales school, one might reasonably object, has in France, at least, a progressivist image. It was a tradition conceived to challenge the rather narrow orthodox political history that dominated the country. This, of course, is fair enough. But one should recall as well that the Annales school went through different phases and that it represents different things in different countries. In France after 1952, the Annales school of the cold war rose up with strong neo-Malthusian tendencies and consequently has become a magnet for demographers, statisticians, and others in the data tradition. It is this newer part of the Annales tradition more than the older more humanistic one that has attracted the neoliberal state in several different countries.

In addition, one might observe that ideas supported by the Annales school that sound as if they are part of the politics of the Left may on closer analysis be ideas that tend to serve the Right. If the Annales school strives toward *total history,* it is not really a corrective to or an engagement with the Marxist concept of social totality but is a trivialization of it. If total history is the tapestry of human experience spread out but linked by trade and technology, if knowledge of total history comes through microhistorical studies, not from theory, because microhistory is decentered and, thus, free from imperializing tendencies, then even theoretically historical knowledge can never be used to challenge any larger structure. What sounds progressive, looked at more closely, is actually a maintenance of the status quo.

If the state pours money into the Annales school, that is, Cambridge, it is not much different than its support for poststructuralist literary criticism, which also goes to Cambridge and Oxford. A little use of Nietzsche, a little attack on tradition, a little recourse to the arcane, these seem to be the common features.[63]

Although it is not possible to work this out in detail here, it is worth noting in a general way that both poststructuralists and Annalistes prefer to emphasize technology and language more than politics. For example, in Baudrilliard's deconstruction of the self, the work of a poststructuralist widely read in the United Kingdom, the author argues that the traditional concept of the self is a false refuge from the modern media. In making this claim, the self as a possible historical agent is denied by the technology of the media and by its use of language. This move places poststructuralism close to the position of the Annaliste Mentalite school and its deconstructive idea of the self.[64]

Yet another area of overlap between poststructuralism and the Annales school comes in their suspicions about teleology. Poststructuralists reject "meta-narrative projects" and, indeed, all narrative projects as teleological, perceiving such projects collectively as "imperialism of the subject." So do the Annalistes. Braudel's master concept, longue durée, is clearly intended as a critique of teleology. It celebrates the catastrophe of inexorable forces of nature, of conjunctures and by implication, the absence of human historical agency, excepting perhaps that of a superman, here to refer to Nietzsche.[65]

On the surface, the apparent influence of the Annales school in British thought has been limited. This is the common assumptiom. Yet, as a recent symposium about British historiography concluded, this may be deceptive. One could include a fair amount of British history writing under this rubric without going wrong. Leaving aside Peter Laslett at Cambridge for a moment, even the School of Lewis Namier, mentioned before, was, according to one author, "Braudelian in spirit."[66]

But even if it turns out that the Annales school in one form or another is influential in the United Kingdom, does this mean that there is a real connection here to hegemony? It does not seem quite sufficient to stop with the point that the Annales school is congruent with the libertarian politics of the state. This does not mean the state chose to use it. More fundamentally, how would something so technical be able to influence the everyday common sense of the culture and, therefore, be worth the investment? One, therefore, has to take the final step and argue, at least hypothetically, for positive gain for the state from supporting this costly work done by a few elite scholars.

I would choose to make this argument, to claim, as I did previously in regard to governmental support for Colin Renfrew's work in prehistory, that the state has an interest in controlling the image of the past, especially given the interest of counterhegemonic elements in this area. Historians in contrast to archeologists are, in general, difficult to control because they do not depend on large sums of money, so if some are found who will cooperate because they need the support, so much the better.

In fact, Renfrew, the preferred archeologist, and Laslett the preferred historian, do share attributes in common that one associates with state intellectuals. Both are critics of the everyday common-sense level of Rankean or Marxist *event history,* the history everyone has access to. Both equally criticize the more conventional ideas of structure, which are also accessible. Both replace what is accessible with what is inaccessible, thereby turning archeology and history into fields for "scientists" only. Renfrew and Laslett also share another useful trait associated with the organization of culture, flexibility. The Annales, like prehistory, can be science or deny science, can be radical and ecological or vociferously anti-Marxist. As the American historian Eugene Genovese noted appropos to this kind of work, the study of the family by numbers pumped into a computer becomes an end in itself, a substitute for the traditional concern of historians, social change.[67]

As the state in effect turned against the majority of the traditional profession after 1970, many historians increasingly alienated by the political situation have apparently become sympathetic with the counterhegemonic movements, and this has had some consequences for the history they write.

Thus in the years since 1970, while many writers of traditional narrative history have revealed how bad the present is compared to the past, many writers of social history have probed deeper and deeper into the history of the counterhegemonic movements and cultures and many writers of political economy have continued their critical analysis of life under capitalism. The growing opposition to Thatcherism spurred this writing forward.

In the 1970s and 1980s came a deepening appreciation in historical circles of Christopher Hill's work on the seventeenth century. Hill had been for a generation one of the major figures in social history and political economy and without question the leading interpreter of English history of the seventeenth century. It scarcely seems a coincidence that this appreciation of him coincided with the resurgence of Puritanism, which was also one of his major themes.[68]

In the same period, other work in history took even more openly counterhegemonic stances. A variety of historians both positivist and Marxist have created or are creating a genre they call popular culture. In journals such as *Cultural Studies* from Birmingham and *History Workshop* from Ruskin College, Oxford, in the writings of Raphael Samuel and of many others now appears an analysis of the English subaltern classes, serving as an impetus, some writers believe, for a renewed *populist Marxism*.

The most prominent of the counterhegemonic scholars of the past twenty years have been E. P. Thompson and Stuart Hall. Thompson has played a leading role in European Nuclear Disarmament (END) and the Campaign for Nuclear Disarmament in Britain. His work on the making of the British working class has become the single best-known work in British social history.[69] For Thompson, the connection between the two parts of his work was obvious. The radical craftsmen and artisans in the eighteenth century created the British working class in a struggle to retain control over their own work, whereas the present-day peace movement is a similar popular democratic movement over questions of control. Thompson is by no means alone; even more famous is Stuart Hall, another scholar-activist.[70] Hall is unique in contemporary British scholarship for his analysis of the British state from the late nineteenth century up through Thatcher. Hall is unique as well for his understanding of the making and unmaking of alliances in modern British history. Peace and disarmament, the issues Thompson used to organize the middle class, are important, but ultimately it will be the mobilization of the working class and the racial undercaste allied together that will challenge the power structure.

Whatever the next few years bring for the British history profession, this period can only be characterized as extraordinary, one in which the state has refused its historians, one in which many historians have consequently become active in building a challenge to the state.

To introduce bourgeois democracy as a distinct historical road with its attributes seeks thereby to challenge the position of the dominant paradigm that democracy is best understood as the universal human ideal, one most closely approximated by a handful of countries more loosely termed democracies. I argue rather that democracies were hegemonies based on rule by race, rationalized by a chosen people ideology, that history has a role to play in such a hegemony, and that in Britain this role was played by the Whig view of history.

The specificity of the United Kingdom can be found in the long-term acceptance of the system by the working class as represented by the Labour party. This differentiates the United Kingdom from the United States, the example taken up in chapter 10. It also explains why the great area of critical thought in British historiography is class while its blind spot is race and gender, which are, as one writer proclaimed, "hidden from history."

10

Bourgeois Democracy in the United States of America, 1877–1990

A second example of the hegemony termed *bourgeois democracy* is the United States, 1877–1990. As with previous chapters, this one is divided into four sections: this interpretation situated in relation to others,[1] a description of the political economy of the United States from 1877 to 1990, a look at the organization of culture as part of that political economy, and an analysis of the writing of history by Americans as part of that organization of culture.

The claim made here that the modern history of the United States is best characterized as that of a bourgeois democracy is not controversial, assuming one follows the more conventional formulations outlined in chapter 9. A chosen people came to America as an "Errand in the Wilderness," following the story of Moses, the Old Testament figure who left the corruption of Egypt behind. North America, like the Sinai Desert, is a land of freedom, and this freedom permits the chosen people to strengthen their resolve. A corollary to this formulation is that North America is not populated with people whose existence makes a difference.

With the passage of time arose another strand from within the dominant paradigm, one more concerned with the modern here and now. It took the form of a positivist or Marxist historiography. It, too, took for granted the idea of election, emphasizing merely the contemporary manifestations of chosenness over the myth of origins, i.e., Zion.

This raised the related questions Where should one begin modern history? and What status should modernity have? The answers worked out by American historians range anywhere from the Civil War to World War I, anywhere from simply another chapter in American civilization to a unique phase transcending national boundaries such as one understands from phrases like "global village" or "end of history."

287

Specialists in the formation of the modern nation-state typically portray their subject through precise internalist categories: the era after 1877 is variously termed the Gilded Age (1877–1900), the birth of the new South (1877–1900), the development of the West (1865–1900) and of national politics (1877–1900). This is followed by the Progressive era, "rise to world power" (1896–1920), and the emergence of America as a great power, a period also coinciding with the age of world wars. After World War I comes the era of Coolidge prosperity, the Great Depression, the New Deal, cold war, and so forth. Such work, on the one hand, constitutes a modern history or, on the other, reinforces the chosen people ideology, bringing out the idea of the uniqueness of American history, the consensualist nature of the American experience, and, ultimately, the dependence of Americans on their heritage.

The approach proposed in this chapter sides with the modernists; it is designed to elucidate what the country shares with other democracies and yet how it differs from them. The U.S. state promotes the existence of a racial undercaste; it plays the white worker off against the black. It does so not only in employment but in education and the media, and so forth, which makes the United States a democracy in the sense of the term as it has been developed to this point.[2] But the imposition of democracy was less complete or, at least, has been more resisted than was the case in the United Kingdom. White workers are not predictably racists, and blacks are intent on integration, not on accepting their status as a separate nation. The inability of the state really to *Americanize* the huge immigrant population into race hatred forced it to invest in greater and greater repression. For the first ninety years, 1870s–1960s, repression seemed to work because the country was experiencing continuous growth. Thereafter, challenges by the working class and the civil rights movements drove manufacturers abroad, leaving the country to finance capitalism. The groups emerging on top politically were the Christian Right and the libertarian liberals.

If one adopts this hypothesis, one can then construct American history so that its phases resemble those of other modern democracies. If one chooses the compromise of 1877 as the takeoff point of modern history, what becomes apparent is that the United States had entered a phase of one-class rule or classical liberalism or finance capitalism as many other countries did at about the same time and that this phase lasted until 1932, in other words, covering the time frame of the challenges of the Populists, the Wobblies and others that led up to those during the Great Depression. The phase extending from 1932 to 1970 is found to be one of cross-class rule or corporatism, Communists and others often now for the first time siding with the state. It coincided with a relative predominance of industrial capitalism. For a certain period, notably during the years of World War II and of the cold war, the system was successful in limiting challenges by making demands for greater and greater patriotism. Gradually, however, challenges began to grow to the point where they were less and less easy to confront, especially given the increasing weakness of American industrial competitiveness. Finally, the phase from 1970 to the present marks a return to nineteenth-century liberalism, to a political and economic culture in some senses purer than the original. Finance capitalism in recent times almost totally dominates the rest of the economy. Challenge to this phase returned to the local level.

Each phase has had its characteristic forms of struggle and state regulation, state organization of culture, and repression.[3] In the first phase were third parties, regional and local movements, and the rise of tolerated extra-legal organizations such as the Klu Klux Klan. In the second were legal struggles, such as those around civil rights and trade unionism, and in the third the struggle shifted back to the local and regional level where race often played against class in the allocation of funding in city budgets.

The state's alliances have also influenced the form these struggles took. One could term the American state a regulatory state. It builds up the dominant wings of American capitalism—the international capitalism located on the East Coast and the West Coast and the national capitalism located in the Midwest and the South—and then plays them against each other, thereby gaining its position. Of course, regulationism implies bureaucracy, with the result that much of the struggle in the United States goes on within the confines of the bureaucracy.

In this chapter, I suggest, in sum, an alternative to the American exceptionalist approach, one that argues for the specificity, as opposed to uniqueness, of the United States from among the world's democracies.

The Political Economy of the United States, 1877–1990

If one adopts an approach to the U.S., 1877–1990, that emphasizes the conflict of the ruler (the state and the regional ruling classes) and the ruled (the traditional working class), and the groups that were played off against it (the Afro-Americans and the poor white Southerners), one necessarily collides with a central tenet of the dominant view about 1877. As claimed in the preceding section and in much of the standard scholarship as well, the compromise of 1877 marked the beginning of the modern U.S. with its regulationism perhaps, but above all with its consensus.

Although the Civil War (1860–1865) represented a milestone in the integration of the society, when the capitalist North defeated the slave South, it did not achieve a political solution. The southern elite did not accept the former slaves as fellow citizens. By the 1870s, labor struggles in the East and unrest in the West added to the political instability.

The reformulation of the hegemony in 1877 returned political power to the southern elite and ended federal attempts to reform civil rights in that region. In return, Eastern capitalism gained the South as a labor market and as a source of timber, agriculture, and textile products. The new hegemony, thus, returned to a reliance on regionalism as a prop for racism; it was a system designed to preserve the interests of the historic "North and the South" and to preserve the interests of the state as arbiter or regulator.

Terms such as *region* or *regionalism* have diverse connotations in American historical discourse. Here region is used in a narrow sense to refer to two kinds of socioeconomic entities, the one dominated by East Coast corporate capitalism, the Northeast Corridor, aligned as it was at least before 1970 to the new South and to the major cities of the Midwest and the Pacific Coast. The other region was dominated by national capitalism and was composed of the states commonly characterized as the *Core Culture*. In this chapter, the discussion of the Core Culture is focused on the South because the race issue is close to the surface there. An account placing greater emphasis purely on counterhegemony as part of U.S. history would also include an account of the popular struggle in the far West and in the upper Midwest.

The political strategy that emerged on the highest level is termed here the *regulatory state*. The decision of the rulers to rule through a regulatory state can best be understood in three ways. It was a way in which conflicting interests could be rationalized. Equally, it was a way in which conflicting interests could be encouraged, thereby giving the state more power. Finally, and most importantly, regulationism was a way to deal with class conflict. U.S. capitalism could not or would not buy off the working class as Bismarck could in Germany. It therefore chose to regulate it. The ideal would be a two-party system, one straddling the racial and regional divides.[4]

A power structure thus arose built from the graduates of East Coast schools who became the Civil Service. The South and the West provided the personnel for the military and religious structures; the important positions within each were allocated according to which wing of capitalism had the most strength.

Opposition to this power structure quickly formed along class, regional, and racial lines, trade union movements, populist movements, and civil rights movements. The struggle that ensued between ruler and ruled —and not some consensus—shaped the history that followed.

Trade unions have been part of the challenge to the hegemony from the beginning. At least until 1970, when capitalism had the option of leaving, this challenge was never an easy one for the state. Trade unionists were difficult to attack because they always insisted that they eschewed politics and pursued free-trade unionism. Still, as their critics have noted, their strategies have had a number of consequences, not all of them favorable. They might escape being attacked on political grounds, but they could also be bypassed economically and co-opted culturally. Because of the concentration of the union movement in the North and East, the state could play one region against another around labor issues, and because the unions eschewed formal politics, for example, the overtures of the Communists, the state pursued policies at home and abroad without fear of political opposition.

Imperalism: A Byproduct of Free Trade Unionism—An Aside

Up to this point, the subject of imperialism has been approached indirectly in this book in terms of the perceptions of writers in different hegemonies of what imperialism was, in terms of the propensity of various types of rulers to ally themselves with the imperialist powers, and in passing references to imperialism in discussions of great powerism. One can scarcely present an account of the political economy of the United States that leaves out the dynamics of imperialism in modern history.

If one were to risk a generalization about all the modern imperialist and great power countries of which the United States is one, it would be that theorists have exaggerated the importance of the machinations of Western political elites, the logic of capitalism, and accumulationism and have underestimated the importance of middle-range interpretations of the subject such as the disposition of the working class and of Third World power structures. On this level, what stands out is that in imperialist countries, if the working classes do not make formal political demands, to the contrary, the ruling class can use its silence—if it so chooses—as a form of acquiescence for projects of overseas expansion and exploitation. This appears to be the case even in countries such as the United States where colonialism itself carries a stigma and where imperialism has often been obliged to take the form of interventionism, that is, sending in the Marines as opposed to setting up a colonial bureaucracy.

In the United States, the working class in the late nineteenth century claimed it was eschewing politics, to follow a "free-trade unionist" approach; this stance gave capitalism in the United States significant opportunities. These opportunities were to last while those of rivals such as Great Britain, if greater initially, crumbled quickly with the rise of the Labour party in the early twentieth century.

From the 1930s, the U.S. trade union leadership permitted itself to be co-opted by the state. As it did so, U.S. imperialism developed even faster, the Pax Americana quickly becoming a new world order headed by the United States although as this happened, the number of unionized workers dropped and dropped. In Japan, imperialism also developed, but worker ideology was drawn into a messianism of the ruler cult. In Germany, this was also partly the case.

The role of labor also stands out clearly in the early Soviet Union. Russia was a major imperialist power in the nineteenth century before labor had a voice. In the early years of the Bolshevik Revolution, there was a lull in imperialism as demands of the working class turned the attention of the state inward. Then once again in the Stalinist period, with the formation of the New Class and the state monopolizing the political sphere, imperialism recommenced.

The great victims of imperialism in modern times are the Africans, a point not easily explained by the traditional theories of imperialism. In the midnineteenth century, Africa was not easily distinguishable from India, Southeast Asia or the Middle East; one century later Africa is in the most desperate poverty. Although much of this is explained by the dynamics within Africa, one cannot escape the important role played by the democracies in Africa during the heyday of colonialism and imperialism. How could the destruction of African life have been allowed to happen? The answer would appear to follow from the democracy of the imperialists. In race-divided societies such as the democracies, citizens of color have trouble having their local concerns heard. Regions such as Africa, the embodiment of race in the Western imagination, thus became frontiers where any form of exploitation was and is possible, more so than elsewhere.

Many rulers of tribal-ethnic states, however, and not just those in Africa, have chosen to be collaborators in Western imperialism. Their motives, as noted in previous chapters, are still not well understood. Some, perhaps, feared the coming of surplus Europeans to form settler states on their land more than they feared unequal trade; others felt threatened by their own working classes and were prepared to trade economic peripheralization or colonization for greater personal security. This question needs study. What stands out is the vast network of tribal-ethnic states and their lobbyists in Washington; what stands out equally is the rise of the airborne as the heart of the U.S. military. As the Gulf War showed, a phone call from Kuwait brings the United States into a war. Recall, as well, Somaliland, South Korea, and South Vietnam.

In its modern form, the counterhegemonic challenge in the United States embraced not only trade unionism but populism and civil rights. In the 1870s and 1880s, in what has sometimes been termed *the* Populist movement, regional radicalism became important. In retrospect, it is clear that this movement was one of many such movements, probably not the first and definitely not the last. It flourished in the formative years of the modern state and subsided by the turn of the twentieth century. Other such movements continued to the present day.

Populism's history is the history of the popular struggle in those regions where free trade unionism and ethnic identity were weakest and where, as a consequence, economic, political, and cultural thought on the mass level could be the most unified. When populist movements allied themselves with capitalism, they tended to be rightist, but when they went their own way, they tended to be leftist, that is, counterhegemonic.

During the nineteenth century, the period just alluded to, western and southern populism were counterhegemonic. National capitalism still depended on Eastern capitalism and was less able to appear as an authentic representative of its region. This phase for the South and the West came to an end in the early twentieth century. After 1970, the merger movement once again tied national and international capitalism together and once again progressive populism was on the rise despite the fundamentalist right, this time benefiting as well by the declining power of free trade unionism.

By 1970, the traditional trade unions were clearly on the wane. As early as the 1950s, George Meany, the president of the union movement had spoken for many trade unionists when he told his partner Walter Reuther that there was no profit in organizing workers as poor as the southern farm workers. Given this state of mind, one can, it seems, explain the gap among populists, civil rights advocates, and trade unionists. Meany was the quintessential American trade unionist; he would ask himself how the organization of farm workers would benefit the AFL-CIO. Would an involvement in the rural black South pay, or would it convert the trade union movement into a class movement? Such closemindedness of the leadership was responsible in no small part for its decline.[5]

The civil rights movement is the third center of counterhegemonic struggle within the United States; its distinctiveness lies in the fact that neither the populists nor the trade unionists addressed the issue of race. The modern history of the civil rights struggle began with a phase of intellectual agitation associated with such figures as W. E. B. Du Bois; it included as well various attempts to accommodate the segregationist structure of liberalism through strategies of racial complementarity and through repatriation of black people to Africa. It reached its high point in the period of corporatism. During this period (1932–70), American culture was its most inclusionist, and the state was the most accepting of the idea of collective rights. In this period, The struggle was waged not only on the street but from within the legal system. In the late 1960s as the American ruling class began to feel real challenge, the movement was suppressed.

But why would a ruling class as prosperous as that of the United States feel vulnerable to counterhegemonic movements? What was the rationale for abandoning reformation for the overt repression of the late 1960s? It is difficult to think of a wealthy power structure, I believe, that ever felt secure; more specifically, it seems reasonable to suppose that even small counterhegemonic movements could influence policy given not just the class conflict but also the rivalries and competition built into a regulatory system of ruling. There is always the question—every day—Will the conflicts being promoted by the system get out of hand?

A regulatory state rules, to summarize, by maintaining old divisions and conflicts, such as racial or regional ones, and through them appearing on the scene as the regulator. Its hope through this strategy is to channel conflicts away from their class component toward their racial and regional ones, ultimately leading to a realization among all parties that compromises and regulation are needed. What could the state do when one region—and one form of capitalism—in certain eras was too dominant for much rivalry to exist between it and the other, and hence, where there was not much room for regulation? During such eras—and there were several of them—the power of the state was threatened and its capacity to intervene and to regulate was challenged. For example, from the 1870's–1890's and on until the 1960s, state power was circumscribed by the growing dominance of the East Coast corporate capitalism over the Midwest, southern, and small town national capitalism. Later, after 1970, the state faced new forms of challenges. As a result of the merger of many national and international corporations in that period, one finds not just regional imbalance but the emergence of something new and even more menacing, a somewhat unified ruling class, this time propelled by the core culture, one less in need of a regulatory state than it previously had been.[6]

Standard accounts suggest that the first important milestone in the rise of the modern state was reached in 1883; that year saw the professionalization of the Civil Service and of the Army's Officer Corps.[7] In both domains, civilian and military, professionalization sharply undercut local influences on the federal system in the area of personnel. It also gave governmental employees more autonomy. From the 1880s, as histories of bureaucracy show, the appearance of one regulatory agency or act followed another until the present day.

The regulatory approach was visible in the workplace as well. From the 1870s and 1880s, disputes there were settled not just by force but by force combined with mediation imposed by the different apparati of the state. Among the first movements, which ran afoul of the state and which encountered the new regulatory approach, was the Knights of Labor in the 1870s. The Knights was both a trade union and a populist movement, appealing as it did both to industrial trade unionists and to small farmers across regional and racial lines. The state saw correctly that it was a movement with a radical intent. As a result, it turned on the Knights, seeking to weaken the movement by forcing it to oppose immigration.

By forcing the Knights to oppose immigration, the state introduced an important divisive issue. During the 1880s, business sought to destroy the union movement by introducing large numbers of immigrants. A flood of immigrants arrived; jobs grew insecure. The unions divided on how to respond to this threat. Some wanted to oppose further immigration; others wanted to organize all workers. This dissension led to splits. Other issues of the period, ranging from temperance to civil rights proved equally divisive when they were raised. After the 1886 "offensive against labor," the Knights could no longer hold together. Their decline after the "great southwestern strike" of that year permitted another group, the American Federation of Labor (AFL), to rise.[8]

Much affected by the setbacks to labor in 1886, Samuel Gompers and the other early leaders of the AFL deliberately chose a different strategy from that of their predecessors. Historians of labor have characterized the AFL's strategy as one that disguised class conflict, upheld the Jacksonian ideal of a limited American state, or simply as voluntarism or free-trade unionism. On the major issue of the day, immigration, the AFL initially supported restriction by a literacy test, reflecting the probable rank-and-file sentiment for exclusion. But when the matter arose in Congress and the East Coast establishment overturned the exclusionary measures directed against the Chinese in California, the AFL did not intervene. Its hallmark was and still is prudence. In seeking to explain this prudence, historians have focused on how AFL leaders differed from those in the Knights and on the different bases of the two organizations. The AFL was led by national crafts unions; the Knights were led by municipally based groups inevitably involved in a wider range of social issues than the more guild-oriented membership of the AFL.[9]

Through the 1880s, the leaders of the AFL sought to explore the possibilities that their strategy of free trade unionism afforded them. When, for example, they reached out to Afro-American workers, the capitalist class became alarmed. When they tried to expand their membership base among white workers, they risked splits even from within the existing ranks. Politics inevitably were close to the surface and, in fact, became an issue when Gompers tried to merge the free labor tradition of the Republicans, that is, workers from a Midwest German-American background, with Irish-American workers who were part of the Democratic machines on the East Coast; fights broke out. Gradually, given the relative advantages, there was no choice for the AFL but to gravitate to the East and to the Democratic party.

Was, then, the Democratic party to become the party of labor? Was the United States on the same path as the United Kingdom? Decidedly not. The AFL was outmaneuvered and overpowered through the 1890s. Not adept at party politics, unlike its English counterpart, it found itself forced into a party serving the interests of the capitalists. In the 1896 election, labor lost its last chance to hold its own from outside the system. Thereafter, it was captive to a party, which it required for its protection, a party that at most paid lip service to labor needs.[10]

Yet despite its claims to the contrary, the AFL did have an important if rather ironic influence on the Democratic party; it influenced the party not to stand for welfare. From the perspective of the AFL leadership, welfare made workers dependent on the state and not on the union. For the AFL, trade union power came first, social welfare second. According to a recent study, the welfare state as it finally emerged in the United States was less corporatist, less extensive, and less worker directed than in Europe; and American trade unions, having been at the margins of welfare state formation—indeed opposed to it—have also been at the margin of its expansion and administration.[11] Until today, the notion of social entitlement is still as alien to labor as it is to capital.[12]

After 1896, the limits of free trade-unionism became increasingly apparent; the "trusts" reigned supreme in the work place, seemingly able to dismiss challenges at will. The use of Taylorism on the assembly line—another form of the new regulationism—was spreading, and workers encountered an intensification of factory discipline. In addition, the use of immigrant labor was also spreading. Step out of line and get fired was the common experience. With capitalists setting the agenda, new technology was imposed; production quotas rose as did production itself, but as the history of the International Workers of the World (IWW) and other radical worker groups revealed, rank and file militancy was also on the rise. The fact that the union leadership did not protest the introduction of millions of non-English-speaking immigrants into American factory jobs contributed to its being discredited. As the years went by and the United States involved itself in World War I, movements such as the IWW were able to persuade more and more workers that the war was not their war, it was the capitalists' war.

In 1917, three years into the war, popular protest escalated against it. In that year also was the only armed revolt by citizens against the government in the twentieth century. This revolt took place, significantly, in a western state when tenant farmers near Durant, Oklahoma, started to march on the state capital, Oklahoma City, with the hope of going on to Washington and ending the war.[13] This protest seems important because revolts in the more oppressed regions of the hegemony, that is, the South, the West, and among groups such as blacks, historically frighten the state more than their counterparts in the more privileged regions.

In 1918, the National Association for the Advancement of Colored People (NAACP) founded its first chapter in Mississippi and Arkansas. News began to spread in the Cotton Belt about national and international politics and to stir the winds of change in previously isolated areas.

In 1919, a panicky group of planters in the deep South allowed itself to believe it was about to be attacked and assaulted the inhabitants of the town of Elaine, Arkansas. Some 250 Afro-Americans were killed in the attack. Thereafter, fear of Afro-Americans gathering in their fraternal lodges was the pretext for many lynchings.

By the 1920s, it was clear that neither the northern nor the southern wing of the ruling class was in an easy situation. If the southern ruling class was confronting labor problems, the northern ruling class was finding itself blocked from developing overseas markets by the powerful isolationist currents that swept the country after the war. The introduction of a Federal Bureau of Investigation (FBI) and a program to Americanize the work force seemed to do little to allay the ruler's fears.

In the North, the major problem was overproduction, and it remained overproduction to the end of the Liberal Age. Accepting isolationism and, hence, diminished opportunities abroad, the northern capitalist class, faute de mieux, turned to the task of creating a higher level of consumerism in the United States. How could more and more Americans become consumers? How could consumerism, a capitalist ideology, be made a worker's ideology? How could it be made a lasting part of the "American Way of Life Ideology"? Would it be through welfare?

The example of the United Kingdom, at least until recent years, provided no answers. In the United Kingdom, consumerism was an ideology of the elite, not a national ideology; the working class's allegiance—despite its political ties to capitalism—was to the flag and not to capitalist economics. After World War II, there were, of course, changes. By that time, many British workers had moved to the suburbs out of their old working-class neighborhoods with all that entailed, including some rise in consumerist sentiment. By contrast in the United States, the synergy of capitalism with the American Way of Life ideology did—with a little prodding—turn consumerism into a mass ideology. This needs more study. Perhaps, the American working class was simply more vulnerable. It lacked its own political party; it was easy for the state to mold its thinking.

Antonio Gramsci, writing from prison in Italy, was among the first to analyze northern capitalism in this period. He suggested that working-class consumerism was actually part of a new managerial strategy, that it was being used to divide the working class. He termed this strategy *Fordism,* naming it after Henry Ford. In recent years, his interpretation has gained some ground. [14]

The Liberal Age, however, was still threatened. Even if consumerism did become a part of the American Way of Life and even if nineteenth-century liberalism remained a powerful force, one could claim, nonetheless, that a crisis was in the air by the late 1920s. Trade union struggle, socialism, and communism were making inroads into the national consciousness; populist movements continued in the South.

What brought an end to the Liberal Age was clearly the depression— the crisis from above caused by overproduction and the crisis from below caused by unemployment. The combination of these two separate but related crises forced the state to move toward corporatism and to allow the unions and even the Communists to play a role in it. The year 1932 was not a highwater mark of struggle from below, by any means, but by then the profound poverty in all parts of the United States might well have led to such struggle. With Roosevelt in office, the state set about to divide the poor against each other, to make cross-class alliances in the North, and once again, to abandon the South to its even deeper economic woes.

Corporatism in the United States 1932–1970

The cross-class alliance that emerged in this period between the ruling class and segments of the petty bourgeoisie and the working class took the form of corporatism. As in Italy, so in the United States, the dominant elements as a whole made selective alliances on their own terms, and as in Italy, the state gained the most from doing so.

In this period, corporate capitalism was far more powerful than national capitalism. The incorporation of lower middle-class functionaries and trade unionists into the hegemony was a way for the state to put pressure on corporate capital and to force it to pay for the debacle of the depression. Equally, it was a way for the state to bolster itself in the face of radical protest, which was rapidly rising in the South and parts of the Midwest.[15]

In the South, the level of suffering and the level of violent protest was indeed on the rise, a point that was far more important given the structure of the hegemony than would otherwise be the case. In Harlan County, Kentucky, in 1932, shooting broke out between striking miners and company guards; in 1932, martial law was imposed on miners in Illinois, and in the same year, the governor of North Carolina while surveying the strikes in the hosiery mills there expressed fears of a general strike. Farmers in many states armed themselves to fight the importation of goods priced below market prices. Coal, textile, and longshoresman strikes broke out in other parts of the country as well.

In 1934, H. L. Mitchell, a white southern radical and owner of a dry cleaning establishment in Tyronza, Arkansas, organized the socialist, interracial Southern Tenant Farmers Union (STFU). Arising when and where it did, the challenge of the STFU was significant. The planters still had not mechanized the production of cotton and thus needed cheap labor. It was counterproductive for them to prevent union organizers from carrying on their work even if this would mean that in the long run labor problems might grow even worse than they were in the short run. Tension began to rise in the Mississippi delta as the planter class grew more insecure about their prospects. Lynchings and other provocative acts began to become commonplace. It was against this background that Roosevelt turned to the northern unions, offering them the New Deal to stabilize what could be stabilized.[16]

The consequences of Roosevelt's initiatives for the leadership of the labor movement were profound. In exchange for new rights and privileges, the leadership found itself more co-opted than ever before. For example, for the first time, leaders found themselves committed to preventing union members from raising social and political issues while at work. In return for the performance of such services by trade union leaders, the government passed the National Labor Relations Act (NLRA) of 1935, the act that more than any other gave unions legitimacy. Under the NLRA, workers were, and today still are, obliged to be represented by a single union, approved by the government, which, in effect, eliminates the possibility of minority union representation. Trade unions, once credentialed, therefore become monopolies. But, in effect, employers and the state also gain the power to dominate unions and union policy through their influence over the duly elected officials. Once a union has achieved the legal right to be the exclusive bargaining agent, it can no longer be easily removed by the rank and file. The main threat to a union, or at least to its officers, becomes decertification by an employer's campaign. Good relations with the employer thus becomes more important than good relations with the rank and file.[17]

The power of corporate capital continued to grow. Despite the common image of the New Deal as a period in which the state was the major actor, the initiatives of the state were often pushed aside, especially if they infringed on corporate prerogatives. For example, corporations simply brushed aside antitrust legislation by controlling the regulatory agencies that Roosevelt set up to control the corporations. Even the Supreme Court worked against the New Deal, declaring unconstitutional a number of the laws affecting industry.[18]

One law that escaped the Supreme Court was social security. Social security began in 1935. With the passage of social security, workers in large numbers came to accept once and for all that they had to fund their own retirement. All waged workers had to pay into the pension fund although not all, it turned out, were eligible to collect because for some time, social security excluded most Afro-American and Hispanic workers, women workers, and much of the South, workers who would have nothing to look forward to at retirement.[19]

Federal housing law under Roosevelt deserves mention alongside social security as representative of the period. Between 1930 and 1937, Savings and Loans Institutions lost two billion dollars and could no longer loan money for mortgages. Housing starts plummeted; foreclosures skyrocketed. From 1932 to 1934, the federal government passed a number of acts to counter these trends, guaranteeing mortgages and providing housing credit. These moves stabilized the housing market; in the process, they brought the government deeper into the domain of how people lived. Finally, despite the long-time opposition of the AFL, the federal government entered the field of public housing with the Wagner-Steagall Act of 1937. By 1941, public housing accounted for 10 percent of new housing. From this involvement, it was obvious that the state also could control who would get this housing. Those who would get it, recent studies show, had to be those who fit the state's concept of the normal family.[20]

The coming of World War II provides an interesting contrast between corporatism in the United States and collectivism in the United Kingdom. The United Kingdom did not opt for war when confronted with a dictator and a trade rival, but the United States did. Chamberlain's attempts at appeasement show that conciliation was expected of a collectivist regime wherein more than one class interest had to be considered. By contrast, after Pearl Harbor, Roosevelt declared on behalf of his corporatist regime that "this day shall live in infamy," declaring war shortly thereafter not only on Japan but on all of Japan's allies as well.

Once war was declared, the United Kingdom hoped for reparations to cut its financial losses. By contrast, the objective of the United States became unconditional surrender, which would permit social engineering in the internal affairs of its trade rivals.

Historians often treat wars, especially its victors, as if they were enjoying a respite from the contradictions in national history. This is not entirely realistic. In general, contradictions, noted as having existed before the war, in fact, continue; sometimes they do so in an intensified form and prepare the way for an explosion at the end of the war. This was the case both in the North and in the South. So by 1945, with soldiers returning and needing government funding and with unions successfully pressing for more and more benefits, with blacks emerging from the army with expectations of being full citizens, with more workers in 1946 on strike than ever before in U.S. history, and with southern planters threatened by labor problems, the state decided to make the postwar period one of repression.

At this point, it was at its zenith and able to implement such policies. Indeed, from the late 1940s, the old regulationary agencies were nearly eclipsed by a new set of secret institutions, the so-called National Security State, which permitted a segment of the state and ruling class to regulate the policies of the government without allowing its decision making to be part of the public domain. A well-known example of the use of this new regulatory power appeared with the purges carried out by the House Un-American Activities Committee (HUAC).

From the point of view of the state, of all the enemies it had in this period, the most dangerous one and, hence, the most logical target for an attack was the Congress of Industrial Organizations (CIO). By the postwar period, the CIO was well known to include many radicals. In addition, it was the union federation that manifested a capacity for real interracial cooperation, and it was the union federation that was successful in winning union rights in key industrial sectors—steel, autos, and maritime industries. Had the CIO continued, it might gradually have eroded all the essential boundaries of the system from race to region. This was not to happen. By 1946, the leadership during Operation Dixie quickly succumbed to the anti-Communist environment of the South and began to purge or silence its own radicals. As is well known, the attacks of the McCarthyites, which followed in the wake of these events, broke the CIO and cost many people their careers.

McCarthyism was extremely useful to the hegemony. Of course, to do what Joseph McCarthy of the HUAC did by way of smear and innuendo was illegal. This was a problem the state had to overcome, and overcome it, it did. Thus, much of what McCarthy did was made legal because the state pushed through enabling legislation to allow it. The founding piece of legislation for carrying out purges was NSC-68. It presumed a clear and present danger to the United States, thereby creating a context for McCarthy. Further examples of this type of legislation, which served as a background for McCarthy, include the Smith-Connally Act of 1943, which allowed for and still allows federal takeovers of strike-torn industries and the outlawing of union political contributions. This, of course, was a public blow at the CIO. In 1947, a third piece of such legislation, the Taft-Hartley Act, outlawed sympathy strikes; it, too, is still in effect. In 1950, the McCarren Act made it possible for union leaders or bosses to fire suspected Communists. In 1952, the McCarran-Walter Act gave the secretary of labor sweeping power over immigration, and this was and remains one of the keys to the hegemony. With the passage of such legislation, it became obvious even to those not directly caught by McCarthy, that to survive they would have to place themselves under the control of "organized" labor, and this they did.

The question that needs to be addressed is why workers coming back from the war permitted the government to dismember their unions and to accuse their leaders and fellow members of being Communists. Why did the society think that the Soviet Union had to be an enemy after it had been an ally? Why did a cold war come about? Here the English experience is somewhat relevant. In the United Kingdom, cold war ideology had little impact on the working class thought, and there was nothing like McCarthyism. What stands out in a comparative view is once again the lack in the United States of a labor party; the American working class, at least white workers in the North, was as a result more susceptible than its English counterpart to the propaganda of the ruling class. The reason for the absence of a cold war in Britain seems to be that the Labour party remained intact. Only when the party nearly collapsed with the rise to power of

Margaret Thatcher was the British state able to introduce purges and de-monization at all comparable to the U.S. cold war or to McCarthyism.

From 1950, the lack of a labor party and the reluctance of the unions to stand up to the state on political matters gave the state influence almost down to the shop floor, especially in the industrial North. The workers were asked not only to surrender their political rights but their control of the shop floor as well. Accept this and enjoy high wages was the offer, or rather the demand, and, given the high profit levels of American business in this period, employers could easily afford to pay what it took.[21]

Cold War ideology or no cold war ideology, labor struggle carried on in the South. By the end of the war, the STFU had unionized many Afro-American cotton pickers in the delta. Faced with rising labor costs as a consequence of new and improved contract agreements after unionization, the planters escalated the class war by bringing in for the first time non-union Hispanic temporary workers from outside.[22] The fights continued.

During the 1940s and 1950s, the struggles of agricultural workers in another area, California, were also reaching a peak. Once again, Mitchell, this time with Hank Hasiwar, served as an organizer for the union. This time, the union, the National Farm Labor Union, was up against the Di Giorgio Winery, the leading element in California agribusiness and report-edly the largest winery in the world. In a fabled two-year strike in Di Giorgio's towns in Kern County, the union struggle became one of the nation's epic dramas. The young Richard Nixon appeared as Di Giorgio's defender before the California Senate Committee on Un-American Activi-ties and true to character he portrayed the union as a communist threat. The strike was finally broken through the corporation's use of thugs despite the support to the strikers given by the young Ronald Reagan, then presi-dent of the Screen Actors Guild. Reagan then sided with the strikers.

In the long term, the significance of the spread of union struggle to the California fields was the organization it brought to Mexican-Americans. It was, in fact, a Mexican-American leader, Cesar Chavez, who emerged from this strike to rise with AFL-CIO backing in the 1960s to become one of the major labor leaders in the United States.

In 1951, labor struggle spread to yet a third locale, Louisiana, first, to the strawberry fields, two years later to the sugar cane workers, and shortly thereafter to the shrimp fishermen, or "pogy-boat" men. There, in one of the notable triumphs of the decade, the union succeeded in organizing the workers, this time with the legal help of the chief executive of Baltimore County, Baltimore, Maryland, a young lawyer named Spiro T. Agnew, later vice-president of the United States. Again, Hasiwar and Mitchell played important roles as organizers.

So, although the glory days of traditional organizing were fast drawing to a close, still, for all the setbacks past and future, the unions had seen many successes. Union jobs tended to be more stable, to pay higher wages, and to pay real benefits.

Then came capital flight. The leadership decided to retain its traditional apolitical approach to trade unionism no matter what. It is not surprising that the percentage of unionized workers in the country began to fall, a trend that continues until this day.

Even in this bleak period, however, there were some moments of success. When the union leadership allowed itself to support Cesar Chavez's United Farm Workers in California and the National Farm Labor Union, they found themselves on the winning side.[23] This, unfortunately, did not have a profound influence on its thinking. They were too co-opted by their relations with the state, with business, and, in some instances, with organized crime.

By 1970, capital flight was certainly well under way; nearly one-third of annual U.S. car company investments were being made abroad. In this period as well, close to three-quarters of U. S. exports were transactions with overseas branches of U.S. corporations. Tax laws in this period gave generous write-offs to corporations for making the flight abroad.

Large numbers of people in both the North and the South in the 1960s, especially youth, grew frustrated at being abandoned in an economy left to stagnate by capital flight. Their frustrations soon took a political form. Why was the United States fighting in Vietnam? Why did the United States have to deny people their civil rights? Of course, small groups had opposed the U.S. involvement in Vietnam and other places for years, and the struggle for blacks for civil rights was even older, but with a nationwide structural crisis in the economy, the possibility for the first time of a nationwide populist movement of the Left came into being. Many middle-class people, many of them youth, became actively pro–civil rights and anti–the Vietnam War.

Confronted by this challenge from its erstwhile allies, the "best and the brightest," the state saw that there was no longer any utility to a corporatist-approach; regulationism worked better following the strategies of the first Liberal Age. It was not worth risking the erosion of racial and regional boundaries to perpetuate corporatism any longer.

Studies of the politics of the late 1960s show that the 1968 presidential election that brought Richard Nixon to office marked the beginning of the transition from corporatism to liberalism, marking, as well, the birth of a new alliance that was to dominate the years that followed, a conservative alliance led by the two main wings of American capitalism. The year 1970 seems like a fair if slightly arbitrary point to call the dividing point between the old period and the new.

In 1968, the state began to distance itself from its own public sector and to reach out to replace it with new alliances. This reaching out has been called the southern strategy. It involved the promotion of a white backlash against civil rights, a capturing of what Richard Nixon and others were calling the *silent majority*.

Nixon was, of course, no outright opponent of civil rights; his interest was the more pragmatic preservation of the hegemony. Some of the state's regulatory initiatives had failed in the 1960s; he had to show that the state was still in control. Taking his line from Wall Street, he began to claim that welfare and entitlement programs created discontented people and had failed to help. Thus, he and those who followed him—Republicans and Democrats—championed the claims of all those who would turn their backs on the Roosevelt tradition and support a return to reliance on private initiative.

Looking at Nixon in this way, one can at least understand his involvement in such seemingly contradictory policies as his creation of an Office of Minority Business Enterprise in 1969 and the unparalleled assault on the black masses he unleashed, the so-called anticrime measures. It explains as well why the Nixonites got America out of the Vietnam War. The war was not worth it; it gave the counterhegemonic movement too strong an issue.

Between 1968 and 1972, the trade union leadership of the major unions perhaps realized that it, too, could become a target of backlashes of the Right or the Left. It thus decided to identify itself with the silent majority, helping to bring about the shift of many traditional Democratic voters, especially whites, to the Republican party. For example, in 1972, George Meany, a traditional symbol of the unity of labor with the Democratic party, declared himself to be neutral about the candidacy of the Democrat George McGovern.

When recalling the key details of the transition period, one might do well also to recall that the setback to the old hegemony and the reformulation of the new one was marked by the rise of violence by the state and by the changes in law that served somehow to legitimate this violence.

Unprecedented violence against black political movements such as the Black Panthers led to many deaths and arrests. Whites began to shy away; black activists gradually began to give up hope that the hegemony could really change.

Among the changes in law of this period, the Law Enforcement Assistance Act signed by Lyndon Johnson late in 1968 came to assume major importance under Nixon thereafter. As a result of this law, the nation's police forces grew with great rapidity. Another law of the Nixon era of great importance for the future was the State and Local Fiscal Assistance Act of 1972 (the General Revenue Service [GRS]), an act replacing the federally directed Great Society programs of the 1960s, programs whose monies came from Washington. This law of 1972 placed the burden of responsibility for the funding of all public programs squarely on the states.

In comparative terms, the Nixon transition reminds one of that of the earlier president, Rutherford Hayes. Nixon's lukewarm concern with the existing laws as reflected, for example, in his refusal to push forward civil rights in the South parallels Hayes decision to withdraw troops from the South and to accept the racial status quo there in the first Liberal Age. Yet to repeat, Nixon was not an antagonist of black people; neither was Hayes. Both sought stability.

Challenged by the possibility that a new counterhegemonic movement would rise organized around environmental and health issues, Nixon also worked out the general outline of how the state should respond to such challenges, an outline still in force today. To head off challenges to industry in the area of ecology, Nixon relied on regulation. In 1970, the Environmental Protection Agency was created and air and water quality legislation began.[24] A new era—or, if one wishes—an old era had dawned.

Neoliberalism, 1970 to the Present

The collapse of corporatism brought a return to neoliberalism in economics and a return to one-class rule in politics. Capitalism became more unified and as that happened the role of the state, which had been expanding, once again shrank.

As a hypothesis to explain the momentous economic and political changes of this period, it seems reasonable to emphasize first that the old capitalist class of the United States, like that of a number of other countries, had accumulated its wealth primarily through manufacturing and was by the mid-1960s reaching a point where this wealth made it vulnerable. The market for industrial goods was no longer expandable. The more revolutionary and dynamic wing of capitalism, finance capitalism, saw its opportunity to push the manufacturers aside as they appeared to be faltering. Industry was thrown out of the country into cheap labor zones; the center of real wealth became the banks and insurance companies. Observers of the period reported that banks and insurance companies could invest selectively where profit was to be made in the short run whereas industrialists with their heavy investments in their plants could not. To stay competitive the traditional corporations began to restructure, to sell off what was unprofitable and to buy into companies that were profitable no matter what field they might be in. Thus, not without reason has the transition to liberalism been called by many writers the era of mergers. When one looks now at the new restructured corporations with their multitude of new and ever-changing investments, what stands out is another power shift, one which goes a long way toward explaining the dominance of finance capitalism over industrial capitalism. I refer to the rise of a new managerial class at the expense of the traditional owners of the corporations and of other large institutions. Rises in power inside corporations, of course, do not come easily. The owner of a traditional steel mill might not claim to know about the market for his new line of Kleenex, but he would likely relinquish power to his CEO only if he were forced to do so, and, in this period, he was forced to do so. In corporation after corporation, with the decline in value of industrial stock, stockholders began to look to whomever could or would raise profits and, hence, stock payments. Stockholders, not surprisingly, often supported the diversification proposed by managers and rejected the more conservative advice of the traditional owner class, who were thus bypassed.

As the trend toward short-term profit seeking through mergers progressed, new opportunities emerged in the political sphere for the American ruling class. Mergers brought together in new ways business people from the national and international wings of the economy. One thing they found that they had in common was a dislike of the regulatory policies of the state. Could they collude and force the state to deregulate? Could they force the state to go deeper into debt by buying their goods and services? The 1970s and 1980s showed that this was, indeed, possible. The state could be weakened; it could be hemmed in quite well by lobbyists for the private interests.

But was it feasible for corporations to go on randomly expanding simply because they had the money to buy up smaller businesses? This was indeed a possibility because of another feature of the period, the access of the corporations to new telecommunications technology. Could these huge international corporations or, more precisely, conglomerates, which were thrown together by happenstance, have survived without this technology or without the political help? While this is a matter of speculation, it is fair to claim that the changes brought by this period involved much more than simply crushing the civil rights of black people; there was a wider destruction of the civil society as well, possibly even a toying with the idea of changing hegemonies, perhaps shifting to a Russian Road regime.

By the 1980s, the state had been able to divide the society into two tiers composed of those with money and those without. Because those without included some whites and those with included some blacks, the government could claim that from the old society with its racism a new society was arising, one moving toward its dream of being a melting pot of the energetic and thrifty.

Of course, most of what was left in the society were low-paying jobs in the service sector.[25] If one was poor, one was trapped. Youth, white and black, denied a future began to stand out again as a problem as they did in the 1960s. Not only was nothing "trickling down" but this time there was no movement to be joined.[26] Feminism, the only new movement on the rise could not take on such burdens. It chose in any case to stay close to the agenda of the dominant interests.

Did an economic underclass, then, come to replace a racial undercaste? The answer is, of course, negative. If an economic underclass had actually come into being, it would have raised the prospects of class conflict without offering a way to deflect it. Although structural unemployment in the old industrial areas and on the farms kept many whites poor, being an underclass and being an undercaste remained two different things.[27]

When pondering why a shift to finance capitalism should lead to such a breakdown of an organized economy, still—and this is an intriguing point —no purely economic answer emerges. Certainly corporate capitalism confronted competition from the Japanese and the Germans after 1970, but this —even along with pressures from unions and from civil rights demands, from stockholders and CEOs—cannot explain the capitulation to short-term planning at the expense of long-term planning. How did the ruling class of an industrial country decide to forego having an industrial policy or a trade policy to protect the national interest? This decision remains unexplained. It is all the more astonishing because all the other leading industrial states had policies to invest in their work forces, in their technologies, and in their infrastructures. Obviously, this was an option for the American ruling class as well. What was it about the Americans, who took the easy way out, gearing their corporations to make noncompetitive sales of unneeded items, such as weapons to the government, then forcing the government to go into debt to pay for them? The fact that long-term planning was not considered must be explained in terms of politics. What else?

For politicians and businesspeople to consider the long term, they must believe in the long term, the idea of the long run being as much political as it is economic. If they believed in the long run, they would plan for it and accept losses along the way. Was this the case in the United States in 1970? I would say not; the hegemony was in the midst of defeat. Against all odds a black middle class had arisen. From this class, many talented individuals had emerged into national life. To return to American "normalcy," that is, to the older white supremacy of the nineteenth century, the one the traditional hegemonic elements might prefer would mean a radical shrinking of this class or the development of a new racial undercaste to substitute for it; neither option was possible, again for political reasons.

Judging from policies proposed and adopted, most of the ruling class appeared after 1970 not to be able to accept the fact that racist ideology was on the decline over what it had been in the nineteenth century and that this was a time for compromises.[28] A smaller section appeared optimistic that by manipulating immigration policy new groups could be introduced to be played off against blacks, and blacks could thereby be pushed down again.

Of course, some thought the past could be restored through Christian fervor.

But for the majority, having failed to gain their way on their concept of fundamentals, the main policy became one simply of running the society into the ground. Where Roosevelt rescued Americans by turning them into consumers, Reagan rescued capitalism by channeling most of the money in the country into the hands of the top 5 percent of the income ladder so that the money could be taken out of the country. The old Poor Law made a comeback. By the 1980s, welfare was being replaced by workfare; business was gaining access to a great deal of semi-free labor, again making one think of other hegemonies.

Such draconian practices of a ruling class, however, did not go uncontested even when the traditional opposition movements were in disarray. The country remained urban, and large segments of the urban population of the North resisted neoliberalism and kept on voting for liberal Democrats and for welfare; large segments of the South and the West resisted as well. Many in both regions realized that they were being abandoned, and this added new urgency to their criticisms of the schools, the health system, the environment, the wars, and so on.

In addition, the new undercaste-cum-underclass was not like the poor and oppressed of yesterday. It was far more enterprising, or, to put it another way, the forces oppressing it were less effective. Who can ignore its Rap music? Who can ignore its contribution to the illegal economy?

By the 1980s, some would argue that a whole sector of the economy was on the rise, illegal business that included the poor and oppressed along with others, some of whom were working from within the very agencies charged with its interdiction.[29]

Some blame the state for this growing illegal economy; some fear the state is so controlled that it is losing its effectiveness; some blame foreigners for skillfully penetrating the country's economy. Should one invoke the idea of a hegemony shift in the works? This seems excessive. If one takes the principal initiative of the state against illegal business, the War on Drugs, it is a policy that clearly fits the praxis of democracy. In fact, increasingly, scholarship is coming to emphasize that the war is being fought purposefully, not to win but to reorganize society.[30] The point appears to be if one could jail more and more poor black men, one could eventually associate crime itself with black men while generating a source of nonunion labor from within the prisons. Incrementally, one could return to the nineteenth century.

How could such a policy be unpopular? Crime in the street, drug related or otherwise, has touched the lives of so many that such solutions have become attractive in many quarters. Why worry about the causes of crime and poverty? Why not worry just about the behavior of criminals and poor people? The initiative is working; most major cities have gone through a phase in this period of electing law-and-order mayors who articulate such sentiments.

Nonetheless, increasingly, the majority of urbanites as time goes on are becoming aware that only a deeper commitment to welfare and social reinvestment will make a difference in their lives. In the 1980s, the mayors of the major cities emerged as a lobby for urban renewal. SWAT teams cannot fight AIDS or tuberculosis.

The long-term interest of the American ruling class was to keep the South a cheap labor zone. The South was a weak area in the neoliberal strategy. If whites who were already poor were made much poorer, how could they be controlled?

With the influx of industry into the southern economy after 1960, the so-called new South appeared to be on the rise; as noted before, however, this change proved to be short-lived and superficial. As early as the 1970s, many corporations shifted out of the South to the Third World or automated. Even the oil industry, long an anchor of the economy of the Southwest, could not withstand the new competition in the 1970s, and left cities such as Houston and Dallas to take a nosedive. Gradually, throughout the South, banking, real estate, and insurance concerns came to the fore as they did elsewhere, and as this happened, the gap between rich and poor widened rapidly.

In this situation, opportunities arose for other power structures to come into being and to assert themselves on both regional and national levels. Fundamentalism, for example, may not have appealed overall to a majority of Americans, but organized society did. Thus, many Americans went along with the "war" against secular humanism and for family values in the 1970s, 1980's, and 1990s. The South with its problems sometimes served as an initial venue.

Some of the influential—or affluent—centers of fundamentalism were and are Jerry Falwell's Liberty Baptist University in Lynchburg, Virginia; Jimmy Swaggart's church in Baton Rouge; Robert Schuller's church in southern California, the Bakers' ministry in South Carolina, and most famous of all, the television ministry of Oral Roberts in Tulsa, Oklahoma. By the mid-1980s, wealth was becoming a problem. All of them were plagued with scandals. Mass opinion in the form of rumor and gossip was exposing their frailties. With the campaign of Governor Clinton in 1992, much money went back to secular politicians.[31]

Hegemony in the United States involves not only the initiatives of the regional wings of American capitalism but those of the state as well. What were the projects of the state? How has the state maintained itself in recent times?

The era of mergers posed a challenge to the old regulatory strategy, and in some areas, the state had to make concessions to the consolidation of the ruling class. In this period, for example, one finds a job in the foreign service more closely tied to politics and patronage and less to education and training. The presidency suffered a blow with Watergate.

Still, overall from 1970 to 1990, the state, continued to hold its own in three main ways, all of which are recognizable from previous American history. First, leading politicians successfully claimed that terrorism was on the rise and that the state was the country's protector. Second, the state insisted that it was uniquely qualified to lead the country's moral mission for human rights and peace treaties. Third, the state was uniquely qualified to regulate religion and religious sects.

Nearly all presidents from the cold war to the present have found a danger from foreign terrorists. At first, they portrayed them as a Soviet menace, but because the Soviet Union entered a long liberal phase in the 1950s, progressively, the threat was identified as coming from the Third World. In the 1970s, terrorism was commonly associated with Palestinians and with the Islamic trend. It ultimately did not matter to the state who the terrorists were, and it did not matter whether the incidents alleged to be taking place were real or not as long as they dominated the newspaper headlines for a few days. The policy seemed to work even if people knew much was spurious about it because there were, of course, real threats to Americans abroad on occasion. How could it be otherwise? Random investments for short-term profits took Americans everywhere, exposing them as never before to local reprisals.

Perhaps the most commented-on initiative by a president since the 1970s was not in antiterrorism but in human rights—the human rights campaign begun by President Jimmy Carter. On one level, it seems reasonable to interpret this campaign as an expression of the man's values and of those of much of the new South, but its acceptance more broadly in Washington and elsewhere must be explained in terms of state interests. In effect, it seems reasonable to suppose that from the state's point of view, if the banks were going to loan money to Third World countries, this could be an opportunity for the state to establish its position as arbiter of who got the money and on what basis. The position of the state came to be that the recipients had to try to uphold American values, for example, human rights values. If from a corporate point of view a loan was a loan, from the state's point of view, a loan could be said to be upholding morality and opposing the demonic or terrorist regimes in the world.

A third area of state initiatives was in the domain of the so-called intractable political problems, such as the Middle East. It is difficult to escape the conclusion that the state benefited from the Middle East problem —until it was pushed into the peace process—because for years it fit right into the contours of the existing regulatory politics. For years, there have been two sides to the Middle East crisis. One side, represented by the East Coast oil companies, wanted stability in the Middle East, and the other side, represented by the core culture, wanted the Middle East to be a Holy Land. The conflict between these two positions permitted regulation.

As noted before, from the 1950s to the 1970s, the sun belt cities experienced rapid growth, permitting the emergence of much new wealth. These cities, in fact, became very affluent, the surrounding countryside increasingly poor.[32]

During this period, by virtue of their prominence, the newly wealthy businesspeople, the beneficiaries of these changes, had to confront the criticism of the larger community, which once they had been part of but which now they were exploiting through their speculative ventures. To do so, they were clearly in need of a new cultural ethos and this they found in religion. When one looks more closely at these developments as they pertain to the Middle East problem, what stands out is the development of two distinct positions on the Middle East within this southern elite.

In the Southwest, the new South was also a new Right. This new Right did not simply want to acknowledge but to celebrate the separateness of the rich, that is, the separateness of themselves from the rest, in essence to celebrate their chosen-ness as chosen people. In the process of celebrating, the New Right's view of the world underwent a dramatic change from anti-Semitic to philo-Semitic. As a consequence of this change, leading politicians of the Southwest made an unprecedented invitation to Prime Minister Menachem Begin of Israel to visit a Texas church in 1980, and Begin made the equally unprecedented decision to attend. From this period, the traditional anti-Semitic movements of the core culture, such as the Aryan nation, appeared to be more secure in the small towns and in the rural areas than in the cities.[33]

By contrast in the Southeast, the new South politicians, many of whom also were nouveau riche, approached the Middle East problem quite differently. The Southeast was more integrated than was the Southwest, especially cities such as Atlanta. When a politician such as Jimmy Carter emerged from Atlanta, he had a strong record on race relations and a strong desire to have justice done for "both" sides in the Middle East. Thus, in the 1970s progressive Baptists, of which he was one, had begun to meet with Palestinians. In the other part of the sun belt, the Southwest, there was also urban prosperity but no change in racial relations. It is there that pro-Israelism took a kind of frozen pro-Likud—or hardline—shape that led to the invitation of Prime Minister Begin.

In contrast to the South, the East Coast in the 1960s had very different ideas about the Middle East. Corporate capital led by the Seven Sisters formulated U.S. policy toward the Middle East. Its policy was that the U.S. stood for stability in the Middle East. The Zionist lobby maintained that Israel was the key to that stability. As the 1960s progressed, however, the struggle for racial integration in the United States began to alter the politics of the region. In the middle-class *movement circles* that were propelling these changes, the call for Afro-American rights and rights for native Americans began to include a call for justice for the Palestinians, and this was picked up as part of northern liberalism.

By the 1970s, the Middle East problem on the East Coast had once again changed. The movement grew weaker and ceased to be so important; an influential upwardly mobile fraction of finance capitalism, represented by such figures as Michael Milken, the junk bond king, began to make its imprint. While the movement was criticizing Israel and boycotting South Africa, Milken was reported in the 1980s to be helping the finances of Israel's Koor Corporation, one of that country's principal links with South Africa.

These splits between North and South and within each region over the problem in the Middle East gave the state a chance to play an important regulatory role, all the more so given the paradigmatic role of the Middle East in U.S. culture. In this case, the state chose to forge what it termed a special relationship with Israel. As 1990 approached, Milken was in jail and the special relationship had all but broken down, but the strategy of keeping the Middle East as a problem still seemed to have a bit of mileage in it.

The Middle East problem was but one of a number of controversies that the state exploited in this period to reassert its regulatory role. A second such controversy surrounded the regulation of religious television programming. Over a number of years, core culture Christians had tried to buy air time on the major television networks, and the state had blocked them by upholding the separation of church and state doctrine in a way that favored the East Coast. In the 1970s, however, they eventually collected enough money to buy their own television stations and even briefly attempted to buy the Columbia Broadcasting System (CBS), one of the major networks. The controversy over the right to air time began to grow. When the Federal Communications Commission (FCC) tried to regulate the shows aired on Christian stations under the Fairness Doctrine, the Christians fought them in court, arguing that it is the marketplace, ultimately the consumer, and not the government who should judge media content. This position, whatever its merits, was unexpected given their position on pornography. In this instance, the state won; in others, it has been less successful. When the FCC ruled that televangelism was nonprofit, it perhaps, unnecessarily permitted monies collected through solicitation to be untaxed.[34] This decision was criticized.

Not deterred by setbacks, however, the state decided to make the issue of media programming an important regulatory arena because it had the potential to remain an ongoing issue. In 1971, it set up a National Council on Religion and Education to air the differences of opinion on such subjects between the East Coast and the core culture.[35]

A third area of state regulation of a protracted problem deserves mention here as well. Pressured by clergy from the mainstream churches, especially from the core culture, the state has targeted various cult groups as being potentially dangerous and not truly religious. In the 1970s and 1980s, the state went to the courts and to the media, insisting such groups were not "real" churches and as such were a menace to society. In these struggles, it has been successful. The core culture was grateful, the East Coast contemptuous that the core culture would violate the civil liberties of these groups. Possibly, of course, as the government maintains, groups such as the Moonies and the Scientologists pose a potential threat to the hegemony; possibly, they have the skill to cross racial and regional lines or to become third parties. What is clear is that as long as they keep struggling, the state has a role to play.[36]

By 1990, after twenty years of neoliberalism, the dominant power bloc was facing setbacks in all parts of the country: partly, because of its unfavorable international economic position, partly because of its declining ability to organize culture and persuasion. Ruling class homogenization played a role. Bitterness and alienation was on the rise all over the country toward the policies imposed during this period.

This seemed almost predictable. If conglomerates were aligning themselves not just internally in the United States but externally to Japanese and European capitalists, forcing the state to go deeper and deeper in debt, beggaring the population in the process, if Israel could push the state around at will, would there not come a time when the issue of the national debt and of foreign influence could make the organization of culture more difficult?

Many years ago, Gramsci showed in Italy that capitalists would do anything to stay in power including aligning themselves with feudalists. In the United Kingdom and the United States, a different view prevails; there, capitalism itself is believed to be inherently revolutionary and capitalists benefit from this aura of being involved in things that are progressive such as development. Thus, when even something so inherently reactionary as a trickle-down economics creed emerged, the Left in the United States and the United Kingdom were not able to make the point. Still, as economic conditions in the United States and the United Kingdom grew worse for the majority, class struggle began to deepen, even without a well-organized radicalism. A vote for Labour or a vote for the Democrats is a vote for the common person. It is a vote for the environment; it is a vote for national health. These are class issues, indeed, the emerging form of class struggle.

For an organized movement to arise and to become nationwide out of the ongoing diverse struggles, there must be people and groups who can blend the different regional, class, and racial cultures. In the American experience, the most evolved such movements have been the religious Right and the Wobblies, an amalgam of the populist and socialist traditions. The two are quite different. The religious Right wants to maintain the economic status quo of capitalism and reorganize the society; the Wobblies are challengers to capitalism. In its first phase, the Wobblies appeared—and I use this term because they are still so poorly studied—to be moving toward a counterhegemonic struggle. With the coming of World War I and the decision of the major trade unions to side with the state, the Wobblies suffered vicious repression.[37] Although their legacy remains in countless American communities, this legacy is submerged because they cannot at this point compete with the state or the religious Right.

The Organization of Culture in the United States

All hegemonies rely on persuasion as a part of ruling, and they organize their cultural systems to achieve it. In the democracies, the organization of culture reinforces the fundamental racial divisions on which the disguise of class relations depends.[38] In the United States, the organization of culture takes place through the actions of the regulatory agencies and through the patronage given out by the state and the ruling classes in their efforts to steer and to mold the trends in civil society. Their actions and efforts result in the perpetuation of an American way of life.

The American way of life differs from its more elite and more neatly honed counterpart Englishness in its superficial inclusiveness of the practices and beliefs of broader strata of society, that include even a small number of African-Americans. Despite this fact, it shares with Englishness a tendency ultimately to reinforce the generic contradictions of race, class, and gender.

According to this ideology, in America, the same culture is for everyone; immigrants and minorities are welcome as soon as they assimilate it. In England, in both ideology and in fact, not only is culture related to class but to nationhood. The ruling class is able to imagine that the Irish and the Commonwealth people are intrinsically different from themselves—a different nation—and, therefore, unassimilable. The American model appears to fit the needs of a regulatory state: it plays with assimilation and segregation. The English model fits the straight approach: relationships are more fixed.

From 1877 to 1970, the efforts by the American state to organize culture appear to have been quite successful, which was a major factor in the failure of revolutionary movements to develop. During this period, the state exercised considerable influence through its regulatory function in science, social science, and the humanities while on a regional level, the ruling class participated as well through its patronage. Evidence of this success is that schools, churches, television, medicine, law, social work, and so forth, were seen by society at large simply as *professional* domains. After 1970, despite the increasing expenditure of money, the organization of culture worked less well in persuading the mass population to embrace the status quo; more coercion was needed. Let us begin with a consideration of the image of intellectuals understood as the bearers of this culture.

Americans have historically been known for their anti-intellectualism.[39] Intellectuals in the common view are to be distrusted. They are not practical people. Seen from another point of view, however, while Americans ward off much potential criticism they might otherwise have to face through their rejection of intellectuals and intellectualism, they block the development of individuals and groups who might uphold their interests. The state can thus when it so chooses use intellectuals to defend it against the society at large—an Einstein, for example, but not a Rosenberg.[40]

As with Englishness, the American way of life has had three historically dominant formulations in modern history. During the early liberal, or Victorian, phase, the state leaned toward the moralistic side of the Puritan core culture to counterbalance the rapid rise of an East Coast pragmatism.[41] During the corporatist phase, the state tried to widen its appeal, and Roosevelt used the different sides of the Lincoln tradition to rule. Roosevelt, as was Lincoln, was everyone's president. Finally, in the 1970s, the American way of life came to include a curious fusion of fundamentalism and libertarian liberalism.[42]

The state's basic involvement in the organization of culture during these periods took the form of regulation. As the state grew and its regulatory capacities expanded, its experts and bureaucrats inevitably came into view and opened themselves to criticism. As a consequence, politicians have had to try to preempt criticism by voicing a need for bureaucratic reform. Discourse about bureaucratic reform, therefore, is a barometer of the class struggle.[43]

One of the major areas of regulatory involvement of the state in culture has been science. Two reasons for this seem obvious. First, as the country secularized, pragmatism gained ground, and the American metaphysical tradition declined, many Americans came to equate science with truth. This was particularly the case on the East Coast. Second, business found it of interest to have the state involved in science because it needed the backing of the state to create and maintain new markets and technologies. What this particular context for science meant for women, minorities, and even for scientists themselves is beginning now to become a research domain.[44]

A common form of regulation of science that arose with the modern state was the awarding of patent claims for new inventions. Patent claims or patent rights serve as a form of validation; they also define terms of access to new technology. As this form of regulation continued to develop, the government soon found itself involved in yet a second form of regulation, weights and measures, a third, classifying certain scientific research as being in the national interest, and a fourth, directly sponsoring scientific research.

Governmental involvement in the regulation of science often took the form of passing laws and creating regulatory agencies. For example, in 1878, the government established its Coast and Geodetic Survey and in the same year, strengthened its hold in the West by establishing a U.S. Geological Survey. These agencies were followed in a few years by such government creations as the Bureau of American Ethnology and the U.S. Fish Commission. In 1884, many members of Congress thought the time was right for an agency to coordinate governmental support to science. The Allison Commission was set up to investigate this matter. East Coast interests objected. The idea was finally shelved on the grounds that centralized agencies do not serve the general welfare.[45] In 1898, the government upgraded the Department of Agriculture to cabinet level.

World War I gave the state a major opportunity to expand its sphere of regulation in science because of the emergency situation. In 1915, the inventor Thomas A. Edison was appointed by the secretary of the navy to be the head of the Naval Consulting Board, a body charged with improving the technology of weapons. In the same year, the government created a National Advisory Committee for Aeronautics. In 1916 the government founded a National Research Council, a body that remained after the war as part of the National Academy of Sciences. These bodies had the power to encourage business to compete for contracts with the military, and fostering such competition proved to be a lucrative and important way by which the state exerted control over what would be produced and who would get the rewards for producing it.

In the interwar period, with peace restored, industry in the North briefly took over the main task of funding and regulating scientific research. Private foundations also became an important source to which researchers could turn. The contemporary period, one again characterized by the preponderance of the role of the state in science, began during World War II.

From the 1970s, the state was perceived to have grown "too strong" in the view of business; regulation was costing it money. In this period, President Reagan undertook to deregulate the airlines and communication industries, to sell public lands, and to give private companies control of inventions funded by federal money.[46]

If science was in the American context a product of the regulatory function of the state, what kind of science did industry and government produce? Science in the United States, apparently, was practical science. Scientists were particularly encouraged to serve the needs of the defense industry; more speculative basic research came second. Carrying this rather sceptical line of thought into other areas of concern to the state such as, gender and race, the well-being of men was a scientific priority, the well-being of women and minorities less so. How else can one explain the fact that a segment of the scientific community still finds funding to pursue even such lost causes as race research, and birth control still is a failure?

But one might argue as many do that all this is in the process of change; new technology is removing traditional burdens, women and minorities are entering the work force in ever greater numbers. But the statistics do not paint such a rosy picture. A recent study suggests, contrary to what one would think, that with each new generation of labor-saving technology for the housewife comes the demand for ever cleaner, more beautiful homes and children? And, thus, although one would suppose that the new miracle technology would liberate women from housework, it never does. Housework imposed on women today uses up on the average as much time as it did half a century ago before much of this technology had been developed. New technology locks in women much as the old did.[47]

But, are not more women entering science fields? Is not this a transitional problem? The answer appears to be negative; the future of science—the near future, at least—does not appear to hold such changes. Most schools and universities admit students to science programs on the basis of tests of *scientific competence*. Judging from the results of these tests over a long period, one can only conclude that they are continuing to successfully block women and minority students from entering science fields. Given how these tests are designed, white middle class men do better on them, so it is they who enter these fields. If this was not the desired outcome, test makers could design tests that would reverse these trends. In fact, existing pilot projects suggest such changes in tests could be easily designed if the government so wished, but this is not happening.

The record suggests to the contrary that the state has actively gone out of its way, at least on some occasions, to drive women who were in fields such as medicine out of the fields. An example is the well-known campaign of the early twentieth century to deny certification to midwives. This was clearly an initiative of the state because there was no important movement in society demanding the end of midwives. Quite the contrary, there was and continues to be a struggle waged by various groups to ensure their survival.

For better or worse then, the treatment of science as part of regulatory politics has had the consequence not only of making it part of the status quo but of creating some disillusion and scepticism about its progressive possibilities in American thought, perhaps even some disinclination to pursue science as a career. As a consequence, it is natural for students to ask if the state has any real commitment to science? If so, what is it? Is there such a thing as science in the United States? Or is it simply a screen to protect discrete practices and particular paradigms, such as the "medical model," practices and paradigms that, perhaps, only share in common that they turn a profit. In addition, there is much suspicion why the establishment view about science and about even the history of science is so narrowly internalist? Why should an externalist view, a sociology of science, for example, be so threatening? Is it threatening because science itself is so flimsy? Critics, including those concerned with gender and racial issues, are divided on these points as are others, but most would agree that the government's regulation of science has been a most significant part of the organization of culture.[48]

For political economy, at least, one final but important piece of evidence linking the development of science to the organization of culture comes from a comparison of scientists, some of whom were loyal to the assumptions of the status quo, some of whom were disloyal. In Germany in the Nazi period, most scientists appear to have supported the racial ideology of the state. As supporters of their government's view of race, German scientists and professors, the so-called *mandinarate,* were adored by the state. In the United States and the United Kingdom by contrast, where scientists and other professors were critics of the idea of race, even prominent scientists were a political liability or, at least, were made to feel so despite the fact that some of these scientists by virtue of their individual prestige lived to enjoy fame and fortune. A famous and controversial antiracist scientist was the American anthropologist, Franz Boas (d. 1942). Alongside his scientific career, Boas found time to participate in various organizations that opposed racism, including the American Committee Against Fascist Oppression in Germany and the Struggle for Negro Rights.[49]

There were, however, consequences for an oppositional stand on race issues, if not for figures such as Boas personally, then seemingly for the system of which they were a part. Looking at the record, one might conclude that where the state in a democracy found a disaffection with the official policy on race among its scientists and educators it was prone to turn away from them to the mass media. In such countries, for example, the United States, the United Kingdom and postwar Germany, universities and research centers suffered a drop in prestige in relation to the mass media. By contrast, where the scholarly community was largely in accord with the racial ideas of the state, one thinks of Nazi Germany or, until quite recently, of Israel and South Africa, the reverse is the case. In these latter countries, the major universities enjoy unrivaled prestige, and the mass media are much less important.

If science in the United States has long been a particular object of official regulation, so too, if to a lesser extent, are the arts and the social sciences.[50]

The conventional interpretation of the role of the state with regard to the arts and the social sciences tends to be that the state does little and then only recently. There is, no doubt, some truth in this view. It was only with the New Deal that the state came to subsidize the arts at all and then only accidentally as a result of employing unemployed artists through the Work Projects Administration (WPA) for a brief period. True too, that by 1938 the WPA was under attack from Representative Martin Dies and the House Un-American Activities Committee and that in 1943, Roosevelt brought all WPA projects to an end. Furthermore, to this day, the state tries to gather private funds to support many forms of culture in which it has a concern, for example, its support for "amateur" athletes for the Olympics every four years.

Still, government influence in cultural fields has probably been far more pervasive than is commonly admitted, but this is not well studied. Billions of federal dollars have been spent in this century in the construction of drab armylike public buildings. No city is free from them. This architecture is a powerful cultural symbol of what the state is. One considers, too, the influence of the military on music, costumes, sports, food, the legal system, and even hobbies.

In the years after World War II, when the power of the state was unquestionably on the rise, the state set up a National Foundation on the Arts and Humanities (1965), a Corporation for Public Broadcasting and an American Film Institute (1967), and a Historic Sites and Monuments Act (1968).

In the 1970s, official policy toward the arts changed as the power of the now more-consolidated ruling class grew in relation to that of the state. In this period, a class interest in art emerged.

Thus, during the 1976 presidential campaign, the government began to claim that it had a responsibility to subsidize the arts. Government spending on the arts, which was 5 million dollars in 1965 rose to more than 157 million dollars by 1980. In the 1960s and 1970s, the state created a number of new cultural institutions, such as the National Endowment for the Arts, the National Endowment for the Humanities, and, as noted above, the Corporation for Public Broadcasting. In addition, governmental support for cultural work appears to broaden in its scope. Along with elite culture, the state began to support folk art from 1972, the existence of the one reinforcing the existence of the other.[51] Still, the artistic community has drawn little attention from students of hegemony.

In contrast to the state's role as patron in humanistic fields, the state's role with regard to social scientists was more specifically that of employer. This fact alone explains much of what has taken place in American social science, given the power and wealth of the state.[52]

One writer who studied the history of the linkage of the state and social science has argued that it arose before World War I and has had three major features. First, the federal government needed social scientists to work in its agencies to collect statistically valid information on demographic trends and natural resources. It also needed social scientists to teach in its land grant colleges and work in its Agricultural Extension Service programs throughout the country. Second, the federal government needed expert advice on how to carry out reforms promoted by politicians, especially in the progressive period but thereafter as well, and this was acknowleged to be an area for social scientists. Third, the army needed social scientists to study enlistees during World War I.[53]

The coming of corporatism led to an enlargement of the role that social scientists played in the official arena. The country's continuing economic crises required in 1933 a transformation of the statistical agencies into a Central Statistical Board. Those interested in the passage of social security legislation in 1935 also required specific knowledge about American society to argue their case as did most of the politicians involved in the "social engineering" legislation from that time onward to the Kennedy era. In fact, as social engineering became the order of the day, the social scientist gradually emerged from the provider of statistical information to the interpreter of the social order. Social scientists even came to provide much of the ideology for the state in such areas as the cold war and development.

The situation for social science changed, however, in the 1960s. In this period, it experienced a profound crisis as did the state itself. An important turning point in that decade for social scientists was reached after the revelation that some of their number had been involved in Operation Camelot during the Vietnam War. Investigation showed that the work of these social scientists was used to destroy civilians, mislead the American public, and jeopardize the trust needed for future research of any kind in the Third World.

By the 1970s, engagement in covert activity became for the first time widely understood to be a part of professional work. In this period, the Department of Defense became a major employer. Many social scientists accepted their new role; some withdrew. Fierce debates took place within the professions over the ethical implication of these involvements.[54]

As social science's utility to the hegemony diminished, humanists rose to serve the state once again: literary critics. It is too early to assess their chances. What seems clear in the U.S. as in the U.K. is that they are promising a Nietzschean anarchism and making it acceptable to more parts of the country than could previously have been anticipated. They seem to please the state by denying that reality exists outside of language, for, as is well known, the ruling class was quite distressed by social science analysis of social realities, but they seem to limit their own utility by failing to provide a basis for any science, progress, or development whatsoever or a basis for dealing with the fundamentalist wing of the hegemony.

One final but important form of governmental involvement in the organization of culture has come through its regulation of the mass media, a topic already mentioned in several specific contexts. The major piece of legislation that established the government's involvement was the Communications Act of 1934. The passage of this act resulted in the creation of the Federal Communications Commission (FCC). The FCC became one of the most important agencies of the government, regulating not only radio and television but by extension films as well.

In the 1970s when television became a vehicle for popular music— Country and Western, Rock and Roll, Punk Rock, and so forth—the federal government expanded its regulatory role still further cutting into the regional control of the music world that had previously existed in such cities as Detroit and Nashville. Increasingly, by the 1970s as a result of FCC regulations, bands seeking to be on radio and television had to submit to a wide range of political, economic, and cultural controls, including obscenity laws. Most bands have chosen to submit to these controls because there is little real choice; a few of the most interesting did not, and they have attracted a growing following for that reason.[55]

Commentators on government regulation of the media, not without reason, emphasize the immensity of this involvement. One need only look back to the nineteenth century. At that time, large-scale cultural enterprises, for example, the symphonies and operas, developed through private regional subsidies. It was only with the New Deal that the state even began to be involved in subsidies, much less regulation. Clearly, the main line of interpretation goes, the capacity of the state to regulate the content of the mass media today marks a huge advance into a domain that had once been the property of largely self-sufficient regional cultures.

Yet one could equally claim from a historical perspective that the more things change, the more they stay the same. The old patronage went to musicians in the European mold and not to those in the American mold such as jazz musicians. When the state became involved, the situation did not really change. Is it an accident that not only the government but the Hollywood film music industry and the producers of the hit Broadway musicals since the 1930s have eschewed jazz or that jazz musicians have received very little real support even until today?[56] Is it not that Jazz today as in the past has several strikes against it? Is it not the cultural form in which Afro-Americans and women have long played a major role? In addition, are not Jazz musicians given a kind of freedom not even granted virtuosos or athletic stars? Do they not respond to their immediate feelings?

The organization of culture to be sure involves not only the activities of the state, but those of the regional ruling classes as well. If one were to begin such an account in the South, what would inevitably follow would be an account of the role played in the organization of culture by the southern elite through the Southern Baptist Church, the major cultural institution of the South; one would also note the role played by the South in the development of a modern literary criticism.[57] It seems worth pursuing this in some detail because the South needs some credit for developing the dominant forms of state intellectuals that emerged with the decline of the social scientists around 1970.

When examining the role of the Southern Baptist Church in terms of its contribution to the organization of culture, one finds that its outstanding feature has been to tie the individual to the authority of the Bible as interpreted by the pastors of the church. In the Southern Baptist Statements of Faith of 1925 and again of 1963, one finds a reaffirmation of one of the traditional features of the American way of life ideology, the inerrancy of Scripture. Scripture for the Baptists is revelation, and because revelation is God's word, it is not only true but truth itself. Of course, what inerrancy or other doctrines means in a region as vast and varied as the American South or the American core culture varies. Some pastors take inerrancy to cover all aspects of the Bible, including its references to history and science, others limit it to the Bible's references to religious matters. Some prefer a literalist reading; some do not. Some place more weight on the role of the pastor than others, but these are secondary issues. Overall, what stands out is that the Baptist Church through its strong stands on doctrine manages to cross class lines while leaving racial lines intact in the South, even in the occasional churches that are racially integrated.[58]

Not only racial lines, one might add, but regional ones as well are left intact. Through its strong emphasis on doctrine, the Southern Baptist Church stands as a veritable bulwark against northern culture in general.

In a recent work, one Southern Baptist warned his fellow believers to learn from the unfortunate experience of the British Baptist Church when it chose to abandon inerrancy and to accept the ideas of Darwin and of higher criticism, ideas southerners associate with the North. Only the great British Baptist Charles Haddon Spurgeon, this writer thought, fought these corrosive influences but he (Spurgeon) by himself could not prevent the decline of the British Baptist Church after it abandoned its original doctrines.

After the doctrine of inerrancy for Baptists comes the doctrine of the virgin birth of Jesus; this belief is an affirmation of the existence of the deity. Without a deity there is no sinlessness, no atonement, no hope. Although again divisions of opinion crop up and attract attention, the main point is the existence of a core belief that stands as a wall against the claims of science or relativism prevalent in the North.

The southern elite has to the satisfaction of most observers not only succeeded in holding together a church culture but has been able to participate to its advantage in the development of the national secular culture. This deserves comment.

At the turn of the twentieth century, the South's presence in national culture is à la folklore, for example, Mark Twain's *Tom Sawyer* and *Huckleberry Finn,* the approach the motion picture industry adopted. By 1950, conditions had changed; the northern school child might well read William Faulkner. The South was coming to be understood more as tragedy than as farce.[59] Let us examine how this came about.

If in the years after Reconstruction, the South produced many writers educated in the classical tradition, a generation or so later, important changes arrived.[60] Centers of regional culture such as Nashville became the springboard for a new wave of modernist critics and writers, for men and women who were rising to positions of national prominence. As early as the 1920s and 1930s, the first effect of this southern literary assault can be detected on the national level. Initiatives from this period at Vanderbilt University in Nashville as well as from other parts of the South were beginning to lead to a new emphasis nationally on American literature as part of the canon of English literature. The first center in the North that responded to the southern initiative was Columbia University in the 1920s. But soon the idea that American literature had prestige spread throughout the North.

Columbia University, partly as a consequence of its initial acceptance of American literature, chose to seize on its leadership role and in the 1930s to take up the project of producing a dictionary of American English. This it did although the impetus for this work was clearly southern.

Between the 1920s and the 1960s, spurred by the efforts of a number of organizations and individuals in the North and the South, the study of America became a respected part of the dominant culture of the United States, a change in orientation that seems all the more remarkable given the commitment of the intelligentsia to a Western heritage, given the atmosphere of the cold war and given the country's enormous overseas involvements. But it did occur. By the 1960s, a fast-growing set of American Studies programs were spreading all over the country, and the national culture was becoming more integrated.

To form an impression of this phenomenon of American cultural integration, one could do worse than to examine the changing reputation of the now well-known southern novelist William Faulkner. Faulkner's numerous tales of a dying southern planter class beset by insoluble racial problems attracted little critical acclaim when they appeared in the 1930s. In the late 1940s, however, with transplanted southerners such as the literary critic Robert Penn Warren occupying a prominent place in American letters and with a sharp decline of the northern Left, a southern writer such as Faulkner, or, by extension, a painter such as Jackson Pollock, who was originally from the West, could emerge as national figures. In the early years of the cold war, both Faulkner and Pollock were taken to represent American force and violence or American modernism.[61]

In the cold war and through the last years of the corporatist period, literary critics, a number of them southerners, seized on the ever-widening regulationism of the state and began to maintain that not just one writer existed—Faulkner—but many. In fact, the state should uphold a canon of American writers from Poe to James. The heyday of this campaign to have the state accept the idea of a canon coincided with the waning years of corporatism, 1941–70. Clearly, for the state, there must have been pros and cons, which took some time to sort out. Certainly, the existence of a literary canon offers more control of what the society will read than otherwise exists, but it does so at a price. The price is that the state must uphold this particular body of work as opposed to simply regulating what emerges in the different regions. Ultimately, the price was too high. The existence of a canon was not worth it; a canon might homogenize American culture and make regulationism over all more difficult.

Whereas in the United Kingdom, given the long-term alliances of the ruling class, a literary canon and a distinctive form of the English language could serve a useful role in the control of culture, in the United States, this was not the case. The most the U.S. state would truly benefit from was upholding a minimal Anglo-Saxon American language policy, for example, a policy against bilingualism.[62]

Yet, this was not quite all. Although a canon may have been too much of a commitment, the state did want some way to mold culture, some way to play one race's identity against another's. This way came to be known by the 1980s as *multiculturalism*.

To understand multiculturalism as a regulatory activity, the most consistent approach, one must also put it in the larger context of the state's other initiatives toward racial matters. At the time that multiculturalism began to emerge, one can observe a series of moves by the Immigrations Authority to build into American society *buffer races,* such as Hispanics, Middle Easterners, and East Asians, a policy reminiscent of American immigration policy at the turn of the twentieth century. The logic of this policy and the logic of supporting multiculturalism appears to be that by introducing new groups in this cultural environment, one could diminish the ability of the blacks to monopolize a claim to racial oppression without fundamentally conceding anything to these newer groups. Multiculturalism was, thus, a way for whites to overcome their feelings of guilt about blacks through its diffusion. It might even contribute to the relegitimation of white antagonism to blacks. In the 1960s, if a black person robbed a Korean grocer, it was perceived as political. Today, if a black person robs a Korean grocer, one expects the media to pick up its cue from multiculturalism and play on the theme of the need for greater tolerance and mutual cultural acceptance. With a huge Asian buffer race in place, the media will ask, "Why can't black people learn to visit a Chinatown, a Puerto Rico, or an Indian reservation as whites do?"

The organization of culture has played and continues to play a role in hegemony in the United States, along with coercion. By the same token, fields, even important fields, that get in the way of the organization of culture tend in the United States as elsewhere to be ignored. The field of history has suffered that fate to one degree or another.

History Writing in the United States

To this point, the argument in the chapter has been that democracies in general and America in particular are rooted in a chosen people ideology, an ideology that induces them to look to their heritage for their identity as opposed to their history. As a consequence, historians who wish to be influential professionally must try to emphasize heritage. These historians, I have suggested, employ a consensus approach to history, avoiding thereby approaches stressing change and conflict, approaches that might be incompatible with heritage. I have also made clear, however, that on the state level, the impact of history writing has been quite limited. The best-recognized peacetime service of the national professional organization of historians, the AHA, has been to provide the government with librarians and archivists. Historians have played important roles as regional intellectuals, as interpreters of the North, the South, and the West in American history. Finally, the ensconcement of history within civil society has had the further consequence that it becomes a field capable of some independent criticism and reflection. After 1970, this has become apparent with the steady development of a *revisionist* trend in history.

The Growth of Professional History in the Liberal Age

In both the United Kingdom and the United States, the attempt at the professionalization of history met with difficulties not encountered in other professions. Amateur historians held sway, for in neither country was the state in urgent need of the services of professionals.[63]

Whereas the British historians of the Liberal Age finally slid into a small niche within Englishness, their American counterparts never quite did the same. Thus, although the American Historical Association was founded in 1884, it was only after five years of lobbying that its leading figure, the prominent historian Herbert Baxter Adams, secured a congressional charter in 1889 that attached the AHA loosely to the Smithsonian Institution.[64] It took years for historians to achieve their present-day eminence as governmental librarians.

Like their English counterparts in Manchester, the first professional American historians tried to appeal to their state's interest in science as a way to legitimate their attempts to have history recognized as a serious venture. This explains the attempt by the early leadership of the AHA to turn for its self-definition to the German scientific school of historical study of Leopold von Ranke.[65]

The AHA leadership, however, had to contend with the fact that the American state far more than its British counterpart did not want to be locked into specific interpretations, much less specific methodologies; it was, after all, a regulatory state. Gradually, American historians came to accept this position and found other ways of seeking influence. According to a recent article on this subject, the second generation of American professional historians rebelled against Ranke's *metaphysics,* replacing it with a stricter nominalist empiricism. By the end of the Gilded Age, East Coast historians, at least, were teaching their graduate students that historical facts were actually data, that one should sneer at claims of objective truth.[66] In these moves, the article claims, one sees a number of leading historians of the AHA accepting their role as producers of a regional as oppose to a national culture.

When the AHA's initial efforts to expand from a regional cultural base on the East Coast to national status failed, it made some attempt to alter its strategy. In due course, the AHA opened the door to a wider range of historians, strengthening thereby its claim that even without official recognition it was, in fact, a national institution. Thus, it brought to prominence historians such as Frederick Jackson Turner and Vernon A. Parrington, historians who could be seen for all intents and purposes as the leading representatives of the American core culture. Still, the fact that the AHA was largely an upper-class East Coast-oriented group of gentlemen meant that its appeal outside its region, class, and gender was quite limited. Evidence for this point can be inferred from the fact that the competition to the AHA, which did rise, was essentially regional or racial or gender specific in inspiration. For example, in 1907, the Mississippi Valley Historical Association was founded and soon became a competitor to the AHA in the area suggested by its name.[67] Other organizations soon followed.

As in the case of the United Kingdom, so in the United States, another problem for professional history was not just the attitude of the state but also the taste of the readership of history books. Scientific history cost the AHA a popular base among readers; it also separated the AHA from the local historical societies, groups that took their history to be more or less interchangeable with their heritage and came to find a national advocate not in the AHA nor even in the Organization of American Historians (OAH) but in organizations closer to their worldview, such as the Society for the History in the Federal Government and the National Council on Public History. Having staked out the domain of scientific history for itself, the AHA, for all its scientific credentials, could at best claim to be the titular leader of the study of history.[68]

A representative figure of the AHA of the Liberal Age would be an organization man, for example, a J. Franklin Jameson (1859–1937) more than an introducer of new methods and ideas as was John Seeley, his British counterpart. Jameson took over the task of promoting the profession where Herbert Baxter Adams left off in the 1880s. He accepted the fact that the AHA was an outsider to Washington and galvanized political and professional support in whatever way he could to lay the necessary building blocks for the future. To his credit is the creation of an institution of great importance to historians, the National Archives. He was never well known as a teacher nor as a writer. By contrast, John Seeley's fame at Cambridge in the United Kingdom was derived, as noted in chapter 9, from institutionalizing scientific history in the elite educational system.[69]

History in the Corporatist Period: Wars, Consensus, History, and the Humanization of the Elite

The position of the AHA might have been even more insignificant than it was were it not for the fact that the country was involved in major wars. War raised the prestige of the AHA as the government suddenly needed historians who understood Europe. The increased prestige during World War I was followed by a period of decline that lasted until World World II. During World War II, the prestige of the AHA rose again when a number of professional historians worked for the Office of Strategic Services. In this period, historians were finally able to begin to challenge the influence of relativism and to shake off the doubts about professional history that had lingered at least until that time. It was also during the world wars that historians began to teach special courses linking the United States to its allies, courses such as Western Civilization.[70]

The problem for professional history was peacetime. During peacetime, the AHA lost support. If, for example, it sought to maintain a view of history compatible with the world of East Coast business where its influential membership was, it risked undermining its claim that it was upholding a "consensus view" of history, a view that it also needed to cross class, regional, and racial lines.

Could the AHA abandon consensus history? The answer appears to be negative. First, consensus history or at least the lingo of consensus permits a modus vivandi in the profession; it allows for historians from different regional or racial backgrounds to address each other's works under the umbrella of a national organization without becoming involved in political struggles. Second, consensus history serves as an interpretative principle for the writing of history. Its use leads to an agreement among many historians to characterize some periods of American history as part of consensus or as part of conflict. Third, consensus history accomodates heritage.

The costs of pursuing consensus history, however, are also quite clear.

Consensus history imposes not only a certain politics of history but one that works to the advantage of the more traditional forms of history writing and against the newer and now more important ones. How can labor history and even social history fail to bring out conflicts? How can a critical history of the production of knowledge not reveal conflict as well?

In addition, can consensus history, rooted as it is in heritage and specifically in Western heritage be made to appeal to the experience of Afro-Americans or Amerindians? Can one claim to such an audience that there are periods of consensus, or is consensus history really a pledge of allegiance to the racial status quo?

Even for many guild historians, among them most of the Revisionist school and most of these white, middle-class males, the consensus approach leads to biased outcomes. If, for example, one takes the Progressive era to be a "Conflict era" and the 1950s a "Consensus era," one is slanting one's work a priori. Did Charles Beard, a leading historian of the Progressive era, truly make a conflict interpretation of the struggle for American independence, or is this interpretation simply forced on him by later historians by virtue of their paradigm? A close look at Beard's writing suggests that he used the term *class,* but he used it in the sense of social stratification and not in the sense of conflict. His epistemology was positivist; positivism postulates fundamental harmony not conflict. Was this glossed over for one reason or another?

If the Civil War and Reconstruction were periods of conflict, consensus beginning after the Compromise of 1877, then what is the profession to do with a major work that shows that blacks and whites together brought prosperity to the South in the era of Reconstruction, that the economic stagnation of the South began in the era of Jim Crow in the 1880s and thereafter, a period supposedly characterized by consensus and thus progress. This major work, of course, was W. E. B. Du Bois, *Black Reconstruction in America* (1935), a work that has few equals in American historiography either judged by its quality or by its popularity in the mass market, but a work that the AHA, nonetheless, managed to ignore for many years because it was outside its paradigm.

If the years after 1877 were supposed to be part of the consensus and progress phase, what was one to make of the Jim Crow Laws? How was one to interpret the career of Southern radicals such as Tom Watson? And how was one to explain the renewed exploitation by the North of the South? These problems seem to underlie the profession's hesitant response to the writings of another great southern historian, C. Vann Woodward (b. 1908), who raised them. In contrast to Du Bois, the AHA honored Woodward for many years without acknowledging his findings. Thus, one would not learn from many standard histories of the country that in *Tom Watson: Agrarian Rebel* (New York: Macmillan, 1938), Woodward had found that it was the rise of the new South, a part of consensus history, that defeated a progressive Populist, Tom Watson of Georgia, and turned him ultimately to racism. Nor would one learn that in *The Origins of the New South, 1877–1913* (Baton Rouge: Louisiana State Univ. Press, 1951), Woodward had shown that consensus, meaning the "new departure" Democrats, the politicians of the 1870s and beyond, who exploited the South, meant the valorization of a group of individuals who made considerable profits from the use of convict labor.

When one considers the 1950s, another supposed era of consensus, differences among the leading historians seem so pronounced that only a collective acceptance of the idea of consensus seems to cover this over. In this period, by virtue of contemporaneity, Richard Hofstadter, a pragmatist must be juxtaposed to Daniel Boorstin, a historian who found a surface, common-sense meaning in his sources à là positivism, and to Louis Hartz, a historian who was something of a Marxist. Richard Hofstadter has to be read selectively; it is best to forget his famous essay on anti-intellectualism in the United States, the essay so useful for understanding the American way of life ideology. In that essay, Hofstadter showed that anti-intellectualism was an institutionalized and ongoing factor throughout modern American history. It conflicted with intellectualism not only in times historians term periods of conflict but in periods of consensus as well. Even more ironic is the encounter with Louis Hartz. Louis Hartz had concluded from a quasi-Marxist analysis that there was no conflict in modern America. Perhaps, because of this conclusion, Hartz's Marxism was overlooked, and he became a leading source for the Consensus school.[71]

The 1950s from a more common-sense perspective was scarcely an era of consensus; it was the McCarthy era, a period of purges. In this period, a number of individual historians, perhaps terrified by what was happening, decided to turn on their colleagues. In this traumatic era in which a number of historians lost their jobs for the crime of having been Marxists or having thought in terms of conflict models in the past, a few rose in status. Daniel Boorstin, the historian, who was termed by one student of the purges, the principle "namer of names," became the doyen of consensus history.[72]

By the late 1960s, the intellectual atmosphere in the United States was undergoing a sea change. Both the state and much of professional structure tied to it were in crisis. The Civil Rights movement and the Vietnam War protests were in progress. In view of the divisive potentialities of these events for the AHA, many leading historians refused to take sides on issues of the day and tried to make this refusal their guiding principle. As the decade rolled on and the issues loomed larger and larger, however, taking sides could scarcely be avoided. In this sitation, many leading historians appeared to prefer a pyrrhic victory over a change in strategy. Thus, in university after university by the early 1970s, the administration, driven by student pressure, pushed open the door of the history department to new faces and new views. The Old Guard of the AHA; not surprisingly, simply termed this "the breakdown of consensus."[73]

Conflict and consensus have served as major categories for the interpretation of United States history for the majority of prominent American historians during the era of corporatism. This was much less the case for historians in the United Kingdom in the analogous period, political economy being better established.

For the collectivism period in the United Kingdom, one might well choose Eric Hobsbawm as a representative figure of the history profession. His work on labor aristocracy and his thesis of the industrial revolution as a watershed in human history had become important intellectual categories for a generation of historians molded by the Labour party tradition. The analogous figure in the history profession for the corporatist period in the United States, obviously would not be a historian in economic or labor history, Hobsbawm's specialization. One might more accurately choose a historian within the consensus tradition who tried to humanize the culture of the elite more or less as FDR did the economy of the elite. Such a figure could be Perry Miller (1905–1963), the historian of Puritan New England. Perry Miller's studies of the Puritan texts *Orthodoxy in Massachusetts* (1933) and *The New England Mind: The Seventeenth Century* (1939) removed the stigma commonly associated with figures such as Cotton Mather, giving the Puritans a human face.[74]

History in the Era of Neoliberalism: 1970 and Beyond

From the vantage point of the 1970s, any observer would note that the profession was more diverse than previously. Significant numbers of women and minorities had become professors. The developments of the 1960s, no doubt, are the major explanation for this. A secondary explanation, less often alluded to, were the developments of the 1970s. A tokenistic acceptance of diversity was built into the libertarianism that was emerging. However one chooses to interpret the change, according to one student of the subject, a "disproportionate" number of senior historians chose to retire in the late 1960s and the early 1970s. And, thereafter, the profession shifted its focus away from its traditional concern with state and political history to society and social history.[75] It is this change that awaits evaluation. To what extent, given the absence of a labor party, did it mark a kind of qualitative development as opposed to simply another breakdown of consensus?

In the United Kingdom, the transition out of collectivism found the history profession split with many leading figures remaining in opposition both to official history and official politics. By contrast, in the United States, the transition seems more genteel, at least if one tries to judge from the dominant historical scholarship of the period.[76] Although the scholarship may have addressed new themes, it retained by and large the older concept of consensus as the professional ideal. With a few exceptions, its leaders retained as well the older faith in the political order. The change, perhaps, was that revisionism or Neo-Marxism began to become important in this period.

In both countries, public history and heritage was on the rise. In the United Kingdom, public history and heritage had had little prestige during the period in which the Labour party played an effective role, but in the 1970s and 1980s, with the emergence of a de facto one-party system, this orientation to history experienced rapid growth as a result in part of a sudden growth of official support. In the United States during the same period, a growth of public history and heritage also took place but this increase was less dramatic than it was in the United Kingdom. These fields had been steadily growing for more than one century, a point worth reflecting on in view of the supposed watershed of 1970.

Indeed, what applies to public history applies more widely as well. For the studies of early America, it might actually be incorrect to argue that a breakdown of consensus or a watershed has yet to take place, at least among the best-known historians. True, this was the period that produced integrated and, of course, conflictual histories of whites and Indians in a field that had previously been divided between Puritan history and Indian ethnography.[77] Yet, notwithstanding these achievements, it is equally clear that no major displacement of Perry Miller, the preeminent figure of the last generation, had taken place as a result of this newer work. Instead, the works of Perry Miller, the "philosophical historian" of the field, were left intact; the new social historians simply added their insights. Thus, the image of the Puritans in recent writing is now more of a social movement than a literary and religious movement. But at least up to this point, the Puritans are not perceived as a social movement formed out of the dialectics of their relations with the Indians. Rather, one discerns in newer scholarship the preservation not only of the old boundaries but of some direct continuity with the work of previous generations of historians.[78] Where then is the breakdown of consensus?

The American Revolution has also long been part of the consensus approach to history; in recent work, it continues to be so. Although today social historians have begun to take up the subject, they are unlikely to allow a return to the era of Charles and Mary Beard, that they term the "period of controversy." An important architect of the consensus approach to the Revolution at the end of the interwar period was the Harvard historian Daniel Boorstin. Boorstin, *The Lost World of Thomas Jefferson* (1948), has been heralded as "ending" the "period of controversy." Whereas the aforementioned Charles Beard, a social and economic historian writing in the 1920s in the progressive era, had argued that class interests underlay the American upper-class quest for freedom, subsequent studies, in Boorstin's view, called Beard's perspective into question. As a consequence of these later studies, Boorstin was able to reintroduce the older idea of patriotic ideology as a causal factor that explained why the affluent American revolutionaries did what they did. Following Boorstin, another continuator of the consensus approach was Bernard Bailyn. Whereas Boorstin had noted in the work just cited that the study of Jefferson's tradition was still "mired in ideology," Bernard Bailyn twenty years later was able to remedy this situation. In his *The Ideological Origins of the American Revolution* (1967), Bailyn argued that surface wrangling has covered over an underlying consensus found in the language of the texts.[79] In these two specialties at least, consensus lives on, social history or no social history.

In the interpretation of the Civil War, consensus history, which had dominated the field, grew weaker. This older history had postulated that the war was a discrete and possibly even unnecessary struggle in a century otherwise characterized by consensus, a view that remained in the profession until 1970, when according to standard accounts, it was pushed aside by the black and women historians who entered the field. At a closer glance, this judgment does not seem quite precise. This view was not challenged by blacks and women historians but by revisionist historiography. Some of the black and women historians who entered the field were revisionists, but some were not. Revisionist historians postulate for the Civil War an inevitability of conflict given the contradictory features of the prevailing political and economic system.

For more recent periods, consensus history continued to dominate but important works of revisionism began to appear, making for something of a convergence between English and American historywriting. Revisionist historians tend to emphasize the power of American capitalism as a major explanation for what transpired in modern American history. In doing so, they shed light on the motivations of the ruling class as they found it in the 1970s. Still, there were blinders, which blocked the development of a deeper revisionism. Often enough a northern regional approach to American history underlay these new attempts at political economy. In fact, from Charles Beard and the era of communist historiography, revisionists had downplayed the politics of rule and the role of the state and made race and region simply a part of the superstructure. There are, however, a few notable exceptions.[80]

Eugene D. Genovese (b. 1930–) is the major historian of the slave South and the leading revisionist historian of the contemporary period. Over a long and productive career, Genovese has wrestled with a field divided in the extreme between those who see nineteenth-century southern history as a minor part of American history, a field defined around the North and those who see it as largely separate. A recent commentator on Genovese finds that his work represents a unique fusion of these perspectives. In *The Political Economy of Slavery* (1961), Genovese argued—against the rather northern-centered tradition of American Marxism—insisting that the plantation South has to be studied both in terms of its own dynamics and its relationship to the national economy. The North could not simply modernize the South; politics and social customs were involved. The slave system, a social as well as an economic system, although often enough unprofitable, was one that the planter South was unwilling to abandon. Yet, nonetheless, it drew to an end for a variety of internal and external reasons, not the least of which was debt. By the 1970s, Genovese's ideas about the nature of the American system—North and South—had deepened still further. In *Roll Jordan, Roll: The World the Slaves Made* (1972), he turned to Gramsci's theory of hegemony, moving away from the more economistic Marxist writers of the 1950s and 1960s, such as Maurice Dobbs, replacing their problematic with one that emphasized the culture of hegemony and of counterhegemony drawn from *Prison Notebooks*. In *Roll Jordan, Roll,* the hegemonic planter culture took the form of planter paternalism toward the blacks. This culture, Genovese showed, in the context of a hegemony weakened by its economic problems was increasingly ineffectual. It could not prevent a counterhegemonic struggle from gaining ground in the religious culture of the field hands, a struggle that Genovese terms *protonationalist.*

When comparing Genovese to the historians of the United Kingdom, one is struck by the similarity of his positions to those of the English historical sociologist Stuart Hall. Both represent the tradition of nation-based Marxism in their respective countries; both struggle with the economism of the dominant internationalist Marxism. For Stuart Hall, much of the last twenty years has been spent analyzing the state. As the working class has committed itself to supporting the state, race remains submerged. By contrast, Genovese has been able to go further and explore the language and forms of counterhegemony in race and class.[81]

In this chapter, I argued that the modern democracy dated from 1877, that it was based economically on two main types of capitalism, corporate and national, that situated between them as a regulator was the state, and that out beyond was a civil society and beyond that a racial undercaste. Using a regulatory state approach, the American power structure has shown little or no enthusiasm for cultural orthodoxies or canons. Thus, on the whole, the American Historical Association has been a useful source of archivists, librarians, being neither equipped to participate in heritage production, which is the most efficient way to uphold the dominant paradigm, nor to endorse a critical approach to history, which would entail going against it.[82]

The larger point of the chapter is that the history of the United States appears to fit into the wider study of capitalist nation-states and that it reveals a clear ongoing struggle between ruler and ruled that in most regards, is scarcely exceptional.

11

Conclusion

In the preceding chapters, I set out to develop the methodology for a history of the modern world, following the logic of social history and political economy. This seems a reasonable idea given the direction the discipline of history is moving, challenging in that it has not been done before, feasible in that some general recognition of Eurocentrism as a problem—the big obstacle for these fields—is becoming apparent in general thought, and necessary given my situation as a professor. How would such a work be grounded in theory? How could it be carried out?

Much of what I was trying to analyze political economists would term eras of finance capitalism, and for better or worse I was trying to do so from the vantage point of living in one. In some ways, this was slightly awkward because political economy theory had long been based on the study of industrial capitalism and now was, consequently, somewhat out of kilter. During the last third of the twentieth century, and partly as a result, other theory had become important. Why not, then, benefit from the situation? Not everyone lives to see orthodoxies in disarray! Thus arose the idea of merging parts of Gramsci and Foucault to critique Eurocentrism and then of using social history to go beyond it.

How does one go beyond Eurocentrism? How can one move the center of gravity of world history to where the mass populations are and having arrived there, how can one make these mass populations a significant part of the subject of world history? These are weighty matters; they deserve to be discussed.

Yet, one suspects, they are not being discussed; a majority of historians probably believe that a solution to these problems already exists and that for this reason further concern with them is unnecessary. The solution historians would point to is the world systems model. According to the logic of this model, a majority of the world's population is construed to be a part of the periphery. I rejected this solution because I do not believe that the majority can be part of a periphery or that this particular majority can be very well explained in terms of a capitalist world market because it is composed of peasants and urban slum dwellers, that is, groups that are largely outside of the market. Even the use of these terms underscores the point that historians have not yet approached this subject.

As the writings of Gramsci and more recently of Foucault have shown, power is widely diffused in human society and, this being the case, the real dialectics of modern society remain to be worked out. History today and even political economy, given the legacy of Eurocentrism, remain still too close to the elite-mass concept of dynamics for one to appreciate the role of ordinary people in history.

To compound the problem, traditional historiography rests not only on long-established socioeconomic ideas, such as core, periphery, elite, and mass but on long-established cultural assumptions as well, for example, on the idea—or *an* idea—of modernity; this, therefore, requires some rethinking as well. Almost inevitably, one's idea of modernity, like one's ideas of core, periphery, elite, and mass, helps one locate where history is and why it should be there and why something else—the traditional, the primitive or the peripheral—is not there and should not be there. How can the idea of modernity be made to serve a project in which one construes history to be the study of people? The first idea that occurred to me was that in such a study, it would be useful to conceive of modernity emerging more as a permutation of most of what went before in the world than as a negation of most of it; a majority would never repudiate its past that quickly. The choice seemed to be to abandon the concept of modernity or to enlarge it. To abandon it seemed illogical given the continuing existence of the nation-state system that had given rise to it. The resolution reached, therefore, was one of trying to enlarge it. Thus, rather than equating modernity with Europe or the culture of positivism a là the European Enlightenment or the logic of industrial capitalism or equating it with the idea of progress, which are common practices, I tried to show that modernity was rooted in a dialectic of positivism and nonpositivism, a dialectic sustained in different ways by different nation-states. The richer the dialectic, I assumed, the richer was the modernity; the weaker the dialectic, the flatter and more presentist the modernity.

Working out such ideas entailed what historians call a revisionist approach. Something had to be found to replace the dominant paradigm of "Europe and the rest." My revisionism took the form of dropping the idea of today's Europe as bourgeois democracy, an outgrowth of the Enlightenment/industrialist version of modernity. Modern Europe is too diverse to be the heir of any one tradition and as a result, a more precise unit of analysis than that of Europe as bourgeois democracy—against which the rest of the world would be juxtaposed—was to embrace Europe as the congeries of individual countries with different hegemonies of which the continent is composed. When one analyzes individual countries, what becomes possible is a middle-level historical sociology that compares countries with similar hegemonies to one another whether they are in Europe, in the Third World, or in both.

How then should one begin such a book? Where does modernity, so construed, begin? How much does it take in? One generation ago, the English historian and political economy theorist Erik Hobsbawm resolved the problem of a takeoff point for modern history by using the eighteenth-century industrial revolution in England. For a social history of the world written today, the resolution to this problem appears to lie in the discovery that modernity as embodied in the capitalist nation-state system began one century later in the 1860s-1880s. It began not with the rise but with the spread of capitalism within countries—mainly finance capitalism in that period—which resulted in a major reformulation of the political strategies of rule and, thus, in a new political economy. For the first time, political elites had to devise comprehensive strategies to diffuse class conflict, the mass struggle typifying modern history having begun.

In the book, I identify four and only four major strategies of rule that emerged in this period, each with its characteristic forms of cultural dialectics out of which emerged the various rationalities, sciences, arts, literatures, histories, and common sense of modern cultures, each with images of the other, which would guide its foreign relations. As this took place, counterhegemonic movements also emerged, struggling to tear these hegemonies down. The world as a whole became at this point a decentered totality comprising a large number of countries conforming to these four hegemonies.

The discovery that there are only four stable forms of hegemony appears to open the door in the short term not only to studies of a wider range of countries than I attempted here but to studies of issues framed by their involvement in these different hegemonies. It is, perhaps, this last point that has the greatest novelty and, thus, deserves the most attention. I refer in this conclusion to a number of research topics that range from women's studies, race studies, Jewish studies, and so on, all of which were touched on in this work but which would benefit from the application of a systematic comparative approach. I also recall here several topics that emerged, which were of great importance but were dropped, for example, the comparative study of violence and the study of "mixed-road" hegemonies. They require more theoretical refinement than was possible at this point. I end this book with reflections on who apart from academicians might find this type of work useful. It might aid in the conduct of diplomacy or in human rights work, I conclude.

The book began with a study of the Russian Road a form of hegemony in which rulers disguise class conflict with caste ideology. In such regimes, one's membership in the ruling caste—the nomenklatura or the party—has an objective meaning that caste lacks in countries in which it is secondary, where one finds it riddled with subcastes as in India. I chose two countries to represent the Russian Road, Russia/the Soviet Union and Iraq. The first example was of interest because of its role in Europe and the world at large and because from among the countries one could term Russian Road, it is by far the best studied. Iraq served as a useful foil in such discussions while contributing some issues on its own because of orientalism. Iraq, too, has its nomenklatura, its shrine towns, its religious elite, for the most part little-studied by historians; Iraq, too experimented with greatpowerism.

The traditional preoccupation of scholars with great powers and with their role in history is to a degree no doubt justified; the concern here was what the term would mean for a world history that was not Eurocentric. The conclusion reached was that underlying the dominant usage of the term with all it implies about strong economy and advanced technology was a social historical meaning that a great power was a country of whatever hegemony that had enough class collaboration between workers and rulers to allow for growth, technological change, and expansionism, that such countries were few in number, would tend to be in the core of the world market, and would tend to be the most combative countries in the world. This work affords a look at the rise and fall not only of the USSR as a great power but of Iraq and the United Kingdom as well. The three serve as contrasting examples to that of the United States where decline is still incipient.

Japan posed certain challenges for this study and was not given the space that it deserves. The hegemony of Japan appears to be a mixture of two different roads: there are elements of the Russian Road in the relationship of the Tokyo elite to the rest but there is much else as well. This ruling caste betrays racist sentiments toward lesser races that are not altered even when such groups live and work in Japan, mastering the language and culture of the dominant caste. One associates such sentiments with the racism of tribal-ethnic states. Future studies building on this one ought to be able to show that as a result Japan—and possibly China as well—probably warrant a characterization as a mixed road. They warrant a more complicated form of political economy analysis than the one presented here.

Most other countries appear much simpler to study; they may combine hegemonies but they do so in such a way that only one is clearly predominant. For example, one finds subordinated but accepted elements of tribalism in the Soviet Union and the United States, but these countries are definable in terms of what is dominant. Egypt is Italian Road, but it has subordinated elements of the Russian Road in its language policy and in its efforts at bureaucratic centralization.

Nigeria and Indonesia remain question marks. Possibly, they are also examples of mixed-road hegemonies, and for that reason they were not taken up. Nigeria appears in most work as a tribal-ethnic state like many other African countries. In its southern University towns, however, Nigeria supports a positivist culture in fields such as history that vastly surpasses that of most other tribal-ethnic states. Could the geographical south in Nigeria be—as it is in Brazil—the analytical North of an Italian Road state? Is the interpretation of Nigeria through ethnicity alone a way of hiding the oppression of the analytical South, that is, the mass population of the Hausas in the geographical north? Have not the Hausas been forced to migrate in search of work continuously over the twentieth century? Is not the modern class structure, rule by law, civil society, and so forth, concentrated in the geographical south? In Indonesia as well this may be the case. On the one hand, there is the Northern capitalism of Java versus the Southern feudalism of Bali, on the other, the veneer, at least, of tribalism reflected among other places in the war of annihilation against regions such as West Timor.

Adopting a Russian Road approach, one finds in Iraq as in Russia, rule by caste as the basis of the hegemony. Baghdad is secular like Moscow; the religious leadership is in the shrine towers; Najaf is like Kazan. This strategy of disguising class conflict draws attention to the importance of the Shi'ite hierarchy, who move from their relative obscurity in standard histories to become part of the ruling caste, their various initiatives in favor of autocracy and against liberalism serving as a corroboration of similar findings about the political role of the Russian Orthodox church.

Furthermore, Iraq's hegemony took its contemporary form in response to the spread of capitalism in the latter years of the Ottoman empire in the 1870s. The standard, rather Eurocentric, scholarship that credits modernization to the British in the 1920s is largely incorrect because in the nineteenth century the format of the Russian Road was already evident. For example, from the late nineteenth century, one can observe the ruler's practice of "sheltering" Baghdad from the mass population and of encouraging the production of a cosmopolitan and internationalist urban high culture and of a folklorized culture in the rest of the country, and so on.

Greatpowerism, the phenomenon discussed before, began one generation or more later in Iraq than it did in the Soviet Union. What stood out as the apparent explanation for the difference in time was the combative nature of the Iraqi mass population in comparison to its rather collaborationist counterpart in the Soviet Union. For a period of about twenty years, 1970–1990, this changed. Today, after the Gulf War, the Iraqi state, once again back in the Third World, faces significant rural, ethnic, and class challenges, whereas the Soviet state, for all one reads about its internal problems, faces much less. It is still closer to being a great power than is Iraq.

The example of Iraq highlights the fact that there are alternatives to orientalism for the interpretation of Middle Eastern countries. This point seems necessary to mention because there has been so little successful challenge to the dominant paradigm in the study of that region.

An analysis of caste or nomenklatura explains much in Russian Road regimes; surprisingly, it explains very little elsewhere, for example, in Italian Road regimes such as India, where the dominant scholarship dwells on it.

Italian Road regimes share in common a strategy of disguising class conflict by playing off regional cultures against each other. Other forms of contradiction employed by the state are secondary.

As Gramsci demonstrated in the example of Italy, the ruling class played the more-capitalist North off against the less-capitalist South. This approach, it turns out, was used not only in Italy but in a number of other countries as well, including the countries considered here, India and Mexico.

When examining Italy through a Gramscian lens, several interesting points emerge. First, contrary to long-held views of writers in the dominant paradigm, one finds that the northern exploitation of the South has never ended. It has carried on from the late nineteenth century to the present day, at times more visibly so than at others. In the immediate postwar period, the harshness of this interregional exploitation was papered over as a result of development aid money and of the remittances of southern workers sent from their jobs in northern Europe. In more recent years, however, the contradiction has once again become more visible with the contraction of the northern European economies and with the forced return of many southern workers to Italy.

Thus, although interpreters in the dominant paradigm appear to entertain a somewhat Gramscian view of the South in their accounts of the late nineteenth century, they seem reluctant to pursue this line of interpretation past World War II, leaving unexplained the continuing role of standard features of the hegemony—the Mafia in the South, the Northern League in the North, and so on.

Second, an Italian Road approach to Italian history makes clear that the dominant paradigm's interpretation of Italian culture as liberal culture is a weak one. A number of ideologies compete in Italy. The Liberal Age in Italy, the age of supposed liberal predominance, was by all accounts an extremely unstable one. It was prolonged by colonial adventures and by World War I; it collapsed easily in the face of a fairly small challenge by workers in and around Turin. Such points at least bring into question the continuing scholarly emphasis on the liberal nature of Italy. Is this simply part of the traditional Eurocentrism?

Third, an Italian Road interpretation of Italian history makes clear the involvement of Italian communism in the dominant paradigm. Italian Eurocommunism, often heralded as a final accommodation of the undemocratic Left to democracy, becomes instead the betrayer of the southern peasantry.

A second example of an Italian Road regime considered was that of India. In taking India as Italian Road, what was most important was that the Southern Question could move in a geographical sense and that a counterhegemonic movement along the lines Gramsci had actually discussed could, in fact, bring about a crisis in hegemony.

Although the established scholarship on India does distinguish between North and South in terms of language, culture, and agricultural practices, and although it does note the departure of masses of poor South Indians in search of work abroad in the late nineteenth and early twentieth centuries, it does not find the existence of a Southern Question. This seems a bit odd, given the scholarly recognition of a distinct northern cultural identity that is now so well documented. Does not the North picture itself to be an offshoot of the Aryan migrations and, thus, "like Europe" and the center of modern Indian history as well? Despite all this, there is no Southern Question; the dominant paradigm reigns supreme. Depending on the writer's focus, modern India is either the result of British democracy or of being a subcontinent too large to rule or of being a society organized around caste.

One reason for this continuing consensus among historians may well be that the Southern Question in India is sufficiently different from its counterpart in Italy to not be readily recognizable as such. If the Tamilnadu region of the late nineteenth century is a parallel to South Italy, this is not the case by the interwar period. By this later period, one notices a vigorous capitalist development in the region around Madras and in other parts of the old South and a rising standard of living. One also notices that the older culture of abstract philosophy and art was beginning to yield to one built on a rising positivism. Meanwhile, beginning in the same period, West Bengal underwent a decline and involution. Calcutta lost its importance as the Raj waned and as capitalism spread widely across North India. Bihar, too, underwent a slump from which it has yet to recover and began to export its youth as cheap agricultural labor to the farms of the Punjab and Uttar Pradesh, regions analogous to the Piedmont of northern Italy. India thus reveals a movement or at least a partial movement of the Southern Question from the South to the Northeast.

The example of India contributes to an Italian Road interpretation in the issue of counterhegemony. In general, counterhegemonic movements as led by communist parties in the Italian Road states resulted in Eurocommunism, that is, they became reformist movements that accepted the premises of the status quo of the North. In India, whereas one trend of the communist movement adopted such positions, the other did not, adopting instead the alliance of workers and peasants. This stance gave prominence and importance to a range of movements, some in West Bengal, some elsewhere, some rural, and some urban, which have been responsible for the contemporary crisis of the Indian state. As Italy underwent development and a welfare state, the hegemony in India began to unravel. It is not that India is too large to govern, as the dominant paradigm maintains, but that oppositionists have found an effective way to struggle through movements that have a regional emancipation dimension whether through communism or, more recently, through communalist movements.

In between the cases of Italy and India, one can situate the case of Mexico. Mexico is also of interest because of the Southern Question there and the ambivalent relation of the Left to it. Mexico is of interest as well because the writers in the dominant paradigm deny it an internal dynamic and prefer to interpret it through its linkage to Spain or to the United States.

An Italian Road interpretation of Mexico is quite revisionist but somehow needlessly so. Much evidence suggests that the organization of official institutions works to perpetuate a dualism between a South and a North, an Indian compared to a Mexican, a peasant compared to a citizen, noncapitalist compared to capitalist, custom compared to law. These are the dichotomies promoted in the familiar descriptions but not integrated into the theorization inspired by the dominant paradigm. Rather, the cart is put before the horse. Southern soil, it is asserted, was worn out because of long use dating back to Mayan times, but that does not lead the standard scholarship to wonder if the North might find it easy to use the South as cheap migrant labor for that reason. Indian culture in the South and in the Central Highlands may be more religious, but does this explain or justify the North monopolizing secular culture and higher education for Northern youth? Is it a necessary consequence of regional dominance that one assumes that history only takes place in the dominant region? Whatever the case, the South remains in standard scholarship a land of legend give or take the occasional outbreaks in which it asserts itself. If the Zapatista movement of 1994 opposes NAFTA and calls for regional autonomy in the South in the name of Zapata, it remains simply a random and somewhat quixotic event for writers in the dominant paradigm.

And, why should it be otherwise, if there is no challenge? In Mexico, only at very rare moments, as in the early 1930s, did a trade unionist politician such as Lombardo Toledano manage to combine the Southern Question, which was the Indian Question, with the labor question, which was the North. For the most part, the Mexican Left was northern centered and Eurocommunist. As a consequence, as the Southern Indian peasantry lost its land, it was forced to migrate to the slums of cities such as Mexico City or to look for work in the United States, much as its counterparts had to in other Italian Road regimes.

A third form of hegemony is the tribal-ethnic state, a strategy of rule in which gender becomes the central disguise of class conflict and loyalties are those that are blood based. In such states, official ideology promotes a notion of extreme difference between men and women, blunting class conflict by giving oppressed men a stake in the system while valorizing and rationalizing the idea that women should be outside of politics and history.

These points bear repeating because here the Eurocentric map of world history and national history breaks down altogether and such countries are given over to the students of current events or anthropology.

In choosing the Belgian Congo/Zaire, what was of interest was the approach adopted by the ruling class of this country to cultural persuasion and to international relations.

In standard studies of countries such as the Belgian Congo/Zaire, all one reads about is violence and coercion, and often enough, such features are used to justify excluding the country from serious historical study. The country is uncivilized; it is still a frontier. Yet clearly the social reproduction in such countries takes place through persuasion as well as through violence or coercion. Consider, for example, the role of the Catholic church, the mass media, the music, and so on. This raises a question that I hope others will care to pursue. Is violence and coercion perceived as such by scholars only when it is on the surface? What about violence located, for example— to draw from Foucault—in bureaucratic as opposed to military practices? Is violence ultimately to be defined by style?

In Zaire what does seem certain, is the development over the twentieth century of a form of hegemonic cultural praxis termed here gnosis. Following such a form of praxis, it is better that loyalty be inchoate-tribal, familial, or party-oriented, not credential based. Give or take the postulate of the man-woman dichotomy, which is fixed, the rest of culture should be made subject to deconstruction to head off possibly subversive loyalties. Fields such as modern medicine thus are played off against traditional medicine; fields such as history are played off against folklore studies; language is developed around poetry not prose; religion is developed around mysticism, not scholastic theology. The organization of the culture as a whole benefits from a degree of controlled chaos, a ruler scarcely needing to build up professions and risk the development of unwanted and irrelevant loyalties such as professional loyalties.

The study of the Belgian Congo/Zaire as a representative of a tribal-ethnic hegemony also is useful for understanding the formation of foreign policy of quite a number of countries. To retain power without succumbing to developmentalism, countries such as the Belgian Congo/Zaire depend on alliances that link their ruling classes to the ruling class of a powerful foreign country either in a colonial or a neocolonial relationship. In forming these alliances, these ruling classes offer the work forces and the mineral wealth of their countries in return for political and military support to keep them in power. Often their support is quite total. On occasion, they go so far as to underwrite the reelection of their main allies abroad and to follow their foreign policy initiatives through the United Nations, the world banking system, and elsewhere, assuming of course, they receive the support they want. Seen from the perspective of a great power such as the United States, this seemingly explains the high plurality that it can expect in United Nation votes, on the one hand; it also explains the often unceasing interventionism in the affairs of these countries that it must engage in, on the other. Examples of postwar Britain and France serve to indicate that the working classes cannot be induced to perform these services forever.

The choice of Albania as a foil to the Belgian Congo/Zaire introduces a variant of gnosis and of international relations in a communist mirror. In Albania as in the Belgian Congo/Zaire, gnosis does not question the extreme social conservatism around women but seeks to destabilize other ideologies, especially those linked to positivism. Although the two countries are by no means identical, there are—for a generation raised on the importance of the distinction between Communist and non-Communist— a surprisingly large number of commonalities.

Hoxha, the leader and theoretician of Albanian communism, may have named his party the Albanian Party of Labor, but as his writing shows, he was not anxious to promote a philosophy with an objectivist basis, such as a working class, any more than Mobutu was. Most of his theoretical focus was, thus, placed on the obscure machinations of world imperialism, communism becoming the culture for gnosis as Mobutuism was in Zaire. The study of Hoxha along with the study of other regime intellectuals from the tribal-ethnic states such as Kim Il Sung, Cabral, and Ho Chi Minh offers interesting prospects for social historians.

The study of Albanian foreign relations corroborates points made earlier in connection with that of the Belgian Congo/Zaire. It also introduces a point not previously encountered. For example, while Hoxha's regime served as a client state both for the Soviet Union and for China, unlike Zaire, it was also able to abandon clientelist relations, to withdraw from the world market, and to function in isolation. Seemingly, it is only the tribal-ethnic states, examples apart from Albania being South Yemen and Guinea-Bissau, which have been able to escape in this manner for various periods.

In Zaire, Albania, and other tribal-ethnic states in recent years, many rulers face difficulty in the neoliberal economy of today's world. Although not all tribal-ethnic states are beset by civil wars at this point, many are. Indeed, here Albania seems representative of a large number of such states among which are Lebanon, Yugoslavia, Somaliland, the Sudan, Cambodia, Vietnam, Angola, Mozambique, and so on. This frailty of tribal-ethnic states in the face of finance capitalism requires more study. In the instance under discussion, with the advent of liberalism, the leadership and its ideology simply collapsed into its various ethnic components, each with its own ideologies. Albania went overnight from communism to joining the Muslim League and to allowing U.S. spy planes to fly from its territory. Such changes did not hapen in Zaire. In Zaire, given its nationwide and gender-conscious movements such as the opposition churches, these is a stake in the continuation of the country, its long history of secession movements notwithstanding.

Where a contradiction is a primary one, it is fixed irrevocably. Thus, in Albania, one must note how the logic of the prevailing attitudes toward women overcame the best efforts of the Communist organizers to mount a challenge to it. How else can one explain the party's failure when it tried so hard to impose a Russian Road system and to produce emancipated women to participate in the ruling caste? Yet most of the women who emerged in the system even in the communist period did so in the traditional way, that is, through the support of prominent male relatives. And so it is in Sudan, Algeria, and Tunisia, among many other countries whose recent history and current politics is not so different. This leads to one final point; feminists, especially those functioning in weak moments in a tribal-ethnic hegemony, can become and have become major historical figures if they take up the class issue, more or less like the American feminists who take up and combine race and class.

In the last of the four basic forms of hegemony, bourgeois democracy, the rulers play off class against race. The choice of the United Kingdom clarifies how a working class came to accept or be pushed into accepting the idea of a racial undercaste. Finally, it shed light as well on the possibility that once such an idea was in place the ruling class could gradually shift its targeting of a certain group as a racial undercaste from one to another without disrupting the hegemony.

One of the great unknowns in late nineteenth century British labor history was the position the workers would adopt on the Irish Question. There were many people of Irish descent in the English working class. Would, then, the workers side with the nationalists to kick the British out of Northern Ireland? For, if Northern Ireland became part of Ireland, that is, free from the English, the Irish would no longer serve as a suitable racial undercaste for the United Kingdom. This made the British ruling class strongly opposed to the demands of the Catholics in Northern Ireland. And, through some combination of British workers' perception of their own self-interest and of the social and cultural engineering of the politicians, the workers did not support the unification of Ireland. What happened thereafter was even more interesting. The Irish Question, once a central political issue, receded a bit as first Jews and then Commonwealth citizens were made to occupy the racial undercaste niche. Parenthetically, one might ask if the Israeli ruling class, which is today in a situation somewhat analogous to that of the British ruling class around 1900, will figure out how to let go of the Palestinians, and if they do, who then will serve as their replacement as the Israeli racial undercaste.

As this transition in cultural and social engineering took place, it became clear that the primary loyalty of the British working class was to the state and not to the racial undercaste, no matter which one it was. Workers accepted the racism and the colonial policies promulgated by the state and received in return the welfare state. With this solid base of mass support, Britain also became a great power, and a prosperous one. For this reason it did not go to the extremes of killing its undercaste as several other democracies did where there was more economic crisis.

Race, one learns from this study, also varies according to the hegemony. Where the race question is central as in the democracies, it becomes the core of politics. It becomes a part of education, indeed of science. Where the race question is central, the notion of a racial hierarchy is also more fixed. Thus, in the democracies, Creoles, mixed race families, and interracial adoption policies are examples of controversial issues, whereas in the other hegemonies, such subjects are perceived quite variably. In Italy, for example, where race is a subordinate contradiction, it takes on importance when it becomes related to region and culture. For example, it arises when a member of the Northern League claims that Naples is the Africa of Europe. In Russian Road states, race is tied to an evolutionary notion of culture. Russian means more cultured than Tatar. The significance of race, however, is offset in the case of individuals, no matter of what cultural origin, who learn the Russian language and the way of the ruling caste. It was my hypothesis, in fact, that over the past half century, the ruling caste in the Soviet Union gradually filled with non-Russian ethnics and that this is a major political fact of today. The importance of race in this context is on the rise. Finally, in tribal-ethnic states, race takes on yet another set of meanings as defined by blood ties. In this context, one's race can change by virtue of religious conversion or marriage.

The choice of the United States as an example of a bourgeois democracy adds the idea of the buffer race to the analysis of the race/class dialectic found in all the democracies; it also serves as a point from which to recast the study of international relations so as to be beyond Eurocentrism.

The idea of a buffer race emerges from struggles taking place in the United States. Rather than acceding to the racialism of the regime, the working class in the United States remains somewhat at a distance from it. As a result, some, although not all, black people were able to become members of trade unions. This ambivalence of the U.S. working class toward racialism had a number of well-known consequences, foremost among which was the reluctance of the state to extend welfarism and the social contract to the workers. Welfarism consequently was weaker in the

United States than in the majority of other democracies. Second, American blacks could pursue a strategy of integrationism, an option not available to their counterparts in the United Kingdom. For, in the United Kingdom, the majority of the British population think that Commonwealth people constitute a separate "nation"; by contrast, in the United States, most white Americans think blacks constitute a "racial minority." Third, and this is the distinctively new point, the U.S. state developed a "buffer race" strategy. The state through its immigration policy inserted one or more groups, the buffers, into society between blacks and whites to conflict with the interests of both, thereby deflecting the focus on race off the black-white issue, diffusing it into what is now called multiculturalism. The buffer race strategy in the United States is clearly in evidence as far back as the turn of the twentieth century. At that point, large numbers of Italians and Jews came to occupy such a position; a half-century later they were replaced by Middle Easterners, East Asians, and Hispanics. In the media and throughout the educational system, these newer groups effectively present the race problem as they experience it, often nearly drowning out the blacks. After the recent massive expansion of the buffer race after 1970, the civil rights movement as a movement almost died, the country's status as a great power perhaps thereby remaining intact.

Jewish history appears quite different in the different hegemonies. In tribal states, Jews appear to be tribes; in Italian Road states, Jews appear to be cultures; in Russian Road states, Jews appear to be communities seeking linkages to the state; whereas in democracies—at least in normal democracies—their goal is to be part of civil society. This approach to Jewish history through the logic of hegemonies seems to have interesting implications both for understanding the historic Jewish communities and for understanding the different hegemonies as well.

A second feature of U.S. history that stands out is foreign policy, especially foreign policy to collectivist regimes. No doubt, in contrast to the other hegemonies, democracies are the ones most noticeably antagonized by regimes that promote any collectivist ideology, that is, any ideology that deviates from liberal individualism. But nowhere is this more apparent than in the United States, the democracy that could never be sure of the accommodation of its own labor movement. Thus, in the corporatist period in modern world history, the United States in particular felt itself threatened by "enemies." Some of these enemies were bonafide trade rivals, such as Japan and Germany, but others, such as Nasir's Egypt, Peron's Argentina, Sokarno's Indonesia, and even Mussolini's Italy, were not. In these latter cases, the animosity felt by Americans—projections aside—came from a perception of the structures and ideologies of these countries. Democracy, I suggest, is a factor in international relations; so, too, are the other hegemonic forms, and this seems worth pursuing.

Because of the logic of the hegemony, Russian Road states define their foreign policy in terms of maintaining the security of the state. They often fight defensive wars, sacrificing subject populations to save the state. The recent Iraqi strategy in the Gulf War and the Soviet strategy during World War II are along those lines. These states seem to prefer to expand territorially to the areas around them, again, areas affecting their defense, as in Japan's co-prosperity sphere, the Soviet's East Bloc—rather than its Cuba —or Iraq's Kuwait. This contrasts with the style of imperialism of the bourgeois democracies, which seems more global. In reflecting on why this should be the case, there is the factor of opportunity raised previously in reference to the foreign policy of tribal ethnic states, but there is also the difference in hegemonic logic. A racial "other" can be anywhere, but a culture in some relationship to one's own—the Soviet case—cannot. It was, thus, easy for the United Kingdom to have a global empire because of the extremely stable sense of racial difference that existed at home between white and Commonwealth peoples. It was also easy for the United States to do so, but not as easy because of the integrationist tendencies within the country. The other was not as sustainable as an "other" in, for example, the agonizing by the United States over relations with Puerto Rico and the Philippines. The foreign policy of Italian Road states such as Mexico, Egypt, and India has often supported nonalignment, at its core, a policy of countries desiring greater economic self-sufficiency. "We shall not live by foreign bread," a famous phrase attributed to Mussolini, sums up the frustrated developmentalist impulses in the politics and economy of many Italian Road states.

If, then, international relations appears to involve almost predictable forms of encounter among the different hegemonies, and this seems the best way to make sense of a whole set of events in the twentieth century, why not study the proclivities of these different hegemonies and head off their worst features through diplomacy? The answer I suggest by this study is that people in different hegemonies are not likely to share the same "common sense." Such differences make diplomatic negotiations, even in a language that people share, an opportunity for misunderstandings as much as anything else. A positivist understands a declarative statement to stand alone as a contract. A romantic assumes it is modified by ethical issues. A Marxist assumes it is to be understood as part of a totality. And an anarchist assumes it can be deconstructed.

In short, given the prevailing conditions of international communication, where issues are often complicated, would not diplomats benefit from a deep understanding of these hegemonies? Could they learn to translate their thoughts into different logics as they learn to translate their thoughts into different languages?

I now pose the same question to those concerned with human rights. To coexist, countries in the modern world need not only diplomats but an intellectual culture supporting the preservation of human rights.

To this end, I recommend for those so concerned an interest in the production of history. What does it include? What does it leave out? I suggest that if one examines the organization of culture typical of each of the four hegemonies, one finds that although each values history, each differs in what forms of history are to be pursued; for each there are norms and distortions of these norms.

Thus, for example, in Russian Road regimes, one finds that the sought-after forms of history are political and world historical. In such works, often the country is juxtaposed by the author against the West; examples include the Slavophile historians, the Leninist historians, and the Ba'thi historians in modern Iraq. By contrast, social history in the Russian Road is nearly counterhegemonic. Consequently, little is produced. Major themes of concern to the human rights observer, such as the relationship of caste and class, remain unstudied.

In tribal-ethnic states, positivist history plays an even more limited role than it does in Russian Road states. It is reserved for the study of externalities, such as diplomacy, or to provide chronologies. Here, too, social history is counterhegemonic, and not much is produced; gender history or the relationship between gender and class is what remains untouched.

In Italian Road states, the prestigious history writing deals with cultural subjects, often classical and medieval ones. At certain times, however, social history aligned to the interest of the state does assert itself although not in such a way as to illuminate the South.

In bourgeois democracies, history, if not at home, is less resisted than it is elsewhere. Such, at least, is the common impression that one would get from looking at a card catalog in a library. Closer examination suggests that as with other states, the democracies encourage a great deal of political history, but its preferred form of social history is without agency. Agency in the history writing of the democracies, therefore, remains with the elite and certainly not in the racial undercaste. In light of these trends could not the state of history serve as a barometer of how well rulers are dealing with their indigenous populations? Should not the study of history, especially social history, as it appears in the different hegemonies help people interested in monitoring human rights carry out their responsibilities? Would not, then, a break with Eurocentrism as proposed in this book spell the birth of a Golden Age for social history both in the academy and beyond?

What finally does this come to mean for historians? Three things come to mind. First, the argument of the book poses a rather political question for historians. If world history is to be now understood as the outcome of the encounter or collision of different hegemonies, historians are playing roles and making choices that perceptibly matter. Routine acts such as renewing one's membership in a professional society have implications if that professional society is tied to the organization of culture of the state. Does it not follow that historians, or at least many historians, by so doing, play a role in the ongoing maintenance of social stratification? Is their social function limited, as I may have suggested in the previous chapters, to crisis roles, such as service during wars? What should the stance of historians be toward a possible structural involvement with the state? Second, the findings of the book suggest the need for a new priority for the field of history as a whole, on top of those implied in terms of the greater use of comparative approaches and of the need to abate Eurocentrism. This priority arises from the fact that the majority of people in the world still exist outside the structures used by historians to study them, that is, that the majority still exists in residual categories in our minds, categories such as informal sector workers, squatters, peasants, or subsistence farmers. I believe that this fact makes the immediate priority for the discipline an attempt to forge new categories, ones that would permit an evaluation of the role of the majority of the people in shaping the modern world. Third, the findings of the book suggest the need to rethink some prevailing assumptions not just about the social parameters of the discipline but of the temporal ones as well. If we find that most of the world in this, the age of the modern capitalist nation state, is still outside capitalism and barely a part of the nation state, does this not have theoretical implications for the analysis of both and, by extension, for our definition of modernity?

Notes

Bibliography

Index

Notes

1. Eurocentrism and the Study of World History

1. Gran, "The Political Economy of Aesthetics: Modes of Domination in Modern Nation States Seen Through Shakespeare Reception," *Dialectical Anthropology* 17 (1992): 171–188; the critique of Eurocentrism is drawn from my book referred to in the text, *The Islamic Roots of Capitalism: Egypt, 1760–1840* (Austin: Univ. of Texas Press, 1979); idem, "Political Economy as a Paradigm for the Study of Islamic History," *International Journal of Middle East Studies* 11 (1980): 511–26; idem, "Studies of Anglo-American Political Economy: Democracy, Orientalism and the Left," in *Theory, Politics and the Arab World*, ed. Hisham Sharabi (New York: Routledge, 1990), 228–54; idem, "Mafhum Gramshi 'an al-muthaqqaf al-taqlidi salihiyatiha li-dirasa Misr al-hadith," in *Gramshi*, ed. Hilmi Sha'rawi et al., (Damascus, 1991), 353–67; idem, "Organization of Culture and Construction of the Family in the Modern Middle East," in *Family in the Middle East*, ed. Amira Sonbol (Syracuse, N.Y.: Syracuse Univ. Press, 1995), chap. 4 (forthcoming); idem, "Race and Racism in the Modern World: How It Works in Different Hegemonies," in *Transforming Anthropology*, ed. Lee D. Baker and Thomas C. Patterson 5/1–2 (1994): 8–14; see also Samir Amin, *Eurocentrism* (New York: Monthly Review Press, 1989).

2. "Russian Road": The Russian and Soviet Experience, 1861–1990

1. Teodor Shanin, *Late Marx and the Russian Road* (New York: Monthly Review Press, 1983), is a basic statement of Marx's last phase. In this phase, Marx has abandoned a number of the orthodox formulations, signaling a freer approach on his part to historical study generally and to Russian history in particular. For a summary, see Derek Sayer and Philip Corrigan, "Revolution Against the State: The Context and Significance of Marx's Later Writings," *Dialectical Anthropology* 12 (1987): 65–82. In the Western academic studies of Russia, the first to use these insights were the students of peasant studies, such as Teodor Shanin and Moshe Lewin, and the first to generalize these insights for the subject as a whole; Sheila Fitzpatrick, "New Perspectives on Stalinism," *Russian Review* 45 (1986): 357–73. In the 1980, a widening range of post-cold war studies attempt to place Russian history in a comparative framework, among them, Michael Urban, "Conceptualizing Political Power in the USSR: Patterns of Binding and Bonding," *Studies in Comparative Communism* 18, no. 4 (1985): 207–26; Robert Kelley, "Comparing the Incomparable: Politics and Ideas in the United States and the Soviet

Union," *Comparative Studies in Society and History* 26 (1984): 672–708. The term *Russian Road* used here conveys the social dynamic better than the more elite-oriented concept of *Soviet-Type Societies* appearing in the works cited and in *Political Legitimation in Communist States*, ed. H. Rigby and Ferenc Feher (New York: St. Martin's Press, 1982). From the Soviets' own recasting of their modern history, one could cite the odd work of G. Vodolazov, author of an article in the late 1960s, that raised the question of how in 1917; the Communists could have led a proletarian revolution if the proletariat was not ready for it. He invoked Gramsci's writings to explain the aftermath of 1917, cited in Boris Kagarlitsky, *The Thinking Reed: Intellectuals and the Soviet State 1917 to the Present* (London: Verso, 1988), 292. Other examples of Russian Road regimes in the modern world include Turkey, Iran, Peru, and a number of East Bloc countries.

2. For the idea of the religious leadership as "junior partners" in the power structure, see Jerry G. Pankhurst, "The Sacred and the Secular in the USSR," in *Understanding Soviet Society*, ed. Michael Paul Sacks and Jerry G. Pankhurst (Boston: Unwin Hyman, 1988), 172ff.

3. Christel Lane, *The Rites of Rulers: Ritual in Industrial Society: The Soviet Case* (Cambridge: Cambridge Univ. Press, 1981).

4. The role of foreign technology is extensively studied; for a recent account, see Kendall E. Bailes, "The American Connection: Ideology and the Transfer of American Technology to the Soviet Union, 1917–1941," *Comparative Studies in Society and History* 23, no. 3 (1981): 421–48.

5. Scholars have noted the oscillation pattern, but they have frequently explained it as stemming from traits of the rulers as opposed to the self-protective logic of the structure. An example of a more structuralist argument about Communist rulers is Graeme Gill, "Personality Cult, Political Culture and Party Structure," *Studies in Comparative Communism* 17, no. 2 (1984): 111–21; for the image of modern Soviet history as a spiral, see Ivan Yefremov, "Evolution Is an Upward Spiral," *Soviet Literature* 406 (1982): 173–78.

6. From the outside, the appearance is that the ruler is in charge and the system is cohesive. Traditional scholarship has played a role in sustaining the image of political cohesiveness. Recent scholarship, however, suggests that even the most powerful figure, Stalin, rode the waves of his times while words were put in his mouth. Gabor Rittersporn, "Stalin in 1938: Political Defeat Behind the Rhetorical Apotheosis," *Telos* 46 (Winter 1980–1981): 6–42, shows social groups invoking Stalin's name in their fights; the same revisionary position appears in J. Arch Getty, *Origins of the Great Purges: The Soviet Communist Party Reconsidered, 1933–1938* (Cambridge: Cambridge Univ. Press, 1985), conclusion. The general work on the bureaucratization of Russia is Walter Pintner and Don Rowney, eds. *Russian Officialdom: The Bureaucratization of Russian Society from the Seventeenth to the Twentieth Century* (Chapel Hill: Univ. of North Carolina Press, 1980), 250–52, 316–17. Their research shows that in the period I term Russian Road the bureaucracy starts to embody two contradictory elements—trained specialists and regime loyalists. Yet another theme is the cult of the personality. For this cult, a vast literature exists. One form of it, hagiography, has played a major role in the development of Russian literature; Margaret Ziolkowski, *Hagiography and Modern Russian Literature* (Princeton, N.J.: Princeton Univ. Press, 1988). For the evolution of the cult of the personality in recent years into the *collective leadership*, see Nancy Heer, "Political Leadership in Soviet Historiography: Cult or Collective?" in *The Dynamics of Soviet Politics*, ed. Paul Cocks, Robert V. Daniels, and Nancy Whittier Heer, (Cambridge, Mass.: Harvard Univ. Press, 1976), 37.

7. Tim McDaniel, *Autocracy, Capitalism, and Revolution in Russia* (Berkeley: Univ. of California Press, 1988), 1ff.

8. Dmitry Pospielovsky, *The Russian Church under the Soviet Regime, 1917–1982* (New York: St. Vladimir's Seminary Press, 1984), 1: chap. 2, 90, 91, 190–91. The continuing and almost fanatical piety of Russian peasant women, however, was equally legendary. For example, a women's brigade designated to burn a church committed suicide; other examples of

suffering also appeared, ibid., 1:235, 2:442; Gregory Freeze, *The Parish Clergy in Nineteenth Century Russia: Crisis, Reform, Counter-Reform* (Princeton, N.J.: Princeton Univ. Press, 1983).

9. Barbara Holland, ed., *Soviet Sisterhood* (London: Fourth Estate, 1985), 179–209; Michael Paul Sacks, *Women's Work in Soviet Russia: Continuity in the Midst of Change* (New York: Frederick A. Praeger, 1976), 32–33.

10. Teodor Shanin, *Russia as a Developing Society* (London: Macmillan, 1985), 31, 66, 68, 134; see also the comments of Lawrence Langer on Laura Engelstein, *Moscow 1905: Working Class Organization and Political Conflict* in his "Russia in Revolution—Review Article," *Studies in Comparative Communism* 17, no. 2 (1984): 140–41.

11. Barbara Alpern Engel, *Mothers and Daughters: Women of the Intelligentsia in Nineteenth Century Russia* (Cambridge: Cambridge Univ. Press, 1983), chap. 10. This work takes up the pendular swing in relation to intergenerational relations. Christine Johanson, *Women's Struggle for Higher Education in Russia, 1855–1900* (Kingston: McGill-Queens Univ. Press, 1987), chap. 6.

12. Among interesting features of the post-cold war period is the rise of official public opinion polls in the Soviet Union; see Walter D. Connor, "Public Opinion in the Soviet Union," in *Public Opinion in European Socialist Systems,* ed. Walter D. Connor and Zvi Y. Gitelman (New York: Frederick A. Praeger, 1977), chap. 4.

13. Moshe Lewin, *The Making of the Soviet System* (New York: Pantheon, 1983), 86, 98, 164, 176, 178, 180; Daniel Thorniley, *The Rise and Fall of the Soviet Rural Communist Party, 1927–1939* (New York: St. Martin's Press, 1988), conclusion.

14. For the early Stalinist period, see J. K. Zawodny, "Grievances and Sources of Tension During Stalin's Regime as Reported by Soviet Industrial Workers," *Soviet Studies* 14, no. 2 (1962): 158–73. For the evolution to more pragmatic labor relations in the 1950s, see Vladimir Shlapentokh, *Evolution in the Soviet Sociology of Work: From Ideology to Pragmatism,* Carl Beck Papers, no. 404 (Pittsburgh, Pa.: Univ. of Pittsburgh Press 1985); Mary McAuley, *Labour Disputes in Soviet Russia* (Oxford: Clarendon Press, 1969), 40. For the attitude of workers toward free and unfree workers, see Vladimir Andrle, *Workers in Stalin's Russia* (New York: St. Martin's Press, 1988), 202, 204 ff. On labor shortages in the later 1930s and on the attractiveness of seeking other labor markets, see S. Swianiewicz, *Forced Labour and Economic Development* (Oxford: Oxford Univ. Press, 1985), 81ff., 208. Finally, an official, if indirect, acknowledgment of anarchist sentiment among the Russian people emerges in Zhadanov's concern that the liquidation of Sergei Kirov in the purges of 1934 would remind people of the Russian anarchist tradition of People's Will. In general, Soviet studies of Russian populism increased after Stalin; see John E. Bachman, "Recent Soviet Historiography of Russian Revolutionary Populism," *Slavic Review* 29(1970): 599–612.

15. Donald Filtzer, *Soviet Workers and Stalinist Industrialization* (New York: M. E. Sharpe, 1986), chap. 7, esp. 187. The problems that beset the Stakhanovites in the 1930s still remain for various conscientious workers and among them whistle blowers; Bruno Grancelli, *Soviet Management and Labor Relations* (Boston: Allen and Unwin, 1988), 189ff.; McDaniel, op. cit. *Autocracy, Capitalism, and Revolution.*

16. Moshe Lewin, "Society, State, and Ideology During the First Five Year Plan," in *Cultural Revolution in Russia, 1928–1931,* ed. Sheila Fitzpatrick (Bloomington: Indiana Univ. Press, 1978), chap. 2; Fitzpatrick, "New Perspectives" 367, citing evidence from Vera Dunham, *In Stalin's Time: Middle Class Values in Soviet Fiction.*

17. Valerie Bunce, "The Empire Strikes Back: The Evolution of the East Bloc from a Soviet Asset to a Soviet Liability," *International Organization* 39, no. 10 (1985): 1–46, esp. 3ff.

18. For the process of Sovietization, see Michael Rywkin, "National Symbiosis: Vitality, Religion, Identity, and Allegiance," in *The USSR and the Muslim World—Issues in Domestic and Foreign Policy,* ed. Yaacov Ro'i (London: George Allen and Unwin, 1984), 11; Paul Henze, "The Significance of Increasing Bilingualism among Soviet Muslims," ibid., 127. More fanci-

ful and "orientalist" is Marie Broxup, *The Islamic Threat to the Soviet State* (New York: St. Martin's Press, 1983), arguing for the idea of an unchanging Islamic resistance to the Soviets from Sultan Galiev before World War I to Afghanistan. On interethnic marriage, see Wesley Andrew Fisher, *The Soviet Marriage Market* (New York: Frederick A. Praeger, 1980), chap. 7; on changes in another region, the Ukraine, see Boris Lewytzkyj, *Politics and Society in Soviet Ukraine, 1953–1980* (Edmonton, Canada: Univ. of Alberta Press, 1984), 13–25.

19. Sacks, *Women's Work,* 67; for an overview of the new barter economy, see Steven Sampson, " 'May You Live Only by Your Salary!': The Unplanned Economy in Eastern Europe," *Social Justice* 15, nos. 3–4 (1989): 135–159. On the right generally, see Alexander Panov, *The Russian New Right-Wing Ideologies in the Contemporary USSR* (Berkeley: Univ. of California Press/IIS, 1978), 6ff., 21–25, 113. Panov also uses the model of Russian history as "oscillating phases."

20. A possible alternative to the time frame of *past century* is 1917—before and after. The careful and multisided work by the Joint Committee on Slavic Studies, *Continuity and Change in Russian and Soviet Thought* (New York: Russell and Russell, 1955), persuades one otherwise. The deeper breakpoint comes with the Cultural Revolution. James H. Billington, *The Icon and the Axe* (New York: Alfred A. Knopf, 1966), 564ff., specified some of the cultural trends arising with the New Class at that time, including a growth of humor, a resurgence of romantic poetry as in Evtushenko, increased numbers of people involved in protests over previous periods in Russian history, attraction of the West to the younger generation, a perception of the inadequacy of Marxism to deal with modern science, the rise of the scientist as a hero, philo-Semitism, sympathy to the Baltic regions, and, finally, a demand for a more usable history.

21. Vaclav Havel, Steven Lukes, and John Keane, *The Power of the Powerless-Citizens Against the State in Central-Eastern Europe* (Armonk, N. Y.: M. E. Sharpe, 1985), is similar to the works in Third World peasant studies that argue for the powers of the weak. H. Gordon Skilling and Franklyn Griffiths, eds., *Interest Groups in Soviet Politics* (Princeton, N. J.: Princeton Univ. Press, 1971), is an earlier but still important work that characterizes different power centers. Stephen Cohen's writings open the door to these possibilities in American Soviet studies, *Rethinking the Soviet Experience: Politics and History since 1917* (New York: Oxford Univ. Press, 1985); for the explication of persuasion in hegemony, see John Hoffman, *The Gramscian Challenge: Coercion and Consent in Marxist Political Theory* (Oxford: Basil Blackwell, 1984).

22. Jonathan R. Adelman, "Soviet Secret Police," in *Terror and Communist Politics: The Role of the Secret Police in Communist States,* ed. Jonathan R. Adelman (Boulder, Colo.: Westview Press, 1984), chap. 4; for the army, see William C. Fuller, Jr., *Civil-Military Conflict in Imperial Russia, 1881–1914* (Princeton, N. J.: Princeton Univ. Press, 1985). A work dealing with hegemony both as coercion and as persuasion, involving family-state collaboration, is George Avis, ed., *The Making of the Soviet Citizen: Character Formation and Civic Training in Soviet Education* (London: Croom Helm, 1987).

23. James Riordan, *Sport in Soviet Society: Development of Sport and Physical Education in Russia and the USSR* (Cambridge: Cambridge Univ. Press, 1977).

24. Katerina Clark, "Political History and Literary Chronotype: Some Soviet Case Studies," in *Literature and History: Theoretical Problems and Russian Case Studies,* ed. Gary Paul Morson (Stanford, Calif.: Stanford Univ. Press, 1986), 230–246, esp. eq 233, for comments about the decline of the rural-centered novel, the "Scythianist Trend" of the late 1920s. In the 1960s, the resurgence of a ruralist prose movement appeared to overlap with the "new Right," with organizations such as the Society for the Preservation of the Nation and the Russian Society for the Preservation of Historical and Cultural Monuments; John Dunlop, "Ruralist Prose Writers in the Russian Ethnic Movement," in *Ethnic Russia in the USSR: The Dilemma of Dominance,* ed. Edward Allworth (New York: Pergamon, 1979), 85ff. From the media of

the 1970s, programs supporting the cultural dualism continue to come. For example, from the popular radio station, the All-Union Radio's Channel One, came programs such as "Land and People" for the rural population and musical evenings as well.

25. Peter France, *Poets of Modern Russia* (Cambridge: Cambridge Univ. Press, 1982), 188.

26. Wendy Rosslyn, *The Prince, the Fool, and the Nunnery: The Religious Theme in the Early Poetry of Anna Akhmatova* (Amersham, England: Avebury Publishing, 1984), introduction.

27. Gerald Stanton Smith, *Songs to Seven Strings: Russian Guitar Poetry and Soviet "Mass Song"* (Bloomington: Indiana Univ. Press, 1984), ix-x, 1–2. For an example of a purge of musical Westernism, a purge including scholars as well as musicians, see the case in 1949 of the music historian Roman Gruber charged with having emphasized only the West and having ignored the contribution of Slavonic and Central Asian music to Russian music; Boris Schwarz, *Music and Musical Life in Soviet Russia* (Bloomington: Indiana Univ. Press, 1983), 253–54.

28. Bernard Combrie and Gerald Stone, *The Russian Language since the Revolution* (Oxford: Oxford Univ. Press, 1978), 20, 144–45, 156–58. Since Tsarist times, many Russians had migrated to the national areas as colonists; Max Adler, *Marxist Linguistic Theory and Communist Practice: A Sociolinguistic Study* (Hamburg: Helmut Buske, 1980), 112ff.

29. Elizabeth A. Warner, "Collection and Study of Ethnographical Material in Russia," *Folk Life* 22 (1983–84): 107–18; John L. Wieczynski, ed. *The Modern Encyclopedia of Russian and Soviet History* (Gulf Breeze: Academic Press International, 1976), 2:81; 23:229–46; for a tourist book on old Russia, see Alexander Milovsky, *Ancient Russian Cities: A Travel Guide to the Historical and Architectural Monuments and Fine Arts Museums* (Moscow: Raduga Publishers, 1986).

30. Alexander Vucinich, *Empire of Knowledge: The Academy of Sciences of the USSR (1917–1970)* (Berkeley: Univ. of California Press, 1984), chap. 1.

31. Ibid., chaps. 2–3, esp. 126; Peter Kneen, *Soviet Scientists and the State* (London: Macmillan, 1984), 18ff.

32. Dialectical thought comes into Russian culture through the Mensheviks and through returning Russian émigrées. It was strong in the commercial cities of the Baltics, for example, in the leading Menshevik figure, Abram Deborin (1881–1964), and, of course, Lenin. Lenin's great impact on Russia, however, was the Leninism of Stalin and not Lenin himself, the Lenin of the *Philosophical Notebooks;* see James Edie, James P. Scanlan, and Mary-Barbara Zeldin, eds., *Russian Philosophy* (Knoxville: Univ. of Tennessee Press, 1976), 3:354ff. On worldviews and especially on romanticism, see Lauren G. Leighton, "The Great Soviet Debate over Romanticism: 1957–1964," *Studies in Romanticism* 22 (Spring 1983): 41–64. The atmosphere of the traditional scientific analysis of literature is described in an account from *History of World Literature Project,* the Gorky Institute of World Literatures; Yuri Vipper, "National Literary History in *History of World Literature;* Theoretical Principles of Treatment," *New Literary History* 16(1985): 545–58.

33. For a critique of the "Durkheimian idea" of religion as "social cement," see Gregory Freeze, "Handmaiden of the State? The Church in Imperial Russia," *Journal of Ecclesiastical History* 36(1985): 85–102. During the early period of the Revolution, the secular structure clearly had the upper hand. It even tried to create a new more controllable spiritual hierarchy than the church called the League of the Militant Godless and to tax the church as an enterprise.

34. The 1917 Revolution was not the only one in a Russian Road society to turn its back on the religious structure as the vehicle for channeling romantic or religious fervor. In the Turkish Revolution, Kemal Ataturk also closed religious institutions, replacing Ottoman Islam with Kemalism. The 1958 Revolution in Iraq is yet another example.

35. For an explanation of the motifs of the Orthodox faith in terms of the structure and interactions of the traditional Russian family, see Dinko Tomasic, *The Impact of the Traditional*

Russian Culture on Soviet Communism (Glencoe: Free Press, 1953), sec. 3, 228–29, for a comparison of the Russian family to the Ottoman one.

36. Edie, Scanlan, and Zeldin, *Russian Philosphy* 55–75; Samuel Cioran, *Vladimir Solov'ev and the Knighthood of the Divine Sophia* (Waterloo: Wilfrid Laurier Press, 1977), chap. 2; on the chain of influence through the salon, see Forrest A. Miller, "Solov'ev, Vladimir" in Joseph L. Wieczynski, *The Modern Encyclopedia of Russian and Soviet History* (Gulf Breeze, Fla.: Academic International, 1976), 36: 152–55.

37. A common scholarly view is that history has been more important to the Bolsheviki than has other fields. This may be the case, certainly historical materialism pays allegiance to history, but if so, it requires what could be a difficult line of argument, first to disallow the role played in maintaining the hegemonic cultural dualism by other fields, for example, anthropology, engineering, linguistics, or economics, and second, to demonstrate that Soviet history writing was something new, that the older history writing had not been important in the country. See Nancy Heer, *Politics and History in the Soviet Union* (Cambridge: MIT Press, 1971), 13ff. Looking at concrete cases, one might, in fact, find that the two or three historians who did become politically important were isolated cases. The main example that scholars turn to is M. N. Pokrovsky (1868–1932), a figure discussed at some length in the last section. It suffices to note here that Stalin had him purged like many others; George M. Enteen, *The Soviet Scholar-Bureaucrat: M. N. Pokrovskii and the Society of Marxist Historians* (University Park: Pennsylvania State Univ. Press, 1978); from the Tsarist period arose a historian, who at least equaled and perhaps surpassed Pokrovsky's influence with the power structure, V. O. Kliuchevskii (1841–1911). It is, perhaps, noteworthy that Kliuchevskii's master's thesis was entitled "Ancient Russian Hagiographies as Historical Studies"; George Vernadsky, *Russian Historiography: A History* (Belmont: Nordland, 1978), 128–39, but, and this is the main point, to connect his political success to his prestige as a historian seems strained.

38. Joseph L. Black, "The 'State School' Interpretation of Russian History: A Reappraisal of its Genetic Origins," *Jahrbücher für Geschichte Osteuropas* 21 (1973): 509–30; Joseph L. Black, " 'State School' of Russian Historians," in Wieczynski, *Modern Encylopedia of Russian and Soviet History*, 37: 118–25; idem, "Russian Historical Society," *ibid.*, 32:96. Another source suggests that the conflicts between historians and the state came in the second generation; see Vernadsky, *Russian Historiography* 116, 130, 317; Iu P. Bokarev, "Quantitative Methods and Research on the History of the Traditional Soviet Peasantry," in *Soviet Quantitative History,* ed. Don Karl Rowney (Beverly Hills, Calif.: Sage Publications, 1984), introduction, chap. 4.

39. Paul Dukes, "Solov'ev's *History of Russia,*" *Historical Journal* 31, no. 1 (1988): 187–94; Sergei Solov'ev, *History of Russia* (Gulf Breeze: Academic International Press, 1981), 29:xii.

40. A natural place to look is the image of Peter the Great. For Pobesdonestev, Peter was a model, a pragmatic servant of the state; Stalin, too, held this view although it did not emerge during the years of Pokrovsky, who had a phobia about individual influence. A few years after Pokrovsky's death, Berngard B. Kafengauz (1894–1969) wrote a major work to rehabilitate Peter, which was published in 1940; Nicholas V. Riasanovsky, *The Image of Peter the Great in Russian History and Thought* (New York: Oxford Univ. Press, 1985), 216, 257–58.

41. P. I. Molchanov, "Museum of the History of the Don Cossack Host," in Wieczynski, *Modern Encyclopedia of Russian and Soviet History,* 23: 234–35.

42. Forrest A. Miller, "Russian Palestine Society," in Wieczynski, *Modern Encyclopedia of Russian and Soviet History,* 32: 132–34; "Russian Palestine Society of the Academy of Sciences," in Wieczynski, *Modern Encyclopedia of Russian and Soviet History,* 32: 134–35.

43. Alexander Vucinich, *Social Thought in Tsarist Russia* (Chicago: Univ. of Chicago Press, 1976), 155; for the liberal initiatives in Oriental Studies, see Richard Frye, "Oriental Studies in Russia," in *Russia and Asia,* ed. Wayne S. Vucinich (Stanford, Calif.: Hoover Institution Press, 1972), 46–49.

44. For political history, the rise of the New Class has been fairly well-established,

whereas for fields such as the sociology of knowledge or historiography it has not been. Thus, for example, on the birth of the "Brezhnev Generation" as a political consequence of the Cultural Revolution, see Sheila Fitzpatrick, "Cultural Revolution as Class War," Chap. 1 in *Cultural Revolution in Russia 1928–1931*, (Bloomington: Indiana Univ. Press, 1984).

What follows is an assemblage of some of the important elements from among existing works of scholarship on history writing that could be used to overturn the Stalin/post-Stalin periodization and replace it with one using the Cultural Revolution as the turning point in knowledge production. From all this, one concludes that history was not so central to the organization of culture that it simply mirrored what was going on. It remained, except for a few figures and for the Cultural Revolution, liberal positivist and occasionally romantic.

For general orientation, see C. E. Black, "History and Politics in the Soviet Union," in *Rewriting Russian History,* ed. C. E. Black (New York: Frederick A. Praeger, 1956), 3–32; Samuel H. Baron, "The Resurrection of Plekhanovism in Soviet Historiography," *Russian Review* 33 (1974): 386–404.

The rise of the New Class among the nationalities has generally been denied in much modern scholarship, even where the evidence exists; for example, see Lowell Tillett, *The Great Friendship: Soviet Historians on the Non-Russian Nationalities* (Chapel Hill: Univ. of North Carolina Press, 1969), 36ff., on the Ukraine in the early 1930s. On the Soviet Armenian historians, A. M. Hakobian, and Mehendak Artashesi Melikian, see L. Mikirtitchian, "Soviet Historiography of the Armenian Nation," *Caucasian Review* 9 (1959): 98–122, esp. 120. It is also apparent that ethnic nationalist scholarship was a two-edged matter for the New Class. It was useful in relation to those who deny ethnicity in Moscow, but it had to be curbed in favor of Russocentrism to protect the New Class's overall position. This contradictory situation appears in John Besarab, *Pereiaslav 1654: A Historiographical Study* (Edmonton, Canada: Univ. of Alberta Press, 1982), 179, 184ff. Concerning the tercentenary of the 1654 Pereiaslav Accord, Besarab shows in his research that the more recent Ukrainian historians have tended to embrace the traditional Soviet formulation of the event as marking the "reunification" of the Ukrainians and Russians. Recent Polish historiography has adopted a similar Russocentric tack (182). Stalin's rehabilitation of the Ukrainian historian, Ivan Krypiakevych (1886–1967)(187ff.) was in a similar vein. Beyond the traditional nationalities, the New Class of the peripheral regions, such as Central Asia, Siberia, and the Caucasus, today is participating in this scholarship. In the 1930s, this was not yet the case. At that time, historians and archeologists from these regions welcomed the fall of Pokrovsky in 1934 as they thought it would permit them to take an "ethnogenetic" approach to their studies and to put an end to Great Russian cultural diffusionism; V. A. Bulkin, Leo S. Klejn, and G. S. Lebedev, "Attainments and Problems of Soviet Archeology," *World Archeology* 13, no. 3 (1981): 272–95.

Another orientation in history writing, again reflecting the rise of the New Class, emphasizes the subject of liberalism itself in Russian history. An example of such work from 1933 appears in the writings of the well-known Soviet historian, Nikolai Druzhinin. Druzhinin argued that contrary to the views of Pokrovsky there was indeed a progressive element in the liberal participation in the Decembrist Uprising; cited in John Gooding, "The Decembrists in the Soviet Union," *Soviet Studies* 40 (1988): 196–209, esp. 198ff.; Pokrovsky was nearly isolated by the historians who came after him over the nature of the Pugachev uprisings and of other peasant movements of the Tsarist period. Pokrovsky did not think that the Pugachev Uprising was a peasant uprising or an uprising with political objectives. Liberals, especially after his death, took the opposite view. By the 1950s, the new generation of historians was challenging Pokrovsky's interpretation; Leo Yaresh, "The 'Peasant Wars' in Soviet Historiography," *American Slavic and East European Review* 16 (1957): 241–59, esp. 248.

The study of slavery in Russian history, from its origins to its abolition by Peter the Great, was yet another theme dividing Pokrovsky and other historians. The subject of slavery almost inevitably stirs the controversy surrounding the policy of forced labor from the 1930s to the 1950s. Through the 1950s, historians maintained that slavery was unimportant before Peter because the mode of production was feudal. By the 1960s, with forced labor in abeyance, the study of slavery began to develop more objectively; see Richard Hellie, "Recent Soviet Historiography on Medieval and Early Modern Russian Slavery," *Russian Review* 35 (1976): 1–32. In the early 1960s, a leading Soviet historian, Militsa V. Nechkina, working with a team of collaborators, took on one of Pokrovsky's fundamental premises in a critical spirit, the economic determination of political events. Nechkina's group chose to explore the "revolutionary situation" in the years 1859–61, a situation caused in good measure by the political consciousness of the peasantry; Charles C. Adler, Jr., "The 'Revolutionary Situation 1859–1861': The Uses of an Historical Conception," *Canadian Slavonic Studies* 3, no. 2 (1969): 383–99, esp. 388.

45. M. N. Pokrovskii, *Russia in World History* (Ann Arbor: Univ. of Michigan Press, 1970), esp. the editorial introduction by Roman Szporluk, 10–12, 35–39; Hans Hecker, *Russische Universalgschichteschreibung* (Vienna: Verlag R. Oldenbourg, 1983), found that "universal history" dominated Russia from 1860 to 1955 and "world history," history in which the Russian Revolution is the center of gravity, from 1955 to 1965. Pokrovsky was part of the earlier phase. (320).

46. Samuel H. Baron and Nancy Heer, eds., *Windows on the Russian Past* (Columbus: American Association for the Advancement of Slavic Studies, 1977), introduction, 112, 145ff, 158–59; Black, *Rewriting Russian History* chap. 6; other topics of recent interest to Soviet historiography include: the histories of the non-Bolshevik Left, explorations of the Asiatic mode of production, and its application to Russian despotism, and experiments with the epistemologies that go with this revisionism as well. One such experiment in epistemology has been making use of the concept of *multiformity*, a term implying the coexistence of different forms of economic organization at a given historical moment, a term not unlike *Russian Road*.

47. Roy A. Medvedev, *Let History Judge: The Origins and Consequences of Stalinism* (New York: Vintage Books, 1971), 361–63, 416.

3. The "Russian Road" in the Middle East: Iraqi History, 1869–1990

1. Modern Iraqi history begins with the commitment of capitalism to work on a national scale reflected in the liberal reformism of the 1870s. Before that time, capitalism of small scale and east-west transit trade functioned in three separate regions: the north around Mawsil(Mosul), the middle Euphrates cities dominated by Baghdad, and the south, that is, the Gulf, especially the port of Basra.

2. For information tending to challenge the liberal school's view of a socialist transformation in the USSR and Iraq, see Margaret Chadwick et al., *Soviet Oil Exports: Trade Adjustments, Refining Constraints and Market Behaviour* (Oxford: Oxford Univ. Press, 1987), 32, 71–97; for a more general statement about the reemergence of a consumerist capitalism from under a socialist framework, see Samir Amin, *Irak et Syrie* (Paris: Edition de Minuit, 1982); for a statement on the enormous growth of the Iraqi bureaucracy in the 1970s, see Marion Farouk Sluglett, " 'Socialist' Iraq 1963–1978: Towards a Reappraisal," *Orient* 23, no. 2 (1982): 206–19, esp. 210.

3. Clearly, most of the major texts are produced by the liberal school. Among them, is the trilogy by Majid Khadduri, *Independent Iraq: A Study in Iraqi Politics since 1932* (London: Oxford Univ. Press, 1951); *Republican Iraq: A Study in Iraqi Politics since the Revolution of 1958* (London: Oxford Univ. Press, 1969); and *Socialist Iraq: A Study in Iraqi Politics since 1968* (Washington, D.C.: Middle East Institute, 1978); Stephen Longrigg, *Four Centuries of Modern Iraq* (Beirut: Oxford Univ. Press, 1925); idem, *Iraq 1900–1950: A Political, Social, and Economic History* (Beirut: Lebanon Bookshop, 1986); Phoebe Marr, *The Modern History of Iraq* (Boulder, Colo.: Westview Press, 1985); Fadil Husayn, *Mushkilat al-Mawsil* (Baghdad, 1977); idem,

Suqut al-nizam al-malaki fi Al-'Iraq (Baghdad, 1986); Hanna Batatu, *The Old Social Classes and the Revolutionary Movements of Iraq* (Princeton, N.J.: Princeton Univ. Press, 1978).

For this study, the great contribution of the Liberal school is in establishing the comparison between Iraq and Russia: Samir Al-Khalil, *Republic of Fear, The Politics of Modern Iraq* (Berkeley: Univ. of California Press, 1989); Al-Khalil's comparisons of Saddam Husayn and Stalin will remind the reader of Roy Medvedev and his characterizations of Stalin commented on in chapter 2; additionally, "Le Nomenklatura irakienne ou l'organisation du pouvoir en Irak," *Cahiers de L'Orient* 8–9 (1987–88): 341–51, borrows its name from the well-known Russian political directory of that name; a pioneering study of Russian and Soviet literature on modern Arabic literature, with an emphasis on Syria; Majid 'Ala al-Din, *Al-Waqi'iya fi al-adabayn—Al-Sufyati wa al-'Arabi* (Realism in two literatures, Soviet and Arab)(Damascus, 1984). The liberal school in Iraqi also produced a world-oriented historical sociologist of the sort found in Russia and in other Russian Road regimes, 'Ali al-Wardi. See, for example, 'Ali al-Wardi and Fuad Baali, *Ibn Khaldun and Islamic Thought-Styles, A Social Perspective* (Boston: G. K. Hall, 1981).

4. *The Encyclopedia of Modern Iraq* (Baghdad: Arab Encyclopedia Publishing House, 1977), 3 vols.; 'Abd Al-'Aziz al-Duri, *The Rise of Historical Writing among the Arabs* (Princeton, N.J.: Princeton Univ. Press, 1983).

5. Ahmed Sousa, *Mufassal al-'Arab wa al-Yahud fi al-ta'rikh* (A detailed account of the Arabs and Jews in history); (Baghdad: Ministry of Culture, 1981); see also articles in the Iraqi archeological journal *Sumer*.

6. 'Abd Allah Fayyad, *Al-Thawrah al-'Iraqiyah al-Kubra sanata 1920* (The Iraqi revolt of 1920)(Baghdad: Matba'at Dar Al-Salam, 1975); see also the writings of 'Imad Ad-Din Khalil discussed below.

7. Werner Ende, *Arabische Nation und islamische Geschichte: Die Umayyaden im Urteil arabischer Autoren des 20. Jahrhunderts* (Beirut: OIDMG, 1977). For a criticism of the communal school from the vantage point of political economy, see Marion Farouk Sluglett and Peter Sluglett, "Some Reflections on the Present State of Sunni/Shi'i Relations in Iraq," *Bulletin of the British Society for Middle Eastern Studies* 5 (1978): 79–87.

8. 'Isam Al-Khafaji, *Al-Dawla wa al-tatawwur al-ra'smal fi al-'Iraq, 1968–1978* (The state and the development of capitalism in Egypt)(Cairo: Dar al-Mustabal al-'Arabi, 1983); Muhammad Baqir Sadr (the "Gramsci of Iraq"), *Our Philosophy* (London: Muhammadi Trust/KPI, 1987). The major Gramscian-oriented study of Iraq is 'Abd Al-Salaam Yousif, "Vanguardist Cultural Practices: The Formation of an Alternative Cultural Hegemony in Iraq and Chile, 1930's-1970's" (Ph.D. diss., Univ. of Iowa, 1988); see also his "The Struggle for Cultural Hegemony During the Iraqi Revolution," in *The Iraqi Revolution of 1958: The Old Social Classes Revisited,* ed. Roger Louis and Robert Fernea (London: Tavistock, 1991), 172–96. For an explanation of Iraqi politics from the perspective of "combined and uneven development," see Samira Abuel-Haj, "Class Conflict and Political Revolution in Iraq: The Socio-Economic Origins of the 1958 Revolution" (Ph.D. diss., Univ. of California, Los Angeles, 1987). The writings of Ahmad Kamal Mazhar and Peter and Marion Farouk Sluglett discussed below fall into this category.

9. E. Honigmann, "Karbala,' " in *Encyclopedia of Islam,* ed. H. A. R. Gibb et al. (Leiden: Brill, 1978), n.s., 4:638.

10. Ghassan Atiyya, *Iraq: 1908–1921, A Socio-Political Study* (Beirut, 1973), 28–29, 31.

11. Walid Khadduri, "Social Background of Modern Iraqi Politics" (Ph.D. diss., Johns Hopkins Univ., 1970), 67.

12. 'Abd Al-Karim Al-'Allaf, *Baghdad Qadima* (Old Baghdad)(Baghdad, 1960), 127, 146. For more contemporary comments on Baghdad against the countryside, see Habib Ishow, "L'Exode rural en Irak et ses Consequences économiques et sociales," *Afrique et Asie* 136(1983): 27–44. For a contemporary Soviet statement of the same issue, see B. Khomelyansky, "Stabi-

lizing the USSR's Rural Population through Development of the Social Infrastructure," *International Labor Review* 121, no. 1 (1982): 89–100.

13. Albertine Jwaideh, "The Saniya Lands of Sultan Abdul Hamid II in Iraq," in *Arabic and Islamic Studies in Honor of Hamilton A. R. Gibb,* ed. George Makdisi (Cambridge, Mass.: Dept. of Near East Languages and Literatures, 1965), 326–7.

14. Writings on the contribution of Russian Jews to Russia have a similar slant, for example, Lionel Kochan, ed. *The Jews in Soviet Russia since 1917* (New York: Oxford Univ. Press, 1978).

15. Khadduri, "Social Background," 38, 68; *Encyclopaedia Judaica* (Jerusalem: Keter Publishing House, 1971), 4: 89–90; Nissim Rejwan, *The Jews of Iraq* (Boulder, Colo.: Westview Press, 1985), 220.

16. Atiyya, *Iraq,* 62ff.

17. Khadduri, "Social Background," 70.

18. If few Western writers emphasize the political role of religious officials in Russia or Iraq, this is not the case when it comes to Latin America. In Latin America, Peru is an example of a Russian Road regime. The liberation theologian of Peru, Gustavo Gutiérrez, plays the role that Sadr did in Iraq. For a study of him from the American Enterprise Institute in Washington, see Michael Novak, *Liberation South, Liberation North* (Washington, D.C.: AEI, 1981), *im. passim.* An exception from the typical scholarship on Iraq is Chibli Mallat, "Aux Origines de la guerre Iran-Irak: L'Axe Najaf-Teheran," *Les Cahiers de l'Orient* 3 (1986): 119–36, esp. 134, stressing the internal genesis of Iraq launching the war as a result of the intensifying Ba'thi-Shi'i quarrel over power in Iraq. I believe this view is correct.

19. Walid Yusif Qaysi, "Social Background of Modern Iraqi Politics" (Ph.D. diss., Johns Hopkins Univ., 1970), 179. On the rise of the Barzan Clan in Kurdistan, see Robert W. Olson, *The Emergence of Kurdish Nationalism: The Shaykh Sa'id Rebellion, 1880–1925* (Austin: Univ. of Texas Press, 1989).

20. Marion Farouk Sluglett and Peter Sluglett, "Labor and National Liberation: The Trade Union Movement in Iraq, 1920–1958," *Arab Studies Quarterly* 5 (1983): 148.

21. Elie Kedourie, "The Kingdom of Iraq: A Retrospect," in *The Chatham House Version and Other Middle-Eastern Studies* (New York: Frederick A. Praeger, 1970), 269, emphasizes this as the point of systematic change, that is, the end of the "free man," but this is too late.

22. Mohammad Tarbush, *The Role of the Military in Politics: A Case Study of Iraq to 1941* (London: KPI, 1982), 102ff.

23. Edmund Ghareeb, *The Kurdish Question in Iraq* (Syracuse, N.Y.: Syracuse, N.Y. Univ. Press, 1981), 33, notes that Barzani, after colliding with later liberal regimes, spent many years in exile, returning in 1958, another autocratic phase.

24. Tarbush, *Role of the Military,* 146–49. Sidqi received numerous warnings of danger to him especially from women friends. In light of the rise of poor women in autocratic phases in Russian history, this point might be useful for women's history, a field still almost nonexistent for Iraq; Longrigg, *Iraq 1900 to 1950,* 248. Sidqi's integration of labor involved the passage of a fundamental trade union law, Labor Law no. 72 of 1936. It is translated and explicated in Riadh Khadhiri, "Labor and Industry in Iraq," (Master's Thesis, Univ. of Mississippi, 1957), chap. 4.

25. Longrigg, *Iraq 1900 to 1950,* 280ff. In 1939, Prince Ghazi died in an automobile accident. A regent, 'Abdul-Ilah, took power.

26. *Ibid.,* chap. 9.

27. Sluglett and Sluglett, "Labor and National Liberation," 154.

28. Longrigg, *Iraq 1900 to 1950,* 354ff.

29. *Ibid.,* 382; Sluglett and Sluglett, "Labor and National Liberation," *passim.*

30. Marr, *Modern History of Iraq,* 141–43; on the role of the countryside, see Abuel-Haj, "Class Conflict," chap. 2.

31. Khadduri, *Republican Iraq, passim.*

32. Majid Khadduri, "Marriage in Islamic Law," *American Journal of Comparative Law* 26, no. 2 (1978): 213–19.

33. This policy was advocated by the Kurdish progressive trend, Kurdish Democratic party; (KDP) although the nationality solution was Stalinist in inspiration, it met with opposition from the dominantly Stalinist Iraqi Communist party (ICP).

34. Khadduri, *Socialist Iraq, passim;* Marion Farouk-Sluglett and Peter Sluglett, *Iraq since 1958* (London: KPI, 1987), chap. 4.

35. Further research—suggested by the study of Stalinist Russia—might show that the Iraqi security men were "new men" and that they had a class envy of the Communists, many of whom had become established in the previous generation or were workers in the modern sector industries.

36. A number of women colloquial preachers on the theme of Fatima appear at this time. Possibly, deeper research would show a parallel to the lower-class Russian women known for their piety, who served the Russian church in autocratic phases; A. J. Abdulrahman, *Iraqi National Bibliography, 1856–1972* (Basra, 1978), 1:312.

37. With the passage of these laws, the rationale for the existence of an independent ICP becomes open to question from the point of view that most of its planks had been taken over by the Ba'th party. An important symbol of the crisis of the Left was the defection of the famous militant 'Aziz Al-Haj. In this period, he experimented briefly with Maoism and then abandoned the ICP to work for the Ba'th party in 1969; see A. R. Kelidar, "Aziz Al-Haj: A Communist Radical," in *The Integration of Modern Iraq,* ed. A. R. Kelidar (London: Croom Helm, 1979), chap. 11.

38. J. Havel and M. K. Hita, "On Some Aspects of the Development of Agriculture in Iraq," *Agricultura Tropica et Subtropica* 10 (1977): 43–53; N. K. Rashid, "Economic and Non-Economic Elements in Allocating Expenditures in Traditional Agriculture," Department of Economics, Discussion Papers, no. 12 (Univ. of Nottingham, 1977); R. Singh and Y. H. Sadiq, "Student Preferences in the Choice of Elective Subjects as Compared to the Country's Needs for Various Specializations in Agriculture," *Mesopotamian Journal of Agriculture* 12, no. 2 (1977): 1–12; "Drug Trade to U.S." *Facts on File* 30, no. 1534 (March 1970): 194, suggests possible illegal production.

39. Efraim Karsh, *The Iran-Iraq War: A Military Analysis* (London: International Institute for Strategic Studies 1987), 15ff.

40. Donald M. Reid, *Lawyers and Politics in the Arab World, 1880–1960* (Minneapolis, Minn.: Bibliotheca Islamica, 1981), 324ff.

41. 'Abd Allah al-Juburi, *Al-Majma' al-'Ilmi al-'Iraqi, nasha'tuhu, a'dawuhu wa a'maluhu* (The Iraqi Academy, Its creation, membership, and achievements)(Baghdad, 1965).

42. A. Karouni, "Brecht in Irak," in *Brecht 80,* ed. Werner Hecht (Berlin: Henschelverlag Kunst und Gesellschaft, 1980), 57–66, shows the Ba'thi use of epic tragedy by such directors as Dr. Lamice El-Amari, whose own essay appears, 43–54.

43. Salma Khadra Al-Jayyusi, *Trends and Movements in Modern Arabic Poetry* (Leiden: Brill, 1977), vol. 1; Roger Allen, *The Arabic Novel—An Historical and Critical Introduction* (Syracuse, N.Y.: Syracuse Univ. Press, 1982), 54, notes the Iraqi novel, *Al-Duktur Ibrahim* by Dhu'l Nun Ayyub, that treats the student who goes to the West but, unlike the son in Turgenev's work, becomes totally corrupted.

44. *Al-Tali'a al-adabiya* 2, no. 1 (1976): 51, 104, 117, including attacks on Professor 'Umar Al-Talib of Mawsil Univ.; 2, no. 3 (1976): 36–39, for an attack on the Palestinian folklore study of Tawfiq Zayyad.

45. The debasement of language in Russian Road regimes seemingly accompanies the rise of the New Class; for Iraq, see Al-Khalil, *Republic of Fear,* 99–104; for Japan, see Peter Dale, *The Myth of Japanese Uniqueness* (New York: St. Martin's Press, 1986).

. 46. Jabbar Audah Allawi, "Television and Film in Iraq: A Socio-Political and Cultural Study, 1946–1980," (Ph.D. diss., Univ. of Michigan, 1983), 130.

47. For the Russian Road in linguistics, diglossia is an important concept; see Salih Altoma, *The Problem of Diglossia in Arabic: A Comparative Study of Classical and Iraqi Arabic* (Cambridge, Mass.: Harvard Univ. Press, 1969). For the communal school intepretation of Iraq mentioned at the outset of this chapter, see Haim Blanc, *Communal Dialects in Baghdad* (Cambridge, Mass.: Harvard Univ. Press, 1954).

48. Allawi, "Television and Film in Iraq," 106. A key function of the media was to fight the spread of rumors; such is the thesis of a book by a senior Iraqi media personality, 'Abd Al-Jabbar Da'ud, (Media practice) *Fi al-mumarasa al-i'lamiya* (Baghdad: Ministry of Information 1976). In other contexts, the spread of rumor is linked to women's struggle.

49. The trend in modern Iraqi journalism much resembles that in radio, television, and film. Law no. 155 in December 1967 abolished private newspapers in Iraq and gave rise to the "mobilization press." The prestige of journalism declined sharply; journalists became anonymous. see William Rugh, *The Arab Press: News Media and Political Process in the Arab World* (Syracuse, N.Y.: Syracuse Univ. Press, 1979), *passim*.

50. Pierre Martin, "Le clergé chiite en Irak hier et aujourd'hui," *Maghreb Machrek* 115–118 (1987): 29–52. A more detailed study could take up the somewhat similar pantheist philosophical notions of Ma'rifa among the Shi'a of Iraq and Iran and Sobernost among the Orthodox of Russia.

51. Samuel N. Kramer, *History Begins at Sumer* (London: Thames and Hudson, 1958); al-Duri, *Rise of Historical Writing;* 'Imad 'Abd Al-Salam Ra'uf, *Al-Ta'rikh wa al-mu'arrikhun al-'Iraqiyyun fi 'asr al-'Uthmani* (History and Iraqi historians in the Ottoman period)(Baghdad: Dar Al-Wasit lil-Dirasat wa-al-Nashr wa-al-Tawzi,' 1983) esp. 184–301, comments on several hundred writers of history. And although not researched, accounts of the traditional Iraqi cultural salons, the *majalis,* suggest to me a more urban and class-bound cultural life than the poetry *diwans* or majalis of the tribes of Kuwait or Jordan. A study of recent salon life in Baghdad is Ibrahim Al-Samarra'i, *Majalis Baghdad* (Baghdad: al-Maktabah al-'Alamiyah, 1985). This work builds on the older, better-known compilation of Ibrahim Al-Darubi, *Al-Baghdadiyun-akhbaruhum wa majalisuhum* (Baghdad, 1958), that dealt with the salons of the Ottoman period. A book on the salon tradition in Russia is N. L. Brodskogo, *Literaturnye Salony i Kruski* (New York: G. Olms, 1984). For "youthful wishes" from the 1930s that Iraq, that is, the Baghdadis, could play the role of a "Piedmont" or a "Prussia," see Reeva Simon, "The Teaching of History in Iraq Before the Rashid Ali Coup of 1941," *Middle East Studies* 22 (1986): 39, 45. Simon also showed that by 1943 the Iraqis no longer looked to foreign models; two Iraqi historical studies of modern Italy and its unification dating from the 1930s to 1940s are cited in Abdul Rahman, *Iraqi National Bibliography,* 2: 381.

52. Simon, "Teaching of History," 37–51, notes that the early British curriculum was modeled on the late Ottoman one with its emphasis on language and national history, that the British "lost control" of education to the Pan-Arabism represented by Sati' Al-Husri, and that Husri himself had "shifted pedagogical gears" to fit the liberal 1920s in Iraq. To fit the liberal age in Iraq, Husri dropped his earlier concern for minorities and for language differences and became concerned with a more homogeneous Arab national culture. History, he argued, required a sculptor to mold the facts to fit nationalism. Some evidence for the application of this policy can be gleaned from the changing emphases in textbooks in different phases. In the liberal phase, the heroes in the textbooks were fewer and more culturally diverse, that is, not just military heroes. The reverse was true in autocratic phases such as the Bakr Sidqi period in 1936. In liberal phases, Iraqi history took precedence over Arab and foreign history. By 1943, even the later Ottoman reformers Midhat Pasha and Nadhim Pasha were included. The reverse was true in autocratic phases.

53. 'Abbas al-'Azzawi, *Ta'rikh al-'Iraq bayna al-ihtilalayn* (The History of Iraq between

two occupations, 1257 and 1917)(Baghdad: Matba'at Baghdad, 1935–56), 8 vols.; a second monumental work was 'Abd Al-Razzaq Hasani, *Ta'rikh al-wizarat al-'Iraqiya* (History of the cabinets of Iraq)(Beirut, 1965–67), 6 vols. in 4; a third would be the major scholarly production on the Arabs before Islam, another long-term achievement, Jawad 'Ali, *Al-Mufassal fi ta'rikh al-'Arab qabla al-Islam* Beirut: Dar al-'Ilm lil-Malayin, (1968), 10 vols.

54. Salih Al-'Ali, *Al-Tanzimat al-ijtima'iya wa al-iqtisadiya fi al-Basra fi al-qarn al-awwil al-Hijri* (Social and economic organizations in Basra in the first Islamic century)(Beirut: Dar Al-Tali'ah lil-tiba'ah wa-al-Nashr, 1969). 2d. ed.

55. Husayn, *Suqut al-nizam*. Elite political histories in Iraq have been written for a long time. One work of the later nineteenth century is Ibrahim Haydari's *'Unwan al-majd fi bayan ahwal Baghdad wa al-Basra wa al-Najd* (On Baghdad, Basra, and Najd)(Baghdad: Dar Manshurat al-Basri, 1962). Haydari identifies history with the events in the lives of prominent individuals and families, which he presented.

56. Karl Jahn, "Universalgeschichte im islamischen Raum," in *Mensch und Weltgeschichte,* ed. A. Randa (Salzburg: forschungs gespräche des Internationalen forschungcentrums für grundfragen der wissenschaften Salzburg # 7, 1969), 143–70, makes one aware that modern genres of historical writing have a long prehistory in Islamic culture. A number of writers, most notably Maxime Rodinson, have looked at the Middle East as generally having a "premodern" modernity. For example, Rodinson found capitalism to be a part of classical Islamic culture. See also my *Islamic Roots of Capitalism: Egypt 1760–1840* (Austin: Univ. of Texas Press, 1979).

57. Al-Wardi and Baali, *Ibn. Khaldun;* see also Al-Wardi, *Dirasah fi tabi'a al-mujtama' al-'Iraqi* (On the nature of Iraqi society)(Baghdad: Matba'at al-'Ani, 1966); Al-Wardi's major work is his *Lamahat ijtima'iyah min ta'rikh al-'Iraq al-hadith* (Social features of modern Iraqi history)(Baghdad, Matba'at al-irshad, 1969-), 6 vols.

58. Figures such as Al-Duri, 'Umar, and today Nizar Al-Hadithi have all used medieval history to attack the leftist critics of their own day. For them, the Zanj were not revolutionaries, and the 'Abbasids were not despots. The 'Abbasid empire was Arab; it owed nothing to "foreign" influence. 'Umar's views are collected in his *Al-Ta'rikh al-Islami wa fikr al-qarn al-'ishrin* (Islamic history and twentieth-century thought)(Beirut: Mu'assasat al-Matbu'at al-'Arabiya, 1980) See also his recent *Al-Judhur al-ta'rikhiya li'l-wizara al-'Abbassiya* (Historical roots of the 'Abbassid office of prime minister)(Baghdad, 1986). For Nizar 'Abd Al-Latif Al-Hadithi, see *Al-Umma wa al-dawlah fi siyasat al-Nabi wa al-Rashidin* (Nation and state in the policy of the Prophet Muhammad and the rightly guided caliphs) (Baghdad: N.A.L. Al-Hadithi, 1987). For a discussion of Al-Duri and Shu'ubiya, see Al-Khalil, *Republic of Fear.* 217. Although Pokrovsky, the Soviet historian, maintained in a somewhat similar spirit that the Pugachev Revolt was not revolutionary, it remains to be worked out if the Zanj can be an Iraqi parallel.

59. Faysal Samir also wrote a major book on the Zanj, *Thawrat al-Zanj* (Baghdad: Dar al-Qari, 1954, 1971).

60. Saddam Husayn, *Hawla kitabat al-ta'rikh* (Baghdad: Al-Maktaba Al-Wataniya 1979), 109ff. Nuri al-Qaysi, a university administrator and party official, wrote a similar book about literature, *Al-Adib wa al-iltizam* (The writer and commitment)(Baghdad, 1979).

61. Tariq Al-Janabi, "Islamic Archeology in Iraq. Recent Excavations at Samarra'," *World Archeology* 14, no. 3 (1982): 305–27. For the wider political economy of Mesopotamian archeology, see Vincenzo Strika, "Rívalità e ricércà archeòlogiche europà in Mesopotamia," *Islam, stòria e civiltà* 2 (1983): 166–77.

62. From interviews in Baghdad 1980, 1982.

63. Besides Toynbee, the other figure of general interest to the journal was Ibn Khaldun, a historian who also wrote universal history. All the trends in the New Class vie to control the interpretation of Ibn Khaldun. Although most of the familiar commentaries, for example,

those by 'Ali al-Wardi and Muhsin Mahdi, are liberal, there is the Islamically oriented historian from Mawsil, 'Imad Ad-din Khalil. Khalil linked Ibn Khaldun to Islam in his *Ibn Khaldun Islamiyan* (Beirut: Al-Maktab Al-Islami 1983), whereas the Socialist, 'Abd Al-Razzaq Muslim Majid, linked him to Marx in his *Dirasat Ibn Khaldun fi daw' al-nazariya al-ishtirakiya* (Study of Ibn Khaldun in the light of socialist theory)(Baghdad: Ministry of Information, 1976). A brief survey of studies in Arabic on Ibn Khaldun suggests that for writers in Russian Road and Tribal Road regimes, the theory of Ibn Khaldun explains the failure of history to progress and the inevitability of phases and cycles. For writers in the Italian Road, such as the Egyptian students of Ibn Khaldun, the appeal is more of Ibn Khaldun as the father of a more positivist, evolutionary sociology.

64. As a scholar, Al-Najjar is known for *Al-Ta'rikh al-siyasi li-Imara 'Arabistan al-'Arabiyah, 1897–1925* (The political history of the emirate of Arab Arabistan 1897–1925)(Cairo: Dar al-Ma'arif, 1971).

65. Khalil, "Proposals in Teaching and Frameworks of history," *Adab al-Rafidayn* 1 (1971): 165–93; More recently, Khalil wrote, *Hawla i'adat kitabat al-tarikh al-Islami* (How to construe Islamic history texts)(Al-Dawhah: Dar al-Thaqafah, 1986).

66. Yvonne Yazbeck Haddad, *Contemporary Islam and the Challenge of History* (Albany, N.Y.: SUNY Press, 1982), 188ff. Khalil's text here was drawn from his *Al-Tafsir Al-Islami li-l-ta'rikh* (Islamic commentary on history)(Baghdad: Maktabat Dar Al-Anwar, 1978). It takes up a number of themes, among them a detailed analysis and critique of Toynbee. In *'Imad Ad-Din Zankhi* (Beirut: Al-Dar al-'ilmiya, 1971), Khalil chose a topic he hoped would be an inspirational part of Muslim history, but he felt constrained by the methodology permitted the author of an masters thesis in Baghdad University. "Scientific History" had no place for aesthetics, literature or poetry. This worldview carried over into his judgment of writers in the field of his study. He liked Étienne's Dény's approach to Nasir ad-Din more than that of Bernard Lewis or H. A. R. Gibb, who he said were specialized, meaning they studied their subject without any interaction with it. Somewhat ahead of his times, Khalil introduced feminist history in his treatment of Zankhi's wife. In another essay, Khalil called for a revival of theater as the finest way to express what life is. In this essay, he commented on a number of modernist critics and noted his personal problems with religious censorship, *Fi naqd al-Islami al-mu'asir* (Contemporary Islam Criticism)(Beirut: Al-Mu'assas et al-Risala, 1972), 177ff.

67. Sousa, *Mufassal al'Arab wa al-Yahud.*

68. *Majalla Majma' al-Lughah al-Suryaniya* 2 (1976): 445–467.

69. *Ibid.* 3 (1977): 406 ff. Sebastian Brock, a European expert on Syriac, is quoted to the effect that the reason that Syriac became a literary language was largely because it was chosen as the vehicle for the spread of Christianity in the East. He did not relish its use as a language today because there would certainly be dissension among modern users.

70. Ahmad Suhayl 'Ulaybi, *Thawrat al-Zanj* (Revolution of the Zanj)(Beirut; 1961); Nabih Faris, "Development in Arab Historiography as Reflected in the Struggle Between 'Ali and Mu'awiya," in *Historians of the Middle East,* ed. Bernard Lewis and P. M. Holt (London: Oxford Univ. Press, 1962), 435–41; the Soviets, too, confronted confessional views of Russian history in the émigré scholarship after 1917.

71. Al-Khafaji, *Al-Dawla wa al-tatawwur.*

72. Al-'Azzawi's writings include studies of Iraqi coinage, Iraqi taxation, Iraqi astronomy, Iraqi historians of the medieval period, Iraqi tribes, and theologians of Baghdad. A summary of the views of Al-Duri can be drawn from his *Al-Takwin al-ta'rikhi li-l-umma al-'Arabiya* (Historical formation of the Arab nation) 3d ed. (Beirut: Al-Markaz, 1986).

4. The "Italian Road" in Italy: The Risorgimento to the Present, 1870–1990

1. Other possible examples, such as Egypt, Brazil, Tanzania, or Germany between Bismarck and Weimar, are simply alluded to. The interested reader could refer to Maridi

Nahas, "Hegemonic Constraints and State Autonomy: A Comparative Analysis of Development in Nineteenth Century Egypt, Spain and Italy" (Ph.D. diss., Univ. of California at Los Angeles 1985); Xiao-rong Gu, "Resource, Choice and Power: A Comparative Study in Social Change and Ideological Transformation of Germany (1848–1914), Italy (1861–1963) and Egypt (1919–1983)" (Ph.D. diss., Temple Univ., 1988).

2. This point is not intended to be revisionist. Advaita Vedanta philosophy, which is so often taught in the West as the essence of Hindu thought, is really only one school of philosophy and in some ways is the one most pronounced in its other-worldliness. In India, several schools compete. Another point. Schools of philosophy have their sociological contexts in India as elsewhere. As noted in chapter 5 as part of the argument for making India an example of the Italian Road, the great center of the metaphysical tradition in modern times has been the South.

3. Carlo Levi, *Christ Stopped at Eboli* (New York: Farrar, Straus, 1950), 91; More generally, see Salvatore Salomone-Marino, *Customs and Habits of the Sicilian Peasants* (Rutherford: Fairleigh Dickinson Univ. Press, 1981), chap. 19. Paradoxically, ideas about the immediacy of God and about the cyclical nature of time are well established both in Italian folklore and among the Coptic Christian peasants of Upper Egypt. Here it is helpful to recall that Egypt, too, is an Italian Road state. A Sicilian, who called himself the Grand Copth founded the "Egyptian Order" of the Masonic Lodge. He was Giusèppe Bàlsamo, called Cagliostro, born in Palermo in 1743. To pursue the Egypt-Italy parallel, it is helpful to note that the bulk of the Coptic peasantry is found in Upper Egypt, the region that is the South of Egypt; Samuel Sharpe, *Egyptian Mythology and Egyptian Christianity with Their Influence on the Opinions of Modern Christendom* (London: Carter, 1896), 106ff.

4. Historical affinity among states following the same historical road may in some instances be a feature of the road. For example, in democracies, this is probably the case. Citizens in democracies tend to believe that politicians should make the world safe for democracy. In Italian Road regimes, mutual awareness is a conspicuous fact, but it does not seem to extend beyond that. For the awareness of the Indian national movement of the experiences of its Italian counterpart, see Gita Srivastava, *Mazzini and His Impact on the Indian National Movement* (Allahabad: Chugh Publications, 1982), 188–89, 262; Giusèppe Flòra, "Stùdi Mazziniani in India a Propòsito di un Recènte Volume," *Rasségna Stòrica del Risorgiménto* 70 (1983): 40–45; also his "Surendra Nath Banerjea e Mazzini," ibid. 69 (1982): 297–313. For a recent study published in India, see Ivan Scott, *The Rise of The Italian State: A Study of Italian Politics During the Period of Unification* (Meerut: Sadhna Prakashan, 1980). For Mexico, the connections are more indirect; Arnold Blumberg, "The Italian Diplomacy of the Mexican Empire, 1864–1867," *Hispanic American History Review* 51 (1971): 497–501. On the figure of Porfirio Díaz, a late nineteenth-century ruler of Mexico who practiced a transformist style of politics, there is an Italian edition of his diary translated by L. Bacchi Wilcock and published in 1967; see also Italò Calvino, *Introduzíone a Ocampo, Silvina and Porfiria* (Turin, 1973). Mexican writings include works on Gramsci and a monograph on Italian anthropology; Juan Comas, *La Antropología Italiana a través del Istituto Italiano di Antropología* (Mexico City: Unam, 1978). The figure M. N. Roy played a role as a critic of Stalinist-type Bolshevism in India and Mexico reminiscent of that of Gramsci in Italy. A comparative study of these two figures—Roy and Gramsci—is certainly in order. Finally, one might note that Beníto Mussolini was named for the great Mexican patriot Beníto Juarez, who had fought the Emperor Maxmilian; Luigi Barzini, *The Italians* (New York: Atheneum, 1979), 134. Maxmilian had once been a threat to Italian sovereignty as well.

5. Karl Marx, "Two-Mountain-Crowned Peninsulas," in Karl Marx and Friedrich Engels, *The First Indian War of Independence, 1857–1859* (Moscow: Foreign Languages Publishing House 1959), 14, cited by Victor Kiernan, "Gramsci and the Other Continents," *New Edinburgh Review* 27 (1975): 19–24, esp. 19. By implication, this essay disputes the utility of the more standard uses of Gramsci found in Italy today. For example, Umberto Cerroni,

"Italian Communism's Historic Compromise," *Marxist Perspectives* 1, no. 1 (1978): 126–44, argues that Gramsci has to be reinterpreted in light of fundamental changes in the contemporary world, by which he means the world as it appears at the beginning of the cold war, the world of powerful modern states, so powerful that the age of revolution has come to an end. A rationale for Cerroni's adoption of a Eurocommunist position can certainly be found. The economic growth of Italy in that generation was astonishing. In 1990, Italy's gross national product (GNP) was approximately equal to that of Great Britains; Paul Ginsborg, *A History of Contemporary Italy: Society and Politics, 1943–1988* (New York: Penguin Books, 1990), 1. But is growth development? Does growth of a GNP automatically mean change of the sort that would bring an end to the Southern Question? Ginsborg for one is not a partisan of the Eurocommunist theory of historical rupture. He balances what he writes about change with a strong emphasis on the historical continuity of Italy (1–2). For Cerroni, however, and for many other writers as well, an important part of the "modernization"—hence, continuing utility—of Gramsci involves an abandonment of the idea of the Southern Question. For example, a number of influential postwar Italian sociologists came to perceive the South as a development problem, as a problem of lag, of unequal opportunity as opposed to a question of retarded development to follow Gramsci's traditional formulation; see a representation of their views in a special issue, Paul Piccone, ed., "The 'Southern Question' in Italian Sociology," *International Journal of Sociology* 4, no. 2–3 (1974): 3–203. Although the function of this collection is to show the transition in Italian thought, one nonetheless finds material supportive of the idea of a Southern Question both for the past and for the present. For example, one writer denied the existence of the inequality of regions in Italy (42–43) at the time of the Risorgimento, thus making the Southern Question specifically a part of modern history à la Gramsci; another writer noted the benefit of the fascist period to the South (47); still others find elements in Gramsci's thought of a spontaneist and idealist sort, which they agree are not part of the communist thought of their period (122–23). What is interesting about this well-known collection is that few of the writers—even in presenting such points—argue that the Southern Question is resolved or on the way to being resolved even though they reject Gramsci. As another article shows, the problem of the unequal relations of the North and South, even in a bourgeois democracy such as the United States, is not one that goes away easily even though the regime survives primarily from the exploitation of racial difference more than regional difference; Saul Engelbourg and Gustav Schlachter, "Two 'Souths': The United States and Italy since the 1860's," *Journal of European Economic History* 15, no. 3 (1986): 563–89; the approach adopted here of seeing the Southern Question as spreading North to the slums of northern cities does not appear to be much in favor outside of demographic studies. Writers seem to have forgotten the importance of the southern agricultural worker in the North as early as the 1920s; even then the Southern Question had a northern component. In 1980s, Rome as the meeting point of the South and the North continued to draw southern unskilled workers to its rim and to lose progressively its skilled and professional work force to better paying jobs farther north; Robert C. Fried, *Planning the Eternal City: Roman Politics and Planning since World War Two* (New Haven, Conn.: Yale Univ. Press, 1973), 72–87; Anne-Marie Serond-Babonaux, *De l'Urbs à la ville: Rome croissance d'une capitale* (Aix-en-Provence:EDisud, 1980), 226–52; Ginsborg, *History of Contemporary Italy*, 353, stated that in 1973 migration out of Italy was equaled by reverse migration to Italy; this suggests that the Southern Question was not being displaced by people's departure. A second body of writing that one could use to support the idea that the Southern Question continues to exist is sociological writing on the continuing flourishing of popular religion in contemporary Italy. Because most of this is found in the South, it provides evidence of a kind of sociological continuity with the pre-1948 past that cannot be easily be reconciled with the standard postulates of an economic "miracle." For an overview, see Carlo Prandi, "Religion et classes subalternes en Italie-Trente années de recherches Italiennes," *Archives de Sciences Sociales des Religions* 43, no. 1 (1977): 93–139. A third body of writing that one could use to support the idea that the

Southern Question continues to exist is political writing. Several writers problematize the continuing and distinctive role of southerners in leftist politics; see Grant Amyot: *The Italian Communist Party: The Crisis of the Popular Front Strategy* (New York: St. Martin's Press, 1981), chaps. 9–10; David Forgacs's reintegration of Italian fascism back into Italian social history and out of "the totalitarian, exceptionalist" paradigm is also important. It diminishes the need for the kind of historical rupture that writers such as Cerroni want to invoke for the postwar period; David Forgacs, ed. *Rethinking Italian Fascism* (London: Lawrence and Wishart, 1986). Some of the most telling evidence that the Southern Questions continue to exist comes from local economists writing in such journals as *Review of the Economic Conditions in Italy*. See, for example, Salvatore Vinci and Antonio Cardone, "Fostering Employment in Southern Italy: The Effectiveness of Recent Policies," *RECI* 44, no. 1 (1990): 27–53; Robert Cagliozzi," A Regional or a National Industrial Policy," *RECI* 36, no. 1 (1982): 93–120; Adriano Giannola, "The Industrialization, Dualism, and Economic Dependence of the Mezzogiórno in the 1970's," *RECI* 36, (1982): 67–92; Marcello Poscetti, "Highlights of the 24th Census Report: Phenomena and Trends in Italy in 1990" *RECI* 45 (1991): 81–92; Associazióne per lo Sviluppo dell'indùstria Nel Mezzogiórno, "Recent Economic Trends in the Mezzogiórno," *RECI* 37, (1983): 127–140, among other articles, a number of which are by SVIMEZ, the Association of Southern Industrialists, or by its director, Salvatore Cafiero.

6. C. Scott Littleton, *The New Comparative Mythology: An Anthropological Assessment of the Theories of George Dumezil* (Berkeley: Univ. of California Press, 1966), 17; if it were not for the pervasiveness of orientalism, some writer would surely have noted the "non-Semitic" features of Egypt and, therefore, the possibility of a "Dumezil application" to be found in the castelike system, the godhead, and the female god structure of Fatima and Mary in that country. Egypt is singled out for its feminine components in Jane Smith and Yvonne Haddad, *The Islamic Understanding of Death and Resurrection* (Albany: State Univ. of New York Press, 1981), 158, 180ff.

7. The following draws heavily from Martin Clark, *Modern Italy 1871–1982* (London: Longman, 1984); John A. Davis, ed., *Gramsci and Italy's Passive Revolution* (London: Croom Helm, 1979).

8. The commentary literature on the subject of the factory councils is quite diverse. Some, following the Turino capitalist Olivetti, note how they failed in Germany and Russia and how Gramsci conceived this idea with inadequate knowledge of the Russian Soviets or of syndicalism. R. Bellamy and D. Schecter, *Gramsci and the Italian State* (Manchester: Manchester Univ. Press, 1993). Others find the councils to be integral to Gramsci's mature thought; Franklin Adler, "Factory Councils, Gramsci and the Industrialists," *Telos* 31 (Spring 1977): 67–90; Enzo Rutigliano, "The Ideology of Labor and Capitalist Rationality in Gramsci," ibid., 91–99; Mario Carceres, "Les Fonctions Organiques des conseils d'usine selon la conception gramscienne et leur homologie avec la théorie du blocque historique," *Recherches Sociologiques* 17 (1986): 247–64.

9. Jon S. Cohen, "Fascism and Agriculture in Italy: Policies and Consequences," *Economic History Review* 32, no. 2 (1979): 70–87, especially 70. An exceptional book for comparative studies of Italy despite its diffusionist bias is Maurice F. Neufeld, *Italy, School for Awakening Countries: The Italian Labor Movement in Its Political, Social, and Economic Setting from 1800–1960* (Ithaca, N.Y.: Cornell Univ. Press, 1961).

10. To correct the liberal capitalist slant in the historiography, what is needed is a history of noncapitalism and nonliberalism in modern Italy.

11. Daniel A. Binchy, *Church and State in Fascist Italy* (London: Oxford Univ. Press, 1941); note the degree to which the church as "traditional intellectual" in Gramsci's model can seize the chance to claim a larger part of the hegemony.

12. Richard Webster, *The Cross and the Fasces—Christian Democracy and Fascism in Italy* (Stanford, Calif.: Stanford Univ. Press, 1960), 145.

13. In chapters 5 and 6, I show that in the Cárdenas period, the archbishop of Mexico

City also adopted the tack of mysticism and that leading spiritual figures during Nehru's India did as well. These construction of piety are introduced as parallels to the spirituality of the popes of fascist Italy.

14. John Molony, *The Emergence of Political Catholicism in Italy: Partito Populare 1919–1926* (Totowa: Croom Helm, 1971), 193, 199.

15. S. Agoes, "The Road to Charity Leads to the Picket Lines: The Neo-Thomist Revival and the Italian Catholic Labor Movement," *International Review of Social History* 18, no. 1 (1973): 28–50.

16. Ellen M. Bussey, *The Flight from Rural Poverty: How Nations Cope* (Lexington, KY.: Lexington Books, 1973), 47ff.

17. John Merriman, *Comparative Law: Western European and Latin American Legal Systems* (Indianapolis, Ind.: Bobbs Merrill, 1978), 587ff.; *Encyclopedia Judaica* (Jerusalem: Keter Publishing House, 1971), 9:1134ff.

18. P. A. Allum, *Politics and Society in Post-War Naples* (Cambridge: Cambridge Univ. Press, 1973), 77ff.

19. A writer, who gives considerable detail about his home and family, happens also to be a leading contemporary Communist from South India; see E. M. S. Namboodiripad, *How I Became a Communist* (Trivandrum: Chinta Publishers, 1976).

20. Edward C. Banfield, *The Moral Basis of a Backward Society* (New York: Free Press, 1963).

21. Donald Pitkin, "Marital Property Considerations among Peasants: An Italian Example," *Anthropological Quarterly* 33 (1960): 33–39.

22. Walter Adamson, *Hegemony and Revolution, A Study of Antonio Gramsci's Political and Cultural Theory* (Berkeley: Univ. of California Press, 1980), chap. 3.

23. Amyot, *Italian Communist Party*, 87ff.

24. Maria Antonietta Macciocchi, *Letters from Inside the Italian Communist Party to Louis Althusser* (London: New Left Books, 1973), 27.

25. A major book by a leading northern radical is Antonio Negri, *Marx Beyond Marx—Lessons on the Grundrisse* (South Hadley: Bergin and Garvey, 1984), see esp. the introduction. Despite their many original ideas, Negri and those in his movement do not challenge the regional basis of Italian hegemony.

26. Sidney Tarrow, *Peasant Communism in Southern Italy* (New Haven, Conn.: Yale Univ. Press, 1967), 205.

27. Annarita Buttafuoco, "Italy: The Feminist Challenge," in *The Politics of Eurocommunism: Socialism in Transition*, ed. Carl Boggs and David Plotke (Boston: South End Press, 1980), 197–220.

28. Maria Rosa Cutrufelli, *Des Siciliennes* (Paris: Des Femmes, 1977), 35–38, compares the situation in southern Italy to the situation in Rhodesia, a country where the men are exported to the work zone not so much as an economic strategy but as a political arrangement. Maria Brandon-Albini, *Midi vivant peuple et culture en Italie du Sud* (Paris: Presses Universitaires de France, 1963), takes a Southern Question approach. The developmentalist view appears in Marilyn Yanick Gaetani, *Social Literature on the Southern Italian Problem* (Naples: Faculty of Maritime Economics, 1981).

29. Giacomo Devoto, *The Language of Italy* (Chicago: Univ. of Chicago Press, 1978), 278ff.

30. Bruno Migliorini, *The Italian Language* (London: Faber and Faber, 1984), 409.

31. Giuseppe Cocchiara, *The History of Folklore in Europe* (Philadelphia: Institute for the Study of Human Issues, 1981), 332ff.

32. Ibid., 342.

33. Ibid., 356, 612. Pitre noted the superiority of women in narrative reworkings. Cocchiara generalized the point, stating that most folklore collectors have noted the superiority of

women in terms of memory and of the completeness of renditions. Given that most work on folklore was in the South, this insight by these scholars could be used to substantiate claims made above about the status of women in the South. Claimed to be totally oppressed in the Amoralist Model, they, in fact, exert a profound influence in the culture.

34. Ibid., 519.

35. George Saunders, "Contemporary Italian Cultural Anthropology," *Annual Review of Anthropology* 13 (1984): 447–56.

36. Philip V. Cannistraro, "The Organization of Totalitarian Culture: Culture Policy and the Mass Media in Fascist Italy, 1922–1945" (Ph.D. diss., New York Univ., 1971). A well-known novel is Danilo Dolci, *The Man Who Plays Alone* (New York: Pantheon Books, 1968), 65–86, where the gangster emerges as simply another human being.

37. Philip V. Cannistraro, *Historical Dictionary of Fascist Italy* (Westport, Conn.: Greenwood Press, 1982).

38. *Oxford Classical Dictionary* (Oxford: Oxford Univ. Press, 1949), 808–9.

39. M. V. Taylor, "The Society for the Promotion of Roman Studies, 1910–1960," *Journal of Roman Studies* 50 (1960): 129–34.

40. Marino Berengo, "Italian Historical Scholarship since the Fascist Era," *Daedalus* 100 (1971): 469–84.

41. Edward R. Tannenbaum, "Gioacchino Volpe," in *Historians of Modern Europe,* ed. Hans A. Schmitt (Baton Rouge: Louisiana Univ. Press, 1971), 315–38; another southern colleague on the faculty of Rome, who was a fascist historian, was Pietro Fedele.

42. A. H. McDonald, "Fifty Years of Republican History," *Journal of Roman Studies* 50 (1960): 135–48.

43. M. I. Finley, "The Historical Tradition: The Contribution of Arnaldo Momigliano," in *The Use and Abuse of History,* ed. M. I. Finley (New York: Viking Press, 1971), chap. 4.

44. Wallace K. Ferguson, *The Renaissance in Historical Thought* (Boston: Houghton Mifflin, 1948 [1981]), 314ff. The category of renaissance (al-Nahda) bedevils not only Italian thought but Arab as well. The Arabs, like the Italians, are or were bearers at one point of a supposedly universal culture. The efforts of Arab scholars to place the Greek tradition in a local national context are as controversial in the West as are those of the Italians. One possibility is that the Western attempt to retain a hold on "classical ages," "renaissances," or "enlightenments" could come to an end now that the futility of Eurocentrism has been demonstrated; see Martin Bernal, *Black Athena: The Afroasiatic Roots of Classical Civilization* (New Brunswick, N.J.: Rutgers Univ. Press, 1987). Note, however, that an influential Renaissance specialist has argued that the West cannot do without a renaissance, as a pure type, William J. Bouwsma, "The Renaissance and the Drama of Western History," *American Historical Review* 84, no. 1 (1979): 1–15; a recent American book appears to be leaning in the opposite direction. The author credits the Italian liberal tradition with doing the outstanding scholarship on figures such as Pico Della Mirandola; William G. Craven, *Giovanni Pico Della Mirandola, Symbol of His Age: Modern Interpretations of a Renaissance Philosopher* (Geneva: Librairie Droz, 1981), 5. He notes the importance of the work of Eugenio Garin, a professor at the University of Florence, that has appeared from the 1930s. Garin situates Pico in the intellectual context of his time, reversing the universalizing trend of Jacob Burckhardt and of others who want to take the Renaissance as a pure type.

45. Arnaldo Momigliano, *Essays in Ancient and Modern Historiography* (Middletown, Conn.: Wesleyan Univ. Press, 1977), 2ff.

46. And when Salvemini was pushed out of Italy, the southern peasantry lost its brilliant advocate. Salvemini went to Harvard. In exile in the United States, Salvemini made important discoveries about America. He discovered that the Mazzini Society, including luminaries such as Arturo Toscanini and Lionello Venturi, the art historian, were pro-Mussolini. George T. Peck, "Gaetano Salvemini," in Schmitt, *Historians of Modern Europe,* 206–34.

47. Zeffiro Ciuffoletti, "Nello Roselli: A Historian under Fascism," *Journal of Italian History* 1 (1978): 287–314.

48. Charles F. Delzell, "Adolfo Omodeo: Historian of the Religion of Freedom," in Schmitt, *Historians of Modern Europe,* 123–50.

49. G. Eley, "Reading Gramsci in English," *European Historical Quarterly* 14, no. 4 (1984): 441–78, esp. 454–55.

50. This summary appears in B. Sheik Ali, *History: Its Theory and Method* (Madras: Macmillan, 1978), 350 ff.

51. A. Momigliano, "Historicism in Contemporary Thought," in *Studies in Historiography,* ed. by A. Momigliano (London: Weidenfeld and Nicolson, 1966), 221–38.

52. Berengo, *Italian Historical Scholarship,* 477.

53. Sergio Bertelli, "Local History in Italy," *Local Historian* 11, no. 5 (Feb. 1975): 251–61; for a critical note on the field, see Gino Pasolini, *Guida allo stùdio della stòria* (Bologna, 1970), 4–44.

54. Berengo, *Italian Historical Scholarship,* 474ff.; John Cammett, "Two Recent Polemics on the Character of the Italian Risorgimento," *Science and Society* 27 (1963): 433–57. The rather positivist approach to the history of the CP and its history is brought out in Franco Andreucci and Malcolm Sylvers, "The Italian Communists Write Their History," *Science and Society* 40 (1976): 28–56. For the orthodox leftist position on the Southern Question, see Renato Zangheri, "Moviménto contadino e Stòria d'Itàlia. Riflessióni sulla storiografia del dopoguèrra," *Stùdi Stòrici Stòrica* 17 (1976): 5–33.

55. Burton R. Clark, *Academic Power in Italy: Bureaucracy and Oligarchy in a National University System* (Chicago: Univ. of Chicago Press, 1977), is a criticism of the autocracy within collegiality.

56. Brunello Vigezzi, ed., *Federico Chabod e la 'nuova historiografia' Italiana 1919–1950* (Milan: Jaca Books, 1984).

5. The "Italian Road" in Asia: India, 1861–1990

1. This chapter is indebted to the work accomplished by the Subaltern Group and, in particular, to Partha Chatterjee, *Nationalist Thought and the Colonial World: A Derivative Discourse* (London: Zed Press, 1986); Sumit Sarkar, *Modern India* (New York: St. Martin's Press, 1989).

2. For the evolution of liberal historiography, see Subodh Kumar Mukhopadhyay, *Evolution of Historiography in Modern India, 1900–1960* (Calcutta: K. P. Bagchi, 1981).

3. Louis Dumont, the exponent of the uniqueness of India because of caste.

4. Partha Chatterjee, "Caste and Subaltern Consciousness," in *Subaltern Studies,* ed. R. Guha (New York: Oxford Univ. Press, 1989), 6:169–209.

5. On Backward Caste legislation, for example, for Bihar, Myron Weiner and Mary Fainsod Katzenstein, with K. V. Narayana Rao, *India's Preferential Policies: Migrants, the Middle Classes, and Ethnic Equality* (Chicago: Univ. of Chicago Press, 1981).

6. Nripendra Kumar Dutt, *Origin and Growth of Caste in India* (Calcutta: K. L. Mukhopadhyay, 1931), 21ff. An important part of the documentation of the Southern Question currently comes from demography and historical demography. The study of migration patterns makes clear that there was a new and permanent outflow in the years following World War I of a mass population from the countryside into the cities of the old South and sometimes into the North, following the deepening of the capitalist development in both regions. Demographic sources also make clear that this was a new phenomenon, that the earlier migrations were cyclical and more temporary; that is, when the South was the "South" migration depended on the perception that there were jobs to be found. With the decline of the Southern Question in the old South around 1935, migration was less cyclical, whereas in West Bengal,

it started to become more cyclical. An example of this new South in formation would be Bihar. See Sugata Bose, "Review of Partha Chatterjee, *Bengal 1920–1947: The Land Question,*" *Indian Economic and Social History Review* 24, no. 3 (1987): 336–39. In 1947–48 in Bombay, one finds the steady growth of a local industrial class, whereas in Calcutta, one finds a lack of growth of the economy, which was, in any case, much more controlled from abroad than was that of Bombay. Bengal was the major source of revenue for the Raj and as a result lacked a class that might have sparked a capitalist development, for example, the peasant proprietor class. Here was debt bondage on the tea plantations and a gradually decreasing expanse of land under irrigation in Bihar and Orissa, whereas in the Punjab from 1925 to 1939 the amount of land irrigated, along with that in Madras, rose as did agricultural productivity. Finally, the Punjab stands out as having the strongest laws against moneylenders; Amiya Kumar Bagchi, "Reflections on Patterns of Regional Growth in India During the Period of British Rule," *Bengal Past and Present* (Jan.-June 1976): 247–89. In another contrast, in the twentieth century in West Bengal, the agriculture steadily grew worse. The soil was less fertile than in the East, the monsoon less predictable, and the crop failures more frequent. On the whole, agriculture was less commercialized than it was in East Bengal; much more was done by sharecroppers and by landless labor, explaining in part the outflow of Bihari laborers to richer areas such as the Punjab. With the coming of independence, the Zamindar class was pushed aside by the moneylenders, who became the new class of rich peasants. Money lending continued as did violent political struggles from the Tebhaga revolts in 1946–47 to the Naxil-bari revolts of 1967; Willem Van Schendel, *Three Deltas: Accumulation and Poverty in Rural Burma, Bengal and South India* (New Delhi: Sage, 1991), chaps. 4–5. For changes in internal migration as opposed to, or in addition to, regional involution, note the decline of the move-ment of the Tamil Nadu work force to the North from as early as 1911 see Lalita Chakravarty, "Emergence of an Industrial Labour Force in a Dual Economy: British India, 1880–1920," *Indian Economic and Social History Review* 15, no. 3 (1979): 267, 323, map B. For evidence of the recent influx into the Punjab of Biharis and others seeking casual work from parts of the new South, see S. Hajra, *Bihar and Punjab—A Study in Regional Economic Disparity* (New Delhi: Economic and Scientific Research Foundation 1973), 268–69; A. K. Gupta, *Sociological Implications of Rural to Rural Migration in Punjab* (Allahabad: Vohra Publishers, 1988), chap. 5; versus the Italian flow to Rome, see Alberto Bonaguidi, "Italy" in *International Handbook on Internal Migration,* ed. Charles Nam (Westport, Conn.: Greenwood Press, 1990), chap. 13; the first and only effort to problematize the political and economic elements of what I am terming Bengali *involution* is Chatterjee, *Bengal 1920–1947,* 1: chaps. 15–16.

7. For the new civil society, see S. P. Sen, ed. *The North and the South in Indian History —Contact and Adjustment* (Calcutta: Institute of Historical Studies, 1976). For an analysis of caste, race, and region, see G. S. Ghurye, *Caste and Race in India* (New York: Alfred A. Knopf, 1932), Chap. 5. For changes in the religious institutions as they became part of the new hegemony, see India. Hindu Religious Endowments Commission. *Report of the Hindu Religious Endowments Commission* (New Delhi: Govt. of India, Ministry of Law, 1962), 211; James Preston, *Mother Worship* (Chapel Hill: Univ. of North Carolina Press, 1982), 212; Robert C. Holmes, "State Support and Regulation of Hindu Temples and Maths," (Master's thesis, Univ. of Pennsylvania, 1967), 107ff., 301. For philosophy, see Basant Kumar Lal, *The Indian Philosophical Congress, 1925–1969* (New Delhi: Dept. of Philosophy, Univ. of Delhi, 1975).

8. For comments on the monotheization/masculinization of the godhead, see Rev. John Morrison, *New Ideas in India During the Nineteenth Century* (Chandigarh: Sameer Prakashan, 1977), 70–74, 90ff., which covers Parsees; for the affinity of Hinduism to Catholicism as opposed to Protestant Christianity, see Rajappan D. Immanuel, *The Influence of Hinduism on Indian Christians* (Jabalpur: Leonard Theological College, 1950), 35.

9. The meaning of caste is, not surprisingly, something profoundly influenced by the worldview of the writer. For positivists, for example, M. N. Srinivas, *Social Change in Modern*

India (Berkeley: Univ. of California Press, 1969), chap. 3; Ravindra S. Khare, *The Untouchable as Himself: Ideology, Identity, and Pragmatism among the Lucknow Chamars* (Cambridge: Cambridge Univ. Press, 1984). Caste is an institution of modern society, a part of the contemporary social structure. Political economists tend to tie it to class, stressing subcastes. For the romantic view, the major text is Louis Dumont, *Homo Hierarchus* (Chicago: Univ. of Chicago Press, 1970). The comparativist tradition is prominently represented by A. M. Hocart, *Caste, A Comparative Study* (London: Methuen, 1950); Gerald D. Berreman, "Caste: The Concept of Caste," *International Encyclopedia of the Social Sciences*, ed. David L. Sills (New York: Macmillan, 1968), 2:333–37; Charles Lindholm, "Theories of Caste among Indian Muslims," *Archives Européenes de Sociologie* 26 (1985): 131–41, ties caste to historical context, making it a social outcome of a political economy composed of an Islamic capitalist sector in a noncapitalist Hindu society. Some evidence exists; Rosalind O'Hanlon, *Caste, Conflict and Ideology: Mahatma Jotirao Phule and Low Caste Protest in Nineteenth Century Western India* (Cambridge: Cambridge Univ. Press, 1985), chap. 11.

10. Caste in the Italian context was studied by Màssimo Paci and Corrado Barberis, *La Società italiana classi e casta néllo sviluppo econòmico* (Milan: F. Angeli, 1976). For an anthropological view of caste in Italy, see Leonard W. Moss and Stephen C. Cappannaci, "Estate and Class in a South Italian Hill Village," *American Anthropologist* 64 (1962): 287–300. The persistence of the caste system is taken by some to be the result of the failure of Italian land reform; see Ángel Palerm, a leading Mexican agrarian specialist, in his *Observaciónes sobre la reforma agraria en Italia* (Washington, D.C.: Unión Panamericana, 1963), 111; Alessandro Pizzorno, "Middle Strata in the Mechanisms of Consensus," in *Contemporary Italian Sociology: A Reader,* ed. Diana Pinto (Cambridge: Cambridge Univ. Press, 1981), 101–23. The purity concern among the Italian aristocracy about their blood lines is shown in their socially exclusive associations, academies, institutes, and centers of heraldry and genealogy. For caste in Mexico, note the caste war surrounding the hennequen production. For an ambivalent statement about caste, its persistence and its link to Castillian heritage, by a modern Mexican writer, see José Vasconcelos, *Obras completas* (Mexico City: Libreros Mexicanos Unidos, 1957), 3: 141ff. (the part on Hindu philosophy) (87–335).

11. Caste exists among both Muslims and Hindus in India. Leonard Sinder, *Caste Instability in Moghul India* (Seoul: International Cultural Research Center, 1964), 175, permits one to extrapolate that the weakening of caste during a period of state-sponsored expansion of internal market relations correlated with a rise in the domestication of women. Later in the Mughal period, the ruling class abandoned capitalism for land rent. This period appears to have led to to a reliance on a Muslim, that is, a somewhat exogenous, merchant sector as opposed to an "indigenous" one as one can extrapolate in a commentary on the breakdown of the state's commitment to a mercantilist political economy; Syed Hasan Askari, "Mughal Naval Weakness and Aurangzeb's Attitude Towards the Traders and Pirates on the Western Coast," *Journal of the Bihar Research Society* 46 (1960): 1–15. For the eighteenth-century attempt to maintain caste in the face of general fragmentation of power, see Hiroshi Fukazawa, "State and Caste System—Jati in the Eighteenth Century Maratha Kingdom," *Hitotsubashi Journal of Economics* 9 (1968): 32–44. For the link between caste abandonment and widow remarriage, see V. P. S. Raghuvanshi, "The Institution and Working of Caste in the Latter Part of the Eighteenth Century from European Sources," in *Kunwaz Mohammad Ashraf: An Indian Scholar and Revolutionary, 1903–1962,* ed. Horst Krüger (Berlin: Akademie-Verlag, 1966), 147–75; especially 169–71. British commercial expansion in North India in the nineteenth century brought about a decline of not only the Muslim but of the Hindu merchants as well; Blair B. King, *Partners in Empire: Dwarkanath Tagore and the Age of Enterprise in Eastern India* (Berkeley: Univ. of California Press, 1976). This set of events broadly replicates the pattern shown in my book about Egypt, another Italian Road state with many similarities to India, *Islamic Roots of Capitalism: Egypt 1760–1840* (Austin: Univ. of Texas Press, 1979). Mattison Mines examined

a contemporary Muslim community in South India and found yet another case of the crumbling of caste in an expanding commercial sector, here the region I am terming the old South, "Social Stratification among the Muslim Tamils in Tamilnadu South India," in *Caste and Social Stratification among the Muslims,* ed. Imtiaz Ahmad (Delhi: Manohar Book Service, 1973), 61–72.

12. T. V. Parasuram, *India's Jewish Heritage* (New Delhi: Sagar Publications, 1982), 116; E. Kulke, *The Parsees in India: A Minority as Agent of Social Change* (Delhi: Vikas Publishing, 1974), 238, 247; E. Kulke, *Die Paren/The Parsees* (Freiburg: Materialen des Arnold-Bergstraesser-Instituts für Kulturwissenschaftliche Forschung, 17, 1968), xix; P. A. Wadia, *Parsis Ere the Shadows Thickens* (Bombay, 1949), 140; "Parsi Bureaucracy" (Letter), *Wall Street Journal,* June 10, 1982, 23w. Relatedly, in 1961, the Grand Lodge of India was founded, breaking two centuries of reliance by Indian Free Masons on those of the British Isles. The two foreign deputations who attended this ceremony were from Israel and from Canada; G. S. Gupta, *Free Masonic Movement in India* (New Delhi, 1981), 3ff.

13. Weiner et al., *India's Preferential Policies;* Marc Galanter, "The Problem of Group Membership," *Journal of the Indian Law Institute* 4 (1962): 333–58.

14. Stephen Cohen, "The Untouchable Soldier: Caste, Politics and the Indian Army," *Journal of Asian Studies* 28 (1969): 453–68, claims that the lower castes do not get into the higher officer corps, that northerners dominate the South, and that the army does not integrate but reproduces the social divisions of the society. The Italian army does the same; Gianfranco Pasquino, "The Italian Army: Some Notes on Recruitment," *Armed Forces and Society* 2 (1976): 205–17. Maintenance of the status-quo is also suggested by the fact that the Indian army is the fourth largest in the world and the Italian, the fifth; both armies are known as well for their surplus of officers and for their poor equipment; P. A. Allum, *Italy: Republic Without Government* (New York: W. W. Norton, 1973), 172ff; June Kronholz, "Indian Army," *Wall Street Journal,* September 16, 1981, 1. For caste in the university, see Rajni Kothari, ed., *Caste in Indian Politics* (New Delhi; Orient Longmans, 1970), 83ff.

15. Maria Mies, *Patriarchy and Accumulation on a World Scale* (London: Zed Books, 1986), 146–62.

16. Sushila Mehta, *Revolution and the Status of Women* (New Delhi: Metropolitan, 1982), 207–12.

17. For the general view, see Elizabeth Pleck, *Domestic Tyranny: The Making of Social Policy Against Family Violence from Colonial Times to the Present* (Oxford: Oxford Univ. Press, 1987); for the statistics quoted, see William Stacey and Anton Shupe, *The Family Secret: Domestic Violence in America* (Boston: Beacon, 1983), 2–3; Maria Mies, *Patriarchy and Accumulation,* 150–52.

18. For India, see the journal *Manushi,* for Italy, Maria Weber, "Italy," in *The Politics of the Second Electorate,* ed. Joni Lovenduski and Jill Hills (London: RKP, 1981), 201. For facts about the incidence of Sati, see Kalikinkar Datta, *Educational and Social Amelioration of Women in Pre-Mutiny India* (Patna: Patna Law Press, 1936). For women's attempts to counteract violence in Italy, see Karen Beckwith," Response to Feminism in the Italian Parliament: Divorce, Abortion, and Sexual Violence Legislation," in *The Women's Movements of the United States and Western Europe,* ed. Mary Fainsod Katzenstein and Carol McClurg Mueller (Philadelphia: Temple Univ. Press, 1987), 153–71; P. Allum, "Political Terrorism in Italy," *Journal of the Association of Teachers of Italian* 25 (1978): 5–18.

19. General statements on prostitution appear in Judith Walkowitz, *Prostitution and Victorian Society: Women, Class, and the State* (Cambridge: Cambridge Univ. Press, 1980); Ruth Rosen, *The Lost Sisterhood: Prostitution in America, 1900–1918* (Baltimore, Md.: Johns Hopkins Univ. Press, 1982), xi–xvii. These are supported by the Africanist, Luise White, "Prostitutes, Reformers, and Historians," *Criminal Justice History* 6 (1985): 201–27.

20. Mary Gibson, *Prostitution and the State in Italy, 1860–1915* (New Brunswick, N.J.:

Rutgers Univ. Press, 1986), 223ff; an equally laissez-faire attitude can be found in well-known descriptions of prostitutes in other Italian Road states. One such example is the character Hamida, who appears in one of the most famous Egyptian novels, *Midaq Alley,* written by Naguib Mahfuz. In this novel, Hamida is not portrayed as corrupt, vicious, or glamorous, but simply as another person. A source useful here for comparisons is Evelyn Accad, "The Prostitute in Arab and North African Fiction," in *The Image of the Prostitute in Modern Literature,* ed. Pierre L. Horn and Mary Beth Pringle (New York: Frederick Ungar, 1984), 63–76, esp. 69–71.

21. Julian Roebuck and Patrick McNamara, "Ficheras and Freelancers: Prostitution in a Mexican Border City," *Archives of Sexual Behaviour* 2 (1973): 231–44.

22. Madhu Kishwar, "Gandhi on Women," *Race and Class* 28 (1986): 43–61.

23. Biswanath Joardar, *Prostitution in Historical and Modern Perspectives* (New Delhi: Inter-India Publications, 1985), 142–43.

24. Judith Walkowitz, "Notes on the History of Victorian Prostitution," *Feminist Studies* 1 (1972): 105–14; idem, "Politics of Prostitution," *Signs* 6 (1980): 123–35; idem, "Jack the Ripper," *Feminist Studies* 8 (1982): 543–74.

25. Maurice Hindus, *The Great Offensive* (New York: Harrison Smith and R. Haas, 1933), chap. 11; on Jewish prostitution, see Edward J. Bristow, *Prostitution and Prejudice: The Jewish Fight Against White Slavery* (New York: Schocken Books, 1983), 86–87; also, *Philadelphia Inquirer,* sec. A, 1, July 20, 1987. On Iraq, see the novel of Jabra Ibrahim Jabra, *Hunters in a Narrow Street* (London: Heinemann, 1960); see the commentary of Accad, "Prostitute," 69–71. For prostitution in Baghdad, see Kurkis 'Awwad, *Jamharat al-maraji' al-Baghdadiyah* (Baghdad: Ar-Rabita Press, 1962), under the headings for "al-Mabaghi." A conservative perception of the prostitute as saviour or unifier of society emerges in Tolstoy's *Redemption* and in Badr Shakir al-Sayyab's poem, "The Blind Prostitute." In Russia, liberal reformism was weaker than in the West; Laurie Bernstein, *Sonia's Daughters: Prostitutes and Their Regulation in Imperial Russia,* (Berkeley: Univ. of California Press, 1995).

26. A critic is Tshibanda Wamuela Bujitu, *Femmes libres, femmes enchaînées—La Prostitution au Zaïre* (Lubumbashi: Editions St. Paul-Afrique, 1979), 39; an example of the "normalness" of prostitution appears in Albanian fiction, Ismail Kadare, *The General of the Dead Army* (New York: Grossman, 1972).

27. Sumit Sarkar, *"Popular" Movement and the "Middle" Class Leadership in Late Colonial India: Perspectives and Problems of a History from Below* (Calcutta: K. P. Bagchi, 1983), 71ff, cites Gramsci's observation that Gandhi had made a "naive theorization of the Passive Revolution, one with religious overtones." Sarkar argued that the specificity of India should be found in the landless labor, a group not found in Europe, a group tending to undermine peasant solidarity; Partha Chatterjee, *Nationalist Thought;* 44ff. In India, the more privileged segments of civil society are the base for the "parliamentary road" to the Indian Council of Ministers, that is, from the North, whereas the "organizational road" brings in politicians from "other" parts of the country and through less-predictable channels; Norman Nicholson, "Integative Strategies of a National Elite: Career Patterns in the Indian Council of Ministers," *Comparative Politics* 7 (1975): 533–57. On the dominance of the single party, one finds that Italian Road states tend to both deny and then embrace the phenomenon; K. S. Bhattacharjee, "The Party System in India—One Party Dominance," *Indian Political Science Review* 9 (1975): 189–202.

28. Anandswarup Gupta, *The Police in British India, 1861–1947* (New Delhi: Concept, 1979), xvii, 4, 21, 42ff. In Act 31 of 1860, the government undertook to disarm the civilian population.

29. Ian Copland, *The British Raj and the Indian Princes* (Bombay: Orient Longman, 1982), esp. chap. 4.

30. B. B. Misra, *The Administrative History of India, 1834–1947* (London: Oxford Univ. Press, 1970), 540–43.

31. David Arnold, *Police Power and Colonial Rule in Madras, 1859–1947* (Oxford: Oxford Univ. Press, 1986), introduces the regional specificity of the South.

32. Sarkar, *Modern India*, 230; see also the idea that Curzon attempted a Russian Road regime in 1899, 57–58.

33. Ibid., 189.

34. O. V. Malyarov, *The Role of the State in the Socio-Economic Structure of India* (New Delhi: Vikas Publishing, 1983), 118, 282. Issues of linkage of the party to the state and of the social background of leading cadre permit further comparisons between India and Italy.

In India as in Italy, the CP has wealthy members tied to the state; Giorgio Amendola, "La 'continuità' déllo stato e i limiti dell' antifascismo italiano," *Quadèrni di Crìtica Marxista* 7 (1974); Perry Anderson, *Considerations on Western Marxism* (London: Verso, 1985); Donald Zagoria, "The Social Bases of Indian Communism," in *Issues in the Future of Asia*, ed. Richard Lowenthal (New York: Frederick A. Praeger, 1969), 120.

35. For the economic composition of the syndicate, the twenty largest "business houses," see Stanley Kochanek, *Business and Politics in India* (Berkeley: Univ. of California Press, 1971), 339 ff.

36. A work that mentions the politics of India, Mexico, and Italy in this period is Alan S. Zuckerman, *The Politics of Faction: Christian Democratic Rule in Italy* (New Haven, Conn.: Yale Univ. Press, 1979), 3, chap. 8. In Mexico and India, a conservative purity party has been in opposition, in Mexico, the El Partido Acción Nacional (PAN) party, and in India, the Rashtriya Swayam Sevak Sangh (RSS); G. S. Bhargava, *Indira's India Gate: Latest Study of Political Corruption* (New Delhi: Arnold Heinemann Publishers, 1977).

37. For India, see the journal *Manushi* published in New Delhi; for an example from Italy, see Christiane Veauvy, "Le Mouvement féministe en Italie," *Mediterranean People/Peuples Méditerrannées* (1983): 22–23, 109–30.

38. John A. Vincent, "Differentiation and Resistance: Ethnicity in Valle d'Aosta and Kashmir," *Ethnic and Racial Studies* 5 (1982): 313–25.

39. Thomas R. McGuire, *Politics and Ethnicity of the Río Yaqui* (Tucson: Arizona State Univ. Press, 1986).

40. Sarkar, *Modern India*, 31–52, 439; the Communists, who relied on class analysis models in communal struggles, tended to be defeated.

41. Strong evidence for Madras as a new North can be taken from the rise of a new style of literature and from the rise of a "modern" women's movment there. These reveal the immense social change in Tamilnadu; C. S. Lakshmi, *The Face Behind the Mask: Women in Tamil Literature* (New Delhi: Vikas, 1984); Dharam Paul Sarin, *Influence of Political Movements on Hindi Literature, 1906–1947* (Chandigarh: Panjab University Publication Bureau, 1967), 222. An example of the establishment's recognition of the overcoming of the old North-South divide already cited is Sen, *North and South in Indian History*. For a statement about the rise of modern historiography in a university of the old South, the University of Mysore at Karnatak, see B. Sheik Ali, *History: Its Theory and Method* (Madras, Macmillan, 1978), 458–59.

42. A prize-winning novel translated from Assamese recounts the wooing of peasants away from Gandhism to communism; B. K. Bhattacharya, *Mrityunjay* (New Delhi: Sterling, 1983).

43. Joseph Schwartzberg, Shiva G. Bajpa, et al., *A Historical Atlas of South Asia* (Chicago: Univ. of Chicago Press, 1978).

44. The tribalism of the South has led to some comparative studies on Africa and Southeast Asia, for example, Bernard Cohn, "African Models and Indian History," in *Realm and Region in Traditional India*, ed. Richard G. Fox, Duke Univ. Monographs (Durham: Duke Univ., 1977), 90–116.

45. Ester Boserup, *Women's Role in Economic Development* (London: Earthscan, 1970);

Susan Wadley, ed., *The Power of Tamil Women* (Syracuse, N.Y.: Maxwell School, 1980), 161–62, notes how the birth of the daughter is welcomed more in the South than in the North.

46. The religious ideology of communalism is well known, but not the economic ideology. Is the gradual displacement of the trade union in the Third World by the New International Economic Order (NIEO) leading to wider community-based movements, including communalist ones? The answer will lie with the new urban work force. See, for example, Vijay Joshi and Heather Joshi, *Surplus Labor and the City: A Study of Bombay* (Oxford: Oxford Univ. Press, 1976); B. J. L. Berry, "Comparative Urbanization Strategies," *Ekistics* 42, no. 249 (1976): 130–35; Arvind Narayan Das, *Does Bihar Show the Way? Apathy, Agitation and Alternatives in an Unchanging State* (Calcutta: Research Indian Publications, 1979), 95, on the comparison with Kerala. For Italy, Linda Weiss, "The Italian State and Small Business," *European Journal of Sociology* 25 (1984): 214–41, shows attempts of the Christian Democrats in the age of the NIEO to get a base in the new small shop. Contrast these works with works on the economics of the old South, for examples, in the Indian case, Hugh Tinker, *A New System of Slavery: The Export of Indian Labour Overseas, 1830–1920* (London: Oxford Univ. Press, 1974).

47. For a statement approving the exploitation, see C. H. H. R. Rao, "Uncertainty, Entrepreneurship and Share-Cropping in India," *Journal of Political Economy* 79 (1979): 578–95. For a critique, see Harry Blair, "Rising Kulaks and Backward Classes in Bihar: Social Change in the Late 1970's," *Economic and Political Weekly* 15 (Jan. 12, 1980): 70; also Ben Crow, "Appropriating the Brahmaputra: The Onward March of India's Rich Peasants," *Economic and Political Weekly* 17 (Dec. 25, 1982): 2097–2101. For a statement that Bihar stands at the bottom of the Indian system in agriculture because of "created" disparities, see Veena Singh, *Regional Disparities in Agricultural Development* (New Delhi: Deep and Deep Publications, 1990), 150–51.

48. In India, the government has "found" many sources of "terror." Among these are the Naxalites and the Akali Dal. Outsiders, too, express their alarm when their interests are involved, for example, "Students in India's Northeastern Assam reject Government's Appeal," *New York Times,* June 2, 1980, Section A, 7, col. 6; here the actual focus was the safety of oil shipments. Tenancy issues often lie at the base of the "terror." For Italy, see Russell King, *Land Reform: The Italian Experience* (London: Butterworths, 1973); in chap. 8, he notes that large areas of the Center and the South were omitted from the Italian land reform, that the government actually targeted only a few absentee estates, and that the reform agency became the new padrones, correlating with high crime. Kathleen Gough notes the same problem in land reform in Tamil Nadu for the period 1951–78 in "Modes of Production in South India," *Economic and Political Weekly* 15 (Feb. 2, 1980): 351ff. For the politics of the Janata Kulaks (the Bharatiya Lok Dal), see C. P. Bhambhri, *The Janata Party: A Profile* (New Delhi: National, 1980), 7–8, 100.

49. G. P. Bhattacharjee, *Evolution of the Political Philosophy of M. N. Roy.* (Calcutta: Minerva Associates, 1971), 44, 56, 62, 149.

50. Sally Ray, "Communism in India: Ideological and Tactical Differences among Four Parties," *Studies in Comparative Communism* 5 (1972): 163–80.

51. Communist defensiveness about the land question in Kerala is brought out in an account of Namboodiripad's meeting with Vinoba on Kerala's border in April 1957; Sachidanand, *Sarvodaya in a Communist State* (Bombay: Popular Book Depot, 1961), 33ff. For the life of the Communist leader, E. M. S. Namboodiripad, a famous Malayalam language autobiography that contains interesting personal vignettes about his family, see *How I Became a Communist,* English ed. (Trivandrum: Chinta Publishers, 1976).

52. Gene Overstreet and Marshall Windmiller, *Communism in India* (Berkeley: Univ. of California Press, 1959), 363ff. A recent writer claims that few women play a role in the leadership as compared to the female role in Bengali peasant movements; Peter Custers,

"Women's Role in the Tebhaga Movement," *Economic and Political Weekly* 21 (Oct. 25, 1986): 97–104.

53. Owen M. Lynch, *The Politics of Untouchability: Social Mobility and Social Change in a City of India* (New York: Columbia Univ. Press, 1969), chap. 5.

54. B.R. Ambedkar, *The Untouchables: Who Were They and Why They Became Untouchable?* (New Delhi: Amrit Book Co., 1948); idem, *The Rise and Fall of Hindu Women* (Jullundur: Bheem, Patrika Publications, 1970).

55. One example was B. Shyam Sunder (1908–1975); Sunder fostered a Harijan-Muslim alliance; V. T. Rajshekar Shetty, *Dalit Movement in Karnataka* (Madras: Christian Literature Society, 1978). Sunder like Ambedkar had an international reputation. A current Karnataka figure in this tradition is Laxman G. Havanpur. Is Karnataka like Morelos?

56. Bipan Chandra, "Peasantry and National Integration in Contemporary India," in *National and Left Movements in India,* ed. K. N. Panikkar (New Delhi: Vikas, 1980), 107–45.

57. Nirmala Banerjee, *Women Workers in the Unorganized Sector: The Calcutta Experience* (Hyderabad: Sangam Books, 1985), chap. 9. For the new womens' struggles like Self Employed Women's Association (SEWA) see Devaki Jain, *Women's Quest for Power: Five Indian Case Studies* (Sahibabad: Vikas, 1980). For the failure of the CP to challenge the productivism of the offical women's organizations (Mahila Samajams), see P. M. Mathew and M. S. Nair, *Women's Organizations and Women's Interests* (New Delhi: Ashish Publishing, 1986), 17–18.

58. Dale Riepe, ed. *Asian Philosophy* (New York: Gordon and Breach, 1981), 167–80.

59. Suresht Renjen Bald, *Novelists and Political Consciousness* (Atlantic Highlands: Humanities Press, 1982), 10–12. The author contrasts theosophy of the South with the contemporary early twentieth century Vedantic movement in Bengal; the Vedantists were concerned with the world around them. For comments about idealism in philosophy in Madras, see K. S. Murty, *Philosophy in India* (New Delhi: Motilal Banarsidass, 1985), 125; for Bihar, S. S. Barlingay, S. V. Bokil, R. Sundara Rajan, et al., eds., *A Critical Survey of Research Work in Philosophy in Indian Universities* (Pune: Univ. of Poona, 1986), 99–101.

60. Lawrence Babb, *The Divine Hierachy: Popular Hinduism in Central India* (New York: Columbia Univ. Press, 1975), shows Siva worship as a medieval-like carnival in which the world is overturned.

61. This point is developed in Yogendra Malik, *North Indian Intellectuals: An Attitudinal Profile* (Leiden: Brill, 1979), 23; Nagendra, "Hindi," in *Contemporary Indian Literature and Society,* ed. Motilal Jotwani (New Delhi: Heritage, 1979), 62–63.

62. T. M. Ramachandran, ed. *Fifty Years of Indian Talkies, 1931–1981* (Bombay: Indian Academy of Motion Picture Arts and Sciences, 1981), 63–70, 146–52. The social realism of Satyajit Ray came from Calcutta.

63. Raimundo Panikkar, *The Unknown Christ of Hinduism* (New York: Orbis Books, 1981), 38ff. Panikkar's numerous writings are a major source for comparative studies within the Italian Road, especially for Spain and India.

64. H. C. Srivastava, *The Genesis of Campus Violence in Banaras Hindu Univ. Varanasi* (Allahabad: Indian International Publications, 1974).

65. Satyendra Kishore, *National Integration in India* (New Delhi: Sterling Publishers, 1987), chap. 3.

66. Richard Cashman, "The Phenomenon of Indian Cricket," in *Sport in History: The Making of Modern Sporting History,* ed. Richard Cashman and Michael McKernan (St. Lucia: Univ. of Queensland Press, 1979), 181–205, looks at cricket as an agent of socialization relied on by the state, rating it as superior to other more traditional forms of entertainment/socialization used by the state in India, for example, the religious festival in honor of Ganesha in Bombay, an occasion that does not impose discipline or collectivity.

67. Romen Basu, *Portrait on the Roof* (New Delhi: Sterling, 1980). For science in India, see Ward Morehouse, *Science in India* (Bombay: Popular Prakashan, 1971). For literature in

India, see K. Srinivasa Iyengar, ed. *Indian Literature since Independence* (New Delhi: Sahitya Akademi, 1973).

68. Amiya Dev, *Sudhindranath Datta* (New Delhi: Sahitya Akademi, 1982); Christopher Wagstaff, "The Neo-Avantgarde," in *Writers and Society in Contemporary Italy,* ed. Michael Caesar and Peter Hainsworth (Leamington Spa, Warwickshire: Berg Press, 1984), 35–62. By contrast, traditional romanticism is represented by a doyen of the Indian history profession, S. P. Sen, ed., *History in Modern Indian literature* (Calcutta: Institute of Historical Studies, 1975), preface. He did not find it objectionable that history should reach the masses in romanticized ways or through myths. The task of the historian was simply to do what was possible. This view rather glosses over the way the state can use a willing litarary figure to bypass the serious recognition of the South in an Italian Road country. Examples of this official exploitation in Italy include the southern writers Italo Calvino and Danilo Dolci. An Indian example of a famous reactionary romanticizer of the South was R. K. Narayan; see Tariq Ali, "Midnight's Children," *New Left Review* (Dec. 1986): 87–95. Tariq Ali claimed that Narayan's account of the "sleepy life" in the southern villages made him a favorite of the Colonial Civil Service and that he was a progenitor of the contemporary writer, V. S. Naipaul.

69. For an American statement on modernism, see *Culture Critique* 5 (Winter, 1986–87).

70. Mahadev L. Apte, "Music and Mass Culture in India," in *Mass Culture, Language and Arts in India,* ed. Mahadev L. Apte (Bombay: Popular Prakashan, 1978), 98–120; Umberto Eco, *The Role of the Reader* (Bloomington: Indiana Univ. Press, 1979), chap. 1. For the Indian context, it should be noted that the great players of North India are both Muslims and Hindus. For player-centered as opposed to composer-centered music in Mexico City, for example, the Quanta group of musicians that formed in 1970, seeking "instantaneous musical expression." María Ángeles González and Leonara Saavedra, *Música Mexicana Contemporánea* (Mexico City: Fondo de Cultura Económico, 1982), 119–20.

71. Yogesh Atal, *Social Sciences: The Indian Scene* (New Delhi: Abhinav, 1976), 4, observed that historians created the Indian Council of Historical Research, distinct from the more general Indian Council of Social Science Research.

72. For the contrast to Italy where historians did not have the same oportunities, see Ruggiero Romano, *La Storiografia Italiana oggi* (Rome: L'espresso, 1978), passim. Even the Marxists after World War II appear to deal with small topics and do not challenge the larger canvas of history; Ottavia Cecchi, ed., *La Ricérca stòrica marxista in Itàlia* (Rome: Editori riuniti, 1974).

73. L. P. Vidyarthi, *Rise of Anthropology in India: A Social Science Orientation* (Atlantic Highlands: Humanities Press, 1979), 2 vols., esp. 2:154, 334; Mazharul Islam, *A History of Folktale Collections in India and Pakistan* (Dacca: Bengali Academy, 1970).

74. Surindranath Roy, *The Story of Indian Archaeology, 1784–1947* (New Delhi: Archaeological Survey of India, 1961); B. B. Lal, *Indian Archeology since Independence* (Delhi: Motilal Banarsidass, 1964); a work bringing together museum officials from India, Italy, and Mexico about the problem of foreign art thieves, *The Protection of The Artistic and Archeological Heritage: A View from Italy and India* (Rome: United Nations Social Defense Research Institute, 1976).

75. *Visva-Bharati and Its Institutions* (Santiniketan: Pulinbihari Sen, 1956 [1961]), 30, where Athens is mentioned as the early example of disinterested learning of the East and West; P. C. Mahalanobis, "Our Founder-President in Italy, "*Visva-Bharati Bulletin* 4, no. 3 (1926): 280–306, esp. 292 for Tagore and Croce; for Tagore's quarrels with Gandhi about the utility of modern science and for his trip to meet the Egyptian King Fu'ad, see Krishna Kripalani, *Rabindranath Tagore* (Calcutta: Visva-Bharati, 1980), 337–38, 348.

76. S. P. Sen, ed., *Indian History Congress: Silver Jubilee Souvenir Volume* (Calcutta: Indian History Congress, 1963), passim.

77. In the early issues of the Indian Council of Historical Research *Newsletter* (ICHR) the editor, R. S. Sharma, published a number of analytical articles not generally found in standard

publications such as the *Journal of Indian History*. Later, under different editors, the politics totally shifted toward traditional research. A publication from the Jawaharal Nehru University (JNU) orientation was Amalendu Guha, *Planter-Raj to Swaraj Freedom Struggle and Electoral Politics in Assam, 1826–1947* (New Delhi: ICHR, 1977).

78. S. P. Sen, ed. *Historians and Historiography in Modern India* (Calcutta: Institute of Historical Studies, 1973), 45.

79. W. H. Golay, *The University of Poona 1949–1974* (Poona: Univ. of Poona, 1974), 421.

80. Mukhopadhyay, *Evolution of Historiography*, 23 ff.

81. *Journal of Indian History* 60 (1982): 294.

82. Ibid, 303–4.

83. In Ramesh Chandra Majuandar, *Historiography in Modern India* (New York: Asia Publishing, 1970), 4, he wrote sarcastically about a "great deal of truth in the name of patriotism, communal harmony, national integration and other such high-sounding phrases."

84. Tarasankar Banerjee, "Dr. S. P. Sen: The Historian-organiser a pen picture," *Journal of Indian History* 57 (1979) 451–81, *Quarterly Review of Historical Studies* 19 (1979–80) (Dr. S. P. Sen Memorial Number), ed. N. R. Ray with M. Chattipadhyaya, 3–134.

85. S. P. Sen, ed., *Social Contents of Indian Religious Reform Movements* (Calcutta: Institute of Historical Studies, 1978) tends to whitewash caste.

86. S. P. Sen, ed. *Studies in Modern Indian History; A Region Survey* (Calutta: Institute of Historical Studies, 1969), vii, is a defense of them; for a statement of concern, see Sudhir Chandra, "Modern Indian Historiography: Urgency and Risk of Micro-Studies," *Economic and Political Weekly*, March 18, 1972, 621–22; for a leading example of the new regional history, see the *Journal of Regional History*, 1 (1980), originally from the Department of History of Guru Nanak Dev University in Amritsar. This journal now has an editorial board from a number of universities. Microhistory and regional history are the subject of similar controversies in Mexico and Italy.

87. For a view of current concerns in history more generally, see Vijay C. P. Chaudhary, *Secularism Versus Communalism—An Anatomy of the National Debate on Five Controversial History Books* (Patna: Navdhara Samiti, 1977), 58 ff.

88. For an example of a left-wing globalist outlook, see the "Presidential Address of Section Four" (Countries Other Than India), Indian History Congress, 34th sess., Dec. 1973, published by the author Barun De, the first director of the Centre for Studies in Social Science, in *Itinerario* 10 (1986): 114 ff. For cosmopolitanism, a trend among "southern Intellectuals," see an essay by a Bihari scholar teaching at Princeton University, Gyan Prakash, "Writing Post-Orientalist Histories of the Third World: Perspectives from Indian Historiography," *Comparative Studies in Society and History* 32 (1990): 383–408.

89. Terms like *national capital*, however, must be handled carefully; Dharma Kumar, "Economic History of Modern India," *Indian Economic and Social History Review* 9 (1972): 63–90.

90. The chief representative of the postcolonial trend or neocolonial trend is the Cambridge school; Howard Spodek, "Pluralist Politics in British India: The Cambridge Cluster of Historians of Modern India," *American Historical Review* 84 (1979): 688–707. For the Annales school, see, for example, Roland Lardinois, "Population, Famines et Marché dans l'Historiographie Indienne, "*Annales ESC* (May–June 1987): 577–93. For an overview of paradigms, see Frank Perlin, "Disarticulation of the World: Writing India's Economic History: A Review," *Comparative Studies in Society and History* 31 (1988): 379–87.

91. Romila Thapar, "Ideology and the Interpretation of Early Indian History," in *Society and Change*, ed. K. S. Krishnaswamy and Sachin Chaudhuri. (Bombay: Sameeksha Trust/ Oxford Univ. Press, 1977), 1–20.

92. Utsa Patnaik, "Neo-Populism and Marxism: The Chayanovian View of the Agrarian

Question and Its Fundamental Fallacy," *Social Scientist* 103 (Dec. 1981): 27–52; Suneet Chopra, "Review Article (Ranajit Guha, *Subaltern Studies I*): Missing Correct Perspective," *Social Scientist* 111 (Aug. 1982): 55–63. As a consequence of their paradigm, the JNU group was the target of the textbook controversy during the Janata period. Led by the historian K. K. Datta, the communalist-oriented scholar, rightwing historians managed to block the translation of English language texts from JNU authors into vernacular languages for use in provincial universities; the communalists even briefly had the power to harrass the authors. For details, see Majid Hayat Siddiqi, "History-Writing in India," *History Workshop* 10 (Autumn 1980): 184–90. In India, the challenge over the interpretation of peasant studies or of communalism takes place in history, whereas in Italy and Mexico, it takes place in anthropology; see, for example, the writings of the Italian anthropologist A. M. Cirese, *Ensayos sobre culturas subalternas* (Mexico City: Centro de Investigaciónes y Estudios Superiores en Antropología Social, 1981), here, of course, in a Spanish translation. See also the Italian anthropologist L. M. Lombardi Satriani, *Apropriación y destrucción de la cultura subalterna* (Mexico City, 1978).

93. For an example, see Mohamed Noor Nabi, "The Impact of Sufism on the Bhakti Movement in India," *Indian Journal of Politics* 11 (Aug. 1977): 123–29.

94. "Sardar K. M. Panikkar," *Journal of Indian History* 60 (1982) (Diamond Jubilee Issue): 352; Sardar Panikkar, "A Critical Historian's Interpretation of Indian History," in *Readings in Indian History, Politics, and Philosophy,* ed. K. Satchidananda Murty (London: Allen and Unwin, 1967), 34–37, 106–10, 135–38.

95. B. Sheik Ali, *History, Its Theory and Methods,* 453; Murty, *Readings,* 69ff.

96. A. Nilakanta Sastri is discussed in Subodh Kumar Mukhopadhyay, *Evolution of Historiography,* 104 ff.

97. Somnath Roy, *Recent Historical Studies about Modern Bihar* (Calcutta: J. Roy, 1978).

98. Archives of the Rockefeller Foundation, RG-464R, Patna Univ., History, Datta (1952–57); a less-flattering view finds him benefiting from being from an immigrant Bengali family who spoke English, from currying favor with local politicians, and in his capacity as vice-chancellor of Patna University from 1962 to 1968, opposing student and teacher unions, J. C. Jha, "The Life and Works of Kalikinkar Datta (1905–1982)," *Journal of Indian History* 60 (1982): 277–92.

6. The "Italian Road" in Latin America: Mexico, 1876–1990

1. Barry Carr, "The Peculiarities of the Mexican North, 1880–1928: An Essay in Interpretation," Occasional Papers, no. 4 (Univ. of Glasgow, 1971). The common point of view is that Porfirio Díaz's ties to the South would not lend themselves to allowing a northern capitalist predominance. This view is, however, belied by the concentration of railroad construction in the North; John H. Coatsworth, *Growth Against Development: The Economic Impact of Railroads in Porfirian Mexico* (DeKalb: Northern Illinois Univ. Press, 1981), 178, 183–84, notes the role of the railroads in facilitating internal migration, interelite communication, government ministries to function on a national basis and for giving the state bureaucrats experience in regulation.

2. For the view of the various provinces simply as "other Mexicos" or as "peripheries of Mexican capitalist development," see Gilbert M. Joseph, "From Caste War to Class War: The Historiography of Modern Yucatán (c. 1750–1940)," *Hispanic American Historical Review* 65, no. 1 (1985): 111–34. From this article one can take a number of details to use in a Southern Question type of analysis: the expulsion of the majority of the Yaqui Indians out of the North to the South in the nineteenth century contributed to the alignment of ethnicity and region; the periodization in Yucatán history and national history does not match; and the role of caste is important for an analysis of Yucatán. See Thomas Benjamin and William McNellie, eds., *Other Mexicos: Essays on Regional Mexican History, 1876–1911* (Albuquerque: Univ. of New

Mexico Press, 1984), 46, 78ff, 137, 148, 243, on the transfer of power in a northern state, Chihuahua, from the more traditional Terraza family to Enrique C. Creel, an international financier, on the role of ranchero capitalists in northern Hidalgo, and on the formation of the working class in La Comarca Laguna in north central Mexico. This part of the book stands in contrast to the part discussing the powerbrokers in Puebla, figures, such as the highly authoritarian governor, Mucio P. Martínez, who held his office from 1892 to 1911, and the foreigners who controlled the coffee planatations in Socunusco (Chiapas).

3. An Italian example could be drawn from Frank Snowden, *Violence and Great Estates in the South of Italy: Apulia 1900–1922* (Cambridge: Cambridge Univ. Press, 1986), 94.

4. Friedrich Katz, *The Secret War in Mexico—Europe, the United States, and the Mexican Revolution* (Chicago: Univ. of Chicago Press, 1981), 5.

5. D. A. Brading, *Prophecy and Myth in Mexican History* (Cambridge: Centre of Latin American Studies, 1984), shows the premodern roots of modern Mexico in much the same way that Gramsci started to do in his study of Italian history. Brading makes a number of useful comparisons that touch on Mexico, Spain, Italy, and even Egypt. He insists on the relative uniqueness of Mexico in Latin America.

6. Thomas Benjamin and Marcial Ocasio-Meléndez, "Organizing the Memory of Modern Mexico: Porfirian Historiography in Perspective, 1880–1980's," *Hispanic American Historical Review* 64, no. 2 (1984): 323–64, esp. 358; as in Italy, the liberals split at the birth of the new state; some were pragmatic about the extension of democratic reforms, such as Justo Sierra in his newspaper *La Libertad,* and others, more doctrinnaire liberals, clung to the Constitution of 1857. Charles A. Week, *The Juarez Myth in Mexico* (Tuscaloosa: Univ. of Alabama Press, 1987), 28ff., cites a writer who compares Juarez to the Italian Garibaldi. Internationally, the Porfiriate generally has had a bad reputation for its use of peon labor and debt slavery; see John Kenneth Turner, *Barbarous Mexico,* excerpted in W. Dirk Raat, ed., *Mexico—From Independence to Revolution 1810–1910* (Lincoln: Univ. of Nebraska Press, 1982), chap. 18. For some reason the Raj in India and the landlords in Italy escape such scrutiny.

7. Michael C. Meyer and William L. Sherman, *The Course of Mexican History* (New York: Oxford Univ. Press, 1987), 55–6; for a recent example of this movement of "anthropology into history" that is making the Aztecs and the Mayas visible for comparative history and political economy, see Thomas C. Patterson, *Las sociedades nucleares de Mesoamérica* (Caracas: Historia General de América, forthcoming). For an example of comparative culture, see Werner Müller, "Raum und Zeit in Sprachen und Kalendern Nordamerikas und Alteuropas: Der römische Kalender," *Anthropos* 77(1987): 533–58; earlier, the Chicago school, Robert Redfield and Milton Singer, introduced the idea of the "big tradition" and the "little tradition," using Mexico and India as examples. Gabriel Almond and Sidney Verba, *The Civic Culture: Political Attitudes and Democracy in Five Nations* (Newbury Park, Calif.: Sage Publications, 1989 [1963]), and then recast in the form of an edited volume as *The Civic Culture Revisited* (Newbury Park, Calif.: Sage Publications, 1989), took the United States, Great Britain, Germany, Italy, and Mexico, the last two taken as transitional modernizing examples that differed from the democracies in such categories as alienation, parochialism, political environment, and corruption.

8. An example of the strictures felt by Mexicanists concerning the use of Gramsci can be found in a comment by the well-known professor, John Womack, Jr., noting how Gramsci was rebuffed by Italian historians even in the 1960s, "The Mexican Economy During the Revolution, 1910–1920: Historiography and Analysis," *Marxist Perspectives* 1(1978): 123, 54, citing as a warning to his fellow Mexicanists the article by A. William Salomone, "The Risorgimento Between Ideology and History: The Political Myth of the 'Rivoluzíone Mancata'," *American Historical Review* 68(1962): 38–56. Salomone took exception to the lack of appreciation of the bourgeois revolution of nineteenth-century Italy, to the teleological quality of communist thought in such matters as 'failed revolutions,' and other points stemming from his liberal pluralist methodology. Since Salomone wrote his article, a body of sound academic

scholarship has appeared about Gramsci and on the application of his ideas to Italian history; examples of the scholarship include John Cammett, *Antonio Gramsci and the Origins of Italian Communism* (Palo Alto, Calif.: Stanford Univ. Press, 1967), and of the application, John A. Davis, ed., *Gramsci and Italy's Passive Revolution* (London: Croom Helm, 1979). Meanwhile, in Mexican studies, the translation of Gramsci into Spanish from the Gerratana edition has begun to have an impact. Since 1991, quite a body of writers in Mexico use his theory; see for an overview, José Aricó, *La Cola del diablo: Itinerario de Gramsci en América Latina* (Caracas: Editorial Nueva Sociedad, 1988).

9. The use of the term *Eurocommunism* is Barry Carr's; see, for example, *Mexican Communism, 1968–1983: Eurocommunism in the Americas?* (San Diego, Calif.: Center for United States-Mexican Studies, 1985), examples found in Carlos Sirvent, Christine Buci-Glucksmann et al., eds., *Gramsci y la política* (Mexico City: Universidad Nacional Autónoma de México, 1980). For the Dependency school, see David Barkin, "Mexico's Albatross: The U.S. Economy," in *Modern Mexico,* ed., Nora Hamilton and Timothy F. Harding (Beverly Hills, Calif.: Sage Publications, 1986), 106–27 emphasizes U.S. ownership of Mexican industry and oil interests. For an internal view, see Merrill Rippy, *Oil and the Mexican Revolution* (Leiden: Brill, 1972).

10. Many writers, who choose 1876 stop, however, in 1910, viewing 1910–40 as a period of revolution. Here, I differ, preferring to see 1876–1934 as a liberal phase, meaning a phase of single-class rule, open market capitalism, marked by the relative hegemony of a liberal positivist worldview not withstanding the influence of the southern intellectual in Mexico. A list of writers adopting 1876 as their point of departure appears in the article by Benjamin and Ocasio-Meléndez, "Memory of Modern Mexico" 358–59. Albert L. Michaels and Marvin Bernstein, "The Modernization of the Old Order: Organization and Periodization of Twentieth-Century Mexican History," in *Contemporary Mexico,* ed. James W. Wilkie, Michael C. Meyer, and Edna Monzón de Wilkie (Los Angeles: Univ. of California Press and El Colegio de México, 1976), 687–710, begins with 1876 but approaches corporatism as a "period of transition of power (1932–1946)," Camacho's rule becoming the "Porfiriate restored"; Arnaldo Córdova, "La Transformación del PNR en PRM: El Triunfo del Corporativismo en México," in *Contemporary Mexico,* ed. Wilkie, Meyer, and Monzón de Wilkie, (*Los Angeles Mexico City:* Univ. of California Press and El Colegio de México, 1976), 204–27, adopts the periodization 1934–40. Periodization also depends on whether one does national or regional historiography; for the regional, see Gilbert M. Joseph, *Rediscovering the Past at Mexico's Periphery: Essays on the History of the Modern Yucatan* (University: Univ. of Alabama Press, 1986), in which periodization concerning such issues as Creole racism versus the Mayas, blocked capitalist transformation, debt peonage, the greater exploitation of labor in the South than in the North, the weakness of the southern middle class, the disconnectedness of southern political history from the rest of the national narrative, and so on, do not fit the national framework, nineteenth-century problems that continue today; Leigh Binford, "Political Conflict and Land Tenure in the Mexican Isthmus of Tehuantepec," *Journal of Latin American Studies* 17(1985): 179–200.

11. Martin Stabb, "Indigenism and Racism in Mexican Thought: 1857–1911," *Journal of Inter-American Studies* 1(1959): 405–23, esp. 405.

12. Jean A. Meyer, *The Cristero Rebellion: The Mexican People Between Church and State* (Cambridge: Cambridge Univ. Press, 1975). In one instance, an "oppressed" group staved off defeat through the "politics of religion"; in another, a Yucatán feminist league faced church opposition when it tried to link the woman's question to the Indian question or to construct utopian communities. See also Shirlene Ann Soto, *The Mexican Woman: A Study of Her Participation in the Revolution, 1910–1940* (Palo Alto Calif.: R and E Research Associates, 1979), 63 ff. The Italian counterpart to the Yucatán women would be the feminist anarchosyndicalists, figures such as Maria Rygier; Snowden, *Violence and Great Estates,* 114.

13. Adolfo Gilly, *The Mexican Revolution* (London: Verso Press, 1983), chap. 1, and 49ff., comparing the Indian and Mexican peasantries.

14. Taking internal migration as a political event, it appears possible to correlate it with the degree of longevity of political careers of rulers. In the nineteenth century in countries such as Mexico or Egypt, rulers reigns for many years. Thereafter, as more southerners gave up the struggle on the local level and migrated to the capital city, the terms of the rulers became much shorter. In Italy, this trend is less marked.

15. François-Xavier Guérra, *Le Mexique: De L'Ancien Régime à la Révolution* (Paris: L'Harmattan, 1985), vol. 1, chap. 2, and p. 174, on how the Mexican clergy accepted liberalism better than did their Italian counterparts.

16. Roger D. Hansen, *The Politics of Mexican Development* (Baltimore, Md.: Johns Hopkins Univ. Press, 1971), 147, is an example of an early book stressing the Porfiriate as the basis of modern Mexico.

17. Guillermo Floris Margadant, *An Introduction to the History of Mexican Law* (Dobbs Ferry: Oceana Publications, 1983), chap. 8.

18. J. Lloyd Meacham, *Church and State in Latin America* (Chapel Hill: Univ. of North Carolina Press, 1934), Ch. 16.

19. Guérra, *Le Mexique,* vol. 1: chap. 8, esp. p. 15.

20. For a summary of the early history of the working class, see John Mason Hart, *Revolutionary Mexico: The Coming and Process of the Mexican Revolution* (Berkeley: Univ. of California Press, 1987), chaps. 1 and 2; for the later period, see Lourdes Benería and Martha Roldán, *The Crossroads of Class and Gender: Industrial Housework, Subcontracting and Household Dynamics in Mexico City* (Chicago: Univ. of Chicago Press, 1987).

21. James Cockcroft, *Intellectual Precursors of the Mexican Revolution, 1900–1913* (Austin: Univ. of Texas Press, 1976). For gender issues, see Elizabeth Salas, *Soldaderas in the Mexican Military: Myth and History* (Austin: Univ. of Texas Press, 1990), 45ff. As Arturo Warman rightly pointed out when summarizing an interchange between Zapata and Villa, Zapata was closer to understanding the difference between revolution and seizure of power. Revolution requires understanding and cooperation. Villa refused this. Warman, "The Political Project of Zapatismo," in *Riot, Rebellion, and Revolution: Rural Social Conflict in Mexico,* ed. Friedrich Katz (Princeton, N.J.: Princeton Univ. Press, 1988), esp. 333–34.

22. These themes are introduced in Adolfo Gilly et al., *Interpretaciónes de la revolución mexicana* (Mexico City: Editorial Nueva Imagen, 1979). For a valuable summary of information reintegrating the revolution back into Mexican history, see John Womack, Jr., "The Mexican Economy During the Revolution, 1910–1920: Historiography and Analysis," *Marxist Perspectives* 1(1978): 80–123.

23. John Tutino, *From Insurrection to Revolution in Mexico: Social Bases of Agrarian Violence, 1750–1940* (Princeton, N.J.: Princeton Univ. Press, 1986), 326–47.

24. For an example of the interpretation of the Cárdenas period as corporatist, see Córdova, "La Transformación," noting the base groups brought into the state, the drift toward collective agriculture, and the unionization of government employees. Córdova tied the origins of Cárdenas's state to the revolution because nineteenth-century Mexican socialism was anarchist; still the real cross-class alliance came only in 1934. See also Nora Hamilton, "Mexico: The Limits of State Autonomy," *Latin American Perspectives* 11(Summer 1975): 81–108, esp. 87, 100, emphasizing the constraints Cárdenas faced from U.S. imperialism in attempting a socialist transformation but also noting the options to turn for aid to Japan and Germany.

25. For a discussion of church weakness, see Susan Eckstein, *The Poverty of Revolution* (Princeton, N.J.: Princeton Univ. Press, 1977), 108 ff.; Ivan Vallier, *Catholicism, Social Control, and Modernization.* (Englewood Cliffs, N.J.: Prentice-Hall, 1970). For a discussion of the strategies of the Synarchists in penetrating state power in the 1930s through various government ministries, see Jean Meyer, "Sinarquismo or the Revolutionary Detour of the Right-

Wing," in *Peasantry and National Integration,* ed. Celma Agüero (Mexico City; El Colegio de México, 1981), 237–46.

26. As regards a favored region during and after Cárdenas, see Henry Landsberger and Cynthia Hewitt de Alcantra, "From Violence to Pressure-Group Politics and Cooperation: A Mexican Case Study," in *Two Blades of Grass: Rural Cooperatives in Agricultural Modernization,* ed. Peter Worsley (Manchester: Manchester Univ. Press, 1971), 293–346.

27. For an excellent summary of the early history of gender control, see Jean Franco, *Plotting Women: Gender and Representation in Mexico* (New York: Columbia Univ. Press, 1989), p. 2. For the argument that Mexico is more sexist today than in the past, see Ilene V. O'Malley, *Myth of the Revolution* (Westport, Conn.: Greenwood Press, 1986).

28. Anna Macias, *Against All Odds: The Feminists in Mexico to 1940* (Westport, Conn.: Greenwood Press, 1992), chap. 6.

29. Ward Morton, *Woman Suffrage in Mexico* (Gainesville: Univ. of Florida Press, 1962), 25ff., 51.

30. Patricia Fagen, *Exiles and Citizens, Spanish Republicans in Mexico* (Austin: Univ. of Texas Press, 1973), 66.

31. Roderick Ai Camp, *Intellectuals and the State in Twentieth Century Mexico* (Austin: Univ. of Texas Press, 1985), 140–41.

32. Hamilton, "Mexico."

33. Vicente Camberos Vizcaíno, *Francisco el Grande: Mons. Francisco Orozco y Jimínez* (Mexico City: Editorial Jus, 1966).

34. Joseph G. Trevino, *The Spiritual Life of Archbishop Martínez* (St. Louis: B. Herder Book, 1966), 8. His confessor was known to have worried about maternal influence on him.

35. Following David Harvey, *The Conditions of Postmodernity* (Oxford: Basil Blackwell, 1989).

36. An excellent account of this line is Joe Foweraker and Ann L. Craig, eds., *Popular Movements and Political Change in Mexico* (Boulder, Colo.: Lynne Rienner, 1990).

37. M. B. Wallerstein, *Food for War—Food for Peace: United States Food Aid in a Global Context* (Cambridge: MIT Press, 1980). On migration, see Wayne Cornelius, "Urbanization as an Agent in Latin American Political Stability, the Case of Mexico," *American Political Science Review* 63, no. 2 (1969): 833–85, and Peter Gregory, *The Myth of Market Failure* (Baltimore, Md.: Johns Hopkins Univ. Press, 1986), 146.

38. John J. Bailey, *Governing Mexico: The Statecraft of Crisis Management* (New York: St. Martin's Press, 1988).

39. Latin American and Caribbean Women's Collective, *Slaves of Slaves: The Challenge of Latin American Women* (London: Zed Press, 1980), 125; to contrast, see Jennifer Sebstad, *Women and Self-Reliance: The SEWA Story* (London: Zed Press, 1985).

40. F. Cancian, *The Innovator's Situation: Upper Middle Class Conservatism in Agricultural Communities* (Palo Alto, Calif.: Stanford Univ. Press, 1979), discusses examples of this contradiction, using slightly different vocabulary for Mexico and India; John F. House, *Frontier on the Río Grande: A Political Geography of Development and Social Deprivation* (Oxford: Clarendon Press, 1982), 179. A microanalysis that pins migration on the fate of a particular crop is Ernest Feder, *Strawberry Imperialism: An Enquiry into the Mechanisms of Dependency in Mexican Agriculture* (The Hague: Institute of Social Studies, 1977).

41. Barry Carr, "Marxism and Anarchism in the Formation of the Mexican Communist Party, 1910–1919," *Hispanic American Historical Review* 63, no. 2 (1983): 277–305.

42. James D. Cockcroft, *Intellectual Precursors,* 228; Sheldon B. Liss, *Marxist Thought in Latin America* (Berkeley: Univ. of California Press, 1984), chap. 9.

43. Judith Adler Hellman, "The Role of Ideology in Peasant Politics: Peasant Mobilization and Demobilization in the Laguna Region," *Journal of Inter-American Studies and World Affairs* 25, no. 1 (1983):3–30; the party's most ambitious outreach of the 1930s was to the

peasantry of the Laguna region. Dionicio Encina, ironically, was one of their success stories; Barry Carr, "The Mexican Communist Party and Agrarian Mobilization in the Laguna, 1920–1940: A Worker-Peasant Alliance?" *Hispanic American Historical Review* 67, no. 3 (1987): 387–404.

44. Robert Paul Millon, *Mexican Marxist Vicente Lombardo Toledano* (Chapel Hill: Univ. of North Carolina Press, 1966).

45. Liss, *Marxist Thought in Latin America,* 219.

46. Gerardo Unzueta, *Lombardo Toledano y el Marxismo-Leninismo* (Mexico City: Fondo de Cultura Popular, 1966), 120–21.

47. Millon, *Vicente Lombardo Toledano,* 65 ff.; Arturo Warman, "Indigenist Thought," in *Indigenous Anthropology in Non-Western Countries,* ed. Hussein Fahim (Durham: Carolina Academic Press, 1982), 75–97, esp. 90 ff.

48. For the rise and fall of one of the principal movements of rural challenge, the Veracruz movement of Adalberto Tejeda Olivares, see Heather Fowler Salamini, *Agrarian Radicalism in Veracruz, 1920–1938* (Lincoln: Univ. of Nebraska Press, 1978).

49. Leopoldo Zea, *Positivism in Mexico* (Austin: Univ. of Texas Press, 1968), chap. 2, esp. 20ff., is useful for building an Italian Road argument around positivism, romanticism, and region.

50. Although Unamuno and Croce were friends, commentators point to their differences as the "mature" Croce turned systematizer, for example, Vicente González Martín, *La Cultura Italiana en Miguel de Unamuno* (Salamanca: Univ. de Salamanca, 1978), esp. 267–82.

51. Álvaro Matute, *Lorenzo Boturini y el pensamiento histórico de Vico* (Mexico City: UNAM, 1976); Gustavo Costa, "La Linea Vico-Boturini-Veytia e la storiografia Messicana," *Bollettino del Cèntro di Stùdi Vichiani* 16(1986): 369–73, includes an account of the influence of Vico on the Mexican historian, Mariano Fernández de Echevarría y Veytia (1718–1780); Lois Parkinson Zamora, "Magic Realism and Fantastic History: Carlos Fuentes's 'Terra Nostra' and Giambattista Vico's 'New Science,' " *Reviews of Contemporary Fiction* 8(1988): 249–56. Fuentes actually cites Vico. Vico had been a professor of rhetoric at Naples during the time when Cartesian rationalism and positivism were sweeping Europe. His "new science" represented what in modern lingo would be a radical decentering of the privileged observer-observed relationship that Descartes was championing. For Vico, in contrast to Descartes, the primitive's views of the missionary had the same validity as the missionary's views of the primitive; see Giorgio Tagliacozzo, ed., *Vico and Marx: Affinities and Contrasts* (Atlantic Highlands, N.J.: Humanities Press, 1983), generally, and especially, B. A. Haddock, "Vico and the Crisis of Marxism," 352–67; Edmund E. Jacobitti, "From Vico's Common Sense to Gramsci's Hegemony," 367–87.

52. Fernándo Salmerón, "Mexican Philosophers of the Twentieth Century," México (City): Universidad Nacional, Consejo Técnico de Humanidades, *Major Trends in Mexican Philosophy* (Notre Dame, Ind.: Notre Dame Univ. Press, 1966), 246–87. Bergson's influence in Mexico is the subject of "Ommagio a Henri Bergson," *Humanitas* 14 (1959): 769–852; *Homenaje a Bergson* (Mexico City: Impr. Universitaria, 1941).

53. Mary Kay Vaughn, *The State, Education, and Social Change in Mexico, 1880–1928* (DeKalb: Northern Illinois Univ. Press, 1982), 140–42.

54. Michael A. Weinstein, *The Polarity of Mexican Thought: Instrumentalism and Finalism* (Univ. Park: Pennsylvania State Univ. Press, 1976), 3; a study of the transition to Neo-Kantianism in Mexican philosophy is by Juan Hernández Luna, "Una Polémica en torno al Neokantismo," *Historia Mexicana* 19(1969): 397–417, can be compared to the study of the development of Croce's thought; John Haddox, *Antonio Caso, Philosopher of Mexico* (Austin: Univ. of Texas Press, 1971).

55. Gabriel Careaga, *Los Intelectuales y la política en México* (Mexico City: Editorial Extemporáneos, 1971), 47 ff., argues for a distinction, placing most of the positivists in the Díaz

period, finding their influence on the wane after the revolution. Although this is true of certain famous regime intellectuals who flourished in the heyday of liberalism, positivism actually lived on as bureaucratic logic, and the Atenistas never felt they had conquered it.

56. A writer in this tradition was Miguel Othón de Mendizábal (d. 1946); Benjamin Keen, *The Aztec Image in Western Thought* (New Brunswick, N.J.: Rutgers Univ. Press, 1971), 474–576. The standard work is Carlos García Morá, ed., *La antropología en México* (Mexico City: Instituto Nacional de Antropología e Historia, 1987), 4 vols., see 2:25.

57. John S. Brushwood, *Narrative Innovation and Political Change in Mexico* (New York: Peter Lang, 1989), chap. 3.

58. Jason Wilson, *Octavio Paz* (Boston: Twayne Publishers, 1986), 1. A feature of the southern intellectual is the attraction to but the discomfort in northern intellectual centers, which leads to a life coming and going from them. Such was Croce's life, so, too, the life of the Egyptian literary critic and southern intellectual, Mahmud 'Abbas al-'Aqqad. Paz's experiences in Italy might also be exploited to promote the idea of his "southernness." In "Hymn among the Ruins" (Naples, 1948), Paz takes the uncorrupted landscape of Sicily as his contrast point to the mindless violence of World War II farther north (45). From 1962 to 1968, Paz was Mexico's ambassador to India. This was fortuitous for him because he was also a student of the Orient. Paz's studies of India, like Vasconcelos's, reveal his cosmopolitan side. East and West are found to blend; they are contiguous, separate, but then reflect each other. In some of Paz's poetry, the study further shows, India, meaning Hinduism or Tantric eroticism, becomes intertwined with Paz's own childhood in Mixcoac; Julia A. Kushigan, " 'Ríos en la noche: Fluyen los jardines': Orientalism in the Work of Octavio Paz," *Hispania* 70(1987): 776–86. For the poem "Hymn among the Ruins," see Octavio Paz, *Early Poems 1935–1955* (Bloomington: Indiana Univ. Press, 1973) 94–99.

59. Note his indictment of the Museum of Anthropology; the real history of civilization was in the South before the Aztecs. When the Aztecs arose even before the Spanish arrived, Mexico was already in a postcivilizational phase ruled by force, Octavio Paz, *The Other Mexico: Critique of the Pyramid* (New York: Grove Press, 1972), 109ff.

60. In Italian commentary literature on the *Labyrinth*, a recent writer, while noting Mexican critiques of both the idea of national character literature and of this book in particular, cf., Roger Bartra, *La Jaula de la melancholía. Identidad y metamorfosis del Mexicano* (Mexico City: Grijalbo, 1987), concludes with the observation that the evangelization of Mexico never really sought to eliminate fully the pagan Indian practices noted in this book; Arnaldo Nesti, "Il 'labirinto délla solitùdine' e le identificazióni soteriologische nel Messicano contemporàneo," *Religióni e Società* 5 (1988): 37–56. Luigi Barzini, *The Italians* (New York: Atheneum, 1979) (1964), however, also stresses the importance of spectacle, masks, and deception, the Baroque in Italian character, and even the Southern Question in Italy. Soteriology does not seem so far removed either.

61. Francisco Arce Gurza et al., *Historia de la profesiones en México* (Mexico City: SEP/SESIC; El Colegio de México, 1982); Peter S. Cleaves, *Professions and the State: The Mexican Case* (Tucson: Univ. of Arizona Press, 1987), notes the degree to which nationalism and politicism play a role in professional life.

62. Kaja Finkler, an anthropologist, concludes that the success rate of the spiritualists is "no higher than" that of the biomedical physicians; American doctors do not have to deal with patients who believe in witchcraft or spirit possession; Finkler, *Physicians at Work, Patients in Pain: Biomedical Practice and Patient Response in Mexico* (Boulder, Colo.: Westview Press, 1991), esp. chap. 6 and the conclusion. An older work researched in the U.S. Southwest by Ari Kiev, *Curanderismo: Mexican-American Folk Psychiatry* (New York: Free Press, 1968), accepts as its premise the plurality of epistemologies in medical systems, even for the United States. Witchcraft, he argued, performs a therapeutic function for various people, including some migrants, bereft of the logic of a familiar environment. Curanderos have saved the sanity of

NOTES TO PAGES 182–185 389

many people under the conditions of market capitalism. Another work on differing medical epistemologies is Elliott A. Krause, "Doctors and the State: An Italian/American Comparison," *Research in the Sociology of Health Care* 7(1988): 227–45. The idea of competing medical systems has long been a theme in medical anthropology; see, for example, my article discussing Egypt and India, "Medical Pluralism in Arab and Egyptian History: An Overview of Class Structures and Philosophies of the Main Phases," *Social Science and Medicine* 13b(1979): 339–48. Since the 1970s according to a recent study, the government of India has been subsidizing the employment of alternative medicine, weakening the monopoly of the allopathic medical association; Roger Jeffery, *The Politics of Health in India* (Berkeley: Univ. of California Press, 1988), 185–86; see also Ronald Frykenberg, "Allopathic Medicine, Profession, and Capitalist Ideology in India," *Social Science and Medicine* 15A (1981): 115–25. For Italy, as one source makes clear, the South under conditions of a National Health program is the most neglected in medical resources. Naples, the source claims, is the "Calcutta" of Europe; Alan Maynard, *Health Care in the European Community* (Pittsburgh, Pa.: Univ. of Pittsburgh Press, 1979), 157. For an account of folk healers in Italy, see Lola Romanucci-Ross, "Creativity in Illness: Methodological Linkages to the Logic and Language of Science in Folk Pursuit of Health in Central Italy," *Social Science and Medicine* 23, no. 1 (1986): 1–7; see also Douglas R. Holmes, *Cultural Disenchantments: Worker Peasantries in Northeast Italy* (Princeton, N.J.: Princeton Univ. Press, 1989), chap. 6. This work attracts attention because Holmes acknowledges his indebtedness methodologically for the chapter cited here to a study of north Mexico. Yet another example of cross-cultural awareness in this field could be taken from the work of an Italian researcher who studied in Mexico what is often taken to be a uniquely Latin American peasant condition called *susto,* or fright. This researcher concluded on the basis of his familiarity with south Italian material that susto was the Italian assusto(!); Italo Signorini, "Patterns of Fright: Multiple Concepts of Susto in a Nahua-Ladino Community of the Sierra de Puebla (Mexico)," *Ethnology* 21, no. 4 (Oct. 1982): 313–24, esp. 313.

63. Richard F. Mollica, "From Antonio Gramsci to Franco Basaglia (1924–1980): The Theory and Practice of Italian Psychiatric Reform," *International Journal of Mental Health* 14, no. 2 (1985): 30. This article is part of a special issue called the "Unfinished Revolution in Italian Psychiatry"; *Psychiatry Inside Out: Selected Writings of Franco Basaglia,* ed. Nancy Scheper-Hughes and Anne Lovell (New York: Columbia Univ. Press, 1987).

64. Report in *Enseñanza e Investigación en Psicología* 4, no. 1 (1978): 6–9, as cited in *Psychological Abstracts* 65 (Jan.–June 1981): 421, and other articles in *Enseñanza.* But as events after the passage of Law 180 in 1978 showed, the national organization of Psichiatría Democrática (founded in 1973) would face numerous obstacles in Mexico. For an overview, see Sylvia Marcos et al., eds., *Dossier México sobre alternativas a la psiquiatría* (Mexico City: Ediciónes Nueva Sociología, 1982). This work draws heavily on the writings of the Basaglias, most of which are translated from Italian into Spanish, many among them published in Mexico, for example, Franca Basaglia, *Reflexiónes sobre la mujer* (Puebla: Univ. Autónoma de Puebla, 1986).

65. For an important statement reflecting the dependency school, see Armando Mattelart, *Multinational Corporations and the Control of Culture* (Sussex: Harvester Press, 1979).

66. Richard Ray Cole, "The Mass Media of Mexico: Ownership and Control," (Ph.D. diss., Univ. of Minnesota, 1972), 133, 165.

67. "Obituary," Friday, Aug. 8, 1986, *Philadelphia Inquirer,* sec. B; Camp, *Intellectuals and the State,* Camp, 101, 189.

68. An eminent Mexican historian who writes in this vein is Enrique Florescano, "La influencia del estado en la historiografía," in *Encuentro de Historiadores Latino Americanos y del Caribe* (Caracas, 1977), 1: 350–73; "Le Pouvoir et la lutte pour le pouvoir dans l'historiographie moderne et contemporaine au Mexique," in *Champs de pouvoir et de savoir au Mexique* GRAL, Institut d'Études Mexicaines (Paris: CNRS, 1982), 165–88. "Historia local, historia regional y la formación política del país, in Luis González y González, Jean A. Mayer, and Enrique

Florescano, *Historia Regional y Archivos* (Mexico City: Archivio General de la Nación, 1982), 33–39, emphasizes that the way archives are organized predisposes historians against regional studies. This, coincidentally, is the theme of a recent Italian book, Ilaria Porciani, *"L'Archivio stòrico Italiano": organizzazióne della ricérca ed egemònia moderata nel Risorgiménto* (Florence: L. S. Olschki, 1979). In general, these books are part of the growing body of writing on the relation of the Mexican intellectual and the state; Enrique Krauze, *Los Caudillos culturales en la revolución* (Mexico City: Siglo Veintiuno Editores, 1976); see also GRAL et L'Institut d'études Mexicaine-Perpignan, *Intellectuels et etat au Mexique au XXe siècle* (Paris: CNRS, 1979); *Champs de pouvoir et de savoir;* Louis Panabière, ed., *Pouvoirs et contre-pouvoirs dans la culture Mexicaine* (Paris: CNRS, 1985).

69. Robert A. Potash, "Historiography of Mexico since 1821," *Hispanic American Historical Review* 40(1960): 383–424.

70. Keen, *Aztec Image,* 433.

71. Porrúa, *Diccionario Porrúa de historia, biografía y geografía de México* (Mexico City: Editorial Porrúa, 1986), 2:1955; Academia Mexicana, *Semblanzas de Académicos* (Mexico City: Academia Mexicana, 1975); José Sánchez, *Academias y Sociedades Literarias de México* (Chapel Hill: Univ. of North Carolina Press, 1951); Martín Luis Guzmán, *Academia: Tradición, Independencia, Libertad Discursos* (Mexico City: Companía General de Ediciónes, 1959).

72. For romanticism, see Gurza et al., *Historia de la profesiones.*

73. Porrúa, *Diccionario Porrúa,* 1:903.

74. Jack Ray Thomas, *Biographical Dictionary of Latin American Historians and Historiography* (Westport, Conn.: Greenwood Press, 1984), 214, 294–95.

75. Charles Hale, "The Liberal Impulse: Daniel Cosío Villegas and the *Historia Moderna de México,"* *Hispanic American Historical Review* 54(1974): 479–98; Stanley Ross, "Obituary Daniel Cosío Villegas (1898–1976)" ibid. 57, no. 1 (1977): 91–103.

76. Porrúa, *Diccionario Porrúa,* 1:571.

77. Comité Mexicano de Ciencias Históricas, *Catálogo de tesis sobre historia de México* (Mexico: CMCH, 1976) lists five hundred theses and dissertations completed from 1941 to 1976.

78. John Phelan, "Many Conquests: Some Trends and Some Challenges in Mexican Historiography," *Investigaciones contemporáneos sobre historia de México* (Mexico City, 1971), 125–48.

79. David C. Bailey, "Revisionism and the Recent Historiography of the Mexican Revolution," *Hispanic American Historical Review* 58(1978): 62–79.

80. The information was gathered in previous work from historians at UNAM and El Colegio de México in 1980.

81. For the "continuity of thought" thesis, see Alvaro Matute, *La teoría de la historia en México, 1940–1973* (Mexico City: Secretaría de Educación Pública, 1974), in which he argues that the two main trends in Mexico continue to be positivism represented, for example, by Silvio Zavala and historicism, the romantic metaphysical worldview of Edmondo O'Gorman; Josefina Zoraida Vázquez, *Historia de la Historiografía* (Mexico City: Ediciónes Ateneo, 1978), downplays the distinctiveness of contemporary national schools of history writing.

82. For example, *Primer encuentro Hispano-Mexicano de historiadores* (Madrid: INCE, 1979).

83. Rudolfo Stavenhagen, "Seven Erroneous Theses about Latin America," in *Latin American Radicalism: Documentary Report on Left and Nationalist Movements,* ed. Irving Louis Horowitz, Josué de Castro, and John Gerassi (New York: Vintage Books, 1969), 102–17, argues against overworking the concept of "Primate City," for example, Mexico City, as a way of explaining Mexican political and economic decisions.

84. J. R. Thomas, *Biographical Dictionary,* 183–84.

85. Ibid., 143–44.

86. Edward Mosely and Edward Terry, *Yucután—A World Apart* (Mobile: Univ. of Alabama Press, 1980), chap. 10, and passim.

7. The "Tribal-Ethnic Road" in Europe: Albania, 1878–1990

1. For this road, see Leroy Vail, ed., *The Creation of Tribalism in Southern Africa* (Berkeley: Univ. of California Press, 1991), introduction and chap. 11. In Albanian studies, the model proposed here comes closest to the "Third-Worldist" view of Albania; Elez Biberaj, "Albania and the Third World: Ideological, Political, and Economic Aspects," in *Eastern Europe and the Third World,* ed. Michael Radu (New York: Frederick A. Praeger, 1981), 55–76, but in addition to this Western European countries—Switzerland, Belgium, and Scandanavia are substantially tribal-ethnic—and parts of the Third World are not tribal-ethnic; see Arshi Pipa, "Glasnost in Albania," *Telos* 79 (Spring 1989): 181–203, esp. 197.

2. For gender contradiction in a tribal-ethnic state, portrayed brilliantly in a novel by a Lebanese woman, see Etel Adnan, *Sitt Marie-Rose* (Sausalito: Post-Apollo Press, 1982). For Albania, there is ethnographic literature, more on the Ghegs in the North than on the Tosks of the South. Examples include Berth Danermark et al., "Women, Marriage, and Family—Traditionalism vs. Modernity in Albania," *International Journal of Sociology of the Family* 19 (1989): 19–41; Ian Whitaker, " 'A Sack for Carrying Things': The Traditional Role of Women in Northern Albanian Society," *Anthropological Quarterly* 54, no. 3 (1981): 146–56. Another correlative of gender oppression is forced pronatalism, a policy that in Albania is extreme; Henry Philip David, "Eastern Europe: Pronatalist Policies and Private Behavior," *Population Bulletin* 36, no. 6 (1982): 2–47.

Indirect forms of evidence also substantiate the designation of modern Albania as tribal-ethnic with the added meaning of gender based. Personnel from U.S. hospitals confront the problem of treating patients from Albania and convey in their clinical writings their experiences and insights. Albanians are noted for their obsession with female modesty, reticence about discussions of family planning, predilection for the services of a midwife rather than those of a hospital doctor, and lack of interest in prenatal care.

Other observations concern the reaction of Albanians to the idea of psychiatry; see the article of a hospital administrator, Howard Weinberg, "Staff Overcomes Cultural Barriers to Care," *Hospitals* 49, no. 16 (Aug. 16, 1975): 60–62. Another article reflects on the different ways in which families bond with their newborn children. Albanians in South Italy are among the most immediate and most family intensive even by Italian standards; Lucille F. Newman et al., "Early Human Interaction: Mother and Child," *Primary Care* 3, no. 3 (1976): 491–505, esp. the pages by Janet Schreiber, 499–504.

Another form of indirect evidence can be drawn from studies in comparative law. One such study shows that the tribal-ethnic states of Europe lead the way in giving rights to the child born out of wedlock, whereas in the democracies and in the Italian states, the interest of the child is balanced with the interests of the parents in maintaining the distinction of legitimacy and illegitimacy. Tribal-ethnic states clearly do not want unattached children; in Albania, the court will decide to whom the child is to be awarded in cases in which paternity is not evident; Robert Kiebala and George Naschitz, "The Paternity Suit in Europe," *Buffalo Law Review* 16 (1966–67): 287–305.

3. Partha Chatterjee, "The Nationalist Resolution of the Women's Question," in *Recasting Women: Essays in Colonial History,* ed. Kumkum Sangari and Sudesh Vaid (New Delhi: Kali for Women, 1989), 233–254, esp. 252.

4. Recourse to the writings in "transcultural psychiatry" lends some credence to the idea that schizophrenia is a major problem in at least a number of the contemporary tribal-ethnic states as it is—for whatever reasons—in other kinds of states as well. Ibrahim Sow, the Senegalese scholar, cites a study that indicates it is the major form of chronic mental illness in

tropical Africa; I. Sow, *Anthropological Structures of Madness in Black Africa* (New York: International Universities Press, 1980), 28. In the exhaustive bibliography on Albania compiled by William B. Bland, the only monograph cited in the area of psychiatry was one on the treatment of schizophrenics; Bland, *Albania* (Oxford: Clio Press, 1988), 188. For the opposite view, that schizophrenia would not be likely to occur in primitive societies, see with reference to the Belgian Congo, R. Faris, "Some Observations on the Incidence of Schizophrenia in Primitive Societies," *Journal of Abnormal Social Psychology* 29 (1934): 30-31.

5. Influential writing by overseas Albanian writers includes, Stavro Skendi, *The Albanian National Awakening, 1878-1912* (Princeton, N.J.: Princeton Univ. Press, 1967); Peter Prifti, *Socialist Albania since 1944: Domestic and Foreign Developments* (Cambridge, Mass.: MIT, Press 1978); Arshi Pipa, *Albanian Stalinism: Ideo-Political Aspects* (Boulder, Colo.: East European Monographs, 1990); idem, *The Politics of Language in Socialist Albania* (Boulder, Colo.: East European Monographs, 1989).

6. On the affinity of Albanian communism to Anabaptism, an anarchist, mystical Christian sect found coincidentally in both Albania and the Belgian Congo, see Anton Logoreci, "Albania: The Anabaptists of European Communism," *Problems of Communism* 16, no. 3 (1967): 22-28.

7. For two contrastive works of gnosis, see the Zairian philosophy, V. Y. Mudimbe, *The Invention of Africa—Gnosis, Philosophy, and the Order of Knowledge* (Bloomington: Indiana Univ. Press, 1988); see also the Albanian Albanologist and student of language, Androkli Kostallari, "Le Développement des études Albanologiques en Albanie: Problèmes nouveaux et taches nouvelles," *Studia Albanica* 1, no. 1 (1964): 5-46. Recognition of an Albanian gnosis appears glancingly in Jon Halliday, ed., *The Artful Albanian: Memoirs of Enver Hoxha* (London: Chatto and Windus, 1986), 7 and passim, Arshi Pipa, "Party Ideology and Purges in Albania" *Telos* 59 (Spring 1984): 95, and in an interesting quote: "A Polish literary magazine once accused the Albanian media of speaking what the author of the article called 'Tiranese' which he characterized as a total disregard of the facts, a free transposition of cause and effect, separating words from their real meanings and calling things by names totally alien to them, a whole line of reasoning based on a wholly arbitrary interpretation of reality" (Paul Underwood, "Albania," in *World Press Encyclopedia*, ed. George Thomas Kurian [New York: Facts on File], 1982, 82).

8. Pipa, *Politics of Language, im passim.*

9. Claims about Albania reveal the confusions of outsiders from other hegemonies. Whereas some find Albania to be warlike and dangerous, others find it to be uniquely peaceful, the one country in which Muslims, Christians, and Orthodox peacefully coexist. This was the view of Muhammad Ali, the Indian delegate to the League of Nations, who advocated that Albania should become an independent country. Fan Noli, *Fiftieth Anniversary Book of the Albanian Orthodox Church in America, 1908-1958* (Boston: Albanian Orthodox Church in America, 1960), 117.

10. Samir Amin has called this delinking.

11. Elez Biberaj, *Albania: A Socialist Maverick* (Boulder, Colo.: Westview Press, 1990), is a start.

12. Stavro Skendi, ed., *Albania* (New York: Frederick A. Praeger, 1956), 122, 325-26; Arshi Pipa, "Party Ideology and Purges," 89, 95, notes that among European countries, only in Albania was it predictable for the purger to be purged. Similar claims are made for Zaire.

13. For a work that supports the idea of comparing Albania and North Korea and Kampuchea to each other as opposed to the USSR, see William B. Simons and Stephen White, eds., *The Party Statutes of the Communist World* (The Hague: Martinus Nijhoff, 1984), 25-26, 536; J. S. Roucek, "Criminal Law of Moscow's European Satellites," *International Journal of Legal Research* 2 (1967): 113-29, esp. 113, notes that the constitution of Albania does not borrow the federal structure found in different forms in the USSR and Yugoslavia.

14. Enver Hoxha, *On the Further Revolutionization of the Party and the Whole Life of the Country: Speeches 1971–1973* (Tirana: The "November 8" Publishing House, 1974), 7, 95–96, 100.

15. In both Albania and the Belgian Congo, one finds highly conflictual relations between church and state. For the Roman Catholic church in Albania, see note 53, this chapter; for the church in the Belgian Congo, see, David Northrup, "A Church in Search of a State: Catholic Missions in Eastern Zaire, 1879–1930," *Journal of Church and State* 30(1988): 309–19.

16. Emin Riza, "Les Villes-Musées, Leur valeurs et leur place de nos jours," *Studia Albanica* 14, no. 1 (1987): 129–38.

17. Pipa, "Party Ideology and Purges," 70.

18. Adi Schnytzer, *Stalinist Economic Strategy in Practice: The Case of Albania* (Oxford: Oxford Univ. Press, 1982), chap. 6, notes that while Stalinism was continuously invoked, it was continuously adapted. Halliday, in, *The Artful Albanian,* also hedges on the use of the word *Stalinist* in application to Hoxha, 15–16.

19. Halliday, *Artful Albanian,* 328.

20. In Hoxha's memoirs cited in n. 18, he does not introduce his future wife simply as a leading cadre but as someone loyal to him, ibid., 76–77.

21. For overseas Albanians, see Federal Writer's Project of the Works Progress Administration of Massachusettes, *The Albanian Struggle in the Old World and the New* (Boston: Writer, 1939); for Zairians who were influential in exile and often referred to as such by historians of Zaire, there is the example of Abbé Alexis Kagamé. Beginning in the 1940s, Kagamé gave the Zairians a modernist interpretation of their traditional philosophy. Thomas Kanza, a political thinker, and those of his generation of the 1940s-1960s who lived in Paris and Brussels formulated the ideas of the national struggle for the independent country, then still many years in the future.

22. For the development of different branches of Albanian law for the pre-communist and then for the communist periods, see the chapters written by the Albanian lawyer Kemal Aly Vokopola in Vladimir Gsovski and Kazimierz Grzybowski, *Government, Law, and Courts in the Soviet Union and Eastern Europe* (New York: Frederick A. Praeger 1960), 2 vols., esp. 1:184, 188, 634, where the statute law of the 1920s is praised; 2:970, on military courts in different periods; 972, 974, noting a decline in positive law over the twentieth century as yet another evidence of continuity; 975, 981, 1997, on inheritance law; 1202–4, 1726, and 1731, on some continuity in land reform between the 1930s and the 1950s.

23. Christopher Boehm, "Execution Within the Clan as an Extreme Form of Ostracism," *Social Science Information* 24, no. 2 (1985): 309–21.

24. The line of interpretation followed here emphasizes the continuity of modern Albanian history. The continuity approach in Albanian historiography is called the Ethnogenesis school; see, for example, Pranvera Bogdani, "Les Tendances à l'unification étatique des territoires albanais dans la seconde moitié du XIVᵉ siècle et du début du XVᵉ" *Studia Albanica* 19(1982): 221–31; Alfred Uçi, "La Culture nationale au fil de la lutte pour la liberté et l'indépendance," *Studia Albanica* 25, no. 1 (1988): 19–33; the Modernist school tends to emphasize cultural diffusion over ethnogenesis; Bojka Sokolova, "Les Institutions scolaires et culturelles nationales en Albanie et la formation de l'intelligentsia albanaise a l'époque de la renaissance," *Études Balkaniques* 22, no. 3 (1986): 38–61.

25. A parallel between this period in the Balkans and in Africa emerges from a study of Bismarck and of the various partition plans around 1880. For Albania in this period, see Stavro Skendi, "Beginnings of Albanian Nationalist and Autonomous Trends: The Albanian League, 1878–1881," *American Slavic and East European Review* 12(1953): 219–32; Stefanaq Pollo and Arben Puto, *The History of Albania* (London: Routledge Kegan Paul, 1981), chap. 6.

26. This chronology is drawn from Stavro Skendi, "Albanian Political Thought and Revolutionary Activity," *Süd-Ost Forschungen* 13(1954): 159–99.

27. Stavro Skendi, "The History of the Albanian Alphabet: A Case of Complex Cultural and Political Development," *Balkan Cultural Studies* (Boulder, Colo.: East European Monographs, 1980), chap. 14.

28. Nikolaos A. Stavrou, "Albania," in *Political Parties of Europe: Albania-Norway,* ed. Vincent E. McHale and Sharon Skowronski (Westport, Conn.: Greenwood Press, 1983), 10–17.

29. Gwen Robyns, *Geraldine of the Albanians: The Authorised Biography* (London: Muller, Blond, and White, 1987), 16.

30. Skendi, *Albania,* 190.

31. Pollo and Puto, *History of Albania,* 198, 214, 216.

32. Bernd Jurgen Fischer, *King Zog and the Struggle for Stability in Albania* (Boulder, Colo.: East European Monographs), 198.

33. The life of Prince Leka is a useful example of an elite figure of a tribal-ethnic state dependent on the great powers. This "Chief of the Sons of the Eagle" grew up to be a CIA agent and international weapons smuggler, specializing in Russian and Chinese weapons for a worldwide clientele, including the Arabs, is reputed to have given Ronald Reagan a baby elephant when Reagan was governor of California, and is also reputed to be related to Richard Nixon through his maternal grandmother; see Charles Fenyvesi, *Splendour in Exile: The Ex-Majesties of Europe* (Washington, D.C.: New Republic Books, 1979), 229. Senator Jesse Helms, too, has been a long-time supporter; Gwen Robyns, *Geraldine,* 10. In his personal life, Zog's search for a wife among the nobility, Robyns notes, reflected a certain single-mindedness about virginity (13). Dream interpretation also figures, for example, Geraldine's recollection of her grandmother's advice that came to her in a dream in Albania that she should never read Freud, Nietzsche, or Schopenhauer because they are bad for you; rather one should trust in the Sermon on the Mount (45). Geraldine's office in the palace was designed to deal with the personal problems of petitioners from all over Albania, its power enhanced by her personal tie to the International Red Cross (51). Geraldine also recalled Zog's honoring his six sisters by making them honorary colonels-in-chief of regiments.

34. Margaret Hasluck, *The Unwritten Law in Albania* (Cambridge: Cambridge Univ. Press, 1954), 261; more recently the Code of Lek appeared in translation with notes by Leonard Fox and Shtjefén Gjécov *Kanuni I Leké Dukagjinit: The Code of Leké Dukadjini* (New York: Gjonlekaj Publishing, 1989).

35. Marcelus Redlich, *Albania, Yesterday and Today* (Worcester, Mass.: Albanian Messenger, 1936), 78, 144ff.

36. Fischer, *King Zog,* chap. 8.

37. Pollo and Puto, *History of Albania,* 224.

38. Ramadan Marmullaku, *Albania and the Albanians* (Hamden, Conn.: Archon Books, 1975), 25–26.

39. Prifti, *Socialist Albania,* 105ff., cites Hoxha's statements about women's liberation. Hoxha had as did, Queen Geraldine before him, an active distaste for Nietzsche and Freud. Hoxha believed that those writers promoted the idea that men are active and women passive and that this assumption leads to Nazism in politics and sadism in sex.

40. Article 11 of the Constitution of 1950 stated that no one has the right to use private property against the state and that private property can be limited or expropriated if it is in the public interest to do so; Skendi, *Albania,* 68, 96.

41. Pipa, "Party Ideology and Purges," 78.

42. Elez Biberaj, *Albania and China: A Study of an Unequal Alliance* (Boulder, Colo.: Westview Press, 1986), 97ff., provides a discussion of Chinese economic leverage against Albania.

43. Prifti, *Socialist Albania* 61, 67; Skendi, *Albania,* 210. The fact that the barter market

was declared illegal and abolished in 1956 suggests resistance by the direct producers to the new extractions procedures. In the 1950s, newspaper columnists attacked the state co-ops for their desire for tremendous profits, for hoarding, and for speculation.

44. Ian Whitaker, "Tribal Structure and National Politics in Albania, 1910–1950," in I. M. Lewis, ed., *History and Social Anthropology* (London: Tavistock, 1968), 254ff.

45. André Blanc, "L'Évolution contemporaine de la vie pastorale en Albanie méridionale," *Revue de Géographie Alpine* 51 (1963): 455–56. Despite an enthusiastic commitment to development, Blanc finds a probable lack of change north of Tirana and the persistence of tradition even in the rural South. In a more recent article, an Albanian ethnographer notes the quest of the peasants for the miraculous intervention of God for good harvests and for the cure of ailments along with other miracles. Mark Tirtja, "Survivances religieuses du passé dans la vie du peuples (Objets et lieux de culte)," *Ethnographie Albanaise* (Tiranë: Akademie des Sciences dela RPA, 1976), 49–71. See also Andro Maqi, "Aprons in Albanian Popular Costume from the End of the Nineteenth Century to the First Half of the Twentieth," *Costume* (1986): 44–62. Despite dozens of local permutations, the apron design serves as a defense of tradition against the state. Aprons distinguish married from unmarried women, Muslim (black) from Greek Orthodox (cherry, crimson, and trapeze-shaped). A stock figure in Balkan culture is the figure of the bajalica, or conjurer, who heals with words; see Barbara Kerewsky-Halpern, "Trust, Talk, and Touch in Balkan Folk-Healing," *Social Science and Medicine* 21, no. 3 (1985): 319–25. For an example from another communist country, Romania, see Val Cordun, "Les Saints thaumaturges d'Ada Kaleh," *Turcica* 3 (1971): 101–16; a comment on Albanian healers appears in Edith Durham, *High Albania* (Boston: Beacon Press, 1987), 83, 316. A standard work on Zairian healers is John Janzen, *The Quest for Therapy in Lower Zaire* (Berkeley: Univ. of California Press, 1978).

46. Enver Hoxha, *Revolutionization of the Party*, 106, 110–11, 129, 130, 135, 300–301.

47. Arshi Pipa, "The Political Culture of Hoxha's Albania," in *The Stalinist Legacy: Its Impact on Twentieth-Century World Politics*, ed. Tariq Ali (Boulder, Colo.: Lynne Rienner Publishers, 1985), 435–64, esp. 455–56. For comments on continuity in Albanian history, see Klaus Lange, *Grundzüge der Albanischen Politik* (Munich: R. Trofenik, 1973), 95, 118.

48. For an indication of the continuing existence of the feudal and liberal forces in exile, see Mihail-Dimitri Sturdza, *Dictionnaire Historique et Généalogique des Grandes familles de Grèce, d'Albanie et de Constantinople* (Paris: Mihail-Dimitri Sturdza, 1983).

49. Orjan Sjöberg, "Urban Albania: Developments 1965–1987," in *Albanien im Umbruch,* ed. Franz-Lothar Altmann (Munich: R. Oldenbourg, 1990), 171–224.

50. Robert Elsie, "Modern Albanian Literature," in Sjöberg, *Albanien im Umbruch,* 248; Biberaj, *Albania-A Socialist Maverick,* 63, quotes an official in 1985 who stated that tourism was discouraged to prevent Albanian youth from being influenced by foreign customs.

51. Whitaker, " 'A sack for carrying things,' " other commentary on gender issues includes the following: the claim by Nexhmije Hoxha, the wife of Enver Hoxha, that women are more revolutionary than men, Nexhmije Hoxha, *Some Fundamental Questions of the Revolutionary Policy of the Party of Labor of Albania about the Development of the Class Struggle* (Tirana: "8 Nentori" Publishing House, 1977); on the absence of commentary on women in Hoxha's Memoirs, Halliday, *Artful Albanian,* 13–14; John Kolsti, "From Courtyard to Cabinet: The Political Emergence of Albanian Women," in *Women, State, and Party in Eastern Europe,* ed. Sharon L. Wolchik and Alfred G. Meyer (Durham, N.C.: Duke Univ. Press, 1985), 138–51. It appears that the prominent women are all married (kin linked) to high party officials. Others, such as the television commentator Themi Thomai and Lenka Çuko, the administrator, rose by their competence and by their own party ties.

52. Georges Henri Bousquet, "Notes sur les réformes de l'Islam Albanais," *Revue des Études Islamiques* 9 (1935): 399–410; Margaret Hasluck, "The Non-Conformist Moslems of

Albania," *Muslim World* 15 (1925): 388–98; A. Popovic, "Les Ordres mystiques Musulmans du sud-est Européen dans la période post-Ottomane," in *Les Ordres mystiques dans l'Islam,* ed. A. Popovic and G. Veinstein (Paris: CNRS, 1985), 63–101.

53. Nathalie Clayer, *L'Albanie, Pays des derviches* (Berlin: Osteuropa-Institut der Facien Universität, 1990), 224; A. Popovic, "L'Islam et l'etat dans les pays du sud-est Europe," in *L'Islam et l'état dans le monde Aujourd'hui,* ed. O. Carré (Paris: Presses Universitaires de France, 1982), 133. An obvious parallel to the abolition of the religions in Albania was Mobutu's founding of his Movement Populaire de la Révolution (MPR) as the unique party in 1967 in Zaire. From this step, he then conceived the party's ideology to be an alternative to the gospel. In both countries, the regimes have thought that the Roman Catholic church was a vehicle for international imperialist interference (see n. 15 this chap.).

54. René Epp, "L'Église Catholique en Albanie," *Revue des Sciences Religieuses* 50 (1976): 52–76.

55. Stephen R. Bowers, "Church and State in Albania," *Religion in Communist Lands* 6, no. 3 (1978): 148–52.

56. Kostallari, "Le Développement des études Albanologiques," is an essay in Albanian Albanology, which among other things, is highly critical of contemporary history writing. Concerning the predominance of anarchism in Albania, there is no one source or bibliography. For evidence of anarchism in economics, a sympathetic commentator is the agronomist René Dumont, *Finis les lendemains qui chantent* (Paris: Seuil, 1983). Anarchism in Albanian culture can be observed in such areas as the orientation of the foreign literature translated into Albanian. Among American works translated into Albanian are some by Walt Whitman, Theodore Dreiser, and Mark Twain. Russian authors include Pushkin, Tolstoy, Chekhov, Gogol, and Dostoevski. Other writers include Voltaire, Heine, and Tagore; see Prifti, *Socialist Albania,* 133–34. The anarchist worldview appears in the thought of major Albanian writers as well. An example one could choose would be Bishop Fan Noli. From a recent account of his life, one learns of his exposure to the "orality of culture" from his long years serving as a cantor and, thus, of being a chanter. As a literary translator, Noli has been, in fact, accused of being anarchistic, especially in his *Hamlet* and in his *Don Quixote.* In these works, Noli ignored the formal elements "such as language and style, plot and dialogue, narrative patterns and versification structures." To his biographer, Noli was thus being "one-sided," a one-sidedness that extended to his interpretation of literature as well. Whereas most of Europe is accustomed to Hamlet as irresolute, Noli portrayed Hamlet as a superman, emphasizing his resoluteness and his skill as a diplomat. Even Don Quixote, in Noli's view, took on an anarchist appearance as a champion of old chivalry against the corrupt petty beys of his time. Noli was also drawn to Ibsen's *An Enemy of the People,* bringing to it the insight that in Ibsen's Denmark (another tribal-ethnic road state) an author, such as Ibsen, might well hate bourgeois culture without feeling a tie to the masses. This was arguably Noli's predicament as well. Other pieces of evidence supporting the link between Noli and anarchism could be drawn from his autobiographical sketch in which he refers to leaving "Europe on board a ship with Nietzsche in his hands," from his study of the life of Beethoven (Noli found that Beethoven despised kings, lords, and priests), and from his work on the church. As the head of what became the autocephalous Albanian Orthodox Church, Noli altered the liturgy. An example of Noli's initiatives was his versification of Matthew. See A. Pipa, "Fan Noli as a National and International Figure," *Südost Forschungen* 43(1984): 241–70, esp. 250–51, 252, 262, 269. For the well-known contemporary novelist Ismail Kadare, one could note that in the plot of *The General of the Dead Army,* the best-known modern Albanian novel, the task of the protagonist, an Italian officer searching for war dead in Albania, was to act as an intermediary between the dead and the living. As an "African" conjuror might, the hero quarrels with a Catholic priest over evil spells. Even the priest, however, cannot prevent the germs of the dead from coming back— after twenty years—to kill the living, who pursue them. The world of Albania is described as

if it were an intimidating nether world in which the corpse of Colonel Z, possessed of some evil power, can elude the protagonist; Ismail Kadare, *The General of the Dead Army* (New York: Grossman, 1972).

57. It is, strictly speaking, not correct to term the clarification of the alphabet, the grammar, and the dialect as a "standardization of language" as is the common practice. Standardization is not quite the objective, if one thinks about gnosis, and not quite the outcome, as one can see from the rise of diglossia; Janet Byron, *Selections among Alternatives in Language: Standardization, The Case of Albanian* (The Hague: Mouton, 1976).

58. Skendi, "Albanian Alphabet"; Joan Fultz Kontos, *Red Cross, Black Eagle: A Biography of Albania's American School* (Boulder, Colo.: East European Monographs, 1981).

59. On details of the life, see Noli, *Albanian Orthodox Church;* Pipa, "Fan Noli."

60. Martin E. Huld, "Birds, Beasts and Indo-European Merismatic Compounds in Albanian," *Zeitschrift für Vergleichende Sprachforschung* 96 (1982–83): 152–58, esp. 152, where Albanian is distinguished from other Indo-European languages. For humans in folklore, see Arshi Pipa, "Mythologie de l'Albanie," in *Dictionnaire des Mythologies,* ed. Yves Bonnefoy (Paris: Flammarion, 1981), 1: 5–6.

61. Eric P. Hamp, "Albanian edhe 'And'," in *Bono Homini Donum,* ed. Yoel L. Arbeitman and Allan Bomhard (Amsterdam, John Benjamin B. V., 1981), 127–31; J. Knobloch, " 'Female Speech' in Greek, Armenian, and Albanian," *Journal of Indo-European Studies* 16 (1988): 123–25.

62. His daughter Semiramis, the dean of the College of Natural Sciences at Tiranë, is the wife of the recent Albanian leader Ramiz Alia; Eqrem Çabej, "Alexsandër Xhuvani et la Linguistique Historique Albanaise," *Studia Albanica* 18, no. 2 (1981): 67–71. Could a figure, such as Xhuvani, have survived in another type of hegemony, moving as he did on the basis of personal loyalty from liberalism to fascism to communism?

63. This is the broad theme of Pipa, *Politics of Language;* see also George Messing, "Politics and National Language in Albania," in *Contributions to Historical Linguistics* (Leiden: E. J. Brill, 1980), 3, 270–80.

64. But does mass media overcome diglossia? See Underwood, "Albania" 80–85, on Chinese technical help for Albanian radio.

65. Sources for the 1960s-1970s comment freely on the crisis in development; Peter Prifti, "Albania: Towards an Atheist Society," in *Religion and Atheism in the USSR and Eastern Europe,* ed. Bohdan R. Bociurkin and John Strong (Toronto: Univ. of Toronto Press, 1975), 396, quotes the Albanian folklorist Zihni Sako to the effect that the favorite Albanian folklore figure is Nasrusddin Hoxha, an irreverent religious figure. This is surely regime bravado! Nicholas Pano, "The Albanian Cultural Revolution," *Problems of Communism* 26, (July 1974): 44–57; Annicke Miské, *Des Albanaises* (Paris: Des Femmes, 1976); Peter Prifti, "The Albanian Party of Labor and the Intelligentsia," *East European Quarterly* 8, no. 3 (Fall 1974): 307–35; Julian Birch, "The Albanian Political Experience," in *Political Opposition in One-Party States,* ed. Leonard Shapiro (London: Macmillan, 1972), 179–200, present the problems stemming from development.

66. Materials for this section are drawn from Robert Elsie, *A Dictionary of Albanian Literature* (Westport, Conn.: Greenwood Press, 1986); for Shkodër (Scutari) a more detailed account can be drawn from Stuart E. Mann, *Albanian Literature* (London: Bernard Quaritch, 1955), 63–82.

67. Difficulties in getting the kind of poetry needed are alluded to in Koço Bihiku, "Problèmes du jour de tradition et d'innovation dans notre litiérature du réalisme socialiste," *Studia Albanica* 10, no. 2 (1973): 3–27.

68. Muzafer Korkuti, "Découvrir l'archéologie Albanaise," in *La Très riche Albanie archéologique* Dossiers, histoire et archéologie no. 111, (Dijon: Archéologia, Dec. 1986); on the opening of the Albanian Museum of Natural History in Tirana in 1981, see an article by the director

Burhan Çiraku, "The Albanian Museum of Natural History," *Museum* 36, no. 1 (1984): 49–54.

69. From a conference proceedings published in Tirana in 1971, it appears that expectations concerning archeology were low throughout the early twentieth century, that in 1945, there were only 8 or 9 Illyrian sites, but that later this rose to 170, permitting scholars to speak confidently of the links between ancient Illyria, medieval Arbanon, and modern Albania. A chart reveals that the bulk of the ancient Illyrian fortresses, all of the ancient cities, and most of the total sites were in the South. In the North, the main findings were the medieval fortresses and tumuli. These findings led to a periodization of ancient Albanian history based on Friedrich Engels, *Les Illyriens et la genèse des Albanais*, ed. Muzafer Korkuti, Skënder Anamali, and Jorgji Gjinari (Tiranë: Univ. of Tiranë, 1971), 6, 37, 253; Skënder Anamali, "L'Archéologie Albanaise dans ces 25 ans," *Studia Albanica* 5, no. 2 (1969): 21–34. Along with classical archeology, the state also encouraged the translation of Greek classical poetry, historical epics, and works referring to Illyria; Martin Ferguson Smith, "Classics in Albania" (Ilford U.K.: Albanian Society, 1984).

70. Prifti, *Socialist Albania,* 113ff.

71. Andromaqi Gjergji and Abaz Dojaka, "Un Quart siècle de travaux dans le domaine de l'ethnographie," *Studia Albanica* 5(1969): 57–68; Rrok Zjzi, "L'Ancienne division régionale ethnographique du peuple Albanais," *Ethnographie Albanaise,* (Tiranë: Akademie des Sciences de la RPA, 1976), 7–19; see also Aleks Buda, "L'Ethnographie Albanaise et quelques-uns de ses problèmes," *Studia Albanica* 12, no. 2 (1976): 12–35.

72. Zihni Sako, "Les Voies de développement des études folkloristiques et du folklore Albanais," in *Actes du IIè congrès international des études du sud-est Europe* (Athens, 1973), 471–90, esp. 484–86, 489; for this connundrum see also Alfred Uçi, "Le Folklore Albanais entre le passé et le présent," *Studia Albanica* 12, no. 2 (1976): 12–35.

73. In tribal-ethnic states, where the state itself is weak, the opposite can be true, for example, Beirut.

74. John I. Thomas, "The Evolvement of Communist Education in Albania," (Ph.D. diss., Univ. of Connecticut, 1967).

75. For a list of Albanian historical studies, most of which are on the party, see Erwin Lewin and Willy Steltner, "Bibliographie Albanischer Literatur zur Geschichte Albaniens (1944–1958)," *Jahrbuch für Geschichte des UdSSR und der Volksdemokratischen Länder Europas* 4(1960): 457–75. For an example of a recent work in the genealogical tradition, see the unattributed essay, "Contribution de grande portée pour la nouvelle historiographie Albanaise," *Studia Albanica* 20, no. 1 (1983): 3–17, dwelling on the utility to historians of Hoxha's study, *The Anglo-American Threat to Albania* (Toronto: Marx, Engels, Lenin, Stalin, Institute, 1982). For a validation of the Albanian historical profession in this genealogical vein, see an article by a leading Albanian historian in which he quotes comments by Enver Hoxha praising its historical scholarship; Stefanaq Pollo, "L'Historiographie marxiste-léniniste Albaniase et les chemins de son développement," *Studia Albanica* 18, no. 1 (1979): 3–14. For an example of microhistory or Annaliste history, see also Selami Pulaha, "Aspects de démographie historique des contrées Albanaises pendant les XVe-XVIe siècles," *Studia Albanica* 21, no. 2 (1984): 65–76. For comments on diplomatic history by a leading practitioner, see Arben Puto, "Introduction à l'histoire diplomatique de l'indépendance Albanaise," an essay drawn from his recent monograph and published in *Studia Albanica* 18, no. 1 (1979): 19–64. In this article, he shows the role diplomatic history can play given the great interest of Albanians in imperialism.

76. Aleks Buda, "Quelques questions de l'histoire de la formation du peuple Albanais, de la langue and de la culture," *Studia Albanica* 17(1980): 41–61, explicates ethnogenesis.

77. A bibliography of recent works in Albania up to 1967 shows that nearly every major Albanian interpreter of culture has at least one piece on the figure of Skanderbeg; see Dodona Dhima, "Publications Albanaises à l'occasion du 5e centenaire de la mort de Georges Kastriote

Skanderbeg," *Studia Albanica* 5, no. 2 (1968): 173–95; Kole Luka, *Chansonnier épique Albanais* (Tirana: Académie des Sciences de la RPS d'Albanie, 1983), provides a number of texts on Skanderbeg and on more recent historical themes as well produced by the singers of epics. For the popular attraction to historical epics on even more recent historical themes—the national movement, the opposition to King Zog, and Italian imperialism—and in support of socialism, see Qemal Haxhihasani, "L'Épique populaire histoire Albanaise aux XIX-XXᵉ siècles," *Studia Albanica* 12 (1975): 71–79. For a technical analysis of the form of the epic verse, see Arshi Pipa, *Albanian Folk Verse: Structure and Genre* (Munich: Trofenik, 1978), chap. 9. In Western Europe, Skanderbeg was well-known through the eighteenth century, but thereafter few references appear, compounding the problem of Albanian isolation.

78. Aleks Buda, "Fan S. Noli (1882–1965)," *Studia Albanica* 2, no. 1 (1965): 3–8; V. Gjonaj, "La Vie scientifique—Conférence scientifique à l'occasion du centenaire de la naissance de Fan S. Noli," *Studia Albanica* 19, no. 1 (1982): 240–49. From the analysis of worldviews dominant in different hegemonies, one can examine the structure of national grammars. A recent commentary on the Albanian admirative, a part of the indicative mood, shows that Albanian's indicative mood supports the reportage of facts for which the speaker assumes no responsibility. It is marked by irony, indirection, and uninvolvement. In English or French, this would not be the indicative mood; Victor A. Friedman, *Evidentiality in the Balkans: Bulgarian, Macedonian and Albanian* (Norwood, N.J.: Ablex Publishing, 1986), chap. 10.

79. Skendi, *Albanian National Awakening,* 122–24.

80. A. Ducellier, "L'Orientation des études historiques en république populaire d'Albanie, 1945–1966," *Revue Historique* 237 (Jan.-June 1967): 124–44.

81. Skendi, *Albania,* 282–83.

82. Byron, *Selections among Alternatives* 59.

83. One example was the multivolume *History of the Socialist Construction of Albania, 1944–1975* that Luan Omari and Stefanas Pollo produced under the imprimatur of the Academia e Shkencave e RPS té Shqipérisé, the Popular Socialist Republic of Albania, and the Instituti i Historisé (Tirana; 1983); vol. 4 of this work has been translated into English as Luan Omari and Stefanas Pollo, *Histoire de la Construction Socialiste en Albanie* (Tirana: Academie des Sciences de la RPSA, 1988); see also Pollo and Puto, *History of Albania.*

8. The "Tribal-Ethnic, Road in Africa: Belgian Congo/Zaire, 1885–1990

1. See, Alpha Condé, *Guinée: L'Albanie de l'Afrique ou néo-colonie américaine?* (Paris: Éditions Gît-le Coeur, 1972); Haim Gerber, *Islam, Guerilla War and Revolution* (Boulder, Colo.: Lynn Rienner, 1988); Scandinavian-African connections are yet another way to pursue comparisons among tribal-ethnic states, see Arne Sorenson, "The Scandinavian Concept of History," in Torben Lundbak *African Humanism-Scandinavian Culture—A Dialogue* (Copenhagen: Danish International Development, 1970), 136–39 nn., for example, the popularity of the structuralist anthropologist Claude Lévi-Strauss among Danish historians; Lévi-Strauss is also popular in Zaire. Scholars from the United States and the United Kingdom, however, have attacked Lévi-Strauss, Luc de Heusch, and others for their use of imagination and intuition; Jan Vansina, "Is Elegance Proof? Structuralism and African History," *History in Africa* 10(1983): 307–48, esp. 314; David Pace, *Claude Lévi-Strauss: The Bearer of the Ashes* (Boston: Routledge, Kegan Paul, 1983), 95ff. Crawford Young and Thomas Turner, *The Rise and Decline of the Zairian State* (Madison: Univ. of Wisconsin Press, 1985), 443, n. 55, introduce the possibility of comparing the thought of Mobutu with that of the North Korean leader Kim Il Sung. Considered also is the use of political myth as a source. If, in Bakongo mythology, Zaire was a noble woman who sought her freedom from her Saracen master, was this a Bakongo view of the rise of the modern state and of the destruction of the Congo Arabs?

Young and Turner, *Rise and Decline,* 443, n. 44. Similarly, Ronald Cohen, "Oedipus Rex and Regina: The Queen Mother in Africa," *Africa* 47, no. 1 (1977): 23; Bogumil Jewsiewicki's search for a "new epistème" overlaps here with the formulation of the tribal-ethnic state, "African Historical Studies—Academic Knowledge as 'Usable Past' and Radical Scholarship" (Boulder, Colo.: ACLS/SSRC, 1987), n. 3.

2. An example of the positivist chronology is Mansjumba Mwanyimi-Mbonda, *Chronologie générale de l'histoire du Zaïre* (Kinshasa: Centre de Recherches Pédagogiques, 1985); see Janet MacGaffey, *The Real Economy of Zaire* (Philadelphia: Univ. of Pennsylvania Press, 1991) for the contemporary economy.

3. For other perspectives, refer to the writings of the Faculté de Théologie Catholique at Kinshasa and Tshimpaka Yanga, *La Parenté égyptienne des Peuples du Zaïre* (Lubumbashi: Cactus, 1989).

4. Nzongola-Ntalaja, *Revolution and Counter-Revolution: Essays in Contemporary Politics* (London: Zed, 1987). In modifying here the lineage mode of production, I drew on Peter Geschiere, "Applications of the 'Lineage Mode of Production' in African Studies," *Canadian Journal of African Studies* 19(1985): 81, who notes the problem of projecting this concept with reference to the Congo before the Colonial period.

In criticizing the reified notion of ethnicity found in Marxist and non-Marxist writings, I drew on Aidan Southall, "The Ethnic Heart of Anthropology," *Cahiers d'études africaines* 25, no. 4 (1986): 567–72, esp. 572, an article summarizing Jean-Loup Amselle and Elikia M'Bokolo, eds., *Au coeur de l'ethnie: Ethnies, tribalisme et l'état en Afrique* (Paris: Découverte, 1985).

5. The development of capitalism in a context in which one tribal-ethnic region benefits at the expense of another is spelled out in Robert Harms, *Land Tenure and Agricultural Development in Zaire 1865–1961* (Madison: Land Tenure Center, 1974), which suggests that the land tenure of the Mongo of Equateurial Province was the region most evolved toward capitalism. On the whole in the Congo, the low population density per square mile and the variability of the soil induced the power structure, whether in the era of rubber, ground nuts, or later cotton and rice, simply to extract taxes without altering the relations of production. Other sources on regional favoritism include Edouard Mokila wa Mpimbo, "La Province de l'Équateur," *Courrier Africain* 82–83 (Oct. 30, 1968); idem, "Poids socio-politiques des ressortissants de l'Équateur à Kinshasa," *Courrier Africain* 84 (Nov. 8, 1968). For nonfavored regions see Jean-Luc Vellut, "Rural Poverty in Western Shaba, c. 1890–1930," in *The Roots of Rural Poverty in Central and Southern Africa,* ed. Robin Palmer and Neil Parsons (Berkeley: Univ. of California Press, 1977), chap. 12; see also Bogumil Jewsiewicki, "Unequal Development: Capitalism and the Katangan Economy, 1919–1940," in *"The Roots of Rural Poverty,"* chap. 13.

6. Writers vary slightly in their use of terms, for example, Jean Philippe Peemans, "Accumulation and Underdevelopment in Zaire: General Aspects in Relation to the Agrarian Crisis," in *The Crisis in Zaire: Myths and Realities,* ed. Nzongola-Ntalaja (Trenton, N.J.: Africa World Press, 1986), 67–83, uses the concept of *colonial primitive accumulation* for the years 1885–1945. For the period thereafter comes a fifteen-year rise in prosperity, inflating the local consumption circuit. State controls break down between 1960 and 1970, permitting a rise in rural commerce and a decline in agricultural export. The text follows this line.

7. Bogumil Jewsiewicki, "The Great Depression and the Making of the Colonial Economic System in the Belgian Congo," *African Economic History* 2(Fall 1977): 153–76, takes his subject in a way that includes the postcolonial economic context as well. Studies of the local level even more than on the national level support Jewsiewicki's view of the persistence of traditional power structures through and beyond the independence period; Samba Kaputo, "Phénomène d'ethnicité et conflit ethno-politique dans les centres urbains de l'Afrique Noire. Le cas des Kusu et des Shi dans la ville de Bukavu," *Revue de L'Institut de Sociologie* 49, no. 1 (1976): 149–72.

8. An early example in this field of the rejection of a purely economic approach to the

political economy of colonialism is Bruce Fetter, *Colonial Rule and Regional Imbalance in Central Africa* (Boulder, Colo.: Westview Press, 1983) 26. Another such article and one of importance for understanding hegemony is Thomas M. Callaghy, "External Actors and the Relative Autonomy of the Political Aristocracy in Zaire," *Journal of Commonwealth and Comparative Politics* 21(1983): 61–83. For a critical view of dependency and of unilinear ideas of development, see Wyatt Macgaffey, "The Politics of National Integration in Zaire," *Journal of Modern African Studies* 20, no. 1 (1982): 87–105.

9. For a comment on the continuing competition between Lingala and French for dominance in Kinshasa today, see Mwatha Musanji-Ngalasso, "Usages du français dans un milieu urbain africain: Kinshasa," *Présence Africaine* 33(1988): 105–20.

10. Bogumil Jewsiewicki, "Formation of the Political Culture of Ethnicity in the Belgian Congo," in *Creation of Tribalism in Southern Africa*, ed. Leroy Vail (Berkeley: Univ. of California Press, 1989), 324–49; Bogumil Jewsiewicki and Mumbanza Mwa Bawele, "The Social Context of Slavery in Equatorial Africa During the 19th and 20th Centuries," in *The Ideology of Slavery in Africa*, ed. Paul E. Lovejoy (Beverly Hills, Calif.: Sage Publications, 1981), chap. 3.

11. L. H. Gann and Peter Duignan, *The Rulers of Belgian Africa, 1884–1914* (Princeton, N.J.: Princeton Univ. Press, 1979), chaps. 2–3. An indication of the tribal-ethnic character of the state emerged in legislation in 1898, which decreed that land should be set aside separately for Europeans and for coloreds. This legislation stayed on the books until 1959, George Brausch, *Belgian Administration in the Congo* (Oxford, Institute of Race Relations, 1961), 21–22. Other similar forms of discrimination lasted from the 1940s to 1960 in housing, education, and entertainment facilities.

12. Bogumil Jewsiewicki, "Zaire Enters the World System: Its Colonial Incorporation as the Belgian Congo, 1885–1960," in *Zaire: The Political Economy of Underdevelopment,* ed. Guy Gran (New York: Frederick A. Praeger, 1979), 29–53.

13. Roger Anstey, *King Leopold's Legacy* (Oxford: Oxford Univ. Press, 1966), 47ff.

14. John Higginson, *A Working Class in the Making* (Madison: Univ. of Wisconsin Press, 1989), 42, 54.

15. Anstey, *King Leopold's Legacy,* 63.

16. Higginson, *Working Class,* 115.

17. Jewsiewicki, "Great Depression."

18. The interpretation of Lumumba as a radical stands to be revised. He was welcomed by the Soviets at a time when the Soviets were moving toward détente and liberalism, indicating if anything a probable lack of radicalism. This impression is reinforced by a glance at his earlier career. In 1955, shortly before his ascent to the national leadership, he was the vice-president of the Liberal party at Kisangani. When King Baudoin made his famous visit to the Congo in that year, Lumumba praised Belgian paternalism as good for the masses; George N. Nzongola, "The Bourgeoisie and the Revolution in the Congo," *Journal of Modern African Studies* 8, no. 4 (1970): 511–30, esp. 524, n. 3.

19. Ibid., 527. In Katanga, capitalists used a very sophisticated strategy to control labor —one that not only mixed tribes within work gangs but fused a new supratribal identity from tribal fractions to create a new worker tribe, the Tshanga-Tshanga. Ethnicity mixing proved to be a risky strategy; the Belgians abandoned it and returned to a policy of supporting the spiritual leader of the Lunda, the Mwaant Yaav. In 1955, when King Baudoin visited the Congo, he honored the Mwaant Yaav. In more recent years, Mobutu gave the Mwaant Yaav a civil service rank. See also Jean-Luc Vellut, "Mining in the Belgian Congo," in *History of Central Africa,* ed. David Birmingham and Phyllis M. Martin (London: Longman, 1983), 2: chap. 4; Edouard Bustin, *Lunda under Belgian Rule: The Politics of Ethnicity* (Cambridge, Mass.: Harvard Univ. Press, 1975), 160, 238.

20. Peemans, "Accumulation and Underdevelopment," 67–83.

21. Michael G. Schatzberg, *The Dialectics of Oppression in Zaire* (Bloomington: Indiana Univ. Press, 1988); this writer comes as close as any to the concept of museum city, employed in the chapter on Albania. Lisala (ix) and Kisangani (68) seem like museum cities. On the vulnerability of the regime, see an overview, Kenneth B. Noble, "Pretoria said to advise Zairian army," *New York Times,* Aug. 17, 1991, 2 (int. ed.).

22. Writing on the resistance to the ideology of ethnicity, or at least to the imposition of particular ethnic identities onto different peoples, exists not only for Zaire but for many other countries as well. An example, influential both in early Kimbanguism and among Orthodox Greek dissidents, including Albanians of the early Zoggist period, was the Messianist trend among Greek Orthodox missionaries; Nectaire Hatzimichali, "L'Église orthodoxe grècque et le messianisme en Afrique," *Social Compass* 22, no. 1 (1975): 85–95. Anabaptism from Scandinavia has had its influence in these regions as well.

23. Bruce Fetter, *The Creation of Elisabethville: 1910–1940* (Stanford, Calif.: Hoover Institute, 1976), 138–41.

24. Thomas Kanza, *The Rise and Fall of Patrice Lumumba: Conflict in the Congo* (Cambridge, Mass.: Schenkman Publishing, 1979), 100–121; Mobutu was, of course, linked to U.S. interests.

25. How easily even students could be divided by ethnic appeals, how much more so the uneducated. And this is not something unique to Zaire. In 1985, Hoxha sought to appease his Greek Orthodox constituency, a large part of which was the frustrated youth created by the modern education system, by offering to dig up the bones of Saint Kosma, the Aetolian, and to give them to the Greek authorities; "Bones of Friendship," *The Economist,* Jan. 12, 1985, 42.

26. Barbara A. Yates, "Colonialism, Education, and Work: Sex Differentiation in Colonial Zaire," in *Women and Work in Africa,* ed. Edna G. Bay (Boulder, Colo.: Westview Press, 1982), chap. 6; Francille Wilson, "Reinventing the Past and Circumscribing the Future: Authenticité and the Negative Image of Women's Work in Zaire," *Women and Work in Africa,* chap. 7.

27. Rik Ceyssens, "Mutumbula: Mythe de l'opprimé," *Cultures et Développement* 7(1975): 483–550. Such revolts permitted Congolese to evolve a common culture in opposition to the European colonial one. This process may have contributed to the growing desire of the chiefs and of the other évoluées for Brussels to solidify their status; Jean-Luc Vellut, "Une Image du blanc dans la société coloniale," in *Stéréotypes nationaux et préjugés raciaux aux XIXᵉ et XX siècles* ed. Jean Pirotte (Leuven: Editions Nauwelaerts, 1982), 91–116.

28. René Lemarchand, "The Politics of Penury in Rural Zaire: The View From Bandundu," in *Zaire: The Political Economy of Underdevelopment,* ed. Guy Gran (New York: Frederick A. Praeger, 1979), 240; Kanza, *Rise and Fall of Lumumba,* 117; *Encyclopedia Britannica* (Chicago: Univ. of Chicago Press, 1975), 5:810.

29. Susan Asch, *L'Église de Prophète Kimbangu* (Paris: Karthala, 1983), 287–90.

30. A statement close to this appears by the writer, Anicet Mobe-Fansiama, "L'Éxpression culturelle dans les écoles du Zaïre," *Afrique Littéraire et Artistique,* 64 (1982): esp. 48–49.

31. This is not the standard view. The standard view stresses how powerful the secular administration was compared to its counterparts elsewhere in Africa, the ruler as "philosopher king." The idea of the church as a challenge to the hegemony from within is, thus, not a familiar one; see Marvin Markowitz, *Cross and Sword* (Stanford, Calif.: Hoover Institute, 1973). For a more recent account of the church and the state in conflict, see Michael G. Schatzberg, *The Dialectics of Oppression,* 116ff. For the philosopher king approach, see a quote from Thomas Hodgkin in Crawford Young, *Politics in the Congo* (Princeton, N.J.: Princeton Univ. Press, 1965), 10.

32. Relevant articles on the historical background include, Barbara A. Yates, "Church, State, and Education in Belgian Africa: Implications for Contemporary Third World

Women," in *Women's Education in the Third World: Comparative Perspectives,* ed. Gail Kelly and Carolyn Elliott (Albany: State Univ. of New York Press, 1982), chap. 6; Barbara A. Yates, "Colonialism, Education and Work," chap. 6; Sylvia M. Jacobs, "Their 'Special Mission': Afro-American Women as Missionaries to the Congo, 1894–1937," in *Black Americans and the Missionary Movement in Africa,* ed. Sylvia M. Jacobs (Westport, Conn.: Greenwood Press, 1982), chap. 8; Wilson, "Reinventing the Past"; Terri F. Gould, "Value Conflict and Development: The Struggle of the Professional Zairian Woman," *Journal of Modern African Studies* 16, no. 1 (1988): 133–39. For a study of an alternative church in which women play an important role, see Willy de Craemer, *The Jamaa and the Church: A Bantu Catholic Movement in Zaire* (Oxford: Clarendon Press, 1977). For the more violent side of gender struggle, see the following: Jean S. Lafontaine, "The Free Women of Kinshasa: Prostitution in a City in Zaire," in *Choice and Change,* ed. J. Davis (London: Athalone Press, 1974), 89–113; M. Catherine Newbury, "Ebutumwa Bw'Emiogo: The Tyranny of Cassava, A Women's Tax Revolt in Eastern Zaire," *Canadian Journal of African Studies* 18, no. 1 (1984): 35–55; Afrika Baraza, *Rapes, Tortures, and Execution of Women in Zaire* (Boston: Afrika Baraza, 1982).

33. Mulago gwa Ciralâ M. (Vincent) *La Religion traditionelle des Bantus et leur vision du monde* (Kinshasa; Presses Universitaires du Zaïre, 1973). Another work by the same author picks up the theme of *l'union vitale* in Bantu (*luba*—'thought') and in Catholic mystical theology. See, in addition, the more recent work in the same vein by the Zairian theologian François Kasabele Lumbala, *Alliances avec le Christ en Afrique: Inculturation des rites religieux au Zaïre* (Athens: Éditions historiques S.D. Basilopoulos, 1987). A further indication of the church's power and success is that it is not mentioned in the major party-oriented work on the evils of foreign influence, Mabika Kalanda, *La Remise en question: Base de la décolonisation mentale* (Brussels: Éditions Remarques Africaines 1967). For an expression of secular concerns with the role of religion, see V. Mudimbe, *L'Odeur du Père* (Paris: Présence Africaines, 1982), 58–71. On Vincent Mulago and the Africanization of Catholicism project, see V. Y. Mudimbe, *Parables and Fables* (Madison: Univ. of Wisconsin Press, 1991), 53ff.

34. David Northrup, "A Church in Search of a State: Catholic Missions in Eastern Zaire, 1879–1930," *Journal of Church and State* 30 (1988): 309–19; P. Kisimba Nyembo, *La Parole comme manifestation personnelle de dieu dans les sacrements selon Martin Luther (1483–1546)* (Kinshasa: Faculté de Théologie Catholique, 1988); Wyatt MacGaffey, *Modern Kongo Prophets* (Bloomington: Indiana Univ. Press, 1983).

35. Bogumil Jewsiewicki, "The Formation of the Political Culture of Ethnicity in the Belgian Congo, 1920–1959," in *The Creation of Tribalism in Southern Africa,* ed. Leroy Vail (Berkeley: Univ. of California Press, 1991), chap. 11.

36. David J. Gould, "Local Administration in Zaire and Underdevelopment," *Journal of Modern African Studies* 15, no. 3 (1977): 349–78.

37. Museums have their political objectives. Sarah Brett-Smith, "The Doyle Collection of African Art," *Record of the Art Museum Princeton University* 42, no. 2 (1983): 2–43, gives the odyssey of an American businessman and his wife, who acquired artifacts of the Kuba, Pende, and Tshokwé tribes. Princeton's Doyle collection portrays them as the timeless heart of central Africa. From the Zairian governmental perspective and even from that of the Belgian administration before it, the question of the specific region has more importance than it does for an American audience; Shaje Tsniluila, "Return and Restoration—Inventorying Movable Cultural Property: National Museum Institute of Zaire," *Museum* 153(1978): 50–51. For details of the Institute's acquisition campaigns in Zaire, see Lucien Cahen, ed., *Rapport Institut des musées nationaux* (Kinshasa, 1972). Cahen, like others in Zaire, distinguishes art not just by regional type but by who has power today. For example, he notes the visit of a musicologist, Benoît Quersin, of the French Radio Company (ORTF) to Equateur Province to tape "modern" Ekonda music (33). Not all U.S. involvements are the same. In 1981, the directors of the National Gallery of Art in Washington construed the national myth of Zaire (as the heir to the

Kongo Kingdom) to arise from the northern and western parts of the country, making it the theme of a major exhibit of Bakongo culture. See Robert Farris Thompson and Joseph Cornet, *The Four Moments of the Sun: Kongo Art in Two Worlds* (Washington, D.C.: National Gallery of Art, 1981). What the museum realized was that Equateur Province was the place to stress for all developments.

38. Sully Faik et al., *La Francophonie au Zaïre* (Lubumbashi: Éditions Impala, 1988); Johannes Fabian, *Language and Colonial Power—The Appropriation of Swahili in the Former Belgian Congo 1880–1938* (Cambridge: Cambridge Univ. Press, 1986); Eyamba G. Bokamba, "Authenticity and the Choice of a National Language: The Case of Zaire," *Studies in the Linguistic Sciences* 6, no. 2 (Fall 1976): 23–65; Lufuluabo Mukeba, "Some Aspects of Bilingualism and Bilingual Education in Zaire," in *International Handbook of Bilingualism and Bilingual Education,* ed., Christina Bratt Paulston (Westport, Conn.: Greenwood Press, 1988), chap. 27. More broadly, social control involves not only the use of language policy but also of censorship; see, for example, *World Press Encyclopedia* 2: 1108–9; see also, Bakwa Muelan Zambi, "Communication in Zaire," *Educational Broadcasting International* 9(1976): 147–49.

39. Daniel Cahen, "Histoire de la recherche archéologique au Zaire," *Études d'Histoire Africaine* 9–10 (1977–78): 33–6; Muya Kamwanga, "Les industries préhistoriques de la plaine de Kinshasa," ibid.: 49–62.

40. For the quarrel on the periodization of Zairian literature, P. Ngandu Nkashama, "La Littérature Zaïroise: Problématique d'une écriture," *Zaïre-Afriques* 116 (1977): 379ff.; work written by Mukala Kadima-Nzuji, *La littérature Zaïroïse de langue Française* (Paris: Karthala, 1984); for commentary on the theatre, P. Ngandu Nkashama, "Le théâtre et la dramaturgie du masque au Zaïre," *Culture Française* 3–4 (1982–83): 58–76. Authenticity in theatre remains unclear. The mobilization possibilities that result from sending troupes to the countryside is noted by a spokesman, Unionmwan Edebiri, "Le théâtre Zaïrois à la recherche de son authenticité," *Afrique Littéraire et Artistique* 40(1976): 76. One might also note some formal similarities between Albanian and Zairian music. Ethnomusicology in Zaire shows a wide range of musical instruments, strings, woodwinds, and percussion, and it also contains reports of traditional court ensembles not too different than those reported in the Balkans. Musical composition in South Albania is termed part of the earliest stratum of vocal polyphony, the later development of which in Western Europe was functional harmony, or major and minor scale systems. The origins of functional harmony are found in the interval of the third; the third as a musical interval is also found in central African music. From the same formal base, the Albanian state promoted a folk orchestra and the Zairian business community promoted the pop commercial groups in Kinshasa. For Albanian music, see Stanley Sadie, ed., *The New Grove Dictionary of Music and Musicians* (London: Macmillan, 1980), 1: 197–202; Tony Reed, "Various Artists," *Melody Maker,* April 16, 1988, 36; for Zaire, Rose Brandel, *The Music of Central Africa: An Ethnomusicological Study* (The Hague: Martinus Nijhoff, 1973), 18ff.; Michel Lonoh, *Essai de commentaire de la musique Congolaise moderne* (Kinshasa: Ministère de la Culture et des Arts, n.d.). For Nietzsche's influence on a Western student of African music, see John Miller Chernoff, *African Rhythm and African Sensibility: Aesthetics and Social Action in African Musical Idioms* (Chicago: Univ. of Chicago Press, 1979). For anarchism in literature, see Bernard Mouralis, *Les Contre-littératures* (Paris: Presses Universitaires de France, 1975); idem, "Vincent Mudimbe et le savoir ethnologique," *L'Afrique Littéraire et Artistique* 58 (1981): 112–25.

41. B. E. Botombele, *Cultural Policy in the Republic of Zaire* (Paris: UNESCO, 1976).

42. *Hommage à Grand Kallé* (Kinshasa: Éditions, Lokole, 1985).

43. John M. Janzen, *The Quest for Therapy in Lower Zaire* (Berkeley: Univ. of California Press, 1978), chap. 12; see also Zola Ni Vunda, "La Science en Afrique ou les tribulations d'une science africaine," *Canadian Journal of African Studies* 13(1979): 211–21; Gilles Bibeau, "New Legal Rules for an Old Art of Healing: The Case of Zairian Healers' Associations," *Social Science and Medicine* 16(1982): 1843–49; Ellen Corin, "Vers une réappropriation de la

dimension individuelle en psychologie africaine," *Canadian Journal of African Studies* 14, no. 1 (1980): 135–56, focusing on the ritual of individuation in none other than Équateur Province.

44. Markowitz, *Cross and Sword*.

45. For a turn of the century liberal protest, see Wm. Roger Louis and Jean Stengers, *E. D. Morel's History of the Congo Reform Movement* (Oxford: Clarendon Press, 1968). For a more recent version of the same thing, see Jeffrey M. Elliot and Marvyn Dymally, *Voice of Zaire* (Washington, D.C.: Washington Institute Press, 1990). For an example of the liberal critique among Zairian intellectuals today, see the writings of V. Y. Mudimbe.

46. It is this fact that led to the unusual colloquium published subsequently as a book entitled *Actualités et inactualité des 'Études Bakongo' du P. Van Wing: Actes du colloque de Mayidi (1980)* (Inkisi: Grand Séminaire Mayidi, 1983).

47. A. J. Smet, *Philosophie africaine: Textes choisis* (Kinshasa: Presses Universitaires du Zaïre, 1975), 1, 116–27. One can infer from a recent survey of curricula how important philosophy is for Zairian education compared to that of the other countries, *Teaching and Research in Philosophy: Africa* (Paris: UNESCO, 1984), 185–213. For an interpretation of Mulago's theology, see Mudimbe, *Parables and Fables,* 53–68.

48. The study of history writing in Zaire cannot entirely bracket the question of the cumulative impact of outside scholarship, however low the official commitment to its study may be.

49. The example of Albania suggests that where a country cannot develop—or does not encourage the development of—the narrative in literature, for example, in the novel, it will not have an easy time with history writing either. For a portrayal of the travails of the novel, see Kadima-Nzuji, *La Littérature Zaïroise;* Mbulamwanza Mudimbe-Boyi, "Les Éditions du mont-noir au Zaïre," *Afrique Littéraire et Artistique* 44 (1977): 69–72. For hesitations about the fate of the novel in Zaire, see Jeannick Odier, "Bilan de la littérature Zaïroise depuis l'indépendance," *Afrique Littéraire et Artistique* 35 (1975): 30; Ngandu Nkashama, "La Littérature au Zaïre depuis l'indépendance," *Zaïre-Afrique* 70 (1972): 624.

50. These points and others are developed in Bogumil Jewsiewicki's major article, "African Historical Studies," 1–76. Benoît Verhagen, *Introduction à l'histoire immédiate* (Gembloux, Belgium: Duculot, 1974) was an early attempt to adjust history writing to gnosis that did not find continuators. François Bontinck was an important representative of the document-oriented historians.

51. For a recent example of the polemics surrounding oral history, see Jan Vansina, *Oral Tradition as History* (Madison: Univ. of Wisconsin Press, 1985); for a criticism of Vansina's oral history as too positivist by an influential figure close to the establishment in Zaire, Luc de Heusch, *The Drunken King, or, the Origin of the State* (Bloomington: Indiana Univ. Press, 1982), 8; for a defense of Vansina's work, Robert W. Harms, "The Wars of August: Diagonal Narrative in African History," *American Historical Review* 88 (1983): 816; for an example of a Congolese historical epic, here to return to the Skanderbeg theme of chapter 7, Daniel Biebuyck and Kahombo C. Mateene, eds., *The Mwindo Epic* (Berkeley: Univ. of California Press, 1969).

52. Mbulamwanza Mudimbe-Boyi, "Béatrice du Congo de Bernard Dédié, signe du temps ou pièce à clé?" *L'Afrique Littéraire et Artistique* 35 (1975): 19–26.

53. Wyatt MacGaffey, "The West in Congolese Experience," in *Africa and the West: Intellectual Reponses to European Culture,* ed. Philip D. Curtin (Madison: Univ. of Wisconsin Press, 1972), 49–72; idem, "Zamenga Batukezanga: The Novelist and Ethnographer," *Africana Journal* 13(1982): 91–97. Batukezanga is a littérateur cum historian whose knowledge of village life is obviously immense. In his *Bandoki ou les sorciers,* the theme of live burial as part of negotiations with the next world is important; Odier, "Bilan de la littérature Zaïroise," 34. In the Albanian context, this subject was important as a theme for the novelist Ismail Kadare. See more generally, Zihni Sako, "The Albanian Entombment Ballad and Other Common

Balkan Different Versions," in Institute of Popular Culture (Instituti i Kulturís Popullore), *Questions of the Albanian Folklore* (Tirana: "8 Nevtori Publishing House 1984), 155–65; see also Bogumil Jewsiewicki, "Collective Memory and the Stakes of Power. A Reading of Popular Zairian Historical Discourses" *History in Africa* 13(1986): 202, for comments on the power of the narrative of the "free woman."

54. Jean-Luc Vellut, *Guide de l'étudiant en histoire du Zaïre* (Kinshasa: Editions du Mont Noir, 1974), 41.

55. See an early statement confirming this interest, Ian Cunnison, "History and Genealogy in Conquest States," *American Anthropologist* 59, no. 1 (1957): 20–31.

56. Ndaywel È Nziem, "African Historical Study," in *African Historiographies: What History for Which Africa?* ed. Bogumil Jewsiewicki and David Newbury (Beverly Hills, Calif.: Sage Publications, 1986), chap. 1. The role of François Bontinck in Zaire as a history teacher could be compared to the comparable role of a founding figure of the Moroccan history profession, Germain 'Ayyash. 'Ayyash, like Bontinck, was a teacher of documentary history in a tribal state context.

57. Among the accomplishments of Lubumbashi was the publication of ten volumes of *Études d'histoire africaine* (Lubumbashi: Presses Universitaires du Zaïre, 1970–78) between 1970 and 1978. Archivally based studies emerge in this period as well; J. Stengers, "Belgian Historiography since 1945," in *Reappraisals in Overseas History,* ed. P. C. Emmer and H. L. Wesseling (Leiden: Leiden Univ. Press, 1979), 161–82.

58. Mumbanza Mwa Bawele and Sabakinu Kivilu, "Historical Research in Zaire," in *African Historiographies What History Which Africa,* ed. Bogumil Jewsiewicki and David Newbury (Beverly Hills, Calif.: Sage Publications, 1986), 226; Benoît Verhaegen, "L'Histoire au Zaïre: Enseignement, recherches, publications," *Revue Belge d'Histoire Contemporaine* 8(1977): 291–314.

59. Best known was Benoît Verhaegen, *Introduction à l'histoire immédiate,* a genealogy of antihistory, or anarchist history, derived from Mao Tse-Tung, the antipsychology of Laing, and a group of writers in Kinshasa around 1970, including Mudimbe. Verhaegen makes the immediate connection between observer and observed the basis for his methodological critique of traditional positivist history writing. V. Y. Mudimbe comments on Verhaegen's work in *L'Odeur du père,* 172–182.

60. Bawele and Kivilu, "Historical Research in Zaire," 226; Ndaywel È Nziem, "Les Archives du Zaïre en question," *Zaïre-Afrique* 124 (1978): 207–13.

61. Mumbanza Mwa Bawele, "Authenticité, histoire et développement," in *Authenticité et développement,* ed. L'Union des écrivains Zaïrois (Kinshasa: Présence Africaine, 1982), 149–94, esp. 156, 166, 182. The author is now the director of Centre d'études et de recherches documentaires sur l'Afrique Centrale (CERDAC) a professor of social history at Lubumbashi as well.

62. CERDAC, ed., *Enseignement de l'histoire au Zaïre-actes du colloque organisé par le CERDAC Lubumbashi 1978* (Lubumbashi; CERDAC, 1982), included complaints about CERDAC's financial problems, the frustration from the low esteem in which students hold history teachers, and the mechanical way in which history is traditionally taught. Another polemical collection from Lubumbashi takes the position that there should be no favorite regions in the writing of Zairian history; Epanya S. Tshund'olela et al., *Histoire du Zaïre* (Lubumbashi: CERDAC, 1981), 1. A writer taking a comparative view of history teaching in Africa noted that UNAZA was unique for its concern simply with art history and political history; Atieno Odhiambo, "The Content of History Education in East, Central and Southern Africa," in *The Teaching of History in African Universities,* ed. E. J. Alagoa (Port Harcourt: University of Lagos, 1977), 49–64.

9. Bourgeois Democracy in Great Britain, 1880–1990

1. Quintin Hoare and Geoffrey Nowell-Smith, eds., *Selections from the Prison Notebooks of Antonio Gramsci* (London: Lawrence and Wishart, 1971), 277–320, combines "Americanism" with the economics of the assembly line which he called Fordism; Alain Lipetz, "Towards Global Fordism?" *New Left Review* 132(Mar. 1982): 33–47, provides a contemporary definition of Fordism as a capitalist strategy of maintaining a continuously self-transforming labor force that adds to accumulation—with the changing technology—by tying wages and prices to each other. Many writers in the Gramsci tradition, however, approach the question of hegemony more through politics than through the division of labor; Roger Simon, *Gramsci's Political Thought* (London: Lawrence and Wishart, 1982), chap. 7. For an overview on the crisis of British political economy thought, see Keith Nield, "A Symptomatic Dispute? Notes on the Relation Between Marxian Theory and Historical Practice in Britain," *Social Research* 47(1980): 479–506.

2. For a critique of the dominant paradigm concerning democracy, see Peter Bachrach, *The Theory of Democratic Elitism: A Critique* (Boston: Little, Brown, 1967); see also my article "Race and Racism in the Modern World: How it Works in Different Hegemonies," *Transforming Anthropology* 5, nos. 1–2 (1993): 8–14.

3. Two schools of thought dominate the interpretation of the racial undercaste in the bourgeois democracies: one emphasizes the idea of progress through social integration as measured by the passage of time; the other disputes this view, pointing toward withdrawal and national independence. These two schools of thought are well established in writings on the Irish in Northern Ireland, Amerinds, Afro-Americans, Hispanics, and East Asians in the United States, Palestinians, and South African blacks. A useful study of American black thought that gives a history of these trends is Harold Cruse, *The Crisis of the Negro Intellectual* (New York: Morrow, 1967); a well-known book in the United Kingdom on the nationalist side is Michael Hechter, *Internal Colonialism: The Celtic Fringe in British National Development, 1536–1966* (Berkeley: Univ. of California Press, 1975). A writer who has introduced the subject as a theme in comparative history is George Marsh Fredrickson, *White Supremacy: A Comparative Study in American and South African History* (New York: Oxford Univ. Press, 1981), a work emphasizing South Africa and the cotton South. Fredrickson's argument is useful. I prefer to take South Africa and the United States as a whole and second, I would focus less on race relations than on system's maintenance, attempting to clarify how a smaller totality serves or fits within a larger one, here a democracy.

4. For Anglo-Saxonism among historians, see David H. Burton, *American History: British Historians* (Chicago: Nelson-Hall, 1978), *passim*. The study of frontiers is important to all the democracies. It is a major theme in the United States and South Africa. The same holds for historical *exceptionalism*. An important article arguing against exceptionalism in the American working class is Sean Wilentz, "Against Exceptionalism: Class Consciousness and the American Labor Movement," *International Labor and Working Class History* 26(Fall 1984): 1–24.

5. By the 1970s, nineteenth-century liberalism was back; for example, Robert William Fogel and Stanley L. Engerman, *Time on the Cross: The Economics of American Slavery* (Boston: Little, Brown, 1974), argued in a very controversial book for the profitability of unpaid slave labor over paid labor.

6. A well-known book of a leading British historian is Sheila Rowbotham, *Hidden from History: Rediscovering Women in History from the 17th Century to the Present* (New York: Vintage Books, 1976); Elizabeth Pleck, *Domestic Tyranny: The Making of Social Policy Against Family Violence from Colonial Times to the Present* (New York: Oxford Univ. Press, 1987).

7. Ian Harden and Norman Lewis, *The Noble Lie: The British Constitution and the Rule by Law* (London: Hutchinson, 1986), chaps. 1–4; Phil Scranton and Paul Gordon, eds., *Causes for Concern: Questions of Law and Justice* (Middlesex: Penguin Books, 1984), chap. 1.

8. American books, for reasons discussed in the text are clearer on these points than the British ones, for example, David W. Noble, *Historians Against History* (Minneapolis: Univ. of Minnesota Press, 1965).

9. There is a correlation between the generally underproblematized role of politics and the overuse of the term *crisis;* cf. Simon, *Gramsci's Political Thought,* finds an "organic crisis" extending from 1910 to 1945 and then from 1970 onward.

10. The text here follows Stuart Hall, "The Rise of the Representative/Interventionist State," in *State and Society in Contemporary Britain,* ed. Gregor McLennan, David Held, and Stuart Hall (Oxford: Blackwell Press, 1984), chap. 1. Bob Jessop, Kevin Bonnett, Simon Bromley, and Tom Ling, "Thatcherism and the Politics of Hegemony: A Reply to Stuart Hall," *New Left Review* 153(Sep. 1985): 87–101, presents various criticisms of Hall's formulation that do not seem too well focused. The growth of the informal economy in the 1970s is too important to be called "conjunctural" or "unplanned."

11. John Benson, *The Penny Capitalists: A Study of the Nineteenth Century Working-Class Entrepreneurs* (Dublin: Gill and Macmillan, 1983), conclusion; Geoffrey Crossick, ed., *The Lower Middle Class in Britain, 1870–1914* (New York: St. Martin's Press, 1977).

12. Judith Walkowitz, *Prostitution and Victorian Society: Women, Class, and the State* (Cambridge: Cambridge Univ. Press, 1980); Bernard Porter, *The Origins of the Vigilant State: The London Metropolitan Police Special Branch Before the First World War* (London: Weidenfeld and Nicholson, 1987).

13. Thomas William Heyck, *The Dimensions of British Radicalism: The Case of Ireland, 1874–1895* (Urbana: Univ. of Illinois Press, 1974); Margaret Ward, *Unmanageable Revolutionaries: Women and Irish Nationalism* (London: Pluto Press, 1983), chap. 1.

14. Stan Taylor, *The National Front in English Politics* (London: Macmillan, 1982), 5.

15. Stuart Hall and Bill Schwarz, "State and Society, 1880–1930," in *The Hard Road to Renewal: Thatcherism and the Crisis of the Left,* ed. Stuart Hall (London: Verso, 1988), 110ff., cites the imperialist, new liberal, and Fabianist roots of collectivism; George Dangerfield, *The Strange Death of Liberal England* (New York: H. Smith and R. Haas, 1935). For a sketch of the history of Fordism, see Alain Lipietz, *Mirages and Miracles: The Crisis of Global Fordism* (London: Verso, 1987), chap. 2.

16. Benson, *Penny Capitalists,* 135ff.

17. Rom Ramdin, *The Making of the Black Working Class in Britain* (Aldershots, Hants: Gower Publishing, 1987).

18. Jacqueline Bhabha, Francesca Klug, and Sue Shutter, eds., *Worlds Apart: Women under Immigration and Nationality Law* (London: Pluto Press, 1985), 34.

19. Paul B. Rich, *Race and Empire in British Politics* (Cambridge: Cambridge Univ. Press, 1986), chaps. 5–7; an alternative formulation emphasizes the Jewish immigration as parallel to those of the Irish and the Commonwealth. See Catherine Jones, *Immigration and Social Policy* (London: Tavistock Publications, 1970), chap. 4, or Joseph Gorny, *The British Labour Movement and Zionism, 1917–1948* (London: Frank Cass, 1983), 237–39. It does not seem reasonable to assert that the Jews were a racial undercaste in British culture in the full sense of the word. Lord Balfour spoke of the Jews as a nation, and he may have been affected by Jewish poverty in London's East End in his declaration, but British hegemony was never organized around the submersion of the Jews. For the periodization of the Irish Question around the rise and fall of the era of collectivism, information was drawn from Belinda Probert, *Beyond Orange and Green: The Political Economy of the Northern Ireland Crisis* (London: Zed, 1978); Henry Patterson, *Class Conflict and Sectarianism: The Protestant Working Class and the Belfast Labour Movement, 1868–1920* (Belfast: Blackstaff Press, 1980), conclusion.

20. Rowbotham, Chap. 19.

21. Harold Perkins, *The Rise of Professional Society in England since 1880* (London: Routledge, 1989), 251ff.

22. Ibid., 337.

23. Neoliberalism was a general phenomenon from the 1970s. The particular interest of the British case is the pureness of its libertarian orientation. In the U.S. case, libertarianism was worn down by its competition with fundamentalism and liberalism.

24. Richard Hoggart, *The Uses of Literacy* (London: Chatto and Windus, 1957); Barbara Ehrenreich, *Fear of Falling: The Inner Life of the Middle Class* (New York: Pantheon, 1989).

25. Diane Elson, "Imperialism," in *The Idea of the Modern State*, ed. Gregor McLennan, David Held, and Stuart Hall (Milton Keynes, U.K.: Open Univ. Press, 1984), 154–82, esp. 170.

26. Raphael Samuel, "British Marxist Historians, 1880–1980,"p. 1, *New Left Review* 120(Mar. 1980): 21–96, esp. 42ff.; Paul K. Conkin, *Puritans and Pragmatists: Eight Eminent American Thinkers* (Bloomington: Indiana Univ. Press, 1968); Geoff Eley and William Hunt, eds., *Reviving the English Revolution* (London: Verso, 1988), 8–9. For the "remissive" aspect of Puritan culture, see John Carroll, *Puritan, Paranoid, Remissive: A Sociology of Modern Culture* (London: Routledge Kegan Paul, 1977).

27. The authors of a recent study lament Thatcher's contribution to the rise in unsolved crime. They note that the majority of crimes ever solved are solved through the help of the community. They regret the centralization of police authority in recent years, which has taken responsibility away from the communities; Richard Kinsey, John Lea, and Jack Young, *Losing the Fight Against Crime* (Oxford: Basil Blackwell, 1986). The authors no doubt are a bit naïve to equate a "war against crime" with solving crimes. Like the American "war against drugs," the object of the British "war against crime" is simply racial oppression.

28. The Campaign for Nuclear Disarmament is a movement outside the party system, one that has so far incorporated gender issues better than class and racial ones. For a biography of Stuart Hall, one of its leaders, see Robert Gorman, ed., *Biographical Dictionary of Neo-Marxism* (Westport, Conn.: Greenwood Press, 1985), 197–200. For E. P. Thompson, another leader, see Bryan D. Palmer, *The Making of E. P. Thompson* (Toronto: New Hogtown Press, 1981). The view of the present reminds one of the difficulties that faced previous challengers. For example, for the career of James Connolly, who tried to combine Irish and British labor through socialism, see David Howell; *A Lost Left: Three Studies in Socialism and Nationalism* (Chicago: Univ. of Chicago Press, 1986).

29. Stuart Hall, "The Great Moving Right Show," in *The Politics of Thatcherism*, ed. Stuart Hall and Martin Jacques (London: Lawrence and Wishart, 1983), 42–43; Stuart Hall et al., *Policing the Crisis: Mugging, the State and Law and Order* (New York: Holmes and Meier Publishing, 1978). This line of thought merges another component of recent scholarship, the Americanization of Europe trend. Clearly, with the breakdown of collectivism, the individual consumer-cum-Puritan moralist then surfaces; Daniel Snowman, *Britain and America: An Interpretation of Their Culture, 1945–1975* (New York: Harper and Row, 1977). David Bouchier, *Idealism and Revolution: New Ideologies of Liberation in Britain and the United States* (New York: St. Martin's Press, 1978), complements Snowman. Bouchier sets out to argue for differences between the British and American New Lefts, but as his evidence shows, to do this effectively he has to confine his discussion to the era of British collectivism of the 1960s.

30. As the problems of maintaining the imperial order overwhelmed the British, a British insularism arose, a renewed interest in the British countryside and its folklore, especially of the South. Accompanying this trend was a Tudor revivalism and a quest for an English music as manifest in a cult of figures such as Sir Edward Elgar; Philip Dodd, "Englishness and the National Culture," in *Englishness: Politics and Culture, 1880–1920*, eds. Robert Colls and Philip Dodd (London: Croom Helm, 1986), 29ff. In this period as well, Henry Tate opened his gallery of British art; Malcolm Bradbury, *The Social Context of Modern English Literature* (New York: Schocken Books, 1971), chap. 3.

31. Dodd, "Englishness," 1–23, and passim.

32. Ibid., 17–18.

33. Perry Anderson, "Components of the National Culture, *New Left Review* 50 (July 1968): 3–57, esp. 17ff.

34. Stephen G. Jones, "State Intervention in Sports and Leisure in Britain Between the Wars," *Journal of Contemporary History* 22(1987): 163–82.

35. Kenneth Hoover and Raymond Plant, *Conservative Capitalism in Britain and the United States: A Critical Appraisal* (London: Routledge, 1988), 142.

36. Joel Krieger, *Reagan, Thatcher, and the Politics of Decline* (Oxford: Oxford Univ. Press, 1986), 63.

37. Hoover and Plant, *Conservative Capitalism* 141.

38. John Gyford, *The Politics of Local Socialism* (London: George Allen and Unwin, 1985); Sheila Button, "Women's Committees: A Study of Gender and Local Government Policy Formulation," Univ. of Bristol, U.K., School for Advanced Urban Studies, Working Paper no. 45 (1985).

39. Anthony Easthope, *British Post-Structuralism since 1968* (London: Routledge, 1988), chap. 13; Terry Eagleton, *Literary Theory: An Introduction* (Minneapolis: Univ. of Minnesota Press, 1983).

40. C. O. Brink, *English Classical Scholarship: Historical Reflections on Bentley, Porson and Housman* (Cambridge: James Clarke, 1986), 116ff. 198; John Kenyon, *The History Men: The Historical Profession in England since the Renaissance* (London: Weidenfeld and Nicolson, 1983), 171; Colin Renfrew, *Archaeology and Language: The Puzzle of Indo-European Origins* (London: Jonathan Cape, 1987), 285, 288; Glyn Daniel and Colin Renfrew, *The Idea of Prehistory* (Edinburgh: Edinburgh Univ. Press, 1988), 166–67, 171, 173, 180, 193–94. Renfrew's writing seems to presage the entrance of Britain into the European Economic Community in 1992; it also appears to be a cautious line of defense against the claims of Martin Bernal in *Black Athena*, vol. 1 (New Brunswick: Rutgers Univ. Press, 1987) that the civilizations of the Europeans contained many Africans (203). More directly oriented toward controversy is Renfrew's intellectual mentor in these matters, the American scholar Lewis Binford, author of *Bones: Ancient Men and Modern Myths* (1981), an attempt to show that bones and artifacts in African deposits do not belong with each other, cited by Daniel and Renfrew, *Idea of Prehistory*, 187.

41. Shirley Williams, a former cabinet minister and president of the Social and Liberal Democratic party, lists those abuses in "The New Authoritarianism," *Political Quarterly* 60, no. 1 (1989): 4–9; Stuart Hall, "Gramsci's Relevance for the Study of Race and Ethnicity," *Journal of Communication Inquiry* 10, no. 2 (1986): 5–27.

42. Wyn Grant, "The Erosion of Intermediary Institutions," *Political Quarterly* 60, no. 1 (1989): 14–15.

43. Jeremy Tunstall, *The Media in Britain* (New York: Columbia Univ. Press, 1983), 21, 127, 136, 226, 237. Tunstall notes (33) the high level of watchers of television in the United Kingdom in 1954, unsurpassed in the world except for the viewer public in the United States. For an example of the official control of the media, see 56ff. For a more detailed study of governmental manipulation of commonsense in post-war Britain, see William Crofts, *Coercion or Persuasion? Propaganda in Britain after 1954* (London: Routledge, 1989). For a discussion of the patronage of art as a part of the maintenance of social stratification, see Carol Duncan, "Who Rules the Art World," *Socialist Review* 13, no. 4 (July 1983): 99–119.

44. Since Marshall McLuhan, writers have described academia in the age of the media as fossils. This is clearly overstated.

45. Not only have states gotten their way with jingoism on many occasions but with scholarship as well; Ray Billington, *The Historians' Contribution to Anglo-American Misunderstanding* (London: Routledge Kegan Paul, 1966). For the sake of manageability, I do not undertake the study of British local history here, a field that does not bear too directly on the

theme of historians and hegemony. Likewise, the work of imperial historians was deemphasized on the assumption that much of the work done was not in an important sense historical, that it was simply knowledge that the government wanted and that historians among others were employed to provide, for example, Robin Winks, ed., *The Historiography of the British Empire-Commonwealth* (Durham, N.C.: Duke Univ. Press, 1966).

46. Gareth Stedman Jones, "The Pathology of English History," *New Left Review* 46 (Nov. 1967): 29–43.

47. Rosemary Jann, "From Amateur to Professional: The Case of the Oxbridge Historians," *Journal of British Studies* 22, no. 2 (1983): 122–47.

48. In one well-known exchange, David Cannadine represented a Thatcherite point of view against several critics, "British History: Past, Present—and Future?" *Past and Present* 116 (Aug. 1987): 169–91; 119(May 1988): 171–203.

49. Keith Robbins, "*History:* The Historical Association and the National Past," *History* 66(1981): 413–25, notes the role of Alice Stopford Green (1848–1929) in pressing Irish and English universities to take up modern Irish history in the 1930s. A chair in Scottish history dates from 1911, a chair in Welsh history from 1930. Black history in contemporary Britain is yet to be on the agenda.

50. F. J. Byrne, "MacNeill the Historian," in *The Scholar Revolutionary: Eoin MacNeill, 1867–1945, and the Making of the New Ireland,* ed. Francis X. Martin and F. J. Byrne (Shannon: Irish Univ. Press, 1973). MacNeill was not the "best" scholar and was always beset by critics.

51. For accounts of writers, who used history when it became "free," see, for example, E. P. Thompson, Stuart Hall, and the American Eugene Genovese, Richard Johnson, "Edward Thompson and Eugene Genovese, and Social-Humanist History," *History Workshop* 6 (Aug. 1978): 79–100; Perkins, *Rise of Professional Society;* Doris S. Goldstein, "The Organizational Development of the British Historical Profession, 1884–1921," *Bulletin of the Institute of Historical Research* 55(1982): 180–93.

52. Deborah Wormell, *Sir John Seeley and the Uses of History* (Cambridge: Cambridge Univ. Press, 1980), introduction, 44–45, 60, 120–21; Jann, "From Amateur to Professional" 139–40.

53. P. B. M. Blaas, *Continuity and Anachronism* (The Hague: Martinus Nijhoff, 1978), xii. For the history of objectivity in the United States, see Peter Novick, *That Noble Dream: The "Objectivity Question" and the American Historical Profession* (Cambridge: Cambridge Univ. Press, 1988).

54. Frank Turner, "British Politics and the Demise of the Roman Republic: 1700–1939," *Historical Journal* 29, no. 3 (1986): 577–99, esp. 595.

55. Edward Kealey, "Recent Writing about Anglo-Norman England," *British Studies Monitor* 9, no. 1 (1980): 3–22, esp. 16.

56. James Smallwood, "A Historical Debate of the 1960s: World War II Historiography: The Origins of the War, A. J. P. Taylor, and His Critics," *Australian Journal of Politics and History* 26 (1980): 402–10. Taylor, he argues, is like the appeasers of Hitler in the 1930s; he suffers from an inability to understand the totalitarian mind. Fear of appeasement and more recently fear of terrorism are prominent parts of the latter-day Puritan mind that resurfaced in the 1970s. The resulting disarray of traditional liberal political history is the subject of Richard Brent, "Historiographical Review—Butterfield's Tories: 'High Politics' and the Writing of Modern British Political History," *Historical Journal* 30, no. 4 (1987): 943–954; Geoffrey Barraclough, *An Introduction to Contemporary History* (New York: Basic Books, 1964).

57. John Field, "British Historians and the Concept of Labor Aristocracy," *Radical History Review* 19 (Winter 1978): 61–85; Jonathan Zeitlin, "From Labour History to the History of Industrial Relations," *Economic History Review* 60, no. 2 (1987): 159–84.

58. A summary of the ideas exchanged on this subject during the later years of collectiv-

ism shows once again a decisive intellectual victory of Hobsbawm; E. J. Hobsbawm, "The Standard of Living During the Industrial Revolution," *Economic History Review* 16, no. 2 (1963–64): 119–46, with replies by the well-known liberal historian, R. M. Hartwell.

59. David Cannadine, "British History," 171–72; Harvey J. Kaye, *The British Marxist Historians* (Oxford: Polity Press, 1984) 138ff.

60. E. J. Hobsbawm, Christopher Hill, and R. H. Hilton, *"Past and Present*—Origins and Early Years," *Past and Present* 100 (Aug. 1983): 3–28.

61. For "ethnic" history, see Stewart Brown, "Assimilation and Identity in Modern Scottish History," *Journal of British Studies* 25, no. 1 (1986): 119–29. Attempts by the Thatcher government to mandate local history as an alternative to national history appear impractical, according even to a sympathetic reviewer, hence I am not pursuing it here; J. R. Lowerson, "Local and Regional History in Southern Tertiary Education," *Southern History* 2(1980): 228–46.

62. With the rise of a libertarian trend in several Western states, Eurocommunists have sought to accommodate it, for example, the French "new philosopher" trend and the celebrants of the "revolution" in communications; see, for example, Jean-François Lyotard, *The Postmodern Condition: A Report on Knowledge* (Minneapolis: Univ. of Minnesota Press, 1986), 3ff. For a more reliable analysis of the computer revolution, see Barbara Garson, *The Electronic Sweatshop: How Computers Are Transforming the Office of the Future into the Factory of the Past* (New York: Simon and Schuster, 1988); Ellen Meiksins Wood, *The Retreat from Class: A New 'True' Socialism* (London: Verso, 1986), is an overview of the accommodation of Marxism to "social democracy" and libertarianism in the 1970s.

63. François Dosse, *L'Histoire en miettes: Des annales à la nouvelle histoire* (Paris: Éditions la Découverte, 1987), 193ff., 207.

64. Lawrence Grossberg, "History, Politics and Postmodernism: Stuart Hall and Cultural Studies," *Journal of Communication Inquiry* 10, no. 2 (Summer 1986): 61–77. Appropos to Baudrilliard and his pessimism, Stuart Hall noted that Third World liberationists have learned to use the modern media to penetrate Western consciousness.

65. Raphael Samuel, "On the Methods of *History Workshop:* A Reply," *History Workshop* no. 9 (Spring 1980): 162–76, esp. 173–74.

66. Peter Burke, "Reflections on the Historical Revolution in France: The Annales School and British Social History," *Review* 1, no. 3–4 (Winter-Spring 1978): 147–56, see also, 157–63, for the affinity of the Annales tradition with *Past and Present;* Melvyn Dubofsky, the American historian, comments in the same issue about the work of Herbert Gutman and the American "new social history" writers, terming it "Annales-like," 182. The relevance of this point is that the Cambridge school acknowledges its debt to the American "new social history" and the "new economic history." This, thus, appears to be the route of the Annales school to Britain. For an example of a Cambridge school attack on Marxism that followed the Annaliste tradition; Peter Laslett, "A One-Class Society," in *History and Class,* ed. R. S. Neale (Oxford: Basil Blackwell, 1984), 196–221.

67. Gregor McLennan, *Marxism and the Methodologies of History* (London: Verso, 1981), 141; Elizabeth Fox-Genovese and Eugene D. Genovese, *Fruits of Merchant Capital* (New York: Oxford Univ. Press, 1983), 205. A forceful critique of the Annales school appears in the writings of Robert Brenner, the American historian, see eds., T. H. Aston and C. H. E. Philpin, eds., *The Brenner Debate* (Cambridge: Cambridge Univ. Press, 1985).

68. Eley and Hunt, *Reviving the English Revolution.*

69. Kevin Davis, "Thompson, Edward P.," in *Biographical Dictionary of Neo-Marxists,* ed. Robert A. Gorman (Westport, Conn.: Greenwood Press, 1985), 409–11. The intellectual groundwork for a left populism in recent times was laid by Raymond Williams and Richard Hoggart; but see also Paul Jones, " 'Organic' Intellectuals and the Generation of English Cultural Studies," *Thesis Eleven* nos. 5–6(1982): 85–124.

70. Ellen Meiksins Wood, "The Politics of Theory and the Concept of Class: E. P. Thompson and His Critics," *Studies in Political Economy* 9(1982): 52ff; Easthope, *British Post-Structuralism* 100–103. Ellen Wood and several other writers carry this line of critique forward in Harvey J. Kaye and Keith McClelland, eds., *E. P. Thompson: Critical Perspectives* (Philadelphia: Temple Univ. Press, 1990). The main point is not how Thompson drifts away from the determinancy of capitalism to class experience but what he does or does not find in class experience that would help overcome the racial division.

10. Bourgeois Democracy in the United States of America, 1877–1990

1. By exceptionalism, I mean the all-inclusive doctrine of interpretation of America that emphasizes its uniqueness, a doctrine that is as hydra-headed and as broad as such terms as *orientalism*. By exceptionalism in American history, I mean, inter alia, first, a largely unstated acceptance of this doctrine, an acceptance of the idea that the country is the universal and unqualified center of modern history. Second, I mean several specific arguments common to historians that are taken to lend credence to exceptionalism. Among these are the unique intent of the founders of America to enjoy freedom, the safety valve of the frontier, and the "Whiggish" continuity of American experience enveloped for generations in a consensus. The importance of exceptionalism is, obviously, quite enormous for the approach adopted in this book. If truly the only way to approach American history is through exceptionalism, the major lines of thought in the book are probably incorrect. The high stakes explain the length of the chapter. An important contemporary statement of the exceptionalist position places its emphasis on the American sanctification of the founding fathers and of the Constitution and more broadly of the American way of life; Robert N. Bellah, "Civil Religion in America," *Daedalus* 96, no. 1 (Winter 1967): 1–21. Comparative history, a field that potentially calls American exceptonalism into question, does have a place in American history, but a very small one; Raymond Grew, "The Comparative Weakness of American History," *Journal of Interdisciplinary History* 16, no. 1 (1985): 87–101. Among areas where comparative history has played a role is in studies of race: Anglo-Saxonism and black history. See George Reid Andrews, "Review Essay: Comparing the Comparers: White Supremacy in the United States and South Africa," *Journal of Social History* 20 (Spring 1987): 585–99; Shula Marks, "White Supremacy: A Review Article," *Comparative Studies in Society and History* 29, no. 2 (1987): 385–97.

Puritanism is a part of American exceptionalism; see Melvin B. Endy, Jr., "Just War, Holy War, and Millenium in Revolutionary America," *William and Mary Quarterly* 42, no. 1 (1985): 3–25; Sacvan Bercovitch, "How the Puritans Won the American Revolution," *Massachusetts Review* 17, no. 4 (1976): 597–630. Seemingly, when the plantation South, which stood for republicanism in 1776, became subordinated to the industrializing North of the nineteenth century, it shifted without perceptible difficulty to Puritanism as well; Elizabeth Fox-Genovese and Eugene D. Genovese, "The Divine Sanction of Social Order: Religious Foundations of the Southern Slaveholders' World View," *Journal of the American Academy of Religions* 60, no. 2 (1987): 211–33; Abraham I. Katsh, *The Biblical Heritage of American Democracy* (New York: KTAV, 1977), stressing the role of the Old Testament through the colonial period and the Indian wars.

An important attempt to get beyond American exceptionalism is to see America as Italian Road. Whatever its limitations, it may cast some light on the unsettled decades of the midnineteenth century when history was taking its modern form. In this period, one notes the propensity of Americans to send their youth to Berlin, not Cambridge; Germany at the time was Italian Road.

2. The importance of a racial distinction to the official mind can be inferred from the long-term, ongoing attempt to foster race as a scientific category in the United States; John H. Stanfield, *Philanthropy and Jim Crow in American Scholarship* (Westport, Conn.: Greenwood

Press, 1985). One of many policy implications that come out of this mindset touched my life recently when a client of my wife, a white family, essentially was prevented from adopting a black child. For a discussion of the constructedness of race in American history, see Barbara Jeanne Fields, "Slavery, Race, and Ideology in the United States of America," *New Left Review* (June 1990): 95–118. Traditional histories of racism, for example, Thomas F. Gossett, *Race: The History of an Idea in America* (Dallas: Southern Methodist Univ. Press, 1975), tend to conclude in the liberal manner that racism is a "real thing" but like other social ills in America is being overcome. The thesis of an enduring racial undercaste can be found, however, or is at least implied in a number of equally standard traditional works; John Ashworth, "The Jeffersonians: Classical Republicans or Liberal Capitalists?" *Journal of American Studies* 18, no. 3 (1984), 425–35, esp. 433–35. Ashforth, depending on Edmund Morgan, *American Slavery, American Freedom* (New York: Norton, 1975), correlates republicanism and slavery, noting first the danger of a republican system without a racial bond, pointing out second the strength of republican ideology in the South versus federalism in the North, and pointing out third the classical antecedents of modern republicanism in the slave-based societies of antiquity. By implication, at least, he is arguing that the maintenance of a republic after the end of slavery would require a racial undercaste as well. Shifting the emphasis from politics to economics, Marxist accounts emphasize the connection between capitalism and racism. Most do so, however, in a "stageist," or a linear way which permits them to dovetail with the liberal mainstream to which I have just referred. A few, however, do not. These show the ongoing nature of slavery in contemporary capitalism either from studies of the undocumented worker or from internal colonialism. For the standard linear approach relating racial oppression to the economy, see, for example, Robert Blauner, *Racial Oppression in America* (New York: Harper and Row, 1972). Much rarer is the attempt to tie racial oppression to the politics of democracy. This project was initiated by Oliver C. Cox but is still largely undeveloped; see George Snedeker, "Capitalism, Racism and the Struggle for Democracy: The Political Sociology of Oliver C. Cox," *Democracy and Socialism* 7(Fall 1988): 75–96. A recent article on structural racism suggests a way to study a racial undercaste on a national level; Philomena Essed, "Understanding Verbal Accounts of Racism: Politics and Heuristics of Reality Construction," *Text* 8(1988): 5–40. Essed argues that structural racism can be not just institutional but verbal. It can function as verbal attacks on blacks in the ordinary language of whites.

For commentaries on other parts of the racial undercaste, see an article arguing for the potential comparability of blacks and Chinese as parts of the American racial undercaste; Luther W. Spoehr, "Sambo and the Heathen Chinee: Californians' Racial Stereotypes in the late 1870's," *Pacific Historical Review* 62(May 1973): 185–204. On Puerto Ricans and Americanization specifically, see Charles Joseph Beirne, S.J., *The Problem of Americanization in the Catholic Schools of Puerto Rico* (San Juan: Univ. of Puerto Rico, 1975). At least through the interwar period, English Jews were arguably part of the racial undercaste as well. Lord Balfour called for a national home for the Jews, meaning, of course, Palestine, not England; Tony Kushner, *The Persistence of Prejudice: Anti-Semitism in British Society During the Second World War* (Manchester: Manchester Univ. Press, 1989), conclusion.

3. Concepts of the state. Paul Sweezy, the editor of *Monthly Review* tied his concept of the state to the phases of capitalism, the contemporary state reflecting monopoly capitalism; Paul A. Baran and Paul M. Sweezy, *Monopoly Capital: An Essay on the American Economic and Social Order* (New York: Monthly Review Press, 1966). The German Frankfort school Marxists, such as Herbert Marcuse, however, characterize the modern state in terms of its apparatus of control, for example, its mass media. See Herbert Marcuse, *One-Dimensional Man: Studies in the Ideology of Advanced Industrial Society* (Boston: Beacon, 1964). A work, such as the present one, beginning from the premise that the state relies on alliances, bureaucratization, a cultural policy,and persuasion alongside coercion will use a mixture of concepts held by various schools of thought. See, for example, n. 6, this chapter. For the cultural policy of the state, a

useful book is Charles C. Mark, *A Study of Cultural Policy in the United States* (Paris: UNESCO, 1969). Useful books discussing the organization of culture include Robert A. Carlson, *The Americanization Syndrome: A Quest for Conformity* (New York: St. Martin's Press, 1987), chap. 5. For the struggle of an East Coast working class to control the idea of what is American, see Gary Gerstle, *Working-Class Americanism: The Politics of Labor in a Textile City, 1914–1960* (Cambridge: Cambridge Univ. Press, 1989), conclusion.

When hegemonies go through less-successful phases, they tend to resort to more violence, and this appears to have been the case for the United States in the nineteenth century. See for example, Alan Dawley, "E. P. Thompson and the Peculiarities of the Americans," *Radical History Review* 19 (Winter 1978–79): 33–59. "In the years between the railway strikes of 1877 and the Republic Steel Massacre of 1937, the jails are filled with political prisoners whose organizing rights have been violated by injunctions against organizing, arrests for free speech, prosecutions (and executions) for trumped-up capital crimes, "suicides" while in police custody, and wholesale massacres on a scale undreamed of in a radical England. All this is undeniably the lived experience of class struggle (even if the word is expunged)" (52). See also James Holt, "Trade Unionism in the British and U.S. Steel Industries, 1880–1914: A Comparative Study," *Labor History* 18(1977): 5–35, suggesting a very rapid evolution of technology in U.S. steel mills, very high wages, relative to Britain, accessibility of management during work time, but, in contrast to Britain, a violent opposition to trade unionism.

Alongside the trade union movement were the radical populist movements inside and outside organized labor, among which the Wobblies, were most famous. Stressing the anarchist side of the Wobblies is Salvatore Salerno, *Red November/Black November: Culture and Community in the Industrial Workers of the World* (Albany, N.Y.: State Univ. of New York Press, 1989). For a work suggesting literal continuity from Populists to Wobblies in the case of the Western Miners, for example, Ed Boyce, and Bill Haywood and, see Melvyn Dubovsky, *We Shall Be All: A History of the Industrial Workers of the World* (Chicago: Quadrangle Books, 1969), 58–59. For a study of counterhegemonic practice, tying class to race and gender and region, see James F. Pickle, "Race, Class and Radicalism: The Wobblies in the Southern Lumber Industry," in *At the Point of Production: The Local History of the IWW*, ed. Joseph Conklin (Westport, Conn.: Greenwood Press, 1981), 97–111.

4. Articles showing the nontransition of the South include, Barbara Jeanne Fields, "The Nineteenth-Century American South: History and Theory," *Plantation Society* 2, no. 1 (1983): 7–27; and Steven Hahn, "Hunting, Fishing, and Foraging: Common Rights and Class Relations in the Postbellum South," *Radical History Review* 26 (1982): 37–64. One could treat this type of subject matter under the broader rubric of the unequal development of capitalism, but as shown in these articles, much would be lost by the abstraction and by the economism. Further, it begs the question Why was the development unequal? As suggested in these articles, in the South it was unequal partly as a result of local resistance to the reinstitution of "home rule" and partly as a response by the federal government, which was anxious to buffer itself from this struggle. The struggle was known to history as it developed as the Populist movement. Instability from the point of view of the state lay in the fact that poor whites were aligning themselves with blacks and not with rich whites. This reading of the instability undercuts much of the utility of various scholarly efforts to compare the United States to Brazil, Prussia, and Italy or other Italian Road regimes. The primary cultural contradiction in the United States is race; region is second.

5. H. L. Mitchell, *Roll the Union* (Chicago: Charles H. Kerr Publishing, 1987), 76.

6. For a detailed analysis of congressional history, permitting one to extrapolate the different interests of national capital in the Midwest and the South compared to international capital on the East Coast; Elizabeth Sanders, "The Regulatory Surge of the 1970's in Historical Perspective," in *Public Regulation: New Perspectives on Institutions and Policies,* ed. Elizabeth E. Bailey (Cambridge: MIT Press, 1987), 117–50. See also, R. F. Bensel, *Sectionalism and American*

Political Development (Madison: Univ. of Wisconsin Press, 1984). For the rise of the regulatory state, see Robert Higgs, *Crisis and Leviathan: Critical Episodes in the Growth of the American Government* (New York: Oxford Univ. Press, 1987). Higgs is useful in two ways: for his statistics and for his discussion of the crises. From the statistics, it appears that the government employs today three to six times as many people as it did around World War I. The crises he identifies could be viewed as moments of particularly aggravated intercapitalist rivalries, which from the perspective adopted here become opportunities for the state to further regulate.

7. The classic works on the origins of modern America are by C. Vann Woodward, *Reunion and Reaction: The Compromise of 1877 and the End of Reconstruction* (Boston: Little, Brown, 1951), outlines the many shady deals that led up to the compromise and his *Origins of the New South, 1877–1913* (Baton Rouge: Louisiana State Univ. Press, 1951), which makes clear the nonsouthern quality of the new South. His *Origins* along with W. E. B. Du Bois's major work, *Black Reconstruction in America, 1860–1880* (New York: Harcourt Brace, 1935), provide the basic critique of consensus history for this period, providing as well an explanation for why the American state could arise as a regulatory state. For an account of the bureaucratic context that grew up with this new regulatory state, see Stephen Skowronek, *Building a New American State: The Expansion of National Administrative Capacities, 1877–1920* (Cambridge: Cambridge Univ. Press, 1982), 15; Robert H. Wiebe, *The Search for Order, 1877–1920* (New York: Hill and Wang, 1967); Michael E. McGeer, *The Decline of Popular Politics: The American North, 1865–1928* (New York: Oxford Univ. Press, 1986). Bureaucracy and regulation in the American context led to a rise in state repression; Robert Justin Goldstein, *Political Repression in Modern America: From 1870 to the Present* (Cambridge, Mass.: Schenkman Publishing, 1978). Goldstein terms the suppression of organized labor between 1873 and 1937 as severe or more severe than in any other Western country; the use of private armies and police against workers reached unique levels.

8. Leon Fink, "The New Labor History and the Powers of Historical Pessimism: Consensus, Hegemony, and the Case of the Knights of Labor," *Journal of American History* 75(June 1988): 115–36, also offers a critique of the consensus view.

9. A. T. Lane, *Solidarity or Survival? American Labor and European Immigrants, 1830–1924* (Westport Conn.: Greenwood Press, 1987), 76–77. For the mixture of race and class in two major labor struggles, see an account of black struggle in the factories of Winston-Salem and Detroit in the 1940s, Robert Korstad and Nelson Lichtenstein, "Opportunities Found and Lost: Labor, Radicals, and the Early Civil Rights Movement," *Journal of American History* 75, no. 3 (Dec. 1988): 786–811. There were no "forgotten years" of the Black struggle in America, these authors argue. For the antecedents in the rural South of the 1930s to the urban struggles of the 1940s noted above, see Mark D. Naison, "Black Agrarian Radicalism in the Great Depression: The Threads of a Lost Tradition," *Journal of Ethnic Studies* 1, no. 3 (1973): 47–65. For the argument that even with the great black migration out of the deep South, a rural environment of struggle persists to the present day, see the valuable article of Nan Elizabeth Woodruff, "African-American Struggles for Citizenship in the Arkansas and Mississippi Deltas in the Age of Jim Crow," *Radical History Review* 55(1993): 33–51.

10. Higgs, *Crisis and Leviathan*, 103.

11. Fink, "New Labor History," passim.

12. Gwendolyn Mink, *Old Labor and New Immigrants in American Political Development: Union, Party, and State, 1875–1920* (Ithaca, N.Y.: Cornell Univ. Press, 1986), 17, 24, 42, and esp. 263, notes that because suffrage had come early in the United States, partisanship and political integration preceded the rise of trade unions, that is, there was no unifying issue for the American working class.

13. Mitchell, *Roll the Union*, 41.

14. John Foster Bellamy, "The Fetishism of Fordism," *Monthly Review* 39, no. 10 (1988): 14–33; an example of the critique of consumerism is Debora Silverman, *Selling Culture: Bloo-*

mingdale's, Diana Vreeland, and the New Aristocracy of Taste in Reagan's America (New York: Pantheon, 1986).

15. Higgs, *Crisis and Leviathan,* chap. 8 notes unemployment insurance, social security, welfare, agricultural price supports, and the regulation of private security markets.

16. For the Delta, see Woodruff, "African-American Struggles" see also, Frances F. Piven and Richard A. Cloward, *Poor People's Movements: Why They Succeed, How They Fail* (New York: Vintage Books, 1979), 108–10. For a comment on the affinities of the southern black church culture and the politics of the Communist party in Birmingham, Alabama, see Robin D. G. Kelley, " 'Comrades, Praise Gawd For Lenin and Them!': Ideology and Culture among Black Communists in Alabama, 1930–1935," *Science and Society* 52, no. 1 (Spring 1988): 59–82. This is an example of the continuing radical populist tradition; see idem, *Hammer and Hoe: Alabama Communists During the Great Depression* (Chapel Hill: Univ. of North Carolina Press, 1990). Steve Fraser and Gary Gerstle, eds., *The Rise and Fall of the New Deal Order, 1930–1980* (Princeton, N.J.: Princeton Univ. Press, 1990).

17. Steve Fraser, "The 'Labor Question,' " in *Rise and Fall of the New Deal Order, 1930–1980,* ed. Steve Fraser and Gary Gerstle, (Princeton, N.J.: Princeton Univ. Press, 1990), 55–81.

18. The history of trust versus antitrust legislation is probably one of the better ways to chart the struggle between national and international capitalism in the United States. Franklin Delano Roosevelt (FDR) is an interesting figure in this history because of his support for the trusts and for the Congress of Industrial Organizations (CIO), which the smaller industries of national capital tended to oppose. For commentary on this historic conflict in one particular area, coal, see Stanley Vittoz, *New Deal Labor Policy and the American Industrial Economy* (Chapel Hill: Univ. of North Carolina Press, 1987), 80–81, esp. 113. In steel, the CIO and U.S. Steel reached an agreement in 1937 after a long secret negotiation. Little Steel, led by Thomas Girdler, however, set out to smash the CIO; Joseph G. Rayback, *A History of American Labor* (New York: Free Press, 1966), 351–52.

19. Sasha G. Lewis, *Slave Trade Today: America's Exploitation of Illegal Aliens* (Boston: Beacon Press, 1979), 17–19.

20. Richard L. Florida and Marshall M. A. Feldman, "Housing in US Fordism," *International Journal of Urban and Regional Research* 12, no. 2 (1988): 187–210, esp. 189–92.

21. Nelson Lichtenstein, "From Corporatism to Collective Bargaining: Organized Labor and the Eclipse of Social Democracy in the Postwar Era," in *The Rise and Fall of the New Deal Order, 1930–1980,* ed. Steve Fraser and Gary Gerstle (Princeton, N.J.: Princeton Univ. Press, 1990), 122–51; Philip Foner, *Organized Labor and the Black Worker* (New York: International Publishers, 1982), 275ff.; Florida and Feldman, "Housing in US Fordism," 195.

22. Nan Elizabeth Woodruff, "Mississippi Delta Planters and Debates over Mechanization, Labor and Civil Rights in the 1940's," *Journal of Southern History* 60, no. 2 (1994): 263–84.

23. Labor initiatives in the 1960s included the struggles in textiles in which many southern workers participated thanks to union struggles after the passage of the Civil Rights Act of 1964; Barry Bluestone and Bennett Harrison, *The Deindustrialization of America* (New York: Basic Books, 1982), chap. 5; Holly Sklar, ed., *Trilateralism* (Boston: South End Press, 1980), chap. 1; an important microcosm of the larger picture would be the rise of George Wallace, governor of Alabama, a strong supporter of the white working class. Wallace's career and that of labor's in Alabama sharply declined around 1970 with the decline of manufacture; Robert H. Zieger, ed., *Organized Labor in the Twentieth-Century South* (Knoxville: Univ. of Tennessee Press, 1991), 269.

24. Leon Friedman and William F. Levantrosser, eds., *Richard M. Nixon* (Westport, Conn.: Greenwood Press, 1991).

25. For the more conventional "disappearing South" thesis, see, for example, Robert P.

Steed, Laurence W. Moreland, and Tod A. Baker, eds., *The Disappearing South* (Tuscaloosa: Univ. of Alabama, 1990).

26. Art Carey, *The United States of Incompetence* (Boston: Houghton Mifflin, 1991); for the 1960s as a period of too much democracy see Michel Crozier, Samuel Huntington, and Joji Watanuki, *Crisis of Democracy: Report on the Governability of Democracies to the Trilateral Commission* (New York: New York Univ. Press, 1975).

27. Representative commentaries include: Carlton Rochell, *Dreams Betrayed: Working in the Technological Age* (Lexington, Mass.: Lexington Books, 1987); Ruth Schwartz Cowan, *More Work for Mother: The Ironies of Household Technology from the Open Hearth to the Microwave* (New York: Basic Books, 1983). During the same period, as many farmers lost their farms, a mental health crisis arose in the countryside; many farmers were committing suicide. See Osha Gray Davidson, *Broken Heartland: The Rise of America's Rural Ghetto* (New York: Free Press, 1990), 94.

28. Elazar Barkan, *The Retreat of Scientific Racism: Changing Concepts of Race in Britain and the United States Between the Two World Wars* (Cambridge: Cambridge Univ. Press, 1992).

29. For the recent drug trade, Peter D. Scott and Jonathan Marshall, *Cocaine Politics: Drugs, Armies, and the CIA in Central America* (Berkeley: Univ. of California Press, 1991). Drug books on the Reagan years emphasize Afghanistan; for the Johnson years, the emphasis is on Cambodia and Laos. In more recent writing, the link between the state and organized crime in the area of the drug trade is called *"deep* politics." Peter D. Scott, *Deep Politics and the Death of JFK,* (Berkeley: Univ. of Calif. Press, 1993).

30. An ideologue of the New Right is James Q. Wilson, *Thinking about Crime* (New York: Vintage Books, 1985).

31. Michael D'Antonio, *Fall from Grace: The Failed Crusade of the Christian Right* (New York: Farrar, Straus, Giroux, 1989), 66. In addition, Afro-Americans were not intimidated in the South: Richard A. Couto, *Ain't Gonna Let Nobody Turn Me Round: The Pursuit of Racial Justice in the Rural South* (Philadelphia: Temple Univ. Press, 1991); Nancie Caraway, *Segregated Sisterhood: Racism and the Politics of American Feminism* (Knoxville: Univ. of Tennessee Press, 1991).

32. For a discussion of the contemporary South, see Thomas A. Lyson, *Two Sides to the Sunbelt: The Growing Divergence Between the Rural and Urban South* (New York: Frederick A. Praeger, 1989).

33. Marc H. Tanenbaum, Marvin R. Wilson, and A. James Rudin, eds., *Evangelicals and Jews in an Age of Pluralism* (Grand Rapids: Baker Book House, 1984), pt. 5, on proselytism suggests that the rapport between the Zionists and the Fundamentalists has its limitations. Political economists have tended to explain the special relationship, first, as a consequence of the service Israel has rendered to U.S. interests abroad, conflating, however, the differing interests of the state and capital. Second, they have tried to explain the influence of Israel in terms of the influence of the American Jewish community. This approach offers few clues to the rise and decline of the special relationship.

34. Vincent Porter, "The Re-Regulation of Television: Pluralism, Constitutionality, and the Free Market in the USA, France, and the UK," *Media, Culture and Society* 11(1989): 5–27; Razelle Frankl, *Televangelism: The Marketing of Popular Religion* (Carbondale: Southern Illinois Univ. Press, 1987), conclusion. For the growth and then deregulation of the telecommunication industry in the United States and the United Kingdom as industry took it over; Ralph Negrine, ed., *Satellite Broadcasting* (London: Routledge, 1988), chaps. 5, 8. For American Telephone and Telegraph (AT&T), see Alan Stone, *Wrong Number* (New York: Basic Books, 1989).

35. A collection of scholarly essays on this subject has appeared from the J. M. Dawson Institute of Church-State Studies at Baylor University in Waco, Texas; James E. Wood, Jr., *Religion, the State, and Education* (Waco, Tex.: Baylor Univ. Press, 1984), 36.

36. Roy Wallis, "Paradoxes of Freedom and Regulation: The Case of the New Religious Movements in Britain and America," *Sociological Analysis* 48, no. 4 (1988): 355–71.

37. For an overview of change in America through the long-term history of populist movements, see the writings of the prolific Harry C. Boyte, *Commonwealth: A Return to Citizen Politics* (New York: Free Press, 1989).

38. This seems to be the most temperate approach to the subject. Perhaps because of American exceptionalism, many writers take extreme positions. They may stress, for example, the extreme freedom of thought to be found in civil society or, conversely, the extreme role played by coercion in the high per capita prison population. For an example that argues against exceptionalism from a labor history perspective, see Michael Goldfield, "The Color of Politics in the United States: White Supremacy as the Main Explanation for the Peculiarities of American Politics from Colonial Times to the Present," in Dominick LaCapra, ed., *The Bounds of Race: Perspectives on Hegemony and Resistance* (Ithaca, N.Y.: Cornell Univ. Press, 1991), 104ff.; in early American history, the native American people were the racial undercaste for the whites. In the nineteenth century, this gradually changed as Afro-Americans became the racial undercaste. From this point, white writers, among others, gradually formed an increasingly subtle and sympathetic view of native American culture and of native American writers; Michael Castro, *Interpreting the Indian: Twentieth Century Poets and the Native American* (Albuquerque: Univ. of New Mexico Press, 1983). After the Civil Rights movement of the 1960s, the government appears to have attempted a new strategy to resolidify the Afro-American population as a racial undercaste by creating "buffer races," groups whose presence and prominence would disguise the oppression of the Afro-Americans. Prominent in this category in different parts of the country are East Asians, Hispanics, and Middle Easterners.

39. For a history of Americanism as affluence, see a work adopting roughly the same periodization used here, Richard Wightman Fox and T. J. Jackson Lears, eds., *The Culture of Consumption* (New York: Pantheon, 1983); Richard Hofstadter, *Anti-Intellectualism in American Life* (New York: Alfred A. Knopf, 1963).

40. For the view that Jews in the United States are not that assimilated, see the writings of Leonard Dinnerstein, for example, *Uneasy at Home: Antisemitism and the American Jewish Experience* (New York: Columbia Univ. Press, 1987).

41. T.J. Jackson Lears, *No Place of Grace: Anti-Modernism and the Transformation of American Culture* (New York: Pantheon, 1981).

42. William Petersen, Michael Novak, and Philip Gleason, *Concepts of Ethnicity* (Cambridge, Mass.: Belknap Press, 1982), 79ff.

43. The details are drawn from Burton W. Adkinson, *Two Centuries of Federal Information* (Stroudsburg: Dowden, Hutchinson and Ross, 1978). For an intellectual history of the famous regulators, see Thomas K. McCraw, *Prophets of Regulation* (Cambridge, Mass.: Belknap Press, 1984).

44. This is the thesis of David F. Noble, *America by Design: Science, Technology, and the Rise of Corporate Capitalism* (New York: Alfred A. Knopf, 1977).

45. Task Force on Science Policy: *A History of Science Policy in the United States, 1940–1985* 99th H. of R./2d sess./serial R (Washington, D.C., 1986), 7.

46. Ibid. For an example of the involvement of the government in regulating science on an international level, see *Regulation of Transnational Communication,* Michigan Yearbook of International Legal Studies, (New York: Clark Boardman, 1984); for an instance during which the governmental regulatory was in disarray in the 1980s, see William B. Ray, *FCC* (Ames: Iowa State Univ. Press, 1990), chap. 8. Even more sweeping is Jeremy Tunstall, *Communication Deregulation* (Oxford: Basil Blackwell, 1986).

47. Cowan, *More Work for Mother.*

48. Charles Rosenberg, "Science in American Society," *Isis* 74(1983): 356–67.

49. Barkan, *Retreat of Scientific Racism,* 284.

50. Mark, *Cultural Policy*.

51. Dick Netzer, *The Subsidized Muse: Public Support for the Arts in the United States* (Cambridge: Cambridge Univ. Press, 1978), 3–4, 15, 53, 208.

52. Gene M. Lyons, *The Uneasy Partnership: Social Science and the Federal Government in the Twentieth Century* (New York: Russell Sage, 1969), 22ff.; Carlo Antoni, *From History to Sociology* (Detroit, Mich.: Wayne State Univ. Press, 1959).

53. Lyons, *The Uneasy Partnership, passim*.

54. Bitter disciplinary histories emerge in this period, for example, Alvin Gouldner, *The Coming Crisis of Western Sociology* (New York: Basic Books, 1970).

55. David P. Szatmary, *Rockin' in Time: A Social History of Rock and Roll* (Englewood Cliffs, N.J.: Prentice-Hall, 1987), 184ff.

56. Grover Sales, *Jazz: America's Classical Music* (Englewood Cliffs, N.J.: Prentice-Hall, 1984), chap. 5; Nicholas E. Tawa, *Serenading the Reluctant Eagle: American Musical Life, 1925–1945* (New York: Schirmer Books, 1984). Herbert Marcuse and others in the American Frankfurt school have emphasized that the division of labor produced highly specialized one-dimensional men, sharply divided along race and gender lines, who have as a consequence of their narrow life experience vivid and questing imaginations. Films could stir this imagination and induce individuals to seek change. This was also the insight of Bertolt Brecht, the German theorist, in a brief visit to Hollywood. Hollywood, of course, thought otherwise.

57. Aldon Lynn Nielsen, *Reading Race: White American Poets and the Racial Discourse in the Twentieth Century* (Athens: Univ. of Georgia Press, 1988).

58. Nancy Tatum Ammerman, *Baptist Battles* (New Brunswick, N. J.: Rutgers Univ. Press, 1990), chap. 4.

59. Warren French, ed., *The South and Film* (Jackson: Univ. Press of Mississippi, 1981).

60. According to the author of a recent article on the history of classics in the United States, race and gender issues are now subjects being taken up by the field. This marks the probable end of the traditional hegemonic role of the field. Phyllis Culham and Lowell Edmunds, eds., *Classics: A Discipline and Profession in Crisis* (Lanham, Md.: Univ. Press of America, 1989), 305–6, 314, 317; *Arethusa* (Fall 1989), a special issue on Martin Bernal, *Black Athena;* Meyer Reinhold, *Classica Americana* (Detroit, Mich.: Wayne State Univ. Press, 1984), 241, 260.

61. Lawrence H. Schwartz, *Creating Faulkner's Reputation: The Politics of Modern Literary Criticism* (Knoxville: Univ. of Tennessee Press, 1988), 30; Serge Guilbaut, *How New York Stole the Idea of Modern Art: Abstract Expressionism, Freedom, and the Cold War* (Chicago: Univ. of Chicago Press, 1983).

62. For language control in the United Kingdom, see Roger Fowler et al., *Language and Control* (London: Routledge Kegan Paul, 1979). For control of language in the United States, see Cushing Strout, "Tocqueville and the Idea of an American Literature (1941–1971)," *New Literary History* 18 (1986–87): 115–27. For the development of the East Coast high culture, see Lawrence W. Levine, *Highbrow/Lowbrow: The Emergence of Cultural Hierarchy in America* (Cambridge, Mass.: Harvard Univ. Press, 1988).

63. The exception was wartime. For studies of the wartime service of historians, see Jesse Lemisch, *On Active Service in War and Peace: Politics and Ideology in the American Historical Association* (Toronto: New Hogtown Press, 1975); also, Carol Gruber, *Mars and Minerva: World War I and the Uses of Higher Learning in America* (Baton Rouge: Louisiana State Univ. Press, 1975).

64. John Higham, *History: Professional Scholarship in America* (Baltimore, Md.: Johns Hopkins Univ. Press, 1986), 6–20, esp. 14, for the early frustrations of the profession.

65. Michael Kammen, "Moses Coit Tyler: The First Professor of American History in the United States," *History Teacher* 17, no. 1 (1983): 61–87, esp. 71. Tyler (1835–1900), who came to Cornell in 1881, is compared to J. R. Seeley (see chap. 9), presented here as the

individual coming from a religious background but believing the state should carry the torch of public morality (75). The linkage of the state to historical study meant for Seeley that political history was natural, whereas in the United States, it led to literary history, given Tyler's core culture affiliations. John Higham credits Tyler as the founder of intellectual history in the United States and, thus, a forerunner of the efflorescence from Parrington, "The Rise of American Intellectual History," *American Historical Review* 46, no. 3 (Apr. 1951): 453–71, esp. 456.

66. Jurgen Herbst, *The German Historical School in American Scholarship* (Ithaca, N.Y.: Cornell Univ. Press, 1965), 125, comments on the ill-situated versions of the German Mandarins in their American context. On the revolt of the second generation, see Dorothy Ross, "On the Misunderstanding of Ranke and the Origins of the Historical Profession in America," in *Leopold von Ranke and the Shaping of the Historical Discipline*, ed. Georg G. Iggers and James M. Powell (Syracuse, N.Y.: Syracuse Univ. Press, 1990), 154–69, esp. 168–69.

67. For an important example of a regionally based organization, see James L. Sellers, "The Semicentennial of the Mississippi Valley Historical Association," *Mississippi Valley Historical Review* 44(1957): 494–518. The rise of this organization and its change into the Organization of American Historians parallels the declining cultural hegemony of the East Coast. Other examples of regional work can be found among the neo-Turnerians, for example, Ray Allen Billington (1903–1981) for the western frontier, Walter Prescott Webb (1888–1963) for the Great Plains, and Herbert Eugene Bolton, for the Borderlands school; see David J. Weber, "Turner: The Boltonians and the Borderlands," *American Historical Review* 91, no. 1 (1986): 66–81. Apparently, when members of the internationalist wing today criticize the Turnerians for a lack of sensitivity to ethnicity or ecology, they are carrying on their old denial of regionalism in a new form; see William G. Robbins, "The 'Plundered Province' Thesis and the Recent Historiography of the American West," *Pacific Historical Review* 55(1986): 577–97. By contrast, see Howard Lamar, "Much to Celebrate: The Western History Association's Twenty-Fifth Birthday," *Western Historical Quarterly* 17, no. 4 (1986): 397ff. In general, the core culture writers tend to give a more favorable view of the earlier populist movement than do the internationalists; Roger D. Launius, "The Nature of the Populists: An Historiographical Essay," *Southern Studies* 22, no. 4 (1983): 366–85. Yet another view on core culture historiography comes from the local history societies; David J. Russo, *Keepers of Our Past: Local Historical Writing in the United States, 1820's-1930's* (Westport, Conn.: Greenwood Press, 1988).

68. David Glassberg, "History and the Public: Legacies of the Progressive Era," *American Historical Review* 73, no. 4 (1987): 957–80, esp. 957. For further commentary on public history's attempt to take the ground lost by the traditional profession, see G. Wesley Johnson, "Professionalism: Foundation of Public History Instruction," *Public Historian* 9, no. 3 (Summer 1987): 96–110. An interesting debate between government historians and academic historians is aired in "Roundtable: Government-Sponsored Research: A Sanitized Past?" *Public Historian* 10, no. 3 (Summer 1988): 31–58. The premise of the debate is the freedom of the ivory tower and the unfreedom of working for an agency, a premise that needs further discussion. In the lower echelons of government agencies, employment need not make the employee an agent of the state.

Of the rather lackadaisical effort of the American Historical Association (AHA) to woo the South, see David D. Van Tassel, "The American Historical Association and the South, 1884–1913," *Journal of Southern History* 23 (1957): 465–82. Policies introduced in the AHA as early as 1895 defined the contours of the profession to eliminate ties to the local historical societies and to popular historical writers in favor of the university professors, especially those of the major universities; John Higham, "Herbert Baxter Adams and the Study of Local History," *American Historical Review* 89, no. 5 (1984): 1225–39, esp. 1237. These restrictive policies also slowed the entrance of women into the profession because most women historians were employed in smaller colleges and women's schools well into the twentieth century;

Kathryn Kish Sklar, "American Female Historians in Context, 1770–1930," *Feminist Studies* 3 (Fall 1975): 171–84. Sklar's thesis was that women were forced together and that this led in time to the formation of the Berkshire Conference in 1930 (171). The career of Mary Beard, a leading historian of the progressive period is perceived to reflect a number of criticisms of the male-dominated positivism of the profession; Bonnie G. Smith, "The Contribution of Women in Modern Historiography in Great Britain, France, and the United States," *American Historical Review* 89 (1984): 709–32, esp. 731–32.

Yet another professional trend at a distance from the AHA was reflected in the founding of the *Journal of Negro History* in 1916 by Carter G. Woodson; John Hope Franklin, "On the Evolution of Scholarship in Afro-American Historiography," in *The State of Afro-American History*, ed. Darlene Clark Hine (Baton Rouge: Louisiana State Univ. Press, 1986), 14.

In the 1930s, the AHA lost its influence over secondary school education to the newly arising schools of education. During this period, the AHA refused to acknowledge the relevance of social science. Professors of history were very condescending to teachers as well; Truman Beckley Brown, "The American Historical Association and the Schools: A Study of Condescension" (Ph.D. diss., State Univ. of New York, at Buffalo, 1986); James T. Kloppenberg, "Review Article: Objectivism and Historicism: A Century of American Historical Writing," *American Historical Review* 94, no. 4 (1989): 1011–30, esp. 1013–14, a review of Peter Novick, *That Noble Dream: The "Objectivity Question" and the American Historical Profession* (Cambridge: Cambridge Univ. Press, 1988).

Finally, the AHA lost ground to American Studies; see Philip Gleason, "World War II and the Development of American Studies," *American Quarterly* 36, no. 3 (1984): 343–58. While acknowledging the launching of the *American Quarterly* in 1949 and the formation of the American Studies Association in 1951, Gleason emphasizes the importance of the "preinstitutional" phase for American studies as well, noting the seminal influence of Vernon Parrington. American studies, too, is caught up in consensus scholarship as is history itself; Gene Wise, " 'Paradigm Dramas' in American Studies: A Cultural and Institutional History of the Movement," *American Quarterly* 31, no. 3 (1979): 293–337.

69. Victor Gondos, Jr., *J. Franklin Jameson and the Birth of the National Archives, 1906–1926* (Philadelphia: Univ. of Pennsylvania Press, 1981).

70. The contribution of various professors to wartime propaganda in the National Board for Historical Service as pamphleteers, orators, and censors is detailed by George T. Blakey, *Historians on the Homefront: American Propagandists for the Great War* (Lexington: Univ. of Kentucky Press, 1970). The isolationist critique of them in the immediate postwar period is reflected in such core culture works as Harry Elmer Barnes, *The Genesis of the World War: An Introduction to the Problems of War Guilt* (New York: Knopf, 1926), cited by Blakey (135). At least one historian, Guy Stanton Ford, ignored the years of criticism and lived long enough to return to work for the War Department in 1941. By World War II, the government relied more heavily than it had earlier on the mass media. See also n. 63, this chapter.

71. Michael Kraus and David D. Joyce, *The Writing of American History* (Norman: Univ. Oklahoma, 1985), 240ff.; Bernard Sternsher, "The Critical Response to Consensus History," in *Consensus, Conflict, and American Historians* (Bloomington: Indiana Univ. Press, 1975), 70ff. For an account of how the conflict and consensus schools can both claim Hofstadter in their own ways, see Susan Stout Baker, *Radical Beginnings: Richard Hofstadter and the 1930's* (Westport, Conn.: Greenwood Press, 1985), introduction. For comments suggesting the continuity between the progressive era and the consensus era, see the discussion of Hofstadter's attraction to Beard in Ian Tyrrell, *The Absent Marx* (Westport, Conn.: Greenwood Press, 1986), 96. Tyrrell's main point about the unusually co-optative nature of American liberal historiography is another way of casting the argument here about the persistence of consensus; Allen F. Davis and Harold D. Woodman, *Conflict and Consensus in Early American History* 7th ed. (Lexington: D. C. Heath, 1988), 11.

72. Victor S. Navasky, *Naming Names* (New York: Viking, 1980); Socialists in the ranks

of historians have faced numerous purges. For a discussion of leading American historians active in carrying out purges in the 1960s, see Lemisch, *On Active Service*. For a more recent example, see Geoff Eley et al., "The David Abraham Case: Ten Comments From Historians," *Radical History Review* 32(1985): 75–96. For reminiscences of an early purge threatened by Arthur Schlesinger, see Betty L. Fladeland, "Revisionists vs. Abolitionists: The Historiographical Cold War of the 1930's and 1940's," *Journal of the Early Republic* 6(Spring 1986): 1–21, esp. 18–21.

73. Representative views of the Old Guard can be found in Oscar Handlin, *Truth in History* (Cambridge, Mass.: Belknap Press, 1979). Handlin disliked the sectarianism and the declining appreciation for one's teacher, the new style of reviewing books, the style that did not judge them but merely identified the trend, the increase in the number of Ph.D. programs in history, and so forth. On a related note, opposition to generalizations in the writing of history is the theme of several well-known old guard writers, for example, Louis Gottschalk, ed., *Generalization in the Writing of History* (Chicago: Univ. of Chicago Press, 1963); Maurice Mandelbaum, *The Anatomy of Historical Knowledge* (Baltimore, Md.: Johns Hopkins Univ. Press, 1977). Knowledge about the history of the profession largely depends until now on this older generation; Higham, *History,* epilogue; Peter Novick, *That Noble Dream,* chap. 13. Novick's theme of the objectivity question is a useful way to characterize conflict in a given domain of knowledge. Commonly, epistemological differences point to deep political differences, here, probably, to the conflict of national and international capitalism.

74. Wise, " 'Paradigm Dramas,' " 301ff. Wise notes the influence of a visit to the Belgian Congo on Perry Miller's whole subsequent career; he also links him back to Parrington.

75. Melvyn Stokes, "American Liberalism and the Neo-Consensus School," *Journal of American Studies* 20, no. 3 (1986): 449–60. For recent examples of AHA consensus construction, see Hine, *Afro-American History*. Does the AHA aspire to become a regulatory agency?

76. Robert Hewison, *The Heritage Industry: Britain in a Climate of Decline* (London: Methuen, 1987).

77. Leading examples of the new writing would be Gary B. Nash, *Red, White, and Black: The Peoples of Early America* (Englewood Cliffs, N.J.: Prentice-Hall, 1974); James H. Merrell, "Some Thoughts on Colonial Historians and American Indians," *William and Mary Quarterly* 46, no. 1 (1989): 94–119, esp. 96. Another revisionist writer is Francis Jennings. Francis Jennings was the author of three major books between 1975 and 1988 on the misrepresentation of the American Indian in history; see also the work of historical archeologists such as Bruce Trigger, "American Archeology as Native History: A Review Essay," *William and Mary Quarterly* 40, no. 3 (1983): 413–52.

78. David D. Hall, "On Common Ground: The Coherence of American Puritan Studies," *William and Mary Quarterly* 44, no. 2 (1987): 193–229.

79. Colin Gordon, "Crafting a Usable Past: Consensus, Ideology, and Historians of the American Revolution," *William and Mary Quarterly* 46, no. 4 (1989): 671–95. To another observer, the Bailyn School's denial of conflict as a part of the Revolution was no more than a traditional position adopted by Loyalists in response to patriot historians from the period of the Revolution itself; Merrill Jensen, "History and the Nature of the American Revolution," in *The Reinterpretation of Early American History* ed. Ray Billington (San Marino: Huntington Library, 1966) 101–28, esp. 122. Jensen clearly did not agree. Examples of the persistence of a conflict approach can be found in Alfred F. Young, ed., *The American Revolution: Explorations in the History of American Radicalism* (DeKalb: Northern Illinois Univ. Press, 1976). The hallmark of a historical field that is not being reduced to consensus and heritage is that it is open to some degree of intellectual experimentation. According to a wistful-sounding American observer, this is the case with European religious history; Jon Butler, "The Future of American Religious History: Prospectus, Agenda, Transatlantique Problematique," *William and Mary Quarterly* 42, no. 2 (1985): 167–83.

80. Eric Foner, "The Causes of the American Civil War: Recent Interpretations and New

Directions," *Civil War History* 20, no. 3 (1974): 197–214, esp. 199. On Reconstruction, John Hope Franklin, "Mirror for Americans: A Century of Reconstruction History," *American Historical Review* 85, no. 1 (1980): 1–14, gives the impression that little has changed since the nineteenth century in this field. Although clearly writers today are not segregationists, their bias against a conflict model approach makes them overlap heavily with the traditional Dunning School. For example, the trauma of the 1960s is sometimes still called a second Reconstruction. If blacks occupied a more prominent place in this paradigm, it would surely collapse; Armstead L. Robinson, "The Difference Freedom Made: The Emancipation of Afro-Americans," in Hine, *Afro-American History,* 51–90.

81. August Meier and Elliott Rudwick, *Black History and the Historical Profession, 1915–1980* (Urbana: Univ. of Illinois Press, 1986), 258–65. In recent years, as Genovese has strayed from the mainstream Marxism of the North, he has been subject to various criticisms; see for example, Susan F. Feiner, "Property Relations and Class Relations in Genovese and the Modes of Production Controversy," *Cambridge Journal of Economics* 10(1986): 61–75. The writing about Genovese makes clear the unresolved nature of race and region in American radical thought. One of the most famous writers Genovese encountered was Herbert Gutman, a radicalized liberal and staunch upholder of an East Coast regional view of American history. Regrettably, in the standard account of the well-known debate between Gutman and Genovese, the editor gives paramount to the issue of personalities; Ira Berlin, ed., *Power and Culture* (New York: Pantheon, 1987), 55–59; Tyrrell, *Absent Marx,* 209ff., who covers the same ground, is more useful. Influenced by Genovese and carrying his line of thought forward is Barbara Jeanne Fields, *Slavery and Freedom on the Middle Ground: Maryland During the Nineteenth Century* (New Haven: Yale Univ. Press, 1985). She argues that the modern history of Maryland arose from the dual economic system of slave and free, an offshoot of Genovese's picture of the political economy of the United States as a whole. Nan Elizabeth Woodruff, *As Rare as Rain: Federal Relief in the Great Southern Drought of 1930–31*(Urbana: Univ. of Illinois Press, 1985) shows the breakdown of voluntary regional self-help (as an adequate response to crisis), pointing toward the still unresolved problem of race and region.

82. Examples where writers are calling for a more integrated or a more political approach include Eugene D. Genovese, "The Political Crisis of Social History: Class Struggle as Subject and Object," in *Fruits of Merchant Capital,* ed. Elizabeth Fox-Genovese and Eugene D. Genovese (New York: Oxford Univ. Press, 1983), 179–212; J. Morgan Kousser, "Restoring Politics to Political History," *Journal of Interdisciplinary History* 12, no. 4 (Spring 1982): 569–95.

Bibliography

Abou-El-Haj, Rifart. *Formation of the Modern State*. Albany: State Univ. of New York, 1991.

Amin, Samir. *Eurocentrism*. New York: Monthly Review Press, 1989.

———. *Irak et Syrie*. Paris: Edition de Minuit, 1982.

Amselle, Jean-Loup, and Elikia M'Bokolo, eds. *Au coeur de l'ethnie Ethnies, tribalisme et l'état en Afrique*. Paris: Découverte, 1985.

Amyot, Grant. *The Italian Communist Party: The Crisis of the Popular Front Strategy*. New York: St. Martin's Press, 1981.

Aricó, José. *La Cola del diablo: itinerario de Gramsci en América Latina*. Caracas: Editorial Nueva Sociedad, 1988.

Asad, Talal. *Genealogies of Religion*. Baltimore: Johns Hopkins Univ. Press, 1993.

———, ed. *Anthropology and the Colonial Encounter*. London: Ithaca Press, 1973.

Bachrach, Peter. *The Theory of Democratic Elitism: A Critique*. Boston: Little, Brown, 1967.

Barkan, Elazar. *The Retreat of Scientific Racism: Changing Concepts of Race in Britain and the United States Between the Two World Wars*. Cambridge: Cambridge Univ. Press, 1992.

Batatu, Hanna. *The Old Social Classes and the Revolutionary Movements of Iraq*. Princeton, N.J.: Princeton Univ. Press, 1978.

Bellah, Robert N. "Civil Religion in America." *Daedalus* 96, no. 1 (Winter 1967): 1–21.

Bellamy, John Foster. "The Fetishism of Fordism." *Monthly Review* 39, no. 10 (1988): 14–33.

Benería, Lourdes, and Martha Roldán. *The Crossroads of Class and Gender: Industrial Housework, Subcontracting, and Household Dynamics in Mexico City*. Chicago: Univ. of Chicago Press, 1987.

Bernal, Martin. *Black Athena: The Afroasiatic Roots of Classical Civilization*. New Brunswick, N.J.: Rutgers Univ. Press, 1987.

Billington, James H. *The Icon and the Axe*. New York: Alfred A. Knopf, 1966.

Bluestone, Barry, and Bennett Harrison. *The Deindustrialization of America*. New York: Basic Books, 1982.

Boserup, Ester. *Women's Role in Economic Development*. London: Earthscan, 1970.

Bouwsma, William J. "The Renaissance and the Drama of Western History." *American Historical Review* 84, no. 1 (1979): 1–15.

Brondino, Michele, and Labib, Tahar. *Gramsci dans le Monde Arabe*. Tunis: Alif, 1994.

Cammett, John. *Antonio Gramsci and the Origins of Italian Communism*. Palo Alto, Calif.: Stanford Univ. Press, 1967.

Carr, Barry. "Marxism and Anarchism in the Formation of the Mexican Communist Party, 1910–1919." *Hispanic American Historical Review* 63, no. 2 (1983): 277–305.

———. *Mexican Communism, 1968–1983: Eurocommunism in the Americas?* San Diego, Calif.: Center for United States-Mexican Studies, 1985.

———. "The Peculiarities of the Mexican North, 1880–1928: An Essay in Interpretation." Occasional Papers, no. 4. Glasgow: Univ. of Glasgow, 1971.

Cashman, Richard. "The Phenomenon of Indian Cricket," In *Sports in History*, edited by Richard Cashman and Michael McKernan. 181–205. Queensland, Australia: Queensland Univ. Press, 1979.

Castro, Michael. *Interpreting the Indian: Twentieth Century Poets and the Native American*. Albuquerque: Univ. of New Mexico Press, 1983.

Chatterjee, Partha. *Nationalist Thought and the Colonial World: A Derivative Discourse*. London: Zed Press, 1986.

Chaudhary, Vijay C. P. *Secularism versus Communalism: An Anatomy of the National Debate on Five Controversial History Books*. Patna: Navdhara Samiti, 1977.

Cocchiara, Giuseppe. *The History of Folklore in Europe*. Philadelphia: Institute for the Study of Human Issues, 1981.

Cohen, Ronald. "Oedipus Rex and Regina: The Queen Mother in Africa." *Africa* 47, no. 1 (1977): 23.

Cohen, Stephen. *Rethinking the Soviet Experience: Politics and History since 1917*. New York: Oxford Univ. Press, 1985.

Colls, Robert, and Philip Dodd, eds. *Englishness: Politics and Culture, 1880–1920*. London: Croom Helm, 1986.

Cunnison, Ian. "History and Genealogy in Conquest States." *American Anthropologist* 59, no. 1 (1957): 20–31.

Dale, Peter. *The Myth of Japanese Uniqueness*. New York: St. Martin's Press, 1986.

Datta, Kalikinkar. *Educational and Social Amelioration of Women in Pre-Mutiny India*. Patna: Patna Law Press, 1936.

Dinnerstein, Leonard. *Uneasy at Home: Antisemitism and the American Jewish Experience*. New York: Columbia Univ. Press, 1987.

Dubovsky, Melvyn. *We Shall Be All: A History of the Industrial Workers of the World*. Chicago: Quadrangle Books, 1969.

Dumont, Louis. *Homo Hierarchus*. Chicago: Univ. of Chicago Press, 1970.

Duncan, Carol. "Who Rules the Art World?" *Socialist Review* 13, no. 4 (July 1983): 99–119.

Ehrenreich, Barbara. *Fear of Falling: The Inner Life of the Middle Class*. New York: Pantheon, 1989.

Eley, G. "Reading Gramsci in English." *European Historical Quarterly* 14, no. 4 (1984): 441–78.

Encyclopedia Judaica. Vol. 9. Jerusalem: Keter Publishing House, 1971.

Encyclopedia of Modern Iraq. 3 vols. Baghdad: Arab Encyclopedia Publishing House, 1978.

Engelbourg, Saul, and Gustav Schlachter. "Two 'Souths': The United States and Italy since the 1860's." *Journal of European Economic History* 15, no. 3 (1986): 563–89.

Enteen, George M. *The Soviet Scholar-Bureaucrat: M. N. Pokrovskii and the Society of Marxist Historians.* University Park: Pennsylvania State Univ. Press, 1978.

Fenyvesi, Charles. *Splendour in Exile: The Ex-Majesties of Europe.* Washington, D.C.: New Republic Books, 1979.

Ferguson, Wallace K. *The Renaissance in Historical Thought.* Boston: Houghton Mifflin 1981.

Fields, Barbara Jeanne. "Slavery, Race, and Ideology in the United States of America." *New Left Review* June (1990): 95–118.

Fitzpatrick, Sheila. "New Perspectives on Stalinism." *Russian Review* 45(1986): 357–73.

Forgacs, David, ed. *Rethinking Italian Fascism.* London: Lawrence and Wishart, 1986.

Fredrickson, George. *White Supremacy: A Comparative Study in American and South African History.* New York: Oxford Univ. Press, 1981.

Friedman, Victor A. *Evidentiality in the Balkans: Bulgarian, Macedonian, and Albanian.* Norwood, N.J.: Ablex, 1986.

Garson, Barbara. *The Electronic Sweatshop: How Computers Are Transforming the Office of the Future into the Factory of the Past.* New York: Simon and Schuster, 1988.

Genovese, Eugene D." The Political Crisis of Social History: Class Struggle as Subject and Object." In *Fruits of Merchant Capital,* edited by Elizabeth Fox-Genovese and Eugene D. Genovese, 179–212. New York: Oxford Univ. Press, 1983.

Gerber, Haim. *Islam, Guerilla War, and Revolution.* Boulder, Colo.: Lynn Rienner, 1988.

Geschiere, Peter. "Applications of the 'Lineage Mode of Production' in African Studies." *Canadian Journal of African Studies* 19(1985).

Gilly, Adolfo. *The Mexican Revolution.* London: Verso Press, 1983.

Goldstein, Robert Justin. *Political Repression in Modern America: From 1870 to the Present.* Cambridge: Schenkman, 1978.

Gorman, Robert, ed. *Biographical Dictionary of Neo-Marxism.* Westport, Conn.: Greenwood Press, 1985.

Gran, Peter. *The Islamic Roots of Capitalism: Egypt, 1760–1840.* Austin: Univ. of Texas Press, 1979.

———. "Political Economy as a Paradigm for the Study of Islamic History." *International Journal of Middle East Studies* 11(1980): 511–26.

———. "The Political Economy of Aesthetics: Modes of Domination in Modern Nation States Seen Through Shakespeare Reception." *Dialectical Anthropology* 17(1992): 171–88.

Grew, Raymond. "The Comparative Weakness of American History." *Journal of Interdisciplinary History* 16, no. 1 (1985): 87–101.

Gsovski, Vladimir, and Kazimierz Grzybowski. *Government, Law, and Courts in the Soviet Union and Eastern Europe.* 2 vols. New York: Frederick A. Praeger, 1960.

Gu, Xiao-rong. "Resource, Choice, and Power: A Comparative Study in Social Change and Ideological Transformation of Germany (1848–1914), Italy (1861–1963), and Egypt (1919–1983)." Ph.D. diss., Temple Univ., 1988.

Hall, Stuart. "The Great Moving Right Show." In *The Politics of Thatcherism;* edited by Stuart Hall and Martin Jacques, 42–43. London: Lawrence and Wishart, 1983.

———. "The Rise of the Representative/Interventionist State." In *State and Society in Contemporary Britain,* edited by Gregor McLennan, David Held, and Stuart Hall, chap. 1. Cambridge: Polity Press, 1984.

Harvey, David. *The Conditions of Postmodernity.* Oxford: Basil Blackwell, 1989.

Hasluck, Margaret. *The Unwritten Law in Albania.* Cambridge: Cambridge Univ. Press, 1954.

Hatzimichali, Nectaire. "L'Église Orthodoxe Grècque et le Messianisme en Afrique." *Social Compass* 22, no. 1 (1975): 85–95.

Heer, Nancy. *Politics and History in the Soviet Union.* Cambridge: MIT Press, 1971.

Hoare, Quintin, and Geoffrey Nowell-Smith, eds. *Selections from the Prison Notebooks of Antonio Gramsci.* London: Lawrence and Wishart, 1971.

Hobsbawn, Eric. *Industry and Empire.* London: Weidenfeld and Nicolson, 1968.

Hodgson, Marshall. *Venture of Islam.* 3 vols. Chicago: Univ. of Chicago Press, 1973.

Hoffman, John. *The Gramscian Challenge: Coercion and Consent in Marxist Political Theory.* Oxford: Basic Blackwell, 1984.

Hoggart, Richard. *The Uses of Literacy.* London: Chatto and Windus, 1957.

Horn, Pierre L., and Mary Beth Pringle, eds. *The Image of the Prostitute in Modern Literature.* New York: Frederick Ungar, 1984.

Iggers, Georg G., and James M. Powell, eds. *Leopold von Ranke and the Shaping of the Historical Discipline.* Syracuse, N.Y.: Syracuse Univ. Press, 1990.

Jewsiewicki, Bogumil. "African Historical Studies: Academic Knowledge as 'Usable Past' and Radical Scholarship." Boulder, Colo.: ACLS/SSRC, 1987.

———. "Formation of the Political Culture of Ethnicity in the Belgian Congo." In *Creation of Tribalism in Southern Africa,* ed. Leroy Vail, 324–49. Berkeley: Univ. of California Press, 1989.

Johnson, Richard. "Edward Thompson and Eugene Genovese, and Social-Humanist History." *History Workshop* no. 6 (August 1978): 79–100.

Joint Committee on Slavic Studies. *Continuity and Change in Russian and Soviet Thought.* New York: Russell and Russell, 1955.

Kadare, Ismail. *The General of the Dead Army.* New York: Grossman, 1972.

Karouni, A. "Brecht in Irak." In *Brecht 80,* edited by Werner Hecht, 57–66. Berlin: Henschelverlag Kunst und Gesellschaft, 1980.

Katz, Friedrich. *The Secret War in Mexico: Europe, the United States, and the Mexican Revolution.* Chicago: Univ. of Chicago Press, 1981.

Keen, Benjamin. *The Aztec Image in Western Thought.* New Brunswick, N.J.: Rutgers Univ. Press, 1971.

Kiernan, Victor. "Gramsci and the Other Continents." *New Edinburgh Review* 27 (1975): 19–24.

Kolsti, John. "From Courtyard to Cabinet: The Political Emergence of Albanian Women." In *Women, State, and Party in Eastern Europe,* edited by Sharon L.

Wolchik and Alfred G. Meyer, 138–51. Durham, N.C.: Duke Univ. Press, 1985.

Kostallari, Androkli. "Le Développement des études Albanologiques en Albanie: Problèmes nouveaux et taches nouvelles." *Studia Albanica* 1, no. 1 (1964): 5–46.

Levine, Lawrence W. *Highbrow/Lowbrow: The Emergence of Cultural Hierarchy in America*. Cambridge, Mass.: Harvard Univ. Press, 1988.

Lewin, Moshe. *The Making of the Soviet System*. New York: Pantheon, 1983.

Lyons, Gene M. *The Uneasy Partnership: Social Science and the Federal Government in the Twentieth Century*. New York: Russell Sage, 1969.

MacGaffey, Janet. *The Real Economy of Zaire*. Philadelphia: Univ. of Pennsylvania Press, 1991.

Mark, Charles C. *A Study of Cultural Policy in the United States*. Paris: UNESCO, 1969.

Mattelart, Armando. *Multinational Corporations and the Control of Culture*. Sussex: Harvester Press, 1979.

Matute, Álvaro. *La teoría de la Historia en México, 1940–1973*. Mexico City, 1974.

McDaniel, Tim. *Autocracy, Capitalism, and Revolution in Russia*. Berkeley: Univ. of California Press, 1987.

McNeill, William. *The Rise of the West*. Chicago: Univ. of Chicago Press 1963.

Merriman, John. *Comparative Law: Western European and Latin American Legal Systems*. Indianapolis: Bobbs Merrill, 1978.

Meyer, Michael C., and William L. Sherman. *The Course of Mexican History*. New York: Oxford Univ. Press, 1987.

Mies, Maria. *Patriarchy and Accumulation on a World Scale*. London: Zed Press, 1986.

Millon, Robert Paul. *Mexican Marxist Vicente Lombardo Toledano*. Chapel Hill: Univ. of North Carolina Press, 1966.

Mollica, Richard F. "From Antonio Gramsci to Franco Basaglia (1924–1980): The Theory and Practice of Italian Psychiatric Reform." *International Journal of Mental Health* 14, no. 2 (1985): 22–41.

Momigliano, A. "Historicism in Contemporary Thought." In *Studies in Historiography*, edited by A. Momigliano, 221–38. London: Weidenfeld and Nicolson, 1966.

Moore, Barrington. *Social Origins of Dictatorship and Democracy*. Boston: Beacon Press, 1967.

Morrison, John. *New Ideas in India During the Nineteenth Century*. Chandigarh: Sameer Pakashan, 1977.

Mouralis, Bernard. *Les Contre-littératures*. Paris: Presses Universitaires de France, 1975.

Mudimbe, V. Y. *The Invention of Africa: Gnosis, Philosophy, and the Order of Knowledge*. Bloomington: Indiana Univ. Press, 1988.

———. *Parables and Fables*. Madison: Univ. of Wisconsin Press, 1991.

Mukeba, Lufuluabo. "Some Aspects of Bilingualism and Bilingual Education in Zaire." *In International Handbook of Bilingualism and Bilingual Education*, edited by Christina Bratt Paulston, chap. 27. Westport, Conn.: Greenwood Press, 1988.

Nahas, Maridi. "Hegemonic Constraints and State Autonomy: A Comparative

430   BIBLIOGRAPHY

Analysis of Development in Nineteenth Century Egypt, Spain, and Italy."
Ph.D. diss., Univ. of California at Los Angeles. 1985.

Nakamura, Hajime. *A Comparative History of Ideas* London: KPI, 1986.

Neufeld, Maurice F. *Italy, School for Awakening Countries: The Italian Labor Movement in its Political, Social, and Economic Setting from 1800–1960*. Ithaca, N.Y.: Cornell Univ. Press, 1961.

Nield, Keith. "A Symptomatic Dispute? Notes on the Relation Between Marxian Theory and Historical Practice in Britain." *Social Research* 47 (1980: 479–506.

Novick, Peter. *That Noble Dream: The "Objectivity Question" and the American Historical Profession*. Cambridge: Cambridge Univ. Press, 1988.

Palmer, Robin, and Neil Parsons, eds. *The Roots of Rural Poverty in Central and Southern Africa*. Berkeley: Univ. of California Press, 1977.

Patterson, Thomas C. *Las sociedades nucleares de Mesoamérica*. Caracas: Historia General de América, forthcoming.

Pipa, Arshi. "The Political Culture of Hoxha's Albania." In *The Stalinist Legacy: Its Impact on Twentieth-Century World Politics,* edited by Tariq Ali. Boulder, Colo.: Lynn Rienner Publishers, 1985.

Pleck, Elizabeth. *Domestic Tyranny: The Making of Social Policy Against Family Violence from Colonial Times to the Present*. New York: Oxford Univ. Press, 1987.

Popovic, A. "Les Ordres mystiques musulmans du sud-est européen dans la période post-Ottomane." In *Les Ordres mystiques dans l'Islam,* edited by A. Popovic and G. Veinstein, 63–100. Paris: CNRS, 1985.

Porciani, Ilaria. *"L'Archivio stòrico Italiano": Organizzazióne dalla ricérca ed egemonìa moderata nel Risorgiménto*. Florence: L. S. Olschki, 1979.

Radu, Michael, ed. *Eastern Europe and the Third World*. New York: Frederick A. Praeger, 1981.

Rich, Paul B. *Race and Empire in British Politics*. Cambridge: Cambridge Univ. Press, 1986.

Riepe, Dale, ed. *Asian Philosophy*. New York: Gordon and Breach, 1981.

Rowbotham, Sheila. *Hidden from History: Rediscovering Women in History from the 17th Century to the Present*. New York: Vintage Books, 1976.

Sadie, Stanley, ed. *The New Grove Dictionary of Music and Musicians*. London: Macmillan, 1980.

Sadr, Muhammad Baqir. *Our Philosophy*. London: Muhammadi Trust/KPI, 1987.

Salmeron, Fernando. "Mexican Philosophers of the Twentieth Century." In *Main Trends in Mexican Philosophy,* 246–87. Notre Dame: Notre Dame Univ. Press, 1966.

Salomone, William A. "The Risorgiménto Between Ideology and History: The Political Myth of the 'Rivoluzióne Mancata'." *American Historical Review* 68 (1962): 38–56.

Sarkar, Sumit. *"Popular" Movement and the "Middle" Class Leadership in Late Colonial India: Perspectives and Problems of a History from Below*. Calcutta, K. P. Bagchi, 1983.

Sarkar, Sumit. *Modern India*. New York: St. Martin's Press, 1989.

Sayer, Derek, and Philip Corrigan. "Revolution Against eq. the State: The Context and Significance of Marx's Later Writings." *Dialectical Anthropology* 12 (1987): 65–82.

Sen, S. P., ed. *The North and the South in Indian History: Contact and Adjustment.* Calcutta: Institute of Historical Studies, 1976.

Shanin, Teodor. *Late Marx and the Russian Road.* New York: Monthly Review Press, 1983.

————. *Russia as a Developing Society.* London: Macmillan, 1985.

Skowronek, Stephen. *Building a New American State: The Expansion of National Administrative Capacities, 1877–1920.* Cambridge: Cambridge Univ. Press, 1982.

Sorenson, Arne. "The Scandinavian Concept of History." In Torben Lundbak, *African Humanism-Scandinavian Culture, A Dialogue* 136–39. Copenhagen: Danish International Development (Danida), 1970.

Sow, I. *Anthropological Structures of Madness in Black Africa.* New York: International Universities Press, 1978.

Srivastava, Gita. *Mazzini and His Impact on the Indian National Movement.* Allahabad, 1982.

Stanfield, John H. *Philanthropy and Jim Crow in American Scholarship.* Westport, Conn.: Greenwood Press, 1985.

Thomas, Jack Ray. *Biographical Dictionary of Latin American Historians and Historiography.* Westport, Conn.: Greenwood Press, 1984.

Thompson, E. P. *The Making of the English Working Class.* New York: Vintage Books, 1963.

Tyrrell, Ian. *The Absent Marx.* Westport, Conn.: Greenwood Press, 1986.

Vail, Leroy, ed. *The Creation of Tribalism in Southern Africa.* Berkeley: Univ. of California Press, 1991.

Vansina, Jan. *Oral Tradition as History.* Madison: Univ. of Wisconsin Press, 1985.

Verhagen, Benoit. *Introduction a l'histoire immediate.* Gembloux, Belgium: Duculot, 1974.

Walkowitz, Judith. *Prostitution and Victorian Society: Women, Class, and the State.* Cambridge: Cambridge Univ. Press, 1980.

Wallerstein, Immanuel. *Capitalist Agriculture and the Origins of the European World Economy in the Sixteenth Century.* New York: Academic Press, 1974.

Wilentz, Sean. "Against Exceptionalism: Class Consciousness and the American Labor Movement." *International Labor and Working Class History* 26(Fall 1984): 1–24.

Wolf, Eric. *Europe and the People Without History.* Berkeley: Univ. of California Press, 1982.

Wood, Ellen Meiksins. *The Retreat from Class: A New 'True' Socialism.* London: Verso, 1986.

Woodruff, Nan Elizabeth. *As Rare as Rain: Federal Relief in the Great Southern Drought of 1930–31.* Urbana: Univ. of Illinois Press, 1985.

Yates, Barbara A. "Colonialism, Education, and Work: Sex Differentiation in Colonial Zaire." In *Women and Work in Africa,* edited by Edna G. Bay, chap. 6. Boulder, Colo.: Westview Press, 1982.

Yousif, 'Abd Al-Salaam. "Vanguardist Cultural Practices: The Formation of an Alternative Cultural Hegemony in Iraq and Chile, 1930's-1970's." Ph.D. diss., Univ. of Iowa, 1988.

Zea, Leopoldo. *Positivism in Mexico.* Austin: Univ. of Texas Press, 1968.

A Conceptual Index

Albania
  Ghegs, 215, 217
  Enver Hoxha,197, 208
  Ilyrianism, 219
  Fan Noli, 203, 215
  Skanderbeg myth, 221, 222
  Tosks, 215, 216
  tribes, 204, 210, 223
Albanian Party of Labor, 207–10, 218
anthropology. *See* organization of culture
  individual countries
archeology. *See* organization of culture
  individual countries

bourgeois democracy (hegemony)
  interventionist state, 257, 258
  legitimated through "scientizing," 317
  as a political ideal, 255
  as presupposition, 252, 287
  racial underclass, 251, 308
  racism and antiracism among scientists,
    253, 317–18
  resistance to an external sociology of
    science, 318
  strategies of, 254, 255, 260–61
  United Kingdom, 257, 262
  United States—Regulationist State, 290,
    294, 301, 310–13

See also civil society; organization of
  culture

caste
  India, 123–25
  Russian Road examples (nomenklatura),
    24–26
China, 8, 338
civilization, 93, 113, 151
civil society, 133, 159
  citizen, 254, 255
  mass movements (birthplace of), 89–90
colonialism
  Belgian, 225–32
  British, 62–68, 132–37, 347
consumerism
  as development (by the rulers of tribal-
    ethnic states), 292, 343
  by the working class, 171, 297,
    408n. 11
counterhegemony
  individuals
    B. R. Ambedkar (India), 141–42
    Erik Hobsbawm (U.K.), 280–82
    E. M. S. Namboodiripad (India), 141
    M. N. Roy (India), 140–41
    Muhammad Baqir al-Sadr (Iraq), 71–
      72

Indexes serve several functions. My primary purpose in creating a conceptual index is to make clear the interrelationships of principle terms used throughout this study and to help clarify my argument. I hope it will be of some use to those who set out to write or teach modern world history.

433